AF693106

Introduction to Mathematics for Ec...

Massimiliano Porto

Introduction to Mathematics for Economics with R

Springer

Massimiliano Porto
Graduate School of Economics
Kobe University
Kobe, Japan

ISBN 978-3-031-05201-9 ISBN 978-3-031-05202-6 (eBook)
https://doi.org/10.1007/978-3-031-05202-6

This Springer imprint is published by the registered company Springer Nature Switzerland AG
The registered company address is: Gewerbestrasse 11, 6330 Cham, Switzerland

Preface

Lately, more and more books in the field of econometrics, time series, statistics, finance, and machine learning, to name a few examples, include applications with a programming language. I strongly believe that such books increase reader engagement and help strengthen reader understanding. Since mathematics has become a core subject in economics, and it usually represents the first main obstacle for an undergraduate student to a smooth path to graduation, I decided to design a book of mathematics for economics for undergraduate students that includes applications with the **R** programming language.

First of all, why **R**? **R** is a free software environment for statistical computing and graphics. It comes with a very nice integrated development environment (IDE) called **RStudio** that is free as well. On top of that, also the packages developed by the **R** Community to expand **R** capabilities are free. This means that all students around the world can work with **R** without bearing any cost. Furthermore, in spite of being completely free, it is as powerful as property software and widely used in academia and private sector. Finally, as we will see in Sect. 2.2.5, it is possible to view the source code of **R** functions, which I consider a great learning tool. Additionally, for mathematical purpose and in particular linear algebra, I think it is convenient that it starts indexing from 1.[1]

Thus, I decided to design a book of mathematics where coding is a key part. By replicating the code in this book, the reader will learn, for example, how to plot functions, solve systems of linear equations, compute derivatives, and solve differential equations in **R**. Additionally, these concepts will be applied to examples in economics.

However, the key part of coding consists in the reader attempting to write their own function before applying ready-to-use functions made available by the **R** Community. Naturally, on one hand, this makes the book more complicated since the reader needs to learn the control flow of the programming language, that is, the order

[1] If the reader is unfamiliar with any of the concepts in this preface, he/she should not worry since we will cover these concepts in detail in the book.

in which statements and instructions are executed or evaluated, to grasp how we will write functions in this book. On the other hand, I think it will add more value to the learning experience of the reader. In fact, even though it is important to learn how to use the available functions—and usually this is all we need to accomplish a task—it is more challenging, useful, and funny— yes, funny!—to code them from scratch. Additionally, by writing functions, we will test our understanding of mathematical notation. We might think that mathematical notation, that is, the writing system of mathematics, is just a fancy—and complicated—way that mathematicians use to express mathematical concepts. However, as it turns out, that is our starting point to code a function. Let's consider a simple example. In Sect. 2.3.3.1, we will code a function to compute the trace of a square matrix A, in mathematical notation $tr(A) = \sum_i^n a_{ii}$. This expression means that we need to sum the diagonal elements of the matrix A to obtain its trace. For the matrix

$$A = \begin{bmatrix} 3 & 2 \\ 2 & 6 \end{bmatrix}$$

the diagonal elements are 3 and 6 because they correspond to, respectively, the indexes [1, 1] (first row, first column) and [2, 2] (second row, second column). Therefore, we can say that the trace of A is 9, $tr(A) = 9$.

In **R**, we write the A matrix as follows

```
> A <- matrix(c(3, 2,
+               2, 6),
+             nrow = 2,
+             ncol = 2,
+             byrow = T)
> A
     [,1] [,2]
[1,]    3    2
[2,]    2    6
```

Then, we can code our function, `tr()`, that computes the trace for us

```
> tr <- function(X){
+
+   n <- ncol(X)
+   a_ii <- numeric(n)
+
+   for(i in 1:n){
+
+     a_ii[i] <- X[i, i]
+
+   }
+
+   res <- sum(a_ii)
```

```
+
+    return(res)
+
+ }
```

Don't mind now the code, but all we did was to select and store all the diagonal elements of the matrix and then to sum all of them. Does it work? Let's check it

```
> tr(A)
[1] 9
```

This confirms that it works. We just set up a strategy to implement the trace based on its notation. Could we have done better? Definitely. In fact, we could code the notation with just one line as follows

```
> tr <- function(X){
+
+    sum(diag(X))
+
+ }
```

Naturally, this produces the same output

```
> tr(A)
[1] 9
```

This is an example of how we will work throughout this book. Automating a process with a function is an important skill—and it makes *life* easier. Therefore, in this context, whenever feasible, we will build functions as part of the learning process. However, since writing functions is not an easy task, we need first to learn the basics of the **R** language. Chapter 1 is designed for this purpose. It is structured to provide a beginner user of **R** with key information to be ready for understanding the code used in this book. First, we will learn how to launch a project in **RStudio** in Sect. 1.3.1 and open an **R Script** file in Sect. 1.3.2. Section 1.4 explains how to install and load packages in **R** and which packages the reader needs to install and load to replicate the code in this book. These sections contain several screenshots of my computer so that the reader can follow all the steps visually. In Sect. 1.5, we will learn how to read and replicate the code in this book. As I will explain in detail later, I will print the code from the console pane. However, the reader is recommended to write and run the code from the **R Script**. Finally, the chapter ends with examples with **R**. Section 1.6 presents eight key facts regarding the **R** *grammar* I think any beginner should be aware of. Section 1.7 builds a step-by-step example applying the knowledge of the previous section. I would recommend any beginner to grasp those concepts before moving forward.

However, since this is a book designed for undergraduates, I tried to tackle an obstacle that usually concerns students while learning mathematics, that is, the *steps* to the solution of an exercise or of a problem. To this end, all the examples are broken down in simple steps. In each step, we will perform a small part of the whole process to the solution so that all the operations from the setup of the problem to its conclusion are clearly visible. In Chap. 2, for example, we will learn how to compute the determinant of a square matrix. One of the methods we will learn is the Laplace expansion method. Its notation may seem intimidating at first. Therefore, our initial goal is to understand the notation. Then, we implement a step-by-step process for a 3×3 matrix and then for 4×4 matrix. The Laplace expansion method for larger matrices—indeed I would say that already for a 5×5 with no zeros (and we will see why)—is burdensome and time consuming. However, if we understand the process for a 4×4 matrix, the same process naturally extends to larger matrices. And this becomes another case where we can test our understanding of the notation and the process studied by writing a function that performs the Laplace expansion method for any square matrix. Therefore, in Sect. 2.3.8.2, we will write the `laplace_expansion()` function that mimics the algorithm that we manually implemented. Is the Laplace expansion method the most efficient way to compute the determinant of a square matrix? Not really. In Sect. 2.3.9, we will learn that we can compute the determinant with the eigenvalues of the matrix. Thus, it becomes an opportunity to write another function to compute the determinant, `eigen_det()`, that will be much more efficient than `laplace_expansion()` (but in this case we will "cheat" a bit). Finally, we will compare the performance of our functions with the `det()` function that is the **R** base function to compute the determinant.

Therefore, to sum up, the *leitmotiv* in this book is

1. Understand the notation
2. Implement manually the process
3. Code a function that automatizes the process, whenever feasible

Let's talk now about the overall organization of this book. The book is not structured based on economics topics but is based on mathematics topics. Originally, I planned to cover only topics from linear algebra to optimization with equality constraints. However, I decided to briefly introduce optimization with inequality constraints as well as difference and differential equations given the importance of these topics. Ideally, the book just stops before the next big challenging topic you need as graduate student: optimal control theory. Therefore, I finally decided to structure the book in two parts. Part I focuses on the mathematics for static economics. Part II is devoted to dynamic economics. Naturally, all the concepts we learn in Part I form the basis for Part II. In some cases, for example, integration, we will apply those techniques more in Part II than in Part I.

Part I starts with Chap. 2 that covers topics regarding linear algebra. This chapter is the longest in the book and ideally it is divided in two parts. The first part of the chapter focuses on vectors (Sect. 2.2) and matrices (Sect. 2.3). In particular, we will cover vector space (Sect. 2.2.1), operations with vectors, linear independence (Sect. 2.2.8), systems of linear equations (Sect. 2.3.7), and the determinant (Sect. 2.3.8). In the second part of the chapter, we will learn topics such as eigenvalues and eigenvectors (Sect. 2.3.9), diagonalization process (Sect. 2.3.9.1), and definiteness of matrices (Sect. 2.3.12) that we will really apply only later in the book. However, I think it is more productive to learn them in the context of the study of matrices so that the concepts are already familiar when we need to use them. Finally, Sect. 2.3.13 introduces matrix decomposition. We will see examples of spectral decomposition, singular value decomposition, Cholesky decomposition, and QR decomposition.

Chapter 3 starts by reviewing the concept of functions of one variable (Sect. 3.1). Then, we discuss the main functions such as linear (Sect. 3.2), quadratic (Sect. 3.3), cubic (Sect. 3.4), logarithmic and exponential (Sect. 3.6), radical (Sect. 3.7), and rational (Sect. 3.8). From this chapter onward, I would recommend keeping the following keyword in mind: "evaluate at".

Chapter 4 starts by introducing the meaning of the derivatives (Sect. 4.1). However, before continuing the discussion on the derivatives, we take a step back and discuss the concept of the limit of a function (Sect. 4.2). Then, we will learn the rules of differentiation (Sect. 4.6) and the concepts of points of minimum, maximum, and inflection associated with functions (Sect. 4.9). Additional topics are the Taylor expansion (Sect. 4.10) and the L'Hôpital theorem (Sect. 4.11).

Chapter 5 covers integral calculus. First, we will study indefinite integrals and the anti-derivative process (Sect. 5.1). We will cover fundamental integrals (Sect. 5.1.1.1), integration by substitution (Sect. 5.1.1.2), integration by parts (Sect. 5.1.1.3), and partial fractions (Sect. 5.1.1.4). Second, we will study definite integrals with examples of calculation of areas under a curve and between two lines (Sect. 5.2). Finally, we will cover the topic of improper integrals and the case of convergence and divergence (Sect. 5.4).

Chapter 6 covers functions of several variables (Sect. 6.1), partial and total derivatives (Sect. 6.2), and unconstrained optimization (Sect. 6.3). The chapter concludes with a simple example of integration with multiple variables (Sect. 6.4).

Chapter 7 deals with constrained optimization. First, we will learn about optimization with equality constraints (Sect. 7.1) and then with inequality constraints. In this last case, we will focus on the Kuhn-Tucker conditions (Sect. 7.2).

With Chap. 7, we conclude Part I. Part II focuses on difference equations (Chap. 10) and differential equations (Chap. 11). However, it starts with trigonometry (Chap. 8) and complex numbers (Chap. 9). In particular, complex numbers will be first introduced in Chaps. 2 and 3. However, we will discuss them only in Chap. 9. In our context, our interest is limited to build intuition regarding the relations between trigonometry and complex numbers that will be useful to figure out where the solutions of systems of linear difference equations and systems of linear differential equations with complex eigenvalues originate from.

Chapter 10 deals with difference equations. In Sect. 10.1, we will present first-order linear difference equations. In particular, we will discuss solution by iteration (Sect. 10.1.1) and by general method (Sect. 10.1.2). In Sect. 10.2, we will learn how to solve second-order linear difference equations. Section 10.3 is devoted to systems of linear difference equations, while in Sect. 10.4, we will learn how to transform high-order difference equations.

Chapter 11 starts by discussing the solution to differential equations, including the initial value problem (Sect. 11.1.5) and numerical solutions (Sect. 11.1.6). In the case of numerical solutions of differential equations, we will cover two algorithms, the Euler method (Sect. 11.1.6.1) and the Runge-Kutta method (Sect. 11.1.6.2). Then, we will present the methods to solve first-order differential equations such as separation of variables, substitution method for homogeneous-type equations, integrating factor, exact equations, and Bernoulli equations (Sect. 11.2). The remaining part of the chapter is devoted to second-order linear differential equations (Sect. 11.4) and systems of linear differential equations (Sect. 11.5).

Most of these chapters share the same three-part structure. In the first part of the chapter, the mathematical concepts are presented. In the second part, called *Applications in Economics*, we will see where we can encounter in economics the mathematics studied in the chapter. Examples of applications include: network analysis (Sect. 2.4.4), profit maximization (Sect. 4.14.3), ordinary least aquare (Sect. 6.3.4.2), transportation problem (Sect. 7.4.3), computable general equilibrium (CGE) model (Sect. 7.4.4), law of motion for public debt (Sect. 10.5.4), and the Solow growth model (Sect. 11.8.4). The last part of the chapter is an *Exercises* section where the reader can test their understanding. Maybe it was more appropriate to name the Exercises section as "Code Challenge". In fact, in the spirit of this book, the reader will not be asked to solve *standard* exercises but to code functions. For example, in Chap. 2, we will learn the Cramer's rule to solve a system of linear equations. In the Exercises section, the reader is challenged to write a function, `cramer()`, that implements the Cramer's rule. The reader will use again the `cramer()` function in the Exercises section in Chap. 6 to estimate a liner model. Another example, in Chap. 11, we will study differential equations. Before using the `deSolve` package, an **R** package designed to solve differential equations, we will write functions that implement the Euler and Runge-Kutta algorithms to solve first-order differential equations. Then, at the end of the chapter, the reader will be given the Runge-Kutta algorithm to numerically solve second-order differential equations and will be required to write a function that returns a table of values and a plot as solution of the differential equation. Table 1 lists all the functions that we will code in this book with a brief description. However, to be remarked, our main goal for these functions is to test our understanding of the notation and the process. For details about programming in **R** the reader is referred to specific resources.

In addition to writing and using functions, we will make extensively use of **R** packages to plot. Most of the plots will be made by using the `ggplot2` package. However, we will also use other packages for visualization for 3D plots, dynamic plots, and geographical maps. In some cases, we will write functions that have an argument to return a plot as result. For example, the `tangent_line()` function will be just a wrapper, that is, a function that encapsulates the code to reshape and plot tangent lines to a function based on our calculations. This is just to avoid repeating the same code to plot. On the other hand, for example, `iter_de()` is a function that numerically solves difference equations and can return the time path

Table 1 Functions coded in this book

Name	Description
`mtable()`	Compute multiplication tables (Sect. 1.6.7)
`inner_product()`	Compute the inner product between two vectors (Sect. 2.2.3). The replication is left as exercise
`unit_vec()`	Compute the unit vector (Sect. 2.2.5)
`proj_vec()`	Compute the vector projection (Sect. 2.2.7). The replication is left as exercise
`tr()`	Compute the trace of a square matrix (Sect. 2.3.3.1)
`sys_leq()`	Solve system of two linear equations with integer solutions by using a nested loop (Sect. 2.3.7). In the Exercises section, the reader is asked to write another function to solve a system of two linear equations
`geom_det()`	Compute *geometrically* the determinant of a 2×2 matrix and plot a geometric representation of the determinant (Sect. 2.3.8.1.1)
`laplace_expansion()`	Compute the determinant of any square matrix with the Laplace expansion method. We will first build `laplace_expansion3x3()` that applies to 3×3 matrix as a simpler example (Sect. 2.3.8.2)
`LPM()`	Compute the leading principal minor (Sect. 2.3.8.2.1). `bLPM()` is a modified version that computes bordered leading principal minors (Sect. 7.1.4). The replication is left as exercise
`cramer()`	Solve a system of linear equations with the Cramer's rule (Sect. 2.3.8.4). The replication is left as exercise (Sect. 2.5.4)
`eigen_det()`	Compute the determinant of a square matrix by multiplying its eigenvalues (Sect. 2.3.9)
`diagonalization()`	Compute the diagonalization process. The replication is left as exercise (Sect. 2.3.9.1)
`svar()`	Compute the sample variance. The implementation with matrix algebra is left as exercise (Sect. 2.5.6)
`lqc_fn()`	Compute linear, quadratic or cubic functions. By default, it computes $y = f(x) = x$ (Sect. 3.1)
`log_fn()`	Compute logarithmic functions. By default, natural logarithmic functions (Sect. 3.1)
`exp_fn()`	Compute exponential functions with e as base (Sect. 3.1). To be modified as exercise (Sect. 3.9.4)
`radical_fn()`	Compute radical functions (Sect. 3.1)
`slope_linfun()`	Compute the slope of a linear function and return two points if the equation of the line is known; otherwise, with two points return the equation of the line and the slope; it is also possible to plot the graph of the linear function (Sect. 3.2.1)
`quadratic_formula()`	Solve a quadratic equation and plot the corresponding quadratic function (Sect. 3.3.3)
`cub_eq_solver()`	Solve a cubic equation (real roots only) and plot the corresponding function (Sect. 3.4.1)
`pol_fn()`	Compute polynomial functions of any degree (Sect. 3.5)

(continued)

Table 1 (continued)

Name	Description
`comp_int_rate_formula()`	Compute the compound interest rate (Sect. 3.6.6.1)
`future_value()`	Compute the amount of money accumulated at the end of the investment (Sect. 3.6.7.1)
`present_value()`	Compute the amount of money the investor should deposit to obtain a desired amount of money in future (Sect. 3.6.7.1)
`time_invest()`	Compute the time needed for an investment to generate the desired accumulated amount of money (Sect. 3.6.7.1). To be modified as exercise (Sect. 3.9.5)
`vertex_quad()`	Compute the vertex of a quadratic function. The replication of this function is left as exercise (Sect. 3.9.1)
`per_change()`	Compute the percentage change. The replication of this function is left as exercise (Sect. 3.9.2)
`avg()`	Compute the arithmetic mean or the geometric mean. The replication of this function is left as exercise (Sect. 3.9.3)
`LiMiT()`	Compute the limit of a function (Sect. 4.2)
`dfdx()`	Compute numerically the derivative of a function of one variable (Sect. 4.3)
`newton()`	Find the roots of a real-valued function of one variable by using the Newton-Raphson method (Sect. 4.3)
`tangent_line()`	This function is a wrapper to arrange and plot the data (Sect. 4.8)
`total_cost()`	Compute the total cost function of a polynomial (highest degree 3) given quantities as a vector, variable costs, and fixed cost (Sect. 4.14.1)
`marginal_cost()`	Compute the marginal cost (Sect. 4.14.1). As exercise you are asked to write a function that computes both total cost and marginal cost
`y_inter()`	Compute the y intercept (Sect. 4.14.1)
`elas()`	Compute the point elasticity and the arc elasticity (Sect. 4.14.4)
`profit_max()`	Compute the quantity that maximizes profit. The replication of this function is left as exercise (Sect. 4.15.2)
`area_under_curve()`	Compute the area under a curve based on the definition (5.19). The replication is left as exercise (Sect. 5.7)
`angle_conversion()`	Convert the measurement of an angle in degree into radians (default) and vice versa (Sect. 8.1)
`trig_taylor()`	Compute the approximation for sine (default) and cosine functions by using Taylor series (Sect. 9.5)
`iter_de()`	Solve numerically difference equations (by default first-order) by iteration. By setting `graph = TRUE`, the time path of y_t is plotted (Sect. 10.1.1)

(continued)

Table 1 (continued)

Name	Description
`sys_folde()`	Solve numerically systems of first-order linear difference equations (Sect. 10.3.2). The replication of an extended version, `trajectory_de()`, is left as exercise (Sect. 10.3.4)
`sys_folde_diag()`	Solve numerically systems of first-order linear difference equations by applying the diagonalization process. Its replication is left as exercise (Sect. 10.3.3.1)
`cobweb()`	Plot p_t and Q_t from a linear cobweb model (Sect. 10.5.2)
`debt_path()`	Simulate the law of motion for public debt (Sect. 10.5.4)
`ode_euler()`	Solve numerically first-order ordinary differential equations by applying Euler method (Sect. 11.1.6.1). In Sect. 11.7 we rewrite the function in a `deSolve` fashion
`ode_RungeKutta()`	Solve numerically first-order ordinary differential equations by applying Runge-Kutta method (Sect. 11.1.6.2). In Sect. 11.7 we rewrite the function in a `deSolve` fashion
`system_ode_euler()`	Solve numerically systems of two first-order differential equations by using the Euler method (Sect. 11.5). The replication of `system_ode_RungeKutta()` that uses the Runge-Kutta method is left as exercise
`ode2nd_euler()`	Solve numerically second-order ordinary differential equations by applying Euler method (Sect. 11.6). The replication of `ode2nd_RungeKutta()` that uses the Runge-Kutta method is left as exercise

of y_t as plot.[2] Finally, we will make use of some data management techniques in **R**. In particular, we will often reshape data from wide to long because, as we will see, this is the most efficient way to plot with `ggplot()`.

Now that the talk has been done, it is time to start.

Ad maiora

Kobe, Japan Massimiliano Porto

[2] All figures in the book are reproducible. However, the code for some figures is made available in the appendix corresponding to the chapter to make the presentation smoother.

Contents

List of Figures

List of Tables

Chapter 1
Introduction to R

This chapter introduces the reader to **R** (R Core Team 2020) and **RStudio** (RStudio Team 2020). The **R** version used in this book is 4.0.2. You can retrieve the version info by typing `sessionInfo()` in the console pane (Sect. 1.3). Following I print the first lines of the output of `sessionInfo()` in my console pane.[1]

```
> sessionInfo()
R version 4.0.2 (2020-06-22)
Platform: x86_64-w64-mingw32/x64 (64-bit)
Running under: Windows 10 x64 (build 19042)
```

The **RStudio** version used in this book is 1.3.1056. You can retrieve this info by typing the following command in the console pane

```
> rstudioapi::versionInfo()$version
[1] '1.3.1056'
```

Note that even though you use a different version of **R** and **RStudio**, you can still run the code in this book. However, you may observe slight differences in the output. In Sect. 1.6.5, I will discuss a main difference if you use an **R** version before 4.0.0.

1.1 Installing R

R can be installed on different operating system such as Windows, Mac and Linux. The reader is referred to the Comprehensive R Archive Network (CRAN) (http://cran.r-project.org) for the instructions to install **R**.

[1] Do not write > because it is not part of the code—we will return to > in Sect. 1.5.1.

M. Porto, *Introduction to Mathematics for Economics with R*,
https://doi.org/10.1007/978-3-031-05202-6_1

If you have Windows, you may refer to:
https://cran.r-project.org/bin/windows/base/
If you have Mac, you may refer to:
https://cran.r-project.org/bin/macosx/

1.2 Installing RStudio

RStudio is an integrated development environment (IDE) that makes easier to work with **R**. You can download **RStudio Desktop**—Open Source License—at the following page:
https://www.rstudio.com/products/rstudio/download/

1.3 Introduction to RStudio

If you open **RStudio**, you will see a screen like in Fig. 1.1. The interface of **RStudio** is divided in 4 panes.

Console pane: the console pane (1 in Fig. 1.1) is where you write your code, called **command** in **R language**.

Environment/History pane: in the environment/history pane (2 in Fig. 1.1) you can see all the objects you create in **R** and the history of your commands.

Fig. 1.1 RStudio interface

Files, plots, packages,.. pane: the pane number 3 in Fig. 1.1 is where you find your files, the packages you can install to improve the capabilities of **R**, where you can visualize the plots you create etc.

Source pane: the source pane (4 in Fig. 1.1) provides you different ways to write and save your code. This is the pane where we open the **R Script** and write the code in this book.

1.3.1 Launching a New Project

A project is a place to store your work on a particular topic (or project). To create a project follow the procedure as in Figs. 1.2, 1.3, and 1.4.

Click on the **R** symbol in the top hand right corner, click **New Directory** > **New Project** and then write the directory name (`Math_R` for this book) and click **Create project**.[2]

I strongly recommend creating projects whenever you start what you consider a new project, not related to previous projects. For example, observe Fig. 1.5. This figure tells us that currently I am in the working directory `Math_R`. You can see that I have other projects—for example a project about Econometrics in **R**, a project about creating maps in **R** and so on. Those projects are not related to the project `Math_R`. Therefore, for each of them I created a project. For example, if I wanted to switch to the project regarding Econometrics, I would just click

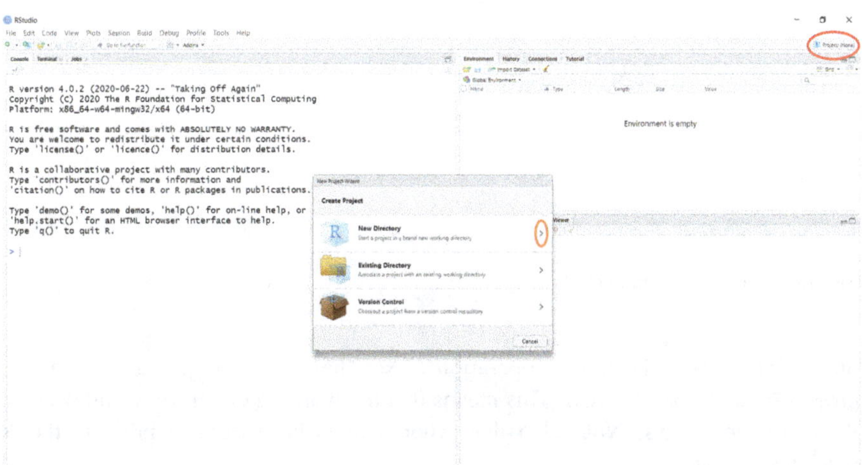

Fig. 1.2 Launch a new project (1)

---

[2] If you have already created a directory, you can click **Existing Directory**.

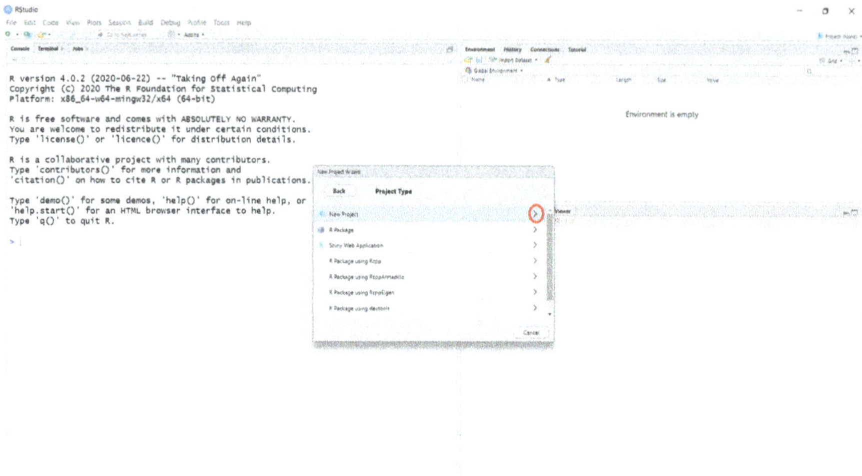

Fig. 1.3 Launch a new project (2)

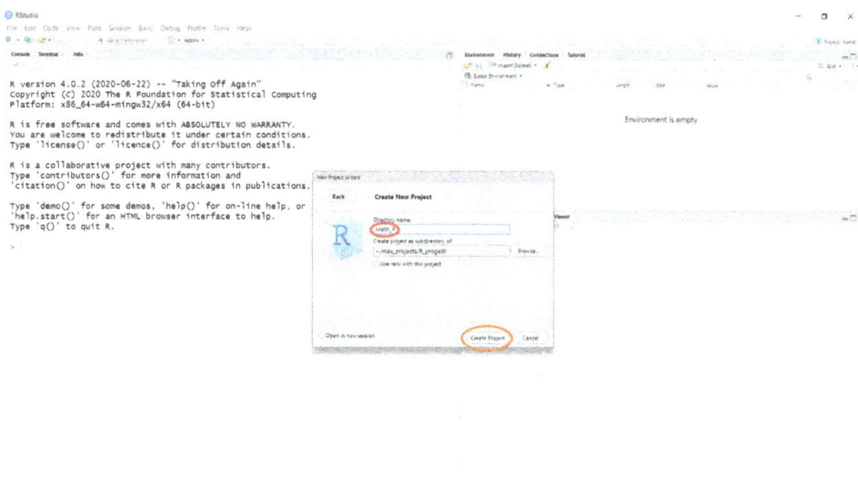

Fig. 1.4 Launch a new project (3)

on `R_Econometrics`. This operation closes the current project and opens the project `R_Econometrics`. This means that my working directory would become `R_Econometrics`. Note also that when you switch between projects the **R** session starts again.

Now let's suppose that you start working without creating a project. In this case you can check your working directory by typing `getwd()` in the command pane. For example, my current working directory is

```
> getwd()
[1] "C:/Users/porto/OneDrive/Documenti/R_progetti/Math_R"
```

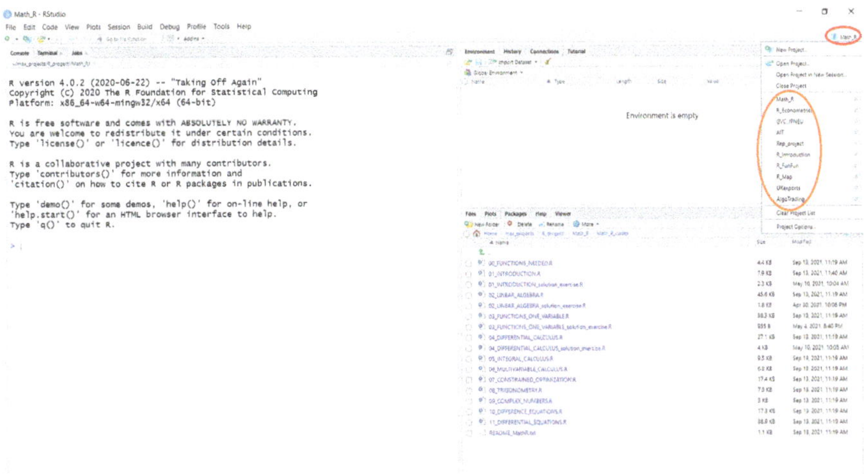

Fig. 1.5 Navigate through projects

If you want to change the working directory, write the new directory path in the brackets of `setwd()` again not really recommended. A better practice when you are already working in **R** without having created a project would be that you associate a project with an existing working directory (refer to Fig. 1.2).

The working directory includes the following files:

- **.RData**: Holds the objects etc in your environment;
- **.RHistory**: Holds the history of what you typed in the console;
- **.RProfile**: Holds specific setup information for the working directory you are in. For example, if you want to disable the scientific notation in **R** and set the number of digits at 4 for your output, you can write `options("scipen"=9999, digits=4)` in **.RProfile** (I did not set it for this book). In this way, this option will be loaded when you open your project.
  - To check if you created the **.RProfile**, write `file.exists("~/.Rprofile")` in the console pane. If you did not, **R** will return the value `FALSE`.
  - By typing `file.edit("~/.Rprofile")` in the console pane you can create the **.RProfile**.

Before continuing, let's create a folder in our working directory called `images`. This folder will contain all the figures that we will create in this book. For this task write `dir.create("images")` in the console pane after creating the `Math_R` project (from now onward I assume that you are in the working directory `Math_R`)

```
> dir.create("images")
```

1.3.2 *Opening an R Script*

We open an **R Script** file in **RStudio** as shown in Fig. 1.6. Before starting working, it is good practice to save it (Fig. 1.7).

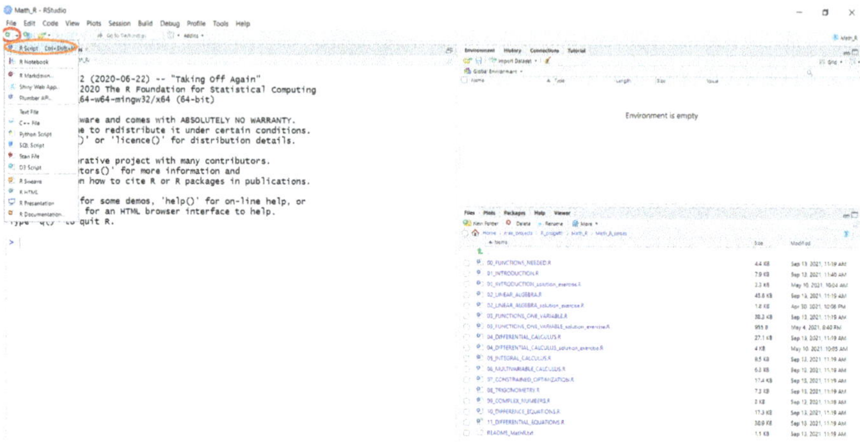

Fig. 1.6 Open an R script

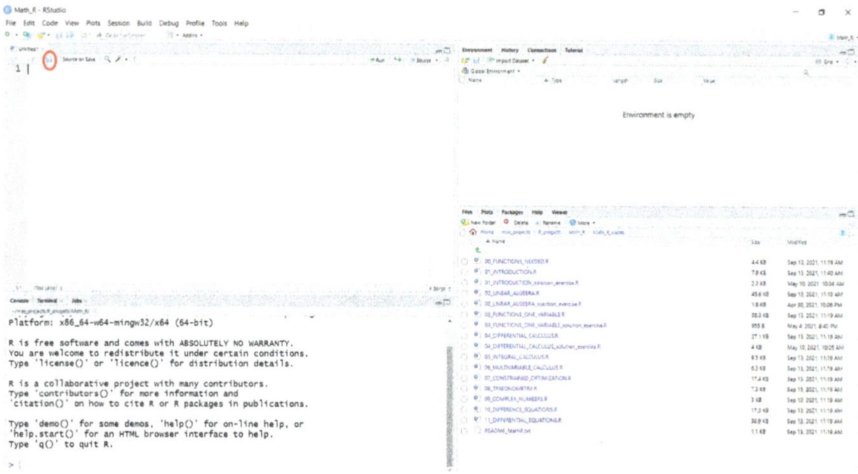

Fig. 1.7 Save an R script

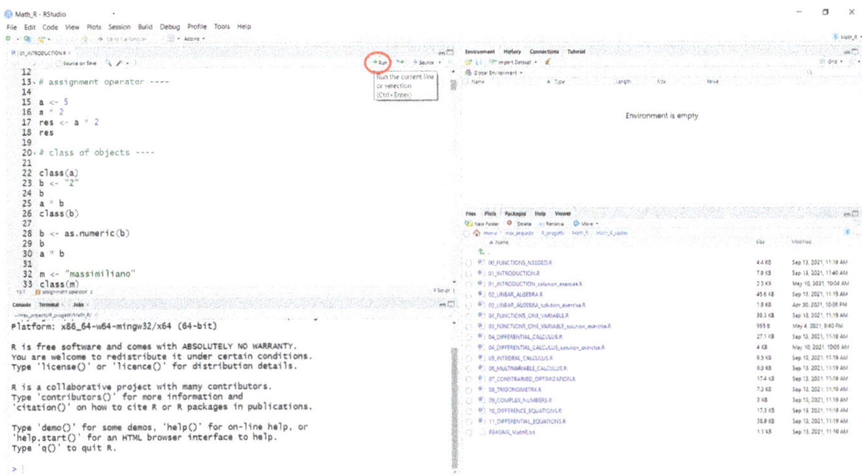

Fig. 1.8 Run button in RStudio

To run a code in the **R Script**, for a single line of code place the mouse pointer before the code, for a block of lines select it, and then click the `Run` button (Fig. 1.8), or press `Ctrl + Enter` on a Windows system.

1.4 Packages to Install

Packages extend the capability of **R**.

To reproduce step by step the code in this book, you need to install the following packages:

- `zoo` (Zeileis & Grothendieck 2005) (version 1.8.8)
- `igraph` (Csardi and Nepusz 2006) (version 1.2.6)
- `ggplot2` (Wickham 2009) (version 3.3.2)
- `deSolve` (Soetaert et al. 2010) (version 1.28)
- `png` (Urbanek 2013) (version 0.1.7)
- `blockmatrix` (Cordano 2014) (version 1.0)
- `manipulate` (Allaire 2014) (version 1.0.1)
- `phaseR` (Grayling 2014) (version 2.1.3)
- `mosaic` (Pruim et al. 2017) (version 1.8.3)
- `mosaicCalc` (Kaplan et al. 2017) (version 0.5.1)
- `data.table` (Dowle and Srinivasan 2017) (version 1.13.2)
- `gifski` (Ooms 2018) (version 0.8.6)
- `nleqslv` (Hasselman 2018) (version 3.3.2)
- `scales` (Wickham 2018) (version 1.1.1)
- `stargazer` (Hlavac 2018) (version 5.2.2)

- Deriv (Clausen and Sokol 2019) (version 4.1.3)
- dplyr (Wickham et al. 2019) (version 1.0.2)
- expm (Goulet et al. 2019) (version 0.999.6)
- ggpubr (Kassambara 2019) (version 0.4.0)
- leaflet (Cheng et al. 2019) (version 2.0.3)
- polynom (Venables et al. 2019) (version 1.4.0)
- pracma (Borchers 2019) (version 2.3.3)
- plot3D (Soetaert 2019) (version 1.3)
- RVenn (Akyol 2019) (version 1.1.0)
- tidyr (Wickham & Henry 2019) (version 1.1.2)
- gganimate (Pedersen and Robinson 2020) (version 1.0.7)
- lpSolve (Berkelaar et al. 2020) (version 5.6.15)
- nloptr (Johnson 2020) (version 1.2.2.2)
- rgl (Murdoch and Adler 2021) (version 0.106.8)

We will talk about these packages when we use them in the next chapters.[3]

1.4.1 How to Install a Package

You install a package in **R** with the function install.packages(). Write the name of the package you want to install in quotation marks. For example,

```
> install.packages("Deriv")
```

You install the package once. If a new version is released, you can update the package by using the function update.packages().

An alternative way—that I prefer—is to install packages in **RStudio** as shown in Figs. 1.9 and 1.10.

1.4.2 How to Load a Package

After you installed the package, you need to load the package in **R** with the library() function to use it. For example,

```
> library("Deriv")
```

You need to load the package you want to use anytime you start a new **R** session. Refer to Appendix A for the list of packages you need to load before replicating the code in the next chapters.

[3] In parenthesis the package version used in this book. For example, to retrieve the package version of nloptr after you installed it: packageVersion("nloptr"). Again, it should be fine to replicate this code even though you have a different version.

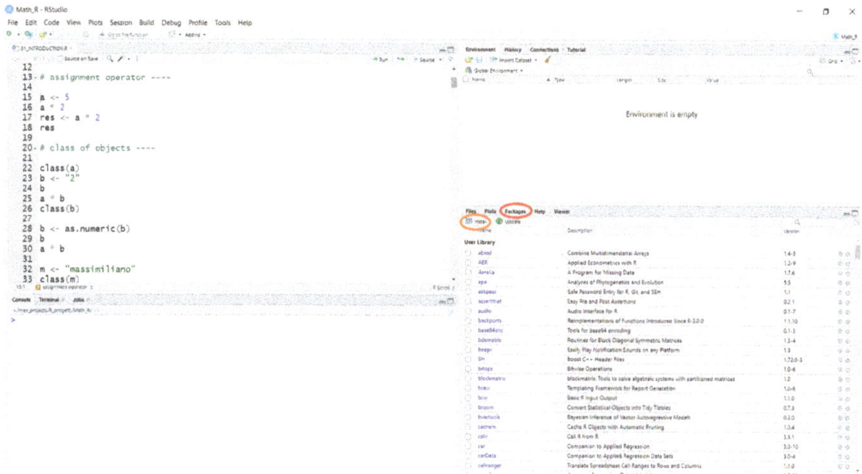

Fig. 1.9 Packages in RStudio

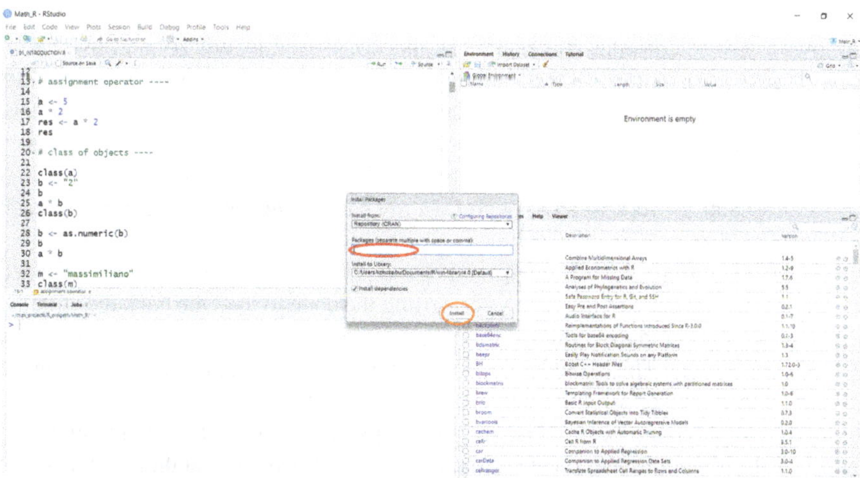

Fig. 1.10 Install packages in RStudio

1.5 Good Practice and Notation

Before starting to replicate the code in this book, make sure you are in the working directory `Math_R`.

Next step is to open an **R Script**. Even though we could write the code directly in the console pane, as we did when we created the folder `images`, it is better to write the code in an **R Script** when we have to write more than one line of code. The commands in an **R Script** can be easily traced back, modified and shared with colleagues. In an **R Script**, it is possible to add comments using `#`. Everything that

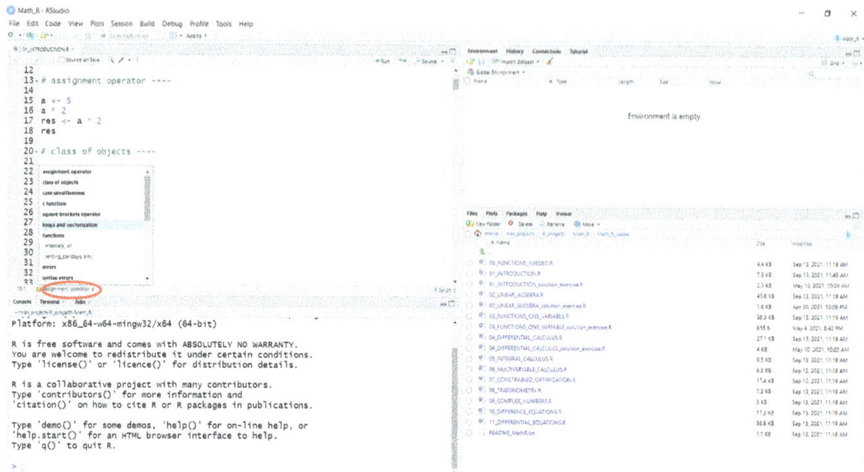

Fig. 1.11 Table of contents in an R script file

follows # will be considered as comment and, consequently, will be not run by **R**. If you want to write multiple lines of comments you may want to use `#'`. Additionally, it is possible to set up a table of contents in an **R Script** file by typing at least four trailing dashes (-), equal signs (=), or pound signs (#). This allows to navigate easily through the script file. For an example refer to Fig. 1.11. Therefore, we can say that it is convenient to work in an **R Script**. In my case, I created an **R Script** for each chapter.

At the beginning of any **R Script**, it is good practice to type the packages needed to implement the code in the file. After writing the code to load the package with the `library()` function, you may add, as comment, a keyword to remind about the use of the package. This would help us to remember the content of the file and make clear to a third person what will be needed to implement the code in the **R Script**.

It is also good practice to describe the project and write short comments in the body of the functions we create. Again this is useful for the author of the script and for a third person who will read the code. However, in this book I will not include any comment in the body of the functions that we will write because I will extensively explain each step of the function in the text.

Finally, a last remark before starting working: to avoid confusion in the text of this book, we will use the following `font` for all the words related to the **R** code we will write. Additionally, all the functions will be written with parenthesis. For example, `sum()` is the base **R** function for summation while `mtable()` is a function that we will write to compute multiplication tables. This notation is adopted to distinguish functions from other type of objects that will be written without parentheses.

1.5.1 How to Read the Code

In this book, to illustrate the code and its outcome, I will print out the code from the console pane, i.e. preceded by >, the prompt symbol. > is not part of the code. It signals that **R** is ready to operate. But keep in mind that I run the code from the **R Script** file. And I suggest you do the same to replicate the code in this book. Let's have a look to see how the two codes look like.

An example of a one line code in **R Script**

```
x <- seq(-10, 10, 0.1)
```

and the same code printed in the console pane

```
> x <- seq(-10, 10, 0.1)
```

For one line of code it may seem that the difference is not so relevant.

Here, an example with two lines of code in **R Script**

```
x <- seq(-10, 10,
         0.1)
```

and the same code printed in the console pane

```
> x <- seq(-10, 10,
+          0.1)
```

Now, note that in the code in the console pane there is a + that is missing in the code in the **R Script** file. Basically, this + is not part of the code. It means that the code is continuing on the following line. It is not needed in the **R Script**.

Let's see another example. The following example is a plot from Chap. 3 generated by using the `ggplot()` function (do not write it now).

This is how the code looks like in the **R Script**

```
ggplot(df) +
  stat_function(aes(x), fun = lqc_fn,
                args = list(a = 1, c = 0)) +
  geom_hline(yintercept = 0) +
  geom_vline(xintercept = 0) +
  theme_minimal() +
  annotate("text", x = 0, y = 45,
           label = "Inflection point")
```

and the same code printed in the console pane

```
> ggplot(df) +
+   stat_function(aes(x), fun = lqc_fn,
+                 args = list(a = 1, c = 0)) +
+   geom_hline(yintercept = 0) +
```

```
+    geom_vline(xintercept = 0) +
+    theme_minimal() +
+    annotate("text", x = 0, y = 45,
+             label = "Inflection point")
>
```

Note that in this case we have one + from the **R Script** file and two + from the console pane. The + in the **R Script** file is part of the code. This is a feature of the `ggplot()` code. On the other hand, the second +, directly below the prompt symbol, >, is not part of our code and it just means that the code continues on the next line. When **R** has finished to run the code, the prompt symbol, >, will appear again meaning that **R** is ready to take a new command.

1.6 8 Key-Points Regarding R

Is **R** hard to learn? If we surf the net to find an answer to this question, it seems that **R** is hard to learn. In this section, I would like to share my own experience in learning **R** with the reader.

R is not the first statistical software I learnt. When I was a PhD student I moved from a property software to **R** to work with two professors of mine who used it. And yes, at the beginning it has been very hard. I was getting errors after errors. I was spending more time to clean the errors than to accomplish my tasks. However, the more errors I solved (mainly thanks to the community of Stack Overflow) the more I started to appreciate **R**. When I got used to the **R** language, I figured out what made it difficult for me at the beginning. Following I list the 8 key-points regarding **R**—with examples—that I think every beginner should grasp when working with **R**.

1.6.1 The Assignment Operator

The assignment operator, `<-`, is used to assign values to variables.

For example, we store 5 in an object, `a`. We can compute operations with `a` as we were dealing directly with 5

```
> a <- 5
> a * 2
[1] 10
```

We can store the result of this multiplication in another object, `res`. In this case, we do not see the result of the operation, that is stored in `res`, unless we run the object

```
> res <- a * 2
> res
[1] 10
```

We can store different kinds of objects, such as functions and plots with `ggplot()`.

1.6.2 The Class of Objects

In **R**, we work with different types of objects. We check the type of object with the `class()` function. For example, the object we generated earlier is `numeric`.

```
> class(a)
[1] "numeric"
```

Now, let's generate an object, `b`, that stores 2. Note that we add quotation marks.

```
> b <- "2"
> b
[1] "2"
```

Let's multiply `a` times `b`. We should get 10 but

```
> a * b
Error in a * b : non-numeric argument to binary operator
```

we get an error. The error says `non-numeric argument to binary operator`. We already know that `a` is `numeric`. What about `b`?

```
> class(b)
[1] "character"
```

As we can see, although `b` stores 2, it stores it as `character` and not as `numeric` because we enclosed it in quotation marks. In the **R** language we cannot multiply a numeric value by a character value and consequently we get the error.[4]

Now it is clear what caused the error. We should have stored 2 as numeric value. Currently, `b` stores something that is very close to a numeric 2. Basically, we need to remove the quotation marks. We have the opportunity to introduce a group of functions that starts with `as.` such as `as.numeric()`, `as.integer()`, `as.character()`, `as.data.frame()`, an so on. These functions coerce a class of an object to another class. In our case, we use the `as.numeric()` function.

[4] We need to specify that this operation does not work in the **R** language. In fact, if you are a Python user you are aware that in Python this is a legit operation that replicates the string many times as determined by the numeric value.

```
> class(b)
[1] "character"
> b <- as.numeric(b)
> b
[1] 2
> a * b
[1] 10
```

We got the expected results. Note that to use this group of functions, the object needs to have the “quality” to be coerced. For example, I store my name in `m`. It is a `character`. In this case we fail the coercion to `numeric` because **R** does not know how to coerce a string of letters to a number.[5]

```
> m <- "massimiliano"
> class(m)
[1] "character"
> m <- as.numeric(m)
Warning message:
NAs introduced by coercion
> m
[1] NA
```

1.6.3 Case Sensitiveness

If we use the same name for an object, the second object overwrites the first object. In the previous section, we wrote

```
> b <- as.numeric(b)
```

In that case, we overwrote the previous `b` that was a `character`. However, observe the following example,

```
> b <- 3
> b
[1] 3
> b <- 2
> b
[1] 2
> B <- 4
> B
[1] 4
> b
[1] 2
```

[5] `NA` stands for `Not Available`. We will return to `Warning message` in Sect. 1.6.8.

The object b initially stores 3. We overwrite it so that it stores 2. On the other hand, if we assign 4 to B this does not affect b. In fact, b and B are two different objects. In other words, **R** is a case sensitive language.

1.6.4 *The c() Function*

The `c()` function is used to concatenate items separated by a comma `,`. For example,

```
> d <- c(1, 2, 3, 4, 5)
> d
[1] 1 2 3 4 5
> e <- c("a", "b", "c", "d", "e")
> e
[1] "a" "b" "c" "d" "e"
```

We can also concatenate the objects we generated. For example, we concatenate the objects d, a, and b. Note that the values of d, a and b are added to the new object, dab, in the order we concatenate them.

```
> dab <- c(d, a, b)
> dab
[1] 1 2 3 4 5 5 2
```

However, note the following

```
> de <- c(d,e)
> de
 [1] "1" "2" "3" "4" "5" "a" "b" "c" "d" "e"
```

Note the quotation marks around the numbers. What is the issue here? This happens because the `c()` function cannot store items with different classes. Consequently, **R** will coerce the different types of items to a common type. In this case, **R** coerced every item to be a `character`. Then, what about if we are not satisfied with this solution? We can use the `list()` function to store the objects in a single object keeping their characteristics.

```
> l <- list(d, e)
> l
[[1]]
[1] 1 2 3 4 5

[[2]]
[1] "a" "b" "c" "d" "e"
```

```
> class(l)
[1] "list"
> class(l[[1]])
[1] "numeric"
> class(l[[2]])
[1] "character"
```

1.6.5 Square Bracket Operator `[ ]`

The square bracket operator `[ ]` has the function to subset, extract, or replace a part of an object such as a vector, a matrix or a data frame. For example, we select the first entry in the `e` object as follows

```
> e[1]
[1] "a"
```

Remember that the **R** language starts indexing from 1. Consequently, `"a"` is extracted because it is stored as the first entry in the `e` object.

If we run the `e` object again, we find that no modification has been made.

```
> e
[1] "a" "b" "c" "d" "e"
```

But as we said, `[ ]` can be used to replace an item from an object. In this case, we have just to assign a new value. For example,

```
> e[1] <- "m"
> e
[1] "m" "b" "c" "d" "e"
```

We replaced the first entry in `e`, i.e. `"a"` with `"m"`. That is, we overwrote the first element of `e`.

Let's rewrite the `e` object as before. Note that this time instead of typing each letter we are selecting them from the built-in object `letters`. Exactly, we are selecting the letters from 1 to (`:`) 5 that correspond to letters from *a* to *e*.

```
> e <- letters[1:5]
> e
[1] "a" "b" "c" "d" "e"
```

We can generate a new object, `e1`, and assign the first value from the `e` object as follows

```
> e1 <- e[1]
> e1
[1] "a"
```

If we want to subset for more that one value, we combine `[ ]` with the `c()` function. For example,

```
> e[c(1, 3)]
[1] "a" "c"
```

subsets for the first element and third element of `e`, that are `"a"` and `"c"`, respectively.

If we want to subset for consecutive values we can use the `:` operator. For example, to select entries from 1 to 3

```
> e[1:3]
[1] "a" "b" "c"
```

This is what we did with the `letters` object.

Until now we worked with one dimension. Let's see a few examples with a data frame that is an object with two dimensions.[6] We use the `data.frame()` function to create a data frame. We name this data frame as `df`. We create it by using `d` and `e` we created earlier. We set the column title for `d` and `e`, `numbers` and `letters`, respectively. Note that to create a data frame it is necessary that the objects we use—in this case `d` and `e`—have the same length, i.e. the same number of items. As `list()`, a data frame allows to store different types of object.

```
> df <- data.frame(numbers = d,
+                  letters = e)
> df
  numbers letters
1       1       a
2       2       b
3       3       c
4       4       d
5       5       e
```

The structure of `df` is rows per columns. Therefore, we need an index for the row and an index for the column. For example, if we want to select `d`, we observe that is located at row number 4 and column number 2. We use again the `[ , ]` but this time we add a comma `,` to separate the row dimension from the column dimension.

```
> df[4, 2]
[1] "d"
```

If we want to select more than one element, we use the `c()` function.

```
> df[4, c(1, 2)]
  numbers letters
```

[6] You may think of a data frame as an Excel spreadsheet.

```
4          4          d
> df[c(3, 5), 2]
[1] "c" "e"
> df[c(3, 5), c(1, 2)]
  numbers letters
3       3       c
5       5       e
```

In the first case, we selected one row, 4, and two column indexes, 1 for `numbers` and 2 for `letters`. In the second case, we selected two row indexes, 3 and 5, and one column index, 2. In the last case we selected two row indexes and two column indexes. What about selecting all the rows for the first column? We leave blank the spot for the row before the comma as follows

```
> df[, 1]
[1] 1 2 3 4 5
```

Consequently, if we leave blank the spot for the columns after the comma, we select all the columns for row indexes. For example,

```
> df[c(2, 4), ]
  numbers letters
2       2       b
4       4       d
```

Note that we can use the name of columns as well to extract the entries for the corresponding column. For example,

```
> df[, "numbers"]
[1] 1 2 3 4 5
> df[2, "letters"]
[1] "b"
```

We can replace an element from a data frame with the same pattern we saw before. Let's replace the entry in the first row and first column with 10.

```
> df[1, 1] <- 10
> df
  numbers letters
1      10       a
2       3       b
3       5       c
4       7       d
5       9       e
```

Additionally, note that `data.frame()` before **R** version 4.0.0 by default converted character vectors to factors. We can replicate it by setting `strings AsFactors = TRUE` in the `data.frame()` function. Let's do it

```
> df <- data.frame(numbers = d,
+                  letters = e,
+                  stringsAsFactors = TRUE)
> df
  numbers letters
1       1       a
2       2       b
3       3       c
4       4       d
5       5       e
```

Note that now `letters` in `df` are stored as `factor`, i.e., categorical variables that take a limited number of different values. `levels` is an attribute that provides the identity of each category.

```
> class(df$letters)
[1] "factor"
> df[4, 2]
[1] d
Levels: a b c d e
```

Sometimes factors can be replaced by character data. We use the `as.character()` function to force it to be `character`. For example,

```
> df$letters <- as.character(df$letters)
> class(df$letters)
[1] "character"
```

Finally, note that we have other two operators acting on vectors, matrices, arrays, lists, and data frames to extract or replace parts: double square brackets `[[ ]]` and $ operators.[7] The most important difference is that `[ ]` can select more than one element whereas the other two select a single element.

```
> l[[1]]
[1] 1 3 5 7 9
```

We extracted the content stored at index 1 of the list `l` we generated earlier.

Let's assign names to the objects stored in the list `l` with the `names()` function. Note that in **R** the order is extremely important. In our case, we assign two names, `numbers` and `letters`. The first name will be assign to the first object stored at index 1 and the second name will be assigned to the second object stored at index 2. Then, we can select the object by name with $

```
> names(l) <- c("numbers", "letters")
> l
$numbers
[1] 1 2 3 4 5
```

[7] $ works for lists and data frames.

```
$letters
[1] "a" "b" "c" "d" "e"

> l$numbers
[1] 1 2 3 4 5
```

With $ operator, we can select the column of a data frame by its name

```
> df$numbers
[1] 1 3 5 7 9
```

In addition, we can use it to create a new column in the data frame by typing $ after the name of the data frame and before the name of the column we choose, and with the values to be assigned to the new column

```
> df$new <- c(0, 1, 0, 1, 0)
> df
  numbers letters new
1       1       a   0
2       3       b   1
3       5       c   0
4       7       d   1
5       9       e   0
```

1.6.6 Loop and Vectorization

Let's suppose we want to compute the multiplication table for 2, i.e, $2 \times 1, 2 \times 2, 2 \times 3, ..., 2 \times 10$. That is, we want to multiply 2 times 1 and print the result. Then, multiply 2 times 2 and print the results, and so on until 2 times 10. Basically, this is a loop. We can generate this kind of loops in **R** with the `for()` function. In the `for()` function we have three keys elements:

- `i` is a syntactical name for a value (as we will see later we can choose any name for it)
- `in` is an operator
- a sequence. In this example, we generate a sequence with the `seq()` function where we indicate the minimum and the maximum value and the increment amount between each value. We store the sequence in the `s` object.
- finally, note that the loop steps are enclosed in curly brackets.

```
> s <- seq(1, 10, 1)
> s
 [1]  1  2  3  4  5  6  7  8  9 10
> for(i in s){
```

```
+   res <- 2 * i
+   print(res)
+ }
[1] 2
[1] 4
[1] 6
[1] 8
[1] 10
[1] 12
[1] 14
[1] 16
[1] 18
[1] 20
```

What is happening? Basically, when the loop starts, `i` is 1. Therefore, `2 * 1` is multiplied, stored in `res` and printed with the `print()` function. Then, the loop moves to the second index in the sequence that in this case is 2. This means that now `i` is 2 and `2 * 2` is multiplied and so on. The loop stops at the end of the sequence, i.e. the last operation is when `i` is 10.

`for()` loop

Loops are generated by the `for()` function.
The structure of a `for()` loop is the following:

```
for(value in sequence){
steps of commands
}
```

where:

- `value`: is an syntactical name for a value. It can be any name as we will see in a following example;
- `in`: is an operator that points where to look for the `value`;
- `sequence`: a vector or a data frame with values to loop over;
- `steps of commands`: the steps of commands you want the loop go through. They are enclosed by { }

However, in **R** we can avoid writing loops like the previous one because we can benefit from the *vectorization* of **R**. We can obtain the same results just multiplying 2 by a vector from 1 to 10 as follows. Note that in this case we use the colon operator `:` to generate the same sequence as before.

```
> n <- 1:10
> n
 [1]  1  2  3  4  5  6  7  8  9 10
> 2 * n
 [1]  2  4  6  8 10 12 14 16 18 20
```

Another kind of loop that is often used is the `while()` loop. The `while()` loop is trickier than the `for()` loop. The main difference is that the `for()` loop iterates over a sequence while the `while()` loop iterates over a conditional statement. The issue is that a sequence can be very long but it is finished, i.e. at the end of the sequence the loop will stop. On the other hand, if we wrongly define the conditional statement or we forget to write the step to modify the conditional statement in the `while()` function, the loop will iterate infinitely times. If this happens, just break the loop by clicking on the `stop` button that will appear in the console pane.

Let's consider a simple example. Let's say we want to print the numbers from 10 to 0 included with a `while()` loop. First, we assign the starting point, 10, to `x`. Then, we write the `while()` loop. The conditional statement in our case is that $x \geq 0$. That is, the loop has to iterate as long as x is greater or equal to 0. Now, keep in mind that we assigned 10 to `x`. That is, `x` is greater than 0. If we do not modify `x` in the `while()` loop so that at a given moment `x` will turn less than 0—and the fulfillment of this condition stops the loop—the loop will run infinitely times because `x` remains greater than 0. Note that also for the `while()` loop the steps of commands are enclosed by `{ }`. In code,

```
> x <- 10
> while(x >= 0){
+   print(x)
+   x <- x - 1
+ }
[1] 10
[1] 9
[1] 8
[1] 7
[1] 6
[1] 5
[1] 4
[1] 3
[1] 2
[1] 1
[1] 0
```

As you can see, in the body of the `while()` function, `print(x)` prints out `x`. Then, we assign a new value to `x` every time the loop iterates. Again, let's go through each step. At the beginning, `x` is 10. Is 10 greater than 0? That's true. The conditional statement is satisfied. Then, `x` is printed, i.e. its value 10 is printed. Before the end of the loop we reassign a value for `x`. In this case we subtract 1 from `x` meaning that `x` becomes 9. Let's ask: is 9 greater than 0? Again, that's true. And again the conditional statement is satisfied and the same steps are implemented. But now, `x` becomes 8. That is still greater than 0. Now let's say that `x` has become 1. Its value is printed and the value 0 is assigned to `x`. The conditional statement that we wrote is true for $x \geq 0$. Meaning that the conditional statement is still satisfied.

Therefore, 0 is printed out. But now x becomes -1. This violates the conditional statement. The conditional statement has turned false and this stops the loop.

If we implement the same task with the `for()` loop

```
> s <- 10:0
> for(i in s){
+   print(i)
+ }
[1] 10
[1] 9
[1] 8
[1] 7
[1] 6
[1] 5
[1] 4
[1] 3
[1] 2
[1] 1
[1] 0
```

As you can see, in this case we already know when the loop will eventually stop. A "side effect" of using a `for()` loop is that at the end of the loop the "unwanted" `i` object is created storing the last value—in this case 0.

`while()` loop

The `while()` loop is another common way to implement loop in **R**. The structure of a `while()` loop is the following:

```
while(conditional statement){
steps of commands
expression that will turn the conditional statement
to false
}
```

where:

- `conditional statement`: the condition that activates the loop;
- `steps of commands`: the steps of commands you want the loop go through. They are enclosed by `{ }`

Again, for this simple task we can avoid using any loop. In fact, by running the sequence `s` we generated we obtain the countdown as well

```
> s
 [1] 10  9  8  7  6  5  4  3  2  1  0
```

1.6.7 Functions

Now, let's continue with the example of the multiplication table and let's say we want to compute the multiplication table for 3 as well. And then for 4, 5, and so on.

```
> 3 * n
 [1]  3  6  9 12 15 18 21 24 27 30
> 4 * n
 [1]  4  8 12 16 20 24 28 32 36 40
> 5 * n
 [1]  5 10 15 20 25 30 35 40 45 50
```

In this code, we can observe that `n` is in common and the output changes based on the the inputs 3, 4, and 5. In this case, we may think to build a function to compute these calculations. We build a function with the `function()` function. We store it in an object, that in this case we call `mtable`.

```
> mtable <- function(x) x * n
```

Our first simple function is now ready. If we want to compute the multiplication table for 2, we just need to write 2 in `mtable()`. This value will be used to replace `x` in `x * n` in the function.

```
> mtable(2)
 [1]  2  4  6  8 10 12 14 16 18 20
```

And, of course, if we want the multiplication table for 5 we write

```
> mtable(5)
 [1]  5 10 15 20 25 30 35 40 45 50
```

We can store the results of a function in an object as well. For example,

```
> mtab10 <- mtable(10)
> mtab10
 [1]  10  20  30  40  50  60  70  80  90 100
```

We can note two critical points of our function. First, `n` is defined outside the environment of the function. Second, `n` is not flexible. What about computing the multiplication table up to 15? and up to 20? We should rewrite `n` each time. Clearly, this would not be efficient. Let's try to fix `mtable()`.

```
> mtable <- function(x, w = 10){
+   n <- 1:w
+   res <- x*n
+   return(res)
+ }
```

We did what we wanted: (1) define `n` inside the environment of the function; and (2) make it flexible. But what did we do? We added a new argument to our function, `w`. Note that inside the function `w` is the end value of a sequence stored in `n` that starts with 1. In addition, we set `w` as a default argument. That is, it is set to 10. This choice depends on the fact that in most of the cases we want the multiplication table up to 10. So we do not want to bother ourselves typing every time 10. But this time, if we want a multiplication table up to 15, we just need to type 15 in the second entry of the function. Finally, note that we enclosed the code in curly brackets { }. We need them when we write the code of a function on multi-levels. However, it would have been more appropriate if we had used the curly brackets also for the first example of `mtable()`.

Functions

You can build your own functions using `function()`. For example, a structure of a function can be the following:

```
name_function <- function(x1, x2){
step1 <- x1 and some operations
step2 <- x2 and some operations
output <- step1 + step2
return(output)
}
```

where:

- `name_function`: you assign the function to an object;
- `function()`: in the parenthesis you type the arguments of the function, `x1` and `x2` in this example;
- `steps of commands`: the steps of commands you want the function go through. They are enclosed by { } ;
- `return()`: is a function that returns the object from inside the function to the workspace.

Basically, you type step by step what the function needs to do. It will take the arguments from inside the parenthesis in `function`.

Now, let's see an example with the fixed `mtable()`. First, let's compute the multiplication table of 2 up to 10.

```
> mtable(2)
 [1]  2  4  6  8 10 12 14 16 18 20
```

And now up to 15.

```
> mtable(2, 15)
 [1]  2  4  6  8 10 12 14 16 18 20 22 24 26 28 30
```

Furthermore, note that the order of the arguments in the function matters unless we explicitly write the argument names. For example,

```
> mtable(15, 2)
[1] 15 30
> mtable(w = 15, x = 2)
 [1]  2  4  6  8 10 12 14 16 18 20 22 24 26 28 30
```

In the first case, 15 takes the place of `x` in `mtable()` while 2 takes the place of `w` in `mtable()`. On the other hand, we do not need to respect the positioning of the arguments if we explicitly write the names of the arguments in the function as in the second case. In other words, "**R** uses either named matching or positional matching to figure out the correct assignment" (Georgakopoulos 2015, p. 28).

Additionally, what I like about functions in **R** is that they can be seen as a neat correspondence of how we state mathematical functions. Let's consider a simple example. The cost, C, of renting a car in dollars depends on the number of days, d, we rent it and how many km, k, we drive. We are just expressing in English a function of two variables, $C = f(d, k)$.[8] Let's say that renting a car costs 30$ per day and 0.15$ per km. We can write the functional form to compute the rental cost as $C = f(d, k) = 30d + 0.15k$. Therefore, what is the cost of renting a car for 2 days and driving it 100 km? Or, in other words, $C = f(d = 2, k = 100)$ (we can omit d and k as well, i.e., $C = f(2, 100)$).

In **R**, we set the function and find the solution as follows

```
> renting_car <- function(days, km){
+   res <- 30*days + 0.15*km
+   return(res)
+ }
> renting_car(2, 100)
[1] 75
```

This means that the cost of renting a car for 2 days and driving it 100 km is $75.

A final remark is that we could safely write `C <- function(d, k)`, and, consequently, `res <- 30*d + 0.15*k` and `C(2, 100)`. Naturally, `renting_car()` and `C()` produce the same results and they are both fine. However, clearly, the former is more readable.

[8] We could add that days and km cannot take negative values because it makes no sense to rent a car for a negative number of days or drive for a negative amount of km. Basically, this turns to be just a domain restriction. We will discuss about functions of one variable and functions of several variables in Chaps. 3 and 6, respectively.

1.6.8 Errors

I want to conclude this section talking about errors. When we make an error, we get an error message in red that can be intimidating and frustrating. When I started to learn **R** I have to admit it was quite discouraging. In addition, I learn **R** after learning a property statistical software that is objectively more user-friendly. Consequently, as a beginner in **R** I was making a lot of errors. As you can imagine, the errors indeed did not discourage me. I got even more passionate about **R** after solving the errors I was doing. I think, indeed, that when we solve errors we really learn how to use **R** (but this can be extended to any software). This short introduction about my experience is just to stress that everyone makes errors, above all at the beginning, and even the most expert users. Here I would like to talk about the most frequent errors I made when I started to learn **R**.

1.6.8.1 Syntax Errors

R is a language and as any language has its own grammar rules. For example, if in English I write "I, want to learn **R**" an English teacher would tell me I made an error because I put a comma between the subject and the verb. And something similar happens in **R**.

We can make "syntax errors" in **R**, i.e. errors due to write a part of code in the wrong place or to forget an essential element of the code. This kind of errors is the most recurrent case and, generally, it is extremely easy to fix. For example,

```
> a <- c(6, 7, 8, 9 10)
Error: unexpected numeric constant in "a <- c(6, 7, 8,
9 10"
```

Basically, we just forgot the comma `,` between 9 and 10.

Let's see another example. In **R**, we use many functions developed by the **R** Community members. All these functions come with documentation regarding their use. We access this documentation by typing a question mark before the name of the function or by using the `help()` function. For example,

```
> ?print
> ?"if"
> help("as.numeric")
```

For example, let's use the `lm()` function to fit a linear model. We generate some random data for the independent variable, `x`, by using the `rnorm()` function and then we generate the dependent variable `y`. We build then a data frame, `df`, with `x` and `y` and we print the first six entries with the `head()` function. Finally, we fit a linear model with the `lm()` function.

```
> x <- rnorm(100)
> y <- 10 + 5*x
> df <- data.frame(x, y)
> head(df)
           x         y
1 -1.1161285  4.419357
2  1.3803809 16.901904
3 -1.7812245  1.093877
4  0.9383783 14.691891
5 -0.4576268  7.711866
6 -1.7358237  1.320882
> model1 <- lm(y, x, data = df)
Error in formula.default(object, env = baseenv()) :
invalid formula
```

However, we got an error. If we investigate the documentation for the `lm()` function, we find out that we incorrectly wrote the formula, i.e. the description of the model. In fact, we should have used the regression operator $\sim$ to separate the dependent variable from the independent variables. We will correctly use the `lm()` function in Sect. 2.4.5.

1.6.8.2 class() Type Errors

This is the kind of error that we encountered when we tried to multiply a numeric value by a character value. If we compare this "class errors" with the "syntax errors", in this case we are correctly writing the code but the objects we use are not appropriate. Let's consider another example.

Let's build a data frame with the `data.frame()` function.

```
> df <- data.frame(a = c(1, 2),
+                  b = c(3, 4))
> df
  a b
1 1 3
2 2 4
```

Now this `df` object looks very similar to a matrix. Let's try to make a matrix multiplication (Sect. 2.3.1.2) with the operator %*%. To investigate the usage of this operator type ?"%*%".

Matrix Multiplication

Description
Multiplies two matrices, if they are conformable. If one argument is a vector, it will be promoted to either a row or column matrix to make the two arguments conformable. If both are vectors of the same length, it will return the inner product (as a matrix).
Usage
x %*% y
Arguments
x, y numeric or complex matrices or vectors.

After reading the documentation for %*%, do you think we can make a matrix multiplication between `df` and `df`? Let's try

```
> df %*% df
Error in df %*% df : requires numeric/complex matrix/
vector arguments
```

As you correctly imagined, we got an error. As the documentation and the error message tell us, the operator %*% requires numeric or complex matrices or vectors. But we have a `data.frame` type object.

```
> class(df)
[1] "data.frame"
```

Since this object is very similar to a matrix, let's try to coerce it to a `matrix` type object by using this time the `as.matrix.data.frame()` function.

```
> df <- as.matrix.data.frame(df)
> class(df)
[1] "matrix" "array"
```

Now, let's compute the matrix multiplication again.

```
> df %*% df
      a  b
[1,]  7 15
[2,] 10 22
```

And as expected now it works.

We should keep in mind that in some cases we can apply operations only with some type of objects. Therefore, it is very important to be aware about the type of objects we are working with.

1.6.8.3 Warning Message

Let's write a conditional statement with the `if()` function. We create an object, `x`, and set it equal to 10. We tell **R** to print `"yes"` *if* `x == 10`.[9] Because `x` is 10, the conditional statement is true and, consequently, the function prints `"yes"`. Then, let's set `x <- 9`. In this case the function does nothing because now `x` is equal to 9 and therefore the conditional statement is false.

```
> x <- 10
> if(x == 10) print("yes")
[1] "yes"
> x <- 9
> if(x == 10) print("yes")
```

But note the following.

```
> x <- 5:15
> x
 [1]  5  6  7  8  9 10 11 12 13 14 15
> if(x == 10) print("yes")
Warning message:
In if (x == 10) print("yes") :
  the condition has length > 1 and
  only the first element will be used
> if(x > 10) print("yes")
Warning message:
In if (x > 10) print("yes") :
  the condition has length > 1 and
  only the first element will be used
```

In these last cases, **R** prints a `Warning message`. We have to make a distinction between error and warning messages in **R**. When we get an error the function does not run. Instead, in the case of the warning message, it runs but **R** tells us something is unexpected.

In the example, the warning message says that `the condition has length > 1`, because we are working with an object that stores multiple values, and that `only the first element will be used`. In this case, the first value is 5 and therefore the function does nothing. But if the first value is 10 we have the following

```
> x <- 10:15
> if(x == 10) print("yes")
[1] "yes"
Warning message:
```

[9] Refer to Table 1.3 for logical operators.

```
In if (x == 10) print("yes") :
  the condition has length > 1 and
  only the first element will be used
```

The function prints "yes" because the first value now is 10. To convince ourselves that the function is really working let's add an `else` expression. Let's rebuild the x object from 5 to 15.

```
> x <- 5:15
> if(x == 10){
+   print("yes")
+ } else{
+   print("no")
+ }
[1] "no"
Warning message:
In if (x == 10) { :
  the condition has length > 1 and
  only the first element will be used
```

And as you can see now the function prints "no" because the first element, 5, is not equal to 10. However, we still get the warning message.

We could work out this warning message by nesting the `any()` function in the `if()` function as follows

```
> x <- 5:15
> if(any(x == 10)) print("yes")
[1] "yes"
```

However, let's say we want something different, i.e. that the function is evaluated at each value of x. A better solution would consist in picking another function. In this case, the `ifelse()` function

```
> ifelse(x == 10, "yes", "no")
 [1] "no"  "no"  "no"  "no"  "no"  "yes" "no"  "no"
     "no"  "no"  "no"
> ifelse(x > 10, "yes", "no")
 [1] "no"  "no"  "no"  "no"  "no"  "no"  "yes" "yes"
     "yes" "yes" "yes"
```

Finally, two pieces of advice. First, if we cannot solve the error after reading the documentation we simply can copy and paste the error or the warning message in a web search engine to look for more explanations and examples. You will find that in most of the cases your question has been already answered by the **R** Community. Second, since most of the **R** Community members communicate in English, it is convenient to set **R** in English. In this way **R** will print the error and warning messages in English. Consequently, we can find more examples for the case we are interested in.

Table 1.1 Math operators

Operator	Description	Example	Output
+	Addition	2 + 5	7
-	Subtraction	5 - 2	3
*	Multiplication	5 * 2	10
/	Division	5/2	2.5
^	Exponentiation	5^2	25
%%	Remainder	5 %% 2	1
%/%	Integer division	5 %/% 2	2

1.6.8.4 No-Error Message Error

In this book, we will code from scratch a number of functions (refer to Table 1). We should be aware about the most difficult errors to deal with that mainly occur when we build our own functions: that is, the function we write runs but it does not do what we programmed it for. The main issue is that because it runs we do not get any error or warning message so we may wrongly think that it properly works. An important check when we build our own function is to test it to replicate well-known results and examples.

1.7 An Example with R

In this section, we will go through some of the main features of **R** with a simple and progressive example. In particular, we will see **R** as calculator, as programming language (interactive mode, loop and functions), as statistical software and as graphical software.

Suppose a student took a test made up of 50 questions. She gets 3 points for each correct answer. In total she gave 43 correct answers. She wants to know her total score. We can make this multiplication in **R**

```
> 43*3
[1] 129
```

In this way, we are using **R** as calculator. Table 1.1 reports the most common operators. In addition, there are some built-in functions that extends the math capability. Refer to Table 1.2.[10]

Continuing with the example, we know that the total score of the student is 129.

However, if you skipped the first lines of the introduction to this section, this number would say nothing to you. Let's see how to reorganize the information.

[10] Note that `sum()`, `min()`, `max()` treat the collection of arguments as the vector. This is not the typical behaviour in **R**. In `cumsum()` and `mean()`, the `c()` function combines values into a vector (Burns 2011, p. 8).

Table 1.2 Math functions

Operator	Description	Example	Output
`sum()`	Sum of vector elements	`sum(5, 2, 3)`	`10`
`cumsum()`	Cumulative sums	`cumsum(c(5, 2, 3))`	`5 7 10`
`min()`	Minima	`min(5, 2, 3)`	`2`
`max()`	Maxima	`max(5, 2, 3)`	`5`
`mean()`	Average	`mean(c(5, 2, 3))`	`3.333333`
`sqrt()`	Square root	`sqrt(25)`	`5`
`abs()`	Absolute value	`abs(-5)`	`5`

We generate an object, `n_correct_answer`, that stores the number of correct answers. We accomplish this task using the assignment operator `<-`. Then, we generate another object, `point`, that stores the points per correct answer. Finally, we multiply these two objects.

```
> n_correct_answer <- 43
> point <- 3
> n_correct_answer * point
[1] 129
```

Now the information is clearer. Let's add a new step. Let's store the result of the multiplication in a new object, `total_score`.

```
> total_score <- n_correct_answer * point
```

Note that now we do not see the output of the operation because it is stored in `total_score`. To see the output, we have to run the object

```
> total_score
[1] 129
```

The number in the brackets points out the position of the printed element. In this case, 129 is the first element. Since we have only one element it may seem not a useful information. Let's see the output of `cumsum(1:25)`, where `:`, the colon operator, generates regular sequences, in this case, from 1 to 25. The output says that 120 is at the 15th index.

```
> cumsum(1:25)
  [1]   1   3   6  10  15  21  28  36  45  55  66  78  91 105
 [15] 120 136 153 171 190 210 231 253 276 300 325
```

Let's continue with the example. Suppose now we want to write a program that allows the students to enter their number of correct answers and calculates the total score. For this task, we use the `readline()` function. `readline()` reads a line from the terminal in interactive use.

We will assign to the object `n_correct_answer` the following input: `readline("Enter your number of correct answers: ")`. Note that the former score of the student will be overwritten.

When we run this object, **R** will ask to enter the input as follows

```
> n_correct_answer <- readline("Enter your number of
  correct answers: ")
Enter your number of correct answers:
```

If a student scored 39 she can enter it as follows.

```
> n_correct_answer <- readline("Enter your number of
  correct answers: ")
Enter your number of correct answers: 39
```

Now we multiply again the number of correct answers by the points, `point`.

```
> total_score <- n_correct_answer * point
Error in n_correct_answer * point :
  non-numeric argument to binary operator
```

But we got an error. The message says that we have a non-numeric argument even though we multiply 39 by 3. Why's that? Let's investigate our objects.

```
> class(point)
[1] "numeric"
```

By using the `class()` function we find out that `point` is a `numeric` class object. Let's check `n_correct_answer`.

```
> class(n_correct_answer)
[1] "character"
```

We found where the problem is. Even though we entered a number, 39, it is returned by the function as a `character`. Basically, we cannot multiply a number by a string. Therefore, we got an error. Let's solve the problem by coercing `n_correct_answer` from `character` to `numeric`. We do this by nesting the previous function in the `as.numeric()` function

```
> n_correct_answer <- as.numeric(
+   readline("Enter your number of correct answers: "))
Enter your number of correct answers: 39
```

Now, let's check again the score of the student.

```
> total_score <- n_correct_answer * point
> total_score
[1] 117
```

This student scored 117. We solved the problem. This example shows that it is important to know the `class` of an object we are dealing with because it can happen that some operations or functions work only with objects with a specific `class`.

Suppose now that we evaluate the tests of 7 students and collect the numbers of correct answers in the tests: 43, 39, 41, 36, 38, 48, 33. We want to calculate their scores.

We can do this by using a loop. First, we generate an object to collect the total score, `total_score`. Second, we collect all the numbers of correct answers in a vector using the `c()` function, `n_correct_answer`. Third, we define the object that stores the points, `point`.[11] Then we use a loop by using the `for()` function, where `i` is a syntactical name and `in` is an operator followed by a sequence. Note that the operations are enclosed in braces. The `print()` function prints out the output. How does the loop work? At the beginning, the `i` element is 43. This is multiplied by `point` and the result is stored in `total_score` and it is printed. Then, the loop starts again. Now the element `i` is 39. This is multiplied by `point` and the result is stored in `total_score` and then it is printed. This is repeated for the length of the sequence. In this case, 7 times.

```
> total_score <- 0
> n_correct_answer <- c(43, 39, 41, 36, 38, 48, 33)
> point <- 3
> for(i in n_correct_answer){
+   total_score <- i * point
+   print(total_score)
+ }
[1] 129
[1] 117
[1] 123
[1] 108
[1] 114
[1] 144
[1] 99
```

We obtained the scores for the 7 students. However, in this case the loop is not the best choice for this computation. We can just use the **R**'s vectorization feature. Basically, we just multiply the vector, `n_correct_answer`, by the scalar, `point`.

---

[11] Note that if you did not remove `point` or clear the objects from the workspace, you do not need to generate again `point` to make the loop work. However, we generate it again to make our work easy to understand. On the other hand, we do not really need to generate `total_score` out of the loop. We could remove it from the workspace with `rm()` and this would not affect the loop. However, when we want to store multiple results it is necessary to initialize it. We will talk again about the initialization of `total_score` in a few pages.

```
> names_stud <- c("Anne", "John", "Bob", "Emma",
+                  "Tony", "Sarah", "James")
> names(n_correct_answer) <- names_stud
> n_correct_answer
 Anne  John   Bob  Emma  Tony Sarah James
   43    39    41    36    38    48    33
> total_score <- n_correct_answer * point
> total_score
 Anne  John   Bob  Emma  Tony Sarah James
  129   117   123   108   114   144    99
```

Note also that we generated an object, `names_stud`, that contains the names of the students. By using the `names()` function, we set the names of `n_correct_answer`. Keep in mind that the order is key in **R**. For example, Anne is stored at index 1 in `names_stud`. Consequently, it is set as name of the item stored at index 1 in `n_correct_answer`.

Let's make another example with `for()` loop. Suppose that the students enter the number of correct answers in turn. We use the `readline()` function inside the loop.

```
> for(students in 1:length(names_stud)){
+   n_correct_answer <- as.numeric(
+   readline("Enter your number of correct answers: "))
+   total_score <- n_correct_answer * point
+   print(total_score)
+ }
Enter your number of correct answers: 43
[1] 129
Enter your number of correct answers: 39
[1] 117
Enter your number of correct answers: 41
[1] 123
Enter your number of correct answers: 36
[1] 108
Enter your number of correct answers: 38
[1] 114
Enter your number of correct answers: 48
[1] 144
Enter your number of correct answers: 33
[1] 99
```

In this example, first note that we use the name `students` as a syntactical name for a variable (basically, you can choose any name even though `i` for the first loop and `j` for the second loop are quite standard). Second, note how the sequence is written. We know that after `in` the sequence begins. We already know the meaning of the `:` operator. Basically, we generated a sequence that starts at 1 and ends at 7. Why seven? Because 7 is the length of the vector `names_stud`. In fact, it contains

7 elements, i.e. 7 students. Run `length(names_stud)` to verify it. `length()` gets or sets the length of vectors (including lists) and factors, and of any other **R** object for which a method has been defined.

```
> length(names_stud)
[1] 7
```

Additionally, instead of inputing the score after `Enter your number of correct answers:` , I write the score after the loop function in the **R Script** file like this

```
43
39
41
36
38
48
33
```

and run each of them them every time `Enter your number of correct answers:` is printed.

In the previous loop, we printed the results. However, in this way they cannot be used. Therefore, this time we run again the same loop but we remove the `print()` function. The results will be stored in `total_score`. Since we have more than one result to store, this time it is necessary to initialize the `total_score` object. In the previous example, we did not really need it because we just printed out each result every time the loop ran. Note that you can initialize the loop in different ways. In this example, we write `total_score <- numeric(length(names_stud))` that returns an object with seven 0, the length of `names_stud`. These zeros will be replaced by the result of each student every time the loop iterates.

In this regard, note how we write `total_score` inside the loop. We use the square brackets `[ ]` to replace the zeros with the results of the students when the loop iterates (more on this in a few lines). However, note that if we do not subset using the square brackets `[ ]` only the last score will be stored because each time the loop runs it will overwrite the previous value.

```
> point <- 3
> names_stud <- c("Anne", "John", "Bob", "Emma",
+                 "Tony", "Sarah", "James")
> total_score <- numeric(length(names_stud))
> total_score
[1] 0 0 0 0 0 0 0
> for(students in seq_along(names_stud)){
+   n_correct_answer <- as.numeric(
+   readline("Enter your number of correct answers:"))
+   total_score[students] <- n_correct_answer * point
+ }
```

```
Enter your number of correct answers: 43
Enter your number of correct answers: 39
Enter your number of correct answers: 41
Enter your number of correct answers: 36
Enter your number of correct answers: 38
Enter your number of correct answers: 48
Enter your number of correct answers: 33
> total_score
[1] 129 117 123 108 114 144  99
```

Finally, note the in `for()` we replaced `for(students in 1:length(x))` with `for(students in seq_along(x))`. `seq_along()` also generates a sequence

```
> seq_along(names_stud)
[1] 1 2 3 4 5 6 7
```

Now let's break the loop down into pieces to analyse what it does.

First, let's again initialize the object to store the results of the loop

```
> total_score <- numeric(length(names_stud))
> total_score
[1] 0 0 0 0 0 0 0
```

When the loop starts, `students` is 1, that is the beginning of the sequence. Therefore, let's replace `students` with 1. The number of correct answers for the first student was 43. Consequently, the total score is replaced at the first entry.

```
> n_correct_answer <- as.numeric(
+   readline("Enter your number of correct answers: "))
Enter your number of correct answers: 43
> total_score[1] <- n_correct_answer * point
> total_score
[1] 129   0   0   0   0   0   0
```

What about if we run this last chunk of code to simulate the second iteration of the loop? Substitute `students` with 2 and give 39 as number of correct answers for the second student and check the output.

Until now the students know their score but they do not know yet if they passed the test. Let's find it out.

First, let's write the information we have, i.e. names of the students who took the test and their number of correct answers, in a data frame. Use the `data.frame()` function to build the data frame named `results_test`.

```
> names_stud <- c("Anne", "John", "Bob", "Emma",
+                 "Tony", "Sarah", "James")
> n_correct_answer <- c(43, 39, 41, 36, 38, 48, 33)
> results_test <- data.frame(names_stud,
```

```
+                                n_correct_answer)
> results_test
  names_stud n_correct_answer
1       Anne               43
2       John               39
3        Bob               41
4       Emma               36
5       Tony               38
6      Sarah               48
7      James               33
```

Now we build a function, `final_test`, that will return the score and the information about if the students passed the test.

```
> final_test <- function(n, data, tot_q,
+                          test_per, point = 3){
+   total_score <- data[, n] * point
+   full_score <- tot_q * point
+   threshold <- full_score * test_per
+   outcome <- ifelse(total_score > threshold,
+                        "PASS",
+                        "FAIL")
+   results_test_1 <- cbind(data, total_score, outcome)
+   return(results_test_1)
+ }
```

The function takes five arguments: `n`, `data`, `tot_q`, `test_per` and `point`. `n` refers to the column in the dataset that contains the number of correct answer. It can be the name of the column as a string or the corresponding column index. In our case, the name of the column in the data frame is `n_correct_answer`. `data` is the name of the dataset with the information about the test. In our case, the name of the dataset is `results_test`. `tot_q` is the total number of questions in the test. `test_per` is the percentage that defines the passing threshold. Note that we set a default value, 3, for `point`. Between the braces, we define the steps of the function. First, we calculate the total score of the students, `total_score` as `n_correct_answer` multiplied by `point`. Note how we select the column with the number of correct answer in the data frame. We will talk about this later. Second, we calculate the maximum score, `full_score`, as `tot_q` multiply by `point`. Third, we calculate the threshold, `threshold`, as `full_score` multiplied by the passing percentage, `test_per`. Fourth, we generate a variable `outcome` that takes value `"PASS"` if the `total_score` is greater than the `threshold`, and `"FAIL"` otherwise. We use the `ifelse()` function to accomplish this task. Then, we combine by columns the dataset, `data`, that represents our dataset, with `total_score` and `outcome` by using the `cbind()` function. We assign this operation to a new object, `results_test_1`. Finally, we will use the `return()` function to return the data frame from inside the function to the workspace.

Now, we are ready to test it. Suppose that only the students who scored more than 80% of the maximum score pass the test. In this case

```
> final_test(n = "n_correct_answer",
+            data = results_test,
+            tot_q = 50,
+            test_per = 0.8)
  names_stud n_correct_answer total_score outcome
1       Anne               43         129    PASS
2       John               39         117    FAIL
3        Bob               41         123    PASS
4       Emma               36         108    FAIL
5       Tony               38         114    FAIL
6      Sarah               48         144    PASS
7      James               33          99    FAIL
```

Let's try the function by replacing the column name for n with the column index, in our case 2

```
> final_test(n = 2,
+            data = results_test,
+            tot_q = 50,
+            test_per = 0.8)
  names_stud n_correct_answer total_score outcome
1       Anne               43         129    PASS
2       John               39         117    FAIL
3        Bob               41         123    PASS
4       Emma               36         108    FAIL
5       Tony               38         114    FAIL
6      Sarah               48         144    PASS
7      James               33          99    FAIL
```

As expected, we obtain the same results. We have only three students who passed the test. Let's lower the percentage to 70%.

```
> final_test(n = "n_correct_answer",
+            data = results_test,
+            tot_q = 50,
+            test_per = 0.7)
  names_stud n_correct_answer total_score outcome
1       Anne               43         129    PASS
2       John               39         117    PASS
3        Bob               41         123    PASS
4       Emma               36         108    PASS
5       Tony               38         114    PASS
6      Sarah               48         144    PASS
7      James               33          99    FAIL
```

In this case, only one student did not pass the test.

Note that we can modify the default value for point as follows:

```
> final_test(n = "n_correct_answer",
+            data = results_test,
+            tot_q = 50,
+            test_per = 0.7,
+            point = 4)
  names_stud n_correct_answer total_score outcome
1       Anne               43         172    PASS
2       John               39         156    PASS
3        Bob               41         164    PASS
4       Emma               36         144    PASS
5       Tony               38         152    PASS
6      Sarah               48         192    PASS
7      James               33         132    FAIL
```

Let's go back to the first case, i.e. an 80% passing percentage. This time let's assign this operation to a new object, results_test_def to calculate some statistics about our data set. Remember that in this case, you have to run the object to see its content.

```
> results_test_def <- final_test(n = "n_correct_answer",
+                                data = results_test,
+                                tot_q = 50,
+                                test_per = 0.8)
> results_test_def
  names_stud n_correct_answer total_score outcome
1       Anne               43         129    PASS
2       John               39         117    FAIL
3        Bob               41         123    PASS
4       Emma               36         108    FAIL
5       Tony               38         114    FAIL
6      Sarah               48         144    PASS
7      James               33          99    FAIL
```

Let's investigate the structure of our dataset with the str() function.

```
> str(results_test_def)
'data.frame': 7 obs. of  4 variables:
 $ names_stud      : chr  "Anne" "John" "Bob" "Emma"...
 $ n_correct_answer: num  43 39 41 36 38 48 33
 $ total_score     : num  129 117 123 108 114 144 99
 $ outcome         : chr  "PASS" "FAIL" "PASS" "FAIL"...
```

Note that n_correct_answer and total_score have numerical values. names_stud and outcome are characters.

Let's find, for example, the average score of the students. We use $ to select the column of interest from the dataset.

```
> mean(results_test_def$total_score)
[1] 119.1429
```

Let's find now the lowest and highest score:

```
> min(results_test_def$total_score)
[1] 99
> max(results_test_def$total_score)
[1] 144
```

A short-cut to obtain this information is through the summary() function.

```
> summary(results_test_def$total_score)
   Min. 1st Qu.  Median    Mean 3rd Qu.    Max.
   99.0   111.0   117.0   119.1   126.0   144.0
```

If we apply it to the whole dataset:

```
> summary(results_test_def)
  names_stud         n_correct_answer  total_score       outcome
 Length:7           Min.   :33.00    Min.   : 99.0   Length:7
 Class :character   1st Qu.:37.00    1st Qu.:111.0   Class :character
 Mode  :character   Median :39.00    Median :117.0   Mode  :character
                    Mean   :39.71    Mean   :119.1
                    3rd Qu.:42.00    3rd Qu.:126.0
                    Max.   :48.00    Max.   :144.0
```

Let's coerce outcome to factors and let's apply again the summary() function to the dataset (refer to Sect. 1.6.5)

```
> results_test_def$outcome <- as.factor(results_test_def$outcome)
> results_test_def$outcome
[1] PASS FAIL PASS FAIL FAIL PASS FAIL
Levels: FAIL PASS
> summary(results_test_def)
  names_stud         n_correct_answer  total_score      outcome
 Length:7           Min.   :33.00    Min.   : 99.0   FAIL:4
 Class :character   1st Qu.:37.00    1st Qu.:111.0   PASS:3
 Mode  :character   Median :39.00    Median :117.0
                    Mean   :39.71    Mean   :119.1
                    3rd Qu.:42.00    3rd Qu.:126.0
                    Max.   :48.00    Max.   :144.0
```

As you can observe, now the summary() function prints how many passed and failed the text in the outcome column.

Now let's suppose we want to show only the personal result scored by the student. There are different ways we can extract information from a data frame. Basically, a data frame has two dimensions like a matrix. We can use the [i, j] indexes for rows and columns, respectively, where the square brackets `[ ]` subset the data frame.

Let's print again the dataset.

```
> results_test_def
  names_stud n_correct_answer total_score outcome
1       Anne               43         129    PASS
2       John               39         117    FAIL
3        Bob               41         123    PASS
4       Emma               36         108    FAIL
5       Tony               38         114    FAIL
6      Sarah               48         144    PASS
7      James               33          99    FAIL
```

We see that student Anne is at row number 1 and column number 1. Therefore, to extract the name of student Anne

```
> results_test_def[1, 1]
[1] "Anne"
```

But if we want to extract all the info for student Anne, i.e. row 1 and all the columns associated

```
> results_test_def[1, ]
  names_stud n_correct_answer total_score outcome
1       Anne               43         129    PASS
```

Basically, we leave blank the space for the column entry after the comma `,`. Therefore, if we want to select only the column with the `total_score` we leave blank the space for the row entry before the comma, `,`

```
> results_test_def[, 3]
[1] 129 117 123 108 114 144  99
```

We can select the data also by column name in a data frame. For example, we could achieve the same previous task as follows:

```
> results_test_def[, "total_score"]
[1] 129 117 123 108 114 144  99
```

The selection of columns with the square bracket operator is alternative to $. However, with the square bracket operator we can select more columns with the `c()` function. For example, to select the first column and third column:

```
> results_test_def[, c(1, 3)]
  names_stud total_score
1       Anne         129
2       John         117
3        Bob         123
```

```
4         Emma         108
5         Tony         114
6        Sarah         144
7        James          99
```

```
> results_test_def[, c("names_stud", "total_score")]
  names_stud total_score
1       Anne         129
2       John         117
3        Bob         123
4       Emma         108
5       Tony         114
6      Sarah         144
7      James          99
```

Consequently, if we want to select more rows:

```
> results_test_def[c(2, 5), ]
  names_stud n_correct_answer total_score outcome
2       John               39         117    FAIL
5       Tony               38         114    FAIL
```

Now suppose we want to find the student who got the highest score:

```
> results_test_def[which.max(results_test_def$total
  _score), ]
  names_stud n_correct_answer total_score outcome
6      Sarah               48         144    PASS
```

Now the notation should be clear. We subset the dataset by the row with the highest total score, i.e. 144, that it is located at row 6, and for all the columns. In fact,

```
> which.max(results_test_def$total_score)
[1] 6
```

Now suppose we want to rename the column names. We use the `colnames()` function.[12]

```
> colnames(results_test_def) <- c("Students", "Correct_Answer",
+                                 "Total_Score", "Outcome")
> results_test_def
  Students Correct_Answer Total_Score Outcome
1     Anne             43         129    PASS
2     John             39         117    FAIL
3      Bob             41         123    PASS
4     Emma             36         108    FAIL
```

[12] Note that it is better to avoid space in the names of the variables.

```
5      Tony              38          114     FAIL
6     Sarah              48          144     PASS
7     James              33           99     FAIL
```

But now we decide we want to change the name of `Outcome` in `PASSFAIL`:

```
> colnames(results_test_def)[
+   colnames(results_test_def) == "Outcome"] <- "PASSFAIL"
> results_test_def
  Students Correct_Answer Total_Score PASSFAIL
1      Anne             43         129     PASS
2      John             39         117     FAIL
3       Bob             41         123     PASS
4      Emma             36         108     FAIL
5      Tony             38         114     FAIL
6     Sarah             48         144     PASS
7     James             33          99     FAIL
```

Let's translate into plain English this line of code. We are telling **R** that "among all column names in the dataset, the one whose name is equal to `Outcome` has to be renamed as `PASSFAIL`".

Note that == is a logical operator that means exact equality. Refer to Table 1.3 for more logical operators.

Let's see how we can replace column names in a different way. Let's change `PASSFAIL` to `PASS/FAIL`. Let's run only `colnames(results_test_def)`. This extracts the column names of the data frame or matrix. We observe that `PASSFAIL` is the 4th entry.

```
> colnames(results_test_def)
[1] "Students"        "Correct_Answer" "Total_Score"    "PASSFAIL"
```

Let's rename it by replacing its 4th entry

```
> colnames(results_test_def)[4] <- "PASS/FAIL"
> results_test_def
  Students Correct_Answer Total_Score PASS/FAIL
1      Anne             43         129      PASS
2      John             39         117      FAIL
3       Bob             41         123      PASS
4      Emma             36         108      FAIL
```

Table 1.3 Logical Operators

Operator	Description
>	Greater than
<	Less than
>=	Greater or equal
<=	Less or equal
==	Exact equality
! =	Inequality

```
5      Tony           38          114        FAIL
6     Sarah           48          144        PASS
7     James           33           99        FAIL
```

Let's generate a new variable, `PASS`, that takes value 1 if the student passed, 0 otherwise. We use again the `ifelse()` function.

```
> results_test_def$PASS <- ifelse(
+   results_test_def$`PASS/FAIL` == "PASS",
+                                    1, 0)
> results_test_def
  Students Correct_Answer Total_Score PASS/FAIL PASS
1     Anne             43         129      PASS    1
2     John             39         117      FAIL    0
3      Bob             41         123      PASS    1
4     Emma             36         108      FAIL    0
5     Tony             38         114      FAIL    0
6    Sarah             48         144      PASS    1
7    James             33          99      FAIL    0
```

Let's conclude this section by plotting some information in the dataset. We will plot using the `ggplot()` function from the `ggplot2` package.

We need to load the package before using it at the beginning of an **R** session. We use the `library()` function to load the package.

```
> library("ggplot2")
```

When we load a package some information about the package may be printed. For the sake of illustration we do not print them.

Now we are ready to use the `ggplot()` function. We will plot a bar plot and a box plot.

First, we will plot the total score of each student. Note again the code printed in the console pane for `ggplot()`. We have two +. One +, directly below the prompt symbol, >, means the the code is continuing on the next line in the console pane. This + is not part of the code we write. The other + is part of the `ggplot()` code and connect the different arguments and options in `ggplot()`.

```
> ggplot(results_test_def, aes(x= Students, y = Total_Score,
+                         fill = `PASS/FAIL`)) +
+       geom_bar(position = "dodge", stat="identity") +
+       ylab("Total Score") + theme_classic() +
+       ggtitle("Total Score for a 50 question test") +
+       theme(legend.position = "bottom")
```

The first entry in `ggplot()` is the dataset. In `aes()` we map the data for the x and y axes. We distinguish the values by whether the students passed the test by using `fill =`. We will return to the meaning of the backticks in `` `PASS/FAIL` `` in a moment. We choose to plot the data as a bar plot using `geom_bar()`. `position`

`= "dodge"` puts the bars side-by-side. With `stat = "identity"` the heights of the bars represent values in the data. `ylab()` sets the label for the y axis. In `ggtitle()` we type the title of the plot. `theme_classic()` is one of the possible options to define the layout of the plot. Finally, in `theme()` we set the position of the legend below the plot. The output is Fig. 1.12.

We can export it as image from **RStudio** as shown in Figs. 1.13 and 1.14

A feature of `ggplot()` is that its output can be stored. For example, if you plot using the built-in function in **R**, i.e. `plot()`, you cannot store its output.

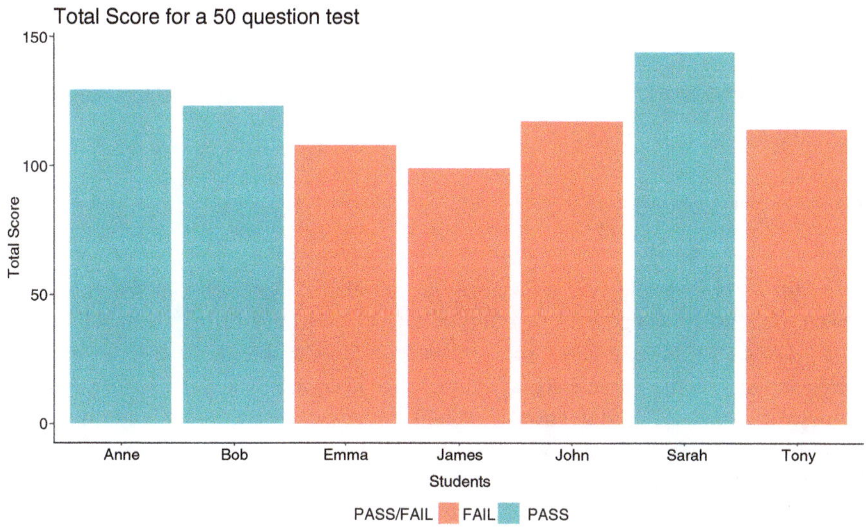

Fig. 1.12 Example of a bar plot

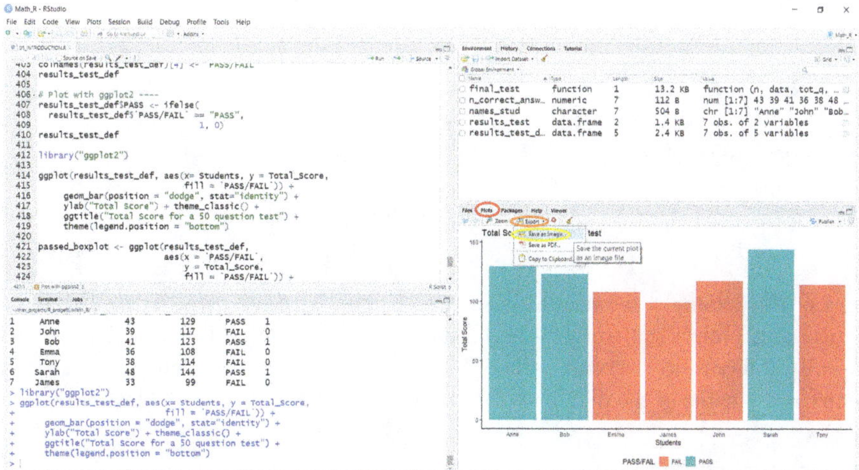

Fig. 1.13 Export plot as image in RStudio (1)

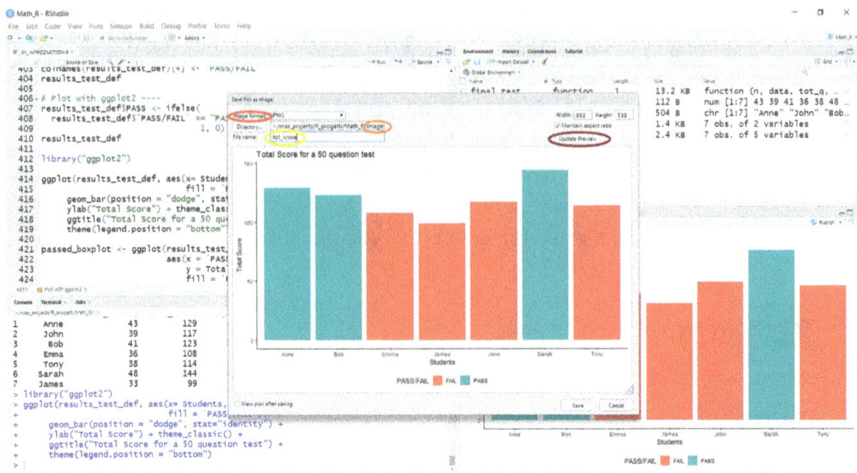

Fig. 1.14 Export plot as image in RStudio (2)

In the next example, we will store the output of a box plot in the following object, `passed_boxplot`. Note the in `aes()`, we have to map `x` and `fill` to `'PASS/FAIL'`. Note that we have to enclose the variable name in `' '` because we included / in the column name. `' '` is also necessary when we write a column name with a space. For this reason, it is better to avoid spaces in the column names. In addition, `xlab("")` removes the title of the *x* axis while `legend.title = element_blank()` removes the title of the legend. Now, we have to run the object to see the plot (Fig. 1.15).

```
> passed_boxplot <- ggplot(results_test_def,
+                          aes(x = 'PASS/FAIL',
+                              y = Total_Score,
+                              fill = 'PASS/FAIL')) +
+   geom_boxplot() +
+   ylab("Total Score") + xlab("") +
+   ggtitle("Boxplot of Results (Fail, Pass)") +
+   theme_bw() +
+   theme(legend.title = element_blank())
> passed_boxplot
```

For this example, we use the `ggsave()` function from `ggplot2` to save the `ggplot2` plot. The first entry is the file name to create on the disk. Note that I specify the path to the `images` folder we created at the beginning. The second entry is the name of the plot we want to save. By default, it saves the last plot.[13]

[13] In the rest of the book I will not print the code to save the images. However, for `ggplot2` plots I use the `ggsave()` function. For other plots, I save them as shown in Figs. 1.13 and 1.14. To save 3D plots, you may use the `rgl.snapshot()` function from the `rgl` package.

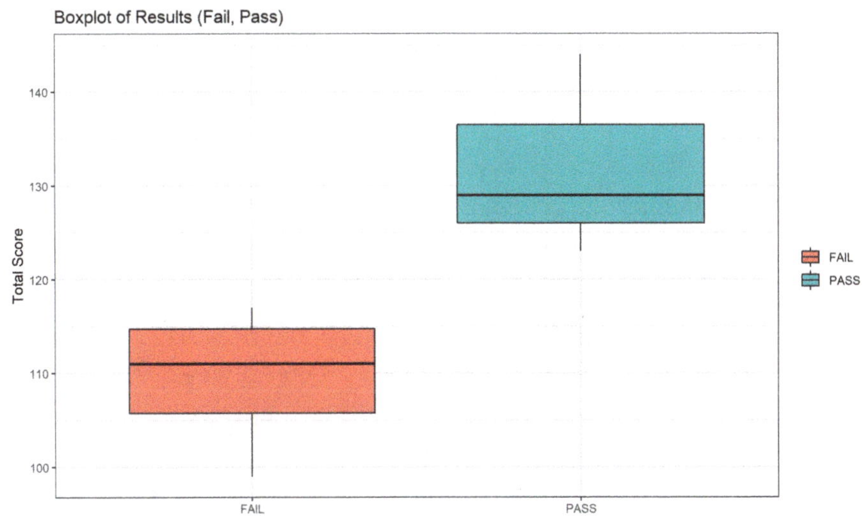

Fig. 1.15 Example of a box plot

```
> ggsave(filename = "images/passes_boxplot.png",
+        plot = passed_boxplot)
Saving 9.28 x 5.6 in image
```

Suppose we want to check the values of the boxplot. First, we can subset the dataset using the `subset()` function. Since the `subset()` function is a built-in function, we do not need to load any package to use it. We create two objects. The first one contains the data only for the students who passed while the second one only for students who did not pass. The first entry in the `subset()` function is the dataset. Then we type the conditional statement. In this case, we subset the dataset if the value in `'PASS/FAIL'` is equal to `"PASS"`. Note again the inclusion of `' '` around the column name. Note that for the object `FAIL` we use the inequality operator `!=`. We could also use `'PASS/FAIL' == "FAIL"` to accomplish the same task. Finally, we apply the `summary()` function to the value in `Total_Score`.

```
> PASS <- subset(results_test_def, 'PASS/FAIL'== "PASS")
> FAIL <- subset(results_test_def, 'PASS/FAIL'!= "PASS")
> PASS
  Students Correct_Answer Total_Score PASS/FAIL PASS
1     Anne             43         129      PASS    1
3      Bob             41         123      PASS    1
6    Sarah             48         144      PASS    1
```

```
> FAIL
  Students Correct_Answer Total_Score PASS/FAIL PASS
2     John             39         117      FAIL    0
4     Emma             36         108      FAIL    0
5     Tony             38         114      FAIL    0
7    James             33          99      FAIL    0
> summary(PASS$Total_Score)
   Min. 1st Qu.  Median    Mean 3rd Qu.    Max. 
  123.0   126.0   129.0   132.0   136.5   144.0 
> summary(FAIL$Total_Score)
   Min. 1st Qu.  Median    Mean 3rd Qu.    Max. 
   99.0   105.8   111.0   109.5   114.8   117.0 
```

We read that the minimum value for PASS is 123, the beginning of the vertical line in Fig. 1.15. The first quartile corresponds to the beginning of the box, 126, while the third quartile corresponds to the end of the box, 136.5. The tick middle line corresponds to the median or middle quartile, 129. The end of the line corresponds to the maximum value, 144.

1.8 Exercise

1.8.1 Exercise 1

The professor noted that the number of correct answers of Tony was 42. Replace the number of correct answer for Tony in `result_test_def`. Modify the other columns where needed as well.

Additionally, two other students took the test. Matt got 40 correct answers. Stephanie scored 138 points. Append the results of these two students to `result_test_def` and plot again the results (do not use the `final_test()` function).

```
> results_test_def
   Students Correct_Answer Total_Score PASS/FAIL PASS
1      Anne             43         129      PASS    1
2      John             39         117      FAIL    0
3       Bob             41         123      PASS    1
4      Emma             36         108      FAIL    0
5      Tony             42         126      PASS    1
6     Sarah             48         144      PASS    1
7     James             33          99      FAIL    0
8      Matt             40         120      FAIL    0
9 Stephanie             46         138      PASS    1
```

1.8.2 Exercise 2

In Sect. 1.6.7, we built `mtable()` to compute the multiplication table for a single value. Rewrite the function so that it can compute the multiplication table for single value and multiple values. Use a `for()` loop for this task. Try to replicate the following outputs:

```
> mtable(7)
 [1]  7 14 21 28 35 42 49 56 63 70
> s <- c(3, 7, 9)
> mtable(x = s, w = 12)
     [,1] [,2] [,3] [,4] [,5] [,6] [,7] [,8] [,9] [,10] [,11] [,12]
[1,]    3    6    9   12   15   18   21   24   27    30    33    36
[2,]    7   14   21   28   35   42   49   56   63    70    77    84
[3,]    9   18   27   36   45   54   63   72   81    90    99   108
> mtable(x = 1:10)
      [,1] [,2] [,3] [,4] [,5] [,6] [,7] [,8] [,9] [,10]
 [1,]    1    2    3    4    5    6    7    8    9    10
 [2,]    2    4    6    8   10   12   14   16   18    20
 [3,]    3    6    9   12   15   18   21   24   27    30
 [4,]    4    8   12   16   20   24   28   32   36    40
 [5,]    5   10   15   20   25   30   35   40   45    50
 [6,]    6   12   18   24   30   36   42   48   54    60
 [7,]    7   14   21   28   35   42   49   56   63    70
 [8,]    8   16   24   32   40   48   56   64   72    80
 [9,]    9   18   27   36   45   54   63   72   81    90
[10,]   10   20   30   40   50   60   70   80   90   100
```

If you already have experience with **R** you probably thought that we do not really need to modify the original `mtable()` function to obtain the previous outputs because we can use the `sapply()` function. Alternatively, we could use the `sapply()` function instead of using a `for()` loop in the revised `mtable()`. And both statements are correct.

`sapply()` is part of the `apply()` family functions that includes `lapply()`, `tapply()`, `vapply()`, and `mapply()`. Basically these functions substitute the loop by applying another function to all elements in an object. For example, the object can be a matrix, an array or a data frame in the case of the `apply()` function; a vector, a data frame and a list in the case of `sapply()` and `apply()`. The difference between `sapply()` and `lapply()` is that the former returns as result a vector, a matrix or a list, while the latter returns a list.

Let's see how to use the `sapply()` function to obtain the previous outputs.

```
> sapply(7, FUN = mtable)
      [,1]
 [1,]    7
 [2,]   14
 [3,]   21
 [4,]   28
 [5,]   35
 [6,]   42
 [7,]   49
```

```
 [8,]   56
 [9,]   63
[10,]   70
> s <- c(3, 7, 9)
> t(sapply(s, FUN = mtable, w = 12))
     [,1] [,2] [,3] [,4] [,5] [,6] [,7] [,8] [,9] [,10] [,11] [,12]
[1,]    3    6    9   12   15   18   21   24   27    30    33    36
[2,]    7   14   21   28   35   42   49   56   63    70    77    84
[3,]    9   18   27   36   45   54   63   72   81    90    99   108
> t(sapply(1:10, FUN = mtable))
      [,1] [,2] [,3] [,4] [,5] [,6] [,7] [,8] [,9] [,10]
 [1,]    1    2    3    4    5    6    7    8    9    10
 [2,]    2    4    6    8   10   12   14   16   18    20
 [3,]    3    6    9   12   15   18   21   24   27    30
 [4,]    4    8   12   16   20   24   28   32   36    40
 [5,]    5   10   15   20   25   30   35   40   45    50
 [6,]    6   12   18   24   30   36   42   48   54    60
 [7,]    7   14   21   28   35   42   49   56   63    70
 [8,]    8   16   24   32   40   48   56   64   72    80
 [9,]    9   18   27   36   45   54   63   72   81    90
[10,]   10   20   30   40   50   60   70   80   90   100
```

The first argument is the vector on which we want to apply the function. The second argument is the name of the function, in our case the `mtable()` we built in Sect. 1.6.7 (note that we do not need to add the parentheses to the name of the function). Following all the arguments we want to pass to the function, w in our case. Additionally, note that I nested `sapply()` in the `t()` function that returns the transpose of the object, typically a matrix or a data frame. At the beginning it results quite tough to get used to the `apply()` functions. My advice is to read them from the end to the beginning. For instance, I would read the last example as "apply the `mtable()` function to the vector $1:10$."

Finally, after reading Chap. 2, return to this exercise. Choose one of the operations we will learn in Chap. 2 to rewrite this function without the loop.

Part I
Introduction to Mathematics for Static Economics

Chapter 2
Linear Algebra

2.1 Set, Group, Ring, Field: Short Overview

In this section we briefly review some key concepts of Linear Algebra before delving into vectors and matrices.

A *set* is collection of objects that are called *elements*. If s is an element of a set S, we write $s \in S$. If M and S are sets and if every elements of M is an element of S, we say that M is a subset of S or M is *contained* in S, $M \subset S$.

If S_1 and S_2 are sets, the *intersection* of S_1 and S_2, $S_1 \cap S_2$, is the set of elements which lie in both S_1 and S_2. On the other hand, the union of S_1 and S_2, $S_1 \cup S_2$, is the set of elements which lie in S_1 or S_2.

We can work with sets in **R** using the `RVenn` package. First, we create the two objects, `S1` and `S2`, that represent the two sets. Second, we convert them into a `Venn` object, `S`, with the `Venn()` function. Because the `Venn()` function requires the vectors to be of the same class, we coerce the class of `S2` to be integer. Then, we compute the intersection with the `overlap()` function, the union with the `unite()` function. Note that for the union we write `RVenn::unite(S)`. We are clearly saying to **R** that we want to use the `unite()` function from the `RVenn` package. This is necessary when there may be functions with the same name from different packages. Therefore, to avoid confusion (and errors) we specify the package.

Finally, we can plot `S` with the `ggvenn()` function or the `setmap()` function. `ggvenn()` is designed for 2 or 3 sets because "Venn diagrams are terrible for showing the interactions of 4 or more sets" (Akyol 2019). `ggvenn()` reports the numbers of elements of intersection and union among sets (Fig. 2.1). `setmap()` shows the presence/absence of the elements among all the sets (Fig. 2.2). At the end we use the `detach()` function to detach the `RVenn` package because we do not use it anymore.

M. Porto, *Introduction to Mathematics for Economics with R*,
https://doi.org/10.1007/978-3-031-05202-6_2

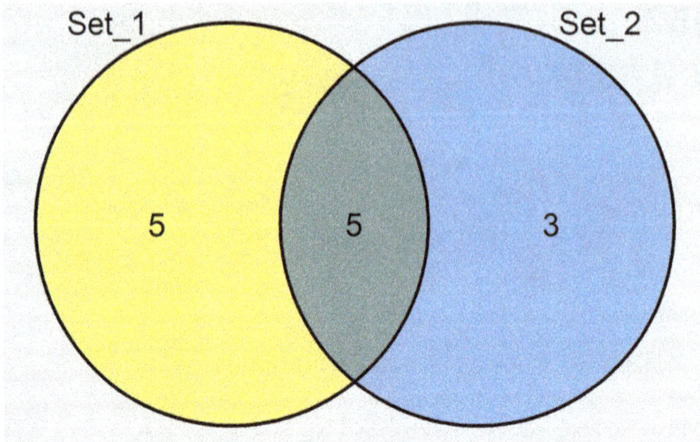

Fig. 2.1 Set

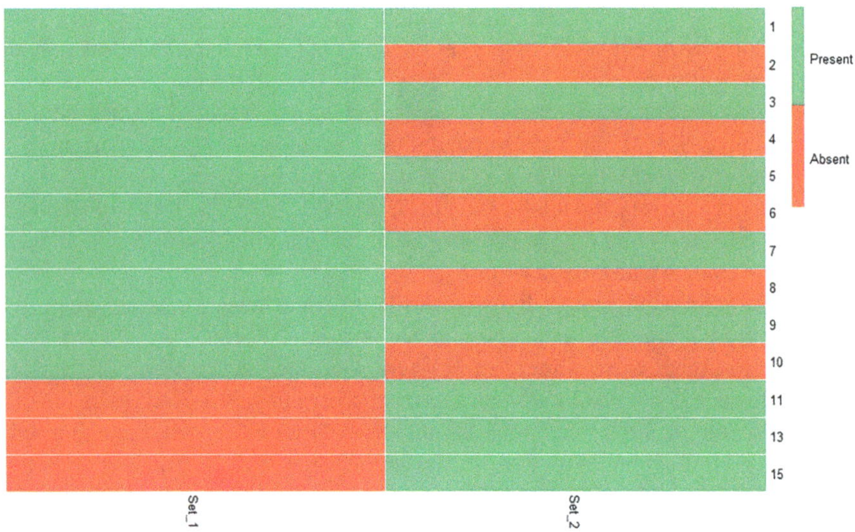

Fig. 2.2 Setmap

```
> S1 <- 1:10
> class(S1)
[1] "integer"
> S2 <- c(1, 3, 5, 7, 9, 11, 13, 15)
> class(S2)
[1] "numeric"
> S2 <- as.integer(S2)
> S <- Venn(list(S1, S2))
> # intersection
```

```
> overlap(S)
[1] 1 3 5 7 9
> # union
> RVenn::unite(S)
 [1]  1  2  3  4  5  6  7  8  9 10 11 13 15
> # plot
> ggvenn(S)
> setmap(S, element_clustering = F, set_clustering = F)
> detach("package:RVenn")
```

Let S and S' be sets. A *mapping* (or *map*) from S to S' is an association which to every element of S associates an element of S', i.e. $f : S \to S'$ that we read as "f is a mapping of S into S'". If $f : S \to S'$ is a mapping, and $x \in S$ then $f(x)$ denotes the element of S' associated to x by f and it is the value of f at x that is also called the *image* of x under f, $x \mapsto f(x)$. The set of all elements $f(x)$ $\forall x \in S$, is called the *image* of f.

A map $f : S \to S'$ is said to be *injective* if whenever $x, y \in S$ and $x \neq y$ then $f(x) \neq f(y)$, or, consequently $f(x) = f(y)$ implies $x = y$. For example, let $f : \mathbb{R} \to \mathbb{R}$ be the mapping $f(x) = x+1$. Then, f is injective because $x+1 = y+1$ implies that $x = y$. On the other hand, $f(x) = x^2$ is not injective because $f(2) = 4$ and $f(-2) = 4$.

A map $f : S \to S'$ is said to be *surjective* if the image $f(S)$ of S is equal to all of S'. This means that given any element $x' \in S'$, there exists an element $x \in S$ such that $f(x) = x'$. We say that f is *onto* S'. For example, let $g : \mathbb{N} \to \mathbb{N}$ be the mapping $g(x) = 2x$, where $\mathbb{N}$ is the set of *natural numbers* that contains the "counting numbers" starting from 1, i.e. 1, 2, 3, ... Then, g is not surjective. In fact, $g(1) = 2$, $g(2) = 4$, $g(3) = 6$ and so on. That is, no elements in $\mathbb{N}$ can be mapped to odd numbers. On the other hand, let g be the mapping from $\mathbb{N}$ to the set of *non-negative even* numbers. Then $g(x) = 2x$ is surjective.

Let S and S' be sets and $f : S \to S'$ a mapping. If f is both injective and surjective is said to be *bijective*. This means that given an element $x' \in S'$, there exists a unique element $x \in S$ such that $f(x) = x'$. (Existence because f is surjective, and uniqueness because f is injective) (Lang 2005, p. 27). Then, if f is surjective and injective (i.e. bijective), it is invertible and we denote as f^{-1} an *inverse mapping* $g : S' \to S$.[1] Figure 2.3 gives a representation of injective, surjective, bijective mapping.[2]

A group G is a set, together with a rule, $*$,[3] which to each pair of elements x, y in G associates an element denoted by xy in G, having the following properties

[1] Most of definitions in this section are based on Lang (2005).

[2] The code used to generate Fig. 2.3 is available in Appendix B.

[3] In general we use $*$ for the two common operations $+$, $\times$. Remember that in abstract algebra we basically have two operations, addition and multiplication, since subtraction and division are, respectively, the inverse operation of addition and multiplication.

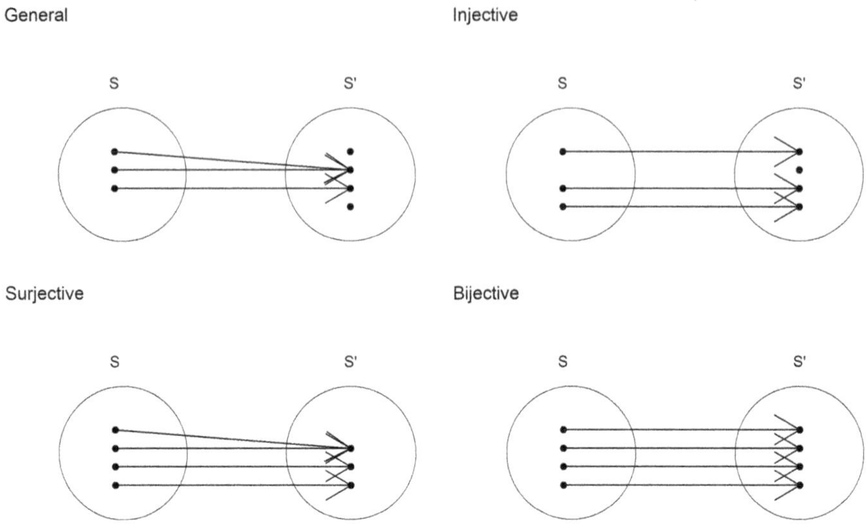

Fig. 2.3 Injection, surjection, bijection

1. Associativity: for all x, y, z in G we have $(x * y) * z = x * (y * z)$;
2. Identity element, e: there exists an element e of G such that $e * x = x * e = x$ for all x in G;
3. Inverse: if x is an element of G, then there exists an element y of G such that $x * y = y * x = e$.

Note that G may not be *commutative*, i.e. $x * y \neq y * x$. However, if G is also commutative it is called *abelian group*.

For example, the integers, $\mathbb{Z} = \{\ldots - 2, -1, 0, 1, 2 \ldots\}$, is a group under addition. In fact,

1. $(2 + 3) + 4 = 2 + (3 + 4)$
2. $0 + 2 = 2 + 0 = 2$
3. $2 + (-2) = -2 + 2 = 0$

Furthermore, we define *trivial* a group consisting of one element. A group in general may have infinitely many elements, or only a finite number. If G has only a finite number of elements, then G is called a *finite group*, and the number of elements of G is called its *order*.

A ring R is a set, whose objects can be added and multiplied satisfying the following conditions:

1. Under addition, R is an additive (abelian) group;
2. Distributive property: for all $x, y, z \in R$ we have $x(y + z) = xy + xz$ and $(y + z)x = yx + zx$;
3. Associativity: for all $x, y, z \in R$, we have associativity $(x * y) * z = x * (y * z)$;

4. Identity element: there exists an element $e \in R$ such that $e * x = x * e = x$ for all $x \in R$.

Note that we do not require multiplication to be commutative. For example, a 2×2 matrix is a type of ring. As we will see, matrix multiplication is not commutative.

We say that K is a field if it satisfies the following conditions:

1. if x, y are elements of K, $x + y$ and $x \times y$ are also elements of K;
2. if $x \in K$, then $-x$ is also an element of K. Furthermore, if $x \neq 0$, then x^{-1} is an element of K;
3. the elements 0 and 1 are elements of K.

For example, the set of all real numbers, $\mathbb{R}$, is a field. On the other hand, the set of all integers, $\mathbb{Z}$, is not a field. This can be verified from property number 2. For example, $5 \in \mathbb{Z}$. However, $5^{-1} = \frac{1}{5} \notin \mathbb{Z}$, i.e. it is not an integer. You can verify that the set of natural numbers $\mathbb{N}$ is not a field either. If K and L are fields and K is contained in L, it is said to be a *subfield* of L. For example, the set of rational numbers, $\mathbb{Q}$, is a subfield of $\mathbb{R}$, and $\mathbb{R}$ is a subfield of the set of complex numbers, $\mathbb{C}$ (Sect. 9.1). The elements of the field K are also called numbers or *scalars*.

2.2 Vectors

2.2.1 *Vector Space*

A vector space V over the field K is a set of objects which can be added and multiplied by elements of K, in such a way that the sum of two elements of V is again an element of V (closure under addition), the product of an element of V by an element of K is an element of V (closure under scalar multiplication). Furthermore, a few properties must apply. We are going to enunciate the properties by applying to the vectors **u**, **v**, and **w** in $\mathbb{R}^2$ (read as "R two").[4]

```
> v <- c(3, 5)
> u <- c(4, 2)
> w <- c(2, 4)
```

2.2.1.1 Properties of Vector Space

The properties of vector space are the following:

1. Associativity of addition
   Given elements **u**, **v**, **w** of V, we have

[4] Each vector in $\mathbb{R}^2$ has two components. The vector space $\mathbb{R}^2$ is represented by the xy plane.

$$(\mathbf{u}+\mathbf{v})+\mathbf{w}=\mathbf{u}+(\mathbf{v}+\mathbf{w})$$

```
> (u + v) + w
[1]  9 11
> u + (v + w)
[1]  9 11
```

2. Identity element of addition
   There is an element of V, denoted by $\mathbf{0}$, such that

$$\mathbf{0}+\mathbf{v}=\mathbf{v}+\mathbf{0}=\mathbf{v}$$

   for all elements of $\mathbf{v}$ of V.

```
> o <- c(0, 0)
> o + v
[1] 3 5
> v + o
[1] 3 5
```

3. Inverse elements of addition
   Given an element $\mathbf{v}$ of V, there exists an element - $\mathbf{v}$ in V such that

$$\mathbf{v}+(-\mathbf{v})=0$$

```
> v1 <- c(-3, -5)
> v + v1
[1] 0 0
```

4. Commutativity of addition
   For all elements $\mathbf{v}$, $\mathbf{w}$ of V, we have

$$\mathbf{v}+\mathbf{w}=\mathbf{w}+\mathbf{v}$$

```
> v + w
[1] 5 9
> w + v
[1] 5 9
```

5. Distributivity of vector sums
   If n is a number, then

$$n(\mathbf{v}+\mathbf{w})=n\mathbf{v}+n\mathbf{w}$$

```
> n <- 5
> n * (v + w)
[1] 25 45
```

```
> n*v + n*w
[1] 25 45
```

6. Distributivity of scalar sums
   If a, b are two numbers, then

$$(a+b)\mathbf{v} = a\mathbf{v} + b\mathbf{v}$$

```
> a <- 2
> b <- 3
> (a + b)*v
[1] 15 25
> a*v + b*v
[1] 15 25
```

7. Associativity of scalar multiplication
   If a, b are two numbers, then

$$(ab)\mathbf{v} = a(b\mathbf{v})$$

```
> (a*b)*v
[1] 18 30
> a*(b*v)
[1] 18 30
```

8. Identity element of scalar multiplication
   For all elements $\mathbf{v}$ of V, we have

$$1 \cdot \mathbf{v} = \mathbf{v}$$

```
> 1 * v
[1] 3 5
```

2.2.1.2 Vector Notation

A vector is an element of a vector space. A vector has magnitude and direction. Vectors can be represented geometrically in two or three dimensions (Sect. 2.2.2).

We may encounter vectors written with different notations.

In Linear Algebra, it is common to write the vectors in column brackets

$$\mathbf{v} = \begin{bmatrix} v_1 \\ v_2 \\ v_3 \\ \vdots \\ v_n \end{bmatrix}$$

For example,

$$\mathbf{v} = \begin{bmatrix} 4 \\ -5 \\ 1 \end{bmatrix}$$

A vector from point A, the initial point or *tail*, to point B, the terminal point or *head*, may be indicated as $\overline{AB}$ or $\overrightarrow{AB}$.

Another way to express a vector is $\overrightarrow{v}$ or $\mathbf{v} = \langle v_1, v_2, v_3 \ldots, v_n \rangle$. For example, $\mathbf{v} = \langle 2, 3, 5, 14, 21 \rangle$ is a vector in $\mathbb{R}^5$.[5]

Another notation uses *unit vectors*, $\hat{i} = \langle 1, 0 \rangle$, $\hat{j} = \langle 0, 1 \rangle$ in two dimensions. In three dimensions, $\hat{i} = \langle 1, 0, 0 \rangle$, $\hat{j} = \langle 0, 1, 0 \rangle$ and $\hat{k} = \langle 0, 0, 1 \rangle$. For example, $\mathbf{v} = 2\hat{i} + 3\hat{j}$.

Finally, we report the definition of vectors in the software language of **R** (to not be confused with the set of real number $\mathbb{R}$). The **R** manual[6] defines vectors as follows:

> **R** operates on named data structures. The simplest such structure is the numeric vector, which is a single entity consisting of an ordered collection of numbers. To set up a vector named x, say, consisting of five numbers, namely 10.4, 5.6, 3.1, 6.4 and 21.7, use the **R** command `x <- c(10.4, 5.6, 3.1, 6.4, 21.7)`.

2.2.2 Vector Representation in Two and Three Dimensions

Let's represent a two-dimensional vector, $\mathbf{v} = \langle 3, 5 \rangle$, in the Cartesian plane (or *Euclidean 2-space*) where the tail of the vector is at the origin (0, 0) and the head at the coordinates (3, 5) (Fig. 2.4). We use `ggplot()` to produce Fig. 2.4. Try to build Fig. 2.4 step by step to see what `ggplot()` does. We will delve into the details of `ggplot()` from next chapter.

```
> ggplot() +
+     theme_minimal() +
+     geom_hline(yintercept = 0, size = 1) +
+     geom_vline(xintercept = 0, size = 1) +
+     xlab("x") + ylab("y") +
+     geom_segment(aes(x = 0,
+                      xend = 3,
+                      y = 0,
+                      yend = 5),
```

[5] $\mathbb{R}^5$ has 5 dimensions, while $\mathbb{R}^2$ has 2 dimensions and $\mathbb{R}^3$ has 3 dimensions. Therefore, $\mathbb{R}^n$ has n dimensions. The number n in $\mathbb{R}^n$ refers to how many numbers are needed to describe each location in an n-space. This n-space is usually referred to as *Euclidean n-space*.

[6] An Introduction to **R**, https://cran.r-project.org/manuals.html.

Fig. 2.4 Vector

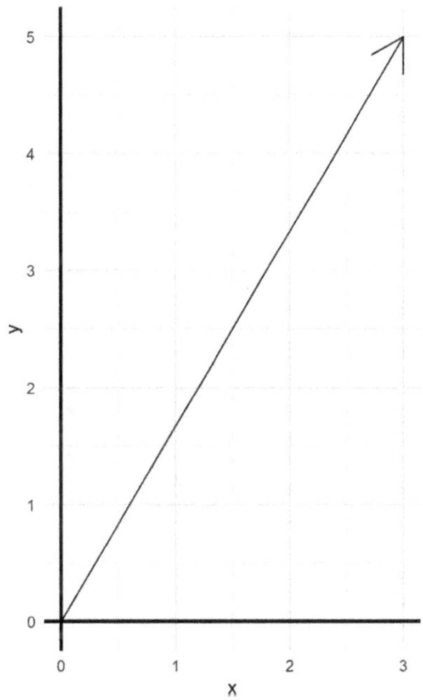


```
+                       arrow = arrow(
+                         length = unit(0.3,
+                                       "inches"))) +
+   coord_equal()
```

As you can observe from Fig. 2.4, we represent the vector as a directed line segment starting from the tail and ending at the head. This represents the direction of the vector. Its length is the magnitude of the vector. Two vectors are the same if they have the same magnitude and direction regardless of their different initial and terminal locations (Fig. 2.5).

```
> ggplot() +
+   theme_minimal() +
+   geom_hline(yintercept = 0, size = 1) +
+   geom_vline(xintercept = 0, size = 1) +
+   xlab("x") + ylab("y") +
+   geom_segment(aes(x = c(0, 2, -2),
+                    xend = c(3, 2+3, -2+3),
+                    y = c(0, 1, 0),
+                    yend = c(5, 1+5, 0+5)),
+                arrow = arrow(
+                  length = unit(0.3,
+                                "inches"))) +
+   coord_equal()
```

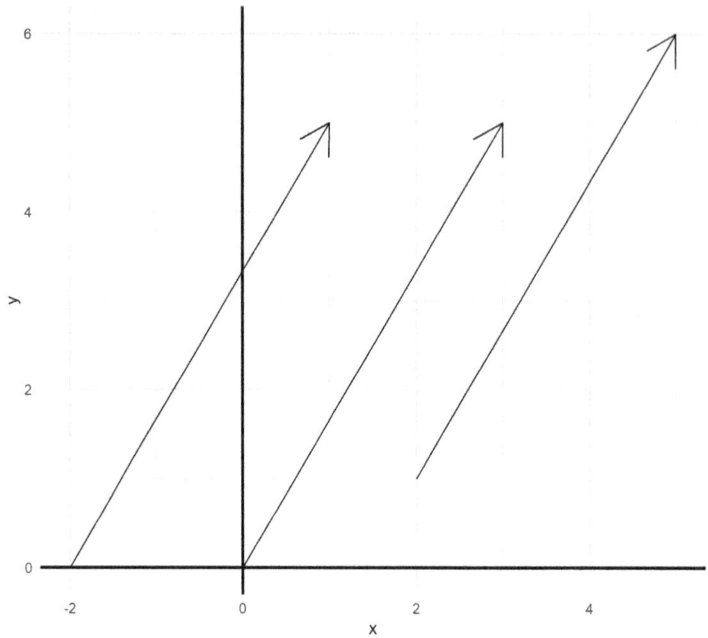

Fig. 2.5 Vectors with same magnitude and direction

Now let's add to Fig. 2.4 a vector $\mathbf{d} = \langle 5, 3 \rangle$, i.e. with tail in the origin and head at the point (5, 3)

```
> ggplot() +
+   theme_minimal() +
+   geom_hline(yintercept = 0, size = 1) +
+   geom_vline(xintercept = 0, size = 1) +
+   xlab("x") + ylab("y") +
+   geom_segment(aes(x = c(0, 0),
+                    xend = c(3, 5),
+                    y = c(0, 0),
+                    yend = c(5, 3)),
+                arrow = arrow(
+                  length = unit(0.3,
+                                "inches"))) +
+   coord_equal()
```

Figure 2.6 clearly shows that the order in which the coordinates are written matters since (3, 5) and (5, 3) do not represent the same point. Therefore, we refer to them as *ordered pairs*. In general, Euclidean n-space consists of ordered n-tuples of numbers, i.e. ordered lists of n numbers.

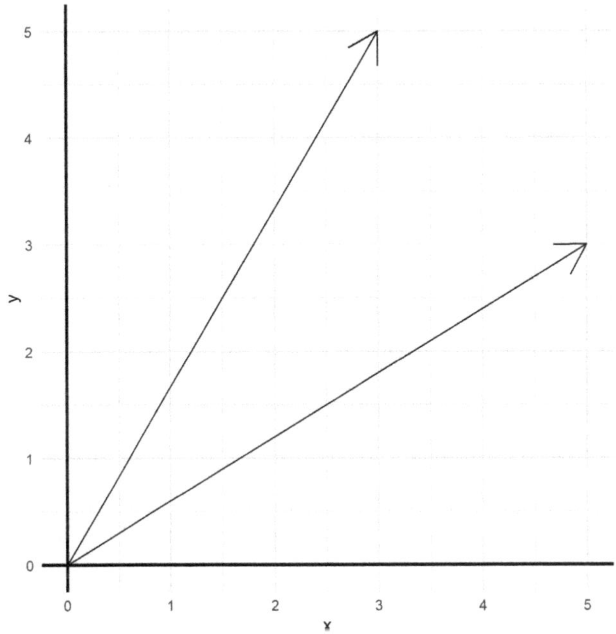

Fig. 2.6 Vectors $\mathbf{v} = \langle 3, 5 \rangle$ and $\mathbf{d} = \langle 5, 3 \rangle$

Let's multiply the vector **v** by a real number, that is called *scalar*. Let's use 2 for this example. Figure 2.7 shows that this scalar multiplication stretches the vector on the same line, i.e. without changing its direction.

```
> v1 <- 2 * v
> v1
[1]  6 10
> ggplot() +
+   theme_minimal() +
+   geom_hline(yintercept = 0, size = 1) +
+   geom_vline(xintercept = 0, size = 1) +
+   xlab("x") + ylab("y") +
+   geom_segment(aes(x = c(0, 0),
+                    xend = c(3, 6),
+                    y = c(0, 0),
+                    yend = c(5, 10)),
+                size = c(1.5, 1),
+                color = c("blue", "red"),
+                arrow = arrow(
+                  length = unit(0.3,
+                                "inches"))) +
```

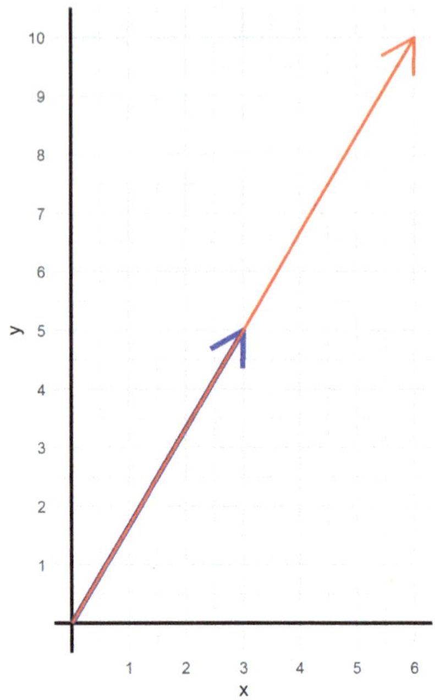

Fig. 2.7 Scalar multiplication

```
+    scale_y_continuous(breaks = 1:10) +
+    scale_x_continuous(breaks = 1:6) +
+    coord_equal()
```

Multiplication by 1 leaves the vector unchanged. On the other hand, multiplication by -1 changes the direction of the vector (Fig. 2.8). In general, a scalar multiplication by a negative number $-n$ reverses the direction and changes the length of the vector.

```
> v2 <- -1 * v
> v2
[1] -3 -5
> ggplot() +
+    theme_minimal() +
+    geom_hline(yintercept = 0, size = 1) +
+    geom_vline(xintercept = 0, size = 1) +
+    xlab("x") + ylab("y") +
+    geom_segment(aes(x = c(0, 0),
+                     xend = c(3, -3),
+                     y = c(0, 0),
+                     yend = c(5, -5)),
+                 size = c(1, 1),
+                 color = c("blue", "red"),
```

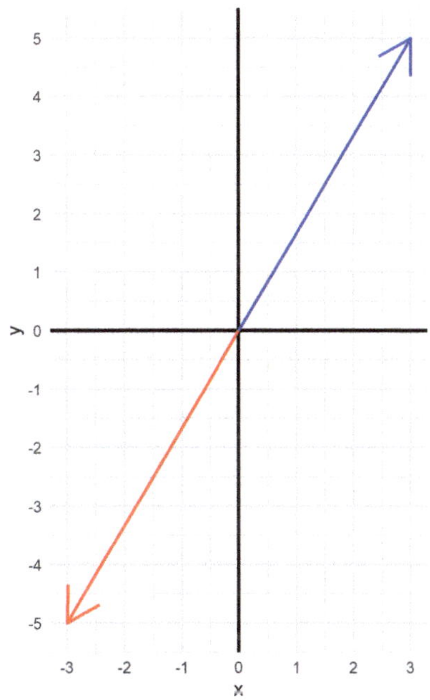

Fig. 2.8 Scalar multiplication by -1

```
+                        arrow = arrow(
+                          length = unit(0.3,
+                                        "inches"))) +
+   scale_y_continuous(breaks = -5:5) +
+   scale_x_continuous(breaks = -3:3) +
+   coord_equal()
```

Let's add the vector **v** to, respectively, $\mathbf{w} = \langle 2, 4 \rangle$, $\mathbf{u} = \langle 4, 2 \rangle$, and $\mathbf{z} = \langle -2, 4 \rangle$ (Fig. 2.9).

```
> w <- c(2, 4)
> vw <- v + w
> vw
[1] 5 9
> u <- c(4, 2)
> uv <- u + v
> uv
[1] 7 7
> z <- c(-2, 4)
> vz <- v + z
> vz
[1] 1 9
> ggplot() +
+   theme_minimal() +
```

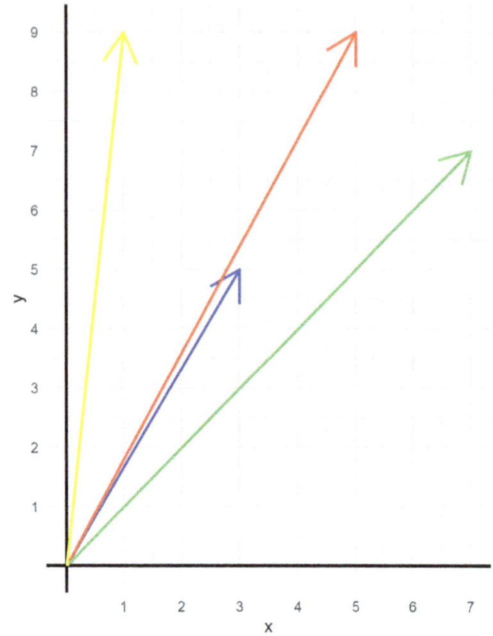

Fig. 2.9 Vector addition

```
+    geom_hline(yintercept = 0, size = 1) +
+    geom_vline(xintercept = 0, size = 1) +
+    xlab("x") + ylab("y") +
+    geom_segment(aes(x = c(0, 0, 0, 0),
+                     xend = c(3, 5, 7, 1),
+                     y = c(0, 0, 0, 0),
+                     yend = c(5, 9, 7, 9)),
+                 size = rep(1, 4),
+                 color = c("blue", "red",
+                           "green", "yellow"),
+                 arrow = arrow(
+                   length = unit(0.3,
+                                 "inches"))) +
+    scale_y_continuous(breaks = 1:9) +
+    scale_x_continuous(breaks = 1:7) +
+    coord_equal()
```

Let's add a dimension to the vector **v**, $\mathbf{v} = \langle 3, 5, 4 \rangle$. We use the `arrows3D()` function from the `plot3D` package to plot a three-dimensional graph (Fig. 2.10).

```
> v <- c(3, 5, 4)
> arrows3D(0, 0, 0,
+          3, 5, 4,
+          ticktype = "detailed")
```

Fig. 2.10 3D vector

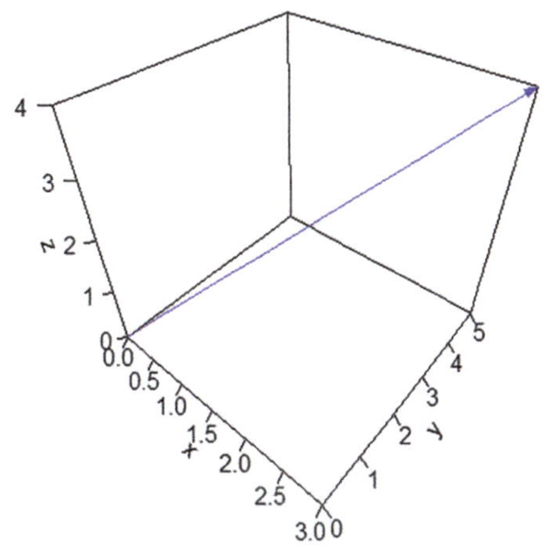

Let's repeat the same operations for the three-dimensional vector. Therefore, let's multiply by 2 (Fig. 2.11). Note that we store the coordinates of points from which to draw in `x0`, `y0`, and `z0` and the coordinates of points to which to draw in `x1`, `y1`, and `z1`

```
> v1 <- 2 * v
> v1
[1]  6 10  8
> x0 <- c(0, 0)
> y0 <- c(0, 0)
> z0 <- c(0, 0)
> x1 <- c(3, 6)
> y1 <- c(5, 10)
> z1 <- c(4, 8)
> cols <- c("blue", "red")
> arrows3D(x0, y0, z0, x1, y1, z1,
+          col = cols,
+          lwd = 2,
+          ticktype = "detailed")
```

Next, we multiply the vector by -1 (Fig. 2.12).

```
> v2 <- -1 * v
> v2
[1] -3 -5 -4
> x0 <- c(0, 0)
> y0 <- c(0, 0)
> z0 <- c(0, 0)
> x1 <- c(3, -3)
```

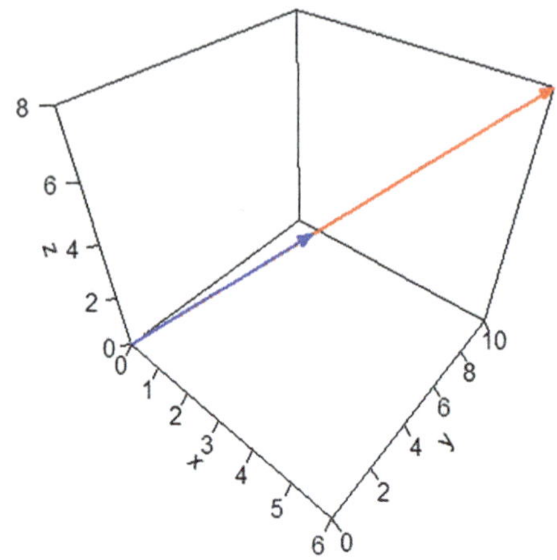

Fig. 2.11 3D scalar multiplication

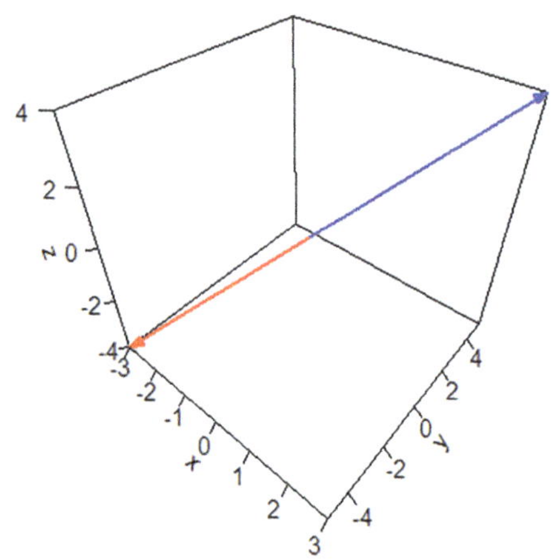

Fig. 2.12 3D scalar multiplication by −1

```
> y1 <- c(5, -5)
> z1 <- c(4, -4)
> cols <- c("blue", "red")
> arrows3D(x0, y0, z0, x1, y1, z1,
+          col = cols,
+          lwd = 2,
+          ticktype = "detailed")
```

Figure 2.13 represents vector addition.

```
> w <- c(2, 4, 3)
> vw <- v + w
> vw
[1] 5 9 7
> u <- c(4, 2, 3)
> uv <- u + v
```

Fig. 2.13 3D vector addition

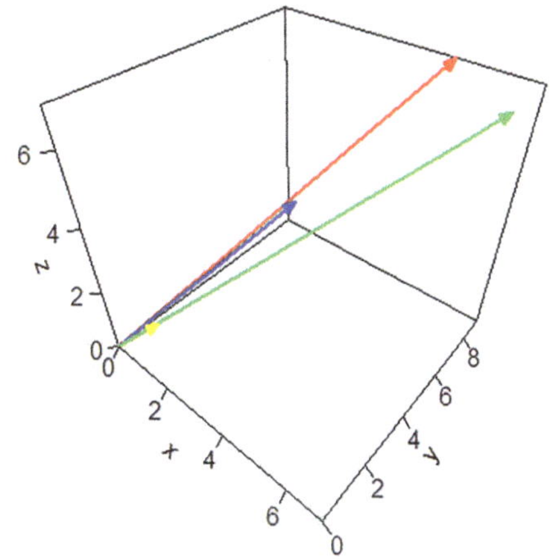


```
> uv
[1] 7 7 7
> z <- c(-2, -4, -3)
> vz <- v + z
> vz
[1] 1 1 1
> x0 <- c(0, 0, 0, 0)
> y0 <- c(0, 0, 0, 0)
> z0 <- c(0, 0, 0, 0)
> x1 <- c(3, 5, 7, 1)
> y1 <- c(5, 9, 7, 1)
> z1 <- c(4, 7, 7, 1)
> cols <- c("blue", "red", "green", "yellow")
> arrows3D(x0, y0, z0, x1, y1, z1,
+          col = cols,
+          lwd = 2,
+          ticktype = "detailed")
```

Note that we can add together two vectors from the same vector space. For example, the addition between $\mathbf{v} = \langle 3, 5 \rangle$ and $\mathbf{u} = \langle 4, 2, 3 \rangle$ is not defined since $\mathbf{v}$ lies in $\mathbb{R}^2$ while $\mathbf{u}$ lies in $\mathbb{R}^3$.

2.2.3 *Inner Product*

In the previous section, we have seen operations like addition and scalar multiplication. Another operation between two vectors of the same dimension is the *inner product*:

$$\mathbf{u} \cdot \mathbf{v} = u_1 v_1 + u_2 v_2 + \ldots + u_n v_n$$

Because the operational notation is a dot, the inner product is also know as the *dot product*. Furthermore, because the result is not a vector but a scalar, the inner product is known as *scalar product* as well. For example, with $\mathbf{u} = \langle 4, 6\rangle$ and $\mathbf{v} = \langle 3, 2\rangle$, the inner product is $4 \cdot 3 + 6 \cdot 2 = 24$. With **R**

```
> u <- c(4, 6)
> v <- c(3, 2)
> uv <- sum(u*v)
> uv
[1] 24
> class(uv)
[1] "numeric"
> uv <- u%*%v
> uv
     [,1]
[1,]   24
> class(uv)
[1] "matrix" "array"
```

Note that we first computed the dot product manually, i.e. we multiplied each corresponding element of the two vectors and then we added them all. Then, we used `%*%` operator. Note that they return the same result but objects with a different class. We will return to the `%*%` operator in Sect. 2.3.1. In the exercise in Sect. 2.5.1, you are asked to write a function that implements the inner product.

2.2.4 Outer Product

The outer product, denoted by $\otimes$, is another algebraic operation between vectors. In this context, we highlight two differences with the inner product:

1. it also applies to two vectors with different dimensions
2. its outcome is a matrix

Therefore, the outer product $\mathbf{u} \otimes \mathbf{v}$, where $\mathbf{u} = \langle u_1, u_2, \cdots, u_m\rangle$ and $\mathbf{v} = \langle v_1, v_2, \cdots, v_n\rangle$, produces the matrix A with m rows and n columns:

$$\mathbf{u} \otimes \mathbf{v} = A = \begin{bmatrix} u_1v_1 & u_1v_2 & \cdots & u_1v_n \\ u_2v_1 & u_2v_2 & \cdots & u_2v_n \\ \vdots & \vdots & \ddots & \vdots \\ u_mv_1 & u_mv_2 & \cdots & u_mv_n \end{bmatrix}$$

For example, given $\mathbf{u} = \langle 1, 2, 3\rangle$ and $\mathbf{v} = \langle 4, 5, 6, 7\rangle$, the outer product $\mathbf{u} \otimes \mathbf{v}$ is

$$\mathbf{u} \otimes \mathbf{v} = \begin{bmatrix} 1\cdot 4 & 1\cdot 5 & 1\cdot 6 & 1\cdot 7 \\ 2\cdot 4 & 2\cdot 5 & 2\cdot 6 & 2\cdot 7 \\ 3\cdot 4 & 3\cdot 5 & 3\cdot 6 & 3\cdot 7 \end{bmatrix} = \begin{bmatrix} 4 & 5 & 6 & 7 \\ 8 & 10 & 12 & 14 \\ 12 & 15 & 18 & 21 \end{bmatrix}$$

In **R**, we can compute the outer product by using the `%o%` operator or the `outer()` function. Following, we show $\mathbf{u} \otimes \mathbf{v}$ by using `%o%` and $\mathbf{v} \otimes \mathbf{u}$ by using `outer()`. Note the different dimensions of the resulting matrices (Sect. 2.3).

```
> u <- c(1, 2, 3)
> v <- c(4, 5, 6, 7)
> u %o% v
     [,1] [,2] [,3] [,4]
[1,]    4    5    6    7
[2,]    8   10   12   14
[3,]   12   15   18   21
> outer(v, u)
     [,1] [,2] [,3]
[1,]    4    8   12
[2,]    5   10   15
[3,]    6   12   18
[4,]    7   14   21
```

2.2.5 Component Form, Magnitude and Unit Vector

Let's suppose we have the initial point $A = (1, 2)$ and the terminal point $B = (4, -3)$ for vector $\overline{AB}$, and the initial point $C = (3, 6)$ and the terminal point $D = (12, -9)$ for vector $\overline{CD}$.

The component form is found by subtracting the coordinates of the initial point from the terminal point.

$$\overline{AB} = \langle B_x - A_x, B_y - A_y\rangle$$

This implies that to find the coordinates of, for example, the terminal point

$$B_x = AB_x + A_x$$

$$B_y = AB_y + A_y$$

Therefore,

$$\overline{AB} = \langle 4 - 1, -3 - 2 \rangle = \langle 3, -5 \rangle$$

$$\overline{CD} = \langle 12 - 3, -9 - 6 \rangle = \langle 9, -15 \rangle$$

Consequently, to find the coordinates of the terminal point B

$$B_x = 3 + 1 = 4$$

$$B_y = -5 + 2 = -3$$

For $\mathbf{v} = \langle 3, -5 \rangle$, the magnitude (*norm* or length) is

$$\|\mathbf{v}\| = \sqrt{v_1^2 + v_2^2} = \sqrt{3^2 + (-5)^2} = \sqrt{34} = 5.83095$$

This can be generalized to $\mathbf{v} = \langle v_1, v_2, \ldots, v_n \rangle$.
In **R**, we use `Norm()` from the `pracma` package to compute the norm.

```
> v <- c(3, -5)
> Norm(v)
[1] 5.830952
```

An arbitrary vector may be converted to a unit vector, $\hat{v}$, which points to the same direction as **v** but with length 1, by dividing it by its norm

$$\hat{v} = \frac{\mathbf{v}}{\|\mathbf{v}\|} = \left(\frac{1}{\|\mathbf{v}\|}\right) < v_1, v_2 >= \frac{1}{\sqrt{34}} < 3, -5 >= \left\langle \frac{3}{\sqrt{34}}, -\frac{5}{\sqrt{34}} \right\rangle$$

We code a function, `unit_vec()`, to compute the unit vector in **R**

```
> unit_vec <- function(vector, p = 2){
+   vhat <- vector/(sum(abs(vector)^p)^(1/p))
+   return(vhat)
+ }
> unit_vec(v)
[1]  0.5144958 -0.8574929
> 3/sqrt(34)
[1] 0.5144958
> -5/sqrt(34)
[1] -0.8574929
> vec1 <- c(3/sqrt(34), -5/sqrt(34))
> Norm(vec1)
[1] 1
```

Note that the denominator in the formula, i.e. the magnitude of the vector, uses a part of the formula in the `Norm()` function. Use `getAnywhere()` to print the code of the `Norm()` function. The possibility of having access to the code of functions in **R** is a great asset.[7]

```
> getAnywhere(Norm())
A single object matching 'Norm' was found
It was found in the following places
  package:pracma
  namespace:pracma
with value

function (x, p = 2)
{
    stopifnot(is.numeric(x) ||
              is.complex(x),
              is.numeric(p),
        length(p) == 1)
    if (p > -Inf && p < Inf)
        sum(abs(x)^p)^(1/p)
    else if (p == Inf)
        max(abs(x))
    else if (p == -Inf)
        min(abs(x))
    else return(NULL)
}
<bytecode: 0x0000000004c73f28>
<environment: namespace:pracma>
```

We could directly use the `Norm()` function in the denominator of the `unit_vec()` function. We use the `require()` function to load the `pracma` package in the `unit_vec()` function. Note that `require()` works as `library()` but it is designed for use inside other functions.

```
> unit_vec <- function(vector, p = 2){
+   require("pracma")
+   vhat <- vector/Norm(vector, p)
+   return(vhat)
+ }
> unit_vec(v)
[1]  0.5144958 -0.8574929
```

[7] For built-in functions such as `summary()` use the `methods()` function to list all the available methods. For example: `methods(summary)` and then `getAnywhere(summary.default)`.

2.2.6 Parallel and Orthogonal Vectors

Two non-zero vectors **u** and **v** are parallel if there is some scalar k such as $\mathbf{u} = k\mathbf{v}$.

For example, let's suppose we have two vectors $\mathbf{u} = \langle 3, -5 \rangle$ and $\mathbf{v} = \langle 9, -15 \rangle$. We note that $\mathbf{v} = 3 \cdot \mathbf{u}$. Additionally, we can test the condition $u_1 \cdot v_2 = v_1 \cdot u_2$

```
> u <- c(3, -5)
> v <- c(9 , -15)
> k <- 3
> v == k*u
[1] TRUE TRUE
> u[[1]]*v[[2]] == v[[1]]*u[[2]]
[1] TRUE
```

Therefore, **u** and **v** are parallel.

The vectors, **u** and **v**, are orthogonal (i.e. they form a 90° angle) if $\mathbf{u} \cdot \mathbf{v} = 0$, i.e. the dot product of the two vectors is zero.

For example, let's check if the following two vectors $\mathbf{u} = \langle 1, 2, 3 \rangle$ and $\mathbf{v} = \langle 2, 1, -4/3 \rangle$ are orthogonal.

We again compute the dot product in two ways.

```
> u <- c(1, 2, 3)
> v <- c(2, 1, -4/3)
> uv <- sum(u*v)
> uv
[1] 0
> class(uv)
[1] "numeric"
> uv <- u%*%v
> uv
     [,1]
[1,]    0
> class(uv)
[1] "matrix" "array"
```

This confirms that they are orthogonal.

Additionally, if $\mathbf{u} \cdot \mathbf{v} > 0$ ($\mathbf{u} \cdot \mathbf{v} < 0$) then the angle between the two vectors is acute (obtuse).

2.2.7 Vector Projection

The vector projection of **u** onto **v** is defined as follows:

$$proj_v u = \frac{\mathbf{u} \cdot \mathbf{v}}{\|\mathbf{v}\|^2}\mathbf{v} \tag{2.1}$$

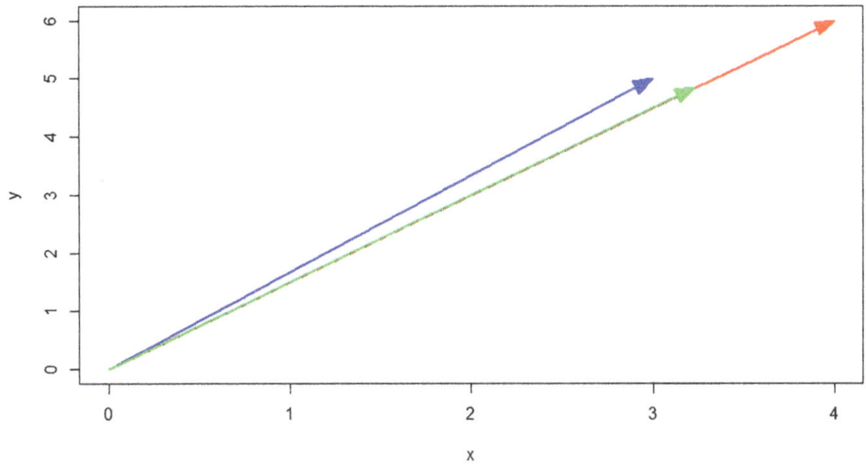

Fig. 2.14 Vector projection

For $\mathbf{u} = \langle 3, 5 \rangle$ and $\mathbf{v} = \langle 4, 6 \rangle$, the projection of $\mathbf{u}$ onto $\mathbf{v}$ is

```
> u <- c(3, 5)
> v <- c(4, 6)
> pvu <- (sum(u*v)/Norm(v)^2)*v
> pvu
[1] 3.230769 4.846154
```

Note that we computed the dot product *manually* to obtain a numeric object. In the exercise in Sect. 2.5.2, you are asked to write a function that computes vector projection.

Let's represent it with the `arrows2D()` function from `plot3D`. The green vector represents $proj_v u$ (Fig. 2.14).

```
> x0 <- c(0, 0, 0)
> y0 <- c(0, 0, 0)
> x1 <- c(3, 4, pvu[1])
> y1 <- c(5, 6, pvu[2])
> cols <- c("blue", "red", "green")
> arrows2D(x0, y0, x1, y1,
+          col = cols,
+          lwd = 2)
```

Let's consider another example with $\mathbf{u} = \langle 1, 2 \rangle$ and $\mathbf{v} = \langle 3, 0 \rangle$. This time we add the orthogonal vector that we compute as $u - proj_v u$. As expected, its dot product with $\mathbf{v}$ is 0 (Fig. 2.15).

```
> u <- c(1, 2)
> v <- c(3, 0)
```

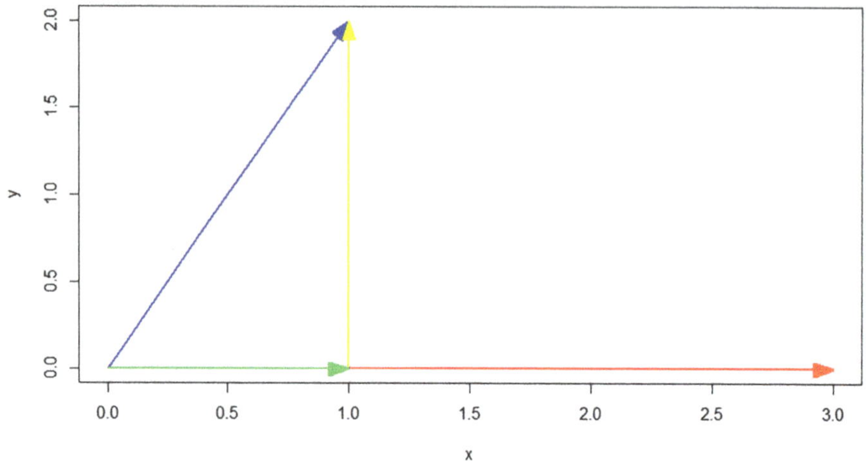

Fig. 2.15 Vector projection and orthogonal vector

```
> pvu <- (sum(u*v)/Norm(v)^2)*v
> pvu
[1] 1 0
> upvu <- u - pvu
> round(sum(upvu * v), 7)
[1] 0
> upvu
[1] 0 2
> x0 <- c(0, 0, 0, 1)
> y0 <- c(0, 0, 0, 0)
> x1 <- c(1, 3, pvu[1], (1+upvu[1]))
> y1 <- c(2, 0, pvu[2], (0+upvu[2]))
> cols <- c("blue", "red", "green", "yellow")
> arrows2D(x0, y0, x1, y1,
+          col = cols,
+          lwd = 2)
```

2.2.8 *Linear Independence*

Let V be a vector space over the field K, and let $\mathbf{v}_1, \mathbf{v}_2, \ldots, \mathbf{v}_n$ be elements of V. We say that $\mathbf{v}_1, \mathbf{v}_2, \ldots, \mathbf{v}_n$ are *linearly dependent* over K if there exist elements $a_1, a_2, \ldots, a_n$ in K not all equal to 0 such that

$$a_1\mathbf{v}_1 + a_2\mathbf{v}_2 + \ldots + a_n\mathbf{v}_n = 0 \tag{2.2}$$

If such numbers do not exist, then we say that $\mathbf{v}_1, \mathbf{v}_2, \ldots, \mathbf{v}_3$ are *linearly independent*.

For example, let's suppose we have $\mathbf{v}_1 = \begin{bmatrix} -1 \\ 2 \\ 0 \end{bmatrix}$, $\mathbf{v}_2 = \begin{bmatrix} 4 \\ 0 \\ 8 \end{bmatrix}$ and $\mathbf{v}_3 = \begin{bmatrix} 3 \\ -1 \\ 5 \end{bmatrix}$.

Let's write Eq. 2.2:

$$a_1\mathbf{v}_1 + a_2\mathbf{v}_2 + a_3\mathbf{v}_3 = 0$$

as

$$a_1 \begin{bmatrix} -1 \\ 2 \\ 0 \end{bmatrix} + a_2 \begin{bmatrix} 4 \\ 0 \\ 8 \end{bmatrix} + a_3 \begin{bmatrix} 3 \\ -1 \\ 5 \end{bmatrix} = \begin{bmatrix} 0 \\ 0 \\ 0 \end{bmatrix} \tag{2.3}$$

From (2.3) we can more easily observe that if the vectors are linearly independent then only the trivial solution exists, i.e. $a_1 = a_2 = a_3 = 0$. Conversely, the vectors are linear dependent if a non-trivial solution exists.

Equation 2.3 can be also written as (Sect. 2.3.7.1)

$$\begin{bmatrix} -1 & 4 & 3 \\ 2 & 0 & -1 \\ 0 & 8 & 5 \end{bmatrix} \begin{bmatrix} a_1 \\ a_2 \\ a_3 \end{bmatrix} = \begin{bmatrix} 0 \\ 0 \\ 0 \end{bmatrix}$$

This linear system is homogeneous because the right hand side is the zero vector. We solve it by setting up an auxiliary matrix and by using row operations to reduce it to echelon form. We will return to these concepts later in this chapter. We use the `echelon()` function from the `matlib` package in **R** to compute it. We set a `V` matrix and the right hand side vector `o`.

```
> v1 <- c(-1, 2, 0)
> v2 <- c(4, 0, 8)
> v3 <- c(3, -1, 5)
> o <- c(0, 0, 0)
> V <- matrix(c(v1, v2, v3), ncol = 3)
> V
     [,1] [,2] [,3]
[1,]   -1    4    3
[2,]    2    0   -1
[3,]    0    8    5
> echelon(V, o)
     [,1] [,2]   [,3] [,4]
[1,]    1    0 -0.500    0
[2,]    0    1  0.625    0
[3,]    0    0  0.000    0
```

This means that $a_1 - 0.5a_3 = 0$, $a_2 + 0.625a_3 = 0$ and for last variable we can set $a_3 = k$, a free variable. In turn, it means that $a_1 = 0.5a_3$, $a_2 = -0.625a_3$, and if we set $a_3 = 2$, it results that $a_1 = 1$, $a_2 = -1.25$ and $a_3 = 2$ are a set of coefficients satisfying Eq. 2.2.

```
> a <- c(1, -1.25, 2)
> V %*% a
     [,1]
[1,]    0
[2,]    0
[3,]    0
```

Therefore, these vectors are linear dependent since a non-trivial solution exists.

Since in this case V is a square matrix, we can compute the *determinant* (*det*) (Sect. 2.3.8). If $det \neq 0$ the vectors are linear independent. In **R**, we use the `det()` function to compute the determinant

```
> det(V)
[1] 0
```

$det = 0$ confirms that they are linear dependent.

Next, we examine a linear independent cases:

```
> v1 <- c(2, 5, 3)
> v2 <- c(1, 1, 1)
> v3 <- c(4, -2, 0)
> o <- c(0, 0, 0)
> V <- matrix(c(v1, v2, v3), ncol = 3)
> V
     [,1] [,2] [,3]
[1,]    2    1    4
[2,]    5    1   -2
[3,]    3    1    0
> echelon(V, o)
     [,1] [,2] [,3] [,4]
[1,]    1    0    0    0
[2,]    0    1    0    0
[3,]    0    0    1    0
> det(V)
[1] 6
```

In this case, we have a trivial solution, i.e. $a_1 = a_2 = a_3 = 0$. Consequently, the vectors are linear independent as confirmed by $det \neq 0$.

Furthermore, note that parallel vectors are linear dependent. For example, the parallel vectors from Sect. 2.2.6

```
> v1 <- c(3, -5)
> v2 <- c(9, -15)
> o <- c(0, 0)
> V <- matrix(c(v1, v2), ncol = 2)
> V
     [,1] [,2]
[1,]    3    9
[2,]   -5  -15
> echelon(V, o)
     [,1] [,2] [,3]
[1,]    1    3    0
[2,]    0    0    0
> round(det(V), 3)
[1] 0
```

Additionally, note that any set of 3 or more vectors in $\mathbb{R}^2$ is linearly dependent and any set of 4 or more vectors in $\mathbb{R}^3$ is linearly dependent. Therefore, we can state that vectors are linearly dependent if there are more vectors than dimensions.

Finally, we define *basis* of V as follows: if elements $\mathbf{v}_1, \mathbf{v}_2, \ldots, \mathbf{v}_n$ of V span[8] V and are linearly independent, then $\mathbf{v}_1, \mathbf{v}_2, \ldots, \mathbf{v}_n$ form a *basis* of V. Or, in other words, a basis is a set of linearly independent vectors from which any other vector in the vector space can be built upon.

For example, let's verify if the vectors $\mathbf{v}_1 = \begin{bmatrix} 1 \\ 1 \end{bmatrix}$ and $\mathbf{v}_2 = \begin{bmatrix} -1 \\ 2 \end{bmatrix}$ form a basis of $\mathbb{R}^2$.

First, we need to verify that they are linear independent.

```
> v1 <- c(1, 1)
> v2 <- c(-1, 2)
> o <- c(0, 0)
> V <- matrix(c(v1, v2), ncol = 2)
> V
     [,1] [,2]
[1,]    1   -1
[2,]    1    2
> echelon(V, o)
     [,1] [,2] [,3]
[1,]    1    0    0
[2,]    0    1    0
> det(V)
[1] 3
```

[8] Or in other words, generate all vectors in a vector space. The span of a set of vectors is the set of all linear combinations of the vectors. For example $span(\mathbf{v}_1, \mathbf{v}_2) = a_1\mathbf{v}_1 + a_2\mathbf{v}_2$.

Then, let (a, b) be an arbitrary element of $\mathbb{R}^2$. We have to show that there exist numbers x, y such that

$$\begin{bmatrix} 1 & -1 \\ 1 & 2 \end{bmatrix} \begin{bmatrix} x \\ y \end{bmatrix} = \begin{bmatrix} a \\ b \end{bmatrix} \tag{2.4}$$

Equation 2.4 can be written as system of linear equations (Sect. 2.3.7)

$$\begin{aligned} x - y &= a \\ x + 2y &= b \end{aligned} \tag{2.5}$$

The solutions of (2.5) are $y = \frac{b-a}{3}$ and $x = \frac{b-a}{3} + a$.

If we pick any element of $\mathbb{R}^2$ for a, b we find the solutions are in $\mathbb{R}^2$. This confirms that $\mathbf{v}_1, \mathbf{v}_2$ form a basis of $\mathbb{R}^2$. The number of vectors in a basis for V is called the dimension of V. Furthermore, we define (x, y) as the coordinates of a, b with respect to the basis.

Finally, we should remark that dependence prevents a system of linear equations from having a unique solution because it means that the system has more *unknowns* than equations (Sect. 2.3.7).

2.3 Matrices

An array of numbers in a field K

$$\begin{bmatrix} a_{11} & a_{12} & a_{13} & \cdot & a_{1n} \\ a_{21} & a_{22} & a_{23} & \cdot & a_{2n} \\ \vdots & \vdots & \vdots & \ddots & \vdots \\ a_{m1} & a_{m2} & a_{m3} & \cdot & a_{mn} \end{bmatrix}$$

is called a matrix in K. It has m number of rows and n number of columns, i.e. it is a $m \times n$ (read "m by n") matrix. We call a_{ij} the *ij*-entry or the *ij*-component of the matrix. For example,

$$A = \begin{bmatrix} 2 & 3 \\ 4 & 6 \\ 6 & 12 \end{bmatrix}$$

A is a 3×2 matrix because $m = 3$ and $n = 2$. The entry a_{11}, i.e. first row and first column, is 2 and the entry a_{22}, i.e. second row and second column, is 6.

If a matrix has an equal numbers of rows and columns, $m = n$, it is called a square matrix. For example,

$$B = \begin{bmatrix} 1 & 2 \\ 3 & 4 \end{bmatrix} \quad C = \begin{bmatrix} 5 & 0 & 2 \\ 4 & 1 & 2 \\ 1 & 12 & -2 \end{bmatrix}$$

B and C are square matrices. B is a 2×2 matrix and C is a 3×3 matrix.

In **R**, we build a matrix using the `matrix()` function. The first entry is the data, `nrow =` is the desired number of rows, `ncol =` is the desired number of columns, and `byrow =` fills the matrix by columns if `FALSE` (default), by rows if `TRUE`. For example,

```
> A <- matrix(c(1, 2 ,3,
+                  4, 5, 6),
+                nrow = 2,
+                ncol = 3)
> A
     [,1] [,2] [,3]
[1,]    1    3    5
[2,]    2    4    6
> A <- matrix(c(1, 2 ,3,
+                  4, 5, 6),
+                nrow = 2,
+                ncol = 3,
+                byrow = T)
> A
     [,1] [,2] [,3]
[1,]    1    2    3
[2,]    4    5    6
> A <- matrix(c(1, 2 ,3,
+                  4, 5, 6),
+                nrow = 3,
+                ncol = 2)
> A
     [,1] [,2]
[1,]    1    4
[2,]    2    5
[3,]    3    6
> A <- matrix(c(1, 2 ,3,
+                  4, 5, 6),
+                nrow = 3,
+                ncol = 2,
+                byrow = T)
> A
     [,1] [,2]
[1,]    1    2
[2,]    3    4
[3,]    5    6
```

2.3.1 Matrix Operations

2.3.1.1 Addition

Addition of matrices is defined only when the matrices to be added have the same size, i.e. same number of rows and columns. For example.

$$A = \begin{bmatrix} a & b \\ c & d \end{bmatrix} \quad B = \begin{bmatrix} e & f \\ g & h \end{bmatrix}$$

We add the entries $a_{ij} + b_{ij}$ for $A + B$. Therefore,

$$A + B = \begin{bmatrix} a+e & b+f \\ c+g & d+h \end{bmatrix}$$

For example,

$$A = \begin{bmatrix} 1 & 2 \\ 3 & 4 \\ 5 & 6 \end{bmatrix} \quad B = \begin{bmatrix} -2 & 3 \\ 5 & -1 \\ 2 & 2 \end{bmatrix}$$

$$A + B = \begin{bmatrix} -1 & 5 \\ 8 & 3 \\ 7 & 8 \end{bmatrix}$$

```
> A <- matrix(c(1, 2 ,3,
+                  4, 5, 6),
+                nrow = 3,
+                ncol = 2,
+                byrow = T)
> A
     [,1] [,2]
[1,]    1    2
[2,]    3    4
[3,]    5    6
> B <- matrix(c(-2, 3,
+                  5, -1,
+                  2, 2),
+                nrow = 3,
+                ncol = 2,
+                byrow = T)
> B
     [,1] [,2]
[1,]   -2    3
```

```
[2,]     5    -1
[3,]     2     2
> A + B
      [,1] [,2]
[1,]    -1    5
[2,]     8    3
[3,]     7    8
```

For subtraction we subtracts the entries. For example, $A - B$

```
> A - B
      [,1] [,2]
[1,]     3   -1
[2,]    -2    5
[3,]     3    4
```

2.3.1.2 Multiplication

Multiplication of a matrix, A, by a number, k, is equal to $kA = (ka_{ij})$. In other words, we multiply each component of A by k. This operation is called *scalar multiplication*. For example,

$$6 \cdot A = \begin{bmatrix} 6 \cdot 1 & 6 \cdot 2 \\ 6 \cdot 3 & 6 \cdot 4 \\ 6 \cdot 5 & 6 \cdot 6 \end{bmatrix} = \begin{bmatrix} 6 & 12 \\ 18 & 24 \\ 30 & 36 \end{bmatrix}$$

```
> 6 * A
      [,1] [,2]
[1,]     6   12
[2,]    18   24
[3,]    30   36
```

For all matrices A, we find that $A + (-1)A = 0$, where 0 is the zero matrix (*null matrix*).

```
> A + (-1*A)
      [,1] [,2]
[1,]     0    0
[2,]     0    0
[3,]     0    0
```

The multiplication between two matrices requires a *conformability condition*, i.e. column dimension of the first matrix A must be equal to the row dimension of the second matrix B. Therefore, we can multiply AB if $A = m \times n$ and $B = n \times p$. This operation is called *matrix multiplication*. For example,

$$A = \begin{bmatrix} a_{11} & a_{12} \end{bmatrix} \quad B = \begin{bmatrix} b_{11} & b_{12} & b_{13} \\ b_{21} & b_{22} & b_{23} \end{bmatrix}$$

A is a 1×2 matrix and B is a 2×3 matrix. Therefore, these matrices can be multiplied as follows:

$$AB = \begin{bmatrix} a_{11}b_{11} + a_{12}b_{21} & a_{11}b_{12} + a_{12}b_{22} & a_{11}b_{13} + a_{12}b_{23} \end{bmatrix}$$

AB is a 1×3 matrix, that is $m \times p$ matrix, the number of rows of the first matrix and the number of columns of the second matrix.

For example,

$$A = \begin{bmatrix} 2 & 5 \end{bmatrix} \quad B = \begin{bmatrix} -2 & 3 & 6 \\ 9 & 0 & 2 \end{bmatrix}$$

$$AB = \begin{bmatrix} -4 + 45 & 6 + 0 & 12 + 10 \end{bmatrix} = \begin{bmatrix} 41 & 6 & 22 \end{bmatrix}$$

Let's see another example where A is a 2×2 matrix and B is a 2×3.

$$A = \begin{bmatrix} 1 & 2 \\ 3 & 4 \end{bmatrix} \quad B = \begin{bmatrix} 5 & 6 & 7 \\ 8 & 9 & 10 \end{bmatrix}$$

Since the number of columns of the first matrix A equals the number of rows of the second matrix B, the multiplication can be computed. Furthermore, we know in advance that the matrix outcome of the multiplication will have 2 rows, the number of rows of the first matrix A, and three columns, the number of columns of the second matrix B.

$$AB = \begin{bmatrix} 5 + 16 & 6 + 18 & 7 + 20 \\ 15 + 32 & 18 + 36 & 21 + 40 \end{bmatrix} = \begin{bmatrix} 21 & 24 & 27 \\ 47 & 54 & 61 \end{bmatrix}$$

Matrix multiplication can be complex to remember at the beginning. In my case, after checking the conformability condition, I used an "arrow" method to memorize it, where the first matrix is represented with as many horizontal arrows as the number of rows of the matrix and the second matrix is represented with as many vertical arrows as the number of columns of the matrix. The length of the arrows is the same because for the first matrix it corresponds to the number of columns and for the second matrix to the number of rows. In fact, we know that the column dimension of the first matrix must be equal to the row dimension of the second matrix. The horizontal arrow is drawn from left to right and the vertical arrows is drawn from top to bottom. This will give the direction of the multiplication where we multiply the first element on the horizontal arrow with the first element of the vertical arrows, the second element on the horizontal arrow with the second element of the vertical arrow and so on. Finally, we sum them up before moving to other arrows combinations.

To make it clearer, let's apply it to the previous example where A is a 2×2 matrix and B is a 2×3. In this case, matrix A is represented with two horizontal arrows and matrix B with three vertical arrows.

$$A = \begin{bmatrix} \rightarrow_1 \\ \rightarrow_2 \end{bmatrix} \quad B = \begin{bmatrix} \downarrow_1 & \downarrow_2 & \downarrow_3 \end{bmatrix}$$

$$AB = \begin{bmatrix} \rightarrow_1\downarrow_1 & \rightarrow_1\downarrow_2 & \rightarrow_1\downarrow_3 \\ \rightarrow_2\downarrow_1 & \rightarrow_2\downarrow_2 & \rightarrow_2\downarrow_3 \end{bmatrix}$$

In **R**, we compute matrix multiplication with `%*%`.

```
> A <- matrix(c(2, 5),
+               nrow = 1,
+               ncol = 2,
+               byrow = T)
> A
     [,1] [,2]
[1,]    2    5
> B <- matrix(c(-2, 3, 6,
+                 9, 0, 2),
+               nrow = 2,
+               ncol = 3,
+               byrow = T)
> B
     [,1] [,2] [,3]
[1,]   -2    3    6
[2,]    9    0    2
> A %*% B
     [,1] [,2] [,3]
[1,]   41    6   22
> A <- matrix(c(1, 2,
+                 3, 4),
+               nrow = 2,
+               ncol = 2, byrow = TRUE)
> A
     [,1] [,2]
[1,]    1    2
[2,]    3    4
> B <- matrix(c(5, 6, 7,
+                 8, 9, 10),
+               nrow = 2,
+               ncol = 3, byrow = TRUE)
> B
     [,1] [,2] [,3]
```

```
[1,]    5    6    7
[2,]    8    9   10
> A %*% B
     [,1] [,2] [,3]
[1,]   21   24   27
[2,]   47   54   61
```

Another example:

```
> A <- matrix(c(-2, 3, 4, 6,
+                4, -4, 3, 0,
+                1, 8, 5, 3),
+              nrow = 3,
+              ncol = 4,
+              byrow = T)
> A
     [,1] [,2] [,3] [,4]
[1,]   -2    3    4    6
[2,]    4   -4    3    0
[3,]    1    8    5    3
> B <- matrix(c(-1, -2,
+                5, 3,
+                5, 4,
+                7, 8),
+              nrow = 4,
+              ncol = 2,
+              byrow = T)
> B
     [,1] [,2]
[1,]   -1   -2
[2,]    5    3
[3,]    5    4
[4,]    7    8
> A %*% B
     [,1] [,2]
[1,]   79   77
[2,]   -9   -8
[3,]   85   66
```

Matrix multiplication is not commutative. Given A and B in the examples, BA cannot be computed. In fact, in the multiplication BA the number of columns of B is not equal to the number of rows of A. If we try BA in **R** we get an error

```
> B %*% A
Error in B %*% A : non-conformable arguments
```

If we multiply two square matrices

$$A = \begin{bmatrix} 2 & 4 \\ 1 & 3 \end{bmatrix} \quad B = \begin{bmatrix} -3 & -4 \\ 3 & 5 \end{bmatrix}$$

we obtain two different results for AB and BA.

```
> A <- matrix(c(2, 4,
+               1, 3),
+             nrow = 2,
+             ncol = 2,
+             byrow = T)
> A
     [,1] [,2]
[1,]    2    4
[2,]    1    3
> B <- matrix(c(-3, -4,
+               3, 5),
+             nrow = 2,
+             ncol = 2,
+             byrow = T)
> B
     [,1] [,2]
[1,]   -3   -4
[2,]    3    5
> A %*% B
     [,1] [,2]
[1,]    6   12
[2,]    6   11
> B %*% A
     [,1] [,2]
[1,]  -10  -24
[2,]   11   27
```

Exceptions to non-commutative multiplication, i.e. $AB = BA$, are due to the fact that one of the two matrices is an identity matrix (Sect. 2.3.3) or an inverse matrix (Sect. 2.3.6).

2.3.1.3 Transpose

The transpose of a $m \times n$ A matrix is a $n \times m$ matrix that is denoted as A^T or A'. Taking the transpose of a matrix consists in interchanging rows into columns and vice versa.

In **R**, we use the `t()` function to compute the transpose. For example,

```
> A <- matrix(c(-2, 3, 4, 6,
+                4, -4, 3, 0,
+                1, 8, 5, 3),
+              nrow = 3,
+              ncol = 4,
+              byrow = T)
> A
     [,1] [,2] [,3] [,4]
[1,]   -2    3    4    6
[2,]    4   -4    3    0
[3,]    1    8    5    3
> t(A)
     [,1] [,2] [,3]
[1,]   -2    4    1
[2,]    3   -4    8
[3,]    4    3    5
[4,]    6    0    3
```

2.3.2 Symmetric Matrix

A square matrix A is said to be symmetric if it is equal to its transpose, i.e. if $A = A^T$. For example,

```
> A <- matrix(c(1, -1, 2,
+                -1, 0, 3,
+                2, 3, 7),
+              nrow = 3,
+              ncol = 3,
+              byrow = T)
> A
     [,1] [,2] [,3]
[1,]    1   -1    2
[2,]   -1    0    3
[3,]    2    3    7
> t(A)
     [,1] [,2] [,3]
[1,]    1   -1    2
[2,]   -1    0    3
[3,]    2    3    7
```

2.3.3 Diagonal Matrix and Identity Matrix

A square matrix A with all its components equal to zero except for the *diagonal* components, $a_{11}, a_{22}, \cdots, a_{nn}$, is said to be a *diagonal matrix*. For example,

$$\begin{bmatrix} 1 & 0 & 0 & 0 \\ 0 & -2 & 0 & 0 \\ 0 & 0 & 3 & 0 \\ 0 & 0 & 0 & 4 \end{bmatrix}$$

In **R**, we generate a diagonal matrix with the `diag()` function.

```
> diag(c(1, -2, 3, 4),
+         ncol = 4,
+         nrow = 4)
     [,1] [,2] [,3] [,4]
[1,]    1    0    0    0
[2,]    0   -2    0    0
[3,]    0    0    3    0
[4,]    0    0    0    4
```

If all the diagonal components of a diagonal matrix are 1, the diagonal matrix is said to be an *identity matrix*

$$\begin{bmatrix} 1 & 0 & 0 & 0 \\ 0 & 1 & 0 & 0 \\ 0 & 0 & 1 & 0 \\ 0 & 0 & 0 & 1 \end{bmatrix}$$

The identity matrix plays a role in matrix multiplication that is similar to the role played by 1 in a regular multiplication with real numbers.

The `diag()` function by default sets value 1 on the main diagonal. Therefore, we can just set the number of rows and columns for the identity matrix

```
> diag(ncol = 4,
+         nrow = 4)
     [,1] [,2] [,3] [,4]
[1,]    1    0    0    0
[2,]    0    1    0    0
[3,]    0    0    1    0
[4,]    0    0    0    1
```

In alternative, the diagonal matrix in **R** can be built by providing only a vector of at least length 2. In this case a matrix with the given diagonal and zero off-diagonal entries is returned. If we provide only a scalar, as we will see later in the book, a square identity matrix of size given by the scalar is returned.

2.3.3.1 Trace of a Square Matrix

The trace of a square matrix A is defined as the sum of the diagonal elements, $\sum_i a_{ii}$.[9] For example,

$$A = \begin{bmatrix} 3 & 2 \\ 2 & 6 \end{bmatrix}, \quad tr(A) = 3 + 6 = 9$$

For

$$B = \begin{bmatrix} 1 & 2 & 3 \\ 4 & 5 & 6 \\ 7 & 8 & 9 \end{bmatrix}, \quad tr(B) = 1 + 5 + 9 = 15$$

Let's build a function to calculate the trace, `tr()`. We use the `stopifnot()` function to check that the matrix supplied to the `tr()` function is square

```
> tr <- function(X){
+
+   stopifnot(nrow(X) == ncol(X))
+   sum(diag(X))
+
+ }
```

Then, we compute the trace and check some of its properties directly with **R**.

```
> A <- matrix(c(3, 2,
+               2, 6),
+             nrow = 2,
+             ncol = 2,
+             byrow = T)
> A
     [,1] [,2]
[1,]    3    2
[2,]    2    6
> tr(A)
[1] 9
> B <- matrix(c(1, 2, 3,
+               4, 5, 6,
+               7, 8, 9),
+             nrow = 3,
+             ncol = 3,
```

[9] $\sum$ is the summation symbol. In this case it is short for $a_{11} + a_{22} + \ldots + a_{nn}$. On the other hand, Π is the product symbol. For example, $\Pi_i a_{ii}$ is short for $a_{11} \cdot a_{22} \cdot \ldots \cdot a_{nn}$.

```
+               byrow = T)
> B
     [,1] [,2] [,3]
[1,]    1    2    3
[2,]    4    5    6
[3,]    7    8    9
> tr(B)
[1] 15
> C <- matrix(c(-2, 3, 4,
+                 4, -4, 3,
+                 1, 2, 5,
+                 -1, -2, 5),
+               nrow = 4,
+               ncol = 3,
+               byrow = T)
> C
     [,1] [,2] [,3]
[1,]   -2    3    4
[2,]    4   -4    3
[3,]    1    2    5
[4,]   -1   -2    5
> tr(C)
 Error in tr(C) : nrow(X) == ncol(X) is not TRUE
> D <- matrix(c(0, 2, 2,
+                 3, 1, -2,
+                 3, 2, 4),
+               nrow = 3,
+               ncol = 3,
+               byrow = T)
> D
     [,1] [,2] [,3]
[1,]    0    2    2
[2,]    3    1   -2
[3,]    3    2    4
> tr(D)
[1] 5
> # properties
> tr(B) + tr(D)
[1] 20
> tr(B + D)
[1] 20
> tr(B%*%D)
[1] 74
> tr(D%*%B)
[1] 74
```

```
> tr(B) == tr(t(B))
[1] TRUE
> 2 * tr(D) == tr(2*D)
[1] TRUE
```

Furthermore, the trace equals the sum of eigenvalues (Sect. 2.3.9).

2.3.4 Triangular Matrix

A square matrix A is a triangular matrix if all entries above or below the main diagonal are 0. More precisely, A is said to be an upper triangular (UT) if $a_{ij} = 0$ for $i > j$; A is said to be a lower triangular (LT) if $a_{ij} = 0$ for $i < j$. The product of two upper (lower) triangular matrices is an upper (lower) triangular matrix.

```
> A <- matrix(c(1, 2, 3,
+               0, 4, 5,
+               0, 0, 6),
+             nrow = 3,
+             ncol = 3,
+             byrow = T)
> A
     [,1] [,2] [,3]
[1,]    1    2    3
[2,]    0    4    5
[3,]    0    0    6
> B <- matrix(c(7, 8, 9,
+               0, 10, 11,
+               0, 0, 12),
+             nrow = 3,
+             ncol = 3,
+             byrow = T)
> B
     [,1] [,2] [,3]
[1,]    7    8    9
[2,]    0   10   11
[3,]    0    0   12
> A %*% B
     [,1] [,2] [,3]
[1,]    7   28   67
[2,]    0   40  104
[3,]    0    0   72
> B %*% A
     [,1] [,2] [,3]
[1,]    7   46  115
```

```
[2,]    0   40  116
[3,]    0    0   72

> A <- matrix(c(1, 0, 0,
+                2, 4, 0,
+                3, 6, 6),
+              nrow = 3,
+              ncol = 3,
+              byrow = T)
> A
     [,1] [,2] [,3]
[1,]    1    0    0
[2,]    2    4    0
[3,]    3    6    6
> B <- matrix(c(7, 0, 0,
+                8, 10, 0,
+                9, 12, 12),
+              nrow = 3,
+              ncol = 3,
+              byrow = T)
> B
     [,1] [,2] [,3]
[1,]    7    0    0
[2,]    8   10    0
[3,]    9   12   12
> A %*% B
     [,1] [,2] [,3]
[1,]    7    0    0
[2,]   46   40    0
[3,]  123  132   72
> B %*% A
     [,1] [,2] [,3]
[1,]    7    0    0
[2,]   28   40    0
[3,]   69  120   72
```

2.3.5 *Idempotent Matrix*

If a matrix that is multiplied by itself does not change, $AA = A$ or $A = A^2 = A^3 = \cdots = A^n$, it is said to be an *idempotent matrix*. The simplest example of an idempotent matrix is the identity matrix.

```
> A <- diag(ncol = 4,
+           nrow = 4)
```

```
> A %*% A
     [,1] [,2] [,3] [,4]
[1,]    1    0    0    0
[2,]    0    1    0    0
[3,]    0    0    1    0
[4,]    0    0    0    1
```

Another example is the matrix

$$A = \begin{bmatrix} 3 & -6 \\ 1 & -2 \end{bmatrix}$$

```
> A <- matrix(c(3, -6,
+                 1, -2),
+               nrow = 2,
+               ncol = 2,
+               byrow = T)
> A
     [,1] [,2]
[1,]    3   -6
[2,]    1   -2
> A %*% A
     [,1] [,2]
[1,]    3   -6
[2,]    1   -2
```

2.3.6 The Inverse of a Matrix

A square matrix A has an inverse matrix, denoted as A^{-1} (read as "A inverse") if $AA^{-1} = I$, that is if A multiplied by its inverse gives as result the identity matrix. This is also true for $A^{-1}A = I$.

The inverse matrix plays the role of division in matrix algebra. We can see similarities with the division with numbers. If a is a number, dividing by a (as long as $a \neq 0$), it is the same as multiplying by $\frac{1}{a}$, that we write as a^{-1} as well.

Let's see an example on how to find an inverse matrix. Let's suppose that the matrix A is the following

$$A = \begin{bmatrix} 1 & 2 \\ 4 & 6 \end{bmatrix}$$

We have another information, the identity matrix

$$I = \begin{bmatrix} 1 & 0 \\ 0 & 1 \end{bmatrix}$$

We need to find A^{-1} that we set as follows

$$A^{-1} = \begin{bmatrix} a & b \\ c & d \end{bmatrix}$$

Therefore,

$$\begin{bmatrix} 1 & 2 \\ 4 & 6 \end{bmatrix} \begin{bmatrix} a & b \\ c & d \end{bmatrix} = \begin{bmatrix} 1 & 0 \\ 0 & 1 \end{bmatrix}$$

From the multiplication AA^{-1} we have the following four equations

$$\begin{aligned} a + 2c &= 1 \\ b + 2d &= 0 \\ 4a + 6c &= 0 \\ 4b + 6d &= 1 \end{aligned} \tag{2.6}$$

Equation 2.6 is a system of four equations with four unknowns. From the second equation $b = -2d$ and from the third equation $a = -\frac{3}{2}c$. Substituting $b = -2d$ in $4b + 6d = 1$, we find that $4(-2d) + 6d = 1$ and consequently $d = -\frac{1}{2}$ and $b = 1$.

Substituting $a = -\frac{3}{2}c$ in $a+2c = 1$, we find that $-\frac{3}{2}c+2c = 1$ and consequently $c = 2$ and $a = -3$.

Therefore,

$$A^{-1} = \begin{bmatrix} -3 & 1 \\ 2 & -\frac{1}{2} \end{bmatrix}$$

In **R**, we use the `solve()` function to find the inverse.

```
> A <- matrix(c(1, 2,
+                4, 6),
+              nrow = 2,
+              ncol = 2,
+              byrow = T)
> A
     [,1] [,2]
[1,]    1    2
[2,]    4    6
> det(A)
[1] -2
> A1 <- solve(A)
> A1
```

```
      [,1] [,2]
[1,]    -3  1.0
[2,]     2 -0.5
```

To verify if it is correct $A^{-1}A = I$.

```
> A %*% A1
      [,1] [,2]
[1,]     1    0
[2,]     0    1
```

Note also that

```
> A1 %*% A
      [,1] [,2]
[1,]     1    0
[2,]     0    1
```

If A and B are invertible, AB is also invertible and $(AB)^{-1} = B^{-1}A^{-1}$. Let's see an example in **R**.

```
> B <- matrix(c(-2, 1,
+                  5, 0),
+                nrow = 2,
+                ncol = 2,
+                byrow = T)
> B
      [,1] [,2]
[1,]    -2    1
[2,]     5    0
> det(B)
[1] -5
> B1 <- solve(B)
> B1
      [,1] [,2]
[1,]     0  0.2
[2,]     1  0.4
> B %*% B1
      [,1] [,2]
[1,]     1    0
[2,]     0    1
> AB <- A %*% B
> AB
      [,1] [,2]
[1,]     8    1
[2,]    22    4
> AB1 <- solve(AB)
> AB1
```

```
     [,1] [,2]
[1,]  0.4 -0.1
[2,] -2.2  0.8
> B1A1 <- B1 %*% A1
> B1A1
     [,1] [,2]
[1,]  0.4 -0.1
[2,] -2.2  0.8
```

Furthermore, $(ABC)^{-1} = C^{-1}B^{-1}A^{-1}$.

```
> C <- matrix(c(4, 2,
+               2, 0),
+             nrow = 2,
+             ncol = 2,
+             byrow = T)
> C
     [,1] [,2]
[1,]    4    2
[2,]    2    0
> det(C)
[1] -4
> C1 <- solve(C)
> C1
     [,1] [,2]
[1,]  0.0  0.5
[2,]  0.5 -1.0
> C %*% C1
     [,1] [,2]
[1,]    1    0
[2,]    0    1
> ABC1 <- solve(A %*% B %*% C)
> ABC1
     [,1]  [,2]
[1,] -1.1  0.40
[2,]  2.4 -0.85
> C1B1A1 <- C1 %*% B1 %*% A1
> C1B1A1
     [,1]  [,2]
[1,] -1.1  0.40
[2,]  2.4 -0.85
```

Note that not all the square matrices are invertible.

```
> A <- matrix(c(3, -6,
+                 1, -2),
+               nrow = 2,
+               ncol = 2,
+               byrow = T)
> A
     [,1] [,2]
[1,]    3   -6
[2,]    1   -2
> det(A)
[1] 0
> solve(A)
Error in solve.default(A) :
  Lapack routine dgesv:
  system is exactly singular: U[2,2] = 0
```

Matrices that do not have an inverse are said to be *singular*. Those with an inverse are said to be *nonsingular*.

2.3.7 System of Linear Equations

Let's consider linear equation (2.7)

$$x + 1 = 4 \tag{2.7}$$

By subtracting 1 on both sides of (2.7), we find that the solution is $x = 3$.
Let's suppose now that the equation is (2.8)

$$x + y = 4 \tag{2.8}$$

If we solve for x we find that

$$x = -y + 4 \tag{2.9}$$

Because we have two *unknowns* we need two equations to find a unique solution (if it exists).

Let's suppose that the second equation is

$$2x + y = 7 \tag{2.10}$$

We can substitute the value we found for x in (2.9) in (2.10)

$$2(-y + 4) + y = 7$$

It results that $y = 1$. We plug this value back into (2.9), $x = -(1) + 4$, to find that $x = 3$.

To check if we are right we can plug the values back into the Eqs. 2.8 and 2.10

$$3 + 1 = 4$$

$$2 \cdot 3 + 1 = 7$$

and verify the equality. This shows that we are correct. We solved a system of two linear equations in two unknowns.

$$\begin{cases} x + y = 4 \\ 2x + y = 7 \end{cases} \tag{2.11}$$

Therefore, to solve a system of linear equations we have to find the values of the unknown that satisfy the equality. Based on this fact, we can write a function, `sys_leq()`, that uses a nested loop to solve simple systems of two linear equations.[10] Note that this function works only with integer solutions (in the exercise in Sect. 2.5.3 you are asked to write another function to solve systems of two linear equations).

Let's analyse how it works. First of all, we need to supply two linear equations written as character to the function. In the body of the function we use the `gsub()` function to replace = with == to evaluate the equality. Then, we implement a nested loop. Note how we write the conditional statement in the `if()` function. Inside the `any()` function, we use `parse()` to return an `expression` to be evaluated with `eval()`. Finally, we store the solutions in `res`. We also set the names for each solutions in `res`.

```
> sys_leq <- function(eq1, eq2){
+
+   EQ1 <- gsub("=", "==", eq1)
+   EQ2 <- gsub("=", "==", eq2)
+
+   for(x in seq(-10, 10, 1)){
+
+     for(y in seq(-10, 10, 1)){
+
```

[10] We will discuss nested loops in more details in Sect. 2.3.8.2.

```
+        if(any(eval(parse(text = EQ1))) &
+           any(eval(parse(text = EQ2)))){
+
+          res <- c("x*" = x, "y*" = y)
+
+        }
+
+      }
+
+    }
+
+    return(res)
+
+ }
```

For example, to solve the previous system of equations

```
> eq1 <- "x + y = 4"
> eq2 <- "2*x + y = 7"
> sys_leq(eq1, eq2)
x* y*
 3  1
```

Another example

```
> eq1 <- "2*x - 4  = -3*y"
> eq2 <- "- y - 7 = -x"
> sys_leq(eq1, eq2)
x* y*
 5 -2
```

2.3.7.1 System of Linear Equations and Matrices

We can solve more efficiently a system of linear equations by using matrices.

Let's write the coefficients of the equations in system (2.11) in a matrix A as follows

$$A = \begin{bmatrix} 1 & 1 \\ 2 & 1 \end{bmatrix}$$

and the constant to the right of the equal sign in a column vector $\mathbf{b}$ as follows

$$\mathbf{b} = \begin{bmatrix} 4 \\ 7 \end{bmatrix}$$

Then, with

$$\mathbf{x} = \begin{bmatrix} x \\ y \end{bmatrix}$$

it follows that

$$A\mathbf{x} = \mathbf{b}$$

and therefore,

$$\mathbf{x} = A^{-1}\mathbf{b}$$

This means that, if A is invertible, we find the solution of the system by multiplying the inverse of A by **b**. In **R**, we use the `solve()` function we used to invert the matrix but adding the **b** column vector.

```
> A <- matrix(c(1, 1,
+               2, 1),
+             nrow = 2,
+             ncol = 2,
+             byrow = T)
> A
     [,1] [,2]
[1,]    1    1
[2,]    2    1
> b <- c(4, 7)
> b
[1] 4 7
> solve(A, b)
[1] 3 1
```

In alternative, we can use functions from the `matlib` package. The `showEqn()` function writes the system of equations from the matrices.

```
> showEqn(A, b)
1*x1 + 1*x2  =  4
2*x1 + 1*x2  =  7
```

The `Solve()` function (capital S), solve the system.

```
> Solve(A, b, fractions = T)
x1    =  3
  x2  =  1
```

A very interesting argument of this function is `verbose = TRUE`. It shows the steps of the Gaussian elimination algorithm to find the solution (Sect. 2.3.7.2).

```
> Solve(A, b, fractions = T,
+         verbose = T)

Initial matrix:
     [,1] [,2] [,3]
[1,] 1    1    4
[2,] 2    1    7

row: 1

 exchange rows 1 and 2
     [,1] [,2] [,3]
[1,] 2    1    7
[2,] 1    1    4

 multiply row 1 by 1/2
     [,1] [,2] [,3]
[1,]    1  1/2  7/2
[2,]    1    1    4

 subtract row 1 from row 2
     [,1] [,2] [,3]
[1,]    1  1/2  7/2
[2,]    0  1/2  1/2

row: 2

 multiply row 2 by 2
     [,1] [,2] [,3]
[1,]    1  1/2  7/2
[2,]    0    1    1

 multiply row 2 by 1/2 and subtract from row 1
     [,1] [,2] [,3]
[1,] 1    0    3
[2,] 0    1    1
x1    =  3
  x2  =  1
```

Finally, it is possible to plot the solution with the `plotEqn()` function (Fig. 2.16).

```
> plotEqn(A, b, xlim = c(-10, 10))
  x1 + x2   =  4
2*x1 + x2   =  7
```

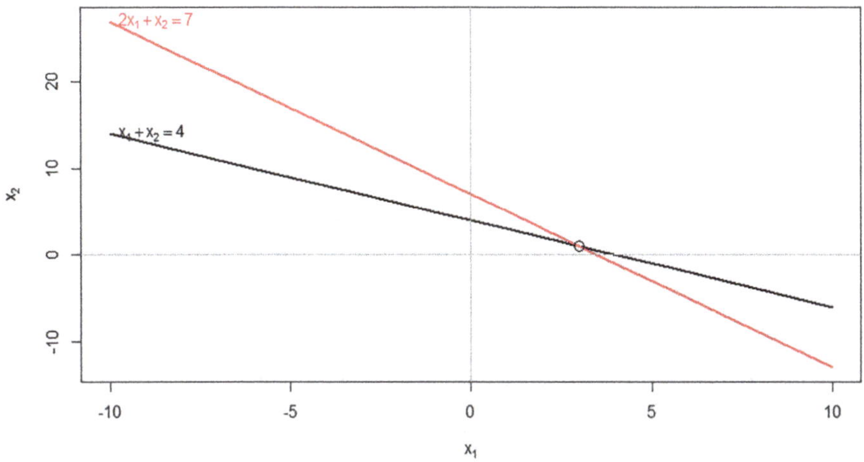

Fig. 2.16 System of two linear equations

As we can see from Fig. 2.16, a unique solution of a system of two linear equations in two unknowns is represented by the point where the two lines cross, that is the point that lies on both lines.

However, it is not said that every system of two linear equations in two unknowns has a unique solution. It may happen that a system as *infinitely* many solutions or *no* solution. The first case happens when the lines generated by the system of equations are parallel to each other and coincide; the second case is given by parallel lines that never cross. An example of the first case is the following system of equations (Fig. 2.17)

$$\begin{cases} x + 2y = 3 \\ 2x + 4y = 6 \end{cases}$$

and of the second case is (Fig. 2.18)

$$\begin{cases} x + 2y = 3 \\ x + 2y = 4 \end{cases}$$

Let's represent them with the `plotEqn()` function.

```
> A <- matrix(c(1, 2,
+               2, 4),
+             nrow = 2,
+             ncol = 2,
+             byrow = T)
> A
```

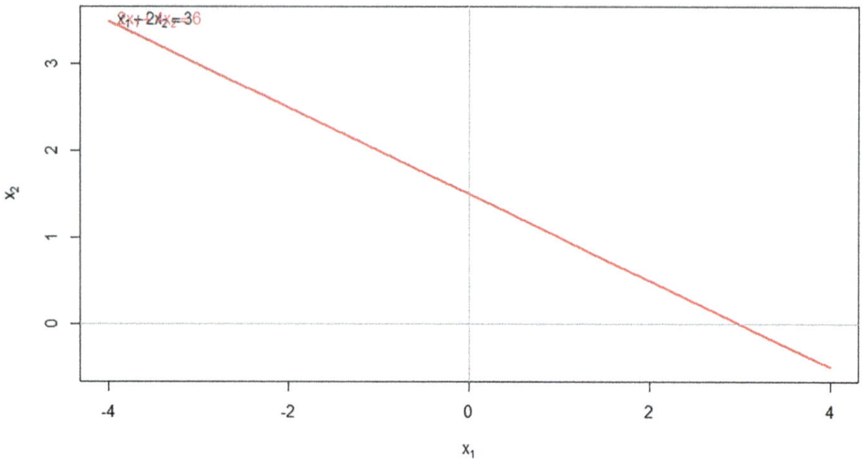

Fig. 2.17 System of two linear equations: infinitely many solutions

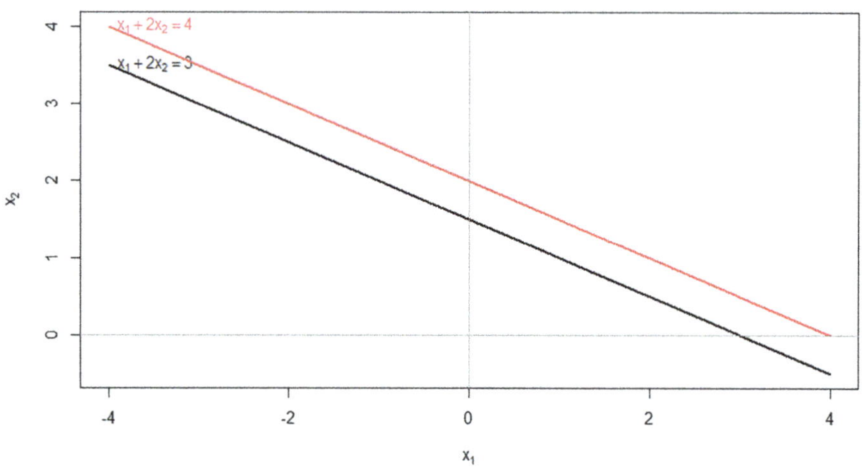

Fig. 2.18 System of two linear equations: no solutions

```
     [,1] [,2]
[1,]    1    2
[2,]    2    4
> b <- c(3, 6)
> plotEqn(A, b)
  x1 + 2*x2  =  3
2*x1 + 4*x2  =  6
> A <- matrix(c(1, 2,
+               1, 2),
+             nrow = 2,
```

```
+                   ncol = 2,
+                   byrow = T)
> A
     [,1] [,2]
[1,]    1    2
[2,]    1    2
> b <- c(3, 4)
> plotEqn(A, b)
x1 + 2*x2  =  3
x1 + 2*x2  =  4
```

What we have said for a system of two linear equations in two unknowns applies to a system of three linear equations in three unknowns as well. In this case, however, we would talk about planes instead of lines. Let's see some examples for a system of three linear equations with a unique solution (Fig. 2.19), with infinitely many solutions (Fig. 2.20), and with no solutions (Fig. 2.21). We plot them with the `plotEqn3D()` function.

$$\begin{cases} 2x + y - z = 4 \\ x - 2y + z = 1 \\ 3x - y - 2z = 3 \end{cases} \tag{2.12}$$

Fig. 2.19 3D system of three linear equations

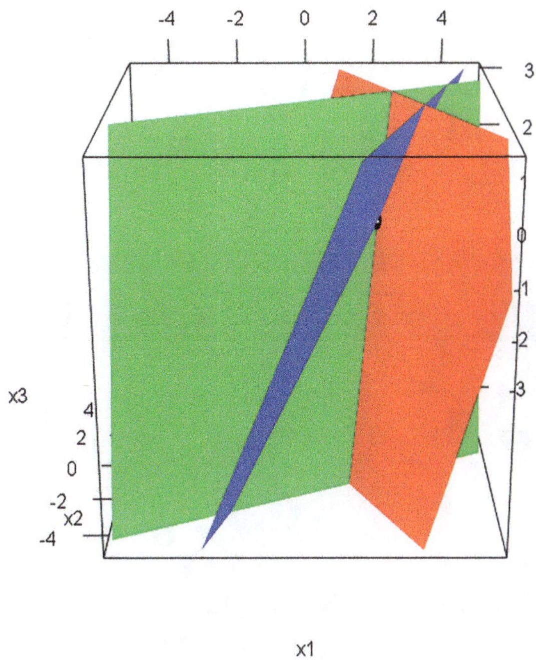

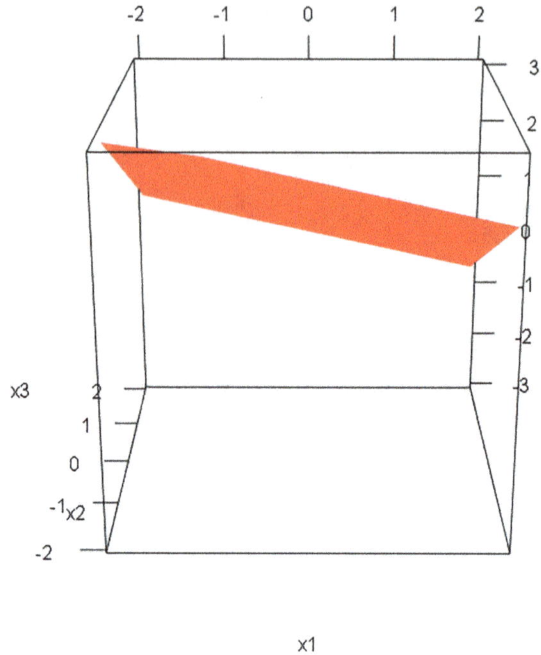

Fig. 2.20 3D system of three linear equations: infinitely many solutions

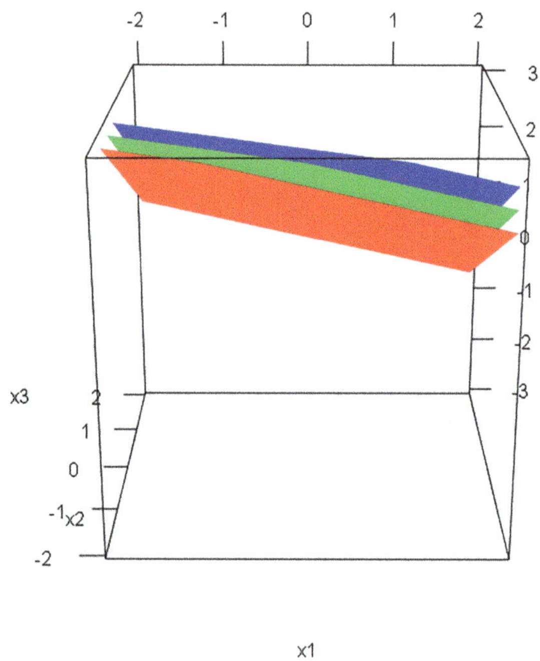

Fig. 2.21 3D system of three linear equations: no solution

```
> A <- matrix(c(2, 1, -1,
+                 1, -2, 1,
+                 3, -1, -2),
+               nrow = 3,
+               ncol = 3,
+               byrow = T)
> A
     [,1] [,2] [,3]
[1,]    2    1   -1
[2,]    1   -2    1
[3,]    3   -1   -2
> b <- c(4, 1, 3)
> showEqn(A, b)
2*x1 + 1*x2 - 1*x3  =  4
1*x1 - 2*x2 + 1*x3  =  1
3*x1 - 1*x2 - 2*x3  =  3
> Solve(A, b, fractions = T)
x1      =  2
  x2    =  1
    x3  =  1

> plotEqn3d(A, b,
+             xlim = c(-5, 5),
+             ylim = c(-5, 5))
```

$$\begin{cases} x + 2y + 3z = 4 \\ 2x + 4y + 6z = 8 \\ 3x + 6y + 9z = 12 \end{cases}$$

```
> A <- matrix(c(1, 2, 3,
+                 2, 4, 6,
+                 3, 6, 9),
+               nrow = 3,
+               ncol = 3,
+               byrow = T)
> A
     [,1] [,2] [,3]
[1,]    1    2    3
[2,]    2    4    6
[3,]    3    6    9
> b <- c(4, 8, 12)
> showEqn(A, b)
1*x1 + 2*x2 + 3*x3  =   4
```

```
2*x1 + 4*x2 + 6*x3  =   8
3*x1 + 6*x2 + 9*x3  =  12
> plotEqn3d(A, b)
```

$$\begin{cases} x + 2y + 3z = 4 \\ x + 2y + 3z = 5 \\ x + 2y + 3z = 6 \end{cases}$$

```
> A <- matrix(c(1, 2, 3,
+               1, 2, 3,
+               1, 2, 3),
+             nrow = 3,
+             ncol = 3,
+             byrow = T)
> A
     [,1] [,2] [,3]
[1,]    1    2    3
[2,]    1    2    3
[3,]    1    2    3
> b <- c(4, 5, 6)
> showEqn(A, b)
1*x1 + 2*x2 + 3*x3  =  4
1*x1 + 2*x2 + 3*x3  =  5
1*x1 + 2*x2 + 3*x3  =  6
> plotEqn3d(A, b)
```

Matrices are very useful to write a large system of equations in a concise way. For example, the following system

$$A = \begin{bmatrix} a_{11} & a_{12} & a_{13} & \cdot & a_{1n} \\ a_{21} & a_{22} & a_{23} & \cdot & a_{2n} \\ \vdots & \vdots & \vdots & \ddots & \vdots \\ a_{m1} & a_{m2} & a_{m3} & \cdot & a_{mn} \end{bmatrix} \quad \mathbf{x} = \begin{bmatrix} x_1 \\ x_2 \\ \vdots \\ x_n \end{bmatrix} \quad \mathbf{b} = \begin{bmatrix} b_1 \\ b_2 \\ \vdots \\ b_n \end{bmatrix}$$

could be written just as $A\mathbf{x} = \mathbf{b}$. Note that before we indicated the unknowns as x, y, and z. However, it is more convenient to indicate them as $x_1, x_2, \ldots, x_n$ because this does not limit us in the number of unknowns to use in the system.

Following an example of a solution of a system of four linear equations with four unknowns.

```
> A <- matrix(c(1, 2, 3, 5,
+               2, 3, 5, 9,
```

```
+                 3, 4, 7, 1,
+                 7, 6, 5, 4),
+               nrow = 4,
+               ncol = 4,
+               byrow = T)
> A
     [,1] [,2] [,3] [,4]
[1,]    1    2    3    5
[2,]    2    3    5    9
[3,]    3    4    7    1
[4,]    7    6    5    4
> B <- c(5, 4, 0, 3)
> showEqn(A, B)
1*x1 + 2*x2 + 3*x3 + 5*x4  =  5
2*x1 + 3*x2 + 5*x3 + 9*x4  =  4
3*x1 + 4*x2 + 7*x3 + 1*x4  =  0
7*x1 + 6*x2 + 5*x3 + 4*x4  =  3
> Solve(A, B, fractions = T)
x1          =  -161/32
  x2        =   271/32
    x3      =   -87/32
      x4    =      1/4
```

In addition, what we have said for the solution of the system of linear equations also holds for larger systems with m linear equations and n unknowns. The number of linear equations, m, and unknowns, n, can help to determine if the system has a unique solution, infinitely many solutions or no solution. In general,

- a system of linear equations with a unique solution must have at least the same number of equations, m, and unknowns, n ($m = n$);
- a system of linear equations with $n > m$ must have either no solution or infinitely many solutions;
- a homogeneous system of linear equations (i.e. with all 0 on the right-hand side of the equation) with $n > m$ must have infinitely many distinct solutions;
- a system of linear equations with $m > n$ may have a right-hand side of the equations for which the system has no solution.

2.3.7.1.1 A Geometric Interpretation

Figures 2.16 and 2.19 represented the equations in two and three dimensions, respectively. In this section, we focus on the geometric interpretation of those systems of linear equations.

In the first system (2.11)

$$A = \begin{bmatrix} 1 & 1 \\ 2 & 1 \end{bmatrix} \quad \mathbf{b} = \begin{bmatrix} 4 \\ 7 \end{bmatrix}$$

we found that

$$\mathbf{x} = A^{-1}\mathbf{b} = \begin{bmatrix} 3 \\ 1 \end{bmatrix}$$

In turn, this means that

$$A\mathbf{x} = \mathbf{b}$$

that is

$$\begin{bmatrix} 1 & 1 \\ 2 & 1 \end{bmatrix} \begin{bmatrix} 3 \\ 1 \end{bmatrix} = \begin{bmatrix} 4 \\ 7 \end{bmatrix}$$

```
> A <- matrix(c(1, 1,
+               2, 1),
+             nrow = 2,
+             ncol = 2,
+             byrow = T)
> A
     [,1] [,2]
[1,]    1    1
[2,]    2    1
> X <- c(3, 1)
> X
[1] 3 1
> b <- A %*% X
> b
     [,1]
[1,]    4
[2,]    7
```

Let's represent the column vectors **x** and **b** with the `arrows2D()` function from the `plot3D` package.

```
> x0 <- c(0, 0)
> y0 <- c(0, 0)
> x1 <- c(3, 4)
> y1 <- c(1, 7)
> cols <- c("blue", "red")
> arrows2D(x0, y0, x1, y1,
+          col = cols,
+          lwd = 2)
```

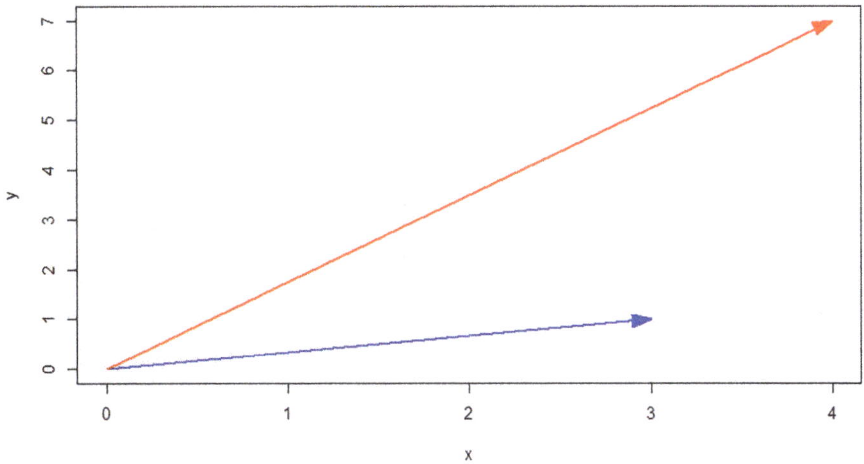

Fig. 2.22 Geometric interpretation of the system of linear equations in Fig. 2.16

Figure 2.22 shows that when $\mathbf{x}$ is multiplied by A it stretches and rotates to $\mathbf{b}$. In the second system (2.12)

$$A = \begin{bmatrix} 2 & 1 & -1 \\ 1 & -2 & 1 \\ 3 & -1 & -2 \end{bmatrix} \quad \mathbf{b} = \begin{bmatrix} 4 \\ 1 \\ 3 \end{bmatrix}$$

we found that

$$\mathbf{x} = A^{-1}\mathbf{b} = \begin{bmatrix} 2 \\ 1 \\ 1 \end{bmatrix}$$

In turn, this means that

$$A\mathbf{x} = \mathbf{b}$$

that is

$$\begin{bmatrix} 2 & 1 & -1 \\ 1 & -2 & 1 \\ 3 & -1 & -2 \end{bmatrix} \begin{bmatrix} 2 \\ 1 \\ 1 \end{bmatrix} = \begin{bmatrix} 4 \\ 1 \\ 3 \end{bmatrix}$$

```
> A <- matrix(c(2, 1, -1,
+               1, -2, 1,
+               3, -1, -2),
+             nrow = 3,
```

```
+                  ncol = 3,
+                  byrow = T)
> A
     [,1] [,2] [,3]
[1,]    2    1   -1
[2,]    1   -2    1
[3,]    3   -1   -2
> X <- c(2, 1, 1)
> b <- A %*% X
> b
     [,1]
[1,]    4
[2,]    1
[3,]    3
```

Let's represent the column vectors **x** and **b** with the `arrows3D()` function from the `plot3D` package.

```
> x0 <- c(0, 0)
> y0 <- c(0, 0)
> z0 <- c(0, 0)
> x1 <- c(2, 4)
> y1 <- c(1, 1)
> z1 <- c(1, 3)
> cols <- c("blue", "red")
> arrows3D(x0, y0, z0, x1, y1, z1,
+          col = cols,
+          lwd = 2,
+          ticktype = "detailed")
```

Figure 2.23 shows that when **x** is multiplied by A stretches and rotates to **b**.

2.3.7.2 Gauss Elimination and Gauss-Jordan Elimination

Elementary row operations are operations over the rows of a matrix used for the Gauss elimination and the Gauss-Jordan elimination. *Elementary row operations* consist in

1. Addition: a constant multiple of any row can be added to any other row
2. Multiplication: a row can be multiplied by a nonzero scalar
3. Switching: any pair of rows can be swapped.

The Gauss elimination and the Gauss-Jordan elimination are used to solve system of liner equations. Let's see the difference between them with an example. We use again system of three linear equations (2.12). The A matrix is

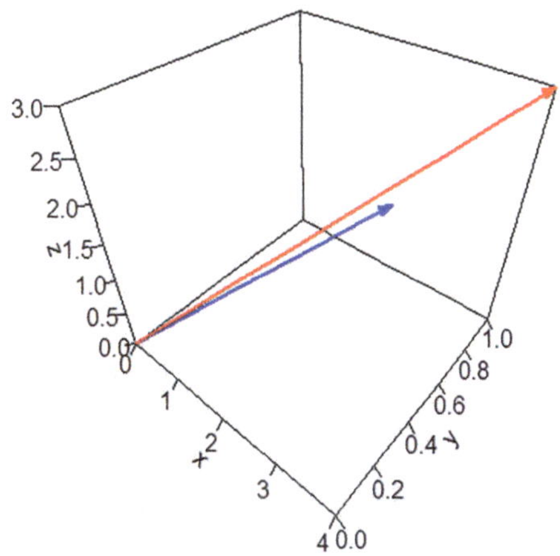

Fig. 2.23 Geometric interpretation of the system of linear equations in Fig. 2.19

$$A = \begin{bmatrix} 2 & 1 & -1 \\ 1 & -2 & 1 \\ 3 & -1 & -2 \end{bmatrix}$$

while the column vector with the constant terms, **b**, is

$$\mathbf{b} = \begin{bmatrix} 4 \\ 1 \\ 3 \end{bmatrix}$$

From A and **b** we build an augmented matrix as follows

$$\begin{bmatrix} 2 & 1 & -1 & 4 \\ 1 & -2 & 1 & 1 \\ 3 & -1 & -2 & 3 \end{bmatrix}$$

We use the `echelon()` function from the `matlib` package to use the Gauss method. Note that we set the argument `reduced = FALSE`.

```
> A <- matrix(c(2, 1, -1,
+               1, -2, 1,
+               3, -1, -2),
+             nrow = 3,
+             ncol = 3,
+             byrow = T)
> A
     [,1] [,2] [,3]
[1,]    2    1   -1
[2,]    1   -2    1
```

```
[3,]    3   -1   -2
> b <- c(4, 1, 3)
> b
[1] 4 1 3
> echelon(A, b, reduced = FALSE,
+         verbose = T,
+         fractions = T)

Initial matrix:
     [,1] [,2] [,3] [,4]
[1,]  2    1   -1    4
[2,]  1   -2    1    1
[3,]  3   -1   -2    3

row: 1

 exchange rows 1 and 3
     [,1] [,2] [,3] [,4]
[1,]  3   -1   -2    3
[2,]  1   -2    1    1
[3,]  2    1   -1    4

 multiply row 1 by 1/3
     [,1] [,2] [,3] [,4]
[1,]    1 -1/3 -2/3    1
[2,]    1   -2    1    1
[3,]    2    1   -1    4

 subtract row 1 from row 2
     [,1] [,2] [,3] [,4]
[1,]    1 -1/3 -2/3    1
[2,]    0 -5/3  5/3    0
[3,]    2    1   -1    4

 multiply row 1 by 2 and subtract from row 3
     [,1] [,2] [,3] [,4]
[1,]    1 -1/3 -2/3    1
[2,]    0 -5/3  5/3    0
[3,]    0  5/3  1/3    2

row: 2

 multiply row 2 by -3/5
     [,1] [,2] [,3] [,4]
[1,]    1 -1/3 -2/3    1
```

```
[2,]     0    1   -1    0
[3,]     0  5/3  1/3    2

 multiply row 2 by 5/3 and subtract from row 3
     [,1] [,2] [,3] [,4]
[1,]    1 -1/3 -2/3    1
[2,]    0    1   -1    0
[3,]    0    0    2    2

row: 3

 multiply row 3 by 1/2
     [,1] [,2] [,3] [,4]
[1,]    1 -1/3 -2/3    1
[2,]    0    1   -1    0
[3,]    0    0    1    1
```

The Gauss elimination method leads to the following matrix

$$\begin{bmatrix} 1 & -\frac{1}{3} & -\frac{2}{3} & 1 \\ 0 & 1 & -1 & 0 \\ 0 & 0 & 1 & 1 \end{bmatrix}$$

Therefore, our system of equations has been reduced to

$$\begin{cases} x - \frac{1}{3}y - \frac{2}{3}z = 1 \\ y - z = 0 \\ z = 1 \end{cases}$$

From here is very simple to find the solutions by back-substitution. We found $z = 1$, consequently $y = 1$ and $x = 2$.

Therefore, the Gauss elimination method leads to a matrix that allows to simply solve the system via back-substitution. We say that this matrix is in *row echelon form*.

If in the `echelon()` function, we set `reduced = TRUE` (or we omit it because it is the default value), we implement the Gauss-Jordan method for the same example.

```
> echelon(A, b,
+           verbose = T,
+           fractions = T)

Initial matrix:
     [,1] [,2] [,3] [,4]
[1,]   2    1   -1    4
```

```
[2,]  1   -2    1    1
[3,]  3   -1   -2    3

row: 1

 exchange rows 1 and 3
     [,1] [,2] [,3] [,4]
[1,]  3   -1   -2    3
[2,]  1   -2    1    1
[3,]  2    1   -1    4

 multiply row 1 by 1/3
     [,1] [,2] [,3] [,4]
[1,]    1 -1/3 -2/3    1
[2,]    1   -2    1    1
[3,]    2    1   -1    4

 subtract row 1 from row 2
     [,1] [,2] [,3] [,4]
[1,]    1 -1/3 -2/3    1
[2,]    0 -5/3  5/3    0
[3,]    2    1   -1    4

 multiply row 1 by 2 and subtract from row 3
     [,1] [,2] [,3] [,4]
[1,]    1 -1/3 -2/3    1
[2,]    0 -5/3  5/3    0
[3,]    0  5/3  1/3    2

row: 2

 multiply row 2 by -3/5
     [,1] [,2] [,3] [,4]
[1,]    1 -1/3 -2/3    1
[2,]    0    1   -1    0
[3,]    0  5/3  1/3    2

 multiply row 2 by 1/3 and add to row 1
     [,1] [,2] [,3] [,4]
[1,]   1    0   -1    1
[2,]   0    1   -1    0
[3,]   0  5/3  1/3    2

 multiply row 2 by 5/3 and subtract from row 3
     [,1] [,2] [,3] [,4]
```

```
[1,]  1    0   -1    1
[2,]  0    1   -1    0
[3,]  0    0    2    2

row: 3

 multiply row 3 by 1/2
      [,1] [,2] [,3] [,4]
[1,]  1    0   -1    1
[2,]  0    1   -1    0
[3,]  0    0    1    1

 multiply row 3 by 1 and add to row 1
      [,1] [,2] [,3] [,4]
[1,]  1    0    0    2
[2,]  0    1   -1    0
[3,]  0    0    1    1

 multiply row 3 by 1 and add to row 2
      [,1] [,2] [,3] [,4]
[1,] 1    0    0    2
[2,] 0    1    0    1
[3,] 0    0    1    1
```

With the Gauss-Jordan method we continue the *elementary row operations* to get an identity matrix from the first columns of the matrix, if the square matrix is full rank (Sect. 2.3.7.3), or a matrix as close as possible to an identity matrix. We say that this matrix is in *reduced row echelon form*.

In our example, the reduced form is

$$\begin{bmatrix} 1 & 0 & 0 & 2 \\ 0 & 1 & 0 & 1 \\ 0 & 0 & 1 & 1 \end{bmatrix}$$

This, as expected, leads to the same solutions: $x = 2$, $y = 1, z = 1$.

The matrix in row echelon form or in reduced row echelon form shows if the system has a unique solution or infinitely many solutions. This is determined by the presence or not of a *free variable* (that is a row of all 0 in the echelon form). If we have a *free* variable as result of the Gauss method or Gauss-Jordan method, the system has infinitely many solutions.

These methods can be used to find the rank of a matrix, the determinant and the inverse of a matrix.

For example, to find the inverse matrix we form the augmented matrix with A and I. Then, we implement *elementary row operations* to get the identity matrix on the left.

For example, given

$$A = \begin{bmatrix} 2 & 1 & 1 \\ 1 & 2 & 1 \\ 1 & 1 & 2 \end{bmatrix}$$

```
> A <- matrix(c(2, 1, 1,
+               1, 2, 1,
+               1, 1, 2),
+             nrow = 3,
+             ncol = 3,
+             byrow = T)
> A
     [,1] [,2] [,3]
[1,]    2    1    1
[2,]    1    2    1
[3,]    1    1    2
> Id <- diag(1, 3, 3)
> Id
     [,1] [,2] [,3]
[1,]    1    0    0
[2,]    0    1    0
[3,]    0    0    1
> echelon(A, Id,
+         verbose = T,
+         fractions = T)

Initial matrix:
     [,1] [,2] [,3] [,4] [,5] [,6]
[1,] 2    1    1    1    0    0
[2,] 1    2    1    0    1    0
[3,] 1    1    2    0    0    1

row: 1

 multiply row 1 by 1/2
     [,1] [,2] [,3] [,4] [,5] [,6]
[1,]   1  1/2  1/2  1/2    0    0
[2,]   1    2    1    0    1    0
[3,]   1    1    2    0    0    1

 subtract row 1 from row 2
     [,1] [,2] [,3] [,4] [,5] [,6]
[1,]    1  1/2  1/2  1/2    0    0
```

```
[2,]    0  3/2  1/2 -1/2    1    0
[3,]    1    1    2    0    0    1

 subtract row 1 from row 3
     [,1] [,2] [,3] [,4] [,5] [,6]
[1,]    1  1/2  1/2  1/2    0    0
[2,]    0  3/2  1/2 -1/2    1    0
[3,]    0  1/2  3/2 -1/2    0    1

row: 2

 multiply row 2 by 2/3
     [,1] [,2] [,3] [,4] [,5] [,6]
[1,]    1  1/2  1/2  1/2    0    0
[2,]    0    1  1/3 -1/3  2/3    0
[3,]    0  1/2  3/2 -1/2    0    1

 multiply row 2 by 1/2 and subtract from row 1
     [,1] [,2] [,3] [,4] [,5] [,6]
[1,]    1    0  1/3  2/3 -1/3    0
[2,]    0    1  1/3 -1/3  2/3    0
[3,]    0  1/2  3/2 -1/2    0    1

 multiply row 2 by 1/2 and subtract from row 3
     [,1] [,2] [,3] [,4] [,5] [,6]
[1,]    1    0  1/3  2/3 -1/3    0
[2,]    0    1  1/3 -1/3  2/3    0
[3,]    0    0  4/3 -1/3 -1/3    1

row: 3

 multiply row 3 by 3/4
     [,1] [,2] [,3] [,4] [,5] [,6]
[1,]    1    0  1/3  2/3 -1/3    0
[2,]    0    1  1/3 -1/3  2/3    0
[3,]    0    0    1 -1/4 -1/4  3/4

 multiply row 3 by 1/3 and subtract from row 1
     [,1] [,2] [,3] [,4] [,5] [,6]
[1,]    1    0    0  3/4 -1/4 -1/4
[2,]    0    1  1/3 -1/3  2/3    0
[3,]    0    0    1 -1/4 -1/4  3/4

 multiply row 3 by 1/3 and subtract from row 2
     [,1] [,2] [,3] [,4] [,5] [,6]
```

```
[1,]    1    0    0  3/4 -1/4 -1/4
[2,]    0    1    0 -1/4  3/4 -1/4
[3,]    0    0    1 -1/4 -1/4  3/4
```

We found the inverse of A. Compare with

```
> solve(A)
      [,1]  [,2]  [,3]
[1,]  0.75 -0.25 -0.25
[2,] -0.25  0.75 -0.25
[3,] -0.25 -0.25  0.75
```

Note that if in `echelon()` we set `fractions = FALSE` we get the matrix with decimal numbers instead of fractions.

2.3.7.3 The Rank of a Matrix

The rank of a matrix A is the maximum number of linearly independent vectors. To find the rank we can reduce the matrix to its row echelon form. The number of non-zero rows is the rank of the matrix. For example,

```
> A <- matrix(c(1, 1,
+               2, 1),
+             nrow = 2,
+             ncol = 2,
+             byrow = T)
> A
     [,1] [,2]
[1,]    1    1
[2,]    2    1
> echelon(A)
     [,1] [,2]
[1,]    1    0
[2,]    0    1
```

The rank is 2. We can use the `Rank()` function from the `pracma` package to find the rank of a matrix. In this example,

```
> Rank(A)
[1] 2
```

Another example

```
> A <- matrix(c(2, 1, -1,
+               1, -2, 1,
+               3, -1, -2),
+             nrow = 3,
```

```
+                 ncol = 3,
+                 byrow = T)
> A
     [,1] [,2] [,3]
[1,]    2    1   -1
[2,]    1   -2    1
[3,]    3   -1   -2
> echelon(A)
     [,1] [,2] [,3]
[1,]    1    0    0
[2,]    0    1    0
[3,]    0    0    1
> Rank(A)
[1] 3
```

In these two examples, the matrices are said to have a *full rank*. If a square matrix of coefficients of a system of linear equations has full rank, the corresponding system has a unique solution.

In the next example, the matrix has rank 1. In fact, there is only one row with non zero rows. If matrix A is not full rank it is said to be *rank deficient*. Note that in this matrix the second column is -2 times the first column.

```
> A <- matrix(c(3, -6,
+                 1, -2),
+               nrow = 2,
+               ncol = 2,
+               byrow = T)
> A
     [,1] [,2]
[1,]    3   -6
[2,]    1   -2
> echelon(A)
     [,1] [,2]
[1,]    1   -2
[2,]    0    0
> Rank(A)
[1] 1
```

Note that the rank of a matrix also applies to non-square matrices. However, more should be said about the rank. The reader is referred to Strang (1988) for a deeper understanding of the rank. Following, two examples of the rank of non-square matrices

```
> A <- matrix(c(-2, 3, 4, 6,
+               4, -4, 3, 0,
+               1, 8, 5, 3),
+             nrow = 3,
+             ncol = 4,
+             byrow = T)
> A
     [,1] [,2] [,3] [,4]
[1,]   -2    3    4    6
[2,]    4   -4    3    0
[3,]    1    8    5    3
> echelon(A)
     [,1] [,2] [,3]      [,4]
[1,]    1    0    0 -1.044199
[2,]    0    1    0 -0.198895
[3,]    0    0    1  1.127072
> Rank(A)
[1] 3
```

```
> A <- matrix(c(-1, -2,
+               5, 3,
+               5, 4,
+               7, 8),
+             nrow = 4,
+             ncol = 2,
+             byrow = T)
> A
     [,1] [,2]
[1,]   -1   -2
[2,]    5    3
[3,]    5    4
[4,]    7    8
> echelon(A)
     [,1] [,2]
[1,]    1    0
[2,]    0    1
[3,]    0    0
[4,]    0    0
> Rank(A)
[1] 2
```

2.3.8 Determinant

Every square matrix A has a number associated called the *determinant*, $det(A)$ or $|A|$, that provides information about the matrix. This information can be used, for example, to solve systems of linear equations and to invert matrices.

The determinant has the following properties (LeCuyer 1978, p.103):

1. If A has a complete row (or column) of zeros, then $det(A) = 0$;
2. If a row (or column) of a matrix A is multiplied by a non-zero constant c, then $det(A)$ is multiplied by c;
3. If a multiple of one row (or column) is added to another row (or column), then the value of $det(A)$ is unchanged;
4. If two rows (or columns) of A are interchanged, then $det(A)$ changes sign (i.e., $det(A)$ is multiplied by -1);
5. If A is a triangular matrix then $det(A)$ is the product of the diagonal elements.

These properties are very important to calculate the determinant of a matrix with the Gauss elimination method. In fact, with this method we calculate the determinant by multiplying the diagonal elements of the matrix in row echelon form. However, we need to adjust the result

- by multiplying it by the inverse of the constant, $\frac{1}{c}$, if we multiplied a row (or column) of a matrix A by a non-zero constant c during the elementary row operations;
- by multiplying it by -1 if we interchanged two rows (or columns) of A during the elementary row operations.

Let's see an example:

```
> A <- matrix(c(1, 1,
+               2, 1),
+             nrow = 2,
+             ncol = 2,
+             byrow = T)
> A
     [,1] [,2]
[1,]    1    1
[2,]    2    1
> Aref <- echelon(A, reduced = F,
+          verbose = T,
+          fractions = T)

Initial matrix:
     [,1] [,2]
[1,] 1    1
[2,] 2    1

row: 1
```

```
 exchange rows 1 and 2
     [,1] [,2]
[1,] 2    1
[2,] 1    1

 multiply row 1 by 1/2
     [,1] [,2]
[1,]    1  1/2
[2,]    1    1

 subtract row 1 from row 2
     [,1] [,2]
[1,]    1  1/2
[2,]    0  1/2

row: 2

 multiply row 2 by 2
     [,1] [,2]
[1,]    1  1/2
[2,]    0    1
> (Aref[1,1] * Aref[2,2] *
+      (-1) * (2) * (1/2))
[1] -1
```

Note that in the last command, we multiplied the diagonal elements of the matrix in row echelon form, `Aref`, by -1 because we exchanged rows 1 and 2, and then we multiplied by 2 because we multiplied row 1 by $\frac{1}{2}$ and finally we multiplied by $\frac{1}{2}$ because we multiplied row 2 by 2.

However, we can compute the determinant of a matrix in **R** just using the `det()` function.

```
> det(A)
[1] -1
```

Other examples:

```
> A <- matrix(c(2, 1, 0, 2,
+               1, -2, 0, 3,
+               3, -1, 0, -2,
+               2, -3, 0, 1),
+             nrow = 4,
+             ncol = 4,
+             byrow = T)
> A
```

```
     [,1] [,2] [,3] [,4]
[1,]    2    1    0    2
[2,]    1   -2    0    3
[3,]    3   -1    0   -2
[4,]    2   -3    0    1
> Aref <- echelon(A, reduced = F,
+                    verbose = T,
+                    fractions = T)

Initial matrix:
     [,1] [,2] [,3] [,4]
[1,] 2     1    0    2
[2,] 1    -2    0    3
[3,] 3    -1    0   -2
[4,] 2    -3    0    1

row: 1

 exchange rows 1 and 3
     [,1] [,2] [,3] [,4]
[1,] 3    -1    0   -2
[2,] 1    -2    0    3
[3,] 2     1    0    2
[4,] 2    -3    0    1

 multiply row 1 by 1/3
     [,1] [,2] [,3] [,4]
[1,]    1 -1/3    0 -2/3
[2,]    1   -2    0    3
[3,]    2    1    0    2
[4,]    2   -3    0    1

 subtract row 1 from row 2
     [,1] [,2] [,3] [,4]
[1,]    1 -1/3    0 -2/3
[2,]    0 -5/3    0 11/3
[3,]    2    1    0    2
[4,]    2   -3    0    1

 multiply row 1 by 2 and subtract from row 3
     [,1] [,2] [,3] [,4]
[1,]    1 -1/3    0 -2/3
[2,]    0 -5/3    0 11/3
[3,]    0  5/3    0 10/3
[4,]    2   -3    0    1
```

```
 multiply row 1 by 2 and subtract from row 4
     [,1] [,2] [,3] [,4]
[1,]    1 -1/3    0 -2/3
[2,]    0 -5/3    0 11/3
[3,]    0  5/3    0 10/3
[4,]    0 -7/3    0  7/3

row: 2

 exchange rows 2 and 4
     [,1] [,2] [,3] [,4]
[1,]    1 -1/3    0 -2/3
[2,]    0 -7/3    0  7/3
[3,]    0  5/3    0 10/3
[4,]    0 -5/3    0 11/3

 multiply row 2 by -3/7
     [,1] [,2] [,3] [,4]
[1,]    1 -1/3    0 -2/3
[2,]    0    1    0   -1
[3,]    0  5/3    0 10/3
[4,]    0 -5/3    0 11/3

 multiply row 2 by 5/3 and subtract from row 3
     [,1] [,2] [,3] [,4]
[1,]    1 -1/3    0 -2/3
[2,]    0    1    0   -1
[3,]    0    0    0    5
[4,]    0 -5/3    0 11/3

 multiply row 2 by 5/3 and add to row 4
     [,1] [,2] [,3] [,4]
[1,]    1 -1/3    0 -2/3
[2,]    0    1    0   -1
[3,]    0    0    0    5
[4,]    0    0    0    2

row: 3

 multiply row 3 by 1/5
     [,1] [,2] [,3] [,4]
[1,]    1 -1/3    0 -2/3
[2,]    0    1    0   -1
[3,]    0    0    0    1
[4,]    0    0    0    2
```

```
 multiply row 3 by 2 and subtract from row 4
     [,1] [,2] [,3] [,4]
[1,]    1 -1/3    0 -2/3
[2,]    0    1    0   -1
[3,]    0    0    0    1
[4,]    0    0    0    0
> (Aref[1, 1] * Aref[2, 2] *
+     Aref[3, 3] * Aref[4, 4] *
+     (-1) * (3) * (-1) * (-7/3) * (5))
[1] 0
```

Note that in this case we can avoid tracking all the steps because according to property 1 the determinant of this matrix is 0. We can verify it:

```
> det(A)
[1] 0

> A <- matrix(c(2, 1, -1,
+                1, -2, 1,
+                3, -1, -2),
+              nrow = 3,
+              ncol = 3,
+              byrow = T)
> A
     [,1] [,2] [,3]
[1,]    2    1   -1
[2,]    1   -2    1
[3,]    3   -1   -2
> Aref <- echelon(A, reduced = F,
+                 verbose = T,
+                 fractions = T)

Initial matrix:
     [,1] [,2] [,3]
[1,] 2     1   -1
[2,] 1    -2    1
[3,] 3    -1   -2

row: 1

 exchange rows 1 and 3
     [,1] [,2] [,3]
[1,] 3    -1   -2
[2,] 1    -2    1
[3,] 2     1   -1
```

```
 multiply row 1 by 1/3
     [,1] [,2] [,3]
[1,]    1 -1/3 -2/3
[2,]    1   -2    1
[3,]    2    1   -1

 subtract row 1 from row 2
     [,1] [,2] [,3]
[1,]    1 -1/3 -2/3
[2,]    0 -5/3  5/3
[3,]    2    1   -1

 multiply row 1 by 2 and subtract from row 3
     [,1] [,2] [,3]
[1,]    1 -1/3 -2/3
[2,]    0 -5/3  5/3
[3,]    0  5/3  1/3

row: 2

 multiply row 2 by -3/5
     [,1] [,2] [,3]
[1,]    1 -1/3 -2/3
[2,]    0    1   -1
[3,]    0  5/3  1/3

 multiply row 2 by 5/3 and subtract from row 3
     [,1] [,2] [,3]
[1,]    1 -1/3 -2/3
[2,]    0    1   -1
[3,]    0    0    2

row: 3

 multiply row 3 by 1/2
     [,1] [,2] [,3]
[1,]    1 -1/3 -2/3
[2,]    0    1   -1
[3,]    0    0    1
> (Aref[1,1] * Aref[2,2] * Aref[3,3] *
+      (-1) * (3) * (-5/3) * (2))
[1] 10
> det(A)
[1] 10
```

```
> A <- matrix(c(-2, 3, 4, 1,
+               4, -4, 3, 0,
+               1, 2, 5, 3,
+               -1, -2, 5, 3),
+             nrow = 4,
+             ncol = 4,
+             byrow = T)
> A
     [,1] [,2] [,3] [,4]
[1,]   -2    3    4    1
[2,]    4   -4    3    0
[3,]    1    2    5    3
[4,]   -1   -2    5    3
> Aref <- echelon(A, reduced = F,
+                 verbose = T,
+                 fractions = T)

Initial matrix:
     [,1] [,2] [,3] [,4]
[1,] -2    3    4    1
[2,]  4   -4    3    0
[3,]  1    2    5    3
[4,] -1   -2    5    3

row: 1

 exchange rows 1 and 2
     [,1] [,2] [,3] [,4]
[1,]  4   -4    3    0
[2,] -2    3    4    1
[3,]  1    2    5    3
[4,] -1   -2    5    3

 multiply row 1 by 1/4
     [,1] [,2] [,3] [,4]
[1,]   1   -1  3/4    0
[2,]  -2    3    4    1
[3,]   1    2    5    3
[4,]  -1   -2    5    3

 multiply row 1 by 2 and add to row 2
     [,1] [,2] [,3] [,4]
[1,]    1   -1  3/4    0
[2,]    0    1 11/2    1
```

```
[3,]    1    2    5    3
[4,]   -1   -2    5    3

 subtract row 1 from row 3
     [,1] [,2] [,3] [,4]
[1,]    1   -1  3/4    0
[2,]    0    1 11/2    1
[3,]    0    3 17/4    3
[4,]   -1   -2    5    3

 multiply row 1 by 1 and add to row 4
     [,1] [,2] [,3] [,4]
[1,]    1   -1  3/4    0
[2,]    0    1 11/2    1
[3,]    0    3 17/4    3
[4,]    0   -3 23/4    3

row: 2

 exchange rows 2 and 3
     [,1] [,2] [,3] [,4]
[1,]    1   -1  3/4    0
[2,]    0    3 17/4    3
[3,]    0    1 11/2    1
[4,]    0   -3 23/4    3

 multiply row 2 by 1/3
     [,1]  [,2]  [,3]  [,4]
[1,]     1    -1   3/4     0
[2,]     0     1 17/12     1
[3,]     0     1  11/2     1
[4,]     0    -3  23/4     3

 subtract row 2 from row 3
     [,1]  [,2]  [,3]  [,4]
[1,]     1    -1   3/4     0
[2,]     0     1 17/12     1
[3,]     0     0 49/12     0
[4,]     0    -3  23/4     3

 multiply row 2 by 3 and add to row 4
     [,1]  [,2]  [,3]  [,4]
[1,]     1    -1   3/4     0
[2,]     0     1 17/12     1
```

```
[3,]    0    0 49/12    0
[4,]    0    0    10    6

row: 3

 exchange rows 3 and 4
     [,1]  [,2]  [,3]  [,4]
[1,]    1    -1   3/4     0
[2,]    0     1 17/12     1
[3,]    0     0    10     6
[4,]    0     0 49/12     0

 multiply row 3 by 1/10
     [,1]  [,2]  [,3]  [,4]
[1,]    1    -1   3/4     0
[2,]    0     1 17/12     1
[3,]    0     0     1   3/5
[4,]    0     0 49/12     0

 multiply row 3 by 49/12 and subtract from row 4
     [,1]   [,2]   [,3]   [,4]
[1,]    1     -1    3/4      0
[2,]    0      1  17/12      1
[3,]    0      0      1    3/5
[4,]    0      0      0 -49/20

row: 4

 multiply row 4 by -20/49
     [,1]  [,2]  [,3]  [,4]
[1,]    1    -1   3/4     0
[2,]    0     1 17/12     1
[3,]    0     0     1   3/5
[4,]    0     0     0     1
> (Aref[1,1]*Aref[2,2]*Aref[3,3]*Aref[4,4] *
+     (-1) * 4 * (-1) * (3) *
+     (-1) * (10) * (-49/20))
[1] 294
> det(A)
[1] 294
```

We can add other properties of the determinant:

6. The determinant of a matrix and its transpose is the same, i.e. $det(A) = det(A^T)$;

7. The determinant of the product of two matrices is equal to the product of the determinants of the two matrices, i.e. $|AB| = |A||B|$;
8. The determinant of the inverse matrix is equal to the reciprocal of the determinant of the matrix, i.e. $|A^{-1}| = \frac{1}{|A|}$.

   For example,

```
> At <- t(A)
> det(At)
[1] 294
> A <- matrix(c(1, 0, 0,
+               2, 4, 0,
+               3, 6, 6),
+             nrow = 3,
+             ncol = 3,
+             byrow = T)
> A
     [,1] [,2] [,3]
[1,]    1    0    0
[2,]    2    4    0
[3,]    3    6    6
> B <- matrix(c(7, 0, 0,
+               8, 10, 0,
+               9, 12, 12),
+             nrow = 3,
+             ncol = 3,
+             byrow = T)
> B
     [,1] [,2] [,3]
[1,]    7    0    0
[2,]    8   10    0
[3,]    9   12   12
> AB <- A %*% B
> det(AB)
[1] 20160
> det(A)*det(B)
[1] 20160
> Ainv <- solve(A)
> det(Ainv)
[1] 0.04166667
> 1/det(A)
[1] 0.04166667
```

Next, we consider other methods to find the determinant of a square matrix.

2.3.8.1 The Determinant of a 2 × 2 Matrix

First we see the case of a 2 × 2 matrix because it represents a special case. Suppose that the square matrix A is the following:

$$A = \begin{bmatrix} a & b \\ c & d \end{bmatrix}$$

In this case, we find the determinant as follows:

$$|A| = ad - bc$$

For example,

$$A = \begin{bmatrix} 1 & 1 \\ 2 & 1 \end{bmatrix}$$

$$|A| = (1 \cdot 1) - (2 \cdot 1) = -1$$

2.3.8.1.1 The Geometric Interpretation of the Determinant

In this section we investigate where the formula $|A| = ad - bc$ comes from. We write a function, `geom_det()`, that geometrically computes the determinant of a 2 × 2 matrix (stored in `res`). Additionally, the function plots the determinant using `ggplot()` (the plot is designed for graphical representation in one quadrant). The plot is stored in `g`. We create a list, `l`, that contains `res` and `g` that are returned as result of the function. The function takes one argument: a 2×2 matrix. We check that the argument is correct with an `if()` function. If the matrix is not a 2 × 2 matrix, the `stop()` function stops the function from running and returns the message `"The matrix needs to be a 2x2 matrix"`. After checking the matrix, the function selects `a`, `b`, `ci`, `d` from the matrix.[11]

```
> geom_det <- function(A){
+
+   if(nrow(A) != 2 || ncol(A) != 2){
+     stop("The matrix needs to be a 2x2 matrix")
+     }
```

[11] I write `ci` instead of `c` to avoid confusion with the `c()` function even though it is not really necessary. However, it is important to know that **R** has reserved words that cannot be used for object names, such as `TRUE`, `FALSE`, `NULL`, `NA`. In addition, remember that `T` and `F` are short for, respectively, `TRUE` and `FALSE`. Consequently, they should be avoided as object names. Refer to the "Reserved words" section in the **R** manual for more details: https://cran.r-project.org/doc/manuals/r-release/R-lang.html.

```
+
+   require("ggplot2")
+
+   a <- A[1,1]
+   b <- A[1,2]
+   ci <- A[2,1]
+   d <- A[2,2]
+
+   x <- c(0, 0, a, ci, a, a+ci, ci, a+ci, a, ci)
+   y <- c(0, 0, b, d, b, b+d,  d, b+d, b, d)
+   xend <- c(a, ci, a+ci, a+ci, a, a+ci, 0, 0, a+ci, ci)
+   yend <- c(b, d, b+d, b+d, 0, 0, d, b+d, b, b+d)
+
+   df <- data.frame(x = x, y = y, xend = xend, yend =
          yend)
+
+   res <- ((a+ci)*(b+d) - (2*(1/2)*a*b) -
+             (2*(1/2)*ci*d) - (2*b*ci))
+   names(res) <- "Determinant"
+
+   g <- ggplot() +
+     geom_hline(yintercept = 0) +
+     geom_vline(xintercept = 0) +
+     geom_segment(data = df[1:4, ], aes(
+       x = x, y = y,
+       xend = xend, yend = yend), size = 1) +
+     geom_segment(data = df[5:10, ], aes(
+       x = x, y = y,
+       xend = xend, yend = yend),
+       size = 1, linetype = "dashed") +
+     theme_void() +
+     annotate("text", x = c(7, -0.2, a/2, a+0.2,
+                              a+0.3, ci, a/2+ci,
+                              a+ci/2, a+ci+0.2, ci+0.2,
+                              ci/2, a+ci + 0.2, -0.2),
+              y = c(-0.2, 9, -0.2, b/2,
+                    b+0.2, d+0.2, b+d+0.2,
+                    -0.2, b+d+0.2, b/2+d,
+                    b+d+0.2, d/2, d/2),
+              label = c("x", "y", "a", "b",
+                        "(a, b)", "(c, d)", "a",
+                        "c", "(a+c, b+d)", "b",
+                        "c", "d", "d"))
+
+   l <- list(determinant = res, plot = g)
```

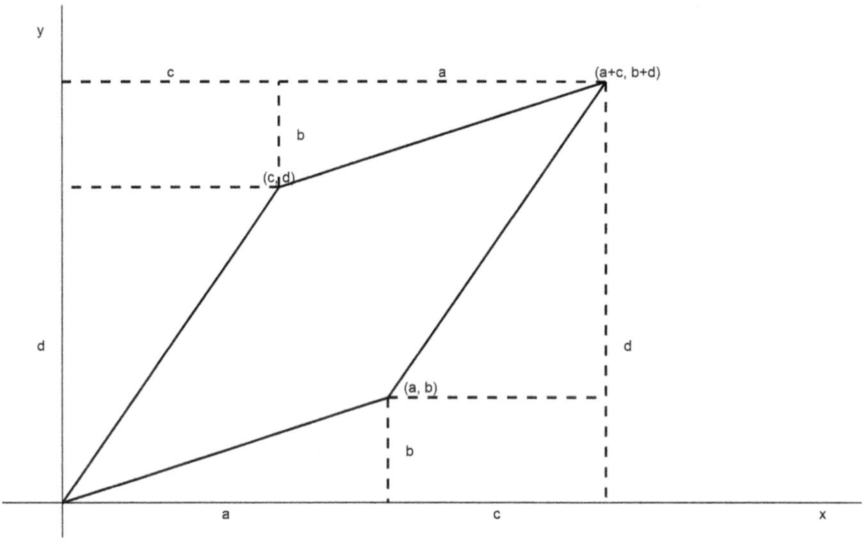

Fig. 2.24 The geometric interpretation of the determinant

```
+     return(1)
+
+   }
```

Figure 2.24 gives a geometric interpretation of the determinant of the matrix A with $a = 3, b = 2, c = 2, d = 6$.

```
> A <- matrix(c(3, 2,
+               2, 6),
+             nrow = 2,
+             ncol = 2,
+             byrow = T)
> A
     [,1] [,2]
[1,]    3    2
[2,]    2    6
> geom_det(A)
$determinant
Determinant
         14

$plot
```

Let's test the function with not 2×2 matrices

```
> B <- matrix(c(1, 2, 3,
+                4, 5, 6,
+                7, 8, 9),
+              nrow = 3,
+              ncol = 3,
+              byrow = T)
> B
     [,1] [,2] [,3]
[1,]    1    2    3
[2,]    4    5    6
[3,]    7    8    9
> geom_det(B)
Error in geom_det(B) : The matrix needs to be a 2x2
matrix
> C <- matrix(c(1, 2, 3,
+                4, 5, 6),
+              nrow = 2,
+              ncol = 3,
+              byrow = T)
> C
     [,1] [,2] [,3]
[1,]    1    2    3
[2,]    4    5    6
> geom_det(C)
Error in geom_det(C) : The matrix needs to be a 2x2
matrix
```

We compute the determinant as the area of the parallelogram. We have all information: we compute the area of the big rectangle and then we subtract the areas of the four right triangles and the area of the two small rectangles, that is

$$\begin{aligned}|A| &= (a+c)(b+d) - 2\left(\frac{1}{2}ab\right) - 2\left(\frac{1}{2}cd\right) - 2bc \\ &= ab + ad + bc + cd - ab - cd - 2bc \\ &= ad - bc\end{aligned} \tag{2.13}$$

If we substitute the values for a, b, c, d we find that

$$\begin{aligned}|A| &= (3+2)(2+6) - 2\left(\frac{1}{2}3 \cdot 2\right) - 2\left(\frac{1}{2}2 \cdot 6\right) - 2(2 \cdot 2) \\ &= 40 - 6 - 12 - 8 \\ &= 14\end{aligned} \tag{2.14}$$

```
> A <- matrix(c(3, 2,
+                 2, 6),
+               nrow = 2,
+               ncol = 2,
+               byrow = T)
> A
     [,1] [,2]
[1,]    3    2
[2,]    2    6
> det(A)
[1] 14
```

Finally, we can say that the determinant of A gives the *signed* area of a parallelogram (or volume of a parallelepiped of a 3×3 matrix) spanned by the column or row vectors of the matrix. If the determinant is negative it shows that the area (or the volume) is flipped over.

2.3.8.2 Laplace Expansion Method

Now, let's consider a technique that allows to find the determinant of an $n \times n$ matrix: the Laplace expansion (also known as *cofactor* expansion). First, we need to introduce two concepts: the *minor* and the *cofactor*.

The minor $|M_{ij}|$ of a matrix A is the determinant of the $(n-1) \times (n-1)$ matrix obtained from A by deleting the *ith* row and *jth* column of A. The cofactor C_{ij} of a matrix A is defined as $C_{ij} = (-1)^{i+j}|M_{ij}|$. To be noted that the transpose of C_{ij} is called the *adjoint* (or *adjugate*) of A and it is denoted as $adj(A)$ (Sect. 2.3.8.3).

Suppose that $A = [a_{ij}]$ is an $n \times n$ matrix and $i, j = \{1, 2, \ldots, n\}$, then the Laplace expansion formula to find the determinant is

$$|A| = a_{i1}C_{i1} + a_{i2}C_{i2} + \ldots + a_{in}C_{in} = a_{1j}C_{1j} + a_{2j}C_{2j} + \ldots + a_{nj}C_{nj} \tag{2.15}$$

where a_{in} and a_{jn} are the values excluded when we compute the minor for the cofactor.

Let's see some examples. A is the following 3×3 matrix:

$$A = \begin{bmatrix} 2 & 4 & 3 \\ -1 & 3 & 0 \\ 0 & 2 & 1 \end{bmatrix}$$

We find the determinant with the Laplace expansion as follows:

$$\begin{bmatrix} \mathbf{2} & & \\ & 3 & 0 \\ & 2 & 1 \end{bmatrix} = 2 \cdot (-1)^{1+1} \begin{vmatrix} 3 & 0 \\ 2 & 1 \end{vmatrix} = 2 \cdot 1 \cdot [(3 \cdot 1) - (2 \cdot 0)] = 6$$

$$\begin{bmatrix} & \mathbf{4} & \\ -1 & & 0 \\ 0 & & 1 \end{bmatrix} = 4 \cdot (-1)^{1+2} \begin{vmatrix} -1 & 0 \\ 0 & 1 \end{vmatrix} = 4 \cdot (-1) \cdot [(-1 \cdot 1) - (0 \cdot 0)] = 4$$

$$\begin{bmatrix} & & \mathbf{3} \\ -1 & 3 & \\ 0 & 2 & \end{bmatrix} = 3 \cdot (-1)^{1+3} \begin{vmatrix} -1 & 3 \\ 0 & 2 \end{vmatrix} = 3 \cdot 1 \cdot [(-1 \cdot 2) - (0 \cdot 3)] = -6$$

Therefore,

$$|A| = 6 + 4 - 6 = 4$$

```
> A <- matrix(c(2, 4, 3,
+               -1, 3, 0,
+               0, 2, 1),
+             nrow = 3,
+             ncol = 3,
+             byrow = T)
> A
     [,1] [,2] [,3]
[1,]    2    4    3
[2,]   -1    3    0
[3,]    0    2    1
> det(A)
[1] 4
```

Next, let's see an example of a 4×4 matrix. In the previous example, we didn't pick up the best row for the cofactor expansion. In fact, it is better to choose a row or a column with most 0. This will make the computation easier. A is the following 4×4 matrix:

$$\begin{bmatrix} -2 & 3 & 4 & 1 \\ 4 & -4 & 3 & 0 \\ 1 & 2 & 5 & 3 \\ -1 & -2 & 5 & 3 \end{bmatrix}$$

Here, we pick up the fourth column because has a 0. Therefore, this time j is fixed and $i = \{1, 2, 3, 4\}$.

$$\begin{bmatrix} & & & \mathbf{1} \\ 4 & -4 & 3 & \\ 1 & 2 & 5 & \\ -1 & -2 & 5 & \end{bmatrix} = 1 \cdot (-1)^{1+4} \begin{vmatrix} 4 & -4 & 3 \\ 1 & 2 & 5 \\ -1 & -2 & 5 \end{vmatrix}$$

From here, we repeat the same steps for the 3×3 matrix:

$$4 \cdot (-1)^{1+1} \begin{vmatrix} 2 & 5 \\ -2 & 5 \end{vmatrix} + (-4) \cdot (-1)^{1+2} \begin{vmatrix} 1 & 5 \\ -1 & 5 \end{vmatrix} + 3 \cdot (-1)^{1+3} \begin{vmatrix} 1 & 2 \\ -1 & -2 \end{vmatrix} = 120$$

Therefore, $a_{14}C_{14} = -120$.
Next, we catch why it is better to pick up row or column with 0.

$$\begin{bmatrix} -2 & 3 & 4 & \\ & & & \mathbf{0} \\ 1 & 2 & 5 & \\ -1 & -2 & 5 & \end{bmatrix} = 0 \cdot \ldots = 0$$

Since we end up multiplying by 0 the result is 0.
The next two steps are the same as the first one.

$$\begin{bmatrix} -2 & 3 & 4 & \\ 4 & -4 & 3 & \\ & & & \mathbf{3} \\ -1 & -2 & 5 & \end{bmatrix} = 3 \cdot (-1)^{3+4} \begin{vmatrix} -2 & 3 & 4 \\ 4 & -4 & 3 \\ -1 & -2 & 5 \end{vmatrix}$$

$$(-2) \cdot (-1)^{1+1} \begin{vmatrix} -4 & 3 \\ 2 & 5 \end{vmatrix} + 3 \cdot (-1)^{1+2} \begin{vmatrix} 4 & 3 \\ -1 & 5 \end{vmatrix} + 4 \cdot (-1)^{1+3} \begin{vmatrix} 4 & -4 \\ -1 & -2 \end{vmatrix} = -89$$

Therefore, $a_{34}C_{34} = -3 \cdot -89 = 267$.
Then,

$$\begin{bmatrix} -2 & 3 & 4 & \\ 4 & -4 & 3 & \\ 1 & 2 & 5 & \\ & & & \mathbf{3} \end{bmatrix} = 3 \cdot (-1)^{4+4} \begin{vmatrix} -2 & 3 & 4 \\ 4 & -4 & 3 \\ 1 & 2 & 5 \end{vmatrix}$$

$$(-2) \cdot (-1)^{1+1} \begin{vmatrix} -4 & 3 \\ 2 & 5 \end{vmatrix} + 3 \cdot (-1)^{1+2} \begin{vmatrix} 4 & 3 \\ 1 & 5 \end{vmatrix} + 4 \cdot (-1)^{1+3} \begin{vmatrix} 4 & -4 \\ 1 & 22 \end{vmatrix} = 49$$

Therefore, $a_{44}C_{44} = 3 \cdot 49 = 147$
Finally, $|A| = -120 + 0 + 267 + 147 = 294$.

Let's build a function to compute the determinant of any square matrix with the Laplace expansion method (excluding the 2 × 2 case). Let's start with a simple case, i.e. a function that only works with a 3 × 3 matrix. We call this function `laplace_expansion3x3()`. The function will return the determinant of a 3×3 matrix. In addition, by setting `info = TRUE`, we will get all the pieces of the Laplace expansion method.

Let's analyse something new in this function. First, we generate a variable `counter` that will count how many times the loop runs. This variable will be used to index the objects in the loop. Second, note that in the loop we subset the A matrix. We set `drop = FALSE` to preserve the original dimensionality. This is always recommended when we subset a 2D object inside the body of a function (Wickham 2019, p. 80). However, note that to compute `L` we subset `A` without setting `drop = FALSE`. In this case, we are fine with a numeric class object. Third, we unlist the `L` list to perform the sum as in the Laplace expansion method by taking the first row fixed.

```
> laplace_expansion3x3 <- function(A, info = FALSE){
+
+   if(nrow(A) != 3 || ncol(A) != 3){
+     stop("The matrix needs to be a 3x3 matrix")
+   }
+
+   n <- dim(A)[1]
+
+   m <- list()
+   M <- list()
+   C <- list()
+   L <- list()
+   counter <- 0
+
+   for(i in 1:n){
+     for(j in 1:n){
+
+       counter <- counter + 1
+       m[[counter]] <- A[-i, -j, drop = FALSE]
+       M[[counter]] <- ((m[[counter]][1,1]*m[[counter]][2,2]) -
+                          (m[[counter]][1,2]*m[[counter]][2,1]))
+       C[[counter]] <- (-1)^(i+j) * M[[counter]]
+       L[[counter]] <- A[i, j] * C[[counter]]
+     }
+
+   }
+
+   LL <- unlist(L)
+   L_det <- sum(LL[1:n])
+   names(L_det) <- "Determinant"
+
+   if(info == FALSE){
+
+     return(L_det)
+
```

```
+     } else{
+
+       INFO <- list(submatrix = m,
+                    minors = M,
+                    cofactor = C,
+                    laplace = L)
+
+       return(INFO)
+
+     }
+
+ }
```

Let's test it with the previous 3×3 matrix

```
> A <- matrix(c(2, 4, 3,
+               -1, 3, 0,
+               0, 2, 1),
+             nrow = 3,
+             ncol = 3,
+             byrow = T)
> A
     [,1] [,2] [,3]
[1,]    2    4    3
[2,]   -1    3    0
[3,]    0    2    1
> laplace_expansion3x3(A)
Determinant
          4
```

The value returned is the determinant of the matrix. We can extract all the information to compute the determinant with the Laplace expansion method as follows

```
> Ainfo <- laplace_expansion3x3(A, info = T)
> Ainfo$submatrix[[1]]
     [,1] [,2]
[1,]    3    0
[2,]    2    1
```

For the sake of illustration, we just extracted the first submatrix the function computed. This is the same first submatrix when we applied the Laplace expansion method at the beginning of this section. Additionally, we stated that the `lapalce_expansion3x3()` function returns the determinant as a result of fixing the first row. To understand this point, we need to understand how the nested loop runs.

Let's print `i` and `j` from the loop of `laplace_expansion3x3()`

```
> for(i in 1:3){
+   for(j in 1:3){
+     print(c(i, j))
+   }
+ }
[1] 1 1
[1] 1 2
[1] 1 3
[1] 2 1
[1] 2 2
[1] 2 3
[1] 3 1
[1] 3 2
[1] 3 3
```

As we can see, after the outer loop starts it moves to the next value in the sequence only after the inner loop completely runs. Consequently, the first three times the loop runs corresponds to fixing the row index in the `laplace_expansion3x3()` function. We can access these results as follows

```
> Ainfo$laplace[1:3]
[[1]]
[1] 6

[[2]]
[1] 4

[[3]]
[1] -6
```

Additionally, since we applied the Laplace expansion to all the rows we can check that indeed that the determinant is always the same no matter what row we fix

```
> Ainfo$laplace[4:6]
[[1]]
[1] -2

[[2]]
[1] 6

[[3]]
[1] 0

> sum(unlist(Ainfo$laplace[4:6]))
[1] 4
```

```
> Ainfo$laplace[7:9]
[[1]]
[1] 0

[[2]]
[1] -6

[[3]]
[1] 10

> sum(unlist(Ainfo$laplace[7:9]))
[1] 4
```

Before building a function that computes the determinant of any square matrix by applying the Laplace expansion (excluding the 2×2 case), let's add a final remark to the nested loop we used. We tracked how many times the loop runs by generating an object `counter`. Note that `counter` has been initialized outside the loop by assigning 0. Every time the loop runs 1 is added to `counter`. Before the loop iterates `counter` equals 0. The first time the loop runs `counter` becomes the result of the sum $0+1$. Consequently, when the loop runs the second time `counter` is the result of the sum $1 + 1$ and so on.

```
> counter <- 0
> for(i in 1:3){
+   for(j in 1:3){
+     counter <- counter + 1
+     print(counter)
+   }
+ }
[1] 1
[1] 2
[1] 3
[1] 4
[1] 5
[1] 6
[1] 7
[1] 8
[1] 9
```

What would happen if we did not initialize `counter` outside the loop? Inside the loop, `counter` is the addition between itself and 1. If we do not assign any value before the loop starts the object `counter` does not exist. This will make **R** generate an error message: `Error in counter: object 'counter' not found` (refer to Sect. 1.7 for the initialization of an object to be used inside a loop).

Let's now build `laplace_expansion()` that computes the determinant of any square matrix.[12] Now it becomes quite tough. For explaining it as well. So while writing the function, I recommend that you keep in mind the steps we followed to solve the 4×4 matrix with the Laplace expansion method at the beginning of this section.

In `laplace_expansion()`, we introduce two functions: `while()` and `rollapply()`. The `while()` function is another function used to generate loop. We need to use extra care when we work with `while()`. In fact, the `for()` function loops over a sequence that we set. On the other hand, the `while()` function implements the loop based on a conditional statement. If the conditional statement is always true, the loop runs infinitely times (Sect. 1.6.6). Let's see practically what it means by observing how we use it in `laplace_expansion()`. We will write

```
while(n > 3){
  counter <- 0
  for(k in 1:length(M)){
    for(j in 1:n){
      counter <- counter + 1
      MM[[counter]] <- M[[k]][-1, -j, drop = FALSE]
       a[[counter]] <- (-1)^(1+j)*M[[k]][1, j]
    }
  }

  aa[[counter]] <- a
  n <- n - 1
  M <- MM
}
```

where `n` corresponds to the number of rows of the matrix. This `while()` function applies only when the matrix we provide to `laplace_expansion()` has more than three rows. Let's suppose we provided a 4×4 matrix. This means that `n` equals 4 that is always greater than 3. This means the loop will run infinitely times because the conditional statement is always true. To avoid this pitfall, in this case we write `n <- n - 1` inside the `while()` loop. That is, every time `while()` runs we subtract 1 from `n`. This means that the conditional statement will become false at a given moment and the loop terminates (if `n` equals 4 after the `while()` loop runs once, if `n` equals 5 after the `while()` loop runs twice and so on). If we forget to make this kind of adjustments when we use `while()` it is not a big deal. We need to stop the function from running and write it again.

The `rollapply()` is a function built in the `zoo` package. `zoo` is a package that is used in particular with time series data. We use `rollapply()` to sum all the determinants the function computes by a given `width`.

[12] Note that the `laplace_expansion()` function returns the determinant of a 2×2 matrix but computed with the basic method.

Let's now describe how the function works. First, the function checks if the matrix we provide is a square matrix. After passing this step, the function checks how many rows the matrix has. If it has 2 rows, it will compute directly the determinant with the formula $ad - bc$. If it has 3 rows, it will compute the determinant as in `laplace_expansion3x3()`. However, we modify this function so that it only expands the first row. In fact, we do not need to expand all the rows and columns to find the determinant. This means that by removing one loop the function will be faster. Finally, we add the code to compute the determinant if the matrix has more than 3 rows.

We need to consider two main points. First, as we saw when we manually expanded a 4×4 matrix, we will have more than one 3×3 matrix. Therefore, the first main step is, regardless the dimension of the matrix we supply to `laplace_expansion()`, to build all the 3×3 matrices. Therefore, `3` will be a key number in the loop. We use the length of the list `M` to control for all the submatrices that we need to build.

Second, we need to consider that first we expand the matrix "forward" but then, after computing all the determinants of the 2×2 matrices, we need to proceed "backward" by multiplying the cofactor with the excluded a_{ij} values when we compute each minors and sum the result. All the a_{1j} values will be grouped and saved in a list `aa` by indexing each level of expansion by `counter`. In one of the last step of the functions, we compute the `H` object that stores the indexes we used. We then use the `rev()` function in the final loop to reverse the arguments of `H`. In fact, we want to compute $a_{1j}C_{1j}$ by using first the last a_{1j} values (going backward). Here the code of `laplace_expansion()`

```
> laplace_expansion <- function(A){
+
+   if(nrow(A) != ncol(A)){
+     stop("The matrix needs to be a square matrix")
+   }
+
+   n0 <- dim(A)[1]
+
+   if(n0 == 2){
+
+     D <- (A[1,1]*A[2,2] - A[1,2]*A[2,1])
+
+     return(D)
+
+   } else if(n0 == 3){
+
+     m <- list()
+     d <- list()
+     C <- list()
+     L <- list()
+
+     for(j in 1:3){
+       m[[j]] <- A[-1, -j, drop = FALSE]
+       d[[j]] <- ((m[[j]][1,1]*m[[j]][2,2]) -
+                    (m[[j]][1,2]*m[[j]][2,1]))
```

```
+       C[[j]] <- (-1)^(1+j) * d[[j]]
+       L[[j]] <- A[1, j] * C[[j]]
+     }
+
+     LL <- sum(unlist(L))
+
+     D <- LL
+
+     return(D)
+
+
+   } else {
+
+     require("zoo")
+
+     n <- n0
+     M <- list()
+     M[[1]] <- A
+
+     MM <- list()
+     a <- list()
+     aa <- list()
+
+     while(n > 3){
+       counter <- 0
+       for(k in 1:length(M)){
+         for(j in 1:n){
+           counter <- counter + 1
+           MM[[counter]] <- M[[k]][-1, -j, drop = FALSE]
+           a[[counter]] <- (-1)^(1+j)*M[[k]][1, j]
+         }
+       }
+       aa[[counter]] <- a
+       n <- n - 1
+       M <- MM
+     }
+
+     m <- list()
+     d <- list()
+     C <- list()
+     L <- list()
+
+     counter <- 0
+     for(k in 1:length(MM)){
+       for(j in 1:3){
+         counter <- counter + 1
+         m[[counter]] <- MM[[k]][-1, -j, drop = FALSE]
+         d[[counter]] <- ((m[[counter]][1,1]*m[[counter]][2,2]) -
+                          (m[[counter]][1,2]*m[[counter]][2,1]))
+         C[[counter]] <- (-1)^(1+j) * d[[counter]]
+         L[[counter]] <- MM[[k]][1, j] * C[[counter]]
+       }
+     }
+
```

```
+       LL <- unlist(L)
+
+       H <- numeric(n0-3)
+       HL <- length(H) - 1
+       H[1] <- n0
+
+       while(n0 > 4){
+         for(w in 1:HL){
+           H[w+1] <- H[w]*(n0-1)
+           n0 <- n0 - 1
+         }
+       }
+
+       counter <- 0
+       for(z in rev(H)){
+         counter <- counter + 1
+         res <- rollapply(LL, width = counter+2,
+                          FUN = sum, by = counter+2)
+         LL <- unlist(aa[[z]])*res
+       }
+
+       D <- (sum(LL))
+
+       return(D)
+
+     }
+ }
```

Let's test it. Additionally, we check the time it takes to run with `system.time()` and we compare it with the `det()` function.

```
> # 2x2
> A <- matrix(c(3, 2,
+               2, 6),
+             nrow = 2,
+             ncol = 2,
+             byrow = T)
> det(A)
[1] 14
> laplace_expansion(A)
[1] 14
> system.time(det(A))
   user  system elapsed
      0       0       0
> system.time(laplace_expansion(A))
   user  system elapsed
      0       0       0
> # 3x3
> A <- matrix(c(2, 4, 3,
+               -1, 3, 0,
```

```
+                0, 2, 1),
+              nrow = 3,
+              ncol = 3,
+              byrow = T)
> det(A)
[1] 4
> laplace_expansion(A)
[1] 4
> system.time(det(A))
   user  system elapsed
      0       0       0
> system.time(laplace_expansion(A))
   user  system elapsed
      0       0       0
> # 4X4
> A <- matrix(c(-2, 3, 4, 1,
+                4, -4, 3, 0,
+                1, 2, 5, 3,
+                -1, -2, 5, 3),
+              nrow = 4,
+              ncol = 4,
+              byrow = T)
> det(A)
[1] 294
> laplace_expansion(A)
[1] 294
> system.time(det(A))
   user  system elapsed
      0       0       0
> system.time(laplace_expansion(A))
   user  system elapsed
      0       0       0
```

These were the determinants of the matrices we computed earlier. For these dimensions of the matrices we do not observe any difference in timing. Let's increase the dimension of the matrix to 7×7 and 8×8 matrices. We generate random matrices for this task.

```
> # 7x7
> N <- 7
> set.seed(1)
> B <- sample(seq(-10, 10), N*N, replace = T)
> A <- matrix(B, nrow = N, ncol = N)
> A
     [,1] [,2] [,3] [,4] [,5] [,6] [,7]
[1,]   -7    8   -4   -6    9    9   -4
```

```
[2,]   -4  -10   -2   -6   -8    9    8
[3,]  -10   10    4   -9   -5    1   -1
[4,]   -9   10   10   -1   -1   -5   -5
[5,]    0   -1   -6    1   -1   -3    3
[6,]    3    3   -2    4   -5    1   -9
[7,]    7   -1    3  -10    4   -5    2
> det(A)
[1] 14683779
> laplace_expansion(A)
[1] 14683779
> system.time(det(A))
   user  system elapsed
      0       0       0
> system.time(laplace_expansion(A))
   user  system elapsed
   0.04    0.02    0.07
> # 8x8
> N <- 8
> set.seed(1)
> B <- sample(seq(-10, 10), N*N, replace = T)
> A <- matrix(B, nrow = N, ncol = N)
> A
     [,1] [,2] [,3] [,4] [,5] [,6] [,7] [,8]
[1,]   -7  -10    4   -1   -1    1    2   -5
[2,]   -4   10   10    1   -5   -5    7    1
[3,]  -10   10   -6    4    4   -4    3   -5
[4,]   -9   -1   -2  -10    9    8   -5   -3
[5,]    0    3    3    9    9   -1  -10   -4
[6,]    3   -1   -6   -8    1   -5    8    0
[7,]    7   -4   -6   -5   -5    3    8    6
[8,]    8   -2   -9   -1   -3   -9   -3   -7
> det(A)
[1] -200800913
> laplace_expansion(A)
[1] -200800913
> system.time(det(A))
   user  system elapsed
      0       0       0
> system.time(laplace_expansion(A))
   user  system elapsed
   0.36    0.03    0.42
```

As expected given the number of matrices generated with the loop, as the matrix gets larger and larger, the performance of `laplace_expansion()` worsens.

2.3.8.2.1 Leading Principal Minor

A submatrix of a square matrix A that is obtained by the simultaneous deletion of the k row and column is called *principal submatrix*. Its determinant is called *principal minor* of A.

For example, given the following 3×3 A matrix

$$A = \begin{bmatrix} a_{11} & a_{12} & a_{13} \\ a_{21} & a_{22} & a_{23} \\ a_{31} & a_{32} & a_{33} \end{bmatrix}$$

the principal minors are (deleting, successively, $k = 1, 2, 3$)

$$\begin{vmatrix} a_{22} & a_{23} \\ a_{32} & a_{33} \end{vmatrix} \quad \begin{vmatrix} a_{11} & a_{13} \\ a_{31} & a_{33} \end{vmatrix} \quad \begin{vmatrix} a_{11} & a_{12} \\ a_{21} & a_{22} \end{vmatrix}$$

Another key concept is that of the *leading principal minors* that are the determinants of the *leading principal submatrices* of an $n \times n$ matrix A. The leading principal submatrix is built by deleting the last $n - k$ rows and $n - k$ columns.

For the previous 3×3 A matrix the leading principal minors are

$$A_1 = \begin{vmatrix} a_{11} \end{vmatrix} \quad A_2 = \begin{vmatrix} a_{11} & a_{12} \\ a_{21} & a_{22} \end{vmatrix} \quad A_3 = \begin{vmatrix} a_{11} & a_{12} & a_{13} \\ a_{21} & a_{22} & a_{23} \\ a_{31} & a_{32} & a_{33} \end{vmatrix}$$

Let's consider an example with the matrix from the previous section.

$$A = \begin{bmatrix} 2 & 4 & 3 \\ -1 & 3 & 0 \\ 0 & 2 & 1 \end{bmatrix}$$

The leading principal submatrices are

$$A_1 = \begin{bmatrix} 2 \end{bmatrix} \quad A_2 = \begin{bmatrix} 2 & 4 \\ -1 & 3 \end{bmatrix} \quad A_3 = \begin{bmatrix} 2 & 4 & 3 \\ -1 & 3 & 0 \\ 0 & 2 & 1 \end{bmatrix}$$

and the leading principal minors are

$$\begin{vmatrix} A_1 \end{vmatrix} = 2 \quad \begin{vmatrix} A_2 \end{vmatrix} = 10 \quad \begin{vmatrix} A_3 \end{vmatrix} = 4$$

Let's build a function, `LPM()`, that computes the leading principal minors. The function takes one argument that needs to be a square matrix

```
> LPM <- function(A){
+
+   stopifnot(nrow(A) == ncol(A))
+
+   n <- dim(A)[1]
+   lpm <- numeric(n)
+
+   for(i in 1:n){
+     lpm[i] <- det(A[1:i, 1:i, drop = FALSE])
+     }
+
+   return(lpm)
+
+ }
```

Let's test it.

```
> A <- matrix(c(2, 4, 3,
+                -1, 3, 0,
+                0, 2, 1),
+              nrow = 3,
+              ncol = 3,
+              byrow = T)
> A
     [,1] [,2] [,3]
[1,]    2    4    3
[2,]   -1    3    0
[3,]    0    2    1
> LPM(A)
[1]  2 10  4
> A <- matrix(c(-2, 3, 4, 1,
+                4, -4, 3, 0,
+                1, 2, 5, 3,
+                -1, -2, 5, 3),
+              nrow = 4,
+              ncol = 4,
+              byrow = T)
> A
     [,1] [,2] [,3] [,4]
[1,]   -2    3    4    1
[2,]    4   -4    3    0
[3,]    1    2    5    3
[4,]   -1   -2    5    3
> LPM(A)
[1]  -2  -4  49 294
```

This is a good example to verify why setting `drop = FALSE` when subsetting in a function is important. In fact, note that the first value selected is A_{11} that is a single value. If we remove `drop = FALSE`, it will be kept as `numeric` and not as `matrix`. This would mean that in the following step the `det()` function will generate an error because `det()` applies to numeric matrix and not numeric values.

```
> class(A[1,1])
[1] "numeric"
> class(A[1,1, drop = FALSE])
[1] "matrix" "array"
> det(A[1,1])
Error in UseMethod("determinant") :
  no applicable method for 'determinant' applied to
  an object of class "c('double', 'numeric')"
> det(A[1,1, drop = FALSE])
[1] -2
```

2.3.8.3 The Determinant and the Matrix Inverse

If A is a square matrix, the determinant tells us if the matrix is invertible. If its determinant is 0, i.e. $|A| = 0$, the matrix has not an inverse. Refer to Sect. 2.3.6 for some examples. If you noted in that section, before inverting the matrix, we calculated the determinant.

We can use the determinant to find the inverse as well.

For a 2×2 A matrix, where $A = \begin{bmatrix} a & b \\ c & d \end{bmatrix}$:

$$A^{-1} = \frac{1}{|A|} \begin{bmatrix} d & -b \\ -c & a \end{bmatrix} \tag{2.16}$$

```
> A <- matrix(c(2, 2,
+               1, 3),
+             nrow = 2,
+             ncol = 2,
+             byrow = T)
> A
     [,1] [,2]
[1,]    2    2
[2,]    1    3
> dA <- det(A)
> dA
[1] 4
> A2 <- matrix(c(3, -2,
+                -1, 2),
```

```
+                 nrow = 2,
+                 ncol = 2,
+                 byrow = T)
> A2
     [,1] [,2]
[1,]    3   -2
[2,]   -1    2
> (1/dA) * A2
      [,1] [,2]
[1,]  0.75 -0.5
[2,] -0.25  0.5
> solve(A)
      [,1] [,2]
[1,]  0.75 -0.5
[2,] -0.25  0.5
```

For a $n \times n$ A matrix,

$$A^{-1} = \frac{1}{|A|} adj(A) \tag{2.17}$$

For example, for

$$A = \begin{bmatrix} 2 & 4 & 3 \\ -1 & 3 & 0 \\ 0 & 2 & 1 \end{bmatrix}$$

the cofactor matrix is given by

$$(-1)^{1+1} \begin{vmatrix} 3 & 0 \\ 2 & 1 \end{vmatrix} = 3$$

$$(-1)^{1+2} \begin{vmatrix} -1 & 0 \\ 0 & 1 \end{vmatrix} = 1$$

$$(-1)^{1+3} \begin{vmatrix} -1 & 3 \\ 0 & 2 \end{vmatrix} = -2$$

$$(-1)^{2+1} \begin{vmatrix} 4 & 3 \\ 2 & 1 \end{vmatrix} = 2$$

$$(-1)^{2+2} \begin{vmatrix} 2 & 3 \\ 0 & 1 \end{vmatrix} = 2$$

$$(-1)^{2+3}\begin{vmatrix}2 & 4\\0 & 2\end{vmatrix} = -4$$

$$(-1)^{3+1}\begin{vmatrix}4 & 3\\3 & 0\end{vmatrix} = -9$$

$$(-1)^{3+2}\begin{vmatrix}2 & 3\\-1 & 0\end{vmatrix} = 3$$

$$(-1)^{3+3}\left|2\ 4\ -\ 1\ 3\right| = 10$$

Thus,

$$C_{ij} = \begin{bmatrix}3 & 1 & -2\\2 & 2 & -4\\-9 & 3 & 10\end{bmatrix}$$

Finally, the adjugate of A is the transpose of the cofactor matrix C of A

$$adj(A) = C^T = \begin{bmatrix}3 & 2 & -9\\1 & 2 & 3\\-2 & -4 & 10\end{bmatrix}$$

Let's now compute the inverse matrix with **R**

```
> A <- matrix(c(2, 4, 3,
+                -1, 3, 0,
+                0, 2, 1),
+              nrow = 3, ncol = 3,
+              byrow = T)
> A
     [,1] [,2] [,3]
[1,]    2    4    3
[2,]   -1    3    0
[3,]    0    2    1
> dA <- det(A)
> C <- matrix(c(3, 1, -2,
+                  2, 2, -4,
+                 -9, 3, 10),
+              nrow = 3, ncol = 3,
+              byrow = T)
> C
     [,1] [,2] [,3]
```

```
[1,]    3    1   -2
[2,]    2    2   -4
[3,]   -9    3   10
> adjA <- t(C)
> adjA
     [,1] [,2] [,3]
[1,]    3    2   -9
[2,]    1    2    3
[3,]   -2   -4   10
> (1/dA)*adjA
      [,1] [,2]  [,3]
[1,]  0.75  0.5 -2.25
[2,]  0.25  0.5  0.75
[3,] -0.50 -1.0  2.50
> solve(A)
      [,1] [,2]  [,3]
[1,]  0.75  0.5 -2.25
[2,]  0.25  0.5 -0.75
[3,] -0.50 -1.0  2.50
```

In both (2.16) and (2.17), we note that if $|A| = 0$ we end up dividing by 0. As a consequence, A has not an inverse.

Let's try to build the intuition behind the relationship between the determinant and the matrix inverse with some verbal logic. To this end, we need four *ingredients*:

1. linear dependence
2. rank
3. the geometric interpretation of the determinant
4. the relation between matrices and linear maps

Suppose that we reduce a square matrix A to its row echelon form and we find that it has a complete row of zeros. This should ring three bells: (1) linear dependence; (2) the matrix has no full rank and (3) the determinant is 0. Now, let's resume the concept of inverse mapping from the real beginning of this chapter. A map $f : A \to A'$ is invertible if f is bijective. However, since the determinant is 0 the dimension collapses to a small dimension. Consequently, f is not bijective and the matrix A is not invertible.

Let's see a numerical example with a graphical representation of a matrix with $|A| = 0$. Figure 2.25 shows that there is no area to compute because the area of the parallelogram has collapsed to 0.

```
> A <- matrix(c(3, -6,
+                1, -2),
+              nrow = 2,
+              ncol = 2,
+              byrow = T)
> A
```

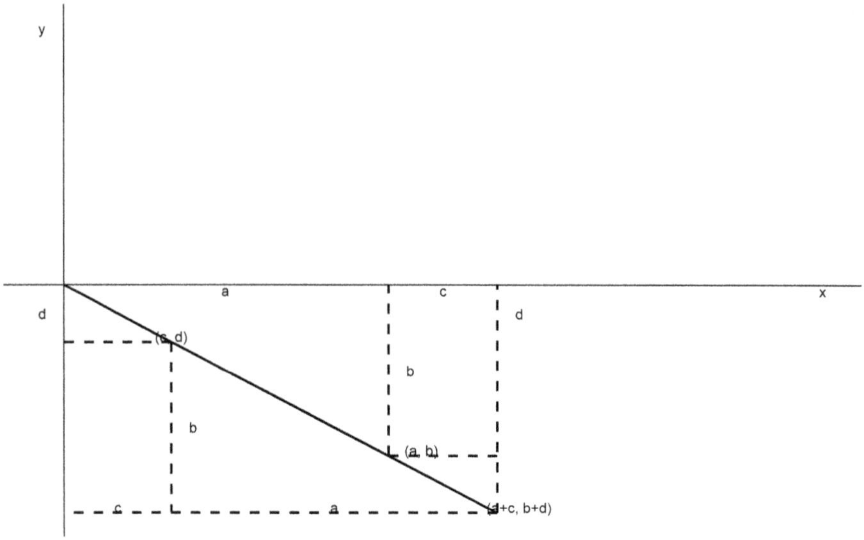

Fig. 2.25 The geometric interpretation of the determinant ($|A| = 0$)

```
      [,1] [,2]
[1,]     3   -6
[2,]     1   -2
> echelon(A)
      [,1] [,2]
[1,]     1   -2
[2,]     0    0
> Rank(A)
[1] 1
> det(A)
[1] 0
> solve(A)
Error in solve.default(A) :
  Lapack routine dgesv:
  system is exactly singular: U[2,2] = 0
> geom_det(A)
$determinant
Determinant
          0

$plot
```

2.3.8.4 Cramer's Rule

If $|A| \neq 0$, the system of equations $A\mathbf{x} = \mathbf{b}$ can be solved applying a technique known as Cramer's rule that use determinants:

$$x_i = \frac{|A(i, \mathbf{b})|}{|A|} \tag{2.18}$$

where x_i represents the solution to the system of equations and $|A(i, \mathbf{b})|$ is the matrix formed by replacing in A the *ith* column with the vector **b**.

Let's use Cramer's rule to solve the system in Sect. 2.3.7.1.

$$\begin{cases} 2x + y - z = 4 \\ x - 2y + z = 1 \\ 3x - y - 2z = 3 \end{cases}$$

In matrix form,

$$A = \begin{bmatrix} 2 & 1 & -1 \\ 1 & -2 & 1 \\ 3 & -1 & -2 \end{bmatrix}, \quad \mathbf{x} = \begin{bmatrix} x \\ y \\ z \end{bmatrix}, \quad \mathbf{b} = \begin{bmatrix} 4 \\ 1 \\ 3 \end{bmatrix}$$

Applying Cramer's rule

$$x = \frac{\begin{vmatrix} 4 & 1 & -1 \\ 1 & -2 & 1 \\ 3 & -1 & -2 \end{vmatrix}}{\begin{vmatrix} 2 & 1 & -1 \\ 1 & -2 & 1 \\ 3 & -1 & -2 \end{vmatrix}} \quad y = \frac{\begin{vmatrix} 2 & 4 & -1 \\ 1 & 1 & 1 \\ 3 & 3 & -2 \end{vmatrix}}{\begin{vmatrix} 2 & 1 & -1 \\ 1 & -2 & 1 \\ 3 & -1 & -2 \end{vmatrix}} \quad z = \frac{\begin{vmatrix} 2 & 1 & 4 \\ 1 & -2 & 1 \\ 3 & -1 & 3 \end{vmatrix}}{\begin{vmatrix} 2 & 1 & -1 \\ 1 & -2 & 1 \\ 3 & -1 & -2 \end{vmatrix}}$$

As we can see, the determinant in the denominator is the same for all the expressions while the column vector `b` shifts from the first column when solving for x, to the second column when solving for y, to the third column when solving for z.

Let's solve it by using **R**.

```
> A <- matrix(c(2, 1, -1,
+               1, -2, 1,
+               3, -1, -2),
+             nrow = 3,
+             ncol = 3,
+             byrow = T)
> A
```

```
     [,1] [,2] [,3]
[1,]    2    1   -1
[2,]    1   -2    1
[3,]    3   -1   -2
> b <- c(4, 1, 3)
> Ax <- A
> Ax[, 1] <- b
> Ax
     [,1] [,2] [,3]
[1,]    4    1   -1
[2,]    1   -2    1
[3,]    3   -1   -2
> Ay <- A
> Ay[, 2] <- b
> Ay
     [,1] [,2] [,3]
[1,]    2    4   -1
[2,]    1    1    1
[3,]    3    3   -2
> Az <- A
> Az[, 3] <- b
> Az
     [,1] [,2] [,3]
[1,]    2    1    4
[2,]    1   -2    1
[3,]    3   -1    3
> x <- det(Ax)/det(A)
> y <- det(Ay)/det(A)
> z <- det(Az)/det(A)
> x
[1] 2
> y
[1] 1
> z
[1] 1
```

In the exercise in Sect. 2.5.4 you are asked to write a function that applies the Cramer's rule to solve a system of linear equations.

2.3.9 *Eigenvalues and Eigenvectors*

Let's build intuition for eigenvalues and eigenvectors while building the steps from the formula to compute them. Our starting point is

$$A\mathbf{v} = \lambda\mathbf{v} \tag{2.19}$$

where A is a square matrix, $\mathbf{v} = \langle v_1, v_2, \ldots, v_n \rangle$ is a vector, called *eigenvector*, and λ is a scalar, called *eigenvalue*.

First, we can note that the left-hand side of Eq. 2.19 is a matrix multiplication. On the right-hand side we have a scalar multiplication. These two sides need to be equal. When we represented the geometric interpretation of the system of linear equations, we saw the transformation caused by multiplying a matrix with a vector (refer to Figs. 2.22 and 2.23). On the other hand, we know that the scalar multiplication stretches, squeezes or inverts the orientation of the vector, always on the same line. Refer to Figs. 2.7, 2.8, 2.11 and 2.12 for some examples. Therefore, given that the two sides of Eq. 2.19 must produce the same outcome, we should ask ourselves: "What is the transformation effect of the matrix multiplication applied to the *eigenvector*?".

Let's continue with the computation of eigenvalues and eigenvectors. First of all, how can we make the two sides of Eq. 2.19 comparable? We should transform the scalar in a matrix without changing the outcome on the right-hand side. We can use the identity matrix to this end. In fact, if we multiply the scalar, λ, times the identity matrix, I, and then we multiply this times the vector $\mathbf{v}$ the result does not change. For example,

```
> s <- 2
> v <- c(3, 6)
> s*v
[1]  6 12
> Id <- diag(2)
> Id
     [,1] [,2]
[1,]    1    0
[2,]    0    1
> sId <- s*Id
> sId
     [,1] [,2]
[1,]    2    0
[2,]    0    2
> sId %*% v
     [,1]
[1,]    6
[2,]   12
```

Therefore, we can rewrite (2.19) as

$$A\mathbf{v} = (\lambda I)\mathbf{v}$$

Let's bring the term on the right-hand side to the left, that is

$$A\mathbf{v} - (\lambda I)\mathbf{v} = 0$$

We can factor out $\mathbf{v}$

$$(A - \lambda I)\mathbf{v} = 0$$

Now let's suppose that $A = \begin{bmatrix} a & b \\ c & d \end{bmatrix}$. This means that

$$A - \lambda I = \begin{bmatrix} a & b \\ c & d \end{bmatrix} - \begin{bmatrix} \lambda & 0 \\ 0 & \lambda \end{bmatrix} = \begin{bmatrix} a - \lambda & b \\ c & d - \lambda \end{bmatrix}$$

Therefore,

$$\begin{bmatrix} a - \lambda & b \\ c & d - \lambda \end{bmatrix} \mathbf{v} = 0$$

The previous expression is true if $\mathbf{v} = 0$. What about if $\mathbf{v} \neq 0$? We find the values of λ that makes the matrix $A - \lambda I$ have determinant equal to 0

$$\begin{vmatrix} a - \lambda & b \\ c & d - \lambda \end{vmatrix} \mathbf{v} = 0$$

Note that $|A - \lambda I|$ is called the *characteristic polynomial* of A.[13] Let's compute $|A - \lambda I| = 0$ to find the eigenvalues, that is

$$\begin{vmatrix} a - \lambda & b \\ c & d - \lambda \end{vmatrix} = 0$$

For this 2×2 matrix, the determinant is

$$(a - \lambda)(d - \lambda) - bc = 0$$

$$ad - a\lambda - d\lambda + \lambda^2 - bc = 0$$

$$\lambda^2 - \lambda(a + d) + ad - bc = 0$$

[13] The eigenvalues and eigenvectors can be also called *characteristic values* and *characteristic vectors*. Other names to refer to them are proper values and proper vectors and latent values and latent vectors.

Solving for λ allows us to find the eigenvalues. Therefore, the eigenvalues are the roots of the characteristic polynomial. We can see that the previous equation could be written as

$$\lambda^2 - \lambda(Tr(A)) + |A| = 0$$

since $a + d$ is the trace of matrix A, and $ad - bc$ is the determinant of matrix A.

Therefore, since in this case we have a polynomial of second degree, we can use the quadratic formula to find the eigenvalues (Sect. 3.3.1)

$$\lambda = \frac{Tr(A) \pm \sqrt{Tr(A)^2 - 4|A|}}{2}$$

Now, to find the eigenvectors, we need to solve the following system of equations

$$\begin{bmatrix} a - \lambda & b \\ c & d - \lambda \end{bmatrix} \begin{bmatrix} v_1 \\ v_2 \end{bmatrix} = \begin{bmatrix} 0 \\ 0 \end{bmatrix}$$

Let's consider an example with a 2×2 matrix.

Example 2.3.1 Find the eigenvalues and eigenvectors for

$$A = \begin{bmatrix} 3 & 2 \\ 2 & 6 \end{bmatrix}$$

Step 1
Set the characteristic polynomial.

$$\begin{vmatrix} 3 - \lambda & 2 \\ 2 & 6 - \lambda \end{vmatrix} = 0$$

$$(3 - \lambda)(6 - \lambda) - 4 = 0$$

$$18 - 3\lambda - 6\lambda + \lambda^2 - 4 = 0$$

$$\lambda^2 - 9\lambda + 14 = 0$$

Step 2
Find the eigenvalues.

$$(\lambda - 7)(\lambda - 2) = 0$$

$$\lambda_1 = 7,\ \lambda_2 = 2$$

Note that the sum of the eigenvalues is 9, that is the trace of A (Sect. 2.3.3.1). In addition, the product of the eigenvalues equals the determinant of the matrix. In this case $7 \cdot 2 = 14$ that is the determinant of A (Sect. 2.3.8.1.1).

Step 3
Find the eigenvectors
For $\lambda = 7$

$$\begin{bmatrix} 3-7 & 2 \\ 2 & 6-7 \end{bmatrix} \begin{bmatrix} v_1 \\ v_2 \end{bmatrix} = 0$$

$$\begin{bmatrix} -4 & 2 \\ 2 & -1 \end{bmatrix} \begin{bmatrix} v_1 \\ v_2 \end{bmatrix} = 0$$

The system of equations is

$$\begin{cases} -4v_1 + 2v_2 = 0 \\ 2v_1 - v_2 = 0 \end{cases}$$

Note that the first equation is equal to -2 times the second equation. If we solve the second equation, we find that

$$2v_1 = v_2$$

Therefore, if $v_1 = \frac{1}{2}$, $v_2 = 1$. The eigenvector is $\mathbf{v} = \begin{bmatrix} \frac{1}{2} \\ 1 \end{bmatrix}$. But if $v_1 = 1$, $v_2 = 2$. $\mathbf{v} = \begin{bmatrix} 1 \\ 2 \end{bmatrix}$ is an eigenvector as well. In general, we choose the *simplest non-zero* eigenvector. The set of all the solutions is called the *eigenspace* of A with respect to 7.

For $\lambda = 2$

$$\begin{bmatrix} 3-2 & 2 \\ 2 & 6-2 \end{bmatrix} \begin{bmatrix} v_1 \\ v_2 \end{bmatrix} = 0$$

$$\begin{bmatrix} 1 & 2 \\ 2 & 4 \end{bmatrix} \begin{bmatrix} v_1 \\ v_2 \end{bmatrix} = 0$$

The system of equations is

$$\begin{cases} v_1 + 2v_2 = 0 \\ 2v_1 + 4v_2 = 0 \end{cases}$$

Note that the second equation is equal to 2 times the first equation. If we solve the first equation, we find that

$$v_1 = -2v_2$$

If $v_2 = 1$, $v_1 = -2$. Therefore, an eigenvector is $\mathbf{v} = \begin{bmatrix} -2 \\ 1 \end{bmatrix}$.

The set of all the solutions is called the *eigenspace* of A with respect to 2. The eigenspace for $\lambda = 7$ has basis $\begin{bmatrix} \frac{1}{2} \\ 1 \end{bmatrix}$ and the eigenspace for $\lambda = 2$ has basis $\begin{bmatrix} -2 \\ 1 \end{bmatrix}$. Any non-zero scalar multiples of these vectors would also be bases.

Let's solve Example 2.3.1 with **R**. We use the `eigen()` function to find the eigenvalues and eigenvectors.

```
> A <- matrix(c(3, 2,
+               2, 6),
+             nrow = 2,
+             ncol = 2,
+             byrow = T)
> A
     [,1] [,2]
[1,]    3    2
[2,]    2    6
> eigen(A)
eigen() decomposition
$values
[1] 7 2

$vectors
          [,1]       [,2]
[1,] 0.4472136 -0.8944272
[2,] 0.8944272  0.4472136
```

Note that **R** returns the eigenvectors normalized to unit length. Let's normalize the results from Step 3 to unit length by imposing the restriction $v_1^2 + v_2^2 = 1$. Therefore, for $\lambda_1 = 7$, we have $2v_1 = v_2$ and consequently

$$(v_1)^2 + (2v_1)^2 = 1$$

$$v_1^2 + 4v_1^2 = 1$$

$$5v_1^2 = 1$$

$$v_1 = \frac{1}{\sqrt{5}}$$

and consequently

$$v_2 = \frac{2}{\sqrt{5}}$$

for $\lambda_2 = 2$, we have $v_1 = -2v_2$ and consequently

$$(-2v_2)^2 + (v_2)^2 = 1$$

$$4v_2^2 + v_2^2 = 1$$

$$5v_2^2 = 1$$

$$v_2 = \frac{1}{\sqrt{5}}$$

and consequently

$$v_1 = -\frac{2}{\sqrt{5}}$$

Therefore, the normalized eigenvectors for $\lambda = 7$ and $\lambda = 2$ are, respectively

$$\begin{bmatrix} \frac{1}{\sqrt{5}} \\ \frac{2}{\sqrt{5}} \end{bmatrix} \quad \begin{bmatrix} -\frac{2}{\sqrt{5}} \\ \frac{1}{\sqrt{5}} \end{bmatrix}$$

```
> v1_norm <- c(1/sqrt(5), 2/sqrt(5))
> v1_norm
[1] 0.4472136 0.8944272
> v2_norm <- c(-2/sqrt(5), 1/sqrt(5))
```

```
> v2_norm
[1] -0.8944272  0.4472136
```

Alternatively, we can use the `unit_vec()` function we built in Sect. 2.2.5 to convert our eigenvectors to the unit eigenvectors.

```
> v1 <- c(1/2, 1)
> v2 <- c(-2, 1)
> unit_vec(v1)
[1] 0.4472136 0.8944272
> unit_vec(v2)
[1] -0.8944272  0.4472136
```

Note that for this example we used a symmetric matrix. For a symmetric matrix, eigenvalues are always real. Additionally, eigenvectors corresponding to distinct eigenvalues of a symmetric matrix are always *orthogonal* (Sect. 2.2.6).

```
> t(v1) %*% v2
     [,1]
[1,]    0
> t(v2) %*% v1
     [,1]
[1,]    0
```

Additionally, the product of normalized vector $v_i'v_i, i = \{1, 2, \ldots, n\}$ must be equal to unity

```
> t(v1_norm) %*% v1_norm
     [,1]
[1,]    1
> t(v2_norm) %*% v2_norm
     [,1]
[1,]    1
```

Normalized eigenvectors are orthogonal to each other as well

```
> t(v1_norm) %*% v2_norm
     [,1]
[1,]    0
> t(v2_norm) %*% v1_norm
     [,1]
[1,]    0
```

Now, let's compare the results of the two sides of Eq. 2.19. First, let's save the eigenvalues in three objects, `lamba`, `l1` and `l2`. Then, we use the eigenvectors we found to compute $A\mathbf{v}$ and $\lambda\mathbf{v}$.

```
> lambda <- eigen(A)[[1]]
> l1 <- lambda[1]
```

```
> l1
[1] 7
> l2 <- lambda[2]
> l2
[1] 2
> A %*% v1
     [,1]
[1,]  3.5
[2,]  7.0
> (l1*Id) %*% v1
     [,1]
[1,]  3.5
[2,]  7.0
> A %*% v2
     [,1]
[1,]   -4
[2,]    2
> (l2*Id) %*% v2
     [,1]
[1,]   -4
[2,]    2
```

As expected, they produce the same results. Then, can we now answer the question we posed at the beginning of this section? Let's represents the eigenvectors with `arrows2D()` from `plot3D`.

```
> x0 <- c(0, 0, 0, 0)
> y0 <- c(0, 0, 0, 0)
> x1 <- c(0.5, -2, 3.5, -4)
> y1 <- c(1, 1, 7, 2)
> cols <- c("blue", "red", "green", "yellow")
> arrows2D(x0, y0, x1, y1,
+          col = cols,
+          lwd = 2)
```

Figure 2.26 shows that the eigenvectors are stretched on the same line after the matrix multiplication.

Let's compare with the eigenvectors normalized to unit vectors (Fig. 2.27).

```
> An1 <- A %*% v1_norm
> An1
         [,1]
[1,] 3.130495
[2,] 6.260990
> (l1*Id) %*% v1_norm
         [,1]
```

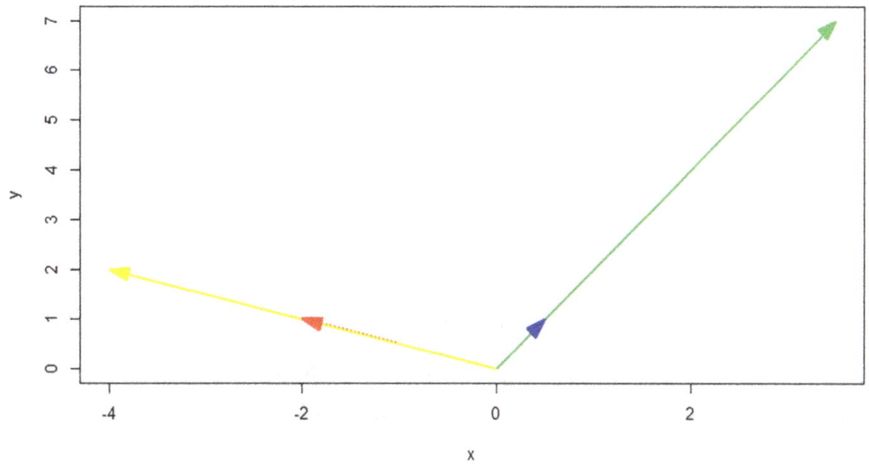

Fig. 2.26 Matrix transformation: eigenvectors

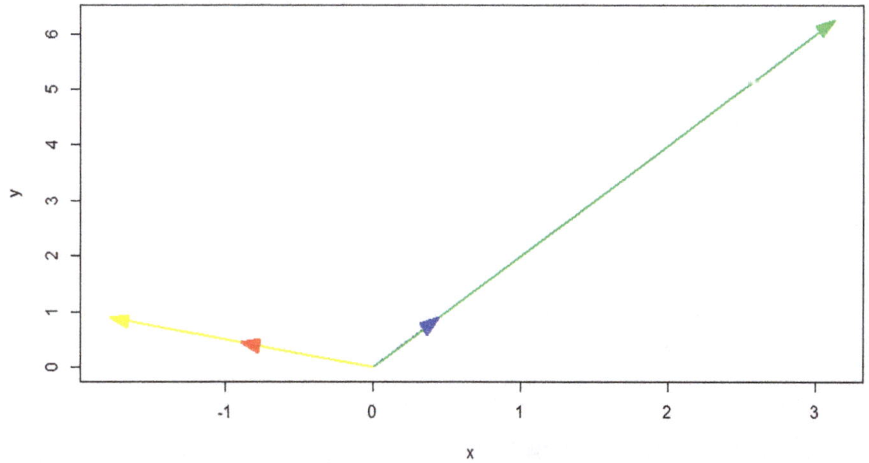

Fig. 2.27 Matrix transformation: eigenvectors (normalized to unit vector)

```
[1,] 3.130495
[2,] 6.260990
> An2 <- A %*% v2_norm
> An2
           [,1]
[1,] -1.7888544
[2,]  0.8944272
> (12*Id) %*% v2_norm
           [,1]
[1,] -1.7888544
```

```
[2,]   0.8944272
> x0 <- c(0, 0, 0, 0)
> y0 <- c(0, 0, 0, 0)
> x1 <- c(v1_norm[1], v2_norm[1], An1[1,1], An2[1,1])
> y1 <- c(v1_norm[2], v2_norm[2], An1[2,1], An2[2,1])
> cols <- c("blue", "red", "green", "yellow")
> arrows2D(x0, y0, x1, y1,
+            col = cols,
+            lwd = 2)
```

Finally, let's compare the multiplication of the A matrix with the eigenvector $\begin{bmatrix} \frac{1}{2} \\ 1 \end{bmatrix}$ and with a *random* vector we choose from a sequence from -5 to 5 with the `sample()` function. The second entry of this function represents the number of items to choose. The `set.seed()` function makes the example reproducible with random number generator functions.

```
> n <- seq(-5, 5, 1)
> set.seed(1)
> z <- sample(n, 2)
> z
[1]  3 -2
> A %*% z
     [,1]
[1,]    5
[2,]   -6
> x0 <- c(0, 0, 0, 0)
> y0 <- c(0, 0, 0, 0)
> x1 <- c(0.5, 3, 3.5, 5)
> y1 <- c(1, -2, 7, -6)
> cols <- c("blue", "red", "green", "yellow")
> arrows2D(x0, y0, x1, y1,
+            col = cols,
+            lwd = 2)
```

Therefore, the multiplication between vector $\mathbf{z}$ and matrix A rotates clockwise and stretches $\mathbf{z}$ (Fig. 2.28).

Let's consider an example with a 3×3 matrix.

Example 2.3.2 Find the eigenvalues and eigenvectors for

$$A = \begin{bmatrix} \frac{1}{2} & \frac{1}{2} & \frac{1}{2} \\ \frac{1}{4} & \frac{1}{2} & 0 \\ \frac{1}{4} & 0 & \frac{1}{2} \end{bmatrix}$$

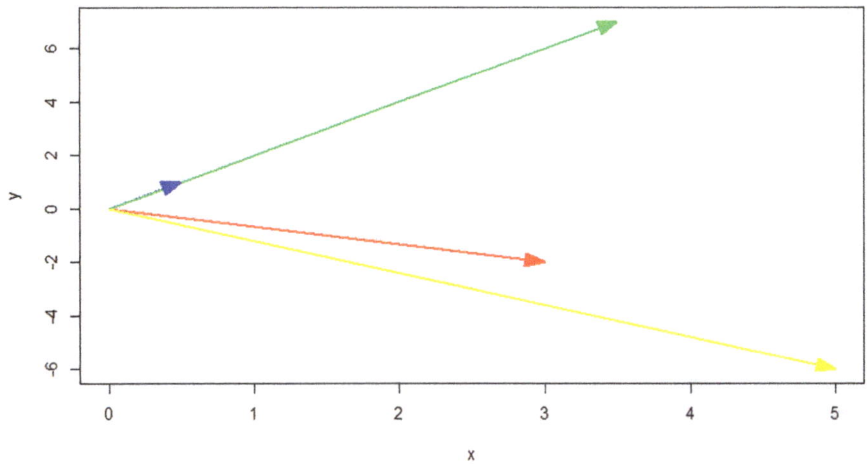

Fig. 2.28 Matrix transformation: eigenvector vs a *random* vector

Step 1
Set the characteristic polynomial

$$\begin{vmatrix} \frac{1}{2}-\lambda & \frac{1}{2} & \frac{1}{2} \\ \frac{1}{4} & \frac{1}{2}-\lambda & 0 \\ \frac{1}{4} & 0 & \frac{1}{2}-\lambda \end{vmatrix} = 0$$

We can use the Laplace expansion (Sect. 2.3.8.2) to compute the determinant. Let's choose row 3 because it has a zero.

$$\frac{1}{4}\cdot(-1)^{3+1}\begin{vmatrix} \frac{1}{2} & \frac{1}{2} \\ \frac{1}{2}-\lambda & 0 \end{vmatrix} + 0\cdot \ldots + \left(\frac{1}{2}-\lambda\right)\cdot(-1)^{3+3}\begin{vmatrix} \frac{1}{2}-\lambda & \frac{1}{2} \\ \frac{1}{4} & \frac{1}{2}-\lambda \end{vmatrix}$$

$$\frac{1}{4}\left(-\frac{1}{4}+\frac{1}{2}\lambda\right)+\left(\frac{1}{2}-\lambda\right)\left(-\lambda+\lambda^2+\frac{1}{8}\right)$$

$$-\frac{1}{16}+\frac{1}{8}\lambda+\frac{1}{8}-\lambda^3+\frac{3}{2}\lambda^2-\frac{5}{8}\lambda+\frac{1}{16}$$

Let's simplify and set the determinant equal to zero

$$-\lambda^3+\frac{3}{2}\lambda^2-\frac{1}{2}\lambda=0$$

This is our characteristic polynomial.

Step 2
Find the eigenvalues

$$-\lambda\left(\lambda^2-\frac{3}{2}\lambda+\frac{1}{2}\right)=0$$

$$-\lambda\left(\lambda-\frac{1}{2}\right)(\lambda-1)=0$$

$$\lambda_1=1,\ \lambda_2=\frac{1}{2},\ \lambda_3=0$$

Step 3
Find the eigenvectors

For $\lambda = 1$

$$\begin{bmatrix}\frac{1}{2}-1 & \frac{1}{2} & \frac{1}{2}\\ \frac{1}{4} & \frac{1}{2}-1 & 0\\ \frac{1}{4} & 0 & \frac{1}{2}-1\end{bmatrix}\begin{bmatrix}u_1\\u_2\\u_3\end{bmatrix}=\begin{bmatrix}0\\0\\0\end{bmatrix}$$

$$\begin{bmatrix}-\frac{1}{2} & \frac{1}{2} & \frac{1}{2}\\ \frac{1}{4} & -\frac{1}{2} & 0\\ \frac{1}{4} & 0 & -\frac{1}{2}\end{bmatrix}\begin{bmatrix}u_1\\u_2\\u_3\end{bmatrix}=\begin{bmatrix}0\\0\\0\end{bmatrix}$$

Let's solve this system with the `echelon()` function (Sect. 2.2.8).

```
> # for lambda = 1
> A_l1 <- matrix(c(0.5-1, 0.5, 0.5,
+                  0.25, 0.5-1, 0,
+                  0.25, 0, 0.5-1),
+                nrow = 3, ncol = 3, byrow = T)
> A_l1
      [,1] [,2] [,3]
[1,] -0.50  0.5  0.5
[2,]  0.25 -0.5  0.0
[3,]  0.25  0.0 -0.5
> echelon(A_l1)
     [,1] [,2] [,3]
[1,]    1    0   -2
[2,]    0    1   -1
[3,]    0    0    0
```

As expected by our discussion in Example 2.3.1 we have a row of zeros. By setting a free variable $u_3 = 1$, we have that $u_1 = 2$ and $u_2 = 1$. Therefore, an eigenvector is $\mathbf{u} = \begin{bmatrix} 2 \\ 1 \\ 1 \end{bmatrix}$

```
> u <- c(2, 1, 1)
```

For $\lambda = \frac{1}{2}$

$$\begin{bmatrix} \frac{1}{2} - \frac{1}{2} & \frac{1}{2} & \frac{1}{2} \\ \frac{1}{4} & \frac{1}{2} - \frac{1}{2} & 0 \\ \frac{1}{4} & 0 & \frac{1}{2} - \frac{1}{2} \end{bmatrix} \begin{bmatrix} v_1 \\ v_2 \\ v_3 \end{bmatrix} = \begin{bmatrix} 0 \\ 0 \\ 0 \end{bmatrix}$$

$$\begin{bmatrix} 0 & \frac{1}{2} & \frac{1}{2} \\ \frac{1}{4} & 0 & 0 \\ \frac{1}{4} & 0 & 0 \end{bmatrix} \begin{bmatrix} v_1 \\ v_2 \\ v_3 \end{bmatrix} = \begin{bmatrix} 0 \\ 0 \\ 0 \end{bmatrix}$$

```
> # for lambda = 1/2
> A_12 <- matrix(c(0.5-0.5, 0.5, 0.5,
+                  0.25, 0.5-0.5, 0,
+                  0.25, 0, 0.5-0.5),
+               nrow = 3, ncol = 3, byrow = T)
> A_12
     [,1] [,2] [,3]
[1,] 0.00  0.5  0.5
[2,] 0.25  0.0  0.0
[3,] 0.25  0.0  0.0
> echelon(A_12)
     [,1] [,2] [,3]
[1,]    1    0    0
[2,]    0    1    1
[3,]    0    0    0
```

Therefore, we have $v_1 = 0$, and by setting $v_3 = 1$, we have $v_2 = -1$. Therefore, an eigenvector is $\mathbf{v} = \begin{bmatrix} 0 \\ -1 \\ 1 \end{bmatrix}$

```
> v <- c(0, -1, 1)
```

For $\lambda = 0$

$$\begin{bmatrix} \frac{1}{2}-0 & \frac{1}{2} & \frac{1}{2} \\ \frac{1}{4} & \frac{1}{2}-0 & 0 \\ \frac{1}{4} & 0 & \frac{1}{2}-0 \end{bmatrix} \begin{bmatrix} w_1 \\ w_2 \\ w_3 \end{bmatrix} = \begin{bmatrix} 0 \\ 0 \\ 0 \end{bmatrix}$$

$$\begin{bmatrix} \frac{1}{2} & \frac{1}{2} & \frac{1}{2} \\ \frac{1}{4} & \frac{1}{2} & 0 \\ \frac{1}{4} & 0 & \frac{1}{2} \end{bmatrix} \begin{bmatrix} w_1 \\ w_2 \\ w_3 \end{bmatrix} = \begin{bmatrix} 0 \\ 0 \\ 0 \end{bmatrix}$$

```
> # for lambda = 0
> A_l3 <- matrix(c(0.5-0, 0.5, 0.5,
+                  0.25, 0.5-0, 0,
+                  0.25, 0, 0.5-0),
+                nrow = 3, ncol = 3, byrow = T)
> A_l3
     [,1] [,2] [,3]
[1,] 0.50  0.5  0.5
[2,] 0.25  0.5  0.0
[3,] 0.25  0.0  0.5
> echelon(A_l3)
     [,1] [,2] [,3]
[1,]    1    0    2
[2,]    0    1   -1
[3,]    0    0    0
```

By setting $w_3 = 1$, we have $w_1 = -2$ and $w_2 = 1$. Therefore, an eigenvetor is $\mathbf{w} = \begin{bmatrix} -2 \\ 1 \\ 1 \end{bmatrix}$.

```
> w <- c(-2, 1, 1)
```

Let's normalize the eigenvectors to the unit length by using the `unit_vec()` function

```
> unit_vec(u)
[1] 0.8164966 0.4082483 0.4082483
> unit_vec(v)
[1]  0.0000000 -0.7071068  0.7071068
> unit_vec(w)
[1] -0.8164966  0.4082483  0.4082483
```

Finally, let's compare our results with the `eigen()` function

```
 A <- matrix(c(0.5, 0.5, 0.5,
+              0.25, 0.5, 0,
+              0.25, 0, 0.5),
```

```
+                nrow = 3, ncol = 3, byrow = T)
> A
     [,1] [,2] [,3]
[1,] 0.50  0.5  0.5
[2,] 0.25  0.5  0.0
[3,] 0.25  0.0  0.5
> eigen(A)
eigen() decomposition
$values
[1]  1.000000e+00  5.000000e-01 -1.665335e-16

$vectors
          [,1]          [,2]       [,3]
[1,] 0.8164966 -3.140185e-16  0.8164966
[2,] 0.4082483 -7.071068e-01 -0.4082483
[3,] 0.4082483  7.071068e-01 -0.4082483
```

Let's conclude this section by writing a new function, `eigen_det()`, to compute the determinant. We can use the property that the product of the eigenvalues of a matrix equals its determinant. In the body of the function we are using the `eigen()` function from which we only select the eigenvalues. Then we use the `prod()` function to multiply the eigenvalues stored in `lambda`. We nest the `prod()` function inside the `Re()` to return only the real part of a complex number (note that in this case the *imaginary* part would be zero—we will deal with complex numbers (and complex eigenvalues) in Chaps. 9 and 10).

```
> eigen_det <- function(A){
+
+   lambda <- eigen(A)$values
+   det <- Re(prod(lambda))
+   return(det)
+
+   }
```

Let's test it with the 8×8 matrix we used to test the `laplace_expansion()` function.

```
> set.seed(1)
> N <- 8
> B <- sample(seq(-10, 10), N*N, replace = T)
> B <- matrix(B, nrow = N, ncol = N)
> eigen_det(B)
[1] -200800913
> system.time(eigen_det(B))
   user  system elapsed
      0       0       0
```

By using the `eigen()` function, that makes the relevant part of the task of the `eigen_det()` function, we wrote a more efficient function to compute the determinant.

2.3.9.1 Diagonalization and Jordan Canonical Form

Suppose that λ_i and λ_j, such that $\lambda_i \neq \lambda_j$, are two eigenvalues of matrix A obtained from $|A - \lambda I| = 0$. Then, there is a matrix $P = \begin{bmatrix} \mathbf{v}^{\lambda_i} \, \mathbf{v}^{\lambda_j} \end{bmatrix}$, i.e. composed of the eigenvectors associated with λ_i and λ_j, such that

$$D = \begin{bmatrix} \lambda_i & 0 \\ 0 & \lambda_j \end{bmatrix} = P^{-1}AP \tag{2.20}$$

Let's check this theorem by continuing Example 2.3.1.

Step 1
Let's form the P matrix. We found the eigenvectors

$$\mathbf{v}^{\lambda_1} = \begin{bmatrix} \frac{1}{2} \\ 1 \end{bmatrix} \quad \mathbf{v}^{\lambda_2} = \begin{bmatrix} -2 \\ 1 \end{bmatrix}$$

Consequently,

$$P = \begin{bmatrix} \frac{1}{2} & -2 \\ 1 & 1 \end{bmatrix}$$

```
> P <- matrix(c(1/2, -2,
+                 1, 1),
+               nrow = 2, ncol = 2,
+               byrow = T)
> P
     [,1] [,2]
[1,]  0.5   -2
[2,]  1.0    1
```

Step 2
Find the inverse of P

```
> P1 <- solve(P)
> P1
     [,1] [,2]
[1,]  0.4  0.8
[2,] -0.4  0.2
```

Step 3
Find D

```
> D <- P1%*%A%*%P
> round(D, 1)
     [,1] [,2]
[1,]    7    0
[2,]    0    2
```

$$D = \begin{bmatrix} 7 & 0 \\ 0 & 2 \end{bmatrix} \tag{2.21}$$

where matrix D is formed with the eigenvalues of matrix A on the main diagonal. Diagonal matrices as in (2.21) are called the *Jordan canonical form* of the original matrix A.[14] Additionally, since $D = P^{-1}AP$, then

$$PDP^{-1} = P\left(P^{-1}AP\right)P^{-1} = A$$

```
> P%*%D%*%P1
     [,1] [,2]
[1,]    3    2
[2,]    2    6
```

Such matrix A is called *diagonalizable* or *not-defective* and the process of finding P and D is called *diagonalization*. Note that not all square matrices are diagonalizable. If A is a $k \times k$ matrix with distinct eigenvalues $\lambda_1, \lambda_2, \ldots, \lambda_k$, then the matrix A is diagonalizable. In the exercise in Sect. 2.5.5 you are asked to write a function that implements this process.

We will return to matrix decomposition methods in Sect. 2.3.13 and to diagonalization and Jordan canonical form in Sect. 10.3.3.

2.3.10 Partitioned Matrix

Partitioned matrix or *block* matrix is a matrix of matrices built in blocks. For example,

[14] I used the `round()` function to print the matrix `D` without scientific notation. The scientific notation is due to the computation of 0.

$$M = \begin{bmatrix} 3 & 2 \\ 2 & 6 \\ - & - \\ 0 & 1 \\ 2 & 3 \\ 4 & 5 \end{bmatrix} = \begin{bmatrix} A \\ B \end{bmatrix}$$

where

$$A = \begin{bmatrix} 3 & 2 \\ 2 & 6 \end{bmatrix}, B = \begin{bmatrix} 0 & 1 \\ 2 & 3 \\ 4 & 5 \end{bmatrix}$$

A partitioned square matrix N is defined as *block diagonal matrix* if the main diagonal blocks are square matrices and the off-diagonal blocks are null matrices. For example,

$$N = \begin{bmatrix} A & 0 \\ 0 & G \end{bmatrix}$$

where

$$G = \begin{bmatrix} 1 & 0 \\ 2 & 3 \end{bmatrix}$$

If partitioned matrices are conformable, they can be added and multiplied. In addition, the inverse of a block diagonal matrix is just the inverse of each block, that is

$$N^{-1} = \begin{bmatrix} A^{-1} & 0 \\ 0 & G^{-1} \end{bmatrix}$$

Partitioned matrices are useful when working with large matrices because they make manipulation more manageable given that it is implemented on the single blocks.

We use the `blockmatrix` package to work with partitioned matrix in **R**. We build the partitioned matrix with the `blockmatrix()` function. To invert a square matrix we use the `solve()` function. To multiply two partitioned matrices—whenever dimensions match up—we use the `blockmatmult()` function. Following some examples.

```
> A <- matrix(c(3, 2,
+                 2, 6),
+              nrow = 2,
+              ncol = 2,
```

```
+               byrow = T)
> A
     [,1] [,2]
[1,]    3    2
[2,]    2    6
> B <- matrix(c(0, 1,
+                 2,  3,
+                 4, 5),
+               nrow = 3,
+               ncol = 2,
+               byrow = T)
> B
     [,1] [,2]
[1,]    0    1
[2,]    2    3
[3,]    4    5
> M <- blockmatrix(names = c("A", "B"),
+                    A = A, B = B,
+                    dim = c(2, 1))
> M
$A
     [,1] [,2]
[1,]    3    2
[2,]    2    6

$B
     [,1] [,2]
[1,]    0    1
[2,]    2    3
[3,]    4    5

$value
     [,1]
[1,] "A"
[2,] "B"

attr(,"class")
[1] "blockmatrix"
> G <- matrix(c(1, 0,
+                 2, 3),
+               nrow = 2,
+               ncol = 2,
+               byrow = T)
> G
     [,1] [,2]
```

```
[1,]    1    0
[2,]    2    3
> N <- blockmatrix(names = c("A", "0",
+                            "0", "G"),
+                  A = A, G = G,
+                  dim = c(2, 2))
> N
$A
     [,1] [,2]
[1,]    3    2
[2,]    2    6

$G
     [,1] [,2]
[1,]    1    0
[2,]    2    3

$value
     [,1] [,2]
[1,] "A"  "0"
[2,] "0"  "G"

attr(,"class")
[1] "blockmatrix"
> S <- matrix(c(3, 2, 0, 0,
+               2, 6, 0, 0,
+               0, 0, 1, 0,
+               0, 0, 2, 3),
+             nrow = 4,
+             ncol = 4,
+             byrow = T)
> S
     [,1] [,2] [,3] [,4]
[1,]    3    2    0    0
[2,]    2    6    0    0
[3,]    0    0    1    0
[4,]    0    0    2    3
> solve(S)
           [,1]       [,2]       [,3]      [,4]
[1,]  0.4285714 -0.1428571  0.0000000 0.0000000
[2,] -0.1428571  0.2142857  0.0000000 0.0000000
[3,]  0.0000000  0.0000000  1.0000000 0.0000000
[4,]  0.0000000  0.0000000 -0.6666667 0.3333333
> solve(N)
$`V1,1`
```

```
           [,1]       [,2]
[1,]  0.4285714 -0.1428571
[2,] -0.1428571  0.2142857

$`V2,2`
           [,1]      [,2]
[1,]  1.0000000 0.0000000
[2,] -0.6666667 0.3333333

$value
     [,1]   [,2]
[1,] "V1,1" "0"
[2,] "0"    "V2,2"

attr(,"class")
[1] "blockmatrix"
> D <- matrix(c(1, 2,
+               3, 2,
+               0, -1,
+               2, 2),
+             nrow = 4,
+             ncol = 2,
+             byrow = TRUE)
> E <- matrix(c(-1, 3,
+               2, 1,
+               4, -2,
+               1, 3),
+             nrow = 4,
+             ncol = 2,
+             byrow = TRUE)
> J <- blockmatrix(names = c("D", "E"),
+                  D = D, E = E,
+                  dim = c(1, 2))
> J
$D
     [,1] [,2]
[1,]    1    2
[2,]    3    2
[3,]    0   -1
[4,]    2    2

$E
     [,1] [,2]
[1,]   -1    3
[2,]    2    1
```

```
[3,]    4   -2
[4,]    1    3

$value
     [,1] [,2]
[1,] "D"  "E"

attr(,"class")
[1] "blockmatrix"
> H <- matrix(c(5, 4, 2,
+               2, 3, 1),
+             nrow = 2,
+             ncol = 3,
+             byrow = TRUE)
> I <- matrix(c(-2, 3, 2,
+               -1, 1, 3),
+             nrow = 2,
+             ncol = 3,
+             byrow = TRUE)
> K <- blockmatrix(names = c("H", "I"),
+                  H = H, I = I,
+                  dim = c(2, 1))
> K
$H
     [,1] [,2] [,3]
[1,]    5    4    2
[2,]    2    3    1

$I
     [,1] [,2] [,3]
[1,]   -2    3    2
[2,]   -1    1    3

$value
     [,1]
[1,] "H"
[2,] "I"

attr(,"class")
[1] "blockmatrix"
> J
$D
     [,1] [,2]
[1,]    1    2
[2,]    3    2
```

```
[3,]    0   -1
[4,]    2    2

$E
     [,1] [,2]
[1,]   -1    3
[2,]    2    1
[3,]    4   -2
[4,]    1    3

$value
     [,1] [,2]
[1,] "D"  "E"

attr(,"class")
[1] "blockmatrix"
> blockmatmult(J, K)
$`V1,1`
     [,1] [,2] [,3]
[1,]    8   10   11
[2,]   14   25   15
[3,]   -8    7    1
[4,]    9   20   17

$value
     [,1]
[1,] "V1,1"

attr(,"class")
[1] "blockmatrix"
> ((D %*% H) + (E %*% I))
     [,1] [,2] [,3]
[1,]    8   10   11
[2,]   14   25   15
[3,]   -8    7    1
[4,]    9   20   17
```

2.3.11 Kronecker Product

The Kronecker product, denoted by $\otimes$, for a 2×2 A matrix and a 3×2 B matrix is defined as follows:

$$A \otimes B = \begin{bmatrix} a_{11}B & a_{12}B \\ a_{21}B & a_{22}B \end{bmatrix} \tag{2.22}$$

Therefore, for

$$A = \begin{bmatrix} 1 & 2 \\ 3 & 4 \end{bmatrix} \quad B = \begin{bmatrix} 5 & 6 \\ 7 & 8 \\ 9 & 10 \end{bmatrix}$$

the Kronecker product is

$$A \otimes B = \left[\begin{array}{cc|cc} 5 & 6 & 10 & 12 \\ 7 & 8 & 14 & 16 \\ 9 & 10 & 18 & 20 \\ \hline 15 & 18 & 20 & 24 \\ 21 & 24 & 28 & 32 \\ 27 & 30 & 36 & 40 \end{array}\right]$$

Thus, the Kronecker product results in a special form of partitioning. In addition, note that the outer product and the Kronecker product share the same operation symbol. However, the former applies to vectors while the latter applies to matrices. For an example of an application of the Kronecker product in Econometrics you may refer to Theil (1983, pp. 17–19).

In **R**, we use the `kronecker()` function:

```
> A <- matrix(c(1, 2,
+                3, 4), nrow = 2,
+              ncol = 2, byrow = T)
> A
     [,1] [,2]
[1,]    1    2
[2,]    3    4
> B <- matrix(c(5, 6,
+                7, 8,
+                9, 10), nrow = 3,
+              ncol = 2, byrow = T)
> B
     [,1] [,2]
[1,]    5    6
[2,]    7    8
[3,]    9   10
> kronecker(A, B)
     [,1] [,2] [,3] [,4]
```

```
[1,]    5    6   10   12
[2,]    7    8   14   16
[3,]    9   10   18   20
[4,]   15   18   20   24
[5,]   21   24   28   32
[6,]   27   30   36   40
```

Compared with the matrix multiplication, the Kronecker product does not require two conformable matrices for the multiplication, that is it can be applied to any $m \times n$ and $p \times q$ matrices.

Let's generate the following matrices *C*, *D*, *E*, *G*, and the scalar *k*:

```
> C <- matrix(c(11, 12,
+                13, 14,
+                15, 16), nrow = 3,
+               ncol = 2, byrow = T)
> C
     [,1] [,2]
[1,]   11   12
[2,]   13   14
[3,]   15   16
> D <- matrix(c(5, 6,
+                7, 8), nrow = 2,
+               ncol = 2, byrow = T)
> D
     [,1] [,2]
[1,]    5    6
[2,]    7    8
> E <- matrix(c(1, 3, 5,
+                2, 4, 6), nrow = 2,
+               ncol = 3, byrow = T)
> E
     [,1] [,2] [,3]
[1,]    1    3    5
[2,]    2    4    6
> G <- matrix(c(0, 1, -8,
+                2, 6, 3,
+                0, 3, 1), nrow = 3,
+               ncol = 3, byrow = T)
> G
     [,1] [,2] [,3]
[1,]    0    1   -8
[2,]    2    6    3
[3,]    0    3    1
> k <- 5
```

Let's check the following properties of the Kronecker product:

(1) Associative

$$A \otimes (B + C) = A \otimes B + A \otimes C$$

$$(B + C) \otimes A = B \otimes A + C \otimes A$$

$$(kA) \otimes B = A \otimes (kB) = k(A \otimes B)$$

$$(A \otimes B) \otimes C = A \otimes (B \otimes C)$$

$$A \otimes 0 = 0 \otimes A = 0$$

(2) Inverse

$$(A \otimes D)^{-1} = A^{-1} \otimes D^{-1}$$

(3) Transpose

$$(A \otimes B)^T = A^T \otimes B^T$$

(4) Mixed-product

$$(A \otimes B)(D \otimes E) = (AD) \otimes (BE)$$

(5) Determinant

Given that A is a $n \times n$ matrix and G is a $m \times m$ matrix, the determinant property states that

$$|A \otimes G| = |A|^m |G|^n$$

```
> # 1 Associative
> kronecker(A, (B + C)) == kronecker(A, B) + kronecker(A, C)
     [,1] [,2] [,3] [,4]
[1,] TRUE TRUE TRUE TRUE
[2,] TRUE TRUE TRUE TRUE
[3,] TRUE TRUE TRUE TRUE
[4,] TRUE TRUE TRUE TRUE
[5,] TRUE TRUE TRUE TRUE
[6,] TRUE TRUE TRUE TRUE
```

```
> kronecker((B + C), A) == kronecker(B, A) + kronecker(C, A)
     [,1] [,2] [,3] [,4]
[1,] TRUE TRUE TRUE TRUE
[2,] TRUE TRUE TRUE TRUE
[3,] TRUE TRUE TRUE TRUE
[4,] TRUE TRUE TRUE TRUE
[5,] TRUE TRUE TRUE TRUE
[6,] TRUE TRUE TRUE TRUE
> all.equal(kronecker(k*A, B),
+           kronecker(A, k*B),
+           (k * kronecker(A, B)))
[1] TRUE
> all.equal(kronecker(kronecker(A, B), C),
+           kronecker(A, kronecker(B, C)))
[1] TRUE
> kronecker(A, 0)
     [,1] [,2]
[1,]    0    0
[2,]    0    0
> kronecker(0, A)
     [,1] [,2]
[1,]    0    0
[2,]    0    0
> # 2 Inverse
> all.equal(solve(kronecker(A, D)),
+           kronecker(solve(A), solve(D)))
[1] TRUE
> # 3 Transpose
> all.equal(t(kronecker(A, B)),
+           (kronecker(t(A), t(B))))
[1] TRUE
> # 4 Mixed-products
> all.equal(kronecker(A, B) %*% kronecker(D, E),
+           kronecker(A%*%D, B%*%E))
[1] TRUE
> # 5 Determinant
> all.equal(det(kronecker(A, G)),
+           (det(A)^dim(G)[1] * det(G)^dim(A)[1]))
[1] TRUE
```

2.3.12 Definiteness of Matrices

We may encounter a matrix that is defined as a *positive definite* matrix. What does that mean? Is there a *negative definite* matrix as well?

In Sect. 2.3.7, we learnt how to write a system of equations in matrix form and how that is convenient in terms of notation. Here, we start our discussion from a different perspective, i.e. functions. We work with the following quadratic function of two variables x and y (Chap. 6):

$$f(x, y) = 3x^2 + 6y^2 + 4xy$$

Let's plot it with the `plotFun()` function from the `mosaic` package. First, we need to generate a function with `function()`. We name the object `fn`. Then, we plot it. Note that we define the limits for the x and y variables with `xlim = range()` and `ylim = range()`. We define the variables names with `xlab =`, `ylab =`, and `zlab =`. Finally, `surface = TRUE` draws a surface plot rather than a contour plot (refer to Sect. 6.1).

```
> fn <- function(x, y){
+      3*x^2 + 6*y^2 + 4*x*y
+    }
> plotFun(fn(x, y) ~ x & y,
+                    xlab = "x",
+                    ylab = "y",
+                    zlab = "f(x, y)",
+                    x.lim = range(-15, 15),
+                    y.lim = range(-15, 15),
+                    surface = T)
```

Figure 2.29 shows that for positive and negative values of x and y the function is positive. Let's check some values of the function. We first generate some values for x and y and then we use these values to generate the `z` object. Then, we collect `x`, `y`, `z` in a data frame, `df`, with `data.frame()`. Finally, we use `head()` and `tail()` to show, respectively, the first six entries and the last six entries of the data

Fig. 2.29 Positive definite matrix

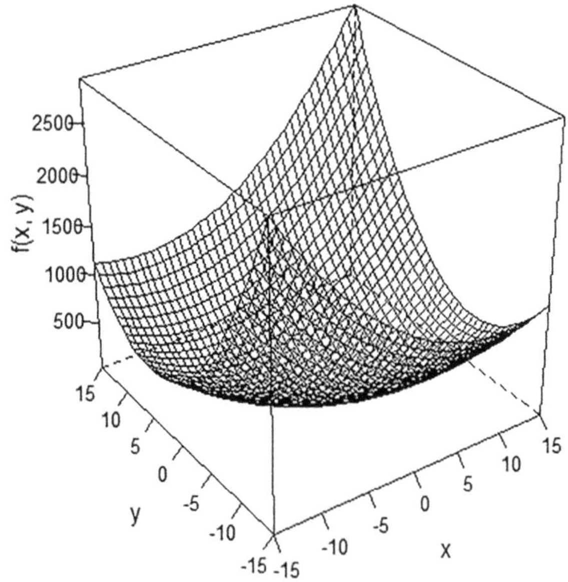

frame `df`. For example, $f(-15, -15) = 2925$, $f(-10, -10) = 1300$, $f(10, 0) = 300$, $f(15, 5) = 1125$.

```
> x <- seq(-15, 15, 1)
> y <- seq(-15, 15, 1)
> z <- fn(x, y)
> df <- data.frame(x, y, z)
> head(df)
    x   y    z
1 -15 -15 2925
2 -14 -14 2548
3 -13 -13 2197
4 -12 -12 1872
5 -11 -11 1573
6 -10 -10 1300
> tail(df)
    x  y    z
26 10 10 1300
27 11 11 1573
28 12 12 1872
29 13 13 2197
30 14 14 2548
31 15 15 2925
```

Where is the connection with matrices? In short, the function we are working with is a quadratic form function that can be represented as a symmetric matrix (Sect. 2.3.2)

$$f(x, y) = \begin{bmatrix} x & y \end{bmatrix} \begin{bmatrix} 3 & 2 \\ 2 & 6 \end{bmatrix} \begin{bmatrix} x \\ y \end{bmatrix}$$

that in notation can be written as $f(\mathbf{w}) = \mathbf{w}^T A\mathbf{w}$.

In our example, $\mathbf{w}$ is a column vector 2×1 and $\mathbf{w}^T$ is its transpose 1×2. A is a 2×2 matrix. Let's multiply it out. First, we multiply $A\mathbf{w}$.

$$\begin{bmatrix} 3 & 2 \\ 2 & 6 \end{bmatrix} \begin{bmatrix} x \\ y \end{bmatrix} = \begin{bmatrix} 3x + 2y \\ 2x + 6y \end{bmatrix}$$

Then, we multiply

$$\begin{bmatrix} x & y \end{bmatrix} \begin{bmatrix} 3x + 2y \\ 2x + 6y \end{bmatrix} = x(3x + 2y) + y(2x + 6y) = 3x^2 + 2xy + 2xy + 6y^2$$

We are back to the initial quadratic form $3x^2 + 6y^2 + 4xy$. Note that the coefficients of the quadratic terms are on the main diagonal. A is a positive definite matrix since $\mathbf{w}^T A\mathbf{w} > 0$ for all non-zero $\mathbf{w}$. We can employ two tests to verify the type of matrix

1. test based on the leading principal minors
2. test based on the eigenvalues

For example,

```
> A <- matrix(c(3, 2,
+                 2, 6),
+               nrow = 2,
+               ncol = 2,
+               byrow = T)
> A
     [,1] [,2]
[1,]    3    2
[2,]    2    6
> det(A)
[1] 14
> LPM(A)
[1]  3 14
> eigen(A)[1]
$values
[1] 7 2
```

A is positive definite if and only if

- all of its leading principal minors are positive
- all of its eigenvalues are positive.

In general, for a $n \times n$ symmetric matrix A, we can distinguish the following types of matrices:

- Positive definite if $\mathbf{w}^T A\mathbf{w} > 0\ \forall \mathbf{w} \neq 0$ in $\mathbb{R}^n$
  - its leading principal minors are positive, $|A_k| > 0$
  - its eigenvalues are positive, $\lambda_i > 0$
- Positive semidefinite if $\mathbf{w}^T A\mathbf{w} \geq 0\ \forall \mathbf{w} \neq 0$ in $\mathbb{R}^n$
  - none of the principal minors (not only the leading principal ones) are negative
  - its eigenvalues are non-negative, $\lambda_i \geq 0$
- Negative definite if $\mathbf{w}^T A\mathbf{w} < 0\ \forall \mathbf{w} \neq 0$ in $\mathbb{R}^n$
  - the leading principal minors alternate the sign as follows: $|A_1| < 0$, $|A_2| > 0$, $|A_3| <= 0$, etc.
  - its eigenvalues are negative, $\lambda_i < 0$

- Negative semidefinite if $\mathbf{w}^T A\mathbf{w} \leq 0 \; \forall \mathbf{w} \neq 0$ in $\mathbb{R}^n$
  - every principal minor of odd order of A is ≤ 0 and every principal minor of even order of A is ≥ 0
  - its eigenvalues are non-positive, $\lambda_i \leq 0$
- A is said to be *indefinite* if it is not included in the previous cases
  - if it does not fit previous definitions in the case of leading principal minors
  - its eigenvalues are positive and negative

In the following examples we consider only the eigenvalue test.

$$B = \begin{bmatrix} 3 & 2 \\ 2 & \frac{4}{3} \end{bmatrix}$$

```
> B <- matrix(c(3, 2,
+               2, 4/3),
+             nrow = 2,
+             ncol = 2,
+             byrow = T)
> B
     [,1]     [,2]
[1,]    3 2.000000
[2,]    2 1.333333
> det(B)
[1] 0
> eigen(B)[1]
$values
[1] 4.333333 0.000000
```

Its eigenvalues are 4.333 and 0. Therefore, B is a positive semidefinite matrix.
The corresponding quadratic form function is $3x^2 + \frac{4}{3}y^2 + 4xy$ that is 0 when $f(4, -6)$.

```
> 3*(4)^2 + (4/3)*(-6)^2 + 4*(4)*(-6)
[1] 0
```

Let's check it in matrix form.

$$[4 \; -6]\begin{bmatrix} 3 & 2 \\ 2 & \frac{4}{3} \end{bmatrix}\begin{bmatrix} 4 \\ -6 \end{bmatrix}$$

After multiplying $B\mathbf{w}$, we multiplying the following

$$[4 \; -6]\begin{bmatrix} 12 & -12 \\ 8 & -8 \end{bmatrix}$$

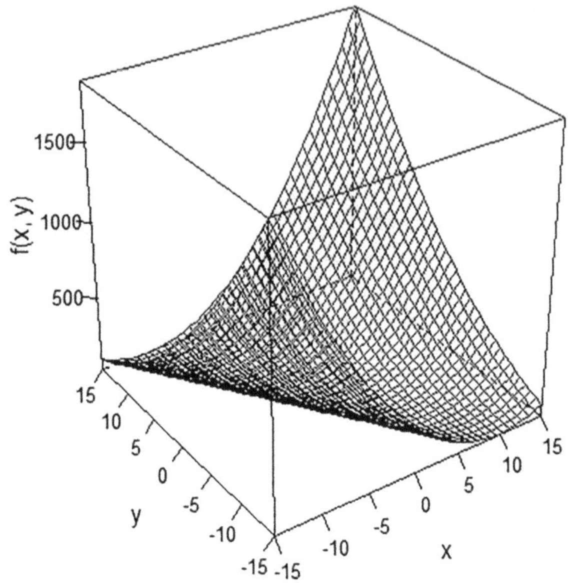

Fig. 2.30 Positive semidefinite matrix

to get

$$4(12-12)-6(8-8)=0$$

Let's give a graphical representation with `plotFun()` (Fig. 2.30).

```
> fn <- function(x, y){
+      3*x^2 + (4/3)*y^2 + 4*x*y
+    }
> plotFun(fn(x, y) ~ x & y,
+                     xlab = "x",
+                     ylab = "y",
+                     zlab = "f(x, y)",
+                     x.lim = range(-15, 15),
+                     y.lim = range(-15, 15),
+                     surface = T)
```

$$D=\begin{bmatrix}-3 & 2\\ 2 & -6\end{bmatrix}$$

```
> D <- matrix(c(-3, 2,
+                 2, -6),
+             nrow = 2,
+             ncol = 2,
```

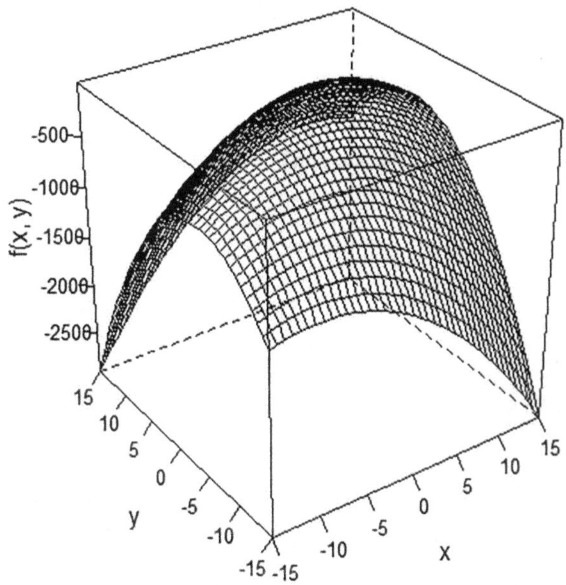

Fig. 2.31 Negative definite matrix

```
+                    byrow = T)
> D
      [,1] [,2]
[1,]    -3    2
[2,]     2   -6
> det(D)
[1] 14
> eigen(D)[1]
$values
[1] -2 -7
```

Its eigenvalues are -2 and -7. Therefore, D is a negative definite matrix. The corresponding quadratic form function is $-3x^2 - 6y^2 + 4xy$ (Fig. 2.31).

```
> fn <- function(x, y){
+        -3*x^2  -6*y^2 + 4*x*y
+     }
> plotFun(fn(x, y) ~ x & y,
+                         xlab = "x",
+                         ylab = "y",
+                         zlab = "f(x, y)",
+                         x.lim = range(-15, 15),
+                         y.lim = range(-15, 15),
+                         surface = T)
```

The matrix E is an example of negative semidefinite matrix since its eigenvalues are 0 and -4.

```
> E <- matrix(c(-2, 2,
+               2, -2),
+             nrow = 2,
+             ncol = 2,
+             byrow = T)
> E
     [,1] [,2]
[1,]   -2    2
[2,]    2   -2
> eigen(E)[1]
$values
[1]  0 -4
```

It corresponds to the quadratic form function $f(x, y) = -2x^2 - 2y^2 + 4xy$. In this case, when $x = y$, $f(x, y) = 0$ (Fig. 2.32).

```
> fn <- function(x, y){
+    -2*x^2 -2*y^2 + 4*x*y
+  }
> plotFun(fn(x, y) ~ x & y,
+                  xlab = "x",
+                  ylab = "y",
+                  zlab = "f(x, y)",
+                  x.lim = range(-15, 15),
+                  y.lim = range(-15, 15),
+                  surface = T)
```

The matrix G is an example of an indefinite form since its eigenvalues are positive and negative.

```
> G <- matrix(c(1, 0,
+               0, -1),
+             nrow = 2,
+             ncol = 2,
+             byrow = T)
> G
     [,1] [,2]
[1,]    1    0
[2,]    0   -1
> eigen(G)[1]
$values
[1]  1 -1
```

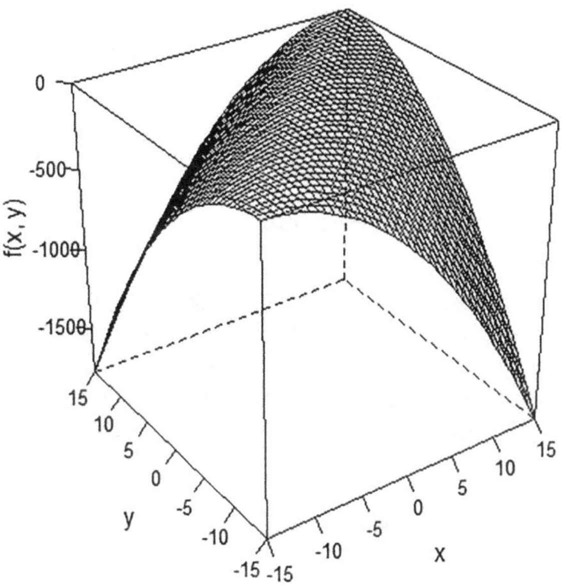

Fig. 2.32 Negative semidefinite matrix

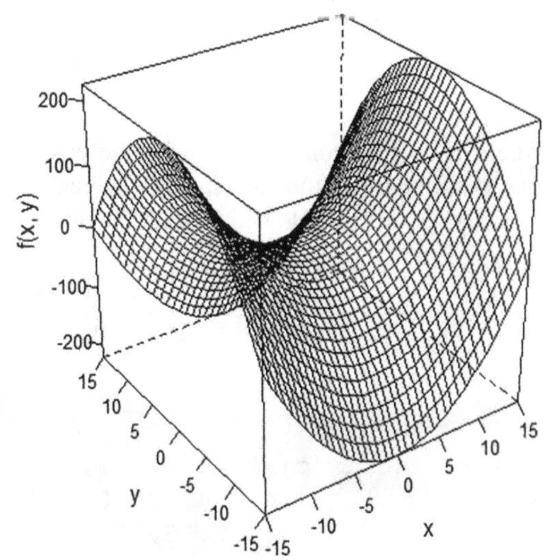

Fig. 2.33 Indefinite form matrix

It corresponds to the quadratic form function $f(x, y) = x^2 - y^2$ (Fig. 2.33)

```
> fn <- function(x, y){
+       x^2 -y^2
+    }
> plotFun(fn(x, y) ~ x & y,
+                       xlab = "x",
+                       ylab = "y",
```

```
+                          zlab = "f(x, y)",
+                          x.lim = range(-15, 15),
+                          y.lim = range(-15, 15),
+                          surface = T)
```

2.3.13 Decomposition

Decomposition methods allow to factorize a matrix as products of matrices. We may want to do this because these matrices provide new information about the original matrix or because they make computation more manageable. In the next sections, we will implement the Spectral decomposition, the Singular Value Decomposition, the Cholesky decomposition and the QR decomposition.

2.3.13.1 Spectral Decomposition

The spectral decomposition (or eigenvalue decomposition) is a technique to factorize a $n \times n$ matrix as follows

$$A = QDQ^{-1} \tag{2.23}$$

where D is a diagonal matrix with the eigenvalues[15] along the diagonal, Q is a matrix formed with the corresponding eigenvectors, and Q^{-1} is its inverse.

Let's see an example with **R** with the matrix

$$A = \begin{bmatrix} -2 & 3 & 4 & 1 \\ 4 & -4 & 3 & 0 \\ 1 & 2 & 5 & 3 \\ -1 & -2 & 5 & 3 \end{bmatrix}$$

```
> A <- matrix(c(-2, 3, 4, 1,
+                4, -4, 3, 0,
+                1, 2, 5, 3,
+                -1, -2, 5, 3),
+              nrow = 4,
+              ncol = 4,
+              byrow = TRUE)
> A
     [,1] [,2] [,3] [,4]
```

[15] All eigenvalues need to be distinct, that is no repeated eigenvalues. If this is the case, the Jordan decomposition generalizes it.

```
[1,]   -2    3    4    1
[2,]    4   -4    3    0
[3,]    1    2    5    3
[4,]   -1   -2    5    3
```

Its spectral decomposition is

```
> D <- diag(eigen(A)$values)
> D
         [,1]      [,2]     [,3]      [,4]
[1,] 8.407216  0.000000 0.000000  0.000000
[2,] 0.000000 -6.692281 0.000000  0.000000
[3,] 0.000000  0.000000 2.432889  0.000000
[4,] 0.000000  0.000000 0.000000 -2.147824
> Q <- eigen(A)$vectors
> Q
          [,1]       [,2]       [,3]       [,4]
[1,] 0.4092104  0.4518831  0.4323711 -0.4938104
[2,] 0.3053133 -0.8512690  0.4267962 -0.3471054
[3,] 0.7170821  0.1614410  0.3386828  0.4441138
[4,] 0.4744722 -0.2123194 -0.7184666 -0.6621420
> Q1 <- solve(Q)
> Q%*%D%*%Q1
     [,1] [,2] [,3]        [,4]
[1,]   -2    3    4 1.00000e+00
[2,]    4   -4    3 1.44329e-15
[3,]    1    2    5 3.00000e+00
[4,]   -1   -2    5 3.00000e+00
```

This decomposition is useful to compute the determinant. In fact,

$$
\begin{aligned}
det(A) &= det(QDQ^{-1}) \\
&= det(Q)\,det(DQ^{-1}) \\
&= det(Q)\,det(D)\,det(Q^{-1}) \\
&= det(D)
\end{aligned}
\tag{2.24}
$$

where we used the properties of the determinant (Sect. 2.3.8). Therefore, the determinant of A can be computed as

```
> det(D)
[1] 294
> all.equal(det(A), det(D))
[1] TRUE
```

Basically, this is the approach that we used to compute the determinant with the `eigen_det()` function.

Additionally, this decomposition can be used to raise the matrix to a power in a faster way. In fact,

$$\begin{aligned} A^n &= (QDQ^{-1})(QDQ^{-1})\dots(QDQ^{-1}) \\ &= (QDID\dots DQ^{-1}) \\ &= QD^nQ^{-1} \end{aligned} \tag{2.25}$$

where the result depends on the fact that the adjacent $\dots Q^{-1})(Q\dots$ are the identity matrix I and $DI = D$. The advantage is that we are raising to the power a diagonal matrix. We will make use of it in Chap. 10.

2.3.13.2 Singular Value Decomposition (SVD)

The Singular Value Decomposition is a technique to factorize a $m \times n$ matrix as follows

$$A = UDV^T \tag{2.26}$$

where U and V are orthogonal, V^T is the transpose of V, and D is a diagonal matrix with the (non-negative) singular values, $D[i, i]$, in decreasing order.

In **R**, we implement the SVD with the `svd()` function. Let's see an example.

Example 2.3.3 Apply the SVD decomposition to the following matrix

$$A = \begin{bmatrix} 5 & 5 & 0 & 1 \\ 5 & 5 & 0 & 2 \\ 5 & 5 & 0 & 3 \\ 3 & 2 & 5 & 4 \\ 1 & 2 & 5 & 5 \\ 0 & 1 & 5 & 5 \end{bmatrix}$$

```
> A <- matrix(c(5, 5, 0, 1,
+               5, 5, 0, 2,
+               5, 5, 0, 3,
+               3, 2, 5, 4,
+               1, 2, 5, 5,
+               0, 1, 5, 5),
+             nrow = 6, ncol = 4,
+             byrow = TRUE)
> A
     [,1] [,2] [,3] [,4]
[1,]    5    5    0    1
[2,]    5    5    0    2
[3,]    5    5    0    3
```

```
[4,]    3    2    5    4
[5,]    1    2    5    5
[6,]    0    1    5    5
> svd(A)
$d
[1] 15.2633366  9.3635395  1.6754202  0.7400338

$u
           [,1]       [,2]        [,3]        [,4]
[1,] -0.3851578 -0.4271824  0.28513239  0.62227908
[2,] -0.4196862 -0.3842846 -0.07877577  0.03454604
[3,] -0.4542146 -0.3413867 -0.44268394 -0.55318700
[4,] -0.4393282  0.2903552  0.74301566 -0.41305241
[5,] -0.4050210  0.4349515 -0.21440534  0.35085396
[6,] -0.3348951  0.5289676 -0.34421345  0.10885154

$v
           [,1]       [,2]       [,3]       [,4]
[1,] -0.5253307 -0.4761289  0.4971917 -0.5001294
[2,] -0.5450241 -0.4041941 -0.2797086  0.6792194
[3,] -0.3862997  0.6697651  0.5503004  0.3152092
[4,] -0.5270189  0.4016755 -0.6096991 -0.4349423
```

The d values are the singular values of A, sorted decreasingly, that show the relative importance of each of the columns in u, that represents the row inputs, and v, that represents the column inputs, in describing the original data.

Following, a step by step SVD procedure for illustration purpose only. Briefly, the procedure consists in finding the eigenvalues and eigenvectors of $A^T A$. The eigenvectors form the columns of V and the square roots of the eigenvalues of $A^T A$ are the singular values of D. After finding V and D, and given A, we find U (note the sign of the eigenvectors computed with the eigen() may be different from svd()—remember that an eigenvector is still an eigenvector if multiplied by -1).[16]

Step 1

Compute $A^T A$. Store this result in tAA.

```
> tA <- t(A)
> tA
     [,1] [,2] [,3] [,4] [,5] [,6]
```

[16] The interested reader may refer to the following links for additional info on SVD in **R**: https://www.r-bloggers.com/singular-value-decomposition-svd-tutorial-using-examples-in-r/ and https://rpubs.com/aaronsc32/singular-value-decomposition-r, and https://towardsdatascience.com/singular-value-decomposition-with-example-in-r-948c3111aa43.

```
[1,]    5    5    5    3    1    0
[2,]    5    5    5    2    2    1
[3,]    0    0    0    5    5    5
[4,]    1    2    3    4    5    5
> tAA <- tA %*% A
> tAA
     [,1] [,2] [,3] [,4]
[1,]   85   83   20   47
[2,]   83   84   25   53
[3,]   20   25   75   70
[4,]   47   53   70   80
```

Step 2
Compute the eigenvectors of `tAA`. Store the result in `V`.

```
> V <- eigen(tAA)[[2]]
> V
           [,1]       [,2]       [,3]       [,4]
[1,] -0.5253307  0.4761289 -0.4971917  0.5001294
[2,] -0.5450241  0.4041941  0.2797086 -0.6792194
[3,] -0.3862997 -0.6697651 -0.5503004 -0.3152092
[4,] -0.5270189 -0.4016755  0.6096991  0.4349423
```

Step 3
Compute the singular values as the square roots of the eigenvalues of `tAA`. Store the result in `D`, as diagonal matrix.

```
> D <- diag(sqrt(eigen(tAA)[[1]]))
> D
         [,1]    [,2]    [,3]      [,4]
[1,] 15.26334 0.00000 0.00000 0.0000000
[2,]  0.00000 9.36354 0.00000 0.0000000
[3,]  0.00000 0.00000 1.67542 0.0000000
[4,]  0.00000 0.00000 0.00000 0.7400338
```

Step 4
Compute the inverse of `D`, `Dinv`.

```
> Dinv <- solve(D)
```

Step 5
Compute U (explanation for the multiplication AV in Sect. 2.3.13.4)

```
> AV <- A %*% V
> U <- AV %*% Dinv
> U
```

```
             [,1]       [,2]        [,3]        [,4]
[1,] -0.3851578  0.4271824 -0.28513239 -0.62227908
[2,] -0.4196862  0.3842846  0.07877577 -0.03454604
[3,] -0.4542146  0.3413867  0.44268394  0.55318700
[4,] -0.4393282 -0.2903552 -0.74301566  0.41305241
[5,] -0.4050210 -0.4349515  0.21440534 -0.35085396
[6,] -0.3348951 -0.5289676  0.34421345 -0.10885154
```

Finally, compare the results of `D`, `U` and `V` with `d`, `u` and `v` from the `svd()` function.

If we multiply `U D` and the transpose of `V` as in (2.26), we obtain the original matrix (we use the `round()` function to print the results without the scientific notation).

```
round(U %*% D %*% t(V), 1)
     [,1] [,2] [,3] [,4]
[1,]    5    5    0    1
[2,]    5    5    0    2
[3,]    5    5    0    3
[4,]    3    2    5    4
[5,]    1    2    5    5
[6,]    0    1    5    5
```

We can recover a single input as well from the decomposed matrices. For example, to recover the entry in row four column three, we compute the following:

```
> sum(svd(A)$d *
+       svd(A)$u[4, ] *
+       svd(A)$v[3, ])
[1] 5
```

2.3.13.3 Cholesky Decomposition

The Cholesky decomposition has different applications. We may encounter it in the solution of system of linear equations and in non linear optimization for example. The Cholesky decomposition consists in factorization of a symmetric positive-definite square matrix into the product of a lower (or upper) triangular matrix and its transpose.

$$A = LL^T \tag{2.27}$$

Let's see a strategy for the Cholesky decomposition. Let's consider the following matrix

$$A = \begin{bmatrix} 3 & 2 \\ 2 & 6 \end{bmatrix}$$

Step 1
Define

$$L = \begin{bmatrix} a & 0 \\ b & c \end{bmatrix} \quad L^T = \begin{bmatrix} a & b \\ 0 & c \end{bmatrix}$$

Step 2
Multiply LL^T to obtain

$$LL^T = \begin{bmatrix} a^2 & ab \\ ab & b^2 + c^2 \end{bmatrix}$$

Note that LL^T is symmetric as well.

Step 3
From (2.27), LL^T is equal to A, that is

$$\begin{bmatrix} 3 & 2 \\ 2 & 6 \end{bmatrix} = \begin{bmatrix} a^2 & ab \\ ab & b^2 + c^2 \end{bmatrix}$$

Proceed by equalising the entries of the matrices.

First, we know that $a^2 = 3$. This means that $a = \sqrt{3}$. Second, $ab = 2 \rightarrow \sqrt{3}b = 2 \rightarrow b = \frac{2}{\sqrt{3}}$. Then, $b^2 + c^2 = 6 \rightarrow \left(\frac{2}{\sqrt{3}}\right)^2 + c^2 = 6 \rightarrow c = \frac{\sqrt{42}}{3}$. Note that we only take the positive value.

Step 4
Replace the values of a, b, c in L and L^T. Consequently,

$$\begin{bmatrix} \sqrt{3} & 0 \\ \frac{2}{\sqrt{3}} & \frac{\sqrt{42}}{3} \end{bmatrix} \begin{bmatrix} \sqrt{3} & \frac{2}{\sqrt{3}} \\ 0 & \frac{\sqrt{42}}{3} \end{bmatrix} = \begin{bmatrix} 3 & 2 \\ 2 & 6 \end{bmatrix}$$

```
> a <- sqrt(3)
> b <- 2/sqrt(3)
> c <- sqrt(42)/3
> L <- matrix(c(a, 0,
+               b, c),
+             nrow = 2,
+             ncol = 2,
+             byrow = T)
> L
```

```
         [,1]     [,2]
[1,] 1.732051 0.000000
[2,] 1.154701 2.160247
> LT <- t(L)
> LT
         [,1]     [,2]
[1,] 1.732051 1.154701
[2,] 0.000000 2.160247
> L %*% LT
     [,1] [,2]
[1,]    3    2
[2,]    2    6
```

In **R** we use the `chol()` function for the Cholesky decomposition.

```
> A <- matrix(c(3, 2,
+               2, 6),
+             nrow = 2,
+             ncol = 2,
+             byrow = T)
> A
     [,1] [,2]
[1,]    3    2
[2,]    2    6
> R <- chol(A)
> R
         [,1]     [,2]
[1,] 1.732051 1.154701
[2,] 0.000000 2.160247
> t(R) %*% R
     [,1] [,2]
[1,]    3    2
[2,]    2    6
```

Note that **R** uses the upper triangular matrix. Consequently, $A = R^T R$.

Let's see an example regarding the solution of a system of linear equations with the Cholesky decomposition. We want to solve $A\mathbf{x} = \mathbf{b}$, where

$$A = \begin{bmatrix} 1 & -1 & 2 \\ -1 & 2 & -2 \\ 2 & -2 & 8 \end{bmatrix} \quad \mathbf{b} = \begin{bmatrix} 2 \\ 1 \\ -4 \end{bmatrix}$$

Let's follow the same strategy as before.

Step 1

$$L = \begin{bmatrix} a & 0 & 0 \\ b & c & 0 \\ d & e & f \end{bmatrix} \quad L^T = \begin{bmatrix} a & b & c \\ 0 & c & e \\ 0 & 0 & f \end{bmatrix}$$

Step 2

$$LL^T = \begin{bmatrix} a^2 & ab & ad \\ ab & b^2 + c^2 & bd + ce \\ ad & bd + ce & d^2 + e^2 + f^2 \end{bmatrix}$$

Step 3

$$\begin{bmatrix} 1 & -1 & 2 \\ -1 & 2 & -2 \\ 2 & -2 & 8 \end{bmatrix} = \begin{bmatrix} a^2 & ab & ad \\ ab & b^2 + c^2 & bd + ce \\ ad & bd + ce & d^2 + e^2 + f^2 \end{bmatrix}$$

Step 4
Following the same procedure as before, we find that $a = 1, b = -1, d = 2, c = 1, e = 0, f = 2$. Therefore,

$$L = \begin{bmatrix} 1 & 0 & 0 \\ -1 & 1 & 0 \\ 2 & 0 & 2 \end{bmatrix} \quad L^T = \begin{bmatrix} 1 & -1 & 2 \\ 0 & 1 & 0 \\ 0 & 0 & 2 \end{bmatrix}$$

From this point we introduce new steps to solve the system.

Step 5
Compute $L\mathbf{s} = \mathbf{b}$, where

$$\mathbf{s} = \begin{bmatrix} g \\ h \\ i \end{bmatrix}$$

Therefore,

$$\begin{bmatrix} 1 & 0 & 0 \\ -1 & 1 & 0 \\ 2 & 0 & 2 \end{bmatrix} \begin{bmatrix} g \\ h \\ i \end{bmatrix} = \begin{bmatrix} 2 \\ 1 \\ -4 \end{bmatrix}$$

Consequently, we obtain

$$g = 2$$

$$-g + h = 1$$

$$2g + 2i = -4$$

and, as a result, $g = 2, h = 3, i = -4$.

Step 6
Compute $L^T \mathbf{w} = \mathbf{s}$, where

$$\mathbf{w} = \begin{bmatrix} x \\ y \\ z \end{bmatrix}$$

$$\begin{bmatrix} 1 & -1 & 2 \\ 0 & 1 & 0 \\ 0 & 0 & 2 \end{bmatrix} \begin{bmatrix} x \\ y \\ z \end{bmatrix} = \begin{bmatrix} 2 \\ 3 \\ -4 \end{bmatrix}$$

That is

$$x - y + 2z = 2$$

$$y = 3$$

$$2z = -4$$

Therefore, the solutions of this system of equations are $x = 9, y = 3, z = -2$. The great advantage is that we did not need to compute the inverse of A.

```
> A <- matrix(c(1, -1, 2,
+               -1, 2, -2,
+                2, -2, 8),
+             nrow = 3,
+             ncol = 3,
+             byrow = T)
> A
     [,1] [,2] [,3]
[1,]    1   -1    2
[2,]   -1    2   -2
[3,]    2   -2    8
> eigen(A)$values
[1] 9.1992994 1.5133878 0.2873128
> R <- chol(A)
> R
     [,1] [,2] [,3]
[1,]    1   -1    2
[2,]    0    1    0
[3,]    0    0    2
> t(R) %*% R
     [,1] [,2] [,3]
[1,]    1   -1    2
[2,]   -1    2   -2
[3,]    2   -2    8
> b <- c(2, 1, -4)
> # check
> solve(A) %*% b
     [,1]
[1,]    9
[2,]    3
[3,]   -2
```

2.3.13.4 QR Decomposition

The QR decomposition is also used in statistical techniques. The QR method decomposes a matrix A as the product of two matrices, an orthogonal matrix Q and an upper triangular matrix R. A can be a square matrix or a $m \times n$ matrix with $m > n$.

$$A = QR \tag{2.28}$$

Here, we will show two examples with square matrices.

For illustration purpose, we show how to *manually* apply the QR composition. We will compute the steps only in **R**. In **R** the QR decomposition is implemented by the `qr()` function.

Example 2.3.4 In this example, we apply the QR decomposition to the following 2×2 matrix

$$A = \begin{bmatrix} 3 & 2 \\ 2 & 6 \end{bmatrix}$$

```
> A <- matrix(c(3, 2,
+               2, 6),
+             nrow = 2,
+             ncol = 2,
+             byrow = T)
> A
     [,1] [,2]
[1,]    3    2
[2,]    2    6
```

We apply the QR decomposition using the Gram-Schmidt process. This process is used to find orthonormal basis for a given set of vectors.

Step 1

Find the orthogonal vectors `q1` and `q2`.

(Note that we use the `unit_vec()` function we coded in Sect. 2.2.5).

$$\mathbf{q}_1 = \frac{\mathbf{v}_1}{||\mathbf{v}_1||}$$

```
> u1 <- A[, 1]
> u1
[1] 3 2
> q1 <- unit_vec(u1)
> q1
[1] 0.8320503 0.5547002
```

$$\mathbf{u}_2 = \mathbf{v}_2 - (\mathbf{q}_1^T \cdot \mathbf{v}_2)\mathbf{q}_1$$

$$\mathbf{q}_2 = \frac{\mathbf{u}_2}{\|\mathbf{u}_2\|}$$

```
> u2 <- A[, 2, drop = FALSE] -
+   as.numeric(t(as.matrix(q1))%*%
+                A[, 2, drop = FALSE])*
+   as.matrix(q1)
> u2
          [,1]
[1,] -2.153846
[2,]  3.230769
> q2 <- unit_vec(u2)
> q2
           [,1]
[1,] -0.5547002
[2,]  0.8320503
```

Let's check that q1 and q2 are orthogonal

```
round(q1 %*% q2, 5)
     [,1]
[1,]    0
```

Step 2
q1 and q2 become the columns of the Q matrix.

```
> Q <- matrix(c(q1, q2),
+             nrow = 2,
+             ncol = 2)
> Q
          [,1]       [,2]
[1,] 0.8320503 -0.5547002
[2,] 0.5547002  0.8320503
```

Step 3
Find R in (2.28).

Since we have A and Q we could invert Q. However, since we know that Q is a square orthogonal matrix, we can take advantage of the nice property $Q^{-1} = Q^T$ and compute the transpose that is much easier and faster to compute.

$$Q^T A = Q^T Q R$$

where $Q^T Q = I$

$$Q^T A = I R$$

$$Q^T A = R$$

```
> R <- round(t(Q)%*%A, 6)
> R
         [,1]     [,2]
[1,] 3.605551 4.992302
[2,] 0.000000 3.882901
```

By multiplying `Q` and `R` we recover the original matrix `A`.

```
> Q%*%R
     [,1] [,2]
[1,]    3    2
[2,]    2    6
```

Let's check the result with the `qr()` function.

```
> res <- qr(A)
> res
$qr
           [,1]      [,2]
[1,] -3.6055513 -4.992302
[2,]  0.5547002  3.882901

$rank
[1] 2

$qraux
[1] 1.832050 3.882901

$pivot
[1] 1 2

attr(,"class")
[1] "qr"
```

In `qr`, the upper triangle contains information on the R of the decomposition and the lower triangle contains information on the Q of the decomposition.

We can recover the components of the composition and the original matrix with `qr.R()` for R, `qr.Q()` for Q and `qr.X()` A.

```
> qr.R(res)
          [,1]      [,2]
[1,] -3.605551 -4.992302
[2,]  0.000000  3.882901
> qr.Q(res)
```

```
           [,1]       [,2]
[1,] -0.8320503 -0.5547002
[2,] -0.5547002  0.8320503
> qr.X(res)
     [,1] [,2]
[1,]    3    2
[2,]    2    6
```

Example 2.3.5 In this example, we apply the QR decomposition to the following 3×3 matrix:

$$B = \begin{bmatrix} 6 & 2 & 4 \\ 3 & 3 & 5 \\ 1 & 2 & 4 \end{bmatrix}$$

```
> B <- matrix(c(6, 2, 4,
+               3, 3, 5,
+               1, 1, 4),
+             3, 3, byrow = T)
> B
     [,1] [,2] [,3]
[1,]    6    2    4
[2,]    3    3    5
[3,]    1    1    4
```

We have the following three vectors: $\mathbf{v}_1 = \langle 6, 3, 1 \rangle, \mathbf{v}_2 = \langle 2, 3, 1 \rangle, \mathbf{v}_3 = \langle 4, 5, 4 \rangle$.

Let's apply the Gram-Schmidt process.

```
> u1 <- B[, 1]
> u1
[1] 6 3 1
> q1 <- unit_vec(u1)
> q1
[1] 0.8846517 0.4423259 0.1474420
> u2 <- (B[, 2, drop = FALSE] -
+          as.numeric(t(as.matrix(q1))%*%
+                       B[, 2, drop = FALSE])*
+          as.matrix(q1))
> u2
           [,1]
[1,] -0.8695652
[2,]  1.5652174
[3,]  0.5217391
> q2 <- unit_vec(u2)
> q2
```

```
              [,1]
[1,] -0.4662524
[2,]  0.8392543
[3,]  0.2797514
```

For the third vector, we have to subtract the projection of $\mathbf{v}_3$ onto $\mathbf{q}_2$ and $\mathbf{q}_1$

$$\mathbf{u}_3 = \mathbf{v}_3 - (\mathbf{q}_2^T \cdot \mathbf{v}_3)\mathbf{q}_2 - (\mathbf{q}_1^T \cdot \mathbf{v}_3)\mathbf{q}_1$$

$$\mathbf{q}_3 = \frac{\mathbf{u}_3}{\|\mathbf{u}_3\|}$$

```
> u3 <- B[, 3, drop = FALSE] -
+    (as.numeric(t(as.matrix(q2))%*%
+                    B[, 3, drop = FALSE])*
+       as.matrix(q2)) -
+    (as.numeric(t(as.matrix(q1))%*%
+                    B[, 3, drop = FALSE])*
+       as.matrix(q1))
> u3
     [,1]
[1,]  0.0
[2,] -0.7
[3,]  2.1
> q3 <- unit_vec(u3)
> q3
              [,1]
[1,]  0.0000000
[2,] -0.3162278
[3,]  0.9486833
```

Let's check that the vectors are orthogonal

```
> round(t(q2) %*% q3, 5)
     [,1]
[1,]    0
> round(t(q3) %*% q1, 5)
     [,1]
[1,]    0
> round(t(q3) %*% q2, 5)
     [,1]
[1,]    0
```

Let's form the Q matrix and compute the R matrix:

```
> Q <- matrix(c(q1, q2, q3),
+                nrow = 3,
```

```
+                 ncol = 3)
> Q
           [,1]       [,2]       [,3]
[1,] 0.8846517 -0.4662524  0.0000000
[2,] 0.4423259  0.8392543 -0.3162278
[3,] 0.1474420  0.2797514  0.9486833
> R <- round(t(Q)%*%B, 6)
> R
        [,1]     [,2]     [,3]
[1,] 6.78233 3.243723 6.340004
[2,] 0.00000 1.865010 3.450268
[3,] 0.00000 0.000000 2.213594
```

Let's check the result:

```
> round(Q%*%R, 6)
     [,1] [,2] [,3]
[1,]    6    2    4
[2,]    3    3    5
[3,]    1    1    4
```

Now let's use the `qr()` function.

```
> res <- qr(B)
> res
$qr
           [,1]       [,2]      [,3]
[1,] -6.7823300 -3.2437230 -6.340004
[2,]  0.4423259 -1.8650096 -3.450268
[3,]  0.1474420  0.3162278  2.213594

$rank
[1] 3

$qraux
[1] 1.884652 1.948683 2.213594

$pivot
[1] 1 2 3

attr(,"class")
[1] "qr"
> qr.R(res)
         [,1]      [,2]      [,3]
[1,] -6.78233 -3.243723 -6.340004
[2,]  0.00000 -1.865010 -3.450268
[3,]  0.00000  0.000000  2.213594
```

```
> qr.Q(res)
           [,1]       [,2]          [,3]
[1,] -0.8846517  0.4662524 -2.775558e-17
[2,] -0.4423259 -0.8392543 -3.162278e-01
[3,] -0.1474420 -0.2797514  9.486833e-01
> qr.X(res)
     [,1] [,2] [,3]
[1,]    6    2    4
[2,]    3    3    5
[3,]    1    1    4
```

The Gram-Schmidt process can be computed with the `gramSchmidt()` function from the `pracma` package. For example:

```
> gramSchmidt(B)
$Q
          [,1]       [,2]          [,3]
[1,] 0.8846517 -0.4662524  2.006191e-16
[2,] 0.4423259  0.8392543 -3.162278e-01
[3,] 0.1474420  0.2797514  9.486833e-01

$R
        [,1]     [,2]     [,3]
[1,] 6.78233 3.243723 6.340004
[2,] 0.00000 1.865010 3.450268
[3,] 0.00000 0.000000 2.213594
```

2.4 Applications in Economics

2.4.1 Budget Set

In Economics, vectors are used to represent commodity bundles

$$\mathbf{x} = (x_1, x_2, \ldots, x_n) \tag{2.29}$$

where x_i is a non-negative amount of commodity i. "We think of consumption bundles as locations in commodity space" (Simon & Blume 1994, p. 202).

We can calculate the price of the bundle by multiplying each commodity by its price $p_i > 0$

$$\mathbf{p} \cdot \mathbf{x} = p_1x_1 + p_2x_2 + \ldots + p_nx_n$$

i.e. we computed the inner product (Sect. 2.2.3).

The consumer can afford this bundle only if $\mathbf{p} \cdot \mathbf{x} \leq Y$, where Y represents her income. The bundle the consumer can purchase is known as the consumer's *budget set*.

Let's represent the standard example from an undergraduate Microeconomics textbook:

$$p_1x_1 + p_2x_2 \leq Y \tag{2.30}$$

where

- x_1 and x_2 represent two goods;
- p_1 represents the price of good x_1 that we suppose it equals \$10 dollars and p_2 represents the price of good x_2 that we suppose it equals \$5 dollars;
- Y represents the weekly income of a consumer that we suppose it equals \$100 dollars.

In **R**, first we generate a `df` object, a data frame with a sequence from 0 to 10 that represents `x1`, `p1`, `p2`, and `Y`. Then, we generate `x2` as function of `x1`.

```
> df <- data.frame(x1 = seq(0, 10, 1))
> p1 <- 10
> p2 <- 5
> Y <- 100
> x2 <- function(x1) Y/p2 - (p1*x1)/p2
```

Now we are ready to plot it with `ggplot()`. Note that we store in `bl_plot` the base plot because we will use it again for the figures in this section. We use `geom_segment()` to draw the budget line (*budget constraint*), i.e. all the combinations of good 1 and good 2 the consumer can afford with \$100 dollars. In `aes()`, `x = Y/p1` and `y = 0` show how many cinema tickets (good x_1 in the example) the consumer can buy if she buys no pizza (10); `xend = 0` and `yend = Y/p2` show how many pizzas (good x_2 in the example) the consumer can buy if she does not go to the cinema (20). Therefore, the budget constraint represents all possible combinations of pizzas and cinema tickets the consumer can buy given her budget. Note that we add a point with `geom_point()` that represents the bundle of 7 cinema tickets and 7 pizzas. As Fig. 2.34 shows, this bundle is in the "not affordable" area because

$$10 \cdot 7 + 5 \cdot 7 = 105 > 100$$

i.e. this bundle costs \$105 dollars, more than the weekly income of our consumer.

```
> bl_plot <- ggplot() +
+   stat_function(data = df,
+                 aes(x1),
+                 fun = x2,
+                 xlim = c(0, 10),
```

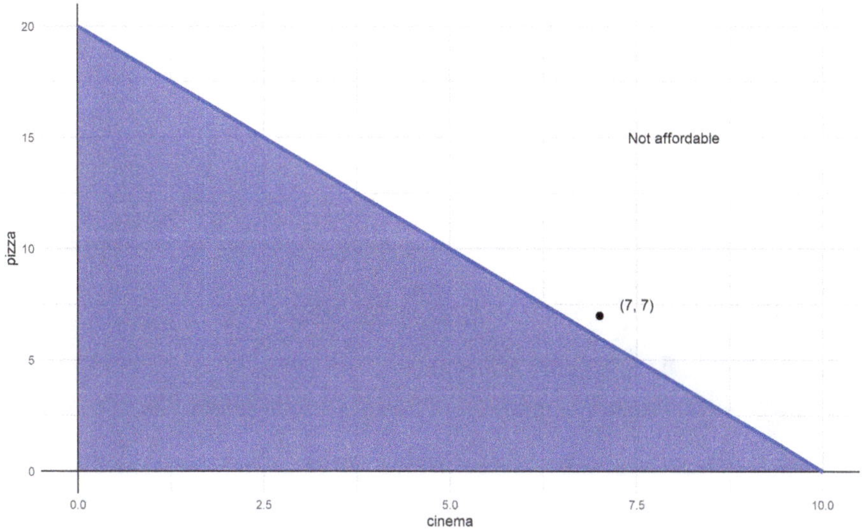

Fig. 2.34 Budget set

```
+                       geom = "area",
+                       fill = "blue",
+                       alpha = 0.5) +
+   geom_point(aes(x = 7,
+                  y = 7),
+               size = 2.5) +
+   xlab("cinema") + ylab("pizza") +
+   theme_minimal() +
+   geom_hline(yintercept = 0) +
+   geom_vline(xintercept = 0)
> bl_plot +
+   geom_segment(aes(x = Y/p1,
+                    y = 0,
+                    xend = 0,
+                    yend = Y/p2),
+                color = "blue",
+                size = 1.5) +
+   annotate("text", x = c(7.5, 8),
+            y = c(7.5, 15),
+            label = c("(7, 7)",
+                      "Not affordable"))
```

What about if the income of the consumer doubles (`Y2`)? Note that we write a new function for good 2, `x2Y2`. This function uses the new level of income.

```
> Y2 <- 2*Y
> x2Y2 <- function(x1) Y2/p2 - (p1*x1)/p2
```

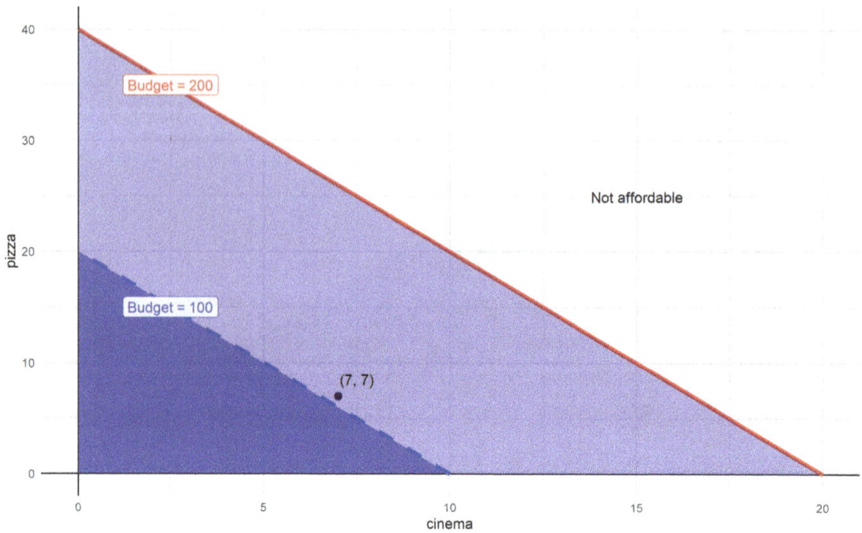

Fig. 2.35 Budget set: effects of increase of income

As for `x2`, we use `x2Y2` as argument of `stat_function()` to fill the area under the function with `geom = "area"`. Figure 2.35 shows that the budget line moves upwards and it is parallel to the previous budget line. The reason is that the increase in the budget of the consumer does not affect the relative price of the cinema ticket in terms of pizza, i.e. the slope of the budget line in the two examples is the same regardless of whether the income is \$100 and \$200. In the example, the cinema ticket is twice as expensive as a pizza. This means that if the consumer wants to go once more time to the cinema she needs to give up two pizzas in the week. This concept is known as *opportunity cost* and it is represented by the slope of the budget line. On the other hand, Fig. 2.35 shows that now the consumer can afford the combination of 7 pizzas and 7 cinema tickets in a week. Note that we used `annotate()` to add the labels of the two budget lines.

```
> bl_plot +
+   geom_segment(aes(x = c(Y/p1, Y2/p1),
+                    y = c(0, 0),
+                    xend = c(0, 0),
+                    yend = c(Y/p2, Y2/p2)),
+                color = c("blue", "red"),
+                size = 1.5,
+                linetype = c("dashed", "solid")) +
+   stat_function(data = df,
+                 aes(x1),
+                 fun = x2Y2,
```

```
+                   xlim = c(0, 20),
+                   geom = "area",
+                   fill = "blue",
+                   alpha = 0.3) +
+     annotate("text", x = c(7.5, 15),
+              y = c(8.5, 25),
+              label = c("(7, 7)",
+                        "Not affordable")) +
+     annotate("label", x =c(2.5, 2.5),
+              y = c(35, 15),
+              label = c("Budget = 200",
+                        "Budget = 100"),
+              color = c("red", "blue"))
```

Finally, we consider the effects of the change in the price of one good on the combination of goods that the consumer can afford with a budget of \$100 dollars. As we can expect, the change in the price of one good affects the relative price of one good in terms of the other. Consequently, it affects the slope of the budget line.

Let's suppose that the price of the ingredients to make a pizza increases leading to an increase in the price of a pizza to \$8 dollars. This rotates the budget line inwards pivoting on the maximum quantity of cinema tickets the consumer can afford. The maximum number of tickets the consumer can afford with \$100 dollars is unchanged because the price of the cinema ticket is unchanged. This means that if the consumer wants to spend all of her income to go to the cinema (i.e. her budget on pizzas is 0) she can go only 10 times in a week. On the other hand, if the consumer wants to spend all of her income on pizzas now she can buy only 12 whole pizzas and not 20 as when a pizza costed \$5 dollars (Fig. 2.36).

```
> p28 <- 8
> x2p28 <- function(x1) Y/p28 - (p1*x1)/p28
> bl_plot +
+     geom_segment(aes(x = c(Y/p1, Y/p1),
+                      y = c(0, 0),
+                      xend = c(0, 0),
+                      yend = c(Y/p2, Y/p28)),
+                  color = c("blue", "red"),
+                  size = 1.5) +
+     stat_function(data = df,
+                   aes(x1),
+                   fun = x2p28,
+                   xlim = c(0, 10),
+                   geom = "area",
+                   fill = "red",
+                   alpha = 0.3) +
+     annotate("text", x = c(7.5, 8),
+              y = c(7.5, 15),
```

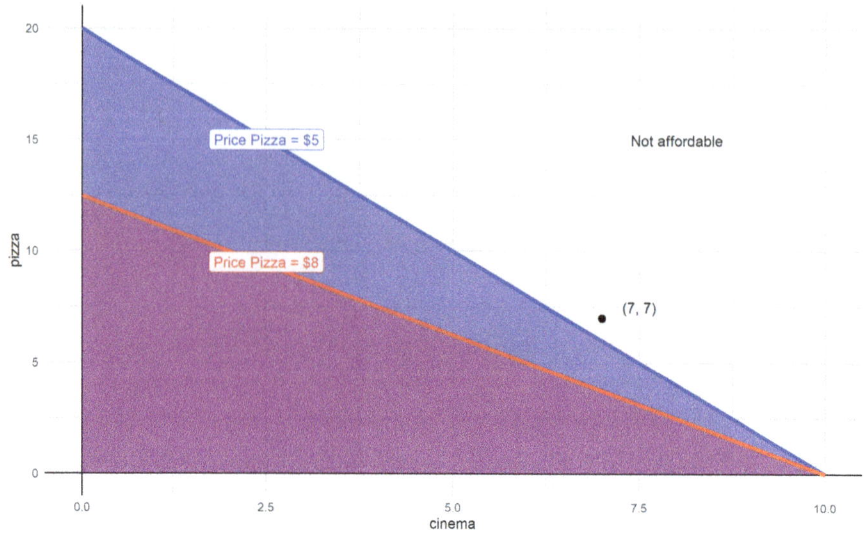

Fig. 2.36 Budget set: effects of increase of price of good 2

```
+              label = c("(7, 7)",
+                        "Not affordable")) +
+    annotate("label", x =c(2.5, 2.5),
+              y = c(15, 9.5),
+              label = c("Price Pizza = $5",
+                        "Price Pizza = $8"),
+              color = c("blue", "red"))
```

2.4.2 *Applying Cramer's Rule to the IS-LM Model*

The IS-LM (Investment Savings-Liquidity preference Money supply) is a macroeconomic model developed by Sir John Hicks based on John Maynard Keynes' *General Theory of Employment, Interest, and Money*. The model explains the interaction between the market of goods (IS) and the money market (LM) to balance the rate of interest and total output.

In a closed economy, the IS equation is

$$Y = C + I + G \tag{2.31}$$

meaning that total spending Y equals the sum of consumption C, investment I, and government expenditure G. In turn, we can express

- consumption as $C = bY$, i.e. the spending by consumers is proportional to total income Y, where $0 < b < 1$ is the *marginal propensity to consume*;
- investment as $I = I^0 - ar$, i.e. investment as a decreasing function of the real interest rate in linear form, where a is the *marginal efficiency of capital*

Substituting these into Eq. 2.31 we obtain the following

$$Y = bY + (I^0 - ar) + G$$

$$Y - bY = I^0 - ar + G$$

$$Y(1 - b) = I^0 - ar + G$$

$$sY + ar = I^0 + G \tag{2.32}$$

where $s = 1 - b$ is called the *marginal propensity to save*. s, a, I^0, G are positive parameters.

The LM equation is

$$M_S = M_d \tag{2.33}$$

meaning that in equilibrium the supply of money M_s equals the demand of money M_d.

M_s is exogenous, i.e. it is determined outside the system. On the other hand, the demand of money can be written as $M_d = M_{dt} + M_{ds}$, i.e. the sum of the *transactions demand* M_{dt} and the *speculative demand* M_{ds}. In turn, we can express

- $M_{dt} = mY$, i.e. the demand for funds increases proportional to the national income;
- $M_{ds} = M^0 - hr$, that expresses a linear relationship regarding the decision of the investor whether to hold money, that is liquid but returns no interest, or bonds, that pay a return rate equal to r.

Substituting these in Eq. 2.33 we obtain

$$M_s = mY + M^0 - hr$$

$$mY - hr = M_s - M^0 \tag{2.34}$$

Therefore, we have a system of two equations and two unknowns, Y, r that represents a closed economy:

$$\begin{cases} sY + ar = I^0 + G \\ mY - hr = M_s - M^0 \end{cases} \tag{2.35}$$

Note that having reduced the system in two equations will make easier to find the solution of the system because we will work with a 2×2 matrix and therefore it will be very easy to compute the determinant. In fact, the system in matrix form is

$$\begin{bmatrix} s & a \\ m & -h \end{bmatrix} \begin{bmatrix} Y \\ r \end{bmatrix} = \begin{bmatrix} I^0 + G \\ M_s - M^0 \end{bmatrix} \tag{2.36}$$

Now we can solve it by using Cramer's rule (Sect. 2.3.8.4):

$$Y^* = \frac{\begin{vmatrix} I^0 + G & a \\ M_s - M^0 & -h \end{vmatrix}}{\begin{vmatrix} s & a \\ m & -h \end{vmatrix}} = \frac{(I^0 + G)h + a(M_s - M^0)}{sh + am}$$

$$r^* = \frac{\begin{vmatrix} s & I^0 + G \\ m & M_s - M^0 \end{vmatrix}}{\begin{vmatrix} s & a \\ m & -h \end{vmatrix}} = \frac{(I^0 + G)m - s(M_s - M^0)}{sh + am}$$

2.4.3 Leontief Input-Output Model

The Input-Output model was first developed by Nobel Prize Professor Leontief to describe the structure of the American economy. Leontief broke up the US economy in sectors and aggregated these sectors into groups by affinity. By organizing these data in *input* needed by these sectors to produce an *output* he obtained information regarding the structure of the economy.

Let's consider a simple example. Suppose we are given the Input-Output table of *Mathland*, a thriving economy. The economy of *Mathland* is made up of three sectors, agriculture, `AGR`, manufacturing, `MFG`, and services, `SER`.

```
> sectors <- c("AGR", "MFG", "SER")
> AGR <- c(200, 400, 150)
> MFG <- c(0, 700, 300)
> SER <- c(0, 300, 150)
> MT <- data.frame(AGR, MFG, SER,
+                  row.names = sectors)
> MT
    AGR MFG SER
AGR 200   0   0
MFG 400 700 300
SER 150 300 150
```

Let's treat the values of these goods in `MT` in monetary terms, for example, millions (mln) of dollars. The rows represent the input of the sectors and the columns the output. Therefore, for example, the agriculture sectors use $200 mln as input from the agriculture sector, $400 mln from the manufacturing sector and $150 mln from the services sector to produce its own output. We can also see that the manufacturing and services sectors do not use any agricultural input to produce their outputs. The manufacturing sector uses $700 mln from its own sector and $300 mln from the services sector to produce its output. The services sector uses $150 mln from its own sector and $300 mln from the manufacturing sector to produce its output.

Let's add that the gross value added, `GVA`, i.e. inputs of the primary factors of the three sectors, such as labour and capital. We append `GVA` to `MT` using the `row.bind.data.frame()` function. Then, we rename the row name for `GVA`.

```
> GVA <- c(50, 4500, 1000)
> MT <- rbind.data.frame(MT, GVA)
> rownames(MT)[4] <- "GVA"
> MT
    AGR  MFG  SER
AGR 200    0    0
MFG 400  700  300
SER 150  300  150
GVA  50 4500 1000
```

Now, let's calculate the total production, `TOT`, as the sum of the values in each column by using the `colSums()` function. Then, we append to `MT` and rename its row name.

```
> TOT <- colSums(MT)
> TOT
 AGR  MFG  SER
 800 5500 1450
> MT <- rbind.data.frame(MT, TOT)
> rownames(MT)[5] <- "TOT"
```

Table 2.1 Transaction table of *Mathland*

	AGR	MFG	SER	D	TOT
AGR	200	0	0	600	800
MFG	400	700	300	4100	5500
SER	150	300	150	850	1450
GVA	50	4500	1000		
TOT	800	5500	1450		

Table 2.2 Basic transaction table

	Sector1	Sector2	Sector3	Final demand	Total domestic production
Sector1	x_{11}	x_{12}	x_{13}	D_1	X_1
Sector2	x_{21}	x_{22}	x_{23}	D_2	X_2
Sector3	x_{31}	x_{32}	x_{33}	D_3	X_3
Gross value added	V_1	V_2	V_3		
Total domestic production	X_1	X_2	X_3		

```
> MT
    AGR  MFG  SER
AGR 200    0    0
MFG 400  700  300
SER 150  300  150
GVA  50 4500 1000
TOT 800 5500 1450
```

This is *Mathland*'s Input-Output table.

The administrators of *Mathland* share with us two additional information about its economy: (1) its a closed economy, i.e. it does not engage in trade with the rest of the world, and (2) the final demand, in \$ millions, of *Mathland*'s consumers of AGR is \$600, MFG is \$4100 and SER is \$850.

```
> D <- matrix(c(600,
+               4100,
+               850))
> D
     [,1]
[1,]  600
[2,] 4100
[3,]  850
```

This last information can be used to build a basic transaction table of *Mathland*'s economy. Table 2.1 represents *Mathland*'s transaction table and Table 2.2 represents its generalization.

These tables show that we have a supply-demand balance:

$$\begin{cases} x_{11} + x_{12} + x_{13} + D_1 = X_1 \\ x_{21} + x_{22} + x_{23} + D_2 = X_2 \\ x_{31} + x_{32} + x_{33} + D_3 = X_3 \end{cases} \tag{2.37}$$

and an income-expense balance:

$$\begin{cases} x_{11} + x_{21} + x_{31} + V_1 = X_1 \\ x_{12} + x_{22} + x_{32} + V_2 = X_2 \\ x_{13} + x_{23} + x_{33} + V_3 = X_3 \end{cases} \tag{2.38}$$

Let's define the Input-Output table in terms of 1 unit of output

$$a_{ij} = \frac{x_{ij}}{X_{ij}} \tag{2.39}$$

For example, a_{11} represents the input required to produce one unit of production of sector 1 from sector 1.

We convert this table in terms of 1 unit of output by dividing each column value by the total output value of the column. We use the `sweep()` function where `2` means that the operation of division, `/`, will be implemented to the columns (`1` for rows). In the first line of code we generate `M` that is our input-coefficient table as a matrix

```
> M <- as.matrix.data.frame(MT)
> M <- sweep(M, 2, M[nrow(M), ], "/")
> M
       AGR        MFG       SER
AGR 0.2500 0.00000000 0.0000000
MFG 0.5000 0.12727273 0.2068966
SER 0.1875 0.05454545 0.1034483
GVA 0.0625 0.81818182 0.6896552
TOT 1.0000 1.00000000 1.0000000
```

This matrix tells us, for example, that we need 0.25 units of `AGR` input to produce 1 unit of `AGR` output. The value for `GPA`, $v_{ij} = \frac{V_{ij}}{X_{ij}}$, can be regarded as an input unit of such production factors.

Let's substitute the input coefficient in (2.39) into (2.37):

$$\begin{cases} a_{11}X_1 + a_{12}X_2 + a_{13}X_3 + D_1 = X_1 \\ a_{21}X_1 + a_{22}X_2 + a_{23}X_3 + D_2 = X_2 \\ a_{31}X_3 + a_{32}X_3 + a_{33}X_3 + D_3 = X_3 \end{cases} \tag{2.40}$$

We know that we can represent the system of equations (2.40) in matrix form:

$$\begin{bmatrix} a_{11} & a_{12} & a_{13} \\ a_{21} & a_{22} & a_{23} \\ a_{31} & a_{32} & a_{33} \end{bmatrix} \begin{bmatrix} X_1 \\ X_2 \\ X_3 \end{bmatrix} + \begin{bmatrix} D_1 \\ D_2 \\ D_3 \end{bmatrix} = \begin{bmatrix} X_1 \\ X_2 \\ X_3 \end{bmatrix} \tag{2.41}$$

where

$$A = \begin{bmatrix} a_{11} & a_{12} & a_{13} \\ a_{21} & a_{22} & a_{23} \\ a_{31} & a_{32} & a_{33} \end{bmatrix}$$

is the input-coefficient matrix.

Let's generate the input-coefficient matrix `A`. We subset the `M` object from row 1 to row 3 (`(nrow(M)-2)`). That is, we keep only the first three rows.

```
> A <- M[1:(nrow(M)-2), ]
> A
       AGR        MFG       SER
AGR 0.2500 0.00000000 0.0000000
MFG 0.5000 0.12727273 0.2068966
SER 0.1875 0.05454545 0.1034483
```

We can write the system of equations in (2.41) as

$$A\mathbf{x} + \mathbf{d} = \mathbf{x} \tag{2.42}$$

where $\mathbf{x} = \begin{bmatrix} X_1 \\ X_2 \\ X_3 \end{bmatrix}$ and $\mathbf{d} = \begin{bmatrix} D_1 \\ D_2 \\ D_3 \end{bmatrix}$.

The left-hand side of (2.42) represents the total demand that includes the demand of input that enters the production process $A\mathbf{x}$ and the demand for consumption $\mathbf{d}$. The left-hand side is equal to right-hand side of (2.42) that represents the total supply.

The administrators of *Mathland* forecast an increase in the demand for agricultural goods to \$800 mln.

```
D[1,1] <- 800
> D
     [,1]
[1,]  800
[2,] 4100
[3,]  850
```

They ask us to compute the corresponding output given the increase in the demand for agricultural goods.

We can solve the system (2.42) as follows:

$$\mathbf{x} - A\mathbf{x} = \mathbf{d}$$

$$(I - A)\mathbf{x} = \mathbf{d}$$

$$\mathbf{x} = (I - A)^{-1}\mathbf{d}$$

where $(I - A)$ is called the Leontief matrix. We know that to be invertible a matrix needs to be nonsingular. What about the Leontief matrix? Should we test for singularity? Luckily, we can avoid this step because a square matrix with the properties that each entry is non-negative and the sum of the entries in each column is less than 1 (both properties satisfied by the Leontief matrix) is invertible and contains only non-negative values.[17]

Let's solve the Input-Output model in **R**.

```
> Id <- diag(3)
> Id
     [,1] [,2] [,3]
[1,]    1    0    0
[2,]    0    1    0
[3,]    0    0    1
> Ainv <- solve(Id - A)
> Ainv
          AGR        MFG       SER
AGR 1.3333333 0.00000000 0.0000000
MFG 0.8421409 1.16260163 0.2682927
SER 0.3300813 0.07073171 1.1317073
> X <- Ainv %*% D
> X
        [,1]
AGR 1066.667
MFG 5668.428
SER 1516.016
```

As check $\mathbf{x} - A\mathbf{x} = \mathbf{d}$:

```
> X - A %*% X
    [,1]
AGR  800
MFG 4100
SER  850
```

[17] The interested reader may refer to Simon and Blume (1994) and Chiang and Wainwright (2005) for insights into the theorem.

We can tell the administrators of *Mathland* that the model establishes a total output of

$$\mathbf{x}^* = \begin{bmatrix} 1066.667 \\ 5668.428 \\ 1516.016 \end{bmatrix}$$

due to the increase in demand for agricultural goods to \$800 mln.

2.4.4 Network Analysis

Matrices are also key in network analysis. The following example is for illustration purpose only. Our goal is to highlight the role played by matrices in network analysis. Let's suppose that we want to analyse the connection among six persons, `P1`, `P2`, `P3`, `P4`, `P5` and `P6`. In particular, we know that

- `P1` is connected with `P4`, `P5` and `P6`
- `P2` is connected with `P4` and `P5`
- `P3` is connected with `P6`

Let's put this information in matrix form. We put the persons in row and column with the same order. We form therefore a 6×6 matrix `P`. If two persons are connected we fill p_{ij} with 1, otherwise with 0. The main diagonal contains 0 because a person is not connected with itself.

Let's build this matrix in **R**. First, we generate an object `persons` that contains the names of the persons. Second, we use the `crossing()` function from the `tidyr` package to generate all combinations of values. We store this operation in a new object `P`. Third, we set the column names of `P` with `colnames()`. Note that the object has `tbl_df` class that is a special class of data frame.[18]

```
> persons <- c("P1", "P2", "P3", "P4", "P5", "P6")
> P <- tidyr::crossing(persons, persons,
+                       .name_repair = "minimal")
> colnames(P) <- c("persons1", "persons2")
> P
# A tibble: 36 x 2
   persons1 persons2
   <chr>    <chr>
 1 P1       P1
 2 P1       P2
```

[18] Here we define `tbl_df` class as a special class of data frame. Refer to Wickham (2019, p. 58) for a discussion about data frames and tibbles.

```
 3 P1       P3
 4 P1       P4
 5 P1       P5
 6 P1       P6
 7 P2       P1
 8 P2       P2
 9 P2       P3
10 P2       P4
# ... with 26 more rows
> class(P)
[1] "tbl_df"     "tbl"        "data.frame"
```

We generate a new variable in the dataset adding a `$` before the name we choose for the variable. We name this variable `connection`. We build it with an `ifelse()` function to show if two persons have a connection (`1`) or not (`0`).

```
> P$connection <- ifelse((P$persons1 == "P1") &
+                        (P$persons2 == "P4") |
+                        (P$persons1 == "P1") &
+                        (P$persons2 == "P5") |
+                        (P$persons1 == "P1") &
+                        (P$persons2 == "P6") |
+                        (P$persons1 == "P2") &
+                        (P$persons2 == "P4") |
+                        (P$persons1 == "P2") &
+                        (P$persons2 == "P5") |
+                        (P$persons1 == "P3") &
+                        (P$persons2 == "P6") |
+                        (P$persons1 == "P4") &
+                        (P$persons2 == "P1") |
+                        (P$persons1 == "P4") &
+                        (P$persons2 == "P2") |
+                        (P$persons1 == "P5") &
+                        (P$persons2 == "P1") |
+                        (P$persons1 == "P5") &
+                        (P$persons2 == "P2") |
+                        (P$persons1 == "P6") &
+                        (P$persons2 == "P1") |
+                        (P$persons1 == "P6") &
+                        (P$persons2 == "P3"),
+                      1, 0)
> P
# A tibble: 36 x 3
   persons1 persons2 connection
```

```
   <chr>     <chr>        <dbl>
 1 P1        P1               0
 2 P1        P2               0
 3 P1        P3               0
 4 P1        P4               1
 5 P1        P5               1
 6 P1        P6               1
 7 P2        P1               0
 8 P2        P2               0
 9 P2        P3               0
10 P2        P4               1
# ... with 26 more rows
```

Next, we need to turn the dataset from a long format to a wide format. We use the `dcast()` function from the `data.table` package. The cast formula takes the form `LHS` ~ `RHS`, ex: `var1 + var2` ~ `var3`. The order of entries in the formula is essential. `value.var` = indicates the name of the column whose values will be filled to cast. The `setDT()` function converts `data.frames` to `data.tables`. This operation is stored in `PP`.

```
> PP <- dcast(setDT(P), persons1 ~ persons2,
+                                 value.var = "connection")
> PP
   persons1 P1 P2 P3 P4 P5 P6
1:       P1  0  0  0  1  1  1
2:       P2  0  0  0  1  1  0
3:       P3  0  0  0  0  0  1
4:       P4  1  1  0  0  0  0
5:       P5  1  1  0  0  0  0
6:       P6  1  0  1  0  0  0
```

Finally, we convert `PP` into a matrix type object. Note that we remove the first column with the names of the persons and then we set the row names with the persons names.[19]

```
> PP <- PP[, -1]
> PP <- as.data.frame(PP)
> rownames(PP) <- persons
> PP <- as.matrix.data.frame(PP)
> PP
   P1 P2 P3 P4 P5 P6
P1  0  0  0  1  1  1
P2  0  0  0  1  1  0
```

[19] Note that there are several packages for network analysis in **R** that would make the previous steps easier. The interested reader may refer to Luke (2015).

```
P3  0  0  0  0  0  1
P4  1  1  0  0  0  0
P5  1  1  0  0  0  0
P6  1  0  1  0  0  0
```

Matrix `PP` is known as *sociomatrix*, i.e. a square matrix where a 1 indicates a tie between two nodes, and a 0 indicates no tie. For example, person `P1` has connections with persons `P4`, `P5` and `P6`. On the other hand, `P1` and `P2` do not have a connection. However, both have connections with persons `P4` and `P5`. By multiplying together the sociomatrix we find the geodesic distance—the distance of the shortest path between two nodes—between all pair of nodes in a network.

```
> PP2 <- PP %*% PP
> PP2
   P1 P2 P3 P4 P5 P6
P1  3  2  1  0  0  0
P2  2  2  0  0  0  0
P3  1  0  1  0  0  0
P4  0  0  0  2  2  1
P5  0  0  0  2  2  1
P6  0  0  0  1  1  2
```

The matrix `PP2` shows how many contacts the persons have in common. The diagonal shows how many matches the persons have in the network.

Let's use the `igraph` package to represent the network. First, we need to convert the `PP` matrix into an `igraph` object. We use the `graph.adjacency()` function from the `igraph` package

```
> Pnet_graph <- graph.adjacency(PP)
> class(Pnet_graph)
[1] "igraph"
```

If we run the `Pnet_graph` we obtain some info such as:

- the graph is directed `D`
- nodes have a name attribute, `N`
- there are 6 nodes and 12 edges

```
> Pnet_graph
IGRAPH d432cbe DN-- 6 12 --
+ attr: name (v/c)
+ edges from d432cbe (vertex names):
 [1] P1->P4 P1->P5 P1->P6 P2->P4 P2->P5
 [6] P3->P6 P4->P1 P4->P2 P5->P1 P5->P2
[11] P6->P1 P6->P3
```

In addition, the `V()` function shows the vertices (nodes) of a graph; the `E()` function shows the edges (i.e. the connections between the nodes); the `degree()`

function shows the number of its adjacent edges, i.e. the sum of the out-degree `out` and in-degree `in`. If we set, for example, `mode = "in"` we only get the number of in-degree. Note that these numbers correspond to those on the main diagonal of `PP2`.

```
> V(Pnet_graph)
+ 6/6 vertices, named, from d432cbe:
[1] P1 P2 P3 P4 P5 P6
> E(Pnet_graph)
+ 12/12 edges from d432cbe (vertex names):
 [1] P1->P4 P1->P5 P1->P6 P2->P4 P2->P5
 [6] P3->P6 P4->P1 P4->P2 P5->P1 P5->P2
[11] P6->P1 P6->P3
> degree(Pnet_graph)
P1 P2 P3 P4 P5 P6
 6  4  2  4  4  4
> degree(Pnet_graph, mode = "in")
P1 P2 P3 P4 P5 P6
 3  2  1  2  2  2
```

We can analyse the prominence of a network member with the *centrality* measure. There are different measures of centrality. Here we will see the *eigenvector centrality* c_i^E. We compute the eigenvector centrality by finding the largest eigenvalue of the adjacency matrix A of the network and its associated eigenvector. Then we scale the eigenvector $\mathbf{v}$ so that its maximum value is equal to 1. The eigenvector centrality c_i^E of vertex i is entry v_i. In **R** we use the `evcent()` function from the `igraph` package.[20]

```
> Pevc <- evcent(Pnet_graph, scale = FALSE)
> Pevc$vector
       P1        P2        P3        P4        P5        P6
0.5576775 0.4082483 0.1494292 0.4440369 0.4440369 0.3250576
> max(eigen(PP)$values)
[1] 2.175328
> which.max(eigen(PP)$values)
[1] 1
> (eigen(PP)$vectors[,1])*-1
[1] 0.5576775 0.4082483 0.1494292 0.4440369 0.4440369 0.3250576
```

Note that with `scale = FALSE` in `evcent()` the result vector has unit length. Let's scale the result to have a maximum score of one (note that `scale = TRUE` is the default value in `evcent()`)

[20] In the manual computation I multiplied the eigenvector by -1 to return the result with the same sign. It is always recommend to use *ad hoc* functions instead of manual computation.

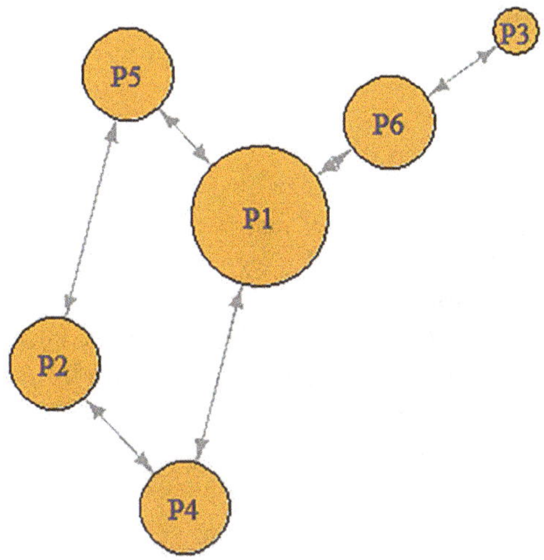

Fig. 2.37 Network analysis

```
> Pevc <- evcent(Pnet_graph)
> Pevc$vector
       P1        P2        P3        P4        P5        P6
1.0000000 0.7320508 0.2679492 0.7962252 0.7962252 0.5828773
```

Thus, based on the eigenvector centrality, `P1` is the most prominent member of this network, followed by `P4` and `P5`.

Finally, let's plot the network using `plot()`. We modify the layout, the vertex size and the edge arrow size. In particular, we scale the vertex size by the size of degree (Fig. 2.37).

```
> plot(Pnet_graph,
+       layout = layout.kamada.kawai,
+       vertex.size = degree(Pnet_graph)*10,
+       edge.arrow.size = 0.6)
```

2.4.5 *Linear Model and the Dummy Variable Trap*

In Econometrics, the dummy variable trap is a scenario where the explanatory variables are perfectly multicollinear. This often happens when we use too many dummy variables (variables that take values 1 or 0) in the model. In this section, we use matrix algebra to grasp these concepts.

Let's start by providing the solution of Ordinary Least Square (OLS) in matrix form:

$$\mathbf{b} = \left(X^T X\right)^{-1} X^T \mathbf{y} \tag{2.43}$$

where

$$X = \begin{bmatrix} 1 & x_{12} & \cdots & x_{1K} \\ \vdots & \vdots & & \vdots \\ 1 & x_{N2} & \cdots & x_{NK} \end{bmatrix} \quad \mathbf{y} = \begin{bmatrix} y_1 \\ \vdots \\ y_N \end{bmatrix}$$

that is, X is a $N \times K$ matrix that includes the intercept and the explanatory variables while $\mathbf{y}$ is a vector that includes the values of the response variables econometricians investigate.[21]

From (2.43), it is evident that $X^T X$ must be invertible. If it is not invertible, we are in the case of *perfect multicollinearity*. A typical case of perfect multicollinearity is when we fall in the *dummy variable trap*. The following example is for illustration purpose only.

Suppose we want to estimate the following model by OLS:

$$wage = \beta_0 + \beta_1 male + u$$

where *wage* is the hourly wage rate of an individual, *male* is a dummy variable that takes value 1 if the individual is male and 0 if is female, and u is the error term.

Let's build some fake data for hourly wage. We use a very naive approach to replicate the *gender wage gap*, the difference in earnings between women and men. First, we create a vector that stores hourly wages from \$0.1 to \$40. We store these values in `s`. Second, we generate two vectors of probability weights for female, `pf`, and for male, `pm`.

```
> s <- seq(0.1, 40, 0.25)
> pf <- c(rep(0.25, 40), rep(0.3, 30),
+         rep(0.2, 50), rep(0.15, 25),
+         rep(0.05, 15))
> pm <- c(rep(0.1, 15), rep(0.25, 20),
+         rep(0.25, 50), rep(0.25, 30),
+         rep(0.15, 45))
```

Third, we use `set.seed()` to make the following analysis reproducible. Finally, we use the `sample()` function to generate the hourly wage sample for female, `wage_f`, and for male, `wage_m`.

```
> set.seed(10)
> wage_f <- sample(s, 100, replace = T, prob = pf)
> mean(wage_f)
[1] 13.875
> wage_m <- sample(s, 100, replace = T, prob = pm)
> mean(wage_m)
[1] 18.71
```

[21] The reader interested in investigating where (2.43) comes from may refer to Strang (1988, pp. 154–162).

Next, we build the dataset. First, we put in `wages` the wages for female and male. Second, we use `rep()` to replicate the value 0 for the first 100 entries and the value 1 for the remaining 100 entries. We store the result in `male`. Note that the order of the entries in `male` is based on the order of the hourly wages in `wage`. That is, `male` is the dummy variable that takes value 1 if the individual is male, 0 if female. Finally, we use the `data.frame()` function to put these data together in `wages`.

```
> wage <- c(wage_f, wage_m)
> male <- c(rep(0, 100), rep(1, 100))
> wages <- data.frame(wage, male)
> head(wages)
   wage male
1  4.35    0
2  9.35    0
3  4.60    0
4 23.60    0
5 12.10    0
6 13.35    0
```

Now we can use the `lm()` function to estimate the model with OLS.[22] Note that ~ is the regressor operator that separates the response variable (or dependent variable) from the explanatory variables (or independent variables). The intercept is included in the model. To remove the intercept you need to write $y \sim x - 1$, where y represents the dependent variable in your model and x represents the independent variable in your model. In addition, you can add more explanatory variables by connecting them with a + (for example, $y \sim x_1 + x_2$). Finally, we indicate in `data =` the dataset that stores the data of our analysis. The estimation is stored in `wages_lm`. We use `summary()` to view the results of the estimation.

```
> wages_lm <- lm(wage ~ male, data = wages)
> summary(wages_lm)

Call:
lm(formula = wage ~ male, data = wages)

Residuals:
    Min      1Q  Median      3Q     Max
-17.610  -7.838  -0.400   6.829  22.225

Coefficients:
            Estimate Std. Error t value Pr(>|t|)
(Intercept)  13.8750     0.9956  13.937  < 2e-16 ***
male          4.8350     1.4079   3.434 0.000724 ***
```

[22] Note that we built `male` as a numeric variable even though it is better to have categorical variables as factors when using the `lm()` function. However, for the purpose of this example it is convenient to have it as numeric.

```
---
Signif. codes:  0 '***' 0.001 '**' 0.01 '*' 0.05 '.' 0.1
                ' ' 1

Residual standard error: 9.956 on 198 degrees of freedom
Multiple R-squared:  0.05621,Adjusted R-squared:  0.05145
F-statistic: 11.79 on 1 and 198 DF,  p-value: 0.0007241
```

The coefficient for the male dummy indicates the expected wage differential between male and female individuals. Therefore, it results that for female the best approximation is \$13.9 and for male is \$18.7.

```
> coef(wages_lm)
(Intercept)        male
     13.875       4.835
> coef(wages_lm)[[1]] + coef(wages_lm)[[2]]*0
[1] 13.875
> coef(wages_lm)[[1]] + coef(wages_lm)[[2]]*1
[1] 18.71
```

As expected, these numbers are exactly equal to the means in the two subsamples (`wage_f` and `wage_m`).

Let's use matrix algebra to estimate the model. We generate `X` that stores the intercept and the dummy variable `male` and `y` that stores the wages. We take the data from `model` that is stored in `wages_lm`.

```
> X <- cbind(1, wages_lm$model[, 2])
> y <- wages_lm$model[, 1]
> b <- solve(t(X)%*%X)%*%t(X)%*%y
> b
       [,1]
[1,] 13.875
[2,]  4.835
```

As expected, we found the same coefficients.

Now let's ask what happens if we include a dummy variable for female too. That is a variable that takes value 1 if the individual is female and 0 if the individual is male.

Let's build it by using the `ifelse()` function. We generate a new variable in the dataset `wages` by using `$` and the name of the variable. Then, in the `ifelse()` function, we write the conditional statement, i.e. if `male == 0`, that attributes value 1 to `female` and 0 otherwise.

```
> wages$female <- ifelse(wages$male == 0, 1, 0)
> head(wages)
  wage male female
1 4.35    0      1
2 9.35    0      1
```

```
3   4.60     0       1
4  23.60     0       1
5  12.10     0       1
6  13.35     0       1
> tail(wages)
     wage male female
195 38.60    1      0
196 27.10    1      0
197  4.60    1      0
198 14.85    1      0
199 35.10    1      0
200 24.10    1      0
```

Now let's estimate the model by including `male`, `female`, and the intercept.

```
> wages_lm_pcoll <- lm(wage ~ male + female,
+                      data = wages)
> summary(wages_lm_pcoll)

Call:
lm(formula = wage ~ male + female, data = wages)

Residuals:
    Min      1Q  Median      3Q     Max
-17.610  -7.838  -0.400   6.829  22.225

Coefficients: (1 not defined because of singularities)
            Estimate Std. Error t value Pr(>|t|)
(Intercept)  13.8750     0.9956  13.937  < 2e-16 ***
male          4.8350     1.4079   3.434 0.000724 ***
female            NA         NA      NA       NA
---
Signif. codes:  0 '***' 0.001 '**' 0.01 '*' 0.05 '.' 0.1
                ' ' 1

Residual standard error: 9.956 on 198 degrees of freedom
Multiple R-squared:  0.05621,Adjusted R-squared:  0.05145
F-statistic: 11.79 on 1 and 198 DF,  p-value: 0.0007241
```

R automatically detects the problem. In fact, it tells us that one coefficient is not defined because of singularities.

But what happened? Let's use matrix algebra to find it out.

We generate again the `X` object but this time we need also to include the column that stores the value for `female`. We add a new step, i.e. we compute the matrix multiplication between the transpose of `X` and `X` itself. We store the result in `XX`. When we try to find the coefficients we encounter an error: "the system is exactly singular".

```
> X <- as.matrix(cbind(1, wages_lm_pcoll$model[, c(2, 3)]))
> XX <- t(X)%*%X
> XX
```

```
         1 male female
1       200  100    100
male    100  100      0
female 100     0    100
> b <- solve(XX)%*%t(X)%*%y
Error in solve.default(XX) :
  Lapack routine dgesv: system is exactly singular:
  U[3,3] = 0
```

This depends on the fact that XX is not invertible. In fact, if we reduce XX to its reduced echelon form with `echelon()`, we find out that

```
> echelon(XX)
     1 male female
[1,] 1    0      1
[2,] 0    1     -1
[3,] 0    0      0
```

that is, we have linear dependency and consequently the matrix is not invertible. Briefly, the point is that including the dummy variables for male and female is redundant.

Observe again the XX matrix. You may have already noticed that the sum of the values in `male` and `female` for each row gives the value of the intercept in the same row, or alternatively, the intercept and `male` predict `female` and the intercept and `female` predict `male`.

Therefore, we need to drop one of the dummy variables, e.g. `female` in this example, to avoid the dummy variable trap. More generally, if we have N categories to analyse, we have to include $N - 1$ in the model.

In the exercise in Sect. 2.5.7, we continue with this example but we will remove the intercept.

2.5 Exercises

2.5.1 Exercise 1

Write a function to compute the inner product without using the operator `%*%`. Replicate the result from Sects. 2.2.3 and 2.2.6

```
> u <- c(4, 6)
> v <- c(3, 2)
> inner_product(u, v)
[1] 24
> u <- c(1, 2, 3)
> v <- c(2, 1, -4/3)
> inner_product(u, v)
[1] 0
```

Make sure that the function stops if the length of the two vectors is different

```
> u <- c(1, 2)
> v <- c(2, 1, -4/3)
> inner_product(u, v)
 Error in inner_product(u, v) : length(u) == length(v)
 is not TRUE
```

2.5.2 Exercise 2

Write a function to compute vector projection based on (2.1) in Sect. 2.2.7. Replicate the following results:

```
> u <- c(3, 5)
> v <- c(4, 6)
> proj_vec(u, v)
[1] 3.230769 4.846154
> u <- c(-1, 4, 2)
> v <- c(1, 0, 3)
> proj_vec(u, v)
[1] 0.5 0.0 1.5
```

2.5.3 Exercise 3

In Sect. 2.3.7, we built the `sys_leq()` function to solve a system of two linear equations by using a nested loop. Indeed, we forced the function to find a solution. Additionally, that function finds a solution only if the solutions are integer. In other words, we really made things complicated and inefficient.

In this exercise the reader is asked to completely rewrite the `sys_leq()` function.

Solve the following system of equations

$$\begin{cases} a_1x + a_2y = a_3 \\ b_1x + b_2y = b_3 \end{cases}$$

and rewrite `sys_leq()` based on its solution. For example, let's solve again system (2.11). My new `sys_leq()` works as follows

```
> sys_leq(a1 = 1, a2 = 1, a3 = 4,
+         b1 = 2, b2 = 1, b3 = 7)
x* y*
 3  1
```

This function has to work for not integer solutions as well. For example, let's slightly change (2.11)

$$\begin{cases} x + 2y = 4 \\ 2x + y = 7 \end{cases}$$

The equilibrium solutions are

```
> sys_leq(a1 = 1, a2 = 2, a3 = 4,
+         b1 = 2, b2 = 1, b3 = 7)
       x*        y*
3.3333333 0.3333333
```

2.5.4 Exercise 4

In Sect. 2.3.8.4, we applied the Cramer's rule to solve a system of linear equations.

In this exercise you are asked to write a function for that task. Replicate the example in Sect. 2.3.8.4.

```
> A <- matrix(c(2, 1, -1,
+               1, -2, 1,
+               3, -1, -2),
+             nrow = 3,
+             ncol = 3,
+             byrow = T)
> A
     [,1] [,2] [,3]
[1,]    2    1   -1
[2,]    1   -2    1
[3,]    3   -1   -2
> b <- c(4, 1, 3)
```

This is the output of my function

```
> cramer(A, b)
x1 x2 x3
 2  1  1
```

Solve the system in four *unknowns* from Sect. 2.3.7.1

```
> A <- matrix(c(1, 2, 3, 5,
+               2, 3, 5, 9,
+               3, 4, 7, 1,
+               7, 6, 5, 4),
+             nrow = 4,
```

```
+                  ncol = 4,
+                  byrow = T)
> A
     [,1] [,2] [,3] [,4]
[1,]    1    2    3    5
[2,]    2    3    5    9
[3,]    3    4    7    1
[4,]    7    6    5    4
> b <- c(5, 4, 0, 3)
> cramer(A, b)
      x1        x2        x3        x4
-5.03125  8.46875 -2.71875  0.25000
```

2.5.5 Exercise 5

Write a function, `diagonalization()`, that implements the diagonalization process as described in Sect. 2.3.9.1. Replicate the result in Sect. 2.3.9.1

```
> A <- matrix(c(3, 2,
+                  2, 6),
+                  nrow = 2,
+                  ncol = 2, byrow = TRUE)
> A
     [,1] [,2]
[1,]    3    2
[2,]    2    6
> round(diagonalization(A), 10)
     [,1] [,2]
[1,]    7    0
[2,]    0    2
```

2.5.6 Exercise 6

The variance is the average of the squared differences from the mean. The sample variance is defined as

$$s_x^2 = \frac{\sum_{i=1}^{n}(x_i - \bar{x})^2}{n-1} \tag{2.44}$$

where x_i represents the individual measurement of the random variable x and $\bar{x}$ represents the mean.

Now let's write a function, svar(), that implements (2.44)

```
> svar <- function(x){
+   dev_x <- x - mean(x)
+   sum_dev_sq <- sum(dev_x^2)
+   res <- sum_dev_sq/(length(x)-1)
+   return(res)
+ }
```

In the first step, we compute dev_x, a vector of deviation of each value of x from the mean of x.[23] In the second step, we sum the square of dev_x. Then, we divide by $n - 1$, where n is given by the length of x. Let's test it and compare with the **R** base function var()

```
> x <- 1:5
> x
[1] 1 2 3 4 5
> var(x)
[1] 2.5
> svar(x)
[1] 2.5
```

Now your task is to rewrite svar() with matrix algebra. In the body of the function you need to replace the second step with matrix algebra operations.

2.5.7 Exercise 7

Let's continue the example on the dummy variable trap in Sect. 2.4.5. This time estimate the model with both male and female but without the intercept, that is:

$$wage = \beta_1 male + \beta_2 female + u$$

First estimate it with the lm() function. Then, obtain the estimates with the OLS in matrix form. Investigate the XX matrix.

Your result should be:

```
> b
          [,1]
male    18.710
female 13.875
```

Are these values familiar? Indeed, these coefficients show the expected wage for male and female, respectively.

---

[23] This exercise was inspired by the example in Dayal (2020, p. 110).

In other words, by removing the intercept we avoided the dummy variable trap as well. However, note that this model (all the categorical variables without the intercept) is not recommended because statistical software tend to compute statistics in different way if the intercept is not included (Verbeek 2004, p.43).

Chapter 3
Functions of One Variable

3.1 What is a Function?

Before delving into the discussion of some of the most common functions, let's refresh the general concept of function. In simple words, how could we define a function? We could say that a function is an instruction to process inputs to generate a *unique* output. For example, we could think of raw inputs that are combined together and processed according to some instructions to produce a unique good. Usually, we indicate the input with x and the output with y. Formally, we write

$$y = f(x) \tag{3.1}$$

where $f()$ indicates the function. We read it as "y equals f of x".[1]

Therefore, we will give an input x to the function. The output will depend on the *instructions* of the function. Let's see an example. And let's do that in **R**. First, let's generate the functions that will accompany us along this chapter

```
> lqc_fn <- function(x, a = 0, b = 0, c = 1, d = 0){
+   # by default linear, y = x
+   a*x^3 + b*x^2 + c*x + d
+ }
> log_fn <- function(x, a = 1, b = 1, c = 1, d = 0, e = 0, ...){
+   #  by default natural logarithmic
+   b*log(a*x^(c) + d, ...) + e
+   }
> exp_fn <- function(x, a = 1, b = 1, c = 0, d = 0, k = 1){
+   a*exp(b*x^k + c) + d
+   }
> radical_fn <- function(x, a = 1, b = 0, c = 0, k = 1){
```

[1] Besides f, we can use other letters to indicate a function such as g, F, G. Greek letters such as ϕ (phi), and ψ (psi), and their capitals, Φ and Ψ respectively, are used as well.

M. Porto, *Introduction to Mathematics for Economics with R*,
https://doi.org/10.1007/978-3-031-05202-6_3

```
+    a*sqrt(x^k + b) + c
+ }
```

lqc_fn() is a function for a polynomial of maximum degree three. That is, we can use it to compute linear, quadratic and cubic functions. By default it is linear. log_fn() by default computes the natural logarithmic function. exp_fn() computes the exponential function. radical_fn() computes the radical function. We will explain all these functions in the respective sections.

Second, we generate our input, x, that contains a sequence of values from -10 to 10. Then, we substitute the x in $y = f(x)$ with our input x, to generate the objects that contain the outputs of the following functions

- $y = f(x) = x$
- $y = f(x) = x^2$
- $y = f(x) = x^3$
- $y = f(x) = \log(x)$
- $y = f(x) = \exp(x)$
- $y = f(x) = \sqrt{x}$

```
> x <- seq(-10, 10, 0.1)
> y_lin <- lqc_fn(x)
> y_qdt <- lqc_fn(x, b = 1, c = 0)
> y_cube <- lqc_fn(x, a = 1, c = 0)
> y_log <- log_fn(x)
Warning message:
In log(a * x^(c) + d, ...) : NaNs produced
> y_exp <- exp_fn(x)
> y_rad <- radical_fn(x)
Warning message:
In sqrt(x + b) : NaNs produced
```

Let's build a dataframe with the input and outputs

```
> df <- data.frame(x, y_lin, y_qdt,
+                    y_cube, y_log,
+                    y_exp, y_rad)
> head(df)
      x y_lin  y_qdt    y_cube y_log        y_exp y_rad
1 -10.0 -10.0 100.00 -1000.000   NaN 4.539993e-05   NaN
2  -9.9  -9.9  98.01  -970.299   NaN 5.017468e-05   NaN
3  -9.8  -9.8  96.04  -941.192   NaN 5.545160e-05   NaN
4  -9.7  -9.7  94.09  -912.673   NaN 6.128350e-05   NaN
5  -9.6  -9.6  92.16  -884.736   NaN 6.772874e-05   NaN
6  -9.5  -9.5  90.25  -857.375   NaN 7.485183e-05   NaN
```

We can observe from the first six entries of the data frame that our x is the same but y varies according to the type of function: linear for y_lin, quadratic

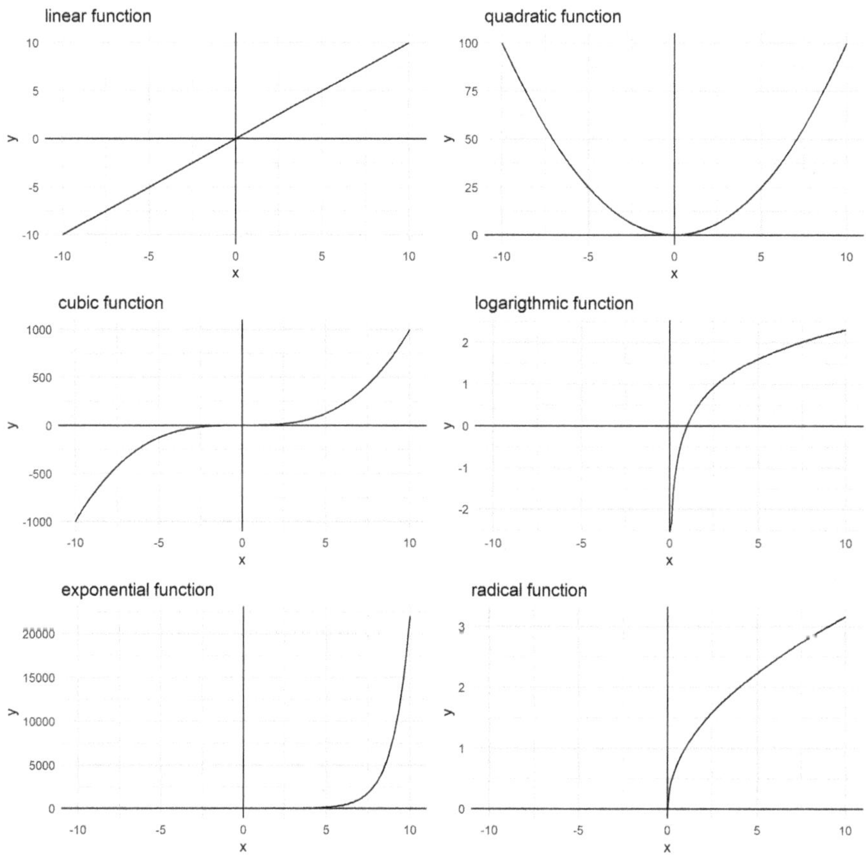

Fig. 3.1 Plot of six functions

for `y_qdt`, cubic for `y_cube`, logarithmic for `y_log`, exponential for `y_exp`, and radical for `y_rad`. The logarithmic function and the radical function, given this input, share the same first 6 entries. However, they behave in a different way as we will see. These functions can be represented in the Cartesian plane. From Fig. 3.1, it is evident that the functions are different. We will return to the meaning of `NaN` later.[2]

In Economics, we use functions to study the relationship between economic variables. In particular, we are interested in studying how the change in the input variable, that is the independent variable (referred in Economics also as the *exogenous variable*), affects the output, that is the dependent variable (referred in Economics also as the *endogenous variable*).

[2] The code used to generate Figs. 3.1, 3.2, and 3.3 is available in the Appendix C.

3.1.1 Domain and Range

Two very important concepts related to functions are *domain* (D) and *range* (W). What are they?

Let's go back to the functions we defined earlier:

- $y = f(x) = x$
- $y = f(x) = x^2$
- $y = f(x) = x^3$
- $y = f(x) = \log(x)$
- $y = f(x) = \exp(x)$
- $y = f(x) = \sqrt{x}$

The domain of the function is the set of all values of the independent variable x at which y is defined. The range of the function is the set of all values of the dependent variable y.

Let's observe again Fig. 3.1. From the graph of the linear function, it is apparent that if we continue adding numbers to our `x` object, the output in the `y_lin` object will continue to extend as well. Therefore, there is no restriction to the value x and y can take from minus infinity to plus infinity. Formally, we write

$$Domain = \{x \mid x \in \mathbb{R}\}$$

that is, the domain is equal to all the x values such that the x values are elements of the real number set, and

$$Range = \{y \mid y \in \mathbb{R}\}$$

that is, the range is equal to all the y values such that the y values are elements of the real number set.

On the other hand, if we observe the graph of the quadratic function, it is clear that the x values can grow to minus and plus infinity but the y values have a minimum value beyond that they cannot go. This value is the vertex of the parabola.[3] In this case, formally we write

$$Domain = \{x \mid x \in \mathbb{R}\}$$

that is, same as before but

$$Range = \{y \mid y \geq y_v\}$$

[3] Note that the parabola opens upwards because the coefficient is positive. If the coefficient were negative, the parabola would open downwards. Therefore, we would have a maximum value beyond that it cannot go. We will discuss quadratic functions in Sect. 3.3.

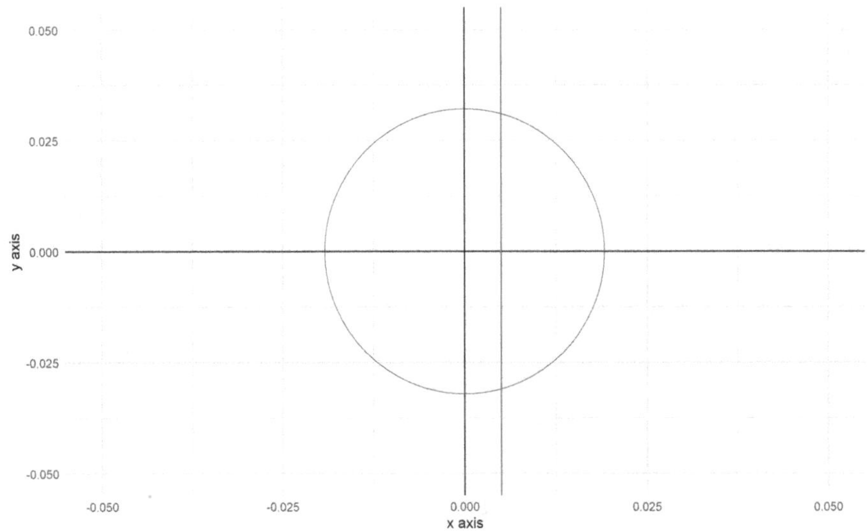

Fig. 3.2 Vertical line test

that is, the range takes all the y values such that y values are greater or equal to y_v, i.e. the y coordinate of the vertex.

If the domain of a function is not specified, it will be understood to consist of all real values of the independent variable for which corresponds a unique real value of the dependent variable.

In simple words, we could say that the domain is all the values that x can be, that is all the valid inputs, while the range is all the values that y can be, that is the possible output. Formally, we can define a function in the following way.

A function is a rule that assigns (maps) a unique element $f(x) \in W$ to every $x \in D$

$$f : D \rightarrow W$$

Figure 3.2 represents a circle in the Cartesian plane. Is the circle, $x^2 + y^2 = 1$, a function? Let's apply the so-called vertical line test (VLT) to answer this question. If we can draw any vertical line that crosses the graph more than once we conclude that the graph does not define a function. From this sketch in Fig. 3.2, we can observe that the vertical line crosses the graph of the circle in two points. This means that for one x value we have two y values. At the real beginning we said that a unique output, i.e. y value, is the outcome of a function. Therefore, the graph of a circle does not represent a function.

On the other hand, two x values can be assigned to a unique y value. For example, in the quadratic function in Fig. 3.1, the same y value is mapped to two values on the x axis, e.g. -5 and 5. We can also have a bijective function, that is for any y value there is one and only one x value. These bijective functions are also called invertible, i.e. for $y = f(x)$ there is a function $f^{-1}(y) = x$ that reverses it. For example, the inverse function of $f(x) = 7x + 3$ is $f^{-1}(y) = \frac{y-3}{7}$, where we basically replaced $f(x)$ with y and solved $y = 7x + 3$ for x. Note, for example, that $f(x = 5) = 7 \cdot 5 + 3 = 38$ and $f^{-1}(y = 38) = \frac{38-3}{7} = 5$. This leads to $f^{-1}(f(x)) = x$. The reverse applies as well $f(f^{-1}(y)) = y$.

In Economics, the *inverse demand function* is the most famous case of an inverse function. To the demand function $Q = f(P)$, that assigns the quantity consumed of a good, Q, to a price of that good, P, corresponds the inverse demand function $P = f^{-1}(Q)$ that assigns a price to each quantity of good consumed. We will return to invertible functions in Chap. 4.

3.1.2 Monotonicity, Boundedness and Extrema

We define a monotonically increasing function as follows:

$$f(x_1) \leq f(x_2) \ \forall x_1, x_2 \in D, x_1 \leq x_2$$

that is a function that is increasing or non-decreasing, while

$$f(x_1) < f(x_2) \ \forall x_1, x_2 \in D, x_1 < x_2$$

is called strictly increasing (it is a strictly monotone function).

On the other hand,

$$f(x_1) \geq f(x_2) \ \forall x_1, x_2 \in D, x_1 \geq x_2$$

is called monotonically decreasing function, that is a function that is decreasing or non-increasing, while

$$f(x_1) > f(x_2) \ \forall x_1, x_2 \in D, x_1 > x_2$$

is called strictly decreasing (it is a strictly monotone function).

Functions can be bounded from above:

$$\exists K : f(x) \leq K \ \forall x \in D$$

We read it as "there exists a K such that f of x is less or equal to K *for all* x in D".

Functions can be bounded from below:

$$\exists K : f(x) \geq K \ \forall x \in D$$

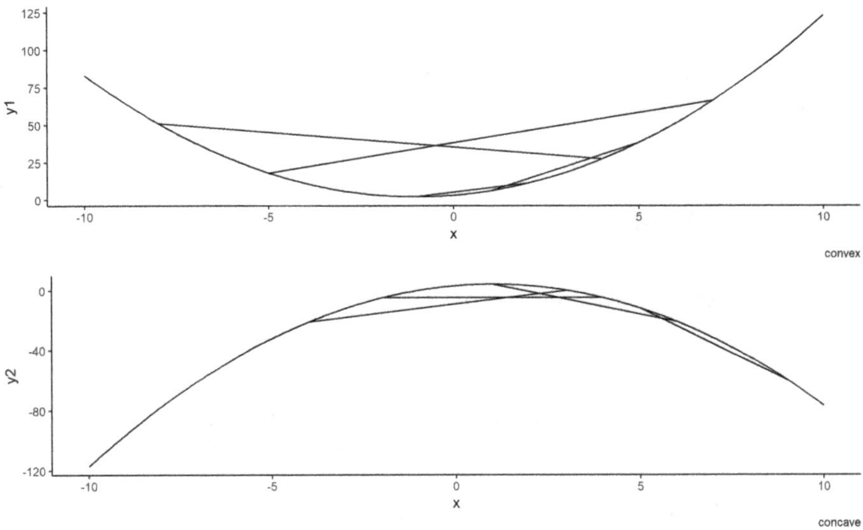

Fig. 3.3 Convex and concave functions

and bounded from above and below:

$$\exists K : |f(x)| \quad \leq K \ \forall x \in D$$

The smallest upper bound K is called *supremum* while the largest lower bound K is called *infimum*.

3.1.3 Convex and Concave Functions

We may distinguish functions based on the curvature of their graph. A function is *strictly* convex (concave) if a straight line that joins any pair of points on the curvature of the graph lies above (below) the curve (Fig. 3.3). If the straight line lies either above (below) the curve or along the curve, we just refer to the function as *convex function* (*concave function*). We may also find that a convex (concave) function is referred to as *concave up* (*concave down*). We will talk again about convexity and concavity of a function in Chap. 6.

3.1.4 Function Operations

- Addition: $(f + g)(x) = f(x) + g(x)$
- Subtraction: $(f - g)(x) = f(x) - g(x)$

- Multiplication: $(fg)(x) = f(x) \cdot g(x)$
- Constant multiplication: $f(kx) = kf(x), k \in \mathbb{R}$
- Division: $(f/g)(x) = f(x)/g(x)$ provided that $g(x) \neq 0$
- Composition: $(g \circ f)(x) = g(f(x))$

3.2 Linear Function

The general form of a linear function is[4]

$$y = f(x) = a + bx \tag{3.2}$$

If $a = 0$, $y = bx$ is a straight line that passes through the origin $(0, 0)$. For example, in Fig. 3.1, the linear function is represented by the function $y = x$, where $b = 1$.

Let's plot the linear functions $y = 3x$, $y = 4 + 3x$, and $y = -4 + 3x$ (Fig. 3.4). First, we generate a data frame that stores the x input that contains the sequence of values from -10 to 10 separated by 1 unit. We use the `seq()` function to generate the sequence. Then, we used `ggplot()` and `stat_function()` to plot the functions. The `aes()` maps the data to the `x` in the data frame `df`. `fun =` takes the `lqc_fn()` we wrote earlier. We use `args()` to pass the additional arguments to our function. In particular, we pass `c` and `d` to model the desired linear function. `color =` and `size =` define the color and size of the lines, respectively. `geom_hline()` and `geom_vline` set an horizontal and vertical line, respectively. `theme_minimal()` is one of the possible ways to define the background of the plot.

```
> df <- data.frame(x = seq(-10, 10, 1))
> ggplot(df) +
+   stat_function(aes(x), fun = lqc_fn,
+                 args = list(c = 3),
+                 color = "blue", size = 1) +
+   stat_function(aes(x), fun = lqc_fn,
+                 args = list(c = 3, d = 4),
+                 color = "red", size = 1) +
+   stat_function(aes(x), fun = lqc_fn,
+                 args = list(c = 3, d = -4),
+                 color = "yellow", size = 1) +
+   geom_hline(yintercept = 0) +
```

[4] Note that a mathematician would refer to (3.2) as an *affine* function and not as a *linear* function. Technically speaking, a linear function is $y = f(x) = bx$. However, since the graph of (3.2) is a straight line we refer to them as linear. In the rest of this book we will not take into account this distinction.

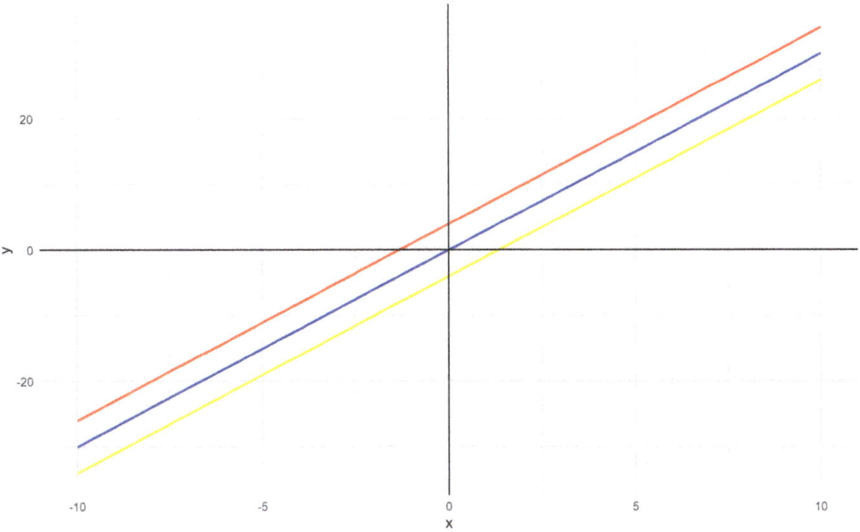

Fig. 3.4 Plot of linear functions

```
+    geom_vline(xintercept = 0) +
+    theme_minimal()
```

The constant, a – d in `lqc_fn()`, shifts the graph of the line upwards (red line) if it is positive and downwards (yellow line) if it is negative (Fig. 3.4).

Lines with a negative b – b corresponds to c in `lqc_fn()` — downward from the left to the right. Figure 3.5 plots $y = 4 - 3x$.

```
> ggplot(df) +
+    stat_function(aes(x), fun = lqc_fn,
+                  args = list(c = -3, d = 4),
+                  size = 1) +
+    geom_hline(yintercept = 0) +
+    geom_vline(xintercept = 0) +
+    theme_minimal()
```

3.2.1 Slope of Linear Function

For

$$y = a + bx$$

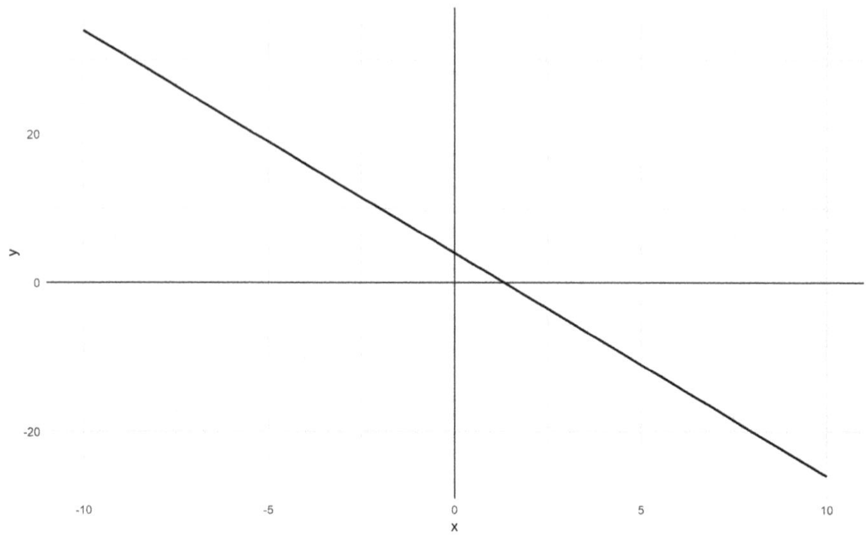

Fig. 3.5 Plot of $y = 4 - 3x$

the slope is

$$\frac{f(x_2) - f(x_1)}{x_2 - x_1} = \frac{y_2 - y_1}{x_2 - x_1} = \frac{\Delta y}{\Delta x} = \frac{rise}{run} = b$$

To see why this is true make the following substitutions:

$$\frac{f(x_2) - f(x_1)}{x_2 - x_1} = \frac{(a + bx_2) - (a + bx_1)}{x_2 - x_1} = \frac{b(x_2 - x_1)}{x_2 - x_1} = b$$

Let's compute the slope in **R**. We write a function, `slope_linfun()`, to compute it. The function `slope_linfun()` can use two methods to compute the slope. The first one, `eq = TRUE`, computes the slope given the equation of the line and two x coordinates. It returns the slope and the coordinates of two points on the line. The second method, `eq = FALSE`, computes the slope given the coordinates of two points. It returns the equation of the line and the slope. In addition, `graph = TRUE` will plot the linear function with `ggplot()`. The arguments of the function are:

- `a` and `b` correspond to $y = a + bx$,
- `x1` and `x2` are two x coordinates,
- `y1` and `y2` are two y coordinates,
- `eq = TRUE` set the method to compute the slope with two x coordinates and the equation of the line;
- `graph` is an option to plot the graph of the linear function.

In the function, we start with the code for `eq = TRUE`. First, we compute the corresponding y coordinates of `x1` and `x2`. Then, we compute the `rise`, the `run` and the `slope`. Finally, we generate an object, `crd`, to contain the results of the coordinates. We use the `paste0()` function that concatenates vectors after converting to character. After computing the slope, we generate an object, `res`, that contains the linear equation and two points. We use `if()` and `else()` to account for different possibilities. Then, we specify the code if `eq = FALSE`, that is we have two points but not the equation of the line. The first step is to compute the slope as before but in this case we already have the y coordinates. We need `a`. We compute it by solving the equation of the line for a and using `x1`, `y1` and the `slope`. We round the result to two decimals with the `round()` function. We do not need to compute `b` because it is the slope. Then, we generate `res` for the case `eq = FALSE`. We do not include the two points because we already know them. Finally, we write the code to plot the linear function. The plot is stored in `g`. At last, `return()` returns the object we generated. Note that `l` uses a `list()` function to store objects with different class. If `graph = FALSE` the function will not show the plot of the linear function (default argument).

```
> slope_linfun <- function(x1, x2,
+                          a = NULL, b = NULL,
+                          y1 = NULL, y2 = NULL,
+                          eq = TRUE,
+                          graph = FALSE){
+   if(eq == TRUE){
+     y1 <- a + b*x1
+     y2 <- a + b*x2
+     rise <- y2 - y1
+     run <- x2 - x1
+     slope <- rise / run
+
+     crd <- paste0("coordinates are ",
+                   "(",x1, ",", y1, ")",
+                   " and ",
+                   "(", x2, ",", y2, ")")
+
+     res <- if(b == 0) {
+       paste0("the slope of y = ", a, " is: ", 0)
+     } else if(a != 0){
+       ifelse(b > 0,
+              paste0("the slope of y = ",
+                     a, " + " , b, "x is: ",
+                     slope),
+              paste0("the slope of y = ",
+                     a, " " , b, "x is: ", slope))
+     } else paste0("the slope of y = ", b, "x is: ",
+                   slope)
```

```
+       res <- list(res, crd)
+     } else if(eq == FALSE){
+
+       rise <- y2 - y1
+       run <- x2 - x1
+       slope <- round(rise / run, 2)
+
+       a <- round(y1 + -1*slope*x1, 2)
+
+       res <- if(slope == 0) {
+         paste0("the slope of y = ", a, " is: ", 0)
+       } else if(a != 0){
+         ifelse(slope > 0,
+                paste0("the slope of y = ",
+                       a, " + " , slope, "x is: ",
+                       slope),
+                paste0("the slope of y = ",
+                       a, " " , slope, "x is: ", slope))
+       } else paste0("the slope of y = ", slope, "x is:",
+                     slope)
+     }
+
+
+     if(graph == FALSE){
+
+       return(res)
+
+     } else{
+
+       require("ggplot2")
+       x <- seq(-10, 10, 0.1)
+       y <- a + slope*x
+       df <- data.frame(x, y)
+
+       g <- ggplot(df, aes(x = x, y = y)) +
+         geom_line() +
+         geom_hline(yintercept = 0) +
+         geom_vline(xintercept = 0) +
+         theme_minimal() +
+         coord_cartesian(xlim = c(-10, 10),
+                         ylim = c(-10, 10))
+
+       l <- list(res, g)
+
+       return(l)
```

```
+
+     }
+ }
```

Now, we are ready to test it. First, let's use different points for the linear function $y = 4 + 3x$.

```
> slope_linfun(2, 6, 4, 3)
[[1]]
[1] "the slope of y = 4 + 3x is: 3"

[[2]]
[1] "coordinates are (2,10) and (6,22)"

> slope_linfun(-1, 6, 4, 3)
[[1]]
[1] "the slope of y = 4 + 3x is: 3"

[[2]]
[1] "coordinates are (-1,1) and (6,22)"

> slope_linfun(10, 6, 4, 3)
[[1]]
[1] "the slope of y = 4 + 3x is: 3"

[[2]]
[1] "coordinates are (10,34) and (6,22)"
```

Let's now use the option `graph = TRUE`.

```
> slope_linfun(4, 6, 2, 4, graph = TRUE)
[[1]]
[[1]][[1]]
[1] "the slope of y = 2 + 4x is: 4"

[[1]][[2]]
[1] "coordinates are (4,18) and (6,26)"


[[2]]

> slope_linfun(0, 7, 1, -5, graph = TRUE)
[[1]]
[[1]][[1]]
[1] "the slope of y = 1 -5x is: -5"
```

```
[[1]][[2]]
[1] "coordinates are (0,1) and (7,-34)"


[[2]]

> slope_linfun(-1, 6, 4, 0, graph = T)
[[1]]
[[1]][[1]]
[1] "the slope of y = 4 is: 0"

[[1]][[2]]
[1] "coordinates are (-1,4) and (6,4)"


[[2]]
```

The respective figures are Figs. 3.6, 3.7, and 3.8.

Graphically, the slope represents the change in y with respect to x on the graph of the line. Lines with positive slope rise as x increases: every increase of 1 in x causes the y value to rise by b. Lines with negative slope fall as x increases: every increase of 1 in x causes the y value to decrease by $-b$. Furthermore, the absolute value of b indicates the degree of steepness of the line. The larger $|b|$ the steeper the line. On the other hand, when the slope is 0, $b = 0$, $y = a$, i.e. the line crosses the y axis and it is parallel to the x axis. Therefore, when x increases by 1, y remains the same.

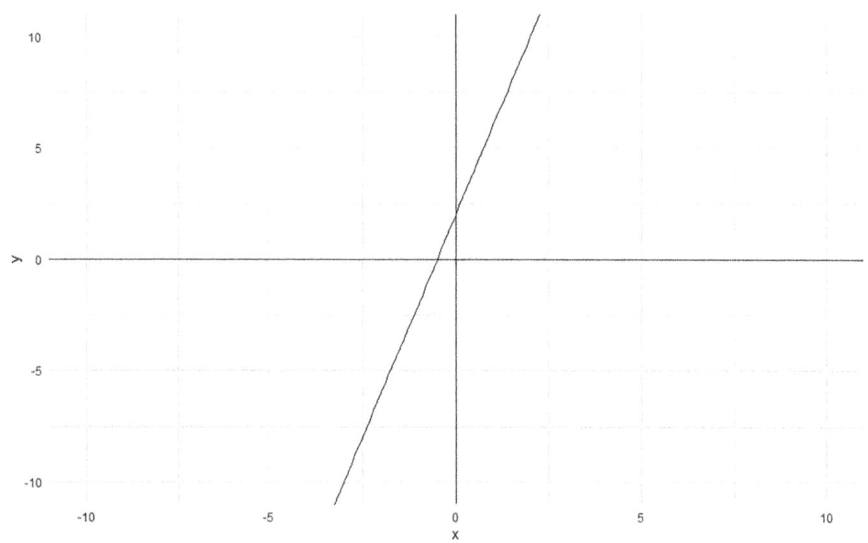

Fig. 3.6 Plot of $y = 2 + 4x$

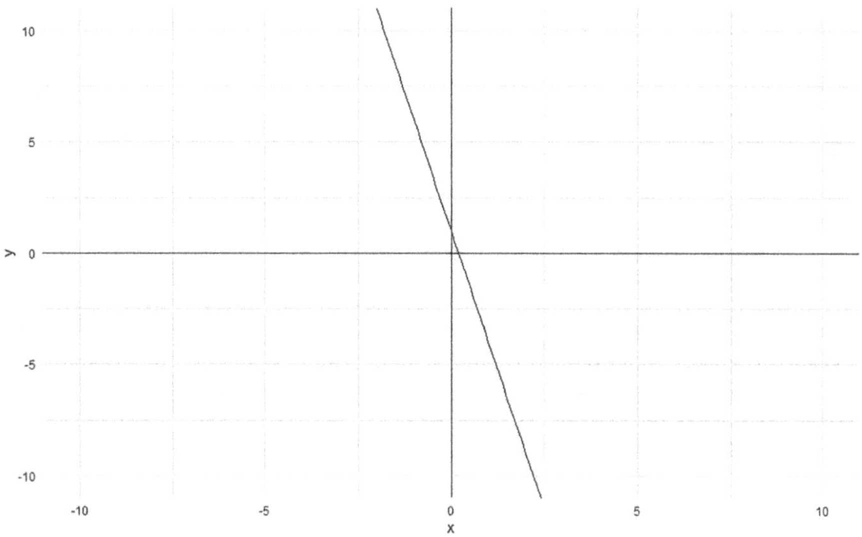

Fig. 3.7 Plot of $y = 1 - 5x$

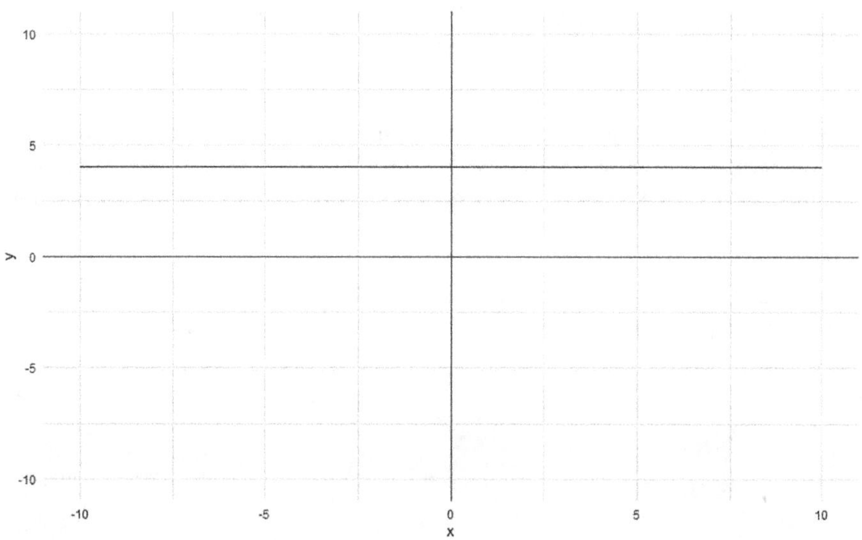

Fig. 3.8 Plot of $y = 4$

Let's try the function with `eq = F`.

```
> slope_linfun(4, 6, y1 = 18, y2 = 26, eq = F)
[1] "the slope of y = 2 + 4x is: 4"
> slope_linfun(0, 7, y1 = 1, y2 = -34, eq = F)
[1] "the slope of y = 1 -5x is: -5"
```

```
> slope_linfun(-1, 6, y1 = 4, y2 = 4, eq = F)
[1] "the slope of y = 4 is: 0"
```

The reader may have noticed that when `eq = T`, we could directly write **b** as the slope. We will talk again about the slope of a function in Chap. 4.

3.2.2 Applications in Economics

Linear functions are popular in Economics because they are easy to handle mathematically and easy to interpret.

In this section, we use a different approach to make plots with `ggplot()`. We assume that we collect the data in a data frame (you may think of a data frame as an Excel spreadsheet). We directly plot the data from the data frame.

3.2.2.1 The Cost Function

A cost function describes the relationship between cost and quantity produced. When the quantity produced changes the cost changes as well. In fact, to increase the quantity produced a firm needs, for example, to increase utilities and raw materials used in the production.

We can decompose the total cost borne by firms in fixed cost (FC), cost that does not vary with the level of production, and variable cost (VC), cost that varies with the amount produced. The amount of change in cost depends on the cost function. We will see three cost functions: linear, quadratic, and cubic. In this section, we start with the linear cost function.

Let's assume that firm *ABC* has fixed cost (FC) for \$5000 and a variable cost (VC) of \$125 per output. We use a linear function to describe the total cost (TC) of firm *ABC*:

$$TC(x) = FC + VC(x)$$

This can be seen as

$$f(x) = a + bx$$

where

- a is the constant, i.e. the fixed cost
- b is the variable cost of \$125 per unit of output x

In our example, it would be

$$TC(x) = 5000 + 125x$$

Let's graph this linear function. Note that we generate a new `x` object as a sequence starting from 0 because we do not consider negative values for quantity produced.

```
> x <- seq(0, 50, 1)
> FC <- 5000
> VC <- 125
> TC <- FC + VC*x
> df <- data.frame(output = x,
+                    total_cost = TC)
> head(df, 10)
   output total_cost
1       0       5000
2       1       5125
3       2       5250
4       3       5375
5       4       5500
6       5       5625
7       6       5750
8       7       5875
9       8       6000
10      9       6125
> ggplot(df, aes(x = output,
+                  y = total_cost)) +
+   geom_line() +
+   geom_hline(yintercept = 0) +
+   geom_hline(yintercept = FC,
+              linetype = "dashed") +
+   geom_vline(xintercept = 0) +
+   theme_minimal() +
+   xlab("Output") +
+   ylab("Total Cost, US dollar") +
+   annotate("text", x = 30, y = c(2500, 6000),
+            label = c("FIXED COST", "VARIABLE COST"))
```

We added in the `ggplot()` code, `xlab()` and `ylab()` to set the label for the x axis and for the y axis, respectively, and `annotate()` to add the text `FIXED COST` and `VARIABLE COST` on the plot. Note that in `annotate()`, `x =` and `y =` indicate the coordinates for the text on the plot. Note that we added another horizontal line that crosses the y axis at the fixed cost amount.

Figure 3.9 shows the decomposition of total cost as the sum of fixed costs and variable costs.

Let's use the `slope_linfun()` we built.

```
> x1 <- df[10, 1]
> y1 <- df[10, 2]
```

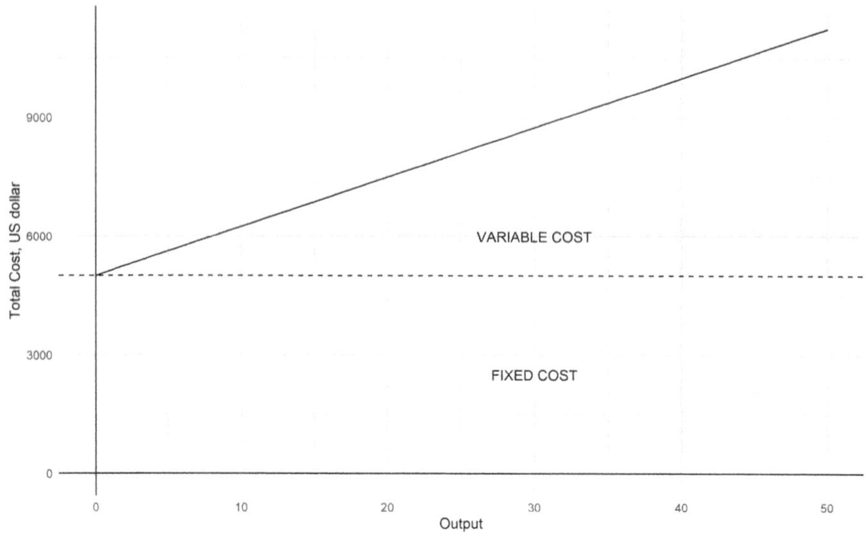

Fig. 3.9 Linear cost function

```
> x2 <- df[11, 1]
> y2 <- df[11, 2]
> x3 <- df[15, 1]
> y3 <- df[15, 2]
> slope_linfun(x1, x2, y1 = y1, y2 = y2, eq = F)
[1] "the slope of y = 5000 + 125x is: 125"
> slope_linfun(x2, x3, y1 = y2, y2 = y3, eq = F)
[1] "the slope of y = 5000 + 125x is: 125"
> slope_linfun(x1, x3, y1 = y1, y2 = y3, eq = F)
[1] "the slope of y = 5000 + 125x is: 125"
```

As we expected, the slope of this cost function is 125. We interpret this slope as a constant marginal cost (see Chap. 4 for marginal cost) . Therefore, a linear constant function is appropriate only for cost structures in which marginal cost is constant.

3.2.2.2 Break-Even

Firm *ABC* sells its product at a price of \$250 each. How many products does *ABC* have to sell to break-even?

Break-even is the point where there is not profit or loss for the firm. In other words, profit has to equal 0. The profit function, that can be formulated in terms of *quantity* (in this case x), is given by

$$\pi(x) = R(x) - C(x) \tag{3.3}$$

where

- π stands for profit
- R stands for revenue, i.e. price times sold quantity
- C stands for cost

Therefore, $\pi(x) = 0$ means that $R(x) - C(x) = 0$. In our example, the profit function would be

$$\pi(x) = 250x - (5000 + 125x)$$

Let's check graphically where firm *ABC* reaches the break-even.

```
> p <- 250
> R <- p * x
> pi <- R - TC
> df <- cbind(df, revenue = R,
+               profit = pi)
> head(df)
  output total_cost revenue profit
1      0       5000       0  -5000
2      1       5125     250  -4875
3      2       5250     500  -4750
4      3       5375     750  -4625
5      4       5500    1000  -4500
6      5       5625    1250  -4375
> tail(df)
   output total_cost revenue profit
46     45      10625   11250    625
47     46      10750   11500    750
48     47      10875   11750    875
49     48      11000   12000   1000
50     49      11125   12250   1125
51     50      11250   12500   1250
```

We add `R` and `pi` to our dataset, `df`, with the `cbind()` function. Additionally we add three columns to map the legend in the `ggplot()` function (later, we show a different and more efficient way to map the legend).

```
> df$R <- "Revenue"
> df$TC <- "Total Cost"
> df$pi <- "Profit"
```

Note that we map the legend in `aes(color = )`. Contrary to Fig. 3.9, we do not add `US dollar` on the title of the *y* axis, but we introduce directly the dollar mark on the ticks of the *y* axis with `scale_y_continuous(labels = scales::dollar)`. Figure 3.10 shows the output.

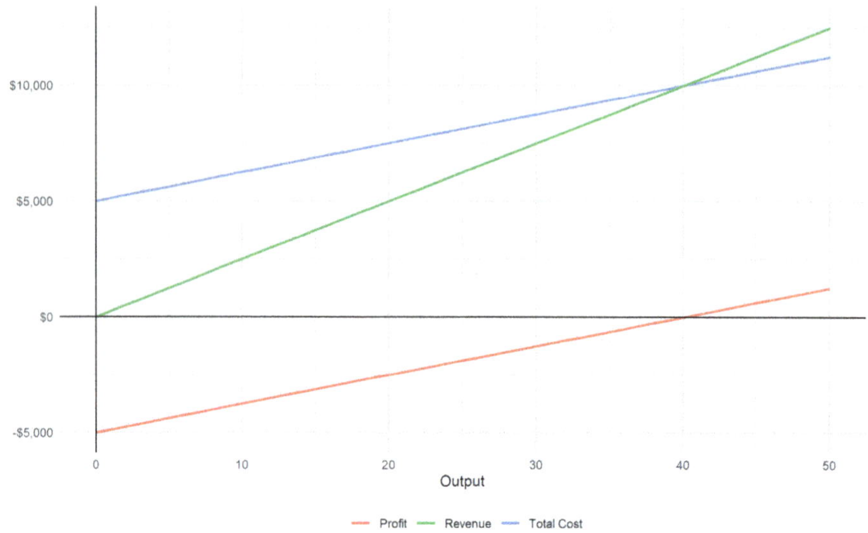

Fig. 3.10 Break-even

Figure 3.10 shows that as long as the revenues are less than the costs, the profits are negative. When the revenue is equal to the cost, the profit is zero. This is represented by the intersection of the revenue line with the cost line, and by the profit line crossing the x axis. At this point the firm is at break-even. After this point, the profits grows according to the shape of the revenue and cost functions.

```
> ggplot(df) +
+   geom_line(aes(x = output, y = total_cost,
+                 color = TC),
+             size = 1) +
+   geom_line(aes(x = output, y = revenue,
+                 color = R),
+             size = 1) +
+   geom_line(aes(x = output, y = profit,
+                 color = pi),
+             size = 1) +
+   geom_hline(yintercept = 0) +
+   geom_vline(xintercept = 0) +
+   theme_minimal() +
+   xlab("Output") + ylab("") +
+   scale_y_continuous(labels = scales::dollar) +
+   theme_minimal() +
+   theme(legend.title = element_blank(),
+         legend.position = "bottom")
```

In this example, firm *ABC* reaches the break-even when it sells exactly 40 of its products.

```
> df[38:42, 1:4]
   output total_cost revenue profit
38     37       9625    9250   -375
39     38       9750    9500   -250
40     39       9875    9750   -125
41     40      10000   10000      0
42     41      10125   10250    125
```

Economic theory tells us that in the long-run firms will enter the industry when price p is above the average cost (AC), $p > AC$, because they can make profits and they will exit the industry when price is below the average cost, $p < AC$, because they will incur in losses. When price is equal to the minimum of the average cost, profits are 0. Therefore, firms will not enter or exit the industry. We are at equilibrium. But why are firms fine with profit equal to zero?

Let's try to get the answer to this question from another perspective, i.e. from Accounting. Table 3.1 shows a simplified version of an income statement of a firm. The income statement, also known as profit and loss statement, is one of the financial statements reported by a firm where it shows profit and loss over a specific accounting period. Let's say that it represents the income statement of firm *ABC*.

As we can see, firm *ABC* paid all the expenses, including wages of the employees (and the owner), and it paid the government as well (taxes). In other words, even though the profit for firm *ABC* is zero, everyone has been paid. This is enough to stay in the industry.

3.2.2.3 Mark-Up and Margin

Imperfectly competitive firms charge a price that exceeds their marginal cost in order to maximize their profits. The amount by which the cost of a product is

Table 3.1 Example of a simplified income statement

Revenue	10,000	–
Wages		
Rent		
Utilities		
Depreciation and amortization		
Interest		
Other expenses		
Total expenses	8000	=
Profit before taxes	2000	–
Taxes	2000	=
Profit after taxes	0	

increased in order to derive the selling price is called mark-up. Sometimes there is some confusion between mark-up and (profit) margin. Are they the same?

From the definition of mark-up we can write:

$$COST \times (1 + MARKUP) = SALESPRICE$$

Let's multiply out and solve for $MARKUP$:

$$COST + COST \cdot MARKUP = SALESPRICE$$

$$COST \cdot MARKUP = SALESPRICE - COST$$

$$MARKUP = \frac{SALESPRICE - COST}{COST} = \frac{PROFIT}{COST}$$

For example, the mark-up of a firm with $SALESPRICE = \$120{,}000$ (revenue) and $COST = \$100{,}000$ is

$$MARKUP = \frac{120{,}000 - 100{,}000}{100{,}000} = 0.2 \rightarrow 20\%$$

Let's check it: $100,000 \times (1 + 0.2) = 120{,}000$

On the other hand, the (profit) margin is sales minus the cost of goods sold. The margin is (derivation left as exercise):

$$MARGIN = \frac{SALESPRICE - COST}{SALESPRICE} = \frac{PROFIT}{SALESPRICE}$$

In our earlier example, the margin is

$$MARGIN = \frac{120,000 - 100,000}{120,000} = 0.166666 \rightarrow 16.666\%$$

Let's check it: $120,000 \times (1 - 0.166666) = 100,000$

Therefore, the mark-up shows the profit related to the cost while the margin shows the profit related to the revenue.

We can find the following relations between mark-up and margin:

$$MARKUP = \frac{MARGIN}{1 - MARGIN}$$

$$MARGIN = \frac{MARKUP}{1 + MARKUP}$$

Example:

$$MARKUP = \frac{0.16666}{1 - 0.16666} = 20\%$$

$$MARGIN = \frac{0.2}{1 + 0.2} = 16.6666\%$$

3.2.2.4 Linear Models in Econometrics

We could use a simple linear model to estimate the relationship between the measure of firm performance (return on equity—roe) and CEO compensation. The econometric model can be specified as follows:

$$salary = \beta_0 + \beta_1 roe + u$$

where *salary* is the compensation of the CEO in thousands dollars, β_0 is the intercept, β_1 is the slope parameter and u is the error term. Let's assume that the following model is estimated:

$$sal\hat{a}ry = 781.225 + 16.443 roe$$

We can graph it as follows (Fig. 3.11):

```
> roe <- seq(0, 100, 1)
> salary <- 781.225 + 16.443 * roe
> df <- data.frame(salary = salary,
+                  roe = roe)
> ggplot(df, aes(x = roe,
+                y = salary)) +
+   geom_line() +
+   geom_hline(yintercept = 0) +
+   geom_vline(xintercept = 0) +
+   theme_minimal() +
+   ylab("salary (in thousands USD)")
```

We can interpret it as follows. When the $roe = 0$, it is estimated that a CEO receives a $\$781,225$ salary (intercept).

Let's compute the slope by using the `slope_linfun()`.

```
> salary1 <- df[1, 1]
> roe1 <- df[1, 2]
> salary2 <- df[2, 1]
> roe2 <- df[2, 2]
> salary50 <- df[50, 1]
> roe50 <- df[50, 2]
```

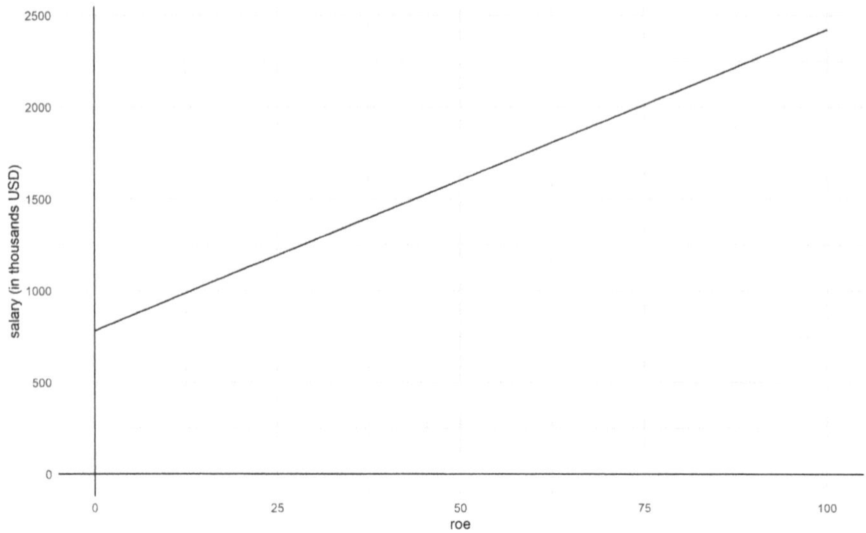

Fig. 3.11 Example: estimation of salary

```
> slope_linfun(roe1, roe2,
+              y1 = salary1, y2 = salary2,
+              eq = F)
[1] "the slope of y = 781.23 + 16.44x is: 16.44"
> slope_linfun(roe1, roe50,
+              y1 = salary1, y2 = salary50,
+              eq = F)
[1] "the slope of y = 781.23 + 16.44x is: 16.44"
```

As expected it is 16.44 (rounded to two decimals). This is interpreted as follows: if the return on equity increases by one percentage point, $\Delta roe = 1$, then salary is predicted to change by about 16.44, or \$16, 443. This simple regression line says that with $roe = 10$, the predicted salary of a CEO would be $\widehat{salary} = 781.225 + 16.443 \cdot (10) = 945.655$, or \$945, 655; with $roe = 20$, the predicted salary of a CEO would be $\widehat{salary} = 781.225 + 16.443 \cdot (20) = 1110.085$, or \$1, 110, 085.[5]

3.3 Quadratic Function

The general form of a quadratic function is

[5] Note that this simple model does not consider other factors that can affect salary.

$$y = f(x) = ax^2 + bx + c \tag{3.4}$$

where a, b, and c are constants and $a \neq 0$.

We need three points to sketch a quadratic function.

Suppose we want to plot:

$$y = x^2 + 2x - 15 \tag{3.5}$$

Let's first use three random points in the range $(-10, 10)$ for the x-axis.

Let's make **R** pick those numbers for us by using the `sample()` function. The first entry is a vector of one o more elements from which to choose. The second entry represents the number of items to choose. Note that we start with the function `set.seed()` to make the example reproducible.

We generate `x` and `y` objects and we store them in a data frame, `df`, with the `data.frame()` function.

```
> set.seed(4)
> x <- sample(-10:10, 3)
> y <- x^2 + 2*x - 15
> df <- data.frame(x = x, y = y)
> df
   x   y
1  0 -15
2  8  65
3 -8  33
```

We reorganize the values in a new data frame as follows:[6]

```
> df2 <- data.frame(x1 = x[1], x2 = x[2], x3 = x[3],
+                   y1 = y[1], y2 = y[2], y3 = y[3])
> df2
  x1 x2 x3  y1 y2 y3
1  0  8 -8 -15 65 33
```

We use both data frames to make Fig. 3.12 with the `ggplot()` function. First, we create a scatter plot with `geom_point()`. We store the plot in an object, `p`. Then, we join these points with `geom_curve()`. We set the color to be blue in `scale_color_manual()` and we remove the legend that is generated with `legend.position = "none"` in `theme()`.

```
> p <- ggplot(df, aes(x, y)) +
+   geom_point(size = 2)
> p +
```

[6] Note that there are functions to reshape a data frame. In the next sections and chapters we will learn two of them. For this simple task we just do manually.

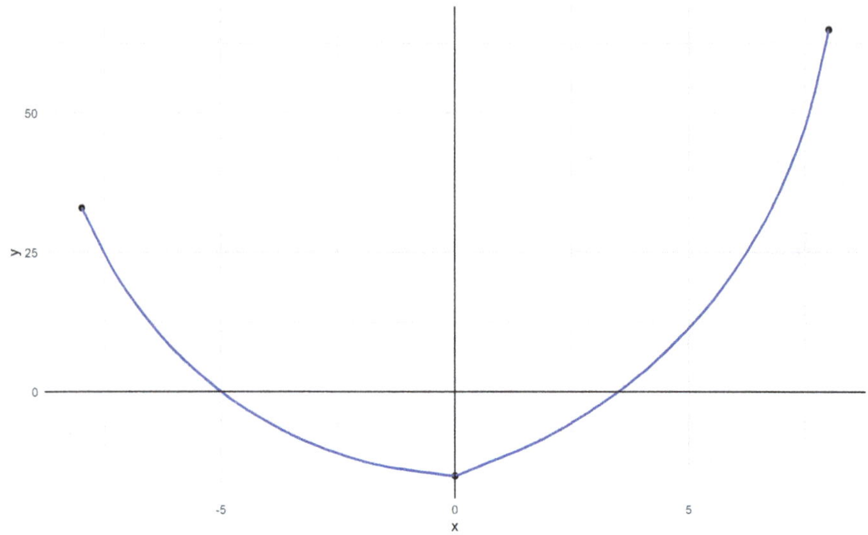

Fig. 3.12 Plot of quadratic function with three random points

```
+    geom_curve(aes(x = x3, xend = x1,
+                   y = y3, yend = y1,
+                   color = "curve"),
+               data = df2, size = 1,
+               curvature = 0.3) +
+    geom_curve(aes(x = x1, xend = x2,
+                   y = y1, yend = y2,
+                   color = "curve"),
+               data = df2, size = 1,
+               curvature = 0.3) +
+    geom_hline(yintercept = 0) +
+    geom_vline(xintercept = 0) +
+    theme_minimal() +
+    scale_color_manual(values = "blue") +
+    theme(legend.position = "none")
```

From Fig. 3.12 we figure out that the $y = x^2 + 2x - 15$ is a concave up function. This is due to the fact that the leading coefficient a is greater than 0 (more on this topic later).

3.3.1 Roots and Vertex

Could we pick up three better points? The answer is yes. We can pick up the roots of the function and the vertex.

We find the roots of the function when $y = 0$, that is we have to solve $x^2 + 2x - 15 = 0$ for x. Therefore, the roots are also called *x-intercept*. We can solve this equation in different ways. For example, in this case we can factor the quadratic equation.

We need two numbers that when multiplied give -15 and when added 2. We can go easily with 3 and 5. However, note the negative sign. The factor is $(x - 3)(x + 5)$. Therefore, $x_1 = -5$ and $x_2 = 3$.

Next method to solve a quadratic equation is to apply the quadratic formula:

$$x = \frac{-b \pm \sqrt{b^2 - 4ac}}{2a} \tag{3.6}$$

where

- a is the coefficient of the leading term; in this example 1.
- b is the coefficient of the second term; in this example 2.
- c is the constant; in this example -15.

If we substitute these values in the formula we obtain $x_1 = -5$ and $x_2 = 3$.

Let's compute the quadratic formula with **R**.

```
> x1 <- (-2 - sqrt(2^2 - (4*1*-15)))/(2*1)
> x1
[1] -5
> x2 <- (-2 + sqrt(2^2 - (4*1*-15)))/(2*1)
> x2
[1] 3
```

Next point to calculate is the vertex. The vertex formula is

$$x_v = -\frac{b}{2a} \tag{3.7}$$

```
> xv <- -2/(2*1)
> xv
[1] -1
```

To find the y coordinate of the vertex, y_v, plug x_v in the equation:

$$y_v\left(x_v = -\frac{b}{2a}\right) = a\left(-\frac{b}{2a}\right)^2 + b\left(-\frac{b}{2a}\right) + c$$

that is, $y_v(x_v = -1) = 1(-1)^2 + 2(-1) - 15 = -16$

In the next line of code, we plug the x value in the equation one by one to find the corresponding y value.

```
> x <- c(x1, x2, xv)
> y <- x^2 + 2*x - 15
> df <- data.frame(x = x, y = y)
> df
   x   y
1 -5   0
2  3   0
3 -1 -16
```

As expected, our three coordinates are $(-5, 0)$, $(3, 0)$ and the vertex $(-1, -16)$.

```
> df2 <- data.frame(x1 = x1, x2 = x2, x3 = xv,
+                   y1 = y[1], y2 = y[2], y3 = y[3])
> df2
  x1 x2 x3 y1 y2  y3
1 -5  3 -1  0  0 -16
```

Plot again the function.

```
> p <- ggplot(df, aes(x, y)) +
+   geom_point(size = 2)
> p +
+   geom_curve(aes(x = x1, xend = x3,
+                  y = y1, yend = y3,
+                  color = "curve"),
+              data = df2, size = 1,
+              curvature = 0.3) +
+   geom_curve(aes(x = x3, xend = x2,
+                  y = y3, yend = y2,
+                  color = "curve"),
+              data = df2, size = 1,
+              curvature = 0.3) +
+   geom_hline(yintercept = 0) +
+   geom_vline(xintercept = 0) +
+   theme_minimal() +
+   scale_color_manual(values = "blue") +
+   theme(legend.position = "none")
```

Figure 3.13 is a better representation than Fig. 3.12. We have the three main points. But it is not precise yet.

A forth point that may help to understand the graph of the quadratic function is the *y-intercept*, i.e. where the parabola crosses the y axis. To find it, we need to set $x = 0$.

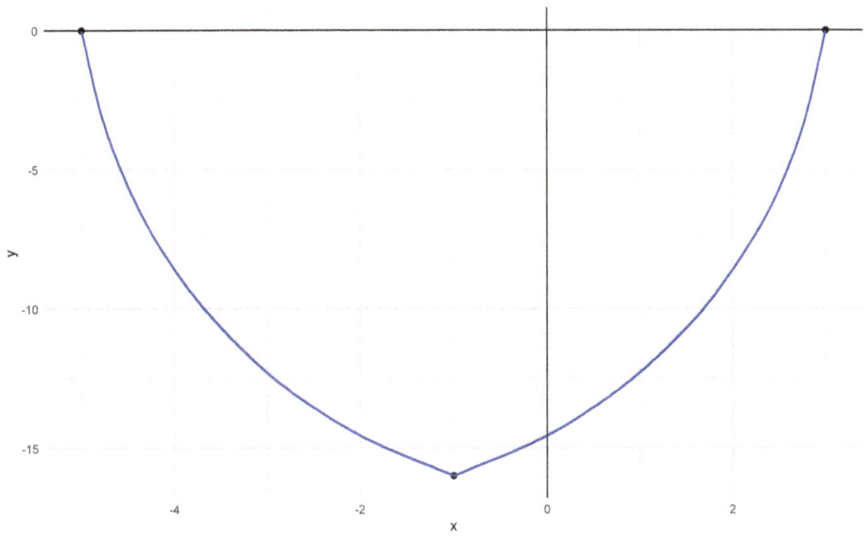

Fig. 3.13 Plot of quadratic function with roots points and vertex point

Therefore, logically, the more coordinates we add, the better the quality of the graph of the function we obtain. If we were to continue with a manual representation of the graph, the *y-intercept* would be the next point to compute. However, we skip this step because in **R** we can easily make a better representation using more coordinates.

3.3.2 The Graph of the Quadratic Function

We use the `lqc_fn()` to plot (3.5). Note that we pass to the function `b` that corresponds to a in (3.4), `c` that corresponds to b in (3.4), and `d` that corresponds to c in (3.4) (Fig. 3.14).

```
> df <- data.frame(x = seq(-10, 10, 0.1))
> ggplot(df) +
+   stat_function(aes(x), fun = lqc_fn,
+                 args = list(b = 1, c = 2,
+                             d = -15),
+                 color = "blue", size = 1) +
+   geom_hline(yintercept = 0) +
+   geom_vline(xintercept = 0) +
+   theme_minimal()
```

Now let's observe the behaviour of the function in detail.

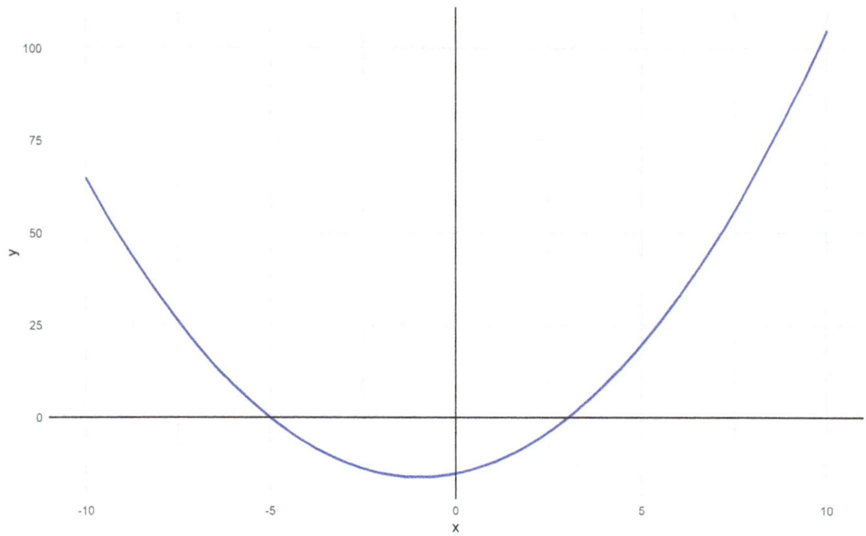

Fig. 3.14 Plot of $y = x^2 + 2x - 15$

The previous function (3.5) is concave up. If the concavity opens upwards or downwards it is determined by the coefficient of the leading term. If $a > 0$ the function is concave up. The vertex represents the minimum value of the quadratic function (*global minimum*). If $a < 0$ the function is concave down. In this case the vertex represents the maximum value of the quadratic function (*global maximum*).

The magnitude of the coefficient determines the width of the openness. The greater the magnitude of the coefficient the narrower is the width. If $0 < |a| < 1$ the width is wider.

Let's represent $y = x^2$ and $y = -x^2$ in **R**. We use different magnitudes for the leading coefficient as well.

We use the `ggarrange()` function to combine the two plots in the same figure (Fig. 3.15).

```
> # plot 1
> p1 <- ggplot(df) +
+   stat_function(aes(x), fun = lqc_fn,
+                 args = list(b = 1, c = 0),
+                 color = "blue", size = 1) +
+   stat_function(aes(x), fun = lqc_fn,
+                 args = list(b = 5, c = 0),
+                 color = "red", size = 1) +
+   stat_function(aes(x), fun = lqc_fn,
+                 args = list(b = 0.5, c = 0),
+                 color = "yellow", size = 1) +
+   geom_hline(yintercept = 0) +
```

```
+   geom_vline(xintercept = 0) +
+   theme_minimal() +
+   labs(caption = "a > 0") +
+   theme(plot.caption =
+           element_text(hjust = 0.5,
+                        size = 12))
> # plot 2
> p2 <- ggplot(df) +
+   stat_function(aes(x), fun = lqc_fn,
+                 args = list(b = -1, c = 0),
+                 color = "blue", size = 1) +
+   stat_function(aes(x), fun = lqc_fn,
+                 args = list(b = -5, c = 0),
+                 color = "red", size = 1) +
+   stat_function(aes(x), fun = lqc_fn,
+                 args = list(b = -0.5, c = 0),
+                 color = "yellow", size = 1) +
+   geom_hline(yintercept = 0) +
+   geom_vline(xintercept = 0) +
+   theme_minimal() +
+   labs(caption = "a < 0") +
+   theme(plot.caption =
+           element_text(hjust = 0.5,
+                        size = 12))
> ggarrange(p1, p2,
+           ncol = 2, nrow = 1)
```

If we add a constant to our function, it shifts the graph upwards by its value, if positive, and shifts the graph downwards by its value, if negative (Fig. 3.16).

```
> # plot 1
> p1 <- ggplot(df) +
+   stat_function(aes(x), fun = lqc_fn,
+                 args = list(b = 1, c = 0),
+                 color = "blue", size = 1) +
+   stat_function(aes(x), fun = lqc_fn,
+                 args = list(b = 1, c = 0,
+                             d = 3),
+                 color = "red", size = 1) +
+   stat_function(aes(x), fun = lqc_fn,
+                 args = list(b = 1, c = 0,
+                             d = -3),
+                 color = "yellow", size = 1) +
+   geom_hline(yintercept = 0) +
+   geom_vline(xintercept = 0) +
+   theme_minimal() +
```

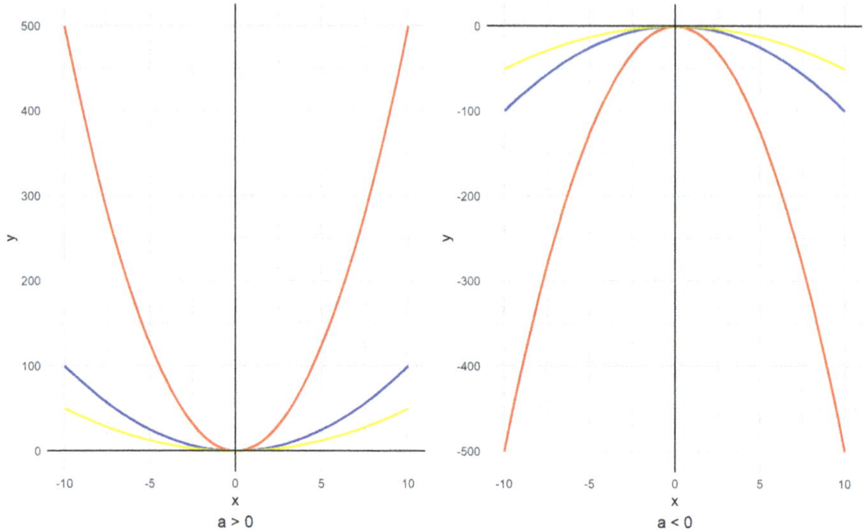

Fig. 3.15 Plot of $y = ax^2$ and $y = -ax^2$

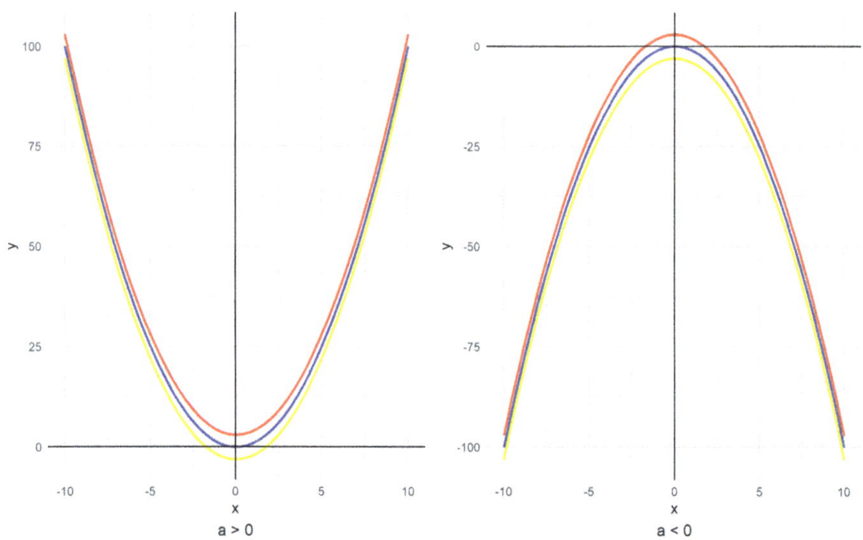

Fig. 3.16 Plot of $y = ax^2 + c$ and $y = -ax^2 + c$

```
+   labs(caption = "a > 0") +
+   theme(plot.caption =
+             element_text(hjust = 0.5, size = 12))
> # plot 2
> p2 <- ggplot(df) +
+   stat_function(aes(x), fun = lqc_fn,
```

```
+                    args = list(b = -1, c = 0),
+                    color = "blue", size = 1) +
+   stat_function(aes(x), fun = lqc_fn,
+                    args = list(b = -1, c = 0,
+                                d = +3),
+                    color = "red", size = 1) +
+   stat_function(aes(x), fun = lqc_fn,
+                    args = list(b = -1, c = 0,
+                                d = -3),
+                    color = "yellow", size = 1) +
+   geom_hline(yintercept = 0) +
+   geom_vline(xintercept = 0) +
+   theme_minimal() +
+   labs(caption = "a < 0") +
+   theme(plot.caption =
+           element_text(hjust = 0.5,
+                        size = 12))
> ggarrange(p1, p2,
+           ncol = 2, nrow = 1)
```

Now let's add the second term to x^2.

When $a > 0$, a negative value for b shifts the graph towards bottom-right and a positive value towards bottom-left. When $a < 0$, a negative value for b shifts the graph towards top-left and a positive value towards top-right (Fig. 3.17). In general, if we write the quadratic function as $y = (x + k)^2$, $k > 0$ shifts the graph leftwards, $k < 0$ shifts the graph rightwards.

```
> # plot 1
> p1 <- ggplot(df) +
+   stat_function(aes(x), fun = lqc_fn,
+                    args = list(b = 1, c = 0),
+                    color = "blue", size = 1) +
+   stat_function(aes(x), fun = lqc_fn,
+                    args = list(b = 1, c = 3),
+                    color = "red", size = 1) +
+   stat_function(aes(x), fun = lqc_fn,
+                    args = list(b = 1, c = -3),
+                    color = "yellow", size = 1) +
+   geom_hline(yintercept = 0) +
+   geom_vline(xintercept = 0) +
+   theme_minimal() +
+   labs(caption = "a > 0") +
+   theme(plot.caption = element_text(hjust = 0.5,
+                                     size = 12))
> # plot 2
> p2 <- ggplot(df) +
```

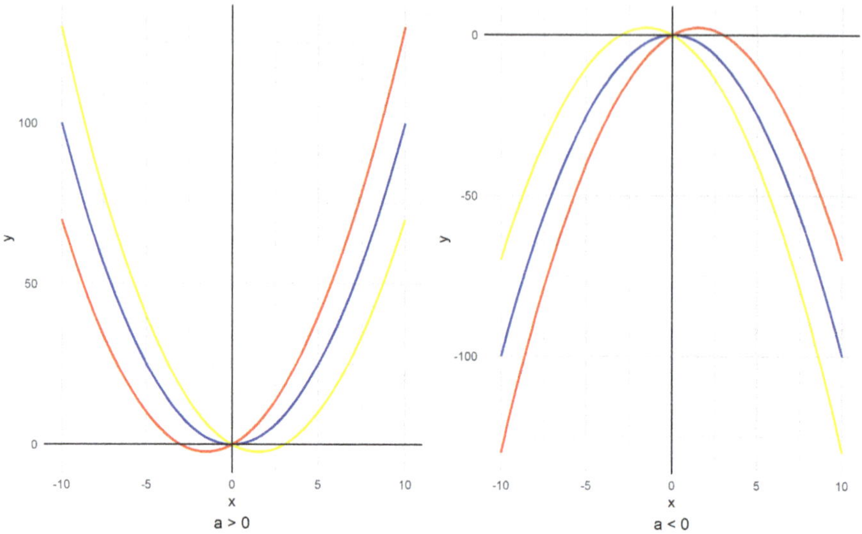

Fig. 3.17 Plot of $y = ax^2 + bx$ and $y = -ax^2 + bx$

```
+   stat_function(aes(x), fun = lqc_fn,
+                 args = list(b = -1, c = 0),
+                 color = "blue", size = 1) +
+   stat_function(aes(x), fun = lqc_fn,
+                 args = list(b = -1, c = 3),
+                 color = "red", size = 1) +
+   stat_function(aes(x), fun = lqc_fn,
+                 args = list(b = -1, c = -3),
+                 color = "yellow", size = 1) +
+   geom_hline(yintercept = 0) +
+   geom_vline(xintercept = 0) +
+   theme_minimal() +
+   labs(caption = "a < 0") +
+   theme(plot.caption =
+           element_text(hjust = 0.5, size = 12))
> ggarrange(p1, p2, ncol = 2, nrow = 1)
```

The following code reproduces Fig. 3.18

```
> # plot 1
> p1 <- ggplot(df) +
+   stat_function(aes(x), fun = lqc_fn,
+                 args = list(b = 1, c = 0),
+                 color = "blue", size = 1) +
+   stat_function(aes(x), fun = lqc_fn,
+                 args = list(b = 1, c = 3,
```

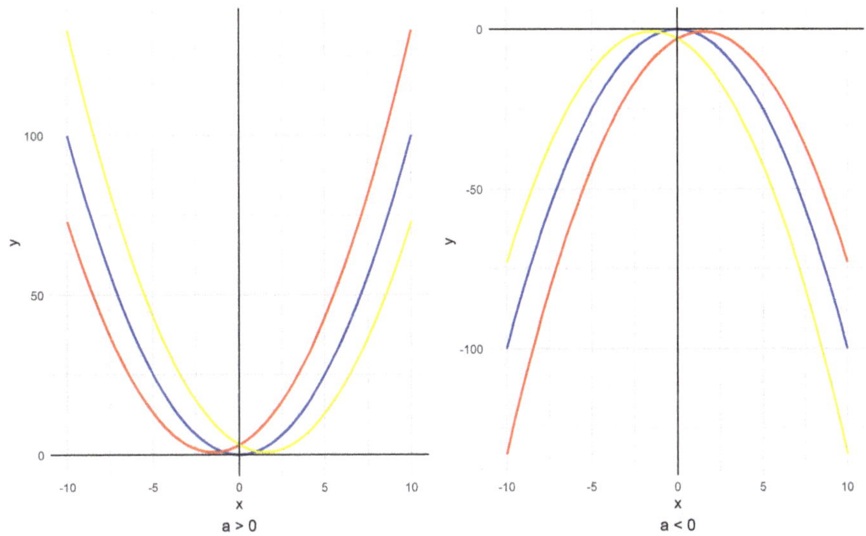

Fig. 3.18 Plot of $y = ax^2 + bx + c$ and $y = -ax^2 + bx + c$

```
+                                   d = 3),
+                        color = "red", size = 1) +
+     stat_function(aes(x), fun = lqc_fn,
+                        args = list(b = 1, c = -3,
+                                   d = 3),
+                        color = "yellow", size = 1) +
+     geom_hline(yintercept = 0) +
+     geom_vline(xintercept = 0) +
+     theme_minimal() +
+     labs(caption = "a > 0") +
+     theme(plot.caption = element_text(hjust = 0.5,
+                                         size = 12))
> # plot 2
> p2 <- ggplot(df) +
+     stat_function(aes(x), fun = lqc_fn,
+                        args = list(b = -1, c = 0),
+                        color = "blue", size = 1) +
+     stat_function(aes(x), fun = lqc_fn,
+                        args = list(b = -1, c = 3,
+                                 d = -3),
+                        color = "red", size = 1) +
+     stat_function(aes(x), fun = lqc_fn,
+                        args = list(b = -1, c = -3,
+                                 d = -3),
+                        color = "yellow", size = 1) +
```

```
+     geom_hline(yintercept = 0) +
+     geom_vline(xintercept = 0) +
+     theme_minimal() +
+     labs(caption = "a < 0") +
+     theme(plot.caption =
+              element_text(hjust = 0.5,
+                                   size = 12))
> ggarrange(p1, p2,
+              ncol = 2, nrow = 1)
```

3.3.3 Discriminant

For any quadratic function we could have:

1. two (distinct) real roots, that is the parabola crosses the x axis in two distinct points as in Fig. 3.14
2. one root (or *repeated* real roots), that is the parabola touches the x axis in only one point as in Fig. 3.18
3. no roots, or better no real roots. In this case the parabola does not cross the x axis.

How do we figure out how many roots the quadratic function has? We need to observe the so called *discriminant*, D , i.e. $b^2 - 4ac$, the number underneath the radical in the quadratic formula.

If

1. $D > 0$, we have two roots, i.e. two solutions to the quadratic equation
2. $D = 0$, we have one root, i.e. one solution to the quadratic equation
3. $D < 0$, we do not have any roots, or better any real roots but two imaginary roots.

Let's see an example with $D < 0$.
Let's analyse the following function, $y = x^2 + 5x + 10$.
First, we observe that it is concave up function given that $a > 0$.
Then, let's compute D.

```
> D <- 5^2 - (4*1*10)
> D
[1] -15
```

Given that $D < 0$, we know that the quadratic function has two imaginary roots. Let's compute them. We use again the quadratic formula but we need to tell **R** that it is working with a complex number. Otherwise, the square root of a negative number will not be computed. We use the `as.complex()` function to accomplish this task.

```
> a <- 1
> b <- 5
> c <- 10
> x1 <- (-b - sqrt(as.complex(b^2 - (4*a*c))))/(2*a)
> x1
[1] -2.5-1.936492i
> x2 <- (-b + sqrt(as.complex(b^2 - (4*a*c))))/(2*a)
> x2
[1] -2.5+1.936492i
```

Our imaginary roots are $x_1 = -2.5 - 1.936492i$ and $x_2 = -2.5 + 1.936492i$, where i is the square root of -1 (we will return to complex numbers and i in Sect. 9.2).

The manual graphical representation is more *complex* than the previous because the parabola does not cross the x axis.

To plot manually the graph, let's start from what we can compute, i.e. the *y-intercept* and the vertex.

```
> x_0 <- 0
> x_v <- -(b/(2*a))
> x_v
[1] -2.5
> y_int <- lqc_fn(x = x_0, b = 1, c = 5, d = 10)
> y_int
[1] 10
> y_v <- lqc_fn(x = x_v, b = 1, c = 5, d = 10)
> y_v
[1] 3.75
```

Next, we compute an arbitrary point symmetrically to the points we know.

```
> x_z <- 2 * x_v
> y_z <- y_int
```

Finally, we follow the same steps we did to plot the graph of the parabola manually.

```
> df <- data.frame(x = c(x_0, x_v, x_z),
+                  y = c(y_int, y_v, y_z))
> df
     x     y
1  0.0 10.00
2 -2.5  3.75
3 -5.0 10.00
> df2 <- data.frame(x1 = x_v, x2 = x_0, x3 = x_z,
+                   y1 = y_v, y2 = y_int, y3 = y_z)
```

```
> df2
    x1 x2 x3   y1 y2 y3
1 -2.5  0 -5 3.75 10 10
```

```
> p <- ggplot(df, aes(x, y)) +
+   geom_point(size = 2)
> p +
+   geom_curve(aes(x = x2, xend = x1,
+                  y = y2, yend = y1,
+                  color = "curve"),
+              data = df2, size = 1,
+              curvature = -0.2) +
+   geom_curve(aes(x = x1, xend = x3,
+                  y = y1, yend = y3,
+                  color = "curve"),
+              data = df2, size = 1,
+              curvature = -0.2) +
+   geom_hline(yintercept = 0) +
+   geom_vline(xintercept = 0) +
+   theme_minimal() +
+   scale_color_manual(values = "blue") +
+   theme(legend.position = "none")
```

Figure 3.19 shows an approximation of the plot of the function $y = x^2 + 5x + 10$. We will give another representation of this plot in Fig. 3.22.

Let's wrap up all we have done in a function, `quadratic_formula()`.

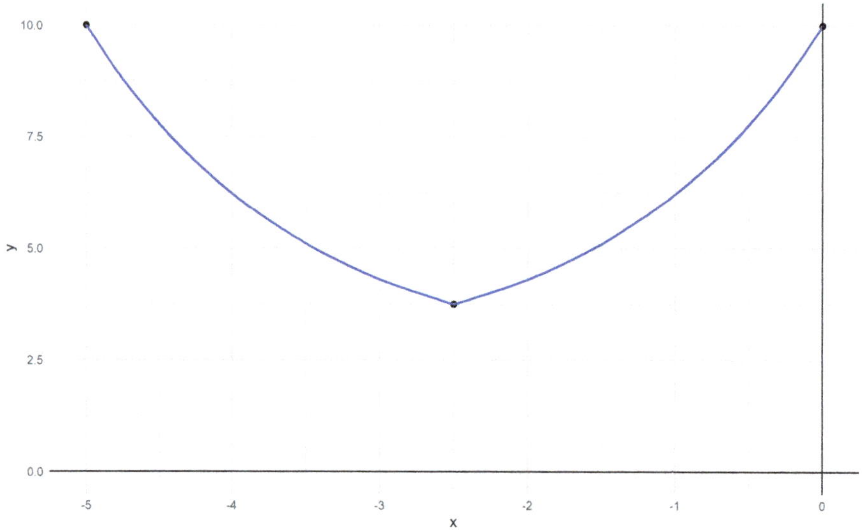

Fig. 3.19 Plot of a quadratic function with no real roots

```
> quadratic_formula <- function(a, b = 0, c = 0,
+                               graph = FALSE){
+   if(a == 0){
+     stop("a cannot be 0")
+   }
+
+   D <- b^2 - 4*a*c
+
+   if(D >= 0){
+
+     x1 <- (-b - sqrt(D)) / (2 * a)
+     x2 <- (-b + sqrt(D)) / (2 * a)
+
+   } else {
+
+     x1 <- (-b - sqrt(as.complex(D))) / (2 * a)
+     x2 <- (-b + sqrt(as.complex(D))) / (2 * a)
+
+   }
+
+   res <- data.frame("x1" = x1,
+                     "x2" = x2,
+                     row.names = "solutions")
+
+   if(graph == FALSE){
+     return(res)
+   } else{
+
+     require("ggplot2")
+     x <- seq(-10, 10, 0.1)
+     y = a*x^2 + b*x + c
+     df <- data.frame(x, y)
+     g <- ggplot(df, aes(x = x, y = y)) +
+       geom_line(color = "blue") +
+       geom_hline(yintercept = 0) +
+       geom_vline(xintercept = 0) +
+       theme_bw()
+
+     l <- list(res, g)
+
+     return(l)
+   }
+ }
```

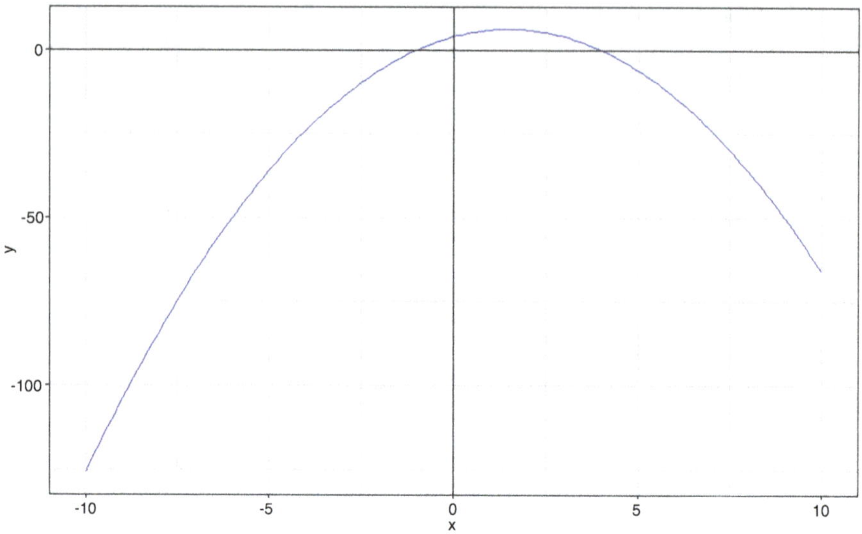

Fig. 3.20 Plot of $y = -x^2 + 3x + 4$

The function takes four inputs, the coefficients of the terms of the quadratic function, a, b and c, and an optional argument, `graph`, to plot the graph of the function.

Note that b, c and *graph* have default values.

First, if $a = 0$, the function stops and produces an error message: "a cannot be 0". This message will be delivered and the function will stop (`stop()` function).

If the function passes this step, it computes the discriminant, D. If `D >= 0`, it computes the real roots. If `D < 0` , it computes the imaginary roots. Note that if we set `graph = TRUE` the plot of the function will be plotted. Let's try the function.

The roots of $y = -x^2 + 3x + 4$ are

```
> quadratic_formula(-1, 3, 4)
          x1 x2
solutions  4 -1
```

Let's print out the graph of the function as well (Fig. 3.20):

```
> quadratic_formula(-1, 3, 4, graph = TRUE)
[[1]]
          x1 x2
solutions  4 -1

[[2]]
```

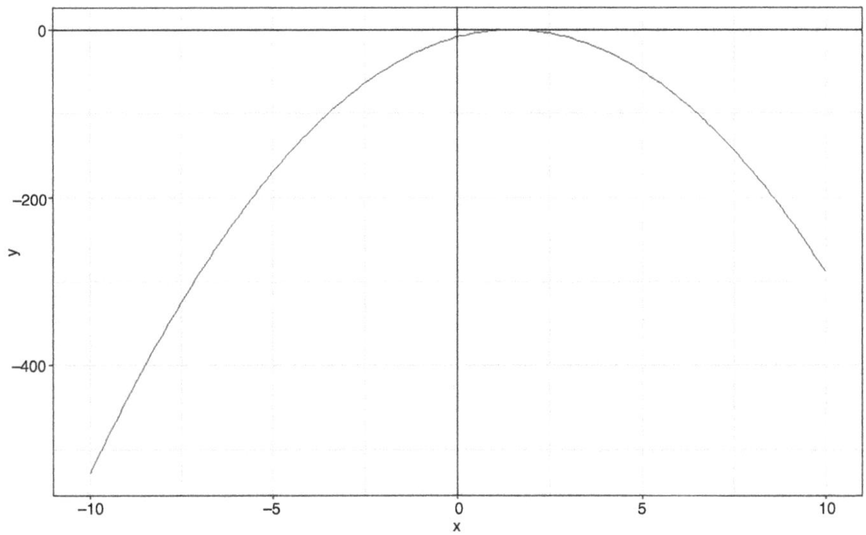

Fig. 3.21 Plot of a quadratic function with one root

Let's try the function with $a = 0$

```
> quadratic_formula(0, 2, 3)
Error in quadratic_formula(0, 2, 3) : a cannot be 0
```

Let's try $y = x^2$

```
> quadratic_formula(1)
           x1 x2
solutions  0  0
```

and $y = -4x^2 + 12x - 9$.

```
> quadratic_formula(-4, 12, -9, graph = TRUE)
[[1]]
           x1  x2
solutions 1.5 1.5

[[2]]
```

In the last two examples, we have the same root for x_1 and x_2. This is an example when $D = 0$. Figure 3.21 shows the graph of $y = -4x^2 + 12x - 9$.

Finally, let's compute again $y = x^2+5x+10$. We already know that this function has imaginary roots. Figure 3.22 shows the graph of this function. Compare with Fig. 3.19.

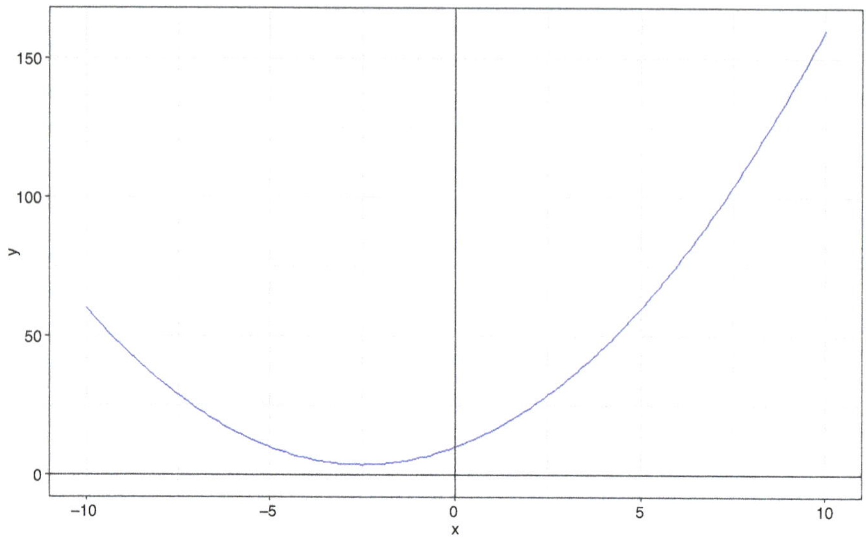

Fig. 3.22 Plot of a quadratic function with no real roots (2)

```
> quadratic_formula(1, 5, 10, graph = TRUE)
[[1]]
                         x1             x2
solutions -2.5-1.936492i -2.5+1.936492i

[[2]]
```

3.3.4 *Applications in Economics*

3.3.4.1 The Cost Function

For the following quadratic cost function:

$$C(x) = 0.01x^2 + x + 10$$

let's plot the total costs, the fixed costs, the variable costs, and the average costs (Fig. 3.23).

Let's first compute the fixed costs, `FC`, the variable costs, `TVC`, and the total costs as the sum of `FC` and `TVC`. Let's store them in `df`.

```
> x <- seq(0, 50, 1)
> FC <- 10
> VC <- 1
> VC2 <- 0.01
```

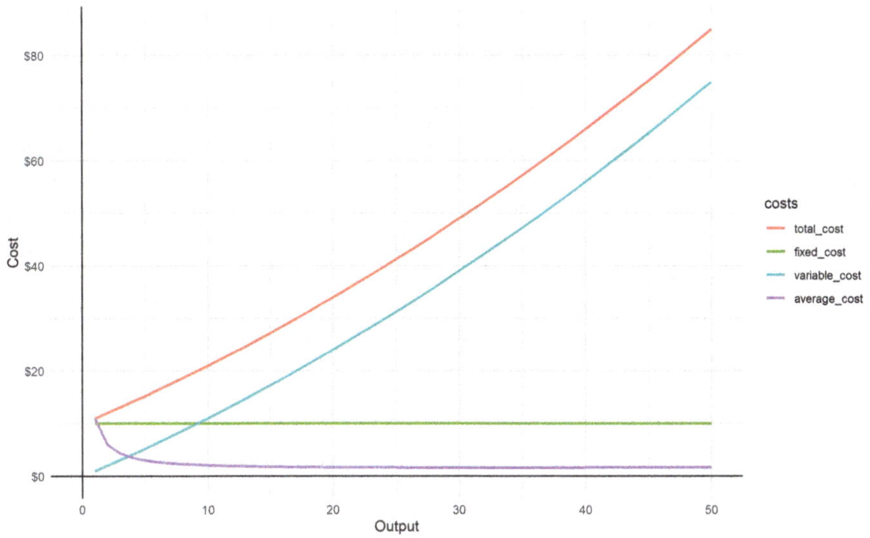

Fig. 3.23 Quadratic cost function

```
> TVC <- VC2*x^2 + VC*x
> TC <- FC + TVC
> df <- data.frame(output = x,
+                  total_cost = TC,
+                  fixed_cost = FC,
+                  variable_cost = TVC)
> head(df)
  output total_cost fixed_cost variable_cost
1      0      10.00         10          0.00
2      1      11.01         10          1.01
3      2      12.04         10          2.04
4      3      13.09         10          3.09
5      4      14.16         10          4.16
6      5      15.25         10          5.25
```

Now, let's compute the average cost (AC) as $AC = TC/x$.

```
> df$average_cost <- df$total_cost / df$output
> head(df)
  output total_cost fixed_cost variable_cost average_cost
1      0      10.00         10          0.00          Inf
2      1      11.01         10          1.01    11.010000
3      2      12.04         10          2.04     6.020000
4      3      13.09         10          3.09     4.363333
5      4      14.16         10          4.16     3.540000
6      5      15.25         10          5.25     3.050000
```

Note that the first value for `average_cost` is not defined because we divided by zero. Thus, let's remove the first row from the dataset to not plot it.

```
> df <- df[-1, ]
```

Next, let's reshape the dataset from wide to long with the `melt()` function from the `data.table` package. This will make easier to map the data in the `ggplot()` function. In the `melt()` function, the argument `id.vars =` is a vector of id variables, i.e., the variables that identify individual rows of data. It can be integer (variable position) or string (variable name). The argument `measure.vars =` is a vector of measured variables. It can be integer (variable position) or string (variable name). We can rename the new variables with `variable.name =` and `value.name =` .

```
> df_l <- melt(setDT(df), id.vars = "output",
+                measure.vars = c("total_cost",
+                                 "fixed_cost",
+                                 "variable_cost",
+                                 "average_cost"),
+                variable.name = "costs",
+                value.name = "USD")
> head(df_l)
   output        costs   USD
1:      1 total_cost 11.01
2:      2 total_cost 12.04
3:      3 total_cost 13.09
4:      4 total_cost 14.16
5:      5 total_cost 15.25
6:      6 total_cost 16.36
> tail(df_l)
   output          costs      USD
1:     45 average_cost 1.672222
2:     46 average_cost 1.677391
3:     47 average_cost 1.682766
4:     48 average_cost 1.688333
5:     49 average_cost 1.694082
6:     50 average_cost 1.700000
```

Finally, let's plot it with `ggplot()`. We use `group =` and `color =` to map the data in `ggplot()`.

```
> ggplot(df_l, aes(x = output,
+                  y = USD,
+                  group = costs,
+                  color = costs)) +
+   geom_line(size = 1) +
+   geom_hline(yintercept = 0) +
+   geom_vline(xintercept = 0) +
```

```
+     theme_minimal() +
+     xlab("Output") +
+     ylab("Cost") +
+     scale_y_continuous(labels = scales::dollar)
```

3.4 Cubic Function

The general form of a cubic function is

$$y = f(x) = ax^3 + bx^2 + cx + d \tag{3.8}$$

where only x^3 is necessary to have a cubic function, i.e. $a \neq 0$. If $a > 0$, the graph starts from negative values of y; if $a < 0$, the graph starts from the positive values of y. A particularity of cubic functions compared with linear and quadratic functions is the *inflection point*. The inflection point is the point where the curvature of the function changes from concave down to concave up, and vice versa (Fig. 3.8).

Before plotting a cubic function $y = x^3$ (Fig. 3.24), let's explain the code for the `lqc_fn()` function. As you may have noted, in the body of the function we wrote a cubic function where `a`, `b`, `c`, and `d` correspond to a, b, c, and d in (3.8). However, we assigned default values for these coefficients in the function: zero for `a`, `b`, and `d`, and 1 for `c`. That is, by default, the `lqc_fn()` function represents the linear function $y = x$.

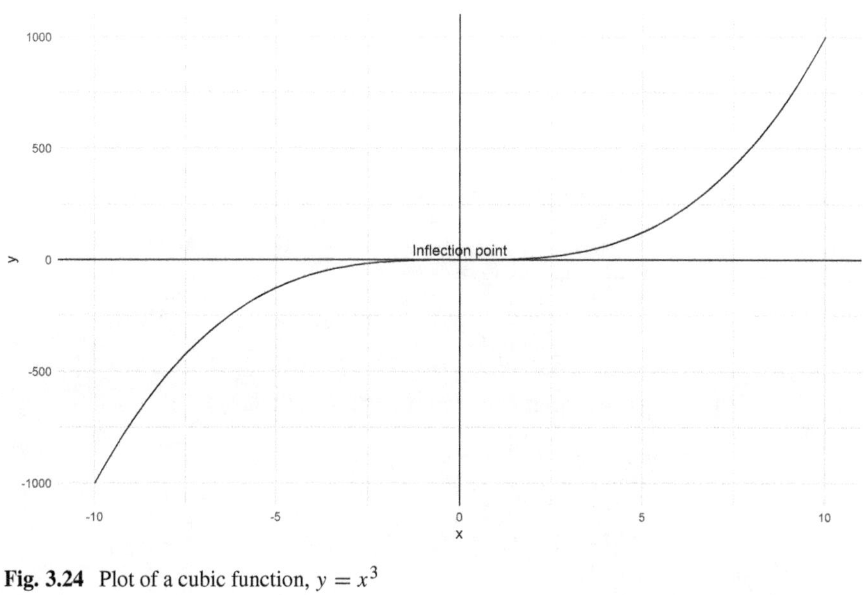

Fig. 3.24 Plot of a cubic function, $y = x^3$

```
> df <- data.frame(x = seq(-10, 10, 0.1))
> ggplot(df) +
+   stat_function(aes(x), fun = lqc_fn,
+                 args = list(a = 1, c = 0)) +
+   geom_hline(yintercept = 0) +
+   geom_vline(xintercept = 0) +
+   theme_minimal() +
+   annotate("text", x = 0, y = 45,
+            label = "Inflection point")
```

The graph is shifted upwards (downwards) if d is positive (negative). To figure out what shifts the graph rightwards or leftwards, we have to reduce the cubic equation to the following form: $(x + k)^3$. If k is positive (negative) the graph shifts leftwards (rightwards). The following code produces Fig. 3.25 where six plots are represented. We use a different approach compared with the approaches we used for Fig. 2.3 and for Fig. 3.1. First, we add variables with the titles we want to add to the plot. We strictly follow the same order of the variables. Then ,we reshape the dataset long with the `melt()` function from the `data.table` package. We use a list in `measure.vars =` to reshape multiple columns. Finally, we use `facet_wrap()` in `ggplot2` to display the individual plots. We introduce `coord_cartesian()` to zoom in/out the plot according to the values in `xlim =` and `ylim =`.

```
> y_1 <- lqc_fn(df$x, a = -1, c = 0)
> y_2 <- lqc_fn(df$x, a = 1, b = -4, c = 0)
> y_3 <- lqc_fn(df$x, a = 1, b = -4, c = 1)
> y_4 <- lqc_fn(df$x, a = 1, b = -4, c = 1, d = 6)
> y_5 <- lqc_fn(df$x, a = -1, b = -4, c = 1, d = 6)
> y_6 <- lqc_fn(df$x, a = 3, b = -4, c = 1, d = 6)
> df <- cbind(df, y_1, y_2, y_3,
+             y_4, y_5, y_6)
> df$ty_1 <- "y = -x^3"
> df$ty_2 <- "y = x^3 - 4x^2"
> df$ty_3 <- "y = x^3 - 4x^2 + x"
> df$ty_4 <- "y = x^3 - 4x^2 + x + 6"
> df$ty_5 <- "y = -x^3 - 4x^2 + x + 6"
> df$ty_6 <- "y = 3x^3 - 4x^2 + x + 6"
> df_l <- melt(setDT(df), id.vars = "x",
+             measure.vars = list(c("y_1", "y_2", "y_3",
+                                   "y_4", "y_5", "y_6"),
+                                 c("ty_1", "ty_2", "ty_3",
+                                   "ty_4", "ty_5", "ty_6")),
+             value.name = c("values", "titles"))
> ggplot() +
+   geom_line(data = df_l, aes(x = x, y = values)) +
+   facet_wrap(vars(titles)) +
+   geom_hline(yintercept = 0) +
+   geom_vline(xintercept = 0) +
+   theme_minimal() +
+   xlab("x") + ylab("y") +
+   coord_cartesian(xlim = c(-5, 5),
+                   ylim = c(-15, 15))
```

3.4.1 How to Solve Cubic Equations

There are different ways to solve a cubic equations. First, if it possible, try to factor out the equation. For example,

$$x^3 - 4x^2 + x + 6 = 0$$

can be factorised as

$$(x + 1)(x - 2)(x - 3) = 0$$

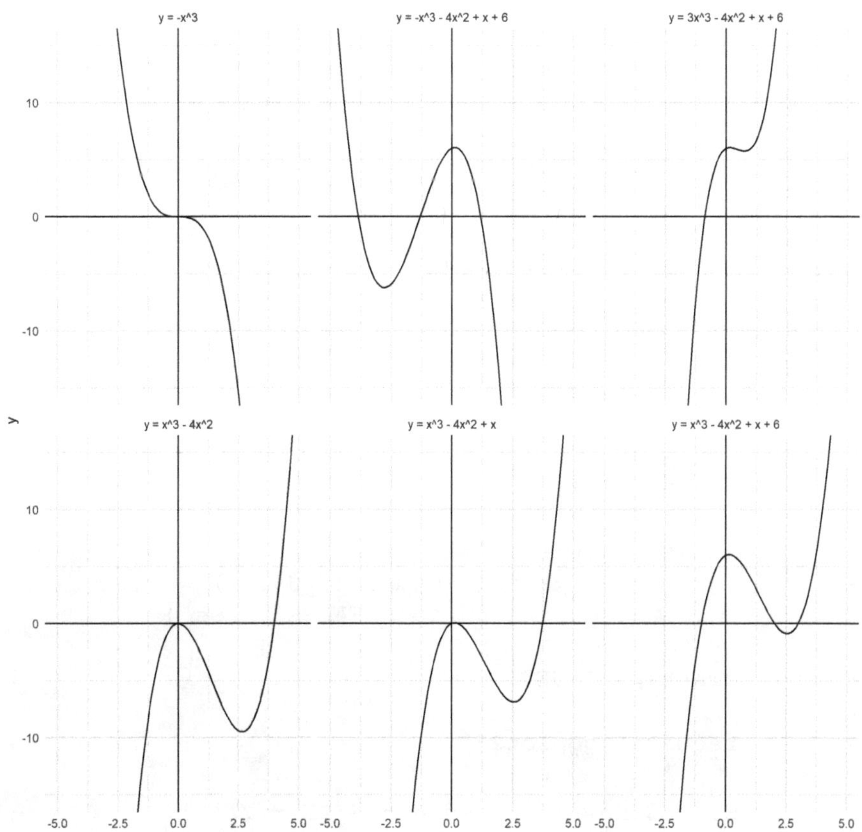

Fig. 3.25 Plot of cubic functions

This means that the equation has three solutions, i.e. three roots: $x_1 = -1, x_2 = 2$ and $x_3 = 3$. The corresponding function is represented in the second row third column in Fig. 3.25.

Second, it is possible to use a table of values. When $y = 0$, we find the roots, i.e. the solutions of the equations. Based on this fact, we code a function, `cub_eq_solver()`, that finds the real roots of a cubic function. Because some results may be approximation, the study of the graph may help understand the solutions of the cubic equation. Therefore, for this function we set the default value `graph = TRUE`.

The difference with `quadratic_formula()` is that we need to extract the values of x when y is 0. We use more points (from -10 to 10 spaced by 0.0001)[7] stored in x. We use the `zapsmall()` function to round the y close to 0 if not. If the number of rows of the object that stores the results, `res`, is greater than 6 we use a loop to increase the digits in the `zapsmall()` (from 2 to 16) such that values get close to 0.

```
> cub_eq_solver <- function(a, b, c, d,
+                              graph = TRUE){
+    if(a == 0){
+       stop("a cannot be 0")
+       }
+
+    x <- seq(-10, 10, 0.0001)
+    y <- a*x^3 + b*x^2 + c*x + d
+    df <- data.frame(x, y)
+
+    res <- df[zapsmall(df$y, 1) == 0, ,
+               drop = FALSE]
+
+    for(i in 2:16){
+
+       ifelse(nrow(res) > 6,
+              res <- df[zapsmall(df$y, i) == 0, ,
+                        drop = FALSE], res)}
+
+    if(graph == TRUE){
+
+       require("ggplot2")
+
+       g <- ggplot(df, aes(x = x, y = y)) +
+          geom_line() +
+          geom_hline(yintercept = 0) +
```

[7] The large number of data points slowdowns the function.

```
+           geom_vline(xintercept = 0) +
+           theme_minimal() +
+           coord_cartesian(xlim = c(-5, 5),
+                           ylim = c(-30, 30))
+
+       l <- list(g, res)
+
+       return(l)
+
+       } else{
+
+           return(res)
+
+       }
+ }
```

Let's try with to solve some cubic equations. For example, $x^3 - 4x^2 + x + 6 = 0$ (Fig. 3.26).

```
> cub_eq_solver(1, -4, 1, 6)
[[1]]

[[2]]
        x y
90001  -1 0
120001  2 0
130001  3 0
```

For example, $x^3 - 6x^2 + 11x - 6 = 0$.

```
cub_eq_solver(1, -6, 11, -6, graph = FALSE)
       x y
110001 1 0
120001 2 0
130001 3 0
```

And $3x^3 + 7x^2 + 12x + 3 = 0$ (Fig. 3.27).

```
> cub_eq_solver(3, 7, 12, 3)
[[1]]

[[2]]
            x             y
97060 -0.2941 -5.070086e-05
```

Other examples:

```
> cub_eq_solver(3, 0, 0, 5, graph = FALSE)
```

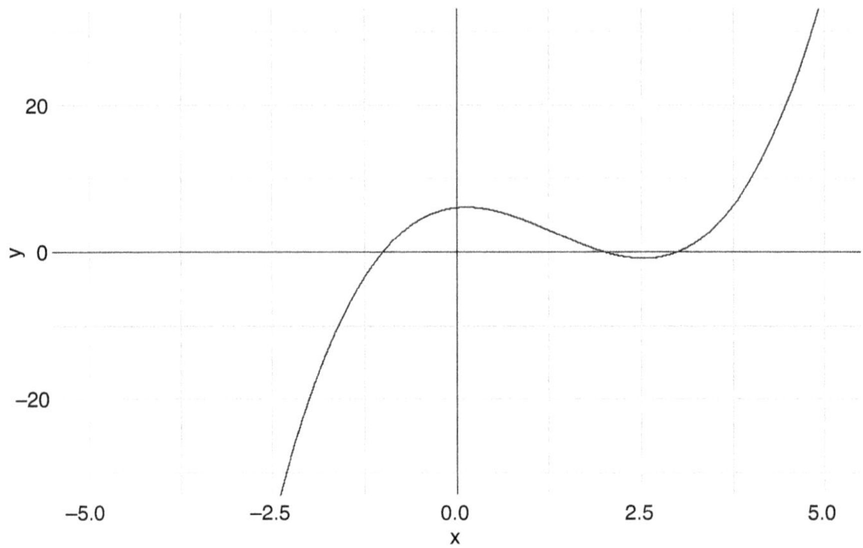

Fig. 3.26 Plot of $y = x^3 - 4x^2 + x + 6$

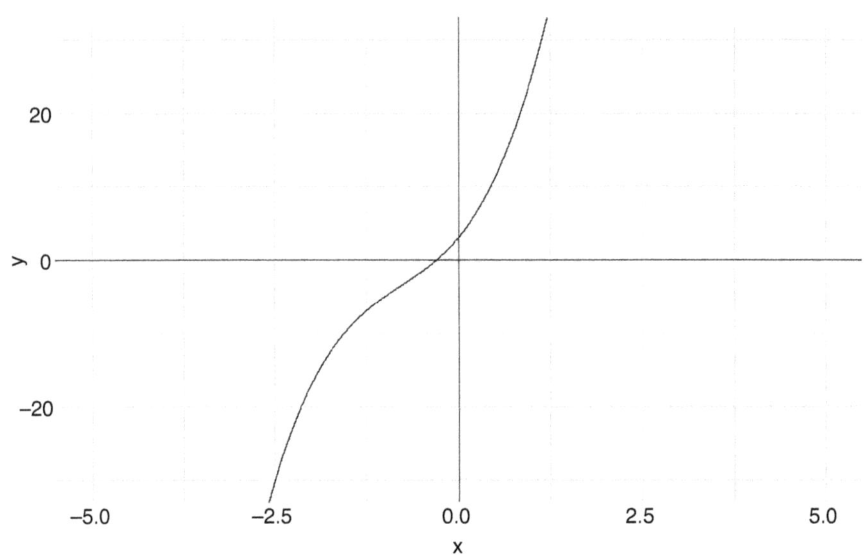

Fig. 3.27 Plot of $y = 3x^3 + 7x^2 + 12x + 3$

```
            x          y
88145 -1.1856 0.00039347
> cub_eq_solver(1, -6, 1, 11, graph = FALSE)
            x              y
```

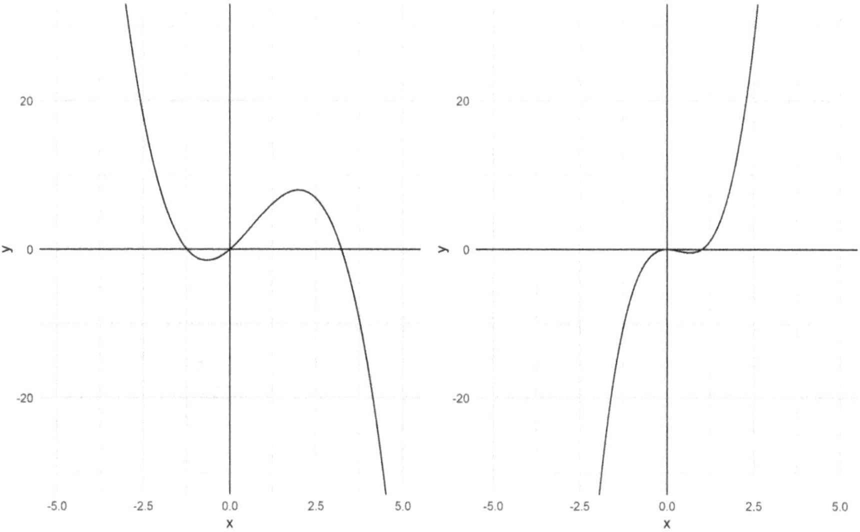

Fig. 3.28 Plot of $y = -x^3 + 2x^2 + 4x$ and $y = 3x^3 - 3x^2$

```
88293   -1.1708 -0.0003364469
117255   1.7254 -0.0001062569
154455   5.4454  0.0001894087
```

The function may provide more approximate results as in the following cases. The plot of the two graphs can help us understand better the solutions. This time we store the output of the function in an object. Then, we select only the plot with the double square brackets, `[[ ]]`, operator. Then, we plot the two graphs side by side using `ggarrange()` (Fig. 3.28).

```
> cube1 <- cub_eq_solver(-1, 2, 4, 0)
> cube1[[2]]
             x            y
87640   -1.2361  0.0001770219
87641   -1.2360 -0.0003757440
100000 -0.0001 -0.0003999800
100001  0.0000  0.0000000000
100002  0.0001  0.0004000200
132362  3.2361 -0.0004634419
> pcube1 <- cube1[[1]]
> cube2 <- cub_eq_solver(3, -3, 0, 0)
> cube2[[2]]
            x           y
100000 -1e-04 -3.0003e-08
100001  0e+00  0.0000e+00
100002  1e-04 -2.9997e-08
```

```
110001  1e+00  0.0000e+00
> pcube2 <- cube2[[1]]
> ggarrange(pcube1, pcube2,
+           ncol = 2, nrow = 1)
```

Finally, other two methods to solve cubic equations are:

- "cubic formula"
- synthetic division

However, these two methods are beyond the scope of this textbook.

In this Section and in Sect. 3.3 we built two simple functions to solve cubic and quadratic equations, respectively.[8] However, we can use better algorithms developed by the **R** Community. For example, we can use the `polynomial()` function from the `polynom` package to construct the polynomial and the `solve()` function to solve them. Note that `polynomial()` takes the coefficients in increasing order and `solve()` returns imaginary roots as well. For example,

```
> p <- polynomial(c(6, 1, -4, 1))
> p
6 + x - 4*x^2 + x^3
> pz <- solve(p)
> pz
[1] -1  2  3
> poly.calc(pz)
6 + x - 4*x^2 + x^3
> p <- polynomial(c(-6, 11, -6, 1))
> p
-6 + 11*x - 6*x^2 + x^3
> pz <- solve(p)
> pz
[1] 1 2 3
> p <- polynomial(c(3, 12, 7, 3))
> p
3 + 12*x + 7*x^2 + 3*x^3
> pz <- solve(p)
> pz
[1] -1.0196196-1.53644i -1.0196196+1.53644i -0.2940941
    +0.00000i
```

Following an example of a polynomial of second degree

```
> p <- polynomial(c(4, 3, -1))
> p
4 + 3*x - x^2
```

[8] In Sect. 4.3 we will write another function for this task.

```
> pz <- solve(p)
> pz
[1] -1  4
```

3.4.2 Applications in Economics

3.4.2.1 The Cost Function

In this example, we plot a traditional cubic cost function. The particularity of a cubic cost function is that total cost first increases at a decreasing rate up to the inflection point and afterwards increases at an increasing rate. This means that we cannot use any cubic function to represent the cost function because a cubic function with a downward-slope segment would imply that a firm would have decreasing costs with a large production while we expect that a larger production entails a higher total cost. Consequently, we need to set the following restrictions on the coefficients of a cubic cost function:

$$a, c, d > 0 \quad b < 0 \quad b^2 < 3ac \tag{3.9}$$

The only intuitive restriction is $d > 0$ since d represents the fixed cost, i.e. costs that the firm bears even though its production (x) is 0. Therefore, d must be a positive amount. The other restrictions require calculus to be shown. We will take them as given for the moment and we will postpone their discussion in Chap. 4.

We will graph the following cubic cost function where `VC3`, `VC2`, `VC1` and `FC` represent, respectively, the coefficients a, b, c, d.

$$TC = VC3 \cdot x^3 - VC2 \cdot x^2 + VC1 \cdot x + FC$$

Let's choose the following coefficients $a = 0.1, b = -0.25, c = 3, d = 100$ and test for the restriction $b^2 < 3ac$.

```
> x <- seq(0, 50, 1)
> FC <- 100
> VC3 <- 0.01
> VC2 <- -0.25
> VC1 <- 3
> # test restriction
> VC2^2 < 3*VC3*VC1
[1] TRUE
```

These coefficients satisfy the coefficient restrictions of (3.9).

We store output, total costs, fixed costs and variables costs in `df`.

```
> TVC <- VC3*x^3 + VC2*x^2 + VC1*x
> TC <- FC + TVC
> df <- data.frame(output = x,
+                  total_cost = TC,
+                  fixed_cost = FC,
+                  variable_cost = TVC)
> head(df)
  output total_cost fixed_cost variable_cost
1      0     100.00        100          0.00
2      1     102.76        100          2.76
3      2     105.08        100          5.08
4      3     107.02        100          7.02
5      4     108.64        100          8.64
6      5     110.00        100         10.00
```

Let's reshape it long but let's keep only output and total_cost.

```
> df_l <- melt(setDT(df), id.vars = "output",
+              measure.vars = c("total_cost"),
+              variable.name = "cost",
+              value.name = "USD")
> head(df_l)
   output       cost    USD
1:      0 total_cost 100.00
2:      1 total_cost 102.76
3:      2 total_cost 105.08
4:      3 total_cost 107.02
5:      4 total_cost 108.64
6:      5 total_cost 110.00
> tail(df_l)
   output       cost    USD
1:     45 total_cost 640.00
2:     46 total_cost 682.36
3:     47 total_cost 726.98
4:     48 total_cost 773.92
5:     49 total_cost 823.24
6:     50 total_cost 875.00
```

Figure 3.29 shows the shape of this cubic function.

```
> ggplot(df_l, aes(x = output,
+                  y = USD)) +
+   geom_line() +
+   geom_hline(yintercept = 0) +
+   geom_vline(xintercept = 0) +
+   theme_minimal() +
+   xlab("Output") +
```

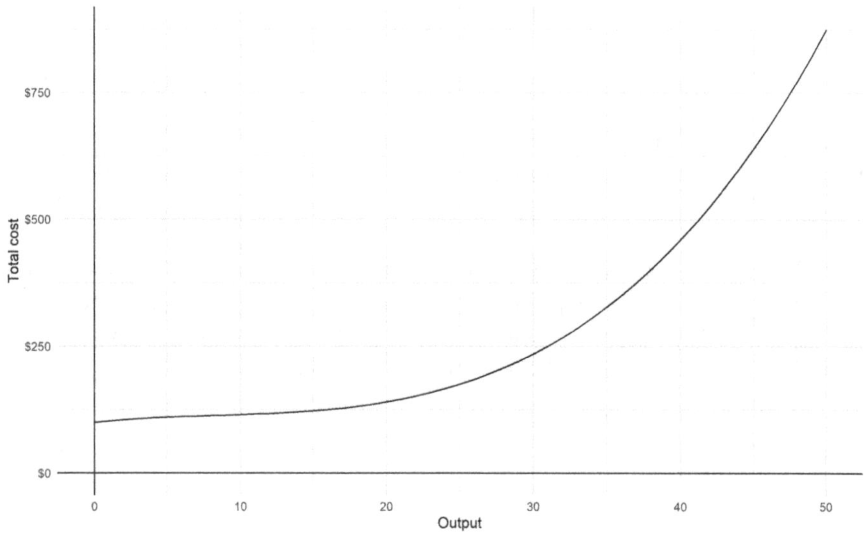

Fig. 3.29 Cubic cost function

```
+    ylab("Total cost") +
+    scale_y_continuous(labels = scales::dollar) +
+    theme(legend.position = "none")
```

3.5 Polynomials of Degree Greater Than Three

Linear functions, quadratic functions, and cubic functions are examples of a broad class of functions that are known as polynomials. A polynomial of *degree n* is defined as follows:

$$y = f(x) = a_n x^n + a_{n-1} x^{n-1} + ... + a_1 x + a_0, \quad a_n \neq 0 \tag{3.10}$$

Let's write a function, `pol_fn()`, based on the notation of (3.10).

```
> pol_fn <- function(x, A, degree){
+
+    a <- paste0("a", degree:0)
+    X <- paste0("x^", degree:0)
+    aX <- paste(a, X, sep = "*")
+    pol <- paste(aX, collapse = "+")
+    res <- eval(parse(text = pol), envir = A)
+    return(res)
+
+ }
```

First note that this function does not take any default values. How does it work? I think that showing the intermediate outputs is clearer than words. I will show the intermediate steps up to `pol` since the last step evaluates the polynomial stored in `pol` where the coefficients are stored in `A` that in our case is created as a list. However, keep in mind that now `degree` does not exist in our environment. This means that if we run the intermediate steps as they are we will get an error, "object not found", because `degree` is required in `a` and `X` but it does not exist. On the other hand, when running the `pol_fn()` function, `x`, `A`, and `degree` will take the values of they respective argument in the `pol_fn()` function. This means that to show the intermediate steps up to `pol` one option is to create `degree` in our environment. The other option is to replace `degree` with the value we would input in the function for `degree`. We will follow this last option.

```
> a <- paste0("a", 4:0)
> a
[1] "a4" "a3" "a2" "a1" "a0"
> X <- paste0("x^", 4:0)
> X
[1] "x^4" "x^3" "x^2" "x^1" "x^0"
> aX <- paste(a, X, sep = "*")
> aX
[1] "a4*x^4" "a3*x^3" "a2*x^2" "a1*x^1" "a0*x^0"
> pol <- paste(aX, collapse = "+")
> pol
[1] "a4*x^4+a3*x^3+a2*x^2+a1*x^1+a0*x^0"
```

As you can see, `pol` just replicates the notation in (3.10) for a polynomial of degree 4.

Next we plot a polynomial of degree four, $y = x^4 + 2x^3 - 3x^2 - x + 5$ (Fig. 3.30), and a polynomial of degree five $x^5 - 3x^4 + 2x^2 - x + 2$ (Fig. 3.31)

```
> df <- data.frame(x = seq(-10, 10, 0.1))
> A4 <- list(a0 = 5, a1 = -1, a2 = -3,
+            a3 = 2, a4 = 1)
> ggplot(df) +
+   stat_function(aes(x), fun = pol_fn,
+                 args = list(A = A4, degree = 4)) +
+   geom_hline(yintercept = 0) +
+   geom_vline(xintercept = 0) +
+   ggtitle("Polynomial of degree 4") +
+   coord_cartesian(xlim = c(-5, 5),
+                   ylim = c(-10, 10)) +
+   theme_minimal() +
+   annotate("text", x = c(-2.4, 1, 0),
+            y = c(-5.5, 3, 5.5),
+            label = c("absolute minimum",
```

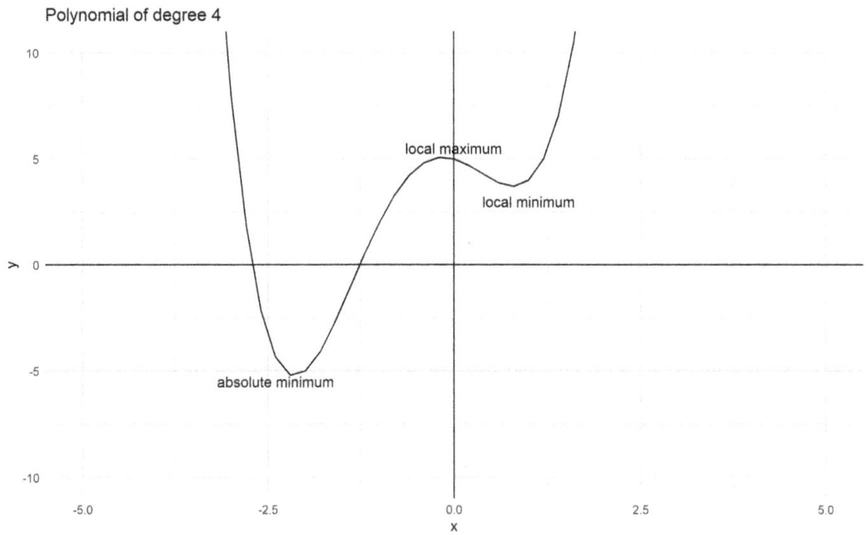

Fig. 3.30 Polynomial of degree four

```
+                               "local minimum",
+                               "local maximum"))
> A5 <- list(a0 = 5, a1 = -1, a2 = 2,
+              a3 = 0, a4 = -3, a5 = 1)
> ggplot(df) +
+   stat_function(aes(x), fun = pol_fn,
+                   args = list(A = A5, degree = 5)) +
+   geom_hline(yintercept = 0) +
+   geom_vline(xintercept = 0) +
+   ggtitle("Polynomial of degree 5") +
+   coord_equal(xlim = c(-10, 10),
+                 ylim = c(-10, 10)) +
+   theme_minimal() +
+   annotate("text", x = c(-0.8, 2.2, 2.5),
+              y = c(6.5, 5.25, -6.5),
+              label = c("local maximum",
+                         "inflection point",
+                         "local minimum"))
```

We will return to maximum, minimum and inflection points of a function in Sect. 4.9. Table 3.2 sums up the number of roots a polynomial of degree n can have.

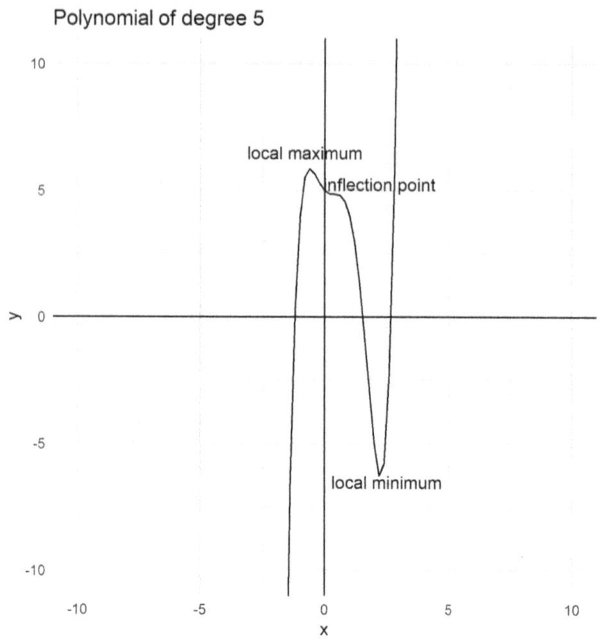

Fig. 3.31 Polynomial of degree five

Table 3.2 Number of roots of a polynomial of degree n

Degree	Min. num. of roots	Max num. of roots
1	1	1
2	0	2
3	1	3
4	0	4
5	1	5
6	0	6

3.6 Logarithmic and Exponential Functions

3.6.1 What is a Logarithm?

Let's warm up for the logarithms. Let's compute very approximately without the use of a calculator, the value of $\log_7(323)$. My answer is 2.something (later we will be more precise). Did you get the answer? Very good. You did not? Let's see why.

I think that difficulties related to the logarithms depend on the fact that not for everyone is clear what the result of a logarithm is. For example, for a division such as $8764.6 \div 227.02$ we could swiftly approximate its result because since primary school we have got what the division operator returns. I think the same happens with the exponents. Everyone knows that $13^{12} = 13 \times 13 \times 13 \ldots$ repeated 12 times. This can also be related to the language where "exponential" is often and clearly used in conversation rather than "logarithmic".

But let's go back to the question: What is the approximate result of $\log_7(323)$? Let's try: $7 \times 7 = 49$. $49 \times 7 = 343$. Since 343 is greater than 323 our approximate result should be 2.something. Why 2? Because we repeated 7 twice. Does not it ring a bell?

3.6.2 Logarithms and Exponents

A logarithm is the power to which a number must be raised in order to get some other number. Or, in other terms, the logarithm is the inverse function to exponentiation.

Let's start by comparing logarithm and exponent.

First, let's compute $2^3 = 2 \times 2 \times 2 = 8$

What would the logarithm base 2 of 8 be? $\log_2(8) = 2 \times 2 \times 2 = 3$. Because we repeated 2 three times. Or, in other words, we need to raise 2 to the power of 3 to get 8.

Clearly, logarithmic and exponential functions are related. Table 3.3 compares the formula for exponents and logarithms; Table 3.4 reports the rules of exponents and logarithms; and Table 3.5 reports the properties of exponents and logarithms.

Note how the rules in Table 3.4 depend on the relations between the two formulas as in Table 3.3. Pay particular attention at $b^{b^y} = b^x$ and $b^{\log_b(x)} = x$. We will discuss the other rules in Sect. 3.6.3. Following, let's observe the properties of exponents and logarithms. First, note that the base must be the same.

The properties of the exponents:

- The product rule says that the product of two exponents is equal to the sum of the exponents.
- The quotient rule says the division of two exponents is equal to the difference of the exponents.

Table 3.3 Formula of exponent and logarithm

Exponent	Logarithm
$b^y = x$	$\log_b(x) = y$

Note: b is the base, y is the exponent, and x is the argument

Table 3.4 Rules of exponents and logarithms and their relations

Exponent	Logarithm
$b^0 = 1$	$\log_b(1) = 0$
$b^1 = b$	$\log_b(b) = 1$
$b^x = b^x$	$\log_b(b^x) = x$
$b^{b^y} = b^x$	$b^{\log_b(x)} = x$
$b^{-y} = \frac{1}{b^y}$	$\log_b\left(\frac{1}{x}\right) = -\log_b(x)$

Table 3.5 Properties of exponent and logarithm

	Exponent	Logarithm
Product	$b^m b^n = b^{m+n}$	$\log_b(MN) = \log_b(M) + \log_b(N)$
Quotient	$\frac{b^m}{b^n} = b^{m-n}$	$\log_b\left(\frac{M}{N}\right) = \log_b(M) - \log_b(N)$
Power	$(b^m)^n = b^{mn}$	$\log_b(M^n) = n\log_b(M)$

- The power rule says that an exponent raise to a power is equal to the multiplication of the exponents.

  Following the properties of the logarithms:

- The product rule says that the logarithm of a product is equal to the sum of the logarithms.
- The quotient rule says that the quotient of a logarithm is equal to the difference of the logarithms.
- The power rule says that the logarithm with the argument raised to a power is equal to that power multiplied by the logarithm.

Let's see now how to compute the logarithms and the exponents in **R**. We compute logarithms in **R** using the `log()` function. The general form is `log(argument, base)`. In our example, the argument is 8 and the base is 2.

```
> log(8, 2)
[1] 3
```

We can compute the exponent using the caret symbol, ^.

```
> 2^3
[1] 8
```

Let's check the properties of exponents and logarithms in **R**.

```
> # properties of exponents
> ## 1) b^m * b^n = b^(m+n)
> 3^5 * 3^2
[1] 2187
> 3^(5+2)
[1] 2187
> ## 2) b^m / b^n = b^(m-n)
> 3^5 / 3^2
[1] 27
> 3^(5-2)
[1] 27
> ## 3) (b^m)^n = b^(m*n)
> (3^5)^2
[1] 59049
> 3^(5*2)
[1] 59049
```

```
> # properties of logarithm
> ## 1) log(M * N) = log(M) + log(N)
> log(3 * 4)
[1] 2.484907
> log(3) + log(4)
[1] 2.484907
> ## 2) log(M/N) = log(M) - log(N)
> log(4/3)
[1] 0.2876821
> log(4) - log(3)
[1] 0.2876821
> ## 3) log(M^n) = n * log(M)
> log(4^3)
[1] 4.158883
> 3 * log(4)
[1] 4.158883
```

After this brief review of the rules and properties of logarithms and exponents, let's try to be more precise about $\log_7(323)$. In particular, let's compute the upper bound and lower bound. We know that $\log_7(323) = y$, that is $7^y = 323$. Let's raise both sides by the power of 3: $(7^y)^3 = 323^3$. This implies that $323^3 = 33698267 < 40353607 = 7^9$. Why 7^9? Because 7^8 is less than 323^3 and consequently it is not an upper bound. Therefore, $7^{3y} < 40353607 = 7^9$. Consequently, $3y < 9$ and $y < 3$. We have found the upper bound. Now, following the same steps for the lower bound but raising both sides by the power of two, $(7^y)^2 = 323^2$, we find that $323^2 = 104329 > 16807 = 7^5$. Why 7^5? Because 7^6 is greater than 323^2 and consequently it is not a lower bound. Therefore, $7^{2y} > 16807 = 7^5$. Consequently, $2y > 5$, and $y > \frac{5}{2}$. That is $y > 2.5$ (or in mixed number form $y > 2\frac{1}{2}$). Finally, $2.5 < y < 3$ should be bounds to $\log_7(323) = y$. In fact, the $\log_7(323) = 2.969126$.

```
> 323^3 < 7^9
[1] TRUE
> 323^3
[1] 33698267
> 7^9
[1] 40353607
> 323^2 > 7^5
[1] TRUE
> 323^2
[1] 104329
> 7^5
[1] 16807
> log(323, 7)
[1] 2.969126
```

3.6.3 The Natural Logarithm

In Economics, when we deal with logarithms we usually deal with a particular kind: the natural logarithm. The natural logarithm of a number x is defined as the base e logarithm of x, i.e. $\log_e(x)$. However, you probably will encounter the natural logarithm as expressed just with log or as ln. In this book, we adopt the notation log for the natural logarithm unless another basis is explicitly indicated. This choice is taken to comply with the notation in **R** where the natural logarithm is computed with the function `log()`.

In Sect. 3.6.2, we learnt the general formula of the logarithm function in **R** and how to compute a logarithm in **R**. Here, we add that `log()` computes the natural logarithm by default. In other words, if we do not explicitly include a base the default base will be e. In fact, the logarithm function usage is defined as `log(x, base = exp(1))`, i.e. `base = exp(1)` is the default value.

Therefore, with

```
> log(8)
[1] 2.079442
```

we compute the natural log of 8.

Finally, note that the rules and properties of the logarithms in Tables 3.3, 3.4, and 3.5 apply to natural log as well. In particular, we often encounter and make use of the rule with natural logarithm $e^{log(x)} = x$ (refer to Sect. 3.6.6.1 for details about e).

3.6.4 The Natural Logarithmic Function

Taking into account the notation as defined in Sect. 3.6.3, the natural logarithmic function is

$$y = f(x) = \log(x) \tag{3.11}$$

Our `log_fn()` function makes use of the `log()` function. With `...` we control for the option `base` in the `log()` function. For example

```
> log(8)
[1] 2.079442
> log_fn(8)
[1] 2.079442
> log(8, 2)
[1] 3
> log_fn(8, base = 2)
[1] 3
```

Let's plot (3.11). Let's store the results in the `df` data frame (we created it in Sect. 3.5). When we try to compute our y, we get a warning message: `NaNs` produced. `NaN` stands for not a number.

```
> df$y <- log_fn(df$x)
Warning message:
In log(a * x^(c) + d, ...) : NaNs produced
```

Let's check it by looking at the first six entries with the `head()` function and at the last six entries with the `tail()` function.

```
> df <- data.frame(x, y)
> head(df)
      x   y
1 -10.0 NaN
2  -9.9 NaN
3  -9.8 NaN
4  -9.7 NaN
5  -9.6 NaN
6  -9.5 NaN
> tail(df)
       x        y
196  9.5 2.251292
197  9.6 2.261763
198  9.7 2.272126
199  9.8 2.282382
200  9.9 2.292535
201 10.0 2.302585
```

It seems that the warning message is related to the negative values of `x`. Let's go on and plot it by using `ggplot()`. We add the number `1`, where the function crosses the x axis, with `annotate()`.

```
> ggplot(df, aes(x = x, y = y)) +
+   geom_line() +
+   geom_hline(yintercept = 0) +
+   geom_vline(xintercept = 0) +
+   theme_minimal() +
+   annotate("text", x = 1, y = 0.1, label = "1")
Warning message:
Removed 100 rows containing missing values (geom_path).
```

`ggplot()` returns a warning message as well: 100 rows have been removed because containing missing values.

From Fig. 3.32, as expected, the missing values are those for $x \leq 0$. This happens because the log function, $y = \log(x)$, is defined only for $x > 0$.

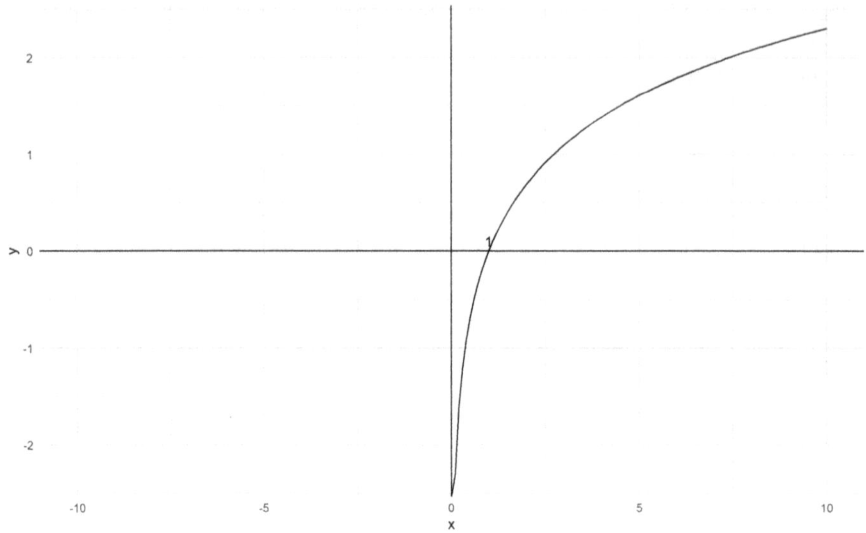

Fig. 3.32 Plot of the logarithm function

But why is the log not defined for negative values of x? The relation with the exponent can help us to get it. Refer to the formulas in Table 3.3. To what number could we raise a base to get a negative x? None. Therefore, $\log(-x)$ is undefined.

But you could think: what about if y is negative? Well, let's review again the property of the exponent

$$b^{-y} = \frac{1}{b^y}$$

Let's try with some numbers.

```
> 2^(-3)
[1] 0.125
> 1/2^3
[1] 0.125
```

We can state that for values of x between 0 and 1, $0 < x < 1$, y is negative.

```
> log(0.125, 2)
[1] -3
```

Note that this is also evident from Fig. 3.32.

But what about $\log(0)$? $\log(0)$ is undefined. Once again let's refer to Table 3.3 and the relation between exponent and logarithm. We can never get zero by raising a number to the power of another number. We can only approach it using an infinitely large and negative power (refer to Sect. 3.6.5.1.4). This is also evident from Fig. 3.32.

From Fig. 3.32, we can infer other facts. For example, when $x = 1$, $y = 0$. Once again let's refer to Table 3.3 and the relation between exponent and logarithm: $b^0 = 1 \Rightarrow \log_b(1) = 0$.

We can recap the following facts about the log function:

- $y = \log(x)$ is defined only for $x > 0$
- $\log(x) < 0$ for $0 < x < 1$
- $\log(1) = 0$
- $\log(x) > 0$ for $x > 1$

Figure 3.33 shows the graphs of the logarithmic function. As we could expect, if we add a negative sign in front of the log the graph flips over the x axis. If we add a constant, the graph shift upwards. If we multiply the function by a constant y grows faster. Finally, if we subtract a constant from its argument the graph is shifted towards right. Note what happens in the example $\log(x - 1)$ (left-bottom panel).

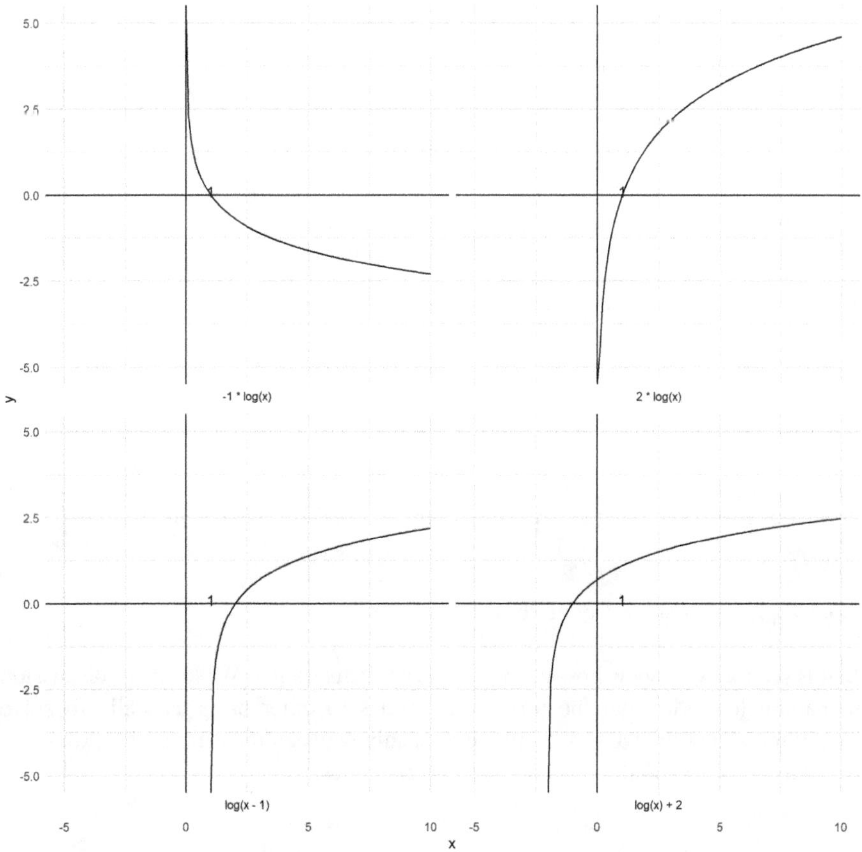

Fig. 3.33 Plots of the logarithm function

The function asymptotically reaches the line $x = 1$ instead of the line $x = 0$, i.e. the y axis.

```
> x <- seq(-10, 10, by = 0.1)
> y1 <- log_fn(x, b = -1)
Warning message:
In log(a * x^(c) + d, ...) : NaNs produced
> y2 <- log_fn(x, d = 2)
Warning message:
In log(a * x^(c) + d, ...) : NaNs produced
> y3 <- log_fn(x, b = 2)
Warning message:
In log(a * x^(c) + d, ...) : NaNs produced
> y4 <- log_fn(x, d= -1)
Warning message:
In log(a * x^(c) + d, ...) : NaNs produced
> df <- data.frame(x, y1, y2, y3, y4)
> df$ty1 <- "-1 * log(x)"
> df$ty2 <- "log(x) + 2"
> df$ty3 <- "2 * log(x)"
> df$ty4 <- "log(x - 1)"
> df_l <- melt(setDT(df), id.vars = "x",
+              measure.vars = list(c("y1", "y2", "y3", "y4"),
+                                  c("ty1", "ty2", "ty3", "ty4")),
+              value.name = c("values", "titles"))
> ggplot() +
+   geom_line(data = df_l, aes(x = x, y = values)) +
+   facet_wrap(vars(titles), nrow = 2, ncol = 2,
+              strip.position = "bottom") +
+   geom_hline(yintercept = 0) +
+   geom_vline(xintercept = 0) +
+   theme_minimal() +
+   xlab("x") + ylab("y") +
+   annotate("text", x = 1, y = 0.1,
+            label = "1") +
+   coord_cartesian(xlim = c(-5, 10),
+                   ylim = c(-5, 5))
Warning message:
Removed 100 row(s) containing missing values (geom_path).
```

3.6.4.1 How to Solve Logarithmic Equation

In this section we review how to solve logarithmic equation. We limit our discussion to natural logarithm but the procedure applies to other basis as well. To solve logarithmic equation we rely on the relationship between logarithms and exponents (refer to Tables 3.4 and 3.5). Let's see two examples.

Example 3.6.1

$$\log(2x - 1) = 7$$

$$e^{\log(2x-1)} = e^7$$

$$2x - 1 = e^7$$

$$2x = e^7 + 1$$

$$x = \frac{e^7 + 1}{2} = 548.8166$$

Example 3.6.2

$$\log(4x) - \log(2) = 5$$

$$\log\left(\frac{4x}{2}\right) = 5$$

$$\log(2x) = 5$$

$$e^{\log(2x)} = e^5$$

$$2x = e^5$$

$$x = \frac{e^5}{2} = 74.20658$$

3.6.5 Applications in Economics

3.6.5.1 Logarithms and Growth

Before diving into the topic of logarithms and growth, let's review some key concepts.

3.6.5.1.1 Ratios, Proportions and Percentages

What is a ratio? The ratio is used to compare the quantities of two different categories. For example, the ratio of female students to male students in a class. Here, female students and male students are the two different categories.

What is a proportion? Proportion is used to find out the quantity of one category over the total. For example, the proportion of female students out of total students in the class.

Let's make an example. Let's suppose our class is made up of 20 students, 12 female students and 8 male students.

The ratio of female students to male students is $12 \div 8 = 1.5$.

```
> 12/8
[1] 1.5
```

The proportion of female students out of total students is $12 \div 20 = 0.6$.

```
> 12/20
[1] 0.6
```

How do we get the percentage? We multiply the proportion by 100, $0.6 * 100 = 60\%$. Therefore, the female students represent the 60% of the total students in the class.

```
> paste0(0.6*100, "%")
[1] "60%"
```

Note that we used the `paste0()` function to paste the result of the multiplication with the percentage symbol, %.[9]

Therefore, a proportion is the decimal form of a percentage. In the following example we convert the percentage to decimal form. For example, suppose there is a 20% import duty on imports of machinery parts. The amount of import duty collected by a state on a \$1,200,000 import in machinery parts is \$240,000, i.e. $0.2 \cdot 1200000 = 240000$

```
> 0.2*1200000
[1] 240000
```

3.6.5.1.2 Measuring the Change

In Economics, we are interested in measuring the change in various quantities. For example, how the gross domestic product (GDP) of a country or the sales of a firm changed with respect to the previous year.

Let's define with x_0 and x_1 the sales of firm XYZ in 2019 and 2020, respectively. Assume that firm XYZ sold goods for \$120,000 in 2019 and for \$150,000 in 2020. What is the relative change (or proportionate change) in its sales?

We use the following formula:

$$\frac{x_1 - x_0}{x_0} = \frac{\Delta x}{x_0} = \frac{x_1}{x_0} - 1 \tag{3.12}$$

[9] Note that if you store this result, `"60%"`, you cannot use for further operations because its class would be a `character` and not a percentage number.

Let's plug our numbers.

$$\frac{150000 - 120000}{120000} = 0.25$$

The relative change is 0.25. Usually, we express this value in percentage form. We just multiply the relative change by 100. Therefore, (3.12) becomes

$$\%\Delta x = 100 \cdot \left(\frac{\Delta x}{x_0}\right) \tag{3.13}$$

where $\%\Delta x$ is read as "the percentage change in x".

Thus, we can say that the sales of firm XYZ increased by 25% in 2020 with respect to 2019.

Let's implement these calculations in **R**. First, we assign the sales values for 2019 and 2020 to two objects, `sales2019` and `sales2020`. Then, we store the relative change in an object `delta_sales`. Finally, we multiply `delta_sales` by 100 and use the `paste0()` function to paste % to the number.

```
> sales2019 <- 120000
> sales2020 <- 150000
> delta_sales <- (sales2020 - sales2019)/
+   sales2019
> delta_sales
[1] 0.25
> paste0(delta_sales*100, "%")
[1] "25%"
```

In the exercise in Sect. 3.9.2 you are asked to write a function that computes the percentage change.

3.6.5.1.3 Percentage Point Change and Percentage Change

Often, in Economics we measure the change between two percentages. We can report the results in two ways.

For example, in 2019, the Japanese VAT was increased to 10 from 8%. How much did the VAT increase?

We can say that the VAT increased by 2% points, $10 - 8 = 2$.

But we could apply (3.13) to percentage as well. In this case, we report the result as a 25% change, $100 * \left(\frac{10-8}{8}\right) = 25\%$.

The former is the percentage point change, i.e., the change in the percentages. The latter is the percentage change, i.e., the change relative to the initial value. They are two different ways to express the same concept.

3.6.5.1.4 Approximations and Logarithms

In Sect. 3.6.3, when we discussed the log(0), we said that we can only approach 0 using an infinitely large and negative power.

In addition, we can state that

$$\log(1 + x) \approx x, \quad \text{for} \quad x \approx 0$$

The quality of the approximation deteriorates as x gets larger.

For example,

$$\log(1 + 0.0001) = 0.00009995$$

$$\log(1 + 0.0002) = 0.00019998$$

$$\log(1 + 0.005) = 0.0049875$$

Furthermore, the difference in logs can be used to approximate proportionate changes. Let x_0 and x_1 be positive values. Then,

$$\log(x_1) - \log(x_0) \approx \frac{x_1 - x_0}{x_0} \tag{3.14}$$

for small changes in x.

If we write $\log(x_1) - \log(x_0) = \Delta log(x)$ and multiply by 100, then

$$100 \cdot \Delta log(x) \approx \%\Delta x \tag{3.15}$$

for small changes in x.

We can show that the difference in logs approximates proportionate changes using calculus (a topic of Chap. 4). Let $y = f(x)$, for some function f. Then, for small changes in x,

$$\Delta y = \frac{dy}{dx} \cdot \Delta x$$

where $\frac{dy}{dx}$ is the derivative of the function f.

If $y = \log(x)$ then $\frac{dy}{dx} = \frac{1}{x}$. With $\frac{dy}{dx}$ evaluated at x_0

$$\Delta y \approx \frac{1}{x_0} \cdot \Delta x$$

or

$$\Delta \log(x) = \frac{\Delta x}{x_0} \tag{3.16}$$

For example, let $x_0 = 20.5$ and $x_1 = 21$. In this case the percentage change in x is:

$$100 \cdot \frac{x_1 - x_0}{x_0} = 100 \cdot \frac{21 - 20.5}{20.5} = 2.439024$$

```
> 100 * ((21 - 20.5)/ 20.5)
[1] 2.439024
```

while the logarithm change in x is:

$$100 \cdot \left[\log(x_1) - \log(x_0)\right] = 100 \cdot \left[\log(21) - \log(20.5)\right] = 2.409755$$

```
> 100 * (log(21) - log(20.5))
[1] 2.409755
```

Now let's try with $x_1 = 22$.
In this case the percentage change in x is:

$$100 \cdot \frac{x_1 - x_0}{x_0} = 100 \cdot \frac{22 - 20.5}{20.5} = 7.317073$$

```
> 100 * ((22 - 20.5)/ 20.5)
[1] 7.317073
```

while the logarithm change in x is:

$$100 \cdot \left[\log(x_1) - \log(x_0)\right] = 100 \cdot \left[\log(22) - \log(20.5)\right] = 7.061757$$

```
> 100 * (log(22) - log(20.5))
[1] 7.061757
```

3.6.5.2 Logarithms and Geometric Mean

Let's start from the review of the concepts of the arithmetic mean (or simply mean or average) and the geometric mean.

The arithmetic mean is the sum of a set of numbers divided by how many numbers constitute the set: $\frac{x_1+x_2+\ldots+x_n}{n}$. For example,

$$\frac{2+8}{2} = 5$$

$$\frac{2+3+7}{3} = 4$$

The geometric mean, on the other hand, is the *nth* root of the product of the numbers in the set: $\sqrt[nth]{x_1 \cdot x_2 \cdot \ldots \cdot x_n}$. For example,

$$\sqrt{2 \cdot 8} = 4$$

$$\sqrt[3]{2 \cdot 3 \cdot 7} = 3.476$$

Note that

$$\sqrt[nth]{x_1 \cdot x_2 \cdot \ldots \cdot x_n} = \left(\Pi_{i=1}^{n} x_i\right)^{\frac{1}{n}} \tag{3.17}$$

Using the logarithm properties, Eq. 3.17 can be rewritten as

$$\exp\left(\frac{1}{n}\sum_{i=1}^{n} \log x_i\right) \tag{3.18}$$

An example of the geometric mean applied through logarithm is the computation of the real effective exchange rate (REER).

The REER is an average of the bilateral real exchange rates (RERs) between the country and each of its trading partners, weighted by the respective trade shares of each partner

$$\text{REER}_i = \Pi_{j=1}^{n} RER_j^{W_j} = \sum_{j=1}^{n} W_j \times RER_j$$

where

- country $j = 1, 2, \ldots N$ are country i's trading partners
- exchange rates are in natural logarithms (in this case we do not "undo" the logarithm (i.e. take the exponential))
- $W_j = \frac{X_j + M_j}{\sum_{j=1}^{n} X_j + \sum_{j=1}^{n} M_j}$

3.6.5.3 Logarithms and Econometrics

3.6.5.3.1 How to Deal with Log(0)

Often, it happens that we have to transform our variable in logarithm but some of its values are 0. For example, we may work with tariffs (τ) in log as independent variable. If for some products a zero-tariff applies, in that case its log would be undefined (Sect. 3.6.3). Therefore, 1 is added to the tariff, $\log(1+\tau)$, so that when the tariff is zero we have $\log(1+0)=0$. Another example is when we have zero-trade flows as dependent variable in the so called *gravity model* that is traditionally estimated in logarithms. The empirical literature proposed different solutions to work with this case. For example, adding a small constant, 1 (dollar), to the value of trade before taking logarithms. However, this solution has been criticized when working with OLS (refer to UNCTAD and WTO 2012, p. 112 for a concise and clear discussion).

3.6.5.3.2 Scale Variables in Charts and Graphs

We can use logarithms to scale variables in charts and graphs. For example, when we have one or few observations much larger than the rest of the data. Another example could be in time series analysis. We may change the scale of the y axis to logarithm to better identify the shape of a trend. In addition, with time series data, we take logarithms to stabilise the variance.

3.6.5.3.3 Logarithms and Regression

We may be in the situation to interpret the coefficients of an OLS model that are in logarithms. Let's see the following three cases: (1) the dependent variable and the independent variable are in log; (2) the dependent variable only is in log; (3) the independent variable only is in log.

Model (1) is known as constant elasticity model, and it takes the following form:

$$\log(y)=\beta_0+\beta_1\log(x)+u$$

In this model, β_1 implies that a 100% change in x generates a $100\cdot\beta_1$ percentage change in y.

Example 3.6.3 We have the following model where salary of CEO is the dependent variable and sales of firm is the independent variable

$$\log(salary)=\beta_0+\beta_1\log(sales)+u$$

where β_1 is the elasticity of salary with respect to sales.

If the estimated model is the following:

$$\log(\hat{salary}) = 3.982 + 0.363\log(sales)$$

we interpret that a 1% increase in firm sales increases CEO salary by about 0.363%.

Model (2) is known as semi-elasticity model and it takes the following form:

$$\log(y) = \beta_0 + \beta_1 x + u$$

In this model, β_1 implies that a one unit change in x generates a $100 \cdot \beta_1$ percentage change in y.

Example 3.6.4 We have the following model where wage is the dependent variable and education is the independent variable.

$$\log(wage) = \beta_0 + \beta_1 education + u$$

where β_1 has a percentage interpretation when it is multiplied by 100.

If the estimated model is the following:

$$\log(\hat{wage}) = 0.467 + 0.078 education$$

we interpret that wage increases by 7.8% for every additional year of education.

Model (3) takes the following form:

$$y = \beta_0 + \beta_1 \log(x) + u$$

In this model, β_1 implies that a 100% change in x generates a β_1 change in y.

Example 3.6.5 We have the following model where hours is the dependent variable and wage is the independent variable.

$$hours = \beta_0 + \beta_1 \log(wage) + u$$

If the estimated model is the following:

$$\hat{hours} = 30 + 40.5\log(wage)$$

we interpret that a 1% increase in wage increases the weekly hours worked by about 0.40, or slightly less than one-half hour.

3.6.6 Exponential Function

The general form of an exponential function is

$$y = f(x) = a \cdot b^{k \cdot x} \tag{3.19}$$

where a, b, k are non-zero constants. Moreover, b is called the *base* of the exponential function and it is required to be positive, $b > 0$, so that the function is defined for all real powers (in fact, if $b < 0$, then $b^{\frac{1}{2}} = \sqrt{b}$ would be not defined—refer to Sect. 3.7.3 for details about the relation between rational exponents and radicals). The most common exponential function in Economics is the exponential function with base e, an irrational number approximately equal to 2.71828 (Sect. 3.6.6.1 for more details). The domain of an exponential function is the set of all real numbers, unless otherwise explicitly restricted.

Figure 3.34 represents the following exponential functions:

$$y = 5^x \quad \text{(b5exp)}$$

$$y = 2^x \quad \text{(b2exp)}$$

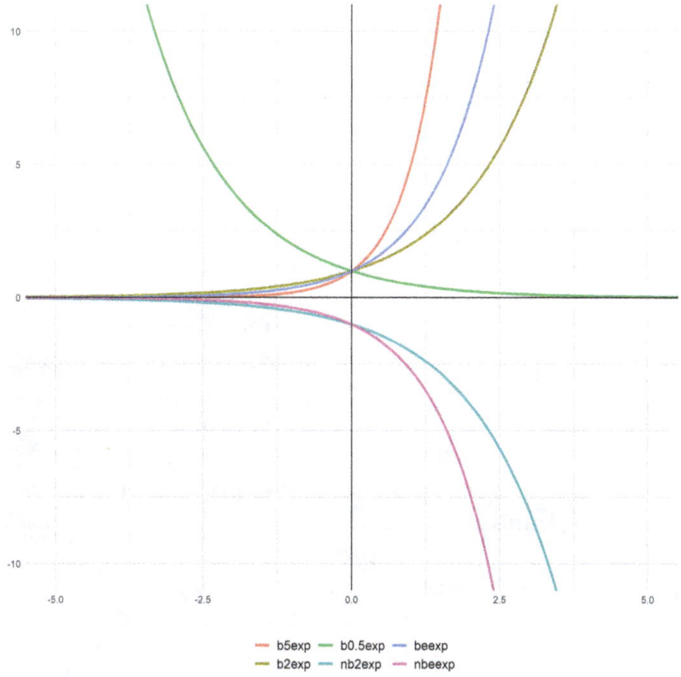

Fig. 3.34 Plot of exponential functions

$$y = 0.5^x \quad \text{(b0.5exp)}$$

$$y = -2^x \quad \text{(nb2exp)}$$

$$y = e^x \quad \text{(beexp)}$$

$$y = -e^x \quad \text{(nbeexp)}$$

Note that regardless of the basis, all exponential functions go through $y = 1$ when $x = 0$ because $b^0 = 1$. The greater the basis the faster the graph grows on the positive quadrant. The negative sign flips the graph over the x axis as in $y = -2^x$ and $y = -e^x$. In this case, the greater the basis the faster the graph decreases. On the other hand, a coefficient between 0 and 1, flips the graph over the y axis. For example, $y = 0.5^x$ can be rewritten as $y = \left(\frac{1}{2}\right)^x$ or $y = 2^{-x}$. It is the mirror image of $y = 2^x$ (Fig. 3.34).

```
> x <- seq(-10, 10, 0.1)
> y_1 <- 5^x
> y_2 <- 2^x
> y_3 <- 0.5^x
> y_4 <- -2^x
> y_exp <- exp(x)
> y_nexp <- -exp(x)
> df <- data.frame(x, "b5exp" = y_1,
+                  "b2exp" = y_2,
+                  "b0.5exp" = y_3,
+                  "nb2exp" = y_4,
+                  "beexp" = y_exp,
+                  "nbeexp" = y_nexp)
> df_l <- melt(setDT(df), id.vars = "x",
+               measure.vars = c("b5exp",
+                                "b2exp",
+                                "b0.5exp",
+                                "nb2exp",
+                                "beexp",
+                                "nbeexp"),
+               variable.name = "exponential")
> ggplot(df_l, aes(x = x,
+                  y = value,
+                  group = exponential,
+                  color = exponential)) +
+   geom_line(size = 1.2) +
+   geom_hline(yintercept = 0) +
+   geom_vline(xintercept = 0) +
+   coord_cartesian(xlim = c(-5, 5),
```

```
+                         ylim = c(-10, 10)) +
+    theme_minimal() + xlab("") + ylab("") +
+    theme(legend.position = "bottom",
+          legend.text = element_text(size = 12),
+          legend.title = element_blank())
```

In Fig. 3.35, we plot the following exponential functions:

$$y = 1^x \quad \texttt{(b1exp)}$$

$$y = 2^{x-1} \quad \texttt{(b2expm1)}$$

$$y = 2^{x+1} \quad \texttt{(b2expp1)}$$

$$y = 2^x + 1 \quad \texttt{(p1b2exp)}$$

$$y = 2^x - 1 \quad \texttt{(m1b2exp)}$$

$$y = 2^{-x} \quad \texttt{(b2expm)}$$

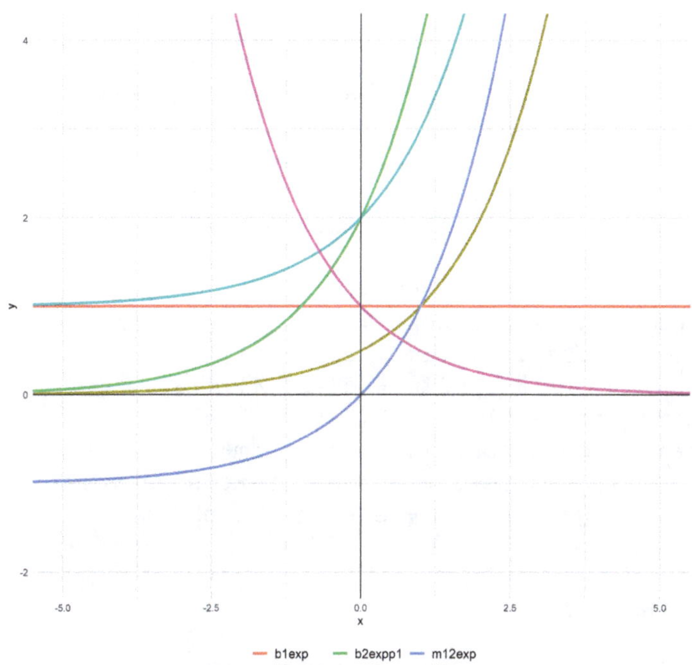

Fig. 3.35 Shifts of the exponential functions

Note that only $y = 1^x$ and $y = 2^{-x}$ pass through $y = 1$ when $x = 0$. We have already seen $y = 2^{-x}$. $y = 1^x$ is a parallel to the x axis because 1 raised to any power is always 1. In the other cases, we can observe that the functions do not pass through $y = 1$ when $x = 0$ because the constant shifts the graph.

```
> y_1 <- 1^x
> y_2 <- 2^(x - 1)
> y_3 <- 2^(x + 1)
> y_4 <- 2^x + 1
> y_5 <- 2^x - 1
> y_6 <- 2^(-x)
> df <- data.frame(x, "b1exp" = y_1,
+                  "b2expm1" = y_2,
+                  "b2expp1" = y_3,
+                  "p1b2exp" = y_4,
+                  "m12exp" = y_5,
+                  "b2expm" = y_6)
> df_l <- melt(setDT(df), id.vars = "x",
+              measure.vars = c("b1exp",
+                               "b2expm1",
+                               "b2expp1",
+                               "p1b2exp",
+                               "m12exp",
+                               "b2expm"),
+              variable.name = "exponential")
> ggplot(df_l, aes(x = x,
+                  y = value,
+                  group = exponential,
+                  color = exponential)) +
+   geom_line(size = 1.2) +
+   geom_hline(yintercept = 0) +
+   geom_vline(xintercept = 0) +
+   coord_cartesian(xlim = c(-5, 5),
+                   ylim = c(-2, 4)) +
+   theme_minimal() + xlab("x") + ylab("y") +
+   theme(legend.position = "bottom",
+         legend.text = element_text(size = 12),
+         legend.title = element_blank())
```

3.6.6.1 What is *e*?

The number e is a mathematical constant that is related to growth and rate of change and it is approximately equal to 2.71828. The number e can be more easily understood from an example from Finance. Let's use the following formula to compute the compound interest rate:

$$\left(1+\frac{r}{m}\right)^m \tag{3.20}$$

where r is the interest rate and m is the time of compounding the interest rate in one period.

Let's assume a 100% interest rate, i.e. $r = 1$ and let's see how much interest we gain on larger and larger compounding. Let's use **R** for this task. We write a function that compounds the interest rate, `comp_int_rate_formula()`, that takes two arguments, the time of compounding, `m`, and the interest rate, `r`, with a default value of 100%. We will return to this function in Sect. 3.6.7.1. We generate a vector, `time`, that includes different time of compounding, from one to one year in seconds.

```
> time <- c(1,2,12,365, 365*24, 365*24*60, 365*24*60*60)
> comp_int_rate_formula <- function(m, r = 1){
+   comp_int_rate <- (1 + r/m)^(m)
+   return(comp_int_rate)
+ }
> comp_int_rate_formula(time)
[1] 2.000000 2.250000 2.613035 2.714567 2.718127
    2.718279 2.718282
```

Note the as `time`, m in (3.20), increases and tends to infinite, the compound interest rate approaches the number e.

Therefore, the number e can be defined as the maximum, continuous compounding interest with a 100% growth in one period.

Formally, we can define e as

$$e = \lim_{n\to\infty}\left(1+\frac{1}{n}\right)^n \tag{3.21}$$

The concept of limit, $\lim_{n\to\infty}$, will be discussed in Chap. 4.

3.6.6.2 How to Solve Exponential Equations

To solve an exponential equation, we rely on the rules of the exponents and logarithms. Let's see some examples.

Example 3.6.6

$$2^x = 7$$

Take the natural log of both sides:

$$\log(2^x) = log(7)$$

Because of the rules of logarithms (Table 3.5), we can move the exponent in front of the logarithm.

$$x \log(2) = \log(7)$$

Therefore,

$$x = \frac{\log(7)}{\log(2)} = 2.807355$$

Example 3.6.7

$$2^{x-1} = 7$$

$$\log(2^{x-1}) = log(7)$$

$$(x-1)\log(2) = \log(7)$$

$$x - 1 = \frac{\log(7)}{\log(2)}$$

$$x = \frac{\log(7)}{\log(2)} + 1 = 3.807355$$

Example 3.6.8

$$2e^{x-1} = 7$$

$$e^{x-1} = \frac{7}{2}$$

$$\log(e^{x-1}) = \log\left(\frac{7}{2}\right)$$

$$x - 1 = \log\left(\frac{7}{2}\right)$$

$$x = \log\left(\frac{7}{2}\right) + 1 = 2.252763$$

Example 3.6.9

$$e^{2x} + 2e^x - 15 = 0$$

This looks like the quadratic equations in Sect. 3.3.1. Indeed, we can solve it through factoring

$$(e^x)^2 + 2(e^x) - 15 = 0$$

$$(e^x - 3)(e^x + 5) = 0$$

Therefore, either

$$e^x = 3$$

$$\log(e^x) = \log(3)$$

$$x = \log(3) = 1.098612$$

or

$$e^x = -5$$

However this last result is not a solution because no number raised to a power gives a negative number.

3.6.7 Applications in Economics

3.6.7.1 Exponential and Investment

An investor deposits an amount of money, P, known as the *principal*, in a bank at a yearly interest rate, r, that is compounded m times per year, t. We use the following formula to compute the amount of money accumulated at the end of the investment, A:

$$A = P\left(1 + \frac{r}{m}\right)^{mt} \tag{3.22}$$

We write the function `future_value()` as follows.

```
> future_value <- function(P, r, m, t){
+         A <- P*(1 + r/m)^(m*t)
+         return(A)
+       }
```

Let's assume that she invests \$10, 000 for 20 years at 6%. Let's see how the total amount changes with a simple interest (note that the simple interest rate formula becomes $P(1 + r)^t$, that is the interest rate is paid annually, $m = 1$), with a 6 month compound interest, with a quarterly compound interest, and with a monthly compound interest rate

```
> future_value(10000, 0.06, 1, 20)
[1] 32071.35
> future_value(10000, 0.06, 2, 20)
[1] 32620.38
> future_value(10000, 0.06, 4, 20)
[1] 32906.63
> future_value(10000, 0.06, 12, 20)
[1] 33102.04
```

If we assume that the interest is compounded continuously $m \to \infty$, therefore

$$\lim_{m\to\infty}\left(1+\frac{r}{m}\right)^{mt} = e^{rt} \tag{3.23}$$

Consequently, the P amount invested at annual rate, continuously compounded grows as follows[10]

$$A = Pe^{rt} \tag{3.24}$$

Therefore, an investment of \$10, 000 at 6% continuously compounded becomes \$33, 201.17 after 20 years.

```
> P <- 10000
> r <- 0.06
> t <- 20
> A <- P*exp(r*t)
> A
[1] 33201.17
```

On the other hand, if the investor would like to know how much she should deposit, *PV*, known as *present value*, to obtain the amount of money, *A*, knowing the *r* interest rate applied, the year, *t*, and time of compounding, *m*, the formula is the following:

$$PV = \frac{A}{\left(1+\frac{r}{m}\right)^{mt}} \tag{3.25}$$

[10] The steps to (3.24) are the following: $P\left[\left(1+\frac{r}{m}\right)^{m/r}\right]^{rt} = P\left[\left(1+\frac{1}{w}\right)^{w}\right]^{rt}$ where $w = \frac{m}{r}$. As $m \to \infty$, $w \to \infty$ and by (3.21) we have Pe^{rt}.

We write the `present_value()` function as follows:

```
> present_value <- function(A, r, m, t){
+         PV <- A / ((1 + r/m)^(m*t))
+         return(PV)
+      }
> present_value(150000, 0.06, 4, 20)
[1] 45583.52
> present_value(200000, 0.06, 4, 20)
[1] 60778.03
> present_value(250000, 0.06, 4, 20)
[1] 75972.54
> present_value(300000, 0.06, 4, 20)
[1] 91167.04
```

Therefore, if an investor would like to have, after 20 years at 6% compounded quarterly,

- a total of $150,000 she should invest $45,583.52
- a total of $200,000 she should invest $60,778.03
- a total of $250,000 she should invest $75,972.54
- a total of $300,000 she should invest $91,167.04

The corresponding continuous-discounting formula of (3.25) is

$$PV = \frac{A}{e^{rt}} = Ae^{-rt} \tag{3.26}$$

where e^{-rt} is known as the *discount factor*.

In the next example, we investigate how long it takes for an investment to generate a wished amount of money, that is we have to solve for t Eq. 3.22 or Eq. 3.24.

For Eq. 3.22, first we divide both sides by P:

$$\frac{A}{P} = \left(1 + \frac{r}{m}\right)^{mt}$$

Then, we take the natural logarithm of both sides:

$$\log\left(\frac{A}{P}\right) = \log\left[\left(1 + \frac{r}{m}\right)^{mt}\right]$$

By using the properties of logarithms (Table 3.5), we can write the exponent in front of the logarithm:

$$\log\left(\frac{A}{P}\right) = mt \cdot \log\left(1 + \frac{r}{m}\right)$$

Finally, we are ready to solve for t:

$$t = \frac{\log\left(\frac{A}{P}\right)}{m \cdot \log\left(1 + \frac{r}{m}\right)} \tag{3.27}$$

In the case of Eq. 3.24, first we divide both sides by P:

$$\frac{A}{P} = e^{rt}$$

Then, we take the natural log of both sides:

$$\log\left(\frac{A}{P}\right) = \log(e^{rt})$$

Because of the relation between logarithm and exponents (Table 3.4), the term on the right hand side becomes as follows:

$$\log\left(\frac{A}{P}\right) = rt$$

Finally, we solve for t:

$$t = \frac{\log\left(\frac{A}{P}\right)}{r} \tag{3.28}$$

Now let's write a function, `time_invest()`, to compute the time needed for an investment to generate the desired accumulated amount of money.

```
> time_invest <- function(A, P, r, m = 1, e = FALSE){
+   t <- log(A/P) / (m * log(1 + r/m))
+
+   t_e <- log(A/P)/r
+
+   ifelse(e == FALSE,
+          return(t),
+          return(t_e))
+ }
```

Now let's suppose the investor wants to know how long an investment will take to double if the interest is 6% with a quarterly, a daily compounding, and a continuous compounding

```
> time_invest(2000, 1000, 0.06, 4)
[1] 11.63888
> time_invest(2000, 1000, 0.06, 365)
[1] 11.5534
> time_invest(2000, 1000, 0.06, e = TRUE)
[1] 11.55245
```

It will take more than 11 years for the investment to double.

To conclude this section, let's check the body of the `time_invest()` function. If you noted, the function computes both `t` and `t_e` even though only one result will be returned based on the method we choose. Because this function is very simple, we may not notice that it is inefficient. However, for more complex functions, this may be critical because the speed of the function heavily slowdowns by computing object we are not requiring to be returned. As exercise, the reader should try to rearrange the function so that it computes and returns only the desired computation based on `e = TRUE` or `FALSE` (Sect. 3.9.5).

3.6.7.2 Exponential Growth and Logistic Growth

An exponential growth function takes the following form

$$N(t) = N_0 e^{rt} \tag{3.29}$$

where N represents a population, N_0 represents the initial population, r is the growth rate and t is the time.

The particularity of the exponential growth is that the population grows without bound. However, in real life, resources are limited. Therefore, it is more plausible that a population grows exponentially until a certain point and then starts to increase at a decreasing rate while approaching the bound. This is modelled with a logistic growth function that takes the following form:

$$N(t) = \frac{K}{1 + \left(\frac{K - N_0}{N_0}\right) e^{-rt}} \tag{3.30}$$

where K is the *carrying capacity*, i.e. the limit of the environment where the population in focus occurs (a large K implies that the environment can support a dense population), r is the *intrinsic growth rate*, N represents a population, N_0 represents the initial population, and t is the time.

Let's suppose that $N_0 = 50$, $K = 10000$, and the population at year 1 is 80, i.e. $N_1 = 80$. From (3.30), we find r by setting (3.30) equal to N_1, that is $t = 1$.

$$80 = \frac{10000}{1 + \left(\frac{10000-50}{50}\right)e^{-r}}$$

$$80 = \frac{10000}{1 + 199e^{-r}}$$

Multiply both sides by the denominator and then divide both sides by 80:

$$80(1 + 199e^{-r}) = 10000$$

$$1 + 199e^{-r} = 125$$

$$199e^{-r} = 124$$

$$e^{-r} = \frac{124}{199}$$

Next take the natural log of both sides:

$$\log(e^{-r}) = \log\left(\frac{124}{199}\right)$$

$$-r = -0.473$$

that is

$$r = 0.473$$

Now that we have found r (we approximate to 0.5), let's substitute it back into (3.30) and let's compute the population after 5 years.

$$N(t = 5) = \frac{10000}{1 + \left(\frac{10000-50}{50}\right)e^{-0.5\cdot 5}}$$

that is $N_5 = 576.87$ (576 if we consider whole numbers only).

We will return to the logistic growth function in Chaps. 4, 5, and 11. Here, we represent the exponential function and the logistic growth function in **R** (Fig. 3.36). Note that we add on the plot the point of maximum growth of the logistic function $\left(\frac{\log\left(\frac{K-N_0}{N_0}\right)}{r}, \frac{K}{2}\right)$. To the left of this point the logistic growth function increases at

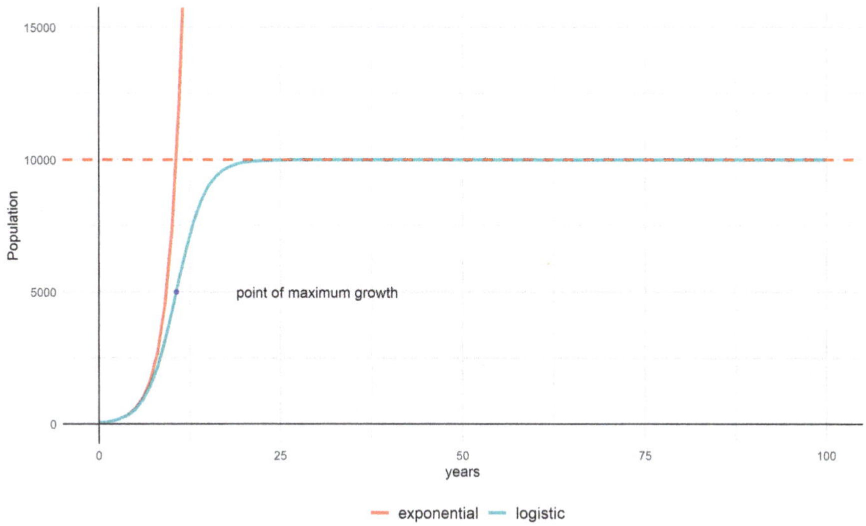

Fig. 3.36 Exponential and logistic growth

an increasing rate; to the right of this point the logistic growth function increases at a decreasing rate.

```
> t <- seq(0, 100, 1)
> N_0 <- 50
> K <- 10000
> r <- 0.5
> N_logi <- K / (1 + ((K - N_0)/N_0) * exp(-r*t))
> head(N_logi)
[1]  50.00000  82.16954 134.75634 220.25024 358.01589
     576.87045
> N_expo <- N_0*exp(r*t)
> head(N_expo)
[1]  50.00000  82.43606 135.91409 224.08445 369.45280
     609.12470
> df <- data.frame(t, "exponential" = N_expo,
+                  "logistic" = N_logi)
> head(df)
  t exponential  logistic
1 0    50.00000  50.00000
2 1    82.43606  82.16954
3 2   135.91409 134.75634
4 3   224.08445 220.25024
5 4   369.45280 358.01589
6 5   609.12470 576.87045
```

```
> df_l <- melt(setDT(df), id.vars = "t",
+              measure.vars = c("exponential",
+                               "logistic"),
+              variable.name = "growth")
> head(df_l)
   t      growth     value
1: 0 exponential  50.00000
2: 1 exponential  82.43606
3: 2 exponential 135.91409
4: 3 exponential 224.08445
5: 4 exponential 369.45280
6: 5 exponential 609.12470
> point_max <- data.frame(x = log((K - N_0)/N_0)/r,
+                         y = K/2)
> point_max
         x    y
1 10.58661 5000
> ggplot(df_l, aes(x = t,
+                  y = value,
+                  group = growth,
+                  color = growth)) +
+   geom_line(size = 1.2) +
+   geom_hline(yintercept = 0) +
+   geom_vline(xintercept = 0) +
+   geom_hline(yintercept = 10000,
+              color = "red",
+              linetype = "dashed",
+              size = 1) +
+   coord_cartesian(ylim = c(0, 15000)) +
+   theme_minimal() +
+   xlab("years") +
+   ylab("Population") +
+   theme(legend.position = "bottom",
+         legend.text = element_text(size = 12),
+         legend.title = element_blank()) +
+   geom_point(aes(x = point_max$x,
+                  y = point_max$y),
+              colour="blue") +
+   annotate("text", x = 30, y = 5000,
+            label = "point of maximum growth")
```

Figure 3.36 shows that the exponential growth function overcomes the bound before 12 years. On the other hand, with the logistic growth function it takes less than 25 years for the population to reach the bound given by the environmental resources but it does not pass it. Note that the exponential growth function has a *J* shape while the logistic growth function has an *S* shape.

3.7 Radical Function

A radical function is a function that contains a *nth* root

$$y = f(x) = \sqrt[n]{x} \tag{3.31}$$

where n is the index of the radicand, the expression under the radical sign.

In Sect. 3.1, we observed that for the logarithm function and for the radical function, the negative values of x produced `NaN`. We have already examined why the domain of the logarithm function is valid for $x > 0$. Now let's examine the domain for the radical function. First, let's compute the following radical functions

$$y = \sqrt{x}$$

$$y = \sqrt[3]{x}$$

$$y = \sqrt[4]{x}$$

$$y = \sqrt[5]{x}$$

$$y = \sqrt[6]{x}$$

Note that if n is omitted in $\sqrt{x}$ it is assumed to be 2. We use the built-in function `sqrt()` to compute the square root; we use the `nthroot()` from the `pracma` package for $n > 2$.

```
> x <- seq(-10, 10, 0.1)
> y_r2 <- sqrt(x)
Warning message:
In sqrt(x) : NaNs produced
> y_r3 <- nthroot(x, 3)
> y_r4 <- nthroot(x, 4)
Error in nthroot(x, 4) :
  If argument 'x' is negative,  'n' must be an odd
  integer.
> y_r5 <- nthroot(x, 5)
> y_r6 <- nthroot(x, 6)
Error in nthroot(x, 6) :
  If argument 'x' is negative, 'n' must be an odd
  integer.
```

```
> df <- data.frame(x = x,
+                  y_r2 = y_r2,
+                  y_r3 = y_r3,
+                  y_r5 = y_r5)
> head(df)
      x y_r2      y_r3      y_r5
1 -10.0  NaN -2.154435 -1.584893
2  -9.9  NaN -2.147229 -1.581711
3  -9.8  NaN -2.139975 -1.578502
4  -9.7  NaN -2.132671 -1.575268
5  -9.6  NaN -2.125317 -1.572006
6  -9.5  NaN -2.117912 -1.568717
> df[x == 0, ]
    x y_r2 y_r3 y_r5
101 0    0    0    0
```

First, observe the different behaviour of the `sqrt()` function and `nthroot()` function. `sqrt()` returns a warning message and produces `NaN` for negative values of `x`. On the other hand, `nthroot()` produces an error message for the negative values of `x` when n is even. From the **R** point of view, this is relevant because when the warning message is produced the function still makes the computation. On the other hand, if an error message is produced the function does not run. From the mathematical point of view, the radical function requires us to consider the domain of the function if the index of the radical is an even number. Since an *even-n* root is only defined for values greater than and or equal to zero, then domain is the set of values of x for which $x \geq 0$.

The following code produces the graph $y = -\sqrt{x}$ (Fig. 3.37) and $y = \sqrt[3]{x}$ (Fig. 3.38).

```
> py_r2 <- ggplot(df,
+                 aes(x = x, y = -1*y_r2)) +
+   geom_line() +
+   theme_minimal() +
+   geom_hline(yintercept = 0) +
+   geom_vline(xintercept = 0) +
+   ylab("y") +
+   coord_cartesian(xlim = c(-5, 5),
+                   ylim = c(-5, 5))
> py_r2
Warning message:
Removed 100 rows containing missing values (geom_path).
> py_r3 <- ggplot(df,
+                 aes(x = x, y = y_r3)) +
+   geom_line() +
+   theme_minimal() +
```

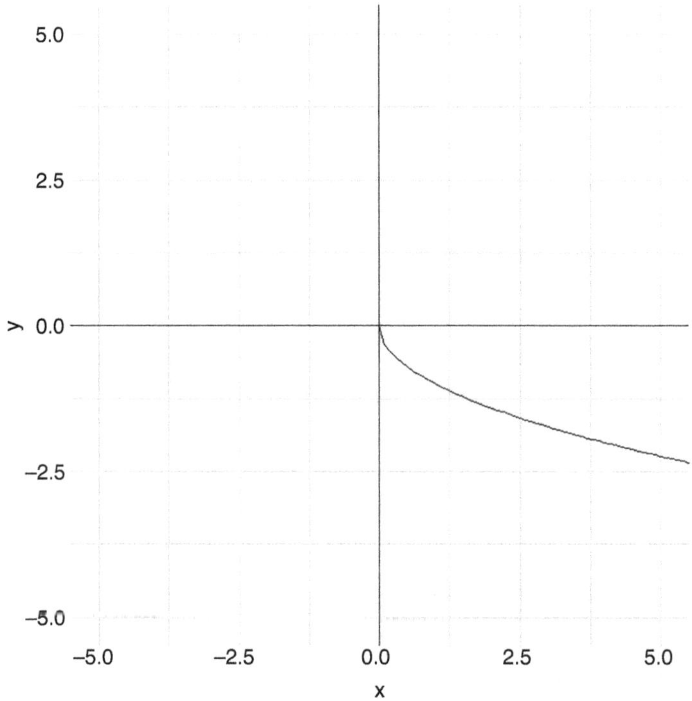

Fig. 3.37 Plot of $y = -\sqrt{x}$

```
+    geom_hline(yintercept = 0) +
+    geom_vline(xintercept = 0) +
+    ylab("y") +
+    coord_cartesian(xlim = c(-5, 5),
+                    ylim = c(-5, 5))
> py_r3
```

For $y = \sqrt{x} + c$, if $c > 0$ the graph shifts upwards by c units; if $c < 0$ the graph shifts downwards by c units. For $y = \sqrt{x + c}$, if $c > 0$ the graph shifts leftwards by c units; if $c < 0$ the graph shifts rightwards by c units (Fig. 3.39).

```
> df <- data.frame(x = seq(0, 10, 0.1))
> pyr <- ggplot(df) +
+   stat_function(aes(x), fun = radical_fn,
+                 color = "blue", size = 1) +
+   stat_function(aes(x), fun = radical_fn,
+                 args = list(c = 3),
+                 color = "red", size = 1) +
+   stat_function(aes(x), fun = radical_fn,
+                 args = list(c = -3),
+                 color = "yellow", size = 1) +
+   geom_hline(yintercept = 0) +
```

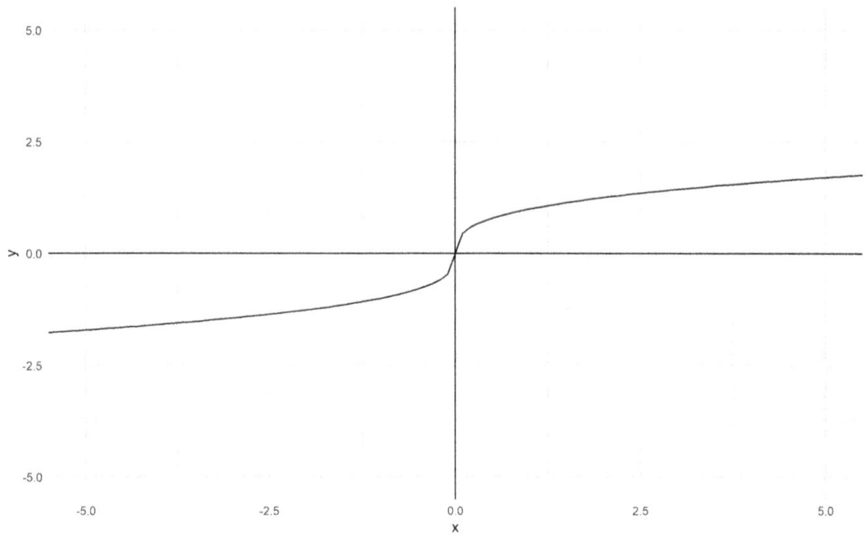

Fig. 3.38 Plot of $y = \sqrt[3]{x}$

```
+   geom_vline(xintercept = 0) +
+   theme_minimal()
> df <- data.frame(x = seq(-10, 10, 0.1))
> pyr2 <- ggplot(df) +
+   stat_function(aes(x), fun = radical_fn,
+                 color = "blue", size = 1) +
+   stat_function(aes(x), fun = radical_fn,
+                 args = list(b = 3),
+                 color = "red", size = 1) +
+   stat_function(aes(x), fun = radical_fn,
+                 args = list(b = -3),
+                 color = "yellow", size = 1) +
+   geom_hline(yintercept = 0) +
+   geom_vline(xintercept = 0) +
+   theme_minimal()
> ggarrange(pyr, pyr2,
+           ncol = 1, nrow = 2)
Warning messages:
1: In sqrt(x + b) : NaNs produced
2: In sqrt(x + b) : NaNs produced
3: In sqrt(x + b) : NaNs produced
4: Removed 50 row(s) containing missing values (geom_path).
5: Removed 35 row(s) containing missing values (geom_path).
6: Removed 65 row(s) containing missing values (geom_path).
```

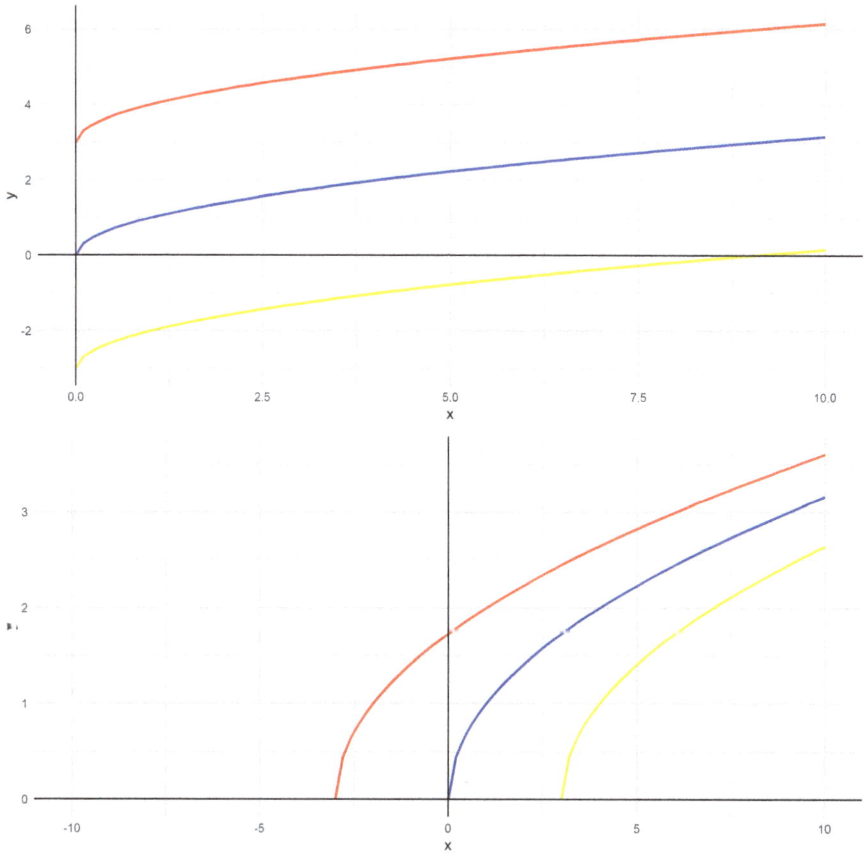

Fig. 3.39 Shift of $y = \sqrt{x}$

3.7.1 *How to Solve Radical Equation*

The strategy to solve a radical equation is to remove the radical sign by raising both sides of the equations to the appropriate power.

Example 3.7.1

$$\sqrt{x-5} = 4$$

$$(\sqrt{x-5})^2 = (4)^2$$

$$x - 5 = 16$$

$$x = 21$$

To check if it is correct, substitute $x = 21$ in the original equation.

$$\sqrt{21-5} = 4$$

$$\sqrt{16} = 4$$

Example 3.7.2

$$\sqrt[3]{x} = 3$$

$$(\sqrt[3]{x})^3 = (3)^3$$

$$x = 27$$

Example 3.7.3 Note, however, that squaring both sides can lead to an *extraneous solution*, i.e. a number that is not a solution of the original equation. For example,

$$x - 2 = \sqrt{x}$$

$$(x-2)^2 = (\sqrt{x})^2$$

$$x^2 - 4x + 4 = x$$

$$x^2 - 5x + 4 = 0$$

$$(x-4)(x-1) = 0$$

Therefore, $x_1 = 1$ and $x_2 = 4$. However, only x_2 is a solution while x_1 is an extraneous solution. Plug these values in the original equation for a check:

$$4 - 2 = \sqrt{4}$$

$$2 = 2$$

$$1 - 2 = \sqrt{1}$$

$$-1 = 1$$

3.7.2 Find the Domain of a Radical Function

Let's see a practical example about how to find the domain for $y = \sqrt{x^2 - 4}$. We need to find where the expression under the radical sign is greater than or equal to zero, $x^2 - 4 \geq 0$. In this case, the solutions for x are -2 and 2. Now let's plug some values less than -2, greater than 2 and between -2 and 2 and let's verify if $x^2 - 4 \geq 0$. If we plug -4, $x^2 - 4 = 12$, i.e. it is greater than 0. If we plug 4, $x^2 - 4 = 12$, i.e. it is greater than 0. If we plug 0, $x^2 - 4 = -4$, i.e. it is less than 0. What about if we plug -2 and 2? As expected, if we plug -2, $x^2 - 4 = 0$, i.e. it is equal to 0. If we plug 2, $x^2 - 4 = 0$, i.e. it is equal to 0. Since the square root of 0 is 0, it is a valid value. Therefore, the domain for $y = \sqrt{x^2 - 4}$ is $(-\infty, -2] \bigcup [2, \infty)$, where the square bracket sign means that the value is included.

Now, let's plot it. As expected, there are no x-values for $-2 < x < 2$ (Fig. 3.40). Note that we use `scale_x_continuous()` to add the numbers from -10 to 10 on the x axis.

```
> ggplot(df) +
+   stat_function(aes(x), fun = radical_fn,
+                 color = "blue", size = 1,
+                 args = list(k = 2, b = -4)) +
+   theme_minimal() +
+   geom_hline(yintercept = 0) +
+   geom_vline(xintercept = 0) +
+   scale_x_continuous(
```

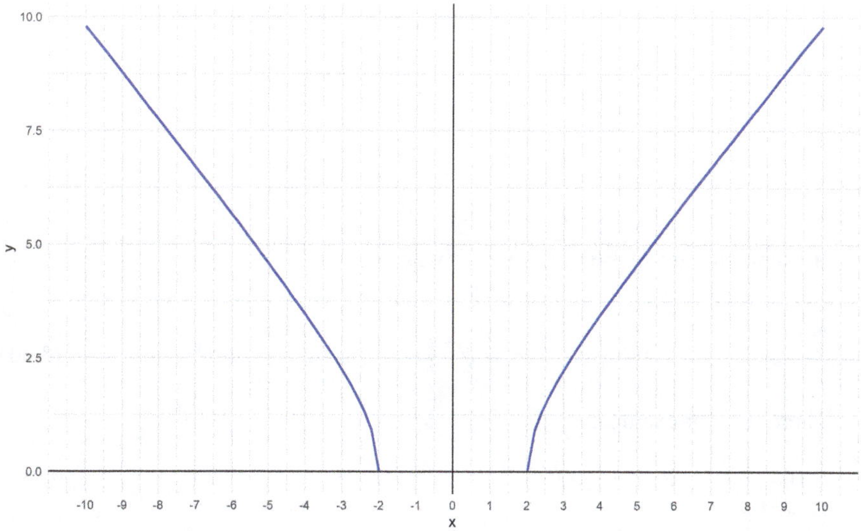

Fig. 3.40 Plot of $y = \sqrt{x^2 - 4}$

```
+       breaks = seq(min(df$x), max(df$x),
+                    by = 1))
Warning message:
In sqrt(x^k + b) : NaNs produced
```

3.7.3 Radicals and Rational Exponents

A radical expression can be written as an exponential expression. This will be useful when computing the derivative of a radical (Chap. 4).

In Eq. 3.32, n is the index of the radicand, a is any number when n is odd and only non-negative real number when n is even, and k is an exponent.

$$\sqrt[n]{a} = a^k \tag{3.32}$$

Let's raise both expression to the n power to eliminate the *nth* root.

$$(\sqrt[n]{a})^n = (a^k)^n$$

$$a = a^{nk}$$

In the next step, we equate the exponents, where 1 is the exponent of a on the left-hand side.

$$1 = nk$$

Solve for k

$$k = \frac{1}{n} \tag{3.33}$$

By substituting (3.33) in (3.32) we obtain

$$\sqrt[n]{a} = a^{\frac{1}{n}} \tag{3.34}$$

Therefore, for example

```
> sqrt(25) == 25^(1/2)
[1] TRUE
> sqrt(28) == 28^(1/2)
[1] TRUE
> nthroot(15, 3) == 15^(1/3)
```

```
[1] TRUE
> nthroot(16, 3) == 2^(4/3)
[1] TRUE
```

Note that in the last line of code we wrote 16 as 2^4.

3.7.4 Applications in Economics

3.7.4.1 Production Function with a Single Input

Let's suppose that a firm uses only labour (L) to produce its output (Q). We could express its production function as

$$Q = f(L)$$

This is an example of a single-input production function.

In Fig. 3.41 we represent the production function $Q = \sqrt{L}$. This is an example of a Cobb-Douglas function with a single output and input. We will discuss about the Cobb-Douglas production function in Chap. 6.

```
> L <- 0:100
> Q <- sqrt(L)
> df <- data.frame(output = Q,
+                  labour = L)
```

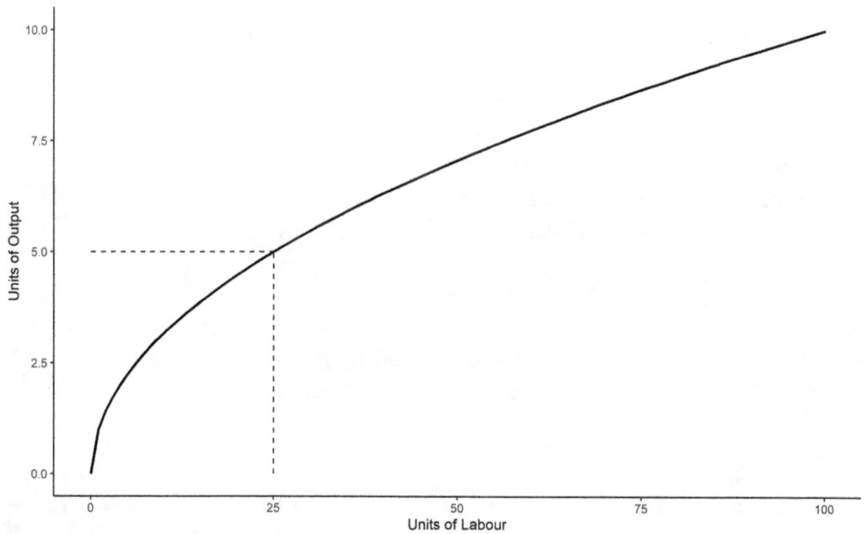

Fig. 3.41 Single input production function

```
> df_s <- data.frame(x = c(25, 0),
+                    y = c(0, 5),
+                    xend = c(25, 25),
+                    yend = c(5, 5))
> ggplot(df, aes(x = labour,
+                y = output)) +
+        geom_line(size = 1) +
+        theme_classic() +
+        ylab("Units of Output") +
+        xlab("Units of Labour") +
+        geom_segment(data = df_s,
+                     aes(x = x,
+                         y = y,
+                         xend = xend,
+                         yend = yend),
+                     linetype = "dashed")
```

If we invert the production function, we get the following function

$$L = g(Q)$$

which tells us the minimum amount of labour L required to produce a given amount of output Q. This function is the *labour requirements function* (Besanko and Braeutigam 2011, p. 203). Therefore, in our example, the *labour requirements function* is $L = Q^2$. Thus, to produce 5 units of output the firm needs 25 units of labour, $25 = 5^2$. Note that in the code we invert the rows in df_s and the coordinates in geom_segment() (Fig. 3.42).

```
> ggplot(df, aes(x = output,
+                y = labour)) +
+     geom_line(size = 1) +
+     theme_classic() +
+     xlab("Units of Output") +
+     ylab("Units of Labour") +
+     geom_segment(data = df_s[c(2, 1), ],
+                  aes(x = y,
+                      y = x,
+                      xend = yend,
+                      yend = xend),
+                  linetype = "dashed")
```

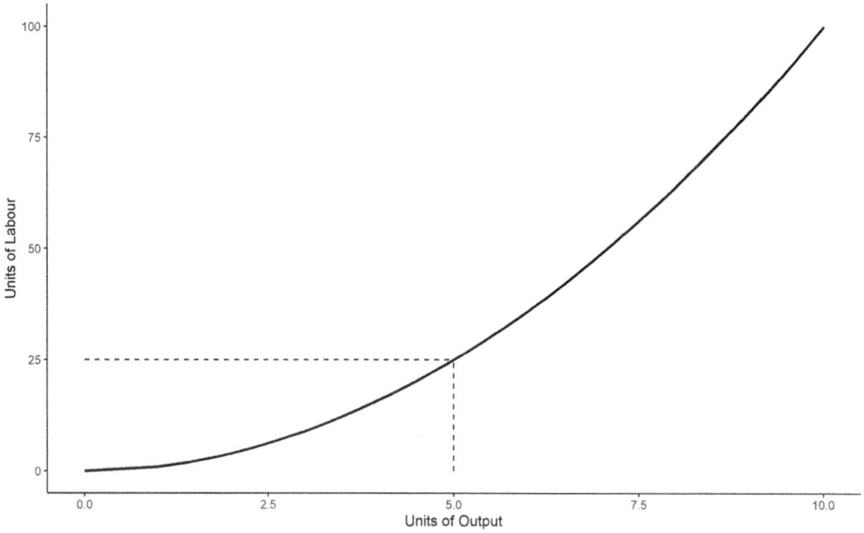

Fig. 3.42 Labour requirement function

3.8 Rational Function

The general form of a rational function is

$$y = \frac{f(x)}{g(x)} \tag{3.35}$$

where $f(x)$ and $g(x)$ are two polynomials.

Let's consider the following case

$$y = \frac{A}{x-h} + k, \ \ x \neq h$$

where A is a constant. The graph of the function shifts upwards or downwards by k units and rightwards or leftwards by h units.

Let's plot the following functions: $y = \frac{4}{x}$, $y = \frac{4}{x-1}$, and $y = \frac{4}{x} + 1$ (Fig. 3.43).

First, we build each functions in **R**. Then, we plot the functions with base **R** functions. We use the `curve()` function to plot the functions and `abline()` to plot the *x-intercept* and *y-intercept*. Note that `bty = "n"` suppresses the box. The option `add = T` overlays the plots.

```
> y_fn <- function(x) 4/x
> y1_fn <- function(x) 4/(x - 1)
> y2_fn <- function(x) 4/x + 1
> curve(y_fn, -10, 10, ylab = "y", bty = "n")
```

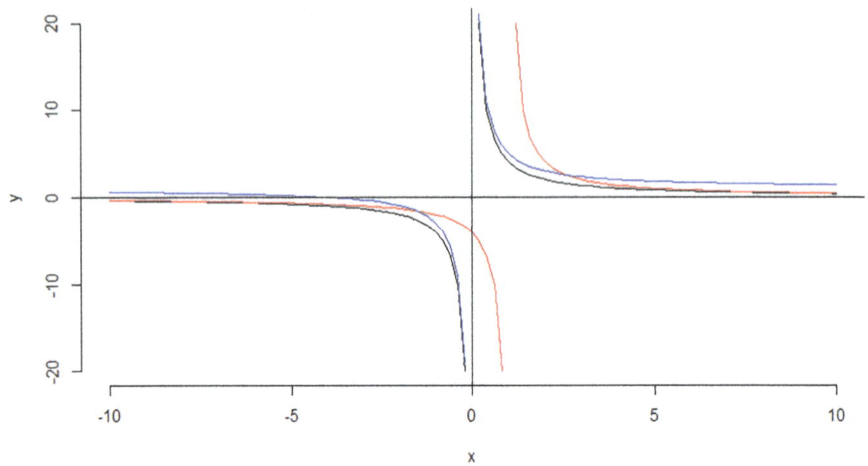

Fig. 3.43 Rational function

```
> curve(y1_fn, -10, 10, ylab = "y", bty = "n",
+         col = "red", add = T)
> curve(y2_fn, -10, 10, ylab = "y", bty = "n",
+         col = "blue", add = T)
> abline(h = 0, v = 0)
```

3.8.1 Intercepts and Asymptotes

We want to plot the function $y = \frac{3-2x}{x-2},\ x \neq 2$.

First, we can rewrite it in the form $y = \frac{A}{x-h} + k,\ x \neq h$ by finding how many multiples of $x - 2$ are in $3 - 2x$ and how much is left over.

$$3 - 2x = 3 - 2(x - 2) = 3 - 2x + 4$$

Therefore, we need to subtract 4

$$3 - 2x + 4 - 4 = -2(x - 2) - 1 = 3 - 2x$$

Therefore,

$$\frac{-2(x-2)-1}{x-2} = -2 - \frac{1}{x-2}$$

or

$$y = -\frac{1}{x-2} - 2,\ x \neq 2$$

We find the *y-intercept* when $x = 0$.

$$y(x = 0) = -\frac{1}{0 - 2} - 2 = -\frac{3}{2}$$

To find the *x-intercept* we set $y = 0$.

$$0 = -\frac{1}{x - 2} - 2$$

$$0 = -1 - 2(x - 2)$$

$$-1 - 2x + 4 = 0$$

$$-2x = -3$$

$$x = \frac{3}{2}$$

Therefore, the coordinates of the *y-intercept* and *x-intercept* are, respectively, $\left(0, -\frac{3}{2}\right)$ and $\left(\frac{3}{2}, 0\right)$. Note that we could have plugged $x = 0$ and $y = 0$ directly in $y = \frac{3-2x}{x-2}$.

The asymptote is $x = 2$.

The following lines of code plot it (Fig. 3.44).

```
> y_fn <- function(x) (3 - 2*x)/(x - 2)
> curve(y_fn, -10, 10, ylab = "y", bty = "n",
+          col = "blue")
```

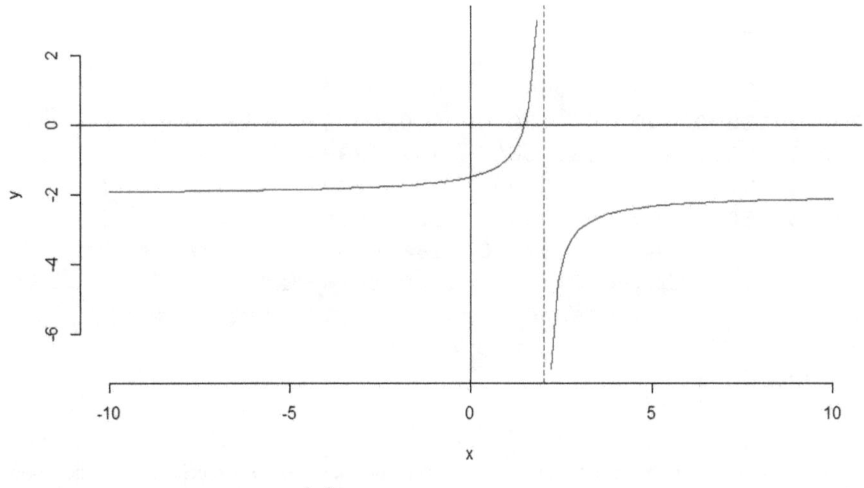

Fig. 3.44 Rational function $y = \frac{3-2x}{x-2}$

```
> abline(h = 0, v = 0)
> abline(v = 2, col = "red",
+        lty = 2)
```

3.8.2 Applications in Economics

3.8.2.1 Indifference Curve

An utility function represents the consumer's preferences over a bundle of goods and it is expressed with a numerical scale. Let's assume that the utility function is given by

$$U = U(x, y) = xy \tag{3.36}$$

Note that here we are dealing with a function of two variables, a topic discussed in Chap. 6.[11] In this context, we want to represent three utility functions. First, we replace U with arbitrary constants. Let's pick up 25, 50, 100. Then, we solve (3.36) for y for each of the three utility levels.

```
> U1 <- 25
> U2 <- 50
> U3 <- 100
> x <- seq(0, 25, 0.1)
> y1 <- U1/x
> y2 <- U2/x
> y3 <- U3/x
> df <- data.frame(x, y1, y2, y3)
> df <- df[-1, ]
> head(df)
    x        y1        y2        y3
2 0.1 250.00000 500.00000 1000.0000
3 0.2 125.00000 250.00000  500.0000
4 0.3  83.33333 166.66667  333.3333
5 0.4  62.50000 125.00000  250.0000
6 0.5  50.00000 100.00000  200.0000
7 0.6  41.66667  83.33333  166.6667
> df_l <- melt(setDT(df), id.vars = "x",
+              measure.vars = c("y1", "y2", "y3"),
+              value.name = "y")
> head(df_l)
```

[11] The utility function to generate these indifference curves, (3.36), is a special case of the Cobb-Douglas function where the exponents of x and y equal 1 (Chap. 6).

```
      x variable         y
1: 0.1        y1 250.00000
2: 0.2        y1 125.00000
3: 0.3        y1  83.33333
4: 0.4        y1  62.50000
5: 0.5        y1  50.00000
6: 0.6        y1  41.66667
```

Let's add `U` in `df_1`. The `with()` function evaluates `x*y` in `df_1`

```
> df_1$U <- with(df_1, x*y)
> head(df_1)
      x variable         y  U
1: 0.1        y1 250.00000 25
2: 0.2        y1 125.00000 25
3: 0.3        y1  83.33333 25
4: 0.4        y1  62.50000 25
5: 0.5        y1  50.00000 25
6: 0.6        y1  41.66667 25
> tail(df_1)
       x variable        y   U
1: 24.5        y3 4.081633 100
2: 24.6        y3 4.065041 100
3: 24.7        y3 4.048583 100
4: 24.8        y3 4.032258 100
5: 24.9        y3 4.016064 100
6: 25.0        y3 4.000000 100
```

Finally, we plot it with `ggplot()` (Fig. 3.45).

```
> ggplot(df_1, aes(x, y,
+                  group = variable,
+                  color = variable)) +
+       geom_line(size = 1) +
+       theme_classic() + ylab("y") +
+       coord_cartesian(xlim = c(0, 20),
+                       ylim = c(0, 20)) +
+       theme(legend.position = "none") +
+       annotate("label", x = c(5, 7, 10),
+                y = c(5, 7, 10),
+                label = c("Utility = 25",
+                          "Utility = 50",
+                          "Utility = 100"),
+                color = c("red", "green", "blue"))
```

Figure 3.45 represents three indifference curves. Along an indifference curve, bundles of goods have the same utility level. The indifference curve with the highest utility level represents the preferred bundle.

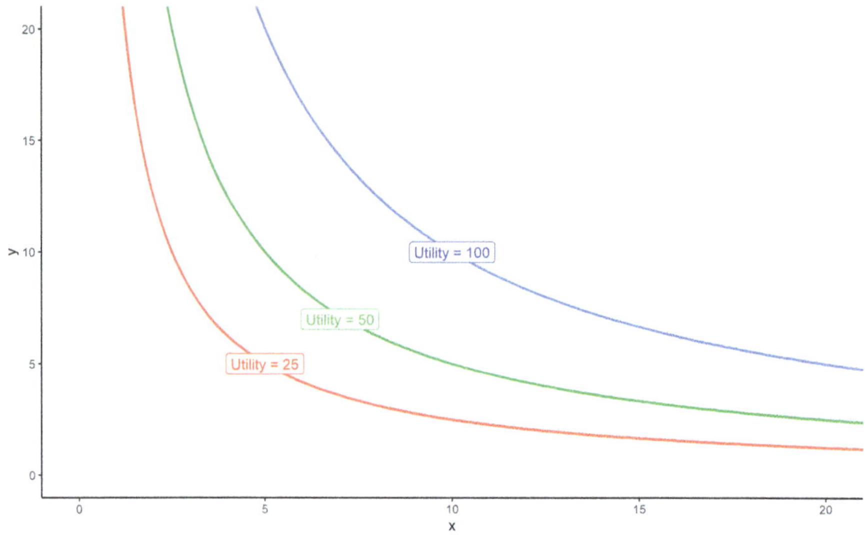

Fig. 3.45 Indifference curve

3.8.2.2 A "Work" Example

The firm PAINT Inc. received a commission to paint the apartments of a residential building. The president of PAINT Inc. send employees (N) to paint the apartments (W). They will need some days (T) to paint all the apartments. We write the relation to complete the job as follows:

$$N \times T = W$$

Therefore,

$$N = \frac{W}{T}$$

Now, let's suppose that the painters use the first day to bring the equipment. Consequently, we need to add one more day to the total time (TT), $TT = T + 1$. Therefore, the relation changes as follows:

$$N \times (TT - 1) = W$$

or

$$N = \frac{W}{TT - 1}$$

Furthermore, let's assume that PAINT Inc. employs an additional employee as bus driver to take the painters to the working place. Therefore, the total number (TN) of workers is $TN = N + 1$. Consequently,

$$TN - 1 = \frac{W}{TT - 1}$$

$$TN = \frac{W}{TT - 1} + 1$$

Let's plot these three cases by assuming a total of 50 apartments to be painted by a 20 days limit.

```
> W <- 50
> TT <- 1:20
> N1 <- W/TT
> N2 <- W/(TT - 1)
> N3 <- W/(TT - 1) + 1
> df <- data.frame(TT, N1, N2, N3)
> head(df)
  TT        N1       N2       N3
1  1 50.000000      Inf      Inf
2  2 25.000000 50.00000 51.00000
3  3 16.666667 25.00000 26.00000
4  4 12.500000 16.66667 17.66667
5  5 10.000000 12.50000 13.50000
6  6  8.333333 10.00000 11.00000
> df <- df[-1, ]
> df_l <- melt(setDT(df), id.vars = "TT",
+              measure.vars = c("N1",
+                               "N2",
+                               "N3"),
+              variable.name = "Nname",
+              value.name = "N")
> ggplot(df_l, aes(x = TT, y = N,
+                  group = Nname,
+                  color = Nname)) +
+   geom_line(size = 1) +
+   theme_classic() +
+   theme(legend.title = element_blank())
```

Figure 3.46 shows that if the job should be finished in 5 days, 10 workers would be needed in case N1, 13 in case N2, and 14 in case N3. On the other hand, for a 10 day deadline, only 5 workers would be needed in case N1, 6 in case N2 and 7 in case N3.

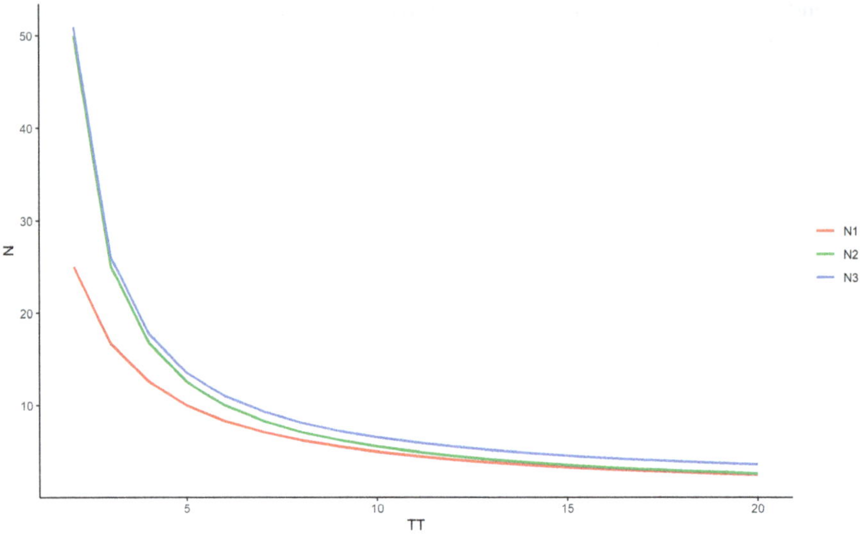

Fig. 3.46 A work example

```
> df[df$TT == 5 |
+        df$TT == 10, ]
   TT N1        N2        N3
1:  5 10 12.500000 13.500000
2: 10  5  5.555556  6.555556
```

3.9 Exercises

3.9.1 Exercise 1

Write a function to compute the vertex of a quadratic function. Replicate the result in Sect. 3.3.1

```
> vertex_quad(1, 2, -15)
[1] "The vertex is: (-1, -16)"
```

3.9.2 Exercise 2

Write a function that computes the percentage change. The function should return NA for the first entry. Replicate the following result

```
> revenue <- c("2017" = 98, "2018" = 100, "2019" = 120,
+              "2020" = 150, "2021" = 90)
```

```
> revenue
2017 2018 2019 2020 2021
  98  100  120  150   90
> per_change(revenue)
                   2018       2019       2020       2021
        NA   2.040816  20.000000  25.000000 -40.000000
```

3.9.3 Exercise 3

Write a function that computes the arithmetic mean (without using the `mean()` function) or the geometric mean based on the chosen method. Replicate the result in Sect. 3.6.5.2

```
> s <- c(2, 3, 7)
> avg(s, method = "arithmetic")
[1] 4
> avg(s, method = "geometric")
[1] 3.476027
```

3.9.4 Exercise 4

Modify the `exp_fn()` from Sect. 3.1 so that it works with bases different from *e* as well. Replicate the following results where the first function uses a base 5 while the second function uses base *e*

```
> s <- c(2, 3, 7)
> exp_fn(s, base = 5)
[1]    25   125 78125
> exp_fn(s)
[1]    7.389056   20.085537 1096.633158
```

3.9.5 Exercise 5

Rewrite the `time_invest()` function so that it computes and returns only the desired output.

Chapter 4
Differential Calculus

4.1 What is the Meaning of Derivatives?

The derivative is the instantaneous rate of change of a function. That is, in the study of functions, the derivative tells how the function is changing. For example, the common interpretation of the first derivative of a function is that it represents the slope of the function. We can interpret the slope as the change in y given the change in x. A positive first derivative (a positive slope) tells us that as x increases y also increases. A negative first derivative (a negative slope) tells us the as x increases y decreases. In Sect. 3.2.1, we reviewed how to compute the slope of a linear function $y = a + bx$. We could use calculus to get the slope. The advantage of using calculus is that we can easily compute the slope of a function different from linear functions as well.

Furthermore, in Sect. 3.5 we identified some critical points of a function such as the minimum of a function, the maximum of a function, and the inflection point. We can use calculus to obtain this information. For example, when the slope is 0, i.e. when the first derivative of the function is equal to zero, $f'(x = x^*) = 0$, the function may have reached a minimum or a maximum. In this case, x^* is known as *critical value* of x while $f(x = x^*)$ is known as the *stationary value* of the function f (or y). The point $(x^*, f(x = x^*))$ is known as *critical point* (or *stationary point*) because this point is situated in a standstill position.

Up to this point, we know we reached a maximum or minimum of the function or we found an inflection point of the function. To know which one we reached, we calculate a second derivative, i.e. the derivative of the derivative. A positive second derivative when the slope is equal to zero tells us the graph of the function at that point is concave up. Therefore, the extremum is established as a local minimum. On the other hand, a negative second derivative when the slope is equal to zero tells us the graph of the function at that point is concave down. Therefore, the extremum is established as a local maximum.

M. Porto, *Introduction to Mathematics for Economics with R*,
https://doi.org/10.1007/978-3-031-05202-6_4

However, there is a third option, i.e. the second derivative is equal to zero. In this case, we have a *necessary* condition to identify an *inflection point*. We also need that the second derivatives of the points immediately at the left and at the right of the point where the second derivative is zero, i.e. in the neighbourhood of that point, have different signs. This implies that the curvature of the function changes in that point (e.g. from concave up to concave down or from concave down to concave up—refer to Fig. 3.24).

What does the second derivative tell us if the first derivative is different from zero?

- If the first derivative is positive and the second derivative is positive, the function increases at an increasing rate;
- If the first derivative is positive and the second derivative is negative, the function increases at a decreasing rate;
- If the first derivative is negative and the second derivative is positive, the function decreases at a decreasing rate (i.e. it is decreasing more slowly);
- If the first derivative is negative and the second derivative is negative, the function decreases at an increasing rate (i.e. it is decreasing faster).

When we take the derivative of a function with respect to time t, we can interpret the function and its derivatives as follows. The function represents a position and its first derivative would tell us how fast it is changing, i.e. its velocity. Its second derivative would represent acceleration or deceleration, that is how fast the velocity increases or decreases.

4.2 The Limit of a Function

Before delving into the derivatives, we need to step back and talk about the limit of a function. Formally, the limit is defined as follows:

$$\lim_{x \to c} F(x) = L \tag{4.1}$$

where $F(x)$ is a function and c and L are real numbers. Equation 4.1 is read as "the limit as x approaches c of $F(x)$ is L". In other words, as x gets closer and closer to c, $F(x)$ gets closer and closer to L. If no such real number L exists we say that the limit does not exist.

An example in **R** can make the concept of the limit clear. Let's suppose we want to find the limit of the following:

$$\lim_{x \to 2} 5x^3$$

First, we generate a vector, a, that contains values from 0.1 to 0.00001. Then, we define the value that x should approach. Finally, we compute the limit by subtracting a from x.

```
> a <- 1/10^(1:5)
> x <- 2
> Fx <- 5*(x-a)^3
> Fx
[1] 34.29500 39.40300 39.94003 39.99400 39.99940
```

As we can observe, as x gets close to 2, $F(x)$ approaches 40.

Furthermore, observe that x is approaching 2 from the left, that is the real number is increasing to 2:

```
> x - a
[1] 1.90000 1.99000 1.99900 1.99990 1.99999
```

To have a limit, the same answer should be provided when x approaches 2 from the right, that is the number is decreasing to 2:

```
> x + a
[1] 2.10000 2.01000 2.00100 2.00010 2.00001
> Fx <- 5*(x+a)^3
> Fx
[1] 46.30500 40.60300 40.06003 40.00600 40.00060
```

As we can observe from this case too, as x gets close to 2, $F(x)$ approaches 40. Figure 4.1 gives a graphical representation.[1]

Next, we build a function to compute the limit, `LiMit()`. The first entry of the function is an expression, `expr`, in quotation marks that represents the limit we want to compute. The second entry, `x`, is the value x approaches. The third entry is `z` that represents the end of the sequence of exponents in `a`, a vector that contains smaller and smaller values. If `LEFT = TRUE`, the function computes the limit from the left. If `LEFT = FALSE`, the function computes the limit from the right. In the body of the function, the `gsub()` function substitutes `x` with `(x - a)` if `LEFT == TRUE`. It searches the value to substitute in `expr`. If `LEFT == FALSE`, it substitutes `x` with `(x + a)`. This outcome is saved in `res`. Then, we use the functions `eval()` and `parse()` to coerce `res` in a numeric class. In particular, `parse()` returns the parsed but unevaluated expressions in an expression and `eval()` evaluates an **R** expression in a specified environment.

```
> LiMiT <- function(expr, x,
+                    z = 7,
+                    LEFT = TRUE) {
+
```

[1] The code used to generate Figs. 4.1, 4.2, 4.3, 4.4, 4.5, 4.6, and 4.13 is available in Appendix D.

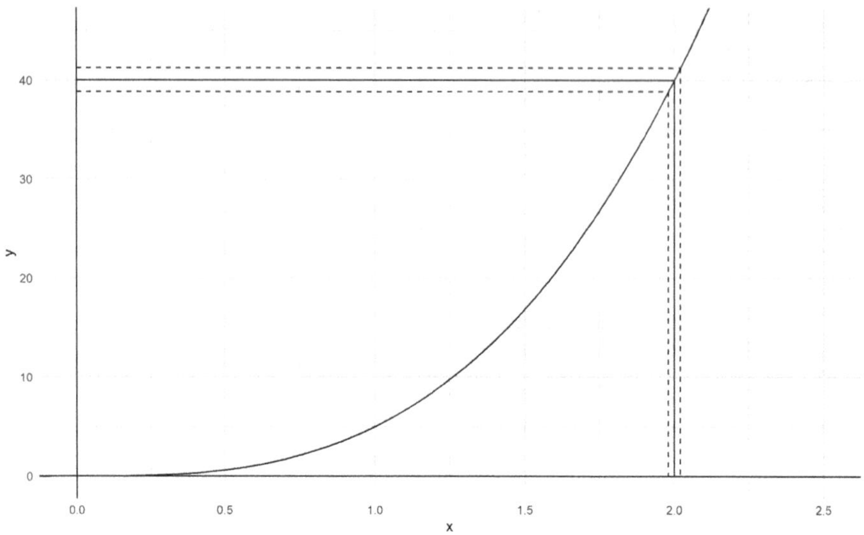

Fig. 4.1 Plot of $\lim_{x \to 2} 5x^3$

```
+     a <- 1/10^(1:z)
+
+     if(LEFT == TRUE){
+       res <- gsub("x", "(x-a)", expr)
+     } else{
+       res <- gsub("x", "(x+a)", expr)
+     }
+
+     res <- eval(parse(text = res))
+     return(res)
+
+ }
```

Finally, we test it. We compute $\lim_{x \to 2} 3x^2$. It results that as x gets closer and closer to 2 from the left and from the right, $3x^2$ approaches 12. Note that we nest the function in `format()` to expand the decimals.[2]

```
> format(LiMiT("3*x^2", 2), nsmall = 20)
[1] "10.83000000000000007105" "11.88030000000000008242"
[3] "11.98800300000000262912" "11.99880002999999994984"
[5] "11.99988000029999923868" "11.99998800000300036572"
[7] "11.99999880000003038560"
```

[2] Note also that for very large numbers of digits or decimals the results printed by **R** may not be completely accurate.

```
> format(LiMiT("3*x^2", 2, LEFT = FALSE), nsmall = 20)
[1] "13.23000000000000042633" "12.12029999999999674287"
[3] "12.01200299999999998590" "12.00120003000000323823"
[5] "12.00012000030000081097" "12.00001200000300194404"
[7] "12.00000120000002823417"
```

For the rest of the examples we are going to use `z = 5` to give the idea of the limit.

Then, we compute $\lim_{x \to 3} \frac{2x+1}{x^2}$. It results that as x gets closer and closer to 3 from the left and from the right, $\frac{2x+1}{x^2}$ approaches 0.7777.

```
> LiMiT("(2*x + 1)/x^2", 3, 5)
[1] 0.8085612 0.7807519 0.7780742 0.7778074 0.7777807
> LiMiT("(2*x + 1)/x^2", 3, 5, LEFT = FALSE)
[1] 0.7492196 0.7748259 0.7774816 0.7777481 0.7777748
```

Then, we compute $\lim_{x \to 1} \frac{3}{x-1}$. Note that as x gets closer and closer to 1 from the left, $F(x)$ becomes smaller and smaller. On the other hand, as x gets closer and closer to 1 from the right, $F(x)$ becomes larger and larger. This implies that the limit does not exist.

```
> LiMiT("3/(x-1)", 1, 5)
[1] -3e+01 -3e+02 -3e+03 -3e+04 -3e+05
> LiMiT("3/(x-1)", 1, 5, LEFT = FALSE)
[1] 3e+01 3e+02 3e+03 3e+04 3e+05
```

Let's see another example with a fraction. Let's compute $\lim_{x \to 1} \frac{x^2-1}{x-1}$. Note that $F(x = 1) = \frac{0}{0}$, that is indefinite. We write that $\lim_{x \to c} F(x) \neq F(c)$. However, the limit can still be evaluated. In fact, as x gets closer and closer to 1, $F(x)$ gets closer and closer to 2.

```
> LiMiT("(x^2 - 1)/(x - 1)", 1, 5)
[1] 1.90000 1.99000 1.99900 1.99990 1.99999
> LiMiT("(x^2 - 1)/(x - 1)", 1, 5, LEFT = FALSE)
[1] 2.10000 2.01000 2.00100 2.00010 2.00001
```

This is confirmed by a simple algebraic manipulation:

$$\frac{x^2 - 1}{x - 1} = \frac{(x - 1)(x + 1)}{x - 1} = x + 1$$

Then,

$$\lim_{x \to 1} x + 1 = 2$$

Next we compute the limit of $F(x) + G(x)$ and $F(x) \cdot G(x)$ where to make the explanation clearer $F(x) = 2x^2 + 1$ and $G(x) = \frac{3x^2}{2}$. Let's use the `LiMiT()`

function to compute the individual limits and then the limit of the addition and the limit of the multiplication of the two functions as x gets closer and closer to 3.

```
> LiMiT("2*x^2 + 1", 3, 5)
[1] 17.82000 18.88020 18.98800 18.99880 18.99988
> LiMiT("2*x^2 + 1", 3, 5, LEFT = F)
[1] 20.22000 19.12020 19.01200 19.00120 19.00012
> LiMiT("3*x^2 / 2", 3, 5)
[1] 12.61500 13.41015 13.49100 13.49910 13.49991
> LiMiT("3*x^2 / 2", 3, 5, LEFT = F)
[1] 14.41500 13.59015 13.50900 13.50090 13.50009
> LiMiT("(2*x^2 + 1) + (3*x^2 / 2)", 3, 5)
[1] 30.43500 32.29035 32.47900 32.49790 32.49979
> LiMiT("(2*x^2 + 1) + (3*x^2 / 2)", 3, 5, LEFT = F)
[1] 34.63500 32.71035 32.52100 32.50210 32.50021
> LiMiT("(2*x^2 + 1) * (3*x^2 / 2)", 3, 5)
[1] 224.7993 253.1863 256.1672 256.4667 256.4967
> LiMiT("(2*x^2 + 1) * (3*x^2 / 2)", 3, 5, LEFT = F)
[1] 291.4713 259.8464 256.8332 256.5333 256.5033
```

It results that as x gets closer and closer to 3, $F(x)$ gets closer and closer to 19; $G(x)$ gets closer and closer to 13.5; $F(x)+G(x)$ gets closer and closer to 32.5; and $F(x) \cdot G(x)$ gets closer and closer to 256.5. We note that $19 + 13.5 = 32.5$ and $19 \cdot 13.5 = 256.5$. Figure 4.2 gives a graphical representation of these results.

Therefore, we can summarize these results as follows.

Let $F(x), G(x) : D \to \mathbb{R}$, and let $L, M \in \mathbb{R}$ be such that

$$\lim_{x\to c} F(x) = L$$

and

$$\lim_{x\to c} G(x) = M$$

Then,

$$\lim_{x\to c} (F(x) + G(x)) = L + M$$

and

$$\lim_{x\to c} (F(x) \cdot G(x)) = L \cdot M$$

Furthermore, the same is true for the following:

$$\lim_{x\to c} (F(x) - G(x)) = L - M$$

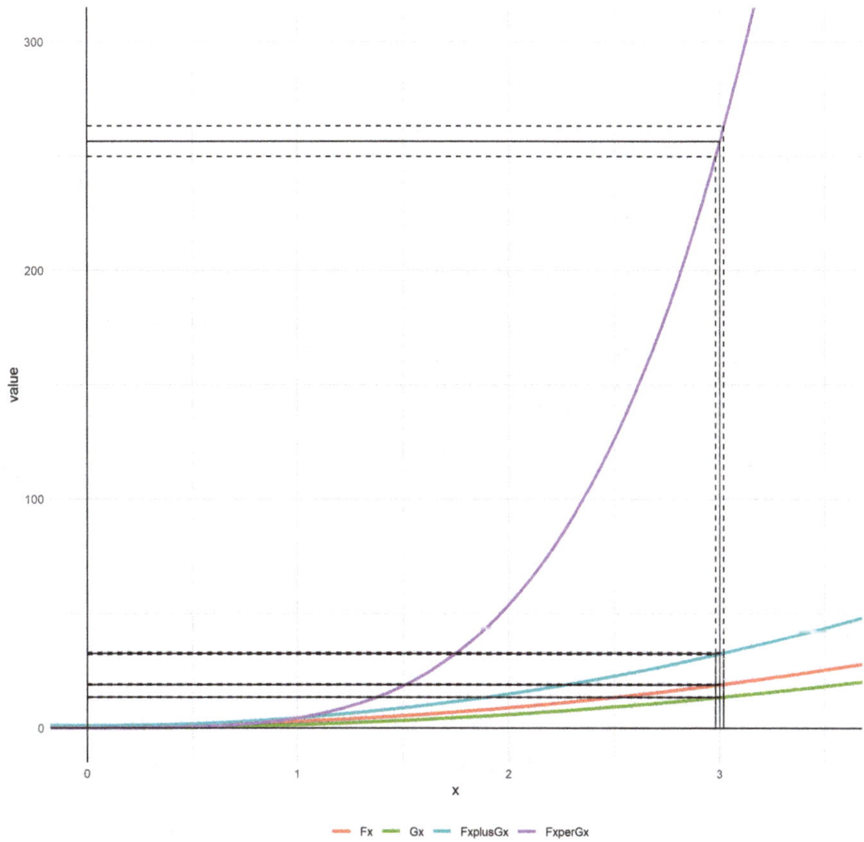

Fig. 4.2 Plot of the limit of $F(x) + G(x)$ and $F(x) \cdot G(x)$

$$\lim_{x \to c} kF(x) = kL$$

where k is a constant.

$$\lim_{x \to c} \frac{F(x)}{G(x)} = \frac{L}{M}, M \neq 0$$

$$\lim_{x \to c} [F(x)]^n = L^n$$

where n is any real number.

$$\lim_{x \to c} \sqrt[n]{F(x)} = \sqrt[n]{L}$$

4.3 Limits, Derivatives and Slope

In this section we examine the relationship among limits, derivatives and slope of a function. Figure 4.3 highlights that the slope changes continuously along the function; i.e. the slope is different for each point along the function.

Figure 4.4 shows one tangent line and two secant lines to the function. The secant lines passes through point A and point C and B, respectively.

We know how to compute the slope of a linear function as $\frac{rise}{run} = \frac{\Delta y}{\Delta x}$ (Sect. 3.2.1). Thus, note that as the distance gets closer and closer from point C to point A and from point B to point A, also the slope of the secant line becomes closer and closer to the slope of the tangent line. This "closer and closer" should ring a bell: we are recalling the concept of the limit.

In Fig. 4.5, Δx, dx in the figure, is equal to $(a + \Delta x) - a$ and represents an infinitesimal distance between two points. Δy, dy in the figure, is equal to $f(a + \Delta x) - f(a)$, i.e. the function evaluated at $f(a + \Delta x)$ minus the function evaluated at $f(a)$. Therefore, we can formally define the derivative as follows

$$\lim_{\Delta x \to 0} \frac{rise}{run} = \lim_{\Delta x \to 0} \frac{\Delta y}{\Delta x} = \lim_{\Delta x \to 0} \frac{f(x + \Delta x) - f(x)}{\Delta x} \tag{4.2}$$

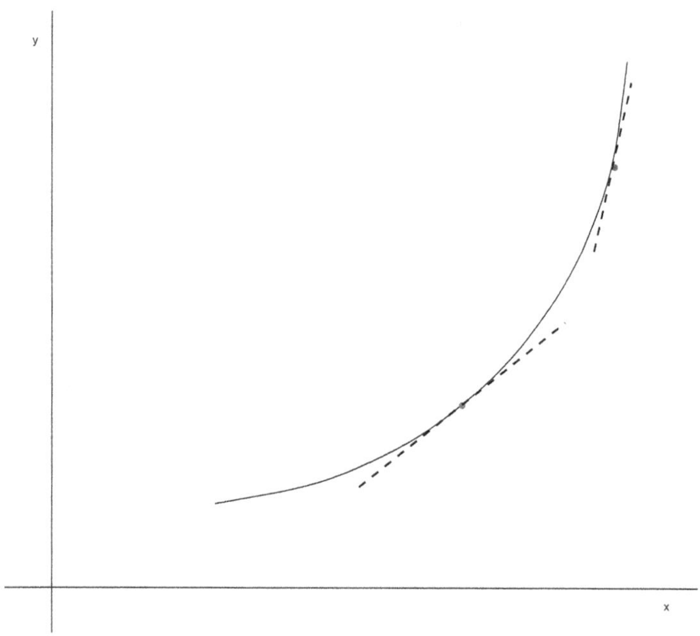

Fig. 4.3 Tangent lines to a function

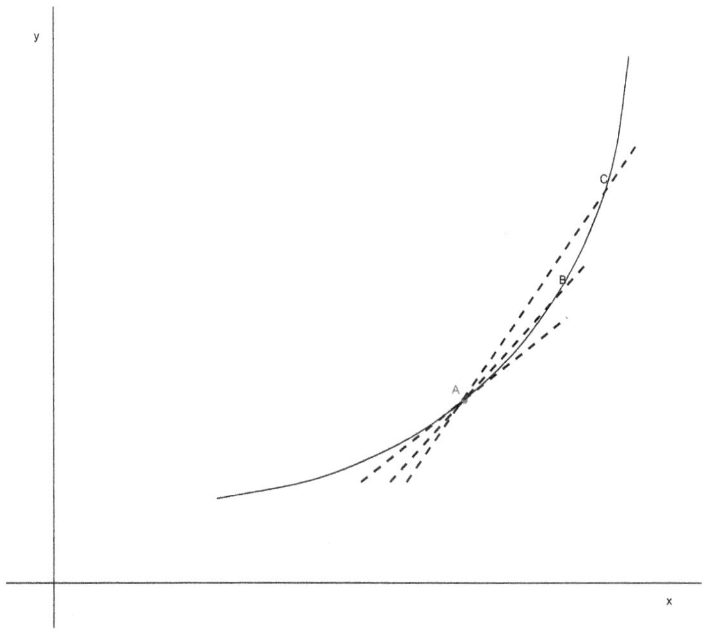

Fig. 4.4 Tangent line and secant lines to a function

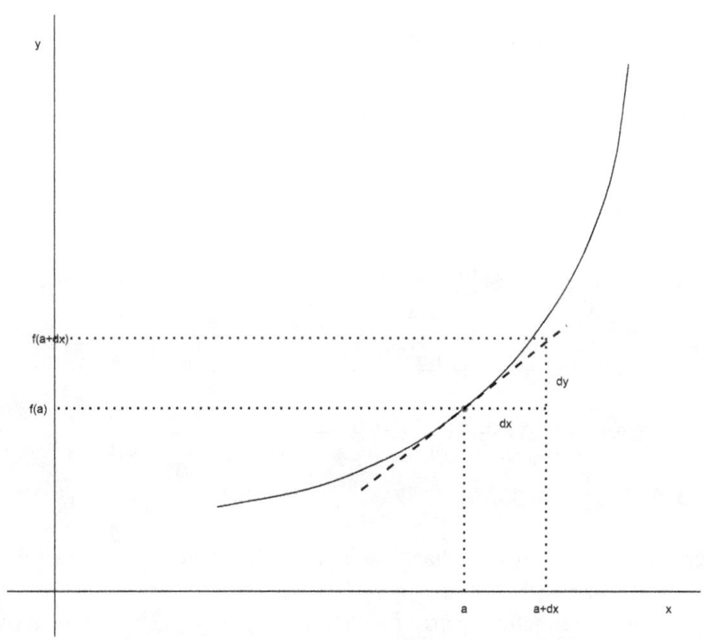

Fig. 4.5 Slope of a function

In Sect. 3.2.1, we found out that the slope of $y = 4 + 3x$ is 3. Now let's apply the definition given by (4.2) to compute the slope.

$$\begin{aligned}
f'(x) &= \lim_{\Delta x \to 0} \frac{f(x + \Delta x) - f(x)}{\Delta x} \\
&= \lim_{\Delta x \to 0} \frac{4 + 3(x + \Delta x) - (4 + 3x)}{\Delta x} \\
&= \lim_{\Delta x \to 0} \frac{4 + 3x + 3\Delta x - 4 - 3x}{\Delta x} \\
&= \lim_{\Delta x \to 0} \frac{3\Delta x}{\Delta x} \\
&= \lim_{\Delta x \to 0} 3 = 3
\end{aligned} \tag{4.3}$$

Note that $f(x)$ is just the function, while $f(x + \Delta x)$ is the function evaluated at this point, i.e. we substituted it for each x. As expected the derivative returns the same slope as we computed in Sect. 3.2.1. As we have seen in Chap. 3, in the case of a linear function the slope is the same for all the values of x. Additionally, note that the constant term, 4 in this example, cancels out since constant terms do not change by definition, i.e. the rate of change of a constant term is zero.

Let's try another example with a non-linear function. Let's compute the derivative of $y = x^2 + x - 1$ applying the definition in (4.2).

$$\begin{aligned}
f'(x) &= \lim_{\Delta x \to 0} \frac{(x + \Delta x)^2 + (x + \Delta x) - 1 - (x^2 + x - 1)}{\Delta x} \\
&= \lim_{\Delta x \to 0} \frac{x^2 + 2x\Delta x + (\Delta x)^2 + x + \Delta x - 1 - x^2 - x + 1}{\Delta x} \\
&= \lim_{\Delta x \to 0} \frac{(\Delta x)^2 + 2x\Delta x + \Delta x}{\Delta x} \\
&= \lim_{\Delta x \to 0} \frac{\Delta x(\Delta x + 2x + 1)}{\Delta x} \\
&= \lim_{\Delta x \to 0} \Delta x + 2x + 1 = 2x + 1
\end{aligned} \tag{4.4}$$

Its derivative is $2x + 1$ that changes based on the values of x. For example, it is 3 at $x = 1$ and 7 at $x = 3$.

Now let's write a function, `dfdx()`, that numerically computes the derivative at a given point based on (4.2)

```
> dfdx <- function(func, x0, deltax = 0.001){
+   (func(x0 + deltax) - func(x0))/deltax
+ }
```

Let's test it for the previous two examples

```
> fn <- function(x){
+   4 + 3*x
+ }
> dfdx(fn, x0 = 1)
[1] 3
> dfdx(fn, x0 = 3)
[1] 3
```

For the second example

```
> fn <- function(x){
+   x^2 + x - 1
+ }
> dfdx(fn, x0 = 1)
[1] 3.001
> dfdx(fn, x0 = 3)
[1] 7.001
```

Our `dfdx()` function confirms that for this linear function the derivative is 3 regardless of the x value, while for the non-linear function the value of the derivative changes with the x value.

4.3.1 Newton-Raphson Method

In Chap. 3, we wrote two functions, `quadratic_formula()` and `cub_eq_solver()`, to find the roots of a quadratic equation and of a cubic equation, respectively. Let's use the concept of the derivative to find the roots of a real-valued function by using the Newton's algorithm. The general idea behind the algorithm is to use tangent lines to the function to get better approximation of the roots.

The Newton's method, also known as Newton-Raphson method, is given by the following iteration process

$$x_{n+1} = x_n - \frac{f(x_n)}{f'(x_n)}, \quad [f'(x_n) \neq 0] \tag{4.5}$$

where the denominator $f'(x_n)$ is the derivative of the function $f(x_n)$ evaluated at x_n, x_n is the approximation of the root, and x_{n+1} is a better approximation of the root as consequence of the iteration process.

Discussing the Newton algorithm is well beyond the scope of this book. Our main purpose here is to check our understanding of the notation of the algorithm and turn the notation into a code. However, let's try to figure out where (4.5) comes from. In approximating the value of the root, we can say that x_{n+1} and x_n differ by an amount Δx

$$x_{n+1} = x_n - \Delta x \tag{4.6}$$

Our goal is to determine Δx. We know that the slope is the rise over the run, where the slope is $f'(x_n)$, the rise is $f(x_n)$—i.e. the derivative of the function and the function evaluated at x_n—and the run is Δx. Therefore

$$f'(x_n) = \frac{f(x_n)}{\Delta x} \tag{4.7}$$

By solving (4.7) for Δx and replacing the outcome in (4.6) we end up with the formula in (4.5).

To be remarked that the Newton's method is an iteration process. For example, let's apply the Newton's algorithm to $x^2 + x - 1 = 0$. Since this is a quadratic equation we know that we can have maximum two roots. Let's find one root. From (4.5), we need

- $f(x)$, that in our example is $x^2 + x - 1$
- $f'(x)$, that is the derivative of $f(x)$. We computed it earlier and we found that it is $2x + 1$
- x_0, that is an initial guess

Let's start by plugging 0 in $f(x)$

$$f(0) = 0^2 + 0 - 1 = -1$$

Now let's try with 1

$$f(1) = 1^2 + 1 - 1 = 1$$

Since we observe that the value of the function changes sign with values 0 and 1, we guess that one root has value between 0 and 1. Therefore, let's set our guess $x_0 = 0$ and let's implement (4.5)

$$x_1 = x_0 - \frac{f(x_0)}{f'(x_0)} = 0 - \frac{0^2 + 0 - 1}{2(0) + 1} = 1$$

$$x_2 = x_1 - \frac{f(x_1)}{f'(x_1)} = 1 - \frac{1^2 + 1 - 1}{2(1) + 1} = 0.6666667$$

$$x_3 = x_2 - \frac{f(x_2)}{f'(x_2)} = 0.6666667 - \frac{0.6666667^2 + 0.6666667 - 1}{2(0.6666667) + 1} = 0.6190476$$

$$x_4 = x_3 - \frac{f(x_3)}{f'(x_3)} = 0.6190476 - \frac{0.6190476^2 + 0.6190476 - 1}{2(0.6190476) + 1} = 0.6180344$$

$$x_5 = x_4 - \frac{f(x_4)}{f'(x_4)} = 0.6180344 - \frac{0.6180344^2 + 0.6180344 - 1}{2(0.6180344) + 1} = 0.6180344$$

As we can see the algorithm converges to 0.6180344. Therefore, $x = 0.6180344$ is one root. We can test it by plugging it in the initial equation

$$0.6180344^2 + 0.6180344 - 1 = 0$$

Note that x_4 and x_5 produces the same seven digits result. However, if we increase the digits to the right of the decimal point we would observe a tiny difference. This difference (Δx), or this "tolerance", is the degree of precision that we set to accept the solution as a root of the equation.

We implement the iteration process given by (4.5) with a function that we call `newton()`. The function takes five arguments:

- `func`: the function for which the root is sought.
- `x0`: an initial guess.
- `deltax`: an infinitesimal distance between two points. By default equal to 0.001.
- `maxIterations`: the maximum number of iterations. By default equal to 500.
- `tolerance`: the desired accuracy (convergence tolerance). By default 12 digits accuracy.

At the beginning, we generate `res` to store the iterations and we initialize `count` to control for the loop. We use a `while()` loop that iterates as long as `count` is less or equal to `maxIterations`. `x1` in the `while()` loop represents x_{n+1} in (4.5). Note that we use the `dfdx()` function to compute the derivative in the denominator. The results are stored in `res`. The condition to stop the loop is that the absolute value of the difference between x_{n+1} (`x1`) and x_n (`x0`) is less than the tolerance level. If the loop continues to iterate, the values of `x0` and `count` are updated. Finally, the function returns the root, if any, the iterations and the number of iterations.

```
> newton <- function(func, x0, deltax = 0.001,
+                    maxIterations = 500,
+                    tolerance = 1e-12){
+
+   res <- numeric(maxIterations)
+   count <- 1
+
```

```
+   while(count <= maxIterations){
+
+     x1 <- x0 - (func(x0)/dfdx(func, x0, deltax))
+     res[count] <- x1
+
+     if(abs(x1 - x0) < tolerance){
+
+       break
+
+     }
+
+     x0 <- x1
+     count <- count + 1
+
+   }
+
+   l <- list("root" = res[count],
+             "iterations" = res[1:count],
+             "number iterations" = count)
+
+   return(l)
+
+ }
```

Let's replicate the previous example

```
> fn <- function(x){
+   x^2 + x - 1
+ }
> r <- newton(fn, x0 = 0)
> r
$root
[1] 0.618034

$iterations
[1] 0.9990010 0.6665557 0.6190635 0.6180349
[5] 0.6180340 0.6180340 0.6180340

$`number iterations`
[1] 7
```

The `newton()` function confirms our solution. However, note that the first terms of the iteration differ from ours. Why is that? The reason is that in our manual computation we used the exact derivative of the function while in `newton()` we compute the derivative with the `dfdx()` function and its approximation `deltax = 0.001`. Nevertheless, we reach the same conclusion.

Additionally, observe that the result for iteration 5, 6, and 7 is the same to seven digits. If we expand the digits

```
> format(r$iterations[5:7], nsmall = 20)
[1] "0.61803398916737795066" "0.61803398875008141999"
[3] "0.61803398874989490253"
```

We observe a tiny difference between those values. Let's check why it stopped after seven iterations by comparing the difference $x_6 - x_5$ and $x_7 - x_6$ with our tolerance threshold

```
> abs(diff(r$iterations[6:5])) < 1e-12
[1] FALSE
> abs(diff(r$iterations[7:6])) < 1e-12
[1] TRUE
```

As we can see, $x_7 - x_6$ fulfils the condition to break the loop.

Let's find the other root by setting $x_0 = -1$

```
> r <- newton(fn, x0 = -1)
> r$root
[1] -1.618034
```

Therefore, the roots of $x^2 + x - 1 = 0$ are 0.618034 and -1.618034.

Let's test `newton()` by replicating some of the results of `quadratic_formula()` and `cub_eq_solver()`.

```
> fn <- function(x){
+    -x^2 + 3*x + 4
+ }
> newton(fn, x0 = 0)
$root
[1] -1

$iterations
[1] -1.333778 -1.019602 -1.000072 -1.000000
[5] -1.000000 -1.000000 -1.000000

$`number iterations`
[1] 7

> newton(fn, x0 = 2)
$root
[1] 4
```

```
$iterations
[1] 7.994006 5.228429 4.202507 4.007623
[5] 4.000013 4.000000 4.000000 4.000000

$`number iterations`
[1] 8
```

This is the result for $y = -x^2 + 3x + 4$. Note that we have to provide different guess to find all the roots. Later on, we will use the **R** base function `uniroot()` to find the roots. In that case, we will select an interval where to search for the roots.

```
> fn <- function(x){
+   x^3 - 4*x^2 + x + 6
+ }
> newton(fn, x0 = 0)
$root
[1] -1

$iterations
 [1] -6.024090 -3.722168 -2.274424 -1.446497
 [5] -1.083321 -1.003729 -1.000006 -1.000000
 [9] -1.000000 -1.000000 -1.000000

$`number iterations`
[1] 11

> newton(fn, x0 = 1)
$root
[1] 2

$iterations
[1] 1.99975 2.00000 2.00000 2.00000 2.00000

$`number iterations`
[1] 5

> newton(fn, x0 = 5)
$root
[1] 3

$iterations
[1] 4.000305 3.412211 3.114868 3.013405
[5] 3.000235 3.000000 3.000000 3.000000 3.000000

$`number iterations`
[1] 9
```

```
> fn <- function(x){
+   3*x^3 + 5
+ }
> newton(fn, x0 = 0)
$root
[1] -1.185631

$iterations
 [1] -1.666667e+06 -1.111111e+06 -7.407407e+05 -4.938271e+05
 [5] -3.292181e+05 -2.194787e+05 -1.463191e+05 -9.754609e+04
 [9] -6.503073e+04 -4.335382e+04 -2.890255e+04 -1.926836e+04
[13] -1.284558e+04 -8.563717e+03 -5.709144e+03 -3.806096e+03
[17] -2.537397e+03 -1.691598e+03 -1.127731e+03 -7.518206e+02
[21] -5.012134e+02 -3.341419e+02 -2.227610e+02 -1.485070e+02
[25] -9.900435e+01 -6.600262e+01 -4.400154e+01 -2.933431e+01
[29] -1.955652e+01 -1.303880e+01 -8.695468e+00 -5.803994e+00
[33] -3.885491e+00 -2.626802e+00 -1.831413e+00 -1.386335e+00
[37] -1.213161e+00 -1.186229e+00 -1.185631e+00 -1.185631e+00
[41] -1.185631e+00 -1.185631e+00

$`number iterations`
[1] 42

> fn <- function(x){
+   -x^3 + 2*x^2 + 4*x
+ }
> newton(fn, x0 = -1)
$root
[1] -1.236068

$iterations
[1] -1.333890 -1.244453 -1.236131 -1.236068
[5] -1.236068 -1.236068 -1.236068

$`number iterations`
[1] 7

> round(newton(fn, x0 = 1)$root, 1)
[1] 0
> newton(fn, x0 = 3)
$root
[1] 3.236068

$iterations
[1] 3.272554 3.236775 3.236069 3.236068
[5] 3.236068 3.236068
```

```
$`number iterations`
[1] 6
```

To conclude this digression in the Newton's algorithm, note that

- the Newton's algorithm can find the roots of differentiable functions (not exclusively polynomial functions as in our examples)
- convergence is not guaranteed
- there are other algorithms to find the roots of a function

We will return to the Newton's algorithm in Sect. 4.10.2.

4.4 Notation of Derivatives

Different equivalent notations are used to express derivatives in Mathematics. For the function $y = f(x)$, we may find the first derivative expressed as follows

$$\frac{dy}{dx}$$

$$\frac{df}{dx}(x) = \frac{d}{dx}f(x) = \frac{df(x)}{dx}$$

$$f'$$

$$f'(x)$$

The second derivative (i.e. the derivative of a derivative) may be expressed as follows:

$$\frac{d^2y}{dx^2}$$

$$\frac{d^2f}{dx^2}$$

$$f''$$

$$f''(x)$$

Higher derivatives follows the same pattern. For example, $\frac{d^3y}{dx^3}$ is the third derivative.

In addition, we introduce here a different notation that we will encounter in multivariable calculus (Chap. 6), i.e. when an endogenous variable depends on two or more exogenous variables. For example, for $z = f(x, y)$ we may find the first derivative expressed as follows:

$$f' = \frac{df}{dx} = f_x$$

$$f_{\prime} = \frac{df}{dy} = f_y$$

$$\frac{\partial f}{\partial x}$$

$$\frac{\partial f}{\partial y}$$

And the second derivative as:

$$f'' = \frac{d^2 f}{dx^2} = f_{xx}$$

$$f_{\prime\prime} = \frac{d^2 f}{dy^2} = f_{yy}$$

$$\frac{\partial^2 f}{\partial x^2}$$

$$\frac{\partial^2 f}{\partial y^2}$$

Furthermore, a different notation is used for the derivative of the function with respect to time t. We may encounter this notation in differential equations (Chap. 11) and dynamic models. For example,

$$\frac{dx(t)}{dt} = \dot{x}$$

where t denotes the real-valued time argument and $x(t)$ denotes some variable which depends on t. With this notation, $\ddot{x}$ denotes the second derivative.

Finally, the value of the derivative of y evaluated at a particular point a can be expressed as follows:

$$\left.\frac{dy}{dx}\right|_{x=a}$$

4.5 Differentials

In Sect. 4.3 we defined a derivative of a function of one variable $y = f(x)$ as

$$\frac{dy}{dx} = \lim_{\Delta x \to 0} \frac{\Delta y}{\Delta x} \tag{4.8}$$

Consequently,

$$\frac{dy}{dx} \neq \frac{\Delta y}{\Delta x}$$

because they differ by an amount

$$\frac{\Delta y}{\Delta x} - \frac{dy}{dx} = \delta \tag{4.9}$$

Additionally, by (4.8), $\delta \to 0$ as $\Delta x \to 0$.

By rearranging (4.9) and multiplying both sides of the equation by Δx we have

$$\Delta y = \frac{dy}{dx}\Delta x + \delta \Delta x \tag{4.10}$$

that tells us how y changes, Δy, as consequence of the change in x, Δx.

By ignoring $\delta \Delta x$,

$$\Delta y = \frac{dy}{dx}\Delta x \tag{4.11}$$

the right-hand side in (4.11) works as an approximation of the change in y that gets better and better as Δx gets smaller and smaller.

Furthermore, by rearranging (4.10) we have

$$\Delta y = \left(\frac{dy}{dx} + \delta\right)\Delta x$$

$$\frac{\Delta y}{\Delta x} = \frac{dy}{dx} + \delta$$

$$\frac{dy}{dx} = \frac{\Delta y}{\Delta x} - \delta$$

and by (4.9) and (4.8)

$$\frac{dy}{dx} = f'(x)$$

Finally, by considering $\frac{dy}{dx}$ a separable mathematical entity and by solving for dy we have

$$dy = f'(x)\,dx \tag{4.12}$$

where dy and dx are called differentials of y and x, respectively, where dy is the dependent variable that depends both on x and dx, and dx is the independent variable. This process of finding dy is called *differentiation*. We will return to differentials in Chapter 6.

4.6 Rules of Differentiation

In Sect. 4.3, we computed the derivative applying the general definition. However, we can compute the derivative in an easier way by applying some rules. In the next sections, we will state the main rules with some examples.

4.6.1 Power Rule

$$y = x^n \rightarrow \frac{dy}{dx} = n \cdot x^{n-1}$$

Example 4.6.1

$$y = x^3 \rightarrow \frac{dy}{dx} = 3 \cdot x^{3-1} = 3x^2$$

$$y = cx^n \rightarrow \frac{dy}{dx} = c \cdot n \cdot x^{n-1}$$

where c is a constant.

Example 4.6.2

$$y = 5x^3 \rightarrow \frac{dy}{dx} = 5 \cdot 3 \cdot x^{3-1} = 15x^2$$

What about the derivative of a constant? The derivative of a constant is 0. A tricky way to see it with the power rule is the following:

$$y = c = cx^0 \rightarrow \frac{dy}{dx} = c \cdot 0 \cdot x^{0-1} = 0$$

because $x^0 = 1$, $c = cx^0$ and any number multiplied by 0 is 0.

Example 4.6.3

$$y = 5 = 5x^0 \rightarrow \frac{dy}{dx} = 5 \cdot 0 \cdot x^{0-1} = 0$$

Example 4.6.4

$$y = 5x^{-3} \rightarrow \frac{dy}{dx} = 5 \cdot (-3) \cdot x^{-3-1} = -15x^{-4}$$

$$y = -15x^{-4} \rightarrow \frac{dy}{dx} = (-15) \cdot (-4) \cdot x^{-4-1} = 60x^{-5}$$

Therefore, we computed the second derivative of $y = 5x^{-3}$, or

$$y = 5x^{-3} \rightarrow \frac{d^2y}{dx^2} = 60x^{-5}$$

Example 4.6.5

$$y = x^2 + 2x - 15 \rightarrow \frac{dy}{dx} = 2x + 2$$

$$y = \frac{1}{x} = x^{-1} \rightarrow \frac{dy}{dx} = (-1) \cdot x^{-1-1} = -x^{-2} = -\frac{1}{x^2}$$

$$y = 3x^5 - 4x^4 + \frac{1}{x^3} = 3x^5 - 4x^4 + x^{-3}$$

$$\rightarrow \frac{dy}{dx} = 3 \cdot 5 \cdot x^{5-1} - 4 \cdot 4 \cdot x^{4-1} + 1 \cdot (-3) \cdot x^{-3-1}$$

$$= 15x^4 - 16x^3 - 3x^{-4} = 15x^4 - 16x^3 - \frac{3}{x^4} \tag{4.13}$$

4.6.2 Product Rule

$$\frac{d}{dx}[f(x) \cdot g(x)] = fg^{'} + f^{'}g$$

Suppose $y = (x^4 + 2x^3)(4x^3 + 6x^2)$. According to the product rule, we first multiply the first function

$$(x^4 + 2x^3)$$

times the derivative of the second function, i.e.

$$\frac{dy}{dx} = 4 \cdot 3 \cdot x^{3-1} + 6 \cdot 2 \cdot x^{2-1} = 12x^2 + 12x$$

and then add the derivative of the first function, i.e.

$$\frac{dy}{dx} = 4 \cdot x^{4-1} + 2 \cdot 3 \cdot x^{3-1} = 4x^3 + 6x^2$$

times the second function

$$(4x^3 + 6x^2)$$

Putting all together we have

$$\begin{aligned}\frac{dy}{dx} &= (x^4 + 2x^3)(12x^2 + 12x) + (4x^3 + 6x^2)(4x^3 + 6x^2)\\ &= (x^4 + 2x^3)(12x^2 + 12x) + (4x^3 + 6x^2)^2\\ &= 28x^6 + 84x^5 + 60x^4 \end{aligned} \tag{4.14}$$

4.6.3 Quotient Rule

$$\frac{d}{dx}\left[\frac{f(x)}{g(x)}\right] = \frac{gf^{'} - fg^{'}}{(g)^2}$$

Suppose $y = \frac{x^4+2x^3}{4x^3+6x^2}$. According to the quotient rule, we first multiply the denominator function

$$4x^3 + 6x^2$$

times the derivative of the numerator function, i.e.

$$\frac{dy}{dx} = 4 \cdot x^{4-1} + 2 \cdot 3 \cdot x^{3-1} = 4x^3 + 6x^2$$

and then subtract the numerator function

$$x^4 + 2x^3$$

times the derivative of the denominator function, i.e.

$$\frac{dy}{dx} = 4 \cdot 3 \cdot x^{3-1} + 6 \cdot 2 \cdot x^{2-1} = 12x^2 + 12x$$

and finally divide all by the square of the denominator function, i.e.

$$(4x^3 + 6x^2)^2$$

Putting all together, we have

$$\begin{aligned}\frac{dy}{dx} &= \frac{(4x^3 + 6x^2)(4x^3 + 6x^2) - (x^4 + 2x^3)(12x^2 + 12x)}{(4x^3 + 6x^2)^2} \\ &= \frac{x^2 + 3x + 3}{(2x + 3)^2}\end{aligned} \tag{4.15}$$

4.6.4 Chain Rule

Chain rule applies when we have a composite function as $f(g(x))$. Its derivative is

$$\frac{d}{dx}[f(g(x))] = f'(g(x))g'(x)$$

The key to apply the chain rule is to distinguish the inner function from the outer function.

For example, for $h(x) = (x^4 + 2x^3)^2$, $g(x) = x^4 + 2x^3$ is the inner function and $f(x) = (x)^2$ is the outer function evaluated at the inner function.

Therefore, let's start from the outer function where in this case we just apply the power rule from Sect. 4.6.1, i.e. $2 \cdot (x^4 + 2x^3)^{2-1}$.

Then, we work with the inner function, i.e. $4 \cdot x^{4-1} + 2 \cdot 3 \cdot x^{3-1}$. Multiplying the two terms from the outer and inner functions we have

$$\frac{dy}{dx} = 2(x^4 + 2x^3)(4x^3 + 6x^2)$$

Example 4.6.6

$$y = \frac{1}{(x^4 + 2x^3)^2} = (x^4 + 2x^3)^{-2}$$

Consequently, the derivative is

$$\frac{dy}{dx} = (-2)(x^4 + 2x^3)^{-3}(4x^3 + 6x^2) = -\frac{2(4x^3 + 6x^2)}{(x^4 + 2x^3)^3}$$

4.6.4.1 Implicit Differentiation

$$y = f(x) \quad \text{given as} \quad F(x, y) = c \rightarrow f'(x) = -\frac{F_x(x, y)}{F_y(x, y)}$$

A particular application of the chain rule is used in the case of the so called *implicit differentiation*. We may use implicit differentiation when it is not convenient to represent an equation as a standard function where y is function of x.

Let's see an example with $2x^4 + y^3 = 1$. It is not in the *standard* format where y is function of x. Because y is not *explicitly* defined as a function of x we say that we take an *implicit differentiation*.

To differentiate with respect to x, first differentiate both sides with respect to x.

$$\frac{d}{dx}(2x^4 + y^3) = \frac{d}{dx}1$$

Note that the right hand side of the equation is 0 because it is a derivative of a constant. Therefore,

$$\frac{d}{dx}(2x^4 + y^3) = 0$$

Because the derivatives of a sum is the sum of the derivatives, we can rewrite the left hand side as

$$\frac{d}{dx}(2x^4) + \frac{d}{dx}(y^3) = 0$$

The first term is simple. The derivative of $2x^4$ with respect to x is $8x^3$.

Now let's apply the chain rule to $\frac{d}{dx}(y^3)$, where we take the derivative of the outer function $(y)^3$ times the derivative of the inner function $\frac{d}{dx}y$, i.e. $3y^2 \cdot \frac{dy}{dx}$.

Putting all together, we have

$$8x^3 + 3y^2\frac{dy}{dx} = 0$$

Next, solve for $\frac{dy}{dx}$

$$\frac{dy}{dx} = -\frac{8x^3}{3y^2}$$

Applying directly the formula[3] $-\frac{F_x(x,y)}{F_y(x,y)}$

$$-\frac{2x^4 + y^3}{2x^4 + y^3} = -\frac{8x^3}{3y^2}$$

4.6.5 *Radicals Differentiation*

$$y = \sqrt[n]{x} = x^{\frac{1}{n}} \rightarrow \frac{dy}{dx} = \frac{1}{n}x^{\frac{1}{n}-1}$$

Example 4.6.7

$$y = \sqrt{x} = x^{\frac{1}{2}} \rightarrow \frac{dy}{dx} = \frac{1}{2}x^{\frac{1}{2}-1} = \frac{1}{2x^{\frac{1}{2}}}$$

Example 4.6.8

$$y = \sqrt[3]{2x+1} = (2x+1)^{\frac{1}{3}} \rightarrow \frac{dy}{dx} = \frac{1}{3}(2x+1)^{\frac{1}{3}-1} \cdot 2 = \frac{2}{3(2x+1)^{\frac{2}{3}}}$$

4.6.6 *Logarithmic Differentiation*

In this section, we will focus on the differentiation of natural logarithms.

$$y = \log(x)$$

[3] We will return to the technique in Chap. 6.

By taking the exponential of both sides

$$e^y = x \tag{4.16}$$

Given that the derivative with respect to y of e^y is e^y (Sect. 4.6.7):

$$\frac{dx}{dy} = e^y$$

Take the reciprocal of both sides

$$\frac{dy}{dx} = \frac{1}{e^y}$$

But given (4.16), consequently we have

$$y = \log(x) \rightarrow \frac{dy}{dx} = \frac{1}{x}$$

Example 4.6.9

$$y = \log(x^2 + 3) \rightarrow \frac{dy}{dx} = \frac{1}{x^2 + 3} \cdot 2x$$

We used the chain rule, i.e. the derivative of the outer function, log, times the derivative of the inner function, $x^2 + 3$.

Logarithmic properties prove to be very useful for differentiation.

Example 4.6.10

$$y = \log 4x \rightarrow \frac{dy}{dx}\log(4) + \frac{dy}{dx}\log(x) = \frac{1}{x}$$

Example 4.6.11

$$y = \log\frac{x^2 + 3}{x + 1} \rightarrow \frac{dy}{dx}\log(x^2 + 3) - \frac{dy}{dx}\log(x + 1) = \frac{2x}{x^2 + 3} - \frac{1}{x + 1}$$

Example 4.6.12

$$y = \log\left[(2x - 1)^3\right] = 3\log(2x - 1) \rightarrow \frac{dx}{dy} = \frac{6}{2x - 1}$$

4.6.7 Exponential Differentiation

$$y = e^x \rightarrow \frac{dy}{dx} = e^x$$

The derivative of e^x is e^x itself. This means that the slope is the same as the function value (the y-value) for all points on the graph.

Example 4.6.13

$$y = e^{-x} \rightarrow \frac{dy}{dx} = -e^{-x}$$

Example 4.6.14

$$y = e^{5x^2} \rightarrow \frac{dy}{dx} = 10xe^{5x^2}$$

Note that in both examples we used the chain rule.

4.6.7.1 Exponential Growth and Logistic Growth

In Sect. 3.6.7.2, we introduced the exponential growth and the logistic growth. Let's differentiate those functions to get the rate of growth.

In the case of the exponential growth, the general equation is (3.29) that we rewrite here for convenience:

$$N(t) = N_0 e^{rt}$$

Let's differentiate N with respect to t.

$$\frac{dN}{dt} = rN_0 e^{rt}$$

Note that $N = N_0 e^{rt}$, therefore,

$$\frac{dN}{dt} = rN \tag{4.17}$$

that tells us the as the population, N, increases, the rate at which population increases, $\frac{dN}{dt}$, increases as well.

In the case of the logistic growth, the general equation is (3.30) that we rewrite here for convenience:

$$N(t) = \frac{K}{1 + \left(\frac{K - N_0}{N_0}\right) e^{-rt}}$$

For convenience we set $\frac{K-N_0}{N_0} = A$.

$$N(t) = \frac{K}{1 + Ae^{-rt}} \tag{4.18}$$

Let's rewrite (4.18) as follows

$$N = K(1 + Ae^{-rt})^{-1}$$

Note that we can apply the chain rule. The outer function is $()^-1$ and the inner function is $1 + Ae^{-rt}$. Therefore,

$$\begin{aligned}\frac{dN}{dt} &= (-1) \cdot K(1 + Ae^{-rt})^{-2} \cdot (-rAe^{-rt}) \\ &= \frac{rKAe^{-rt}}{(1 + Ae^{-rt})^2} \\ &= r \cdot \frac{K}{1 + Ae^{-rt}} \cdot \frac{Ae^{-rt}}{1 + Ae^{-rt}} \end{aligned} \tag{4.19}$$

Note that the second term is equal to *N*. Therefore, we write

$$\frac{dN}{dt} = r \cdot N \cdot \frac{Ae^{-rt}}{1 + Ae^{-rt}}$$

Note that the third term can be rewritten as $1 - \frac{1}{1+Ae^{-rt}}$. Let's write (4.18) as

$$N(t) = K \cdot \frac{1}{1 + Ae^{-rt}}$$

We can see that

$$\frac{1}{1 + Ae^{-rt}} = \frac{N}{K}$$

Consequently, we can write $1 - \frac{1}{1+Ae^{-rt}}$ as $1 - \frac{N}{K}$.
Finally,

$$\frac{dN}{dt} = rN\left(1 - \frac{N}{K}\right) \tag{4.20}$$

Equation 4.20 tells us that as N increases $\frac{dN}{dt}$ increases as well. However, in the limit of N that approaches 0, $\frac{N}{K}$ will be approximately 0, and consequently $\left(1 - \frac{N}{K}\right)$ will be 1.

$$\lim_{N \to 0} rN \left(1 - \frac{N}{K}\right) = rN$$

This means that (4.20) will become $\frac{dN}{dt} = rN$, i.e. as (4.17). This means that when N is very small the logistic growth function behaves like the exponential growth function. On the other hand, if N approaches the limit given by the carrying capacity K, $\frac{N}{K}$ will tend to 1, and consequently $\left(1 - \frac{N}{K}\right)$ will be 0.

$$\lim_{N \to K} rN \left(1 - \frac{N}{K}\right) = 0$$

This means that (4.20) will be $\frac{dN}{dt} = 0$, that is the slope of the curve is 0. Refer to Fig. 3.36.

4.6.8 Derivatives of Elementary Functions

Table 4.1 shows the derivative of some elementary functions.

Table 4.1 Derivatives of some elementary functions

$f(x)$	$f'(x)$
$c = const$	0
x	1
x^n	$n \cdot x^{n-1}$
$\frac{1}{x}$	$-\frac{1}{x^2}$
$\frac{1}{x^n}$	$-\frac{n}{x^{n+1}}$
$\sqrt{x}$	$\frac{1}{2\sqrt{x}}$
$\sqrt[n]{x}$	$\frac{1}{n\sqrt[n]{x^{n-1}}}$
x^x	$x^x(\log(x+1)$
e^x	e^x
a^x	$a^x \log(a)$
$\log(x)$	$\frac{1}{x}$
$\log_a(x)$	$\frac{1}{x\log(a)} = \frac{1}{x}\log_a(e)$

4.7 Derivatives and Inverse Functions

In Sect. 3.1.1, we said that the function $f(x) = 7x + 3$ is a bijective function. Consequently, it is invertible. We found that its inverse is $f^{-1}(y) = \frac{y-3}{7}$.

We can use differential calculus to find if a function has an inverse. If the first derivative has always positive (negative) sign regardless of the value of x, the slope of the function is always upward (downward). This means that the function passes the horizontal line test (HLT), i.e. the graph of the function crosses an horizontal line only once.

In our example, the derivative $f'(x) = 7$. This tells us that the function has always an upward sloping and passes the HLT (Fig. 4.6).

The following rule of differentiation for inverse functions applies

$$\frac{dx}{dy} = \frac{1}{\frac{dy}{dx}} \tag{4.21}$$

that is the derivative of the inverse function is the reciprocal of the derivative of the original function.

In our case,

$$\frac{dx}{dy} = \frac{1}{7}$$

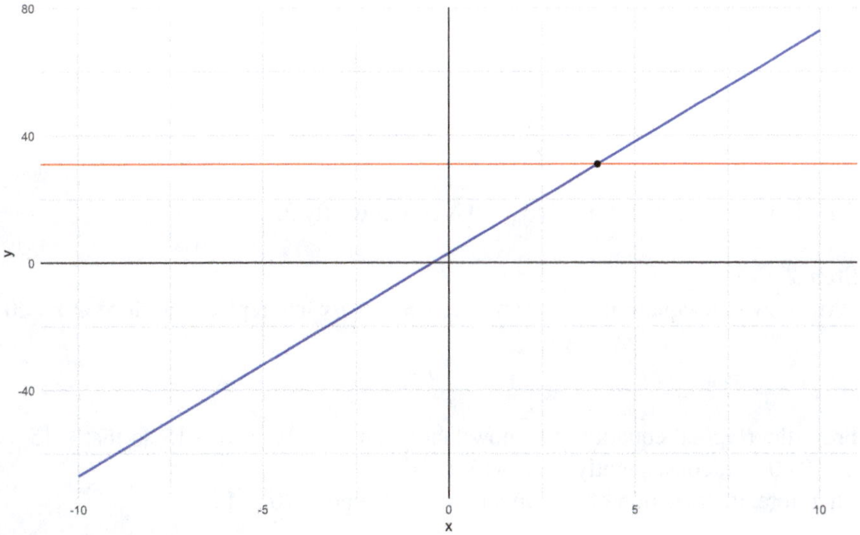

Fig. 4.6 Inverse function and the horizontal line test

This leads to

$$\frac{dx}{dy}\frac{dy}{dx} = 1$$

In our example,

$$\frac{1}{7} \cdot 7 = 1$$

4.8 Tangent Line to the Function

In this section we will learn how to find tangent lines to functions. We start directly with an example. In Sect. 3.3, we plotted the quadratic function $y = x^2 + 2x - 15$. Let's find the tangent lines when $x = 0$ and for other two points, $(4, 9)$ and $(-3, -12)$.

Step 1
Compute the derivative of the function to find the slope of the function at that particular point.

$$\frac{dy}{dx} = 2x + 2$$

Step 2
Evaluate the derivative of the function. In this case, $x = 0$.

$$\left.\frac{dy}{dx}\right|_{x=0} = 2 \cdot 0 + 2 = 2$$

The slope of the tangent line at $x = 0$ is consequently 2.

Step 3
Write down the equation of tangent line, $y = a + bx$ and replace the slope at $x = 0$.

$$y = a + 2x$$

From the original equation we know that when $x = 0$, $y = -15$ so that $-15 = a + 2 \cdot 0$ and, consequently, $a = -15$.
Therefore, the equation of the tangent line at the point $(0, -15)$ is

$$y = 2x - 15$$

Example 4.8.1 Find the equation of the tangent line at the point (4, 9). Let's start from step 2.

$$\frac{dy}{dx}\bigg|_{x=4} = 2 \cdot 4 + 2 = 10$$

The slope of this tangent line is 10. Therefore,

$$y = a + 10x$$

Since (4, 9) is a point of this tangent line, we have

$$9 = a + 10 \cdot 4$$

$$a = -31$$

Therefore, the equation of the tangent line at the point (4, 9) is

$$y = 10x - 31$$

Example 4.8.2 Compute the slope of the tangent line at (−3, −12). Starting from Step 2:

$$\frac{dy}{dx}\bigg|_{x=-3} = 2 \cdot -3 + 2 = -4$$

$$y = a - 4x$$

$$-12 = a - 4 \cdot (-3)$$

$$a = -24$$

$$y = -4x - 24$$

Next, we plot the function and the tangent lines (Fig. 4.7). For this task, we write a function, `tangent_line()`, that encapsulates the code to rearrange and plot the data. We write this `tangent_line()` function to avoid repeating the same code for the next examples. In this function we introduce a different function to reshape the data frame from wide to long, `pivot_longer()` from the `tidyr` package. The question mark `!` in `pivot_longer()` means that we are reshaping

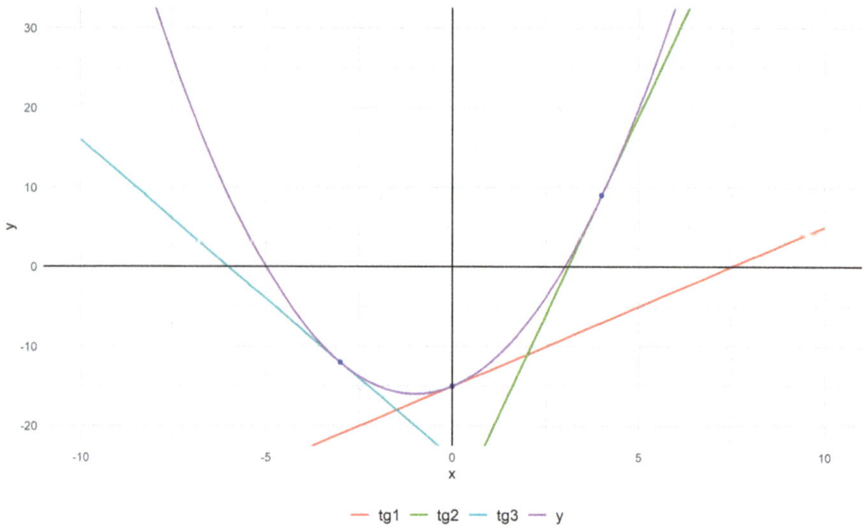

Fig. 4.7 Tangent lines to $y = x^2 + 2x - 15$

all the columns of the data frame with the exception of column x. Note that %>% is a pipe operator that pipes an object forward into a function or call expression.

```
> tangent_line <- function(df_fn, df_points,
+                           XLIM = NULL, YLIM = NULL,
+                           XLAB = "x", YLAB = "y"){
+
+   require("ggplot2")
+   require("tidyr")
+
+   df_l <- df_fn %>% pivot_longer(!x)
+
+   g <- ggplot() +
+     geom_line(data = df_l,
+               aes(x = x, y = value,
+                   group = name,
+                   color = name),
+               size = 0.8) +
+     geom_point(data = df_points,
+                aes(x = x, y = y),
+                color = "blue") +
+     geom_hline(yintercept = 0) +
+     geom_vline(xintercept = 0) +
+     coord_cartesian(xlim = XLIM,
+                     ylim = YLIM) +
```

```
+     theme_minimal() +
+     xlab(XLAB) + ylab(YLAB) +
+     theme(legend.position = "bottom",
+           legend.text = element_text(size = 12),
+           legend.title = element_blank())
+
+   return(g)
+
+ }
```

We need to supply two data frames to the function: one containing the data for the functions (`df_fn`) and another one containing the data for the points (`df_points`). `XLIM` and `YLIM` control the limits for the axes.

```
> x <- seq(-10, 10, 0.1)
> y <- x^2 + 2*x - 15
> tg1 <- 2*x - 15
> tg2 <- 10*x - 31
> tg3 <- -4*x - 24
> df <- data.frame(x, y,
+                  tg1,tg2,tg3)
> df_points <- data.frame(x = c(0, 4, -3),
+                         y = c(-15, 9, -12))
> tangent_line(df, df_points, XLIM = c(-10, 10),
+              YLIM = c(-20, 30))
```

Example 4.8.3 Find the tangent lines to $y = x^3 - 4x^2 + x + 6$ at $x = 0$, point (5, 36) and point (−2, −20) (Fig. 3.26).

Step 1

$$\frac{dy}{dx} = 3x^2 - 8x + 1$$

Step 2
At $x = 0$.

$$\left.\frac{dy}{dx}\right|_{x=0} = 3 \cdot 0^2 - 8 \cdot 0 + 1 = 1$$

The slope of the tangent line is consequently 1.

Step 3
The tangent line is $y = a + 1 \cdot x$. From the original equation we know that when $x = 0$, $y = 6$. Consequently, $6 = a + 1 \cdot 0$, and $a = 6$.

Therefore, the equation of the tangent line at $x = 0$ is

$$y = x + 6$$

We repeat Steps 2 and 3 for the other two points.
At the point (5, 36),

$$\left.\frac{dy}{dx}\right|_{x=5} = 3 \cdot 5^2 - 8 \cdot 5 + 1 = 36$$

$$y = a + 36x$$

$$36 = a + 36 \cdot 5$$

$$a = -144$$

Therefore, the equation of the tangent line at the point (5, 36) is

$$y = 36x - 144$$

At the point (−2, −20),

$$\left.\frac{dy}{dx}\right|_{x=-2} = 3 \cdot (-2)^2 - 8 \cdot (-2) + 1 = 29$$

$$y = a + 29x$$

$$-20 = a - 58$$

$$a = 38$$

Therefore, the equation of the tangent line at point (−2, −20) is

$$y = 29x + 38$$

The following code represent the function and the tangent lines (Fig. 4.8).

```
> x <- seq(-10, 10, 0.1)
> y <- x^3 - 4*x^2 + x + 6
> tg1 <- x + 6
```

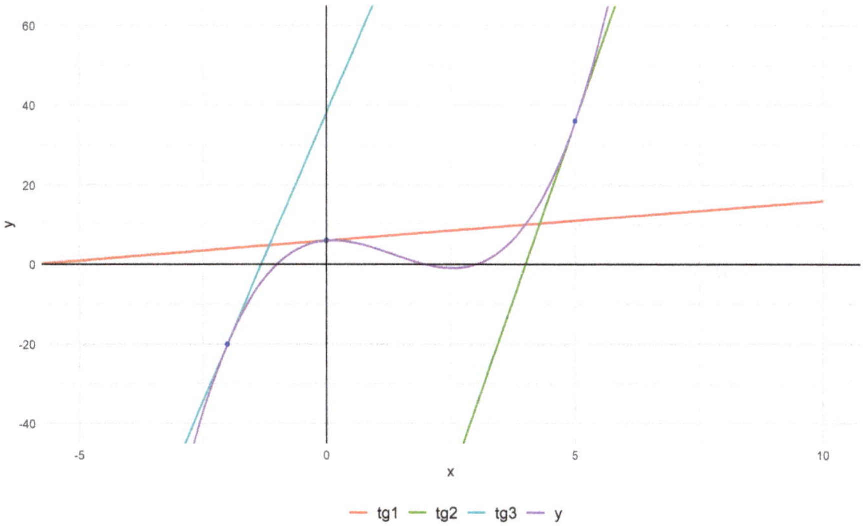

Fig. 4.8 Tangent lines to $y = x^3 - 4x^2 + x + 6$

```
> tg2 <- 36*x - 144
> tg3 <- 29*x + 38
> df <- data.frame(x, y,
+                       tg1, tg2, tg3)
> df_points <- data.frame(x = c(0, 5, -2),
+                              y = c(6, 36, -20))
> tangent_line(df, df_points, XLIM = c(-5, 10),
+                   YLIM = c(-40, 60))
```

Example 4.8.4 Find the tangent lines to $y = \log(x)$ at the points $(1, 0)$ and $(5, 1.609438)$.

Following the same steps as in the previous examples:

$$\frac{dy}{dx} = \frac{1}{x}$$

At the point $(1, 0)$:

$$\left.\frac{dy}{dx}\right|_{x=1} = \frac{1}{1} = 1$$

$$y = a + x$$

$$0 = a + 1$$

$$a = -1$$

$$y = x - 1$$

At the point (5, 1.609438):

$$\left.\frac{dy}{dx}\right|_{x=5} = \frac{1}{5} = 0.2$$

$$y = a + 0.2x$$

$$1.609438 = a + 0.2 \cdot 5$$

$$a = 0.609438$$

$$y = 0.2x + 0.609438$$

Figure 4.9 represents the tangent lines to $y = \log(x)$. Note that for the second point we used the y coordinate with 8 decimals to compute a. This is the value for $y = \log(5)$ that is returned if you print all the dataset `df`.

```
> x <- seq(0, 10, 0.1)
> y <- log(x)
> df <- data.frame(x, y)
> df[x == 1 | x == 5, ]
   x        y
11 1 0.000000
51 5 1.609438
> tg1 <- x - 1
> tg2 <- 0.2*x + 0.60943741
> df <- data.frame(x, y, tg1, tg2)
> df_points <- data.frame(x = c(1, 5),
+                         y = c(0, 1.60943791))
> tangent_line(df, df_points, XLIM = c(0, 10),
+              YLIM = c(-5, 5))
```

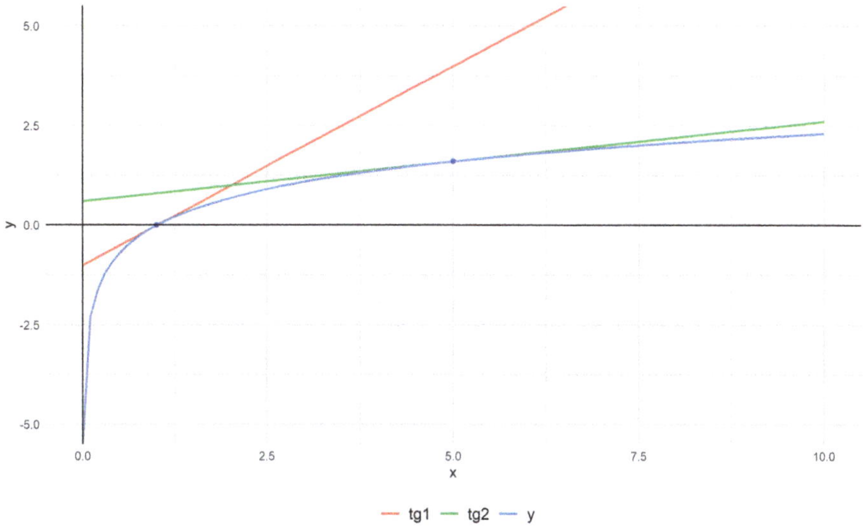

Fig. 4.9 Tangent lines to $y = \log(x)$

Example 4.8.5 Find the tangent lines to $y = e^x$ at the point (0, 1), point (−3, 0.04978706), and point (3, 20.08553692).

Following the same steps as in the previous examples:

$$\frac{dy}{dx} = e^x$$

At the point (0, 1):

$$\left.\frac{dy}{dx}\right|_{x=0} = e^0 = 1$$

$$y = a + x$$

$$a = 1$$

$$y = x + 1$$

At the point (−3, 0.04978706):

$$\left.\frac{dy}{dx}\right|_{x=-3} = e^{-3} = 0.04978706$$

$$y = a + 0.04978706x$$

$$0.04978706 = a + 0.04978706 \cdot (-3)$$

$$a = 0.19914827$$

$$y = 0.04978706x + 0.19914827$$

At the point (3, 20.08553692):

$$\left.\frac{dy}{dx}\right|_{x=3} = e^3 = 20.08553692$$

$$y = a + 20.08553692x$$

$$20.08553692 = a + 20.08553692 \cdot 3$$

$$a = -40.17107924$$

$$y = 20.08553692x - 40.17107924$$

Compare the value of the derivative with the y-value (refer to Sect. 4.6.7). Next we plot the function and the tangent lines (Fig. 4.10).

```
> x <- seq(-10, 10, 0.1)
> y <- exp(x)
> df <- data.frame(x, y)
> df[x == -3 |
+      x == 0 |
+      x == 3, ]
      x           y
71   -3  0.04978707
101   0  1.00000000
131   3 20.08553692
> tg1 <- x + 1
> tg2 <- 0.04978706*x + 0.19914827
> tg3 <- 20.08553962*x - 40.17107924
> df <- data.frame(x, y, tg1, tg2, tg3)
> df_points <- data.frame(x = c(0, -3, 3),
```

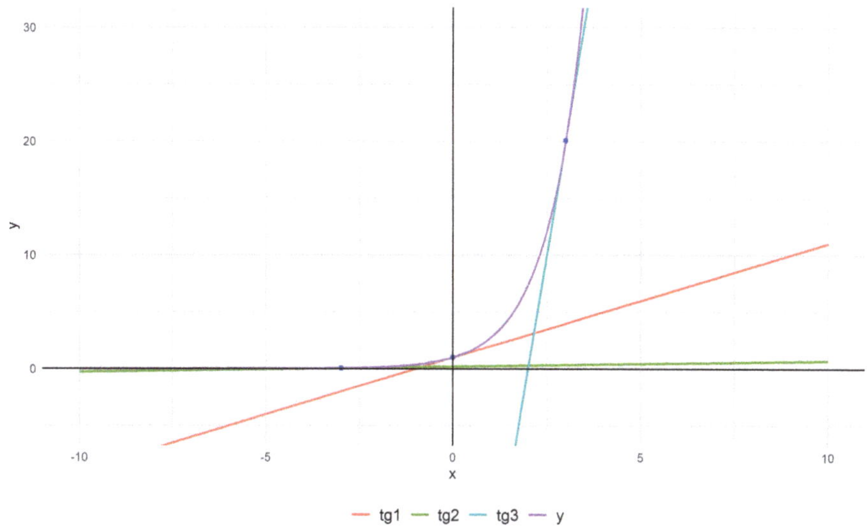

Fig. 4.10 Tangent lines to $y = e^x$

```
+                              y = c(1, 0.04978707,
+                                        20.08553692))
> tangent_line(df, df_points, XLIM = c(-10, 10),
+                 YLIM = c(-5, 30))
```

4.9 Points of Minimum, Maximum and Inflection

Derivatives are useful to find critical values of a function such minimum, maximum and points of inflection.

Let's start with the concept of absolute minimum and maximum of a function over its entire domain. These points are, respectively, the lowest value and the highest value of the function wherever it is defined. However, it should be noted that over the entire domain a function can have an absolute minimum or an absolute maximum or both or neither of the two.

Let's see a practical example by investigating the critical points of the function $y = x^2 + 2x - 15$.

Step 1
Take the derivative of the function.

$$\frac{dy}{dx} = 2x + 2$$

We know that the derivative represents the slope of a function at particular point of the function. At the lowest or at the highest point of the function the slope would be 0, i.e. the tangent line at the point would be a straight line parallel to the x axis.

Step 2
Set the derivative equal to 0, $\frac{dy}{dx} = 0$ and solve for x to find the value of x that makes the slope 0.

$$2x + 2 = 0$$

$$2x = -2$$

$$x = -\frac{2}{2} = -1$$

Step 3
Plug the value for $\frac{dy}{dx} = 0$ in the original function to find the corresponding y coordinate.

$$y(x = -1) = (-1)^2 + 2 \cdot (-1) - 15 = -16$$

Therefore, we have one critical point at $(-1, -16)$. Consequently, the tangent line to the function at that critical point is $y = -16$.

Step 4
Investigate where the function is decreasing or increasing by studying the behaviour of the function at the left and at the right of the critical value -1. First, let's plug a value smaller than -1 in $\frac{dy}{dx}$. Let's go for -2.

$$2 \cdot (-2) + 2 \Rightarrow -4 + 2 \Rightarrow -2 < 0$$

At the left of -1, the slope it is negative, i.e. the function is decreasing. Let's plug now a value greater than -1. Let's go for 0.

$$2 \cdot 0 + 2 \Rightarrow 2 > 0$$

At the right of -1, the slope it is positive, i.e. the function is increasing. We can represent this information as follows

$x < -1$	$x = -1$	$x > -1$
$f'(-2) = -2$	$f'(-1) = 0$	$f'(0) = 2$
$-$	0	+
↘	–	↗

We conclude that the critical point we found, $(-1, -16)$, is the absolute minimum of the function. On the other hand, the function does not have an absolute maximum over its entire domain.

Was this expected? Indeed yes. If you noted, we studied this function in Sect. 3.3.1 where we found the vertex to be $(-1, -16)$. Furthermore, since we are analysing the equation of a parabola we could figure out it was concave up by noting that the leading coefficient is greater than 0, $a > 0$. Therefore, the point $(-1, -16)$ is an absolute minimum.

We can define the absolute maximum and the absolute minimum of a function as follows:

- a function f has an absolute maximum at a point $P(x^*, f(x^*))$ if $f(x^*) \geq f(x)\ \forall x$ in the domain of f.
- a function f has an absolute minimum at a point $P(x^*, f(x^*))$ if $f(x^*) \leq f(x)\ \forall x$ in the domain of f.

Well, nice but in plain English? We can translate the first definition by saying that if the value of the function *evaluated at* the critical value x^* is greater or equal to the value of the function *evaluated at* any x in the domain of the function, then the critical point represents the absolute maximum. That is, the function reaches the maximum value at that critical point. The second definition says that if the value of the function *evaluated at* the critical value x^* is less or equal to the value of the function *evaluated at* any x in the domain of the function, then the critical point represents the absolute minimum. That is, the function reaches the minimum value at that critical point. We will return to these definitions in Sect. 6.3.

Figure 4.11 plots the function with the tangent line to the absolute minimum.

```
> x <- seq(-10, 10, 0.1)
> y <- x^2 + 2*x - 15
> tg0 <- -16
> df <- data.frame(x, y, tg0)
> df_points <- data.frame(x = -1,
+                         y = -16)
> tangent_line(df, df_points,
+              XLIM = c(-10, 10),
+              YLIM = c(-20, 10))
```

Let's see another example with the function $y = -x^3 + 2x^2 + 4x$. We follow the same steps but with we add a new passage in Step 4.

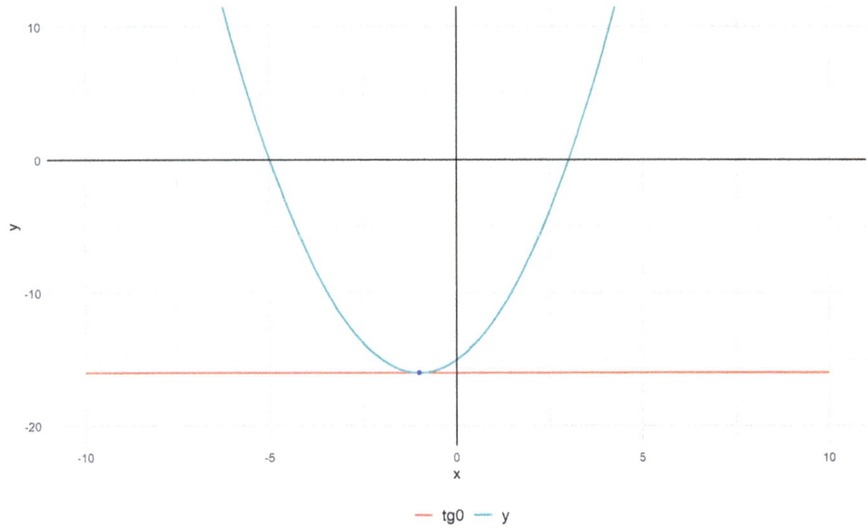

Fig. 4.11 Absolute minimum of $y = x^2 + 2x - 15$

Step 1

$$\frac{dy}{dx} = -3x^2 + 4x + 4$$

Step 2

$$-3x^2 + 4x + 4 = 0$$

$$x_1 = 2, x_2 = -\frac{2}{3}$$

Step 3

$$y(x = 2) = -(2)^3 + 2 \cdot 2^2 + 4 \cdot 2 = 8$$

$$y\left(x = -\frac{2}{3}\right) = -\left(-\frac{2}{3}\right)^3 + 2 \cdot \left(-\frac{2}{3}\right)^2 + 4 \cdot \left(-\frac{2}{3}\right) = -\frac{40}{27}$$

Therefore, our two critical points are $(2, 8)$ and $\left(-\frac{2}{3}, -\frac{40}{27}\right)$ and the tangent lines are $y = 8$ and $y = -\frac{40}{27}$.

Step 4
Investigate where the function is decreasing or increasing by studying the behaviour of the function at the left and at the right of the critical values 2 and $-\frac{2}{3}$.

First, let's plug a value smaller than $-\frac{2}{3}$ in $\frac{dy}{dx}$. Let's go for -1.

$$-3 \cdot (-1)^2 + 4 \cdot (-1) + 4 \Rightarrow -3 < 0$$

At left of $-\frac{2}{3}$ the slope is negative, i.e. the function is decreasing.
Now a value between $-\frac{2}{3}$ and 2. Let's go for 0.

$$-3 \cdot (0)^2 + 4 \cdot (0) + 4 \Rightarrow 4 > 0$$

Between $-\frac{2}{3}$ and 2 the slope is positive, i.e. the function is increasing.
Now a value greater than 2. Let's go for 10.

$$-3 \cdot (10)^2 + 4 \cdot 10 + 4 \Rightarrow -256 < 0$$

At the right of 2 the slope is negative, i.e. the function is decreasing.
We can represent this information as follows

$x < -\frac{2}{3}$	$x = -\frac{2}{3}$	$-\frac{2}{3} < x < 2$	$x = 2$	$x > 2$
$f'(-1) = -3$	$f'(-\frac{2}{3}) = 0$	$f'(0) = 4$	$f'(2) = 0$	$f'(10) = -256$
$-$	0	$+$	0	$-$
↘	$\_$	↗	$-$	↘

Let's now introduce the second derivative test. The second derivative of the function tells about the concavity of the function.

If at $x = x^*$, $f'(x^*) = 0$, the second derivative test tells us that

- y has a local minimum at x^* if $f''(x^*) > 0$
- y has a local maximum at x^* if $f''(x^*) < 0$
- if $f''(x^*) = 0$ a possible inflection point may exist.

Let's apply now the second derivative.

$$\frac{d^2y}{dx^2} = -6x + 4$$

Let's plug the critical values for x.

$$\left.\frac{d^2y}{dx^2}\right|_{x=2} = -6 \cdot 2 + 4 = -8 < 0$$

The second derivative test is negative meaning that the function at point (2, 8) is concave down. Therefore, it is a point of local maximum.

$$\left.\frac{d^2y}{dx^2}\right|_{x=-\frac{2}{3}} = -6 \cdot -\frac{2}{3} + 4 = 8 > 0$$

The second derivative test is positive meaning that the function at point $\left(-\frac{2}{3}, -\frac{40}{27}\right)$ is concave up. Therefore, it is a point of local minimum.

Finally, we set the second derivative equal to zero, $\frac{d^2y}{dx^2} = 0$.

$$\frac{d^2y}{dx^2} = -6x + 4 = 0$$

$$x = \frac{2}{3}$$

This means that when $x = \frac{2}{3}$ we have an inflection point. However, since the critical values we found are different from $x = \frac{2}{3}$ this implies that this point is not a horizontal inflection point but it is a vertical inflection point. By plugging $x = \frac{2}{3}$ in the function we find that this critical point is located at point $\left(\frac{2}{3}, \frac{88}{27}\right)$. Let's test the concavity on either sides of $\frac{d^2y}{dx^2} = 0$. Let's take 0 to the left and 1 to the right.

$$-6 \cdot 0 + 4 = 4 > 0$$

i.e. the function is concave up at left of $\frac{d^2y}{dx^2} = 0$.

$$-6 \cdot 1 + 4 = -2 < 0$$

i.e. the function is concave down at right of $\frac{d^2y}{dx^2} = 0$.

Finally, we can define the relative (or local) maximum and the relative minimum of a function as follows:

- a function has a relative maximum at a point $P(x^*, f(x^*))$ if $f(x^*) \geq f(x)$ for all points $P(x, f(x))$ in the graph near P.
- a function has a relative minimum at a point $P(x^*, f(x^*))$ if $f(x^*) \leq f(x)$ for all points $P(x, f(x))$ in the graph near P.

Figure 4.12 represents the function with the tangent lines at point of local minimum and local maximum and the vertical inflection point .

```
> x <- seq(-10, 10, 0.1)
> y <- -x^3 + 2*x^2 + 4*x
> tg1 <- 8
```

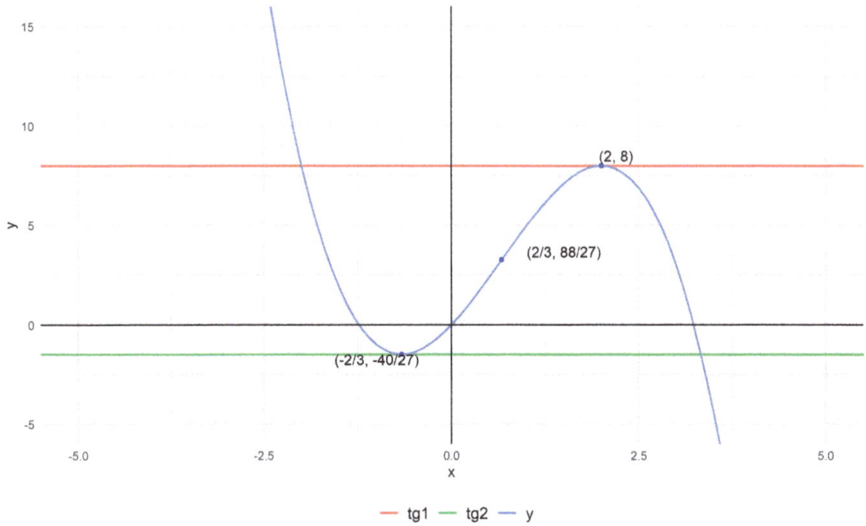

Fig. 4.12 Critical points of $y = -x^3 + 2x^2 + 4x$

```
> tg2 <- -(40/27)
> df <- data.frame(x, y, tg1, tg2)
> df_points <- data.frame(
+   x = c(2, -(2/3), (2/3)),
+   y = c(8, -(40/27), (88/27)))
> tangent_line(df, df_points,
+              XLIM = c(-5, 5),
+              YLIM = c(-5, 15)) +
+   annotate("text", x = c(2.2, -1, 1.5),
+            y = c(8.5, -(40/23), 88/24),
+            label = c("(2, 8)",
+                      "(-2/3, -40/27)",
+                      "(2/3, 88/27)"))
```

Let's consider the same function $y = -x^3 + 2x^2 + 4x$ on the closed interval $[1, 5]$. What would be the conclusion of our analysis?

Let's start by taking the first derivative.

$$\frac{dy}{dx} = -3x^2 + 4x + 4$$

Let's set it equal to 0 and solve for x.

$$-3x^2 + 4x + 4 = 0$$

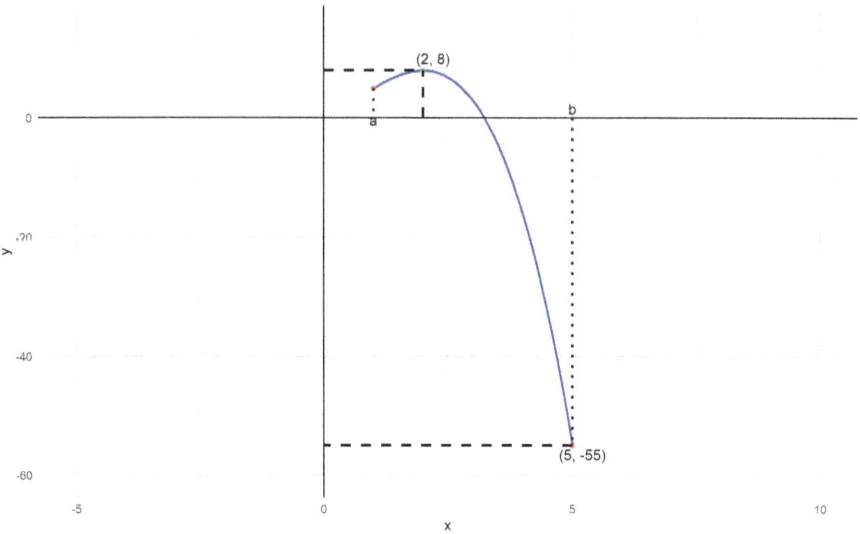

Fig. 4.13 Close interval [1, 5] on $y = -x^3 + 2x^2 + 4x$

$$x_1 = 2, x_2 = -\frac{2}{3}$$

Until this point the analysis is the same as before. However, note that $x_2 = -\frac{2}{3}$ falls outside the interval [1, 5]. Therefore, we consider as critical value only $x_1 = 2$. Additionally, we have to evaluate the function at the single critical value in the interval and at the two endpoints.

$$y(x = 2) = -(2)^3 + 2 \cdot 2^2 + 4 \cdot 2 = 8$$

$$y(x = 1) = -(1)^3 + 2 \cdot 1^2 + 4 \cdot 1 = 5$$

$$y(x = 5) = -(5)^3 + 2 \cdot 5^2 + 4 \cdot 5 = -55$$

From these values we conclude that the absolute maximum occurs at (2, 8) and the absolute minimum occurs at (5, −55) (Fig. 4.13).

This last example shows how the change in the interval affects our analysis.

We can now enunciate the Extreme Value Theorem:

If a function $f(x)$ is continuous on a closed interval $[a, b]$, then $f(x)$ has both a maximum and minimum value on $[a, b]$.

4.10 Taylor Expansion

The *Taylor series* is a series that expresses a function in terms of its derivatives. It provides a good approximation of a function near any point.

The *nth* order Taylor approximation of a differentiable non-linear function $f(x)$ around a point $x = a$ is denoted as

$$f(x) = \frac{f(a)}{0!}(x-a)^0 + \frac{f'(a)}{1!}(x-a)^1 + \frac{f''(a)}{2!}(x-a)^2 + \cdots + \frac{f^n(a)}{n!}(x-a)^n$$

where $n!$, read as *n factorial*, is a shorthand notation for $n! = n(n-1)(n-2)\cdots(3)(2)(1)$, with $n > 0$. For example, $3!$, *three factorial*, equals to $3 \times 2 \times 1 = 6$.

However, note that since $0!$ (by definition) and $1!$ are just 1, as well $(x-a)^0$, the Taylor expansion is generally denoted as

$$f(x) = f(a) + f'(a)(x-a) + \frac{f''(a)}{2!}(x-a)^2 + \cdots + \frac{f^n(a)}{n!}(x-a)^n \tag{4.22}$$

In addition, a Taylor series evaluated at $x = 0$ is known as Maclaurin series:

$$f(x) = f(0) + f'(0)x + \frac{f''(0)}{2!}x^2 + \cdots + \frac{f^n(0)}{n!}x^n \tag{4.23}$$

Furthermore, we can write (4.22) and (4.23) in a more compact way with the summation sign, respectively, as follows:

$$f(x) = \sum_{n=0}^{\infty} \frac{f^n(a)}{n!}(x-a)^n \tag{4.24}$$

$$f(x) = \sum_{n=0}^{\infty} \frac{f^n(0)}{n!}x^n \tag{4.25}$$

Let's see first an example with the Maclaurin series. We will proceed step by step. We will create an **R** object for each step.

Let's find the Maclaurin series for the function

$$f(x) = x^5 - 3x^4 + x^3 + 2x^2 - x + 2$$

```
> x <- seq(-10, 10, 0.01)
> f <- x^5 - 3*x^4 + x^3 + 2*x^2 - x + 2
```

First, we evaluate the function at $x = 0$:

$$f(x=0) = 0^5 - 3 \cdot 0^4 + 0^3 + 2 \cdot 0^2 - 0 + 2 = 2$$

Therefore, the first coefficient we found is 2:

$$f(x) = 2 + f'(0)x + \frac{f^{''}(0)}{2!}x^2 + \frac{f^{'''}(0)}{3!}x^3 + \frac{f^4(0)}{4!}x^4 + \frac{f^5(0)}{5!}x^5$$

```
> n0 <- 2
```

Next, we compute the first derivative and then we evaluate it at $x = 0$:

$$f'(x) = 5x^4 - 12x^3 + 3x^2 + 4x - 1$$

$$f'(x = 0) = 5 \cdot 0^4 - 12 \cdot 0^3 + 3 \cdot 0^2 + 4 \cdot 0 - 1 = -1$$

Therefore, we have

$$f(x) = 2 - x + \frac{f^{''}(0)}{2!}x^2 + \frac{f^{'''}(0)}{3!}x^3 + \frac{f^4(0)}{4!}x^4 + \frac{f^5(0)}{5!}x^5$$

```
> n1 <- 2 - x
```

Next, we compute the second derivative and then we evaluate it at $x = 0$:

$$f^{''}(x) = 20x^3 - 36x^2 + 6x + 4$$

$$f^{''}(x) = 20 \cdot 0^3 - 36 \cdot 0^2 + 6 \cdot 0 + 4 = 4$$

Therefore, we have

$$f(x) = 2 - x + \frac{4}{2!}x^2 + \frac{f^{'''}(0)}{3!}x^3 + \frac{f^4(0)}{4!}x^4 + \frac{f^5(0)}{5!}x^5$$

$$f(x) = 2 - x + 2x^2 + \frac{f^{'''}(0)}{3!}x^3 + \frac{f^4(0)}{4!}x^4 + \frac{f^5(0)}{5!}x^5$$

```
> n2 <- 2 - x + 2*x^2
```

Let's repeat the same steps for $n = 3, n = 4, n = 5$.

$$f^{'''}(x) = 60x^2 - 72x + 6 = 6$$

$$f(x) = 2 - x + \frac{4}{2!}x^2 + \frac{6}{3!}x^3 + \frac{f^4(0)}{4!}x^4 + \frac{f^5(0)}{5!}x^5$$

$$f(x) = 2 - x + 2x^2 + x^3 + \frac{f^4(0)}{4!}x^4 + \frac{f^5(0)}{5!}x^5$$

```
> n3 <- 2 - x + 2*x^2 + x^3
```

$$f^4(x) = 120x - 72 = -72$$

$$f(x) = 2 - x + 2x^2 + x^3 - 3x^4 + \frac{f^5(0)}{5!}x^5$$

```
> n4 <- 2 - x + 2*x^2 + x^3 - 3*x^4
```

$$f^5(x) = 120 = 120$$

$$f(x) = 2 - x + 2x^2 + x^3 - 3x^4 + x^5$$

```
> n5 <- 2 - x + 2*x^2 + x^3 - 3*x^4 + x^5
```

But perhaps at this point you have already noted that we obtained the initial function back. In other words, the Maclaurin series correctly represents the given function.

Now, let's build the dataset with all the steps. We will plot the data by using `ggplot2` package and `gganimate` package to make the plot dynamic. However, first we need to rearrange the data.

```
> df <- data.frame(x, f, n0, n1, n2, n3, n4, n5)
> df_l <- melt(setDT(df), id.vars = c("x", "f"),
+                measure.vars = c("n0", "n1",
+                                 "n2", "n3", "n4", "n5"))
```

We add a new variable to the dataset, `order`, to set the order of the transition in the dynamic plot. We generate it by using a loop. If it is not clear what this loop does, I suggest breaking it down as we did in Sect. 1.7.

```
> order <- numeric(nrow(df_l))
> for(i in 0:5){
+   order[(i*nrow(df)) + 1:nrow(df)] <- rep(i, nrow(df))
+ }
> df_l$order <- order
> head(df_l)
         x         f variable value order
1: -10.00 -130788.0       n0     2     0
2:  -9.99 -130166.6       n0     2     0
```

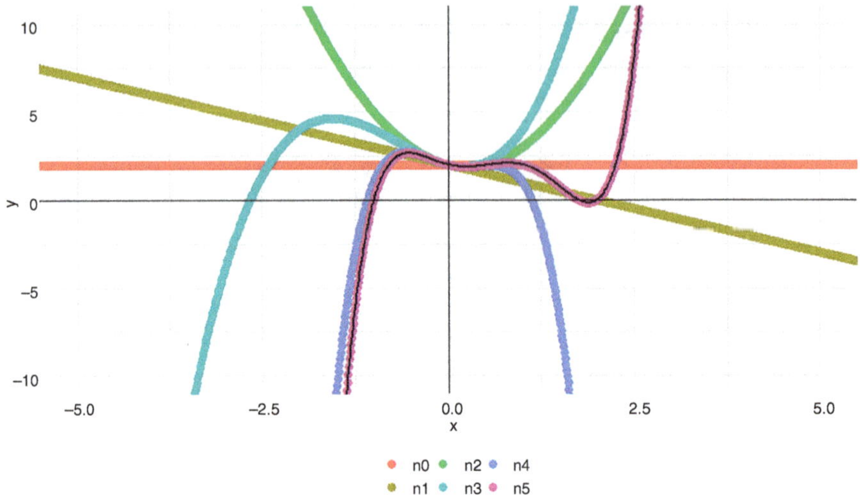

Fig. 4.14 Maclaurin series for $f(x) = x^5 - 3x^4 + x^3 + 2x^2 - x + 2$ (static version of the dynamic plot)

```
3:   -9.98 -129547.5           n0      2      0
4:   -9.97 -128930.8           n0      2      0
5:   -9.96 -128316.5           n0      2      0
6:   -9.95 -127704.5           n0      2      0
> tail(df_l)
       x        f variable     value order
1:   9.95 69295.52       n5 69295.52     5
2:   9.96 69671.55       n5 69671.55     5
3:   9.97 70049.22       n5 70049.22     5
4:   9.98 70428.51       n5 70428.51     5
5:   9.99 70809.43       n5 70809.43     5
6:  10.00 71192.00       n5 71192.00     5
```

Now we are ready to plot it. We add `transition_states()` to the usual `ggplot()` structure to make it dynamic. In the book, it is represented the static version that is generated by removing `transition_states()` (Fig. 4.14). As it appears evident form Fig. 4.14, as n gets larger and larger, we get a better approximation of the function.

```
> ggplot() +
+   geom_point(data = df_l, aes(x = x,
+                        y = value,
+                        group = variable,
+                        color = variable),
+                    size = 3) +
+   geom_line(data = df, aes(x = x, y = f),
```

```
+                       size = 1) +
+     geom_hline(yintercept = 0) +
+     geom_vline(xintercept = 0) +
+     ggtitle("") + ylab("y") +
+     coord_cartesian(xlim = c(-5, 5),
+                       ylim = c(-10, 10)) +
+     theme_minimal() +
+     theme(legend.position = "bottom",
+           legend.title = element_blank()) +
+     transition_states(order,
+       transition_length = 2,
+       state_length = 1)

Frame 100 (100%)
Finalizing encoding... done!
```

What about if we continue with $n > 5$? From the last step:

$$f^6(x) = 0$$

$$f(x) = 2 - x + 2x^2 + x^3 - 3x^4 + x^5 + 0$$

Therefore, for this polynomial $f^n(x) = 0$ for $n > 5$.
Let's expand the same polynomial around $x = 1$.
First, we evaluate the function at $x = 1$:

$$f(x = 1) = 1^5 - 3 \cdot 1^4 + 1^3 + 2 \cdot 1^2 - 1 + 2 = 2$$

Therefore, by replacing in (4.22):

$$f(x) = 2 + f'(a)(x-a) + \frac{f''(a)}{2!}(x-a)^2 + \frac{f'''(a)}{3!}(x-a)^3 + \frac{f^4(a)}{4!}(x-a)^4 + \frac{f^5(a)}{5!}(x-a)^5$$

Next, by computing the first five derivatives and evaluating it at $x = 1$, we find that:

$$f'(x) = 5x^4 - 12x^3 + 3x^2 + 4x - 1$$

$$f'(1) = 5 \cdot 1^4 - 12 \cdot 1^3 + 3 \cdot 1^2 + 4 \cdot 1 - 1 = -1$$

$$f(x) = 2-(x-1)+\frac{f''(a)}{2!}(x-a)^2+\frac{f'''(a)}{3!}(x-a)^3+\frac{f^4(a)}{4!}(x-a)^4+\frac{f^5(a)}{5!}(x-a)^5$$

$$f''(x) = 20x^3 - 36x^2 + 6x + 4$$

$$f''(1) = 20 \cdot 1^3 - 36 \cdot 1^2 + 6 \cdot 1 + 4 = -6$$

$$f(x) = 2 - (x-1) - \frac{6}{2!}(x-1)^2 + \frac{f'''(a)}{3!}(x-a)^3 + \frac{f^4(a)}{4!}(x-a)^4 + \frac{f^5(a)}{5!}(x-a)^5$$

$$f'''(x) = 60x^2 - 72x + 6$$

$$f'''(1) = 60 \cdot 1^2 - 72 \cdot 1 + 6 = -6$$

$$f(x) = 2 - (x-1) - \frac{6}{2!}(x-1)^2 - \frac{6}{3!}(x-1)^3 + \frac{f^4(a)}{4!}(x-a)^4 + \frac{f^5(a)}{5!}(x-a)^5$$

$$f^4(x) = 120x - 72$$

$$f^4(1) = 120 \cdot 1 - 72 = 48$$

$$f(x) = 2 - (x-1) - \frac{6}{2!}(x-1)^2 - \frac{6}{3!}(x-1)^3 + \frac{48}{4!}(x-1)^4 + \frac{f^5(a)}{5!}(x-a)^5$$

$$f^5(x) = 120$$

$$f^5(1) = 120$$

$$f(x) = 2 - (x-1) - \frac{6}{2!}(x-1)^2 - \frac{6}{3!}(x-1)^3 + \frac{48}{4!}(x-1)^4 + \frac{120}{5!}(x-1)^5$$

By simplifying

$$f(x) = 2 - (x-1) - 3(x-1)^2 - (x-1)^3 + 2(x-1)^4 + (x-1)^5$$

and multiplying out the parenthesis we obtain back the initial function $f(x) = 2 - x + 2x^2 + x^3 - 3x^4 + x^5$. This verifies that the Taylor polynomial correctly represents the given function.

In the previous examples, we have shown that the Taylor expansion exactly transformed the given function in its polynomial form. This was due to the fact that we expanded a polynomial function. To apply the Taylor expansion to a differentiable non-linear function that is not a polynomial, we have to introduce the concept of the *remainder*, R. The Taylor formula with *remainder* is

$$f(x) = P_n + R_n \tag{4.26}$$

where P_n equals to (4.22).

Since an arbitrary function can only be approximated to a polynomial form, $f(x) \neq P_n$, we introduce the *remainder* to account for the discrepancy between $f(x)$ and P_n. This means that (4.26) is a generalization of (4.22) where $R_n = 0$. However, we may find the remainder also when we expand a polynomial function into a polynomial of a *lesser* degree. For example, if in the previous example we had expanded the function into a *fourth-degree* polynomial ($n = 4$) we would have had only an approximation. Consequently, it would have been necessary to add the remainder:

$$f(x) = 2 - x + 2x^2 + x^3 - 3x^4 + R_4$$

As an example, let's expand the following non-polynomial function $f(x) = \log(x)$ around the point $x = 1$, with $n = 4$ (Fig. 4.15).

$$f(1) = \log(1) \Rightarrow 0$$

$$f^{'}(x) = \frac{1}{x} \Rightarrow f^{'}(1) = 1$$

$$f^{''}(x) = -\frac{1}{x^2} \Rightarrow f^{''}(1) = -1$$

$$f^{'''}(x) = \frac{2}{x^3} \Rightarrow f^{'''}(1) = 2$$

$$f^4(x) = -\frac{6}{x^4} \Rightarrow f^4(1) = -6$$

$$f(x) = 0 + (x-1) - \frac{1}{2!}(x-1)^2 + \frac{2}{3!}(x-1)^3 - \frac{6}{4!}(x-1)^4 + R_4$$

$$f(x) = -\frac{25}{12} + 4x - 3x^2 + \frac{4}{3}x^3 - \frac{1}{4}x^4 + R_4$$

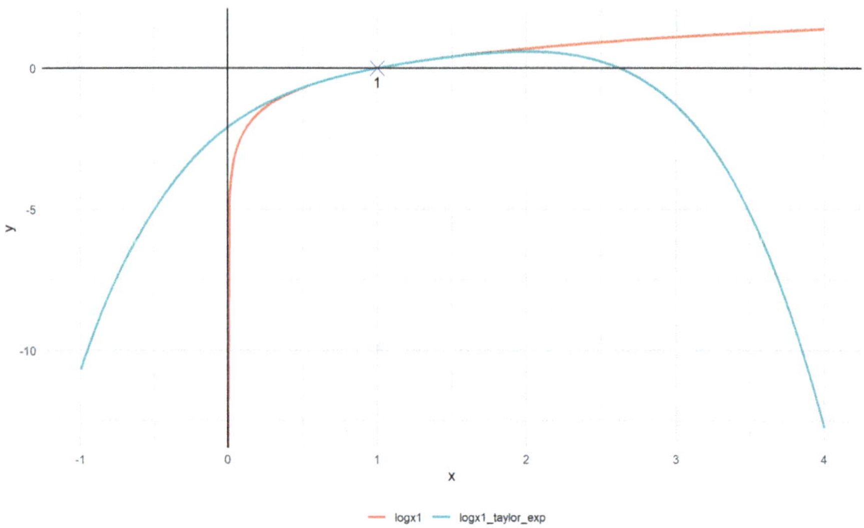

Fig. 4.15 $f(x) = \log(x)$ and its Taylor expansion around the point $x = 1$, with $n = 4$

```
> x <- seq(-1, 4, 0.01)
> logx1 <- log(x)
Warning message:
In log(x) : NaNs produced
> logx1_taylor_exp <- -(25/12) + 4*x - 3*x^2 + (4/3)*x^3
                       - (1/4)*x^4
> df <- data.frame(x, logx1, logx1_taylor_exp)
> df_l <- df %>%
+   pivot_longer(!x)
> ggplot(df_l, aes(x, value,
+                  group = name,
+                  color = name)) +
+   geom_line(size = 1) +
+   geom_point(aes(x = 1, y = 0),
+              size = 5, shape = 4,
+              color = "blue") +
+   geom_hline(yintercept = 0) +
+   geom_vline(xintercept = 0) +
+   theme_minimal() + ylab("y") +
+   theme(legend.position = "bottom",
+         legend.title = element_blank()) +
+   annotate("text", x = 1, y = -0.5, label = "1")
Warning message:
Removed 100 row(s) containing missing values (geom_path).
```

4.10.1 Nth-Derivative Test

The *Nth-derivative* test can be used to determine whether the stationary value of a function is a point of relative maximum, minimum or an inflection point. This test is an application of the development of the Taylor expansion.

The steps to implement the *Nth-derivative test* are the following:

1. Find the critical value where $f'(x = a) = 0$
2. Take successive *Nth-derivative* until $f^N(a) \neq 0$
3. Conclusion:
   (a) if N is an even number and $f^N(a) < 0$, we have a relative maximum
   (b) if N is an even number and $f^N(a) > 0$, we have a relative minimum
   (c) if N is odd, at the point $(a, 0)$ we have an inflection point.

As a remark, we can apply the *Nth-derivative* test provided that a function $f(x)$ has a non-zero derivative at a critical value a.

For example, the stationary value for the function $f(x) = (x - 3)^4$ is

Step 1

$$f'(x) = 4(x - 3)^3 \Rightarrow f'(3) = 0$$

i.e. $x = 3$ is the critical value.

Step 2

$$f''(x) = 12(x - 3)^2 \Rightarrow f''(3) = 0$$

$$f'''(x) = 24(x - 3) \Rightarrow f'''(3) = 0$$

$$f^4(x) = 24 \Rightarrow f^4(3) = 24$$

Step 3
Since $N = 4$ is an even number and $f^4(3) > 0$, we are in case 3 (b), that is the point $(3, 0)$ is a relative minimum.

4.10.2 Newton-Raphson Method

Let's expand a function f around x_n

$$f(x^*) = f(x_n) + f'(x_n)(x_{n+1} - x_n) \tag{4.27}$$

However, if x^* is a root of the function $y = f(x^*) = 0$. To be noted that this is the approach we used to find the roots of a cubic function with the `cub_eq_solver()` function, i.e. we searched for $y = 0$ in the table of values to find the roots. In turn $y = f(x^*) = 0$ means also that (4.27) becomes

$$0 = f(x_n) + f'(x_n)(x_{n+1} - x_n) \tag{4.28}$$

By rearranging (4.28)

$$-f(x_n) = f'(x_n)(x_{n+1} - x_n)$$

$$-\frac{f(x_n)}{f'(x_n)} = x_{n+1} - x_n$$

and finally

$$x_{n+1} = x_n - \frac{f(x_n)}{f'(x_n)}$$

that is (4.5).

4.11 L'Hôpital Theorem

The L'Hôpital theorem allows us to evaluate limits of the form $\left[\frac{0}{0}\right]$ or $\left[\frac{\infty}{\infty}\right]$ by using differential calculus.

Let's suppose we want to evaluate the following limit

$$\lim_{x\to 0^+} \frac{log(x)}{\frac{1}{x}}$$

we would end up to the following indeterminate form $\left[\frac{\infty}{\infty}\right]$.[4]

[4] $\lim_{x\to 0^+}$ means that x approaches zero from the "right" (or positive side). In addition, remember we are using the notation log for natural log unless we write the base.

In this case, we can apply the L'Hôpital theorem that states that

$$\lim_{x \to c} \frac{f(x)}{g(x)} = \lim_{x \to c} \frac{f'(x)}{g'(x)} \tag{4.29}$$

provided that $f(x)$ and $g(x)$ are differentiable on an open interval except possibly at a point c, and if

1. $\lim_{x \to c} f(x) = \lim_{x \to c} g(x) = 0$ or $\pm \infty$, and
2. $g'(x) \neq 0$, and
3. $\lim_{x \to c} \frac{f'(x)}{g'(x)}$ exists.

Therefore,

$$\lim_{x \to 0^+} \frac{log(x)}{\frac{1}{x}} = \left[\frac{\infty}{\infty}\right] \Rightarrow \lim_{x \to 0^+} \frac{\frac{1}{x}}{-\frac{1}{x^2}} = \frac{1}{x} \cdot -x^2 = \lim_{x \to 0^+} (-x) = 0$$

We will see an application in Chap. 6.

4.12 Derivatives with R

We can compute derivatives with **R** by using the `D()` and `deriv()` functions that are base functions in **R** and by using the `Deriv()` function from the `Deriv` package.

First, let's see some examples with the `D()` function. Suppose we want to compute the derivative of $y = x^2$.

```
> y <- expression(x^2)
> dydx <- D(y, "x")
> dydx
2 * x
```

First, we generated an expression containing the derivative we want to compute. We stored this expression in an object, `y`. This will be the first entry of the `D()` function. The second entry of the `D()` function is a character vector, giving the variable name with respect to which derivatives will be computed.

```
> y <- expression(2*x^2 + 3*x^3)
> dydx <- D(y, "x")
> dydx
2 * (2 * x) + 3 * (3 * x^2)
> y <- expression(2*x^2 * 3*x^3)
> dydx <- D(y, "x")
> dydx
2 * (2 * x) * 3 * x^3 + 2 * x^2 * 3 * (3 * x^2)
> y <- expression((2*x^2) / (3*x^3))
> dydx <- D(y, "x")
```

```
> dydx
2 * (2 * x)/(3 * x^3) - (2 * x^2) * (3 * (3 * x^2))/(3 * x^3)^2
> y <- expression(log(x))
> dydx <- D(y, "x")
> dydx
1/x
> y <- expression(exp(x))
> dydx <- D(y, "x")
> dydx
exp(x)
```

We can compute the second derivative as follows:

```
> y <- expression(x^2)
> d2ydx2 <- D(D(y, "x"), "x")
> d2ydx2
[1] 2
```

Now, let's see some examples with the `Deriv()` function from the `Deriv` package.

Note that we can use the same notation that we used for the base functions or write a function or just a string as first input of the function.

```
> y <- expression(x^2)
> dydx <- Deriv(y, "x")
> dydx
expression(2 * x)
> y <- function(x) {x^2}
> dydx <- Deriv(y, "x")
> dydx
function (x)
2 * x
> y <- "x^2"
> dydx <- Deriv(y, "x")
> dydx
[1] "2 * x"
```

Other examples.

```
> y <- "2*x^2 + 3*x^3"
> dydx <- Deriv(y, "x")
> dydx
[1] "x * (4 + 9 * x)"
> y <- "(x^4 + 2*x^3) * (4*x^3 + 6*x^2)"
> dydx <- Deriv(y, "x")
> dydx
[1] "x^4 * ((12 + 12 * x) * (2 + x) + (4 * x + 6)^2)"
> y <- "(x^4 + 2*x^3) / (4*x^3 + 6*x^2)"
```

```
> dydx <- Deriv(y, "x")
> dydx
[1] "1 - x^4 * (12 + 12 * x) * (2 + x)/(x^2 * (4 * x +
                  6))^2"
> y <- "log(x)"
> dydx <- Deriv(y, "x")
> dydx
[1] "1/x"
> y <- "exp(x)"
> dydx <- Deriv(y, "x")
> dydx
[1] "exp(x)"
```

For second derivative we add `nderiv = 2`.

```
> y <- "x^2"
> d2ydx2 <- Deriv(y, "x", nderiv = 2)
> d2ydx2
[1] "2"
```

4.13 Taylor Expansion with R

In **R**, we can compute the Taylor expansion with the `taylor()` function from the `pracma` package.

For example, we can compute the Maclaurin series in the previous example as follows:

```
> f <- function(x) {x^5 - 3*x^4 + x^3 + 2*x^2 - x + 2}
> taylor(f, 0, 5)
[1]  0.9999968 -2.9999993  1.0000027  1.9999999
    -1.0000000  2.0000000
```

The `taylor()` function returns the coefficients of the polynomial.

Following the other two examples with the `taylor()` function.

```
> f <- function(x) {x^5 - 3*x^4 + x^3 + 2*x^2 - x + 2}
> round(taylor(f, 1, 5), 4)
[1]  1 -3  1  2 -1  2
> f <- function(x) {log(x)}
> taylor(f, 1, 4)
[1] -0.2500044  1.3333515 -3.0000281  4.0000192
    -2.0833383
```

4.14 Applications in Economics

4.14.1 Marginal Cost

We define the *marginal cost* as the change in total cost for a given change in quantity. Therefore, with the costs on the y axis and the quantity on the x axis, the marginal cost is the *rise* over the *run* where the *rise* is the change in costs and the *run* is the change in quantity.

$$MC = \lim_{\Delta Q \to 0} \frac{rise}{run} = \lim_{\Delta Q \to 0} \frac{\Delta Costs}{\Delta Quantity} \tag{4.30}$$

Consequently, the marginal cost represents the slope of the cost function. For example, for the following total cost function

$$TC = VC3 \cdot Q^3 - VC2 \cdot Q^2 + VC1 \cdot Q + FC$$

the marginal cost (MC) is:

$$MC = \frac{dTC}{dQ} = 3 \cdot VC3 \cdot Q^2 - 2 \cdot VC2 \cdot Q + VC1$$

Let's plot the marginal costs for the cost function $TC = 0.009Q^3 - 0.5Q^2 + 15Q + 35$ (Fig. 4.16).

From this section we use Q as the notation for the quantity. We use the `Deriv()` function to compute the marginal cost.

```
> FC <- 35
> VC1 <- 15
> VC2 <- -0.5
> VC3 <- 0.009
> TC <- "VC3*Q^3 + VC2*Q^2 + VC1*Q + FC"
> MC <- Deriv(TC, "Q")
> MC
[1] "Q * (2 * VC2 + 3 * (Q * VC3)) + VC1"
```

Let's check the `class()` of `MC`.

```
> class(MC)
[1] "character"
```

We employ the same functions we used for the `LiMiT()` function to use the results of the derivative. The same applies to `TC`.

```
> Q <- seq(0, 50, 1)
> MC <- eval(parse(text = MC))
```

```
> class(MC)
[1] "numeric"
> head(MC)
[1] 15.000 14.027 13.108 12.243 11.432 10.675
> TC <- eval(parse(text = TC))
> head(TC)
[1] 35.000 49.509 63.072 75.743 87.576 98.625
```

In the next step we code three functions: `total_cost()` to compute the total cost, `marginal_cost()` to compute the marginal cost, and `yinter()` to compute the y intercept of a linear function. The outcomes of these three functions will be used to compute the tangent lines to the cost functions. However, first, note how we write the `total_cost()` and the `marginal_cost()` functions. The coefficient of the cubic terms takes the default value of 0. Therefore, these two functions are quadratic by default. Furthermore, note the role of `n = 1` in the `marginal_cost()` function.

```
> total_cost <- function(Q, VC1, VC2, FC, VC3 = 0){
+   TC <- VC3*Q^3 + VC2*Q^2 + VC1*Q + FC
+   return(TC)
+ }
> marginal_cost <- function(Q, VC1, VC2, FC, VC3 = 0,
  n = 1){
+   require("Deriv")
+   tc <- "VC3*Q^3 + VC2*Q^2 + VC1*Q + FC"
+   mc <- Deriv(tc, "Q", nderiv = n)
+   return(eval(parse(text = mc)))
+ }
> yinter <- function(TC, MC, Q){
+   a <- TC - MC*Q
+ return(a)
+ }
```

Now we are ready to find the tangent lines to the cost function at points where $Q = 10$ and $Q = 45$.

```
> Q10 <- 10
> TC10 <- total_cost(Q10, VC1, VC2, FC, VC3)
> TC10
[1] 144
> Q45 <- 45
> TC45 <- total_cost(Q45, VC1, VC2, FC, VC3)
> TC45
[1] 517.625
> MC10 <- marginal_cost(Q10, VC1, VC2, FC, VC3)
> MC10
```

```
[1] 7.7
> MC45 <- marginal_cost(Q45, VC1, VC2, FC, VC3)
> MC45
[1] 24.675
> a10 <- yinter(TC10, MC10, Q10)
> a10
[1] 67
> a45 <- yinter(TC45, MC45, Q45)
> a45
[1] -592.75
> tg10 <- a10 + MC10*Q
> tg45 <- a45 + MC45*Q
```

Then, we need to prepare the data. Since we use `tangent_line()` to plot, we set the column name of `Q` as `x`

```
> df <- data.frame(x = Q,
+                  total_cost = TC,
+                  marginal_cost = MC,
+                  tangent10 = tg10,
+                  tangent45 = tg45)
> df_points <- data.frame(x = c(Q10, Q45),
+                         y = c(TC10, TC45))
```

We add layers to `tangent_line()` to reproduce Fig. 4.16

```
> tangent_line(df, df_points, XLAB = "Output",
+              YLAB = "Cost", YLIM = c(0, 600)) +
+   geom_segment(aes(x = c(Q10, 0, Q45, 0, 0, 0),
+                    y = c(0, TC10, 0, TC45, MC10, MC45),
+                    xend = c(Q10, Q10, Q45, Q45, Q10, Q45),
+                    yend = c(TC10, TC10, TC45, TC45, MC10, MC45)),
+                linetype = c(rep("dotted", 4),
+                             rep("dashed", 2)),
+                color = c(rep("black", 4),
+                          "green", "blue"),
+                size = 1) +
+   scale_y_continuous(labels = scales::dollar)
```

What can we infer from Fig. 4.16? We see that when the firm produces 10 units of output, the total cost is \$144 and the marginal cost is \$7.7. The marginal cost is initially decreasing until the production of the 19th unit. After this unit the marginal cost starts to increase. For example, when the firm produces 45 units of output, the total cost is \$517.65 and the marginal cost is \$24.675.

```
> df[c(10:21, 46), 1:3]
    x total_cost marginal_cost
10  9    136.061         8.187
11 10    144.000         7.700
```

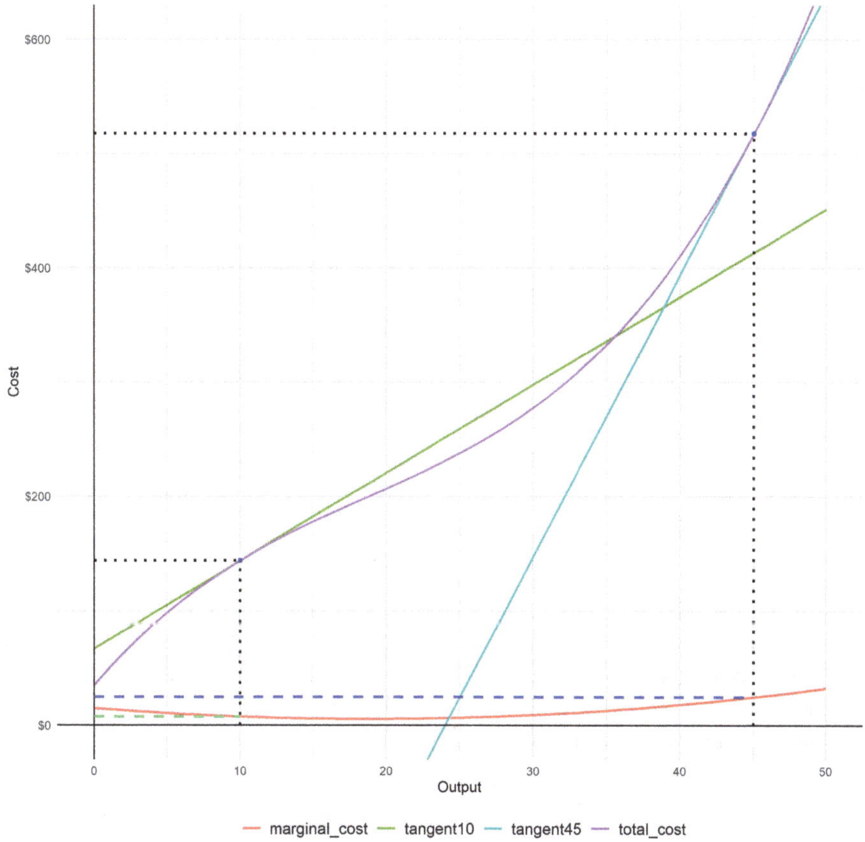

Fig. 4.16 Marginal cost

```
12 11     151.479             7.267
13 12     158.552             6.888
14 13     165.273             6.563
15 14     171.696             6.292
16 15     177.875             6.075
17 16     183.864             5.912
18 17     189.717             5.803
19 18     195.488             5.748
20 19     201.231             5.747
21 20     207.000             5.800
46 45     517.625            24.675
```

But what does this mean? When the firm increases the output, for example, from 10 to 11 units the marginal cost decreases from \$7.7 to \$7.2, i.e. the slope is negative. Since the marginal cost is decreasing the firm has an incentive to increase the production.

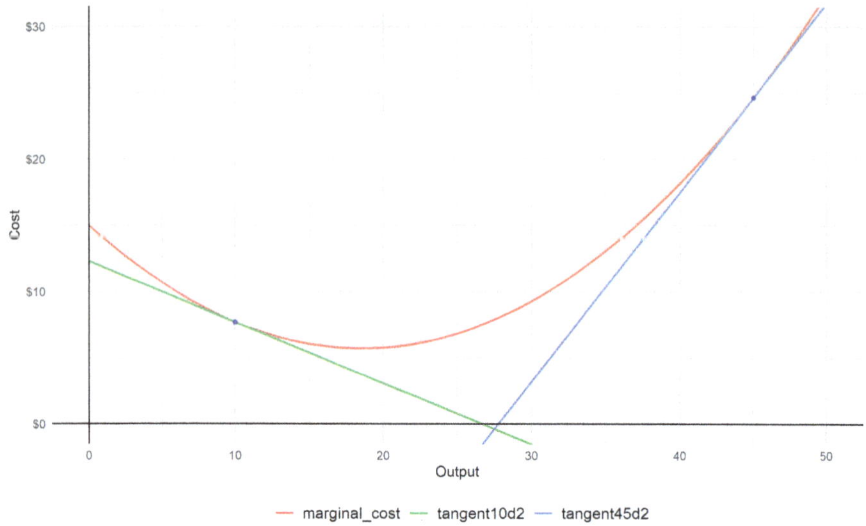

Fig. 4.17 Tangent lines to the marginal cost

Let's plot the tangent lines to the marginal cost curve at the point (Q10, MC10) and at the point (Q45, MC45). In other words, we have to take the second derivative of the total cost function. We set `n = 2` in the `marginal_cost()` function to take the second derivative (Fig. 4.17).

```
> MC10d2 <- marginal_cost(Q10, VC1, VC2, FC, VC3, n = 2)
> MC10d2
[1] -0.46
> MC45d2 <- marginal_cost(Q45, VC1, VC2, FC, VC3, n = 2)
> MC45d2
[1] 1.43
> a10d2 <- yinter(df$marginal_cost[11], MC10d2, Q10)
> a10d2
[1] 12.3
> a45d2 <- yinter(df$marginal_cost[46], MC45d2, Q45)
> a45d2
[1] -39.675
> tg10d2 <- a10d2 + MC10d2*Q
> tg45d2 <- a45d2 + MC45d2*Q
> df2 <- cbind.data.frame(x = df$x,
+                         marginal_cost = df$marginal_cost,
+                         tangent10d2 = tg10d2,
+                         tangent45d2 = tg45d2)
> df_points <- data.frame(x = c(Q10, Q45),
+                         y = c(MC10, MC45))
> tangent_line(df2, df_points, XLAB = "Output",
+              YLAB = "Cost", YLIM = c(0, 30)) +
+   scale_y_continuous(labels = scales::dollar)
```

4.14.1.1 Coefficients of a Cubic Cost Function

In Sect. 3.4.2.1, we set the following restrictions on the coefficients of a cubic cost function, $C(Q) = aQ^3 + bQ^2 + cQ + d$, to prevent the function from bending downward (Eq. 3.9)

$$a, c, d > 0 \quad b < 0 \quad b^2 < 3ac$$

We justified only $d > 0$ since it represents the fixed costs incurred by a firm.

Let's check the other restrictions by starting from the parameter $a > 0$.

To prevent the cubic cost function from bending downward, the absolute minimum of the marginal cost function needs to be positive. Since we are working with a cubic function, the marginal cost, i.e. the first derivative, will be a parabola

$$MC = 3aQ^2 + 2bQ + c \tag{4.31}$$

From Sect. 3.3.2, we know that if $a > 0$, the function is concave up.

By setting $a > 0$ the MC function is concave up. Still, the minimum of the function could be negative. Following the steps from Sect. 4.9, to find the minimum of the function, we set the derivative equal to 0, in this case

$$\frac{dMC}{dQ} = 6aQ + 2b = 0$$

By solving for Q, we find

$$Q^* = -\frac{2b}{6a} \tag{4.32}$$

We know that this is a minimum because the second derivative

$$\frac{d^2MC}{dQ^2} = 6a$$

is greater than 0 because we set $a > 0$.

We now have elements to draw a conclusion for the parameter b. Since the output should be positive, b cannot be positive because $a > 0$. Consequently, we rule out $b > 0$. Still, b could be equal to 0. This would imply that $Q^* = 0$. However, since for the law of diminishing returns $Q^* > 0$, it follows that $b < 0$.

Next, by substituting (4.32) in (4.31) and simplifying, we obtain

$$MC_{min} = 3a\left(-\frac{2b}{6a}\right)^2 + 2b\left(-\frac{2b}{6a}\right) + c = \frac{3ac - b^2}{3a}$$

By rearranging $\frac{3ac-b^2}{3a} = 0$

$$c - \frac{b^2}{3a} = 0 \Rightarrow b^2 = 3ac$$

However, to guarantee the positivity of MC_{min} we need to set $b^2 < 3ac$. Since a square number is always positive, we need $c > 0$.

4.14.2 Marginal Cost and Average Cost

Let's add an additional information about the cost structure of this firm: the average cost (AC). Note that in the code we set the column name for `x` as `output` and we remove the first row of the dataset because the first line includes the division by zero for the AC. Moreover, note what the code `df2[which.min(df2$average_cost),c(1, 2, 5)]` does. Basically, we want to search for the minimum value of the average cost, and we want to compare the results for `output`, `marginal_cost`, and `average_cost`.

```
> colnames(df2)[1] <- "output"
> average_cost <- TC/Q
> df2 <- cbind(df2, average_cost)
> df2 <- df2[-1, ]
> df2$AC <- "AC"
> df2$MC <- "MC"
> df2[which.min(df2$average_cost),
+     c(1, 2, 5)]
   output marginal_cost average_cost
31     30           9.3     9.266667
> ggplot(df2) +
+        geom_line(aes(x = output,
+                      y = average_cost,
+                      color = AC), size = 1) +
+        geom_line(aes(x = output,
+                      y = marginal_cost,
+                      color = MC), size = 1) +
+        xlab("Output") + ylab("Costs") +
+        theme_minimal() +
+        theme(legend.title = element_blank(),
```

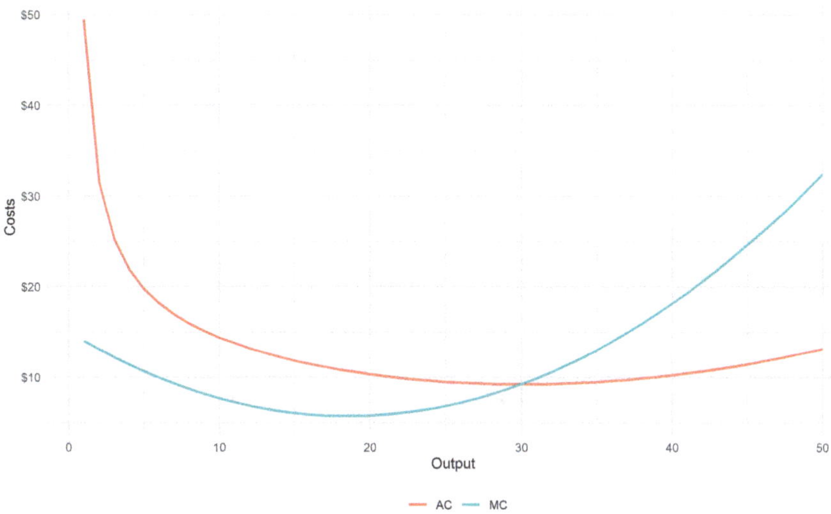

Fig. 4.18 Marginal cost and average cost

```
+             legend.position = "bottom") +
+       scale_y_continuous(labels = scales::dollar)
```

Figure 4.18 shows the relation between marginal cost and average cost. When the marginal cost is lower than the average cost, it draws the average cost downwards. On the other hand, when it is higher than the average cost it pushes the average cost upwards.

4.14.3 *Profit Maximization*

In this section, we will answer the key question: "How many units should a firm produce to maximize its profit?"

Also in this case, calculus helps us find the answer. A firm maximizes its profit when the marginal cost is equal to marginal revenue. We have already seen a definition of the marginal cost. Similarly, we can define the marginal revenue.

We define the *marginal revenue* as the change in total revenue for a given change in quantity. Therefore, with the revenue on the y axis and the quantity on the x axis, the marginal revenue is the *rise* over the *run* where the *rise* is the change in revenue and the *run* is the change in quantity.

$$MR = \lim_{\Delta Q \to 0} \frac{rise}{run} = \lim_{\Delta Q \to 0} \frac{\Delta Revenue}{\Delta Quantity} \tag{4.33}$$

Consequently, the marginal revenue represents the slope of the revenue function.

Now, with these definitions in mind let's put some order. First, let's identify the objective function we want to maximize (we will return to mathematical concepts and definitions in this section in Sect. 6.3). In this case, the objective function is the profit function that can be formulated in terms of quantity Q, the *choice variable*:

$$\pi(Q) = R(Q) - C(Q) \tag{4.34}$$

We have already encountered it in Sect. 3.2.2.2.

The first step is to take the first derivative of (4.34) and set equal to 0

$$\pi'(Q) = R'(Q) - C'(Q) = 0 \quad \text{[first-order condition]} \tag{4.35}$$

Note that $R'(Q)$ is the marginal revenue MR and $C'(Q)$ is the marginal cost MC. Additionally, note that Eq. 4.35 equals to 0 only if $MR = MC$.

Next, to be sure we have indeed reached a maximum and not a minimum, we take the second derivative

$$\pi''(Q^*) = R''(Q^*) - C''(Q^*) \quad \text{[second-order condition]} \tag{4.36}$$

If (4.36) evaluated at the optimal quantity Q^* is less than 0 we conclude we reached a maximum.

Let's start by defining the cost function and the revenue function. However, in this example, we follow a different approach for the cost. Suppose that we do not know the cost function but we observe the following fixed cost and variable costs for a given amount of output.[5]

```
> df
   output fixed_cost variable_cost
1       0         35         0.000
2       1         35        14.509
3       2         35        28.072
4       3         35        40.743
5       4         35        52.576
6       5         35        63.625
7       6         35        73.944
8       7         35        83.587
9       8         35        92.608
10      9         35       101.061
11     10         35       109.000
12     11         35       116.479
13     12         35       123.552
14     13         35       130.273
```

[5] I suggest the reader reading the section before replicating this example.

```
15      14          35          136.696
16      15          35          142.875
17      16          35          148.864
18      17          35          154.717
19      18          35          160.488
20      19          35          166.231
21      20          35          172.000
22      21          35          177.849
23      22          35          183.832
24      23          35          190.003
25      24          35          196.416
26      25          35          203.125
27      26          35          210.184
28      27          35          217.647
29      28          35          225.568
30      29          35          234.001
31      30          35          243.000
32      31          35          252.619
33      32          35          262.912
34      33          35          273.933
35      34          35          285.736
36      35          35          298.375
37      36          35          311.904
38      37          35          326.377
39      38          35          341.848
40      39          35          358.371
41      40          35          376.000
42      41          35          394.789
43      42          35          414.792
44      43          35          436.063
45      44          35          458.656
46      45          35          482.625
47      46          35          508.024
48      47          35          534.907
49      48          35          563.328
50      49          35          593.341
51      50          35          625.000
```

Now let's add the total cost by summing the fixed cost and the variable cost.

```
> df$total_cost <- df$fixed_cost + df$variable_cost
```

Let's suppose that the demand function for the firm's product is the following:

$$Q = 100 - \frac{5}{2}p$$

where Q represents the quantity and p the price. By rearranging the terms we have the inverse demand function as function of Q:

$$p = 40 - \frac{2}{5}Q$$

The revenue, price per quantity sold, is

$$R = pQ = \left(40 - \frac{2}{5}Q\right)Q = 40Q - \frac{2}{5}Q^2$$

```
> df$price <- 40 - (2/5)*Q
> df$revenue <- df$output * df$price
> head(df)
  output fixed_cost variable_cost total_cost price revenue
1      0         35         0.000     35.000  40.0     0.0
2      1         35        14.509     49.509  39.6    39.6
3      2         35        28.072     63.072  39.2    78.4
4      3         35        40.743     75.743  38.8   116.4
5      4         35        52.576     87.576  38.4   153.6
6      5         35        63.625     98.625  38.0   190.0
```

Until now we found the total cost and total revenue per given amount of production. However, we only know the function for total revenue but not for the total cost. Let's plot the data to grasp an idea about the functions. Let's generate a scatter plot with `geom_point()` in `ggplot()` to figure out the shape of the functions (Fig. 4.19).

```
> sp_cost <- ggplot(df) +
+   geom_point(aes(x = output,
+                  y = total_cost)) +
+   ggtitle("Cost function")
> sp_rev <- ggplot(df) +
+   geom_point(aes(x = output,
+                  y = revenue)) +
+   ggtitle("Revenue function")
> ggarrange(sp_cost, sp_rev,
+           ncol = 1, nrow = 2)
```

The cost function loos like a cubic function. Let's use the `splinefun()` function to approximate the functions based on the observed data. We compare the results of our data with the output of `cost_fn()`.

```
> cost_fn <- splinefun(x = df$output,
+                      y = df$total_cost)
> head(df$total_cost, 10)
 [1]  35.000  49.509  63.072  75.743  87.576
 [6]  98.625 108.944 118.587 127.608 136.061
```

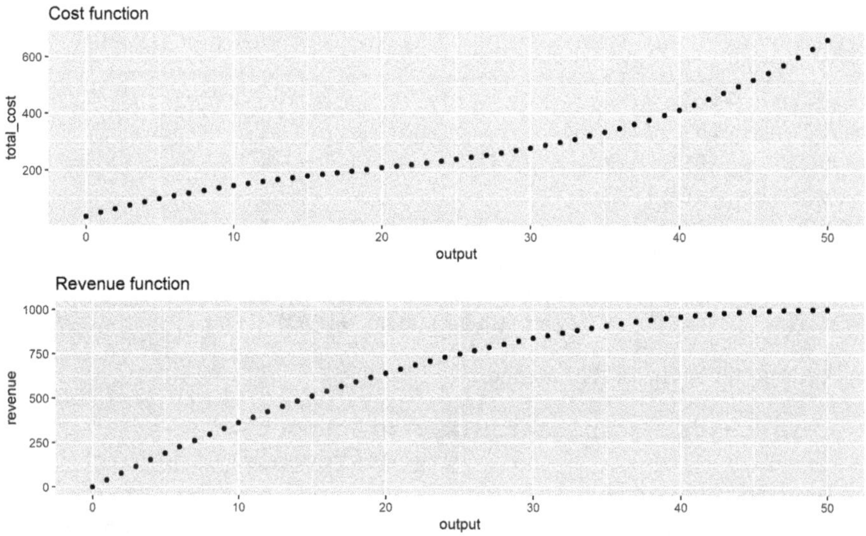

Fig. 4.19 Scatter plot of cost function and revenue function

```
> head(cost_fn(Q), 10)
 [1]  35.000  49.509  63.072  75.743  87.576
 [6]  98.625 108.944 118.587 127.608 136.061
```

But what is the cost function? Let's try to figure out the coefficients. We can extrapolate the coefficients as follows

```
> splinecoef_cost <- get("z", envir = environment
  (cost_fn))
> splinecoef_cost$y[1]
[1] 35
> splinecoef_cost$b[1]
[1] 15
> splinecoef_cost$c[1]
[1] -0.5
> splinecoef_cost$d[1]
[1] 0.009
```

Perhaps these coefficients are familiar to you. Indeed we used the same cost function as in Sect. 4.14.1.[6]

[6] Note that `splinefun()` computes a numerical approximation of the coefficients through cubic (or Hermite) spline interpolation of given data points. We used it since by the plot of the data we figured it out it could be a cubic function. However, keep in mind that the function is not returning a cubic formula such as $f(x) = ax^3 + bx^2 + cx + d$. Here we are extracting only the approximation for the first coefficients. This approximation seems to return the desired coefficients

The dataset for this example has been built as follows

```
> Q <- seq(0, 50, 1)
> FC <- 35
> VC1 <- 15
> VC2 <- -0.5
> VC3 <- 0.009
> VC <- VC3*Q^3 + VC2*Q^2 + VC1*Q
> df <- data.frame(output = Q,
+                  fixed_cost = FC,
+                  variable_cost = VC)
```

Let's do the same for the revenue.

```
> revenue_fn <- splinefun(x = df$output,
+                         y = df$revenue)
> head(df$revenue, 10)
 [1]   0.0  39.6  78.4 116.4 153.6 190.0 225.6 260.4
      294.4 327.6
> head(revenue_fn(Q), 10)
 [1]   0.0  39.6  78.4 116.4 153.6 190.0 225.6 260.4
      294.4 327.6
> splinecoef_rev <- get("z", envir = environment
  (revenue_fn))
> splinecoef_rev$y[1]
[1] 0
> splinecoef_rev$b[1]
[1] 40
> splinecoef_rev$c[1]
[1] -0.4
> round(splinecoef_rev$d[1], 1)
[1] 0
```

Also in this case we found that the coefficients stored at index 1 match the coefficients of the original revenue function.

The `splinfun()` takes an argument, `deriv =`, that allows us to directly compute the derivative. Therefore, from the total cost function and the revenue function we can easily compute the marginal cost and the marginal revenue.

```
> head(cost_fn(Q, deriv = 1))
[1] 15.000 14.027 13.108 12.243 11.432 10.675
```

when the data for x start from 0, i.e. in our case at index 1 $Q = 0$ and the degree of the leading coefficient is at largest 3. One possible alternative would consist in estimating the coefficients by using a polynomial regression model. A degree-3 polynomial fits a cubic curve to the data: `lm(total_cost ~ output + I(output^2) + I(output^3), data = df)`.

```
> head(revenue_fn(Q, deriv = 1))
[1] 40.0 39.2 38.4 37.6 36.8 36.0
```

We plot the marginal cost and the marginal revenue using `stat_function()` in `ggplot()`. `fun =` requires a function and in `args =` we implement the first derivative with `deriv = 1`. We manually change the color for the plot with `scale_color_manual()`

```
> ggplot(data = df,
+          mapping = aes(x = output)) +
+        geom_hline(yintercept = 0) +
+        geom_vline(xintercept = 0) +
+        stat_function(fun = cost_fn,
+                      size = 1,
+                      args = list(deriv = 1),
+                      aes(color = "Marginal cost")) +
+        stat_function(fun = revenue_fn,
+                      size = 1,
+                      args = list(deriv = 1),
+                      aes(color = "Marginal revenue"))+
+        xlab("Quantity") +  ylab("Price") +
+        scale_y_continuous(labels = scales::dollar) +
+        scale_color_manual(values = c("Marginal cost" =
                                        "red",
+                               "Marginal revenue" = "blue"),
+                                name = "Legend") +
+        theme_minimal() +
+        theme(legend.position = "bottom")
```

Figure 4.20 shows the optimal quantity to be produced as the intersection between MC and MR. Therefore, we can also find the optimal output through the intersection of MR and MC. This is an alternative approach to (4.35). In fact, by equating

$$
\begin{aligned}
MR &= 40 - \frac{4}{5}Q \\
MC &= 0.027Q^2 - Q + 15
\end{aligned}
\tag{4.37}
$$

we end up with

$$
-0.027Q^2 + \frac{1}{5}Q + 25 \tag{4.38}
$$

that is the same as $\pi'(Q) = R'(Q) - C'(Q)$.

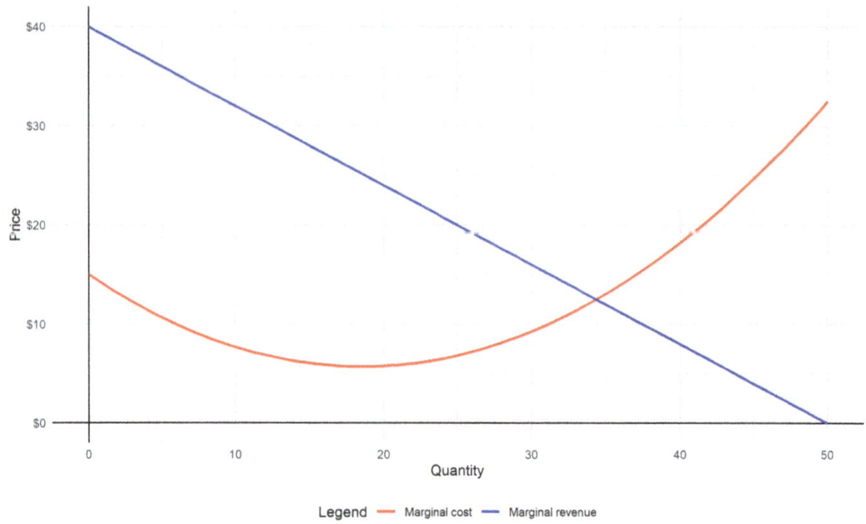

Fig. 4.20 Marginal cost and marginal revenue

But exactly how much is the optimal quantity? We have to set (4.38) equal to 0 and solve for Q. Since this is a quadratic function we can use the `quadratic_formula()` function we built in Chap. 3

```
> quadratic_formula(-0.027, (1/5), 25)
                 x1       x2
solutions 34.35731 -26.9499
```

We have two solutions but we rule out the negative solution since we do not have negative quantities of output.

Let's see another way to do this with the `uniroot()` function. We seek the point where marginal cost and marginal revenue intersect within a given range. In our case, we set all over the possible quantity. The profit is maximized when $MR = MC$ that is when $MR - MC = 0$. This is what we write in the function.

```
> optimalq <- uniroot(function(x) {revenue_fn(x, deriv = 1) -
+                          cost_fn(x, deriv = 1)},
+                        c(1, 50))
> q_opt <- optimalq$root
> q_opt
[1] 34.35731
```

Therefore, 34.4 units is the optimum output. However, let's verify that we indeed reached a maximum.

```
> revenue_fn(q_opt, 2) - cost_fn(q_opt, 2) < 0
[1] TRUE
```

We can conclude that the firm maximizes the profit when it produces 34.4 units of good. But let's check this result in the table of stored data.

```
> df$mc <- cost_fn(Q, deriv = 1)
> df$mr <- revenue_fn(Q, deriv = 1)
> head(df[33:37, c(1, 5, 6, 7, 8)])
   output price revenue     mc   mr
33     32  27.2   870.4 10.648 14.4
34     33  26.8   884.4 11.403 13.6
35     34  26.4   897.6 12.212 12.8
36     35  26.0   910.0 13.075 12.0
37     36  25.6   921.6 13.992 11.2
```

As we can figure out, mc and mr are equal between 34 and 35 units. Since the firm does not produce 34.4 units of good, we should say that the firm maximizes its profit when it produces 35 units. By substituting the optimal quantity Q^* into the profit function (4.34), we can find the maximized profit to be $\pi^* = \pi(Q^*) = 577$

```
> revenue_fn(q_opt) - cost_fn(q_opt)
[1] 576.9693
```

In addition, since the price corresponding to the optimal quantity is $26.3, greater than the marginal cost, we conclude that we represented a monopolistic firm.

```
> p_opt <- 40 - (2/5)*q_opt
> p_opt
[1] 26.25708
```

Before concluding this section, let's add the average cost and the consumer demand to the plot for some additional information.

```
> df$average_cost <- df$total_cost / df$output
> df2 <- df[, c("output", "price", "mc",
+               "mr", "average_cost")]
> head(df2)
  output price     mc   mr average_cost
1      0  40.0 15.000 40.0          Inf
2      1  39.6 14.027 39.2     49.50900
3      2  39.2 13.108 38.4     31.53600
4      3  38.8 12.243 37.6     25.24767
5      4  38.4 11.432 36.8     21.89400
6      5  38.0 10.675 36.0     19.72500
> df2 <- df2[-1, ]
> df2[33:37,]
   output price     mc   mr average_cost
34     33  26.8 11.403 13.6     9.361606
35     34  26.4 12.212 12.8     9.433412
```

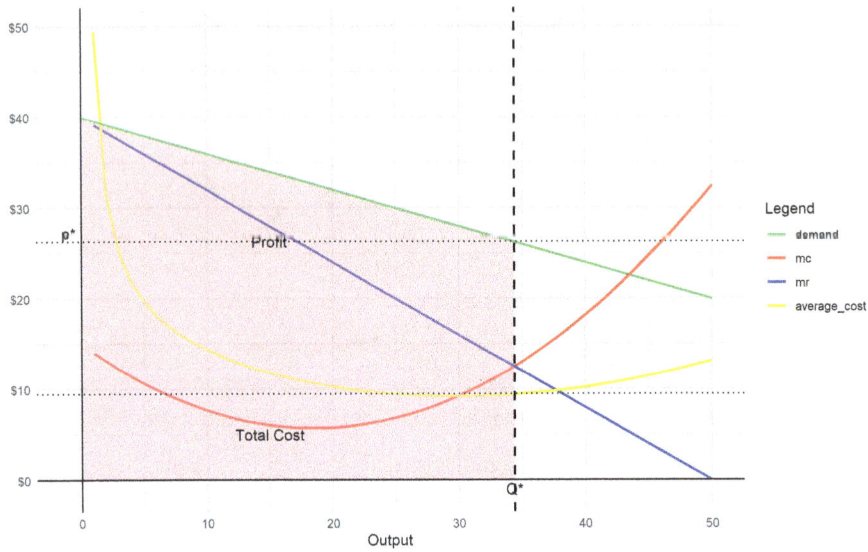

Fig. 4.21 Monopoly graph

```
36         35   26.0 13.075 12.0        9.525000
37         36   25.6 13.992 11.2        9.636222
38         37   25.2 14.963 10.4        9.766946
> demand <- function(output) 40 - (2/5)*output
```

The firm in monopoly does not charge the price where $MC = MR$, but charges p^*, the price the consumers are willing to pay. From this fact, we can compute the total revenue at the optimizing quantity as $TR^* = p^* \cdot Q^*$ The pink area in Fig. 4.21 represents the total revenue. We know that the total cost borne by a firm is $TC = FC + VC$. Since the average cost equals $AC = \frac{TC}{Q} = \frac{FC}{Q} + \frac{VC}{Q}$, at the optimizing quantity $AC = \frac{TC}{Q*}$. Consequently, $TC = AC \cdot Q^*$. This is the area up to the average cost curve in Fig. 4.21. Finally, the difference between total revenue and total cost is the profit of the firm ($\pi = TR - TC$).

```
> TC_opt <- FC + VC3*q_opt^3 + VC2*q_opt^2 + VC1*q_opt
> TC_opt
[1] 325.1533
> AC_opt <- TC_opt/q_opt
> AC_opt
[1] 9.463874
> df_l <- melt(setDT(df2), id.vars = "output",
+              measure.vars = c("price", "mc", "mr",
+                               "average_cost"),
+              variable.name = "var",
+              value.name = "USD")
```

```
> ggplot(df_1, aes(x = output,
+                   y = USD,
+                   group = var,
+                   color = var)) +
+   geom_line(size = 1) +
+   stat_function(data = df_1[1:50,],
+                 mapping = aes(output),
+                 fun = demand,
+                 xlim = c(0, q_opt),
+                 geom = "area",
+                 fill = "pink",
+                 alpha = 0.5,
+                 show.legend = FALSE) +
+   geom_hline(yintercept = p_opt,
+              linetype = "dotted") +
+   geom_hline(yintercept = AC_opt,
+              linetype = "dotted") +
+   geom_vline(xintercept = q_opt,
+              linetype = "dashed",
+              size = 0.8) +
+   geom_hline(yintercept = 0) +
+   geom_vline(xintercept = 0) +
+   theme_minimal() +
+   xlab("Output") + ylab("") +
+   scale_y_continuous(labels = scales::dollar) +
+   scale_color_manual(labels = c("demand", "mc", "mr",
+                                 "average_cost"),
+                      values = c("green",
+                                 "red",
+                                 "blue",
+                                 "yellow"),
+                      name = "Legend") +
+   annotate("text", x = c(q_opt, -1, 15, 15),
+            y = c(-1, p_opt + 1, 5, p_opt),
+            label = c("Q*", "p*", "Total Cost",
+                      "Profit"))
```

4.14.4 Elasticity

Let's say that for a price equal to 20, $p_1 = 20$, a firm sells 15 units of output, $q_1 = 15$, and for a price equal to 15, $p_2 = 15$, the firm sells 35 units of output, $q_2 = 35$.

```
> p1 <- 20
> q1 <- 15
> p2 <- 15
> q2 <- 35
```

With this information, let's find the slope of the inverse demand function $P = f^{-1}(Q)$. We use the `slope_linfun()` function we built in Chap. 3. We use the option `graph = TRUE` to plot the function. However, given that we are dealing with price and quantity, we make the following modification to the plot code in the function:

```
x <- seq(0, 50, 1)
y <- a + slope*x
df <- data.frame(x, y)

g <- ggplot(df, aes(x = x, y = y)) +
  geom_line() +
  geom_hline(yintercept = 0) +
  geom_vline(xintercept = 0) +
  theme_minimal() +
  xlab("Q") + ylab("P") +
  theme(axis.title.y = element_text(angle = 360),
        axis.title.x = element_text(hjust = 1))
```

In `theme()`, we rotate the title of the y axis and we move the title of the x axis to the right. Therefore, we find that the inverse demand function is $P = 23.75 - 0.25Q$ (Fig. 4.22).

```
> slope_linfun(q1, q2, y1 = p1, y2 = p2,
+              graph = T, eq = F)
[[1]]
[1] "the slope of y = 23.75 -0.25x is: -0.25"

[[2]]
```

Substitute $P = 23.75 - 0.25Q$ in the revenue function $R(Q) = PQ$. We find that $R(Q) = (23.75 - 0.25Q)Q = 23.75Q - 0.25Q^2$.

In the next lines of code we generate Figs. 4.23 and 4.24. In the code of Fig. 4.24 we add the `transition_reveal()` function from the `gganimate` package to make the plot dynamic.[7] In addition, we add `geom_point()` to produce a leading point when the plot is animated (note that Fig. 4.24 represents the static plot, i.e. without `transition_reveal()`).

[7] Remember to load `gifski` and `png` packages as well.

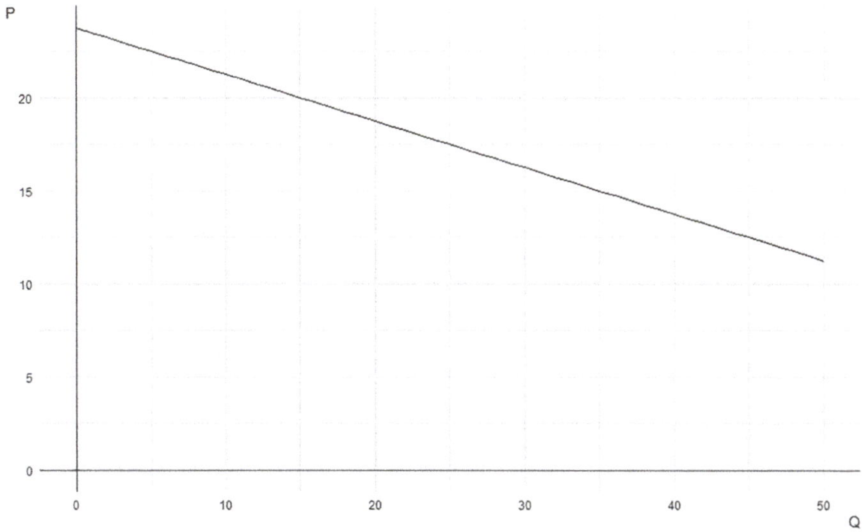

Fig. 4.22 Inverse demand function: $P = 23.75 - 0.25Q$

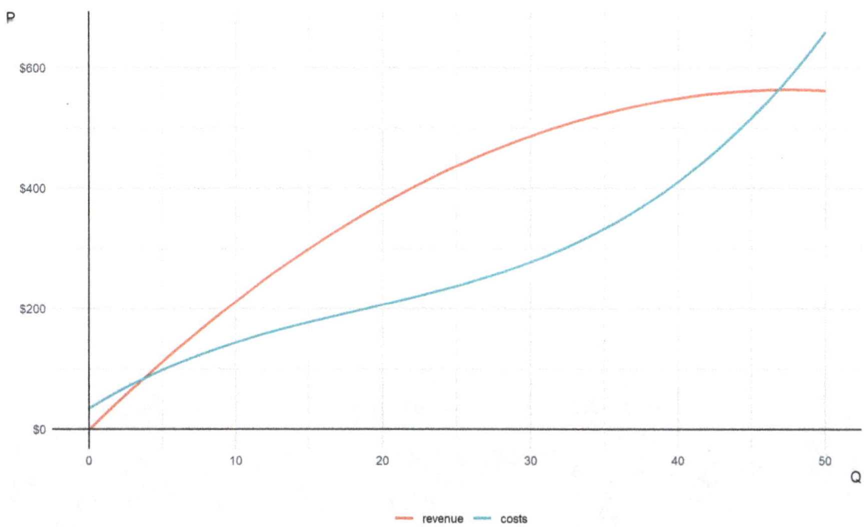

Fig. 4.23 Revenue and total cost

```
> Q <- 0:50
> P <- (23.75 - 0.25*Q)
> R <- P*Q
> TC <- total_cost(Q, VC1, VC2, FC, VC3)
> df <- data.frame(output = Q,
+                  revenue = R,
```

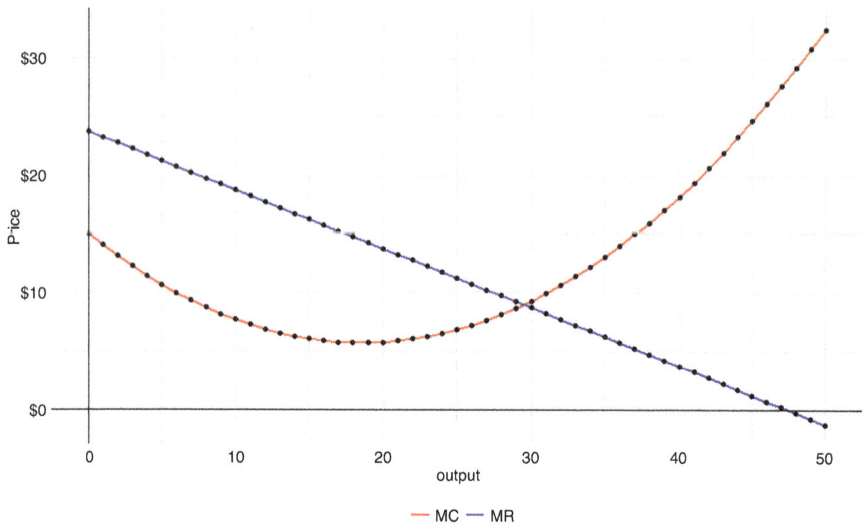

Fig. 4.24 Marginal cost and marginal revenue (static version of the dynamic plot)

```
+                    costs = TC,
+                    price = P)
> df_l <- melt(setDT(df), id.vars = "output",
+                measure.vars = c("revenue",
+                                 "costs"))
> ggplot(df_l, aes(x = output,
+                    y = value,
+                    group = variable,
+                    color = variable)) +
+   geom_line(size = 1) +
+   geom_hline(yintercept = 0) +
+   geom_vline(xintercept = 0) +
+   theme_minimal() +
+   xlab("Q") + ylab("P") +
+   theme(axis.title.y = element_text(angle = 360),
+         axis.title.x = element_text(hjust = 1)) +
+   theme(legend.title = element_blank(),
+         legend.position = "bottom") +
+   scale_y_continuous(labels = scales::dollar)

> MC <- marginal_cost(Q, VC1, VC2, FC, VC3, n = 1)
> revenue_fn <- splinefun(x = df$output,
+                          y = df$revenue)
> MR <- revenue_fn(Q, deriv = 1)
> df <- cbind.data.frame(df, MC, MR)
```

```
> ggplot(df) +
+   geom_line(aes(x = output, y = MC,
+                 color = "MC"),
+             size = 1) +
+   geom_line(aes(x = output, y = MR,
+                 color = "MR"),
+             size = 1) +
+   geom_point(aes(x = output, y = MC)) +
+   geom_point(aes(x = output, y = MR)) +
+   geom_hline(yintercept = 0) +
+   geom_vline(xintercept = 0) +
+   theme_minimal() + ylab("Price") +
+   scale_y_continuous(labels = scales::dollar) +
+   scale_color_manual(values =
+                        c("MC" = "red",
+                          "MR" = "blue")) +
+   theme_minimal() +
+   theme(legend.position = "bottom",
+         legend.title = element_blank()) +
+   transition_reveal(output)

Frame 100 (100%)
Finalizing encoding... done!
```

Finally, we find the output that maximizes the profit where $MC = MR$.

```
> cost_fn <- splinefun(x = df$output,
+                      y = df$costs)
> optimalq <- uniroot(function(x) cost_fn(x, deriv = 1)-
+                       revenue_fn(x, deriv = 1),
+                     c(0, 50))
> optimalq$root
[1] 29.50298
```

Let's observe the following output. We can see that when the `output` is between 29 and 30, the `price` is between 16.50 and 16.25 while `MR` is between 9.25 and 8.75. In other words, the price is higher than the marginal revenue. This means that we are not in the case of a perfect competitive market.

```
> df[27:32, ]
   output revenue   costs price    MC    MR
27     26   448.5 245.184 17.25 7.252 10.75
28     27   459.0 252.647 17.00 7.683 10.25
29     28   469.0 260.568 16.75 8.168  9.75
30     29   478.5 269.001 16.50 8.707  9.25
31     30   487.5 278.000 16.25 9.300  8.75
32     31   496.0 287.619 16.00 9.947  8.25
```

Write the revenue function, `rev_fn()`, as follows

```
> rev_fn  <- function(Q) {23.75*Q - 0.25*Q^2}
> mr <- Deriv(rev_fn, "Q")
> mr
function (Q)
23.75 - 0.5 * Q
> mr(optimalq$root)
[1] 8.998511
```

If we had been in a perfect competitive market, the price, when $P = MR$, would have been \$9.

However, given the inverse demand function `inv_demand_fn()`, the price when $MC = MR$ is \$16.4.

```
> inv_demand_fn <- splinefun(x = Q,
+                            y = P)
> inv_demand_fn(optimalq$root)
[1] 16.37426
> inv_demand_fn_coef <- get("z",
+                       envir = environment(inv_demand_fn))
> inv_demand_fn_coef$y[1]
[1] 23.75
> inv_demand_fn_coef$b[1]
[1] -0.25
```

Let's print again `df`. We see that when $P = 22$, $Q = 7$ and when $P = 20$, $Q = 15$. So what is the price elasticity of the demand?

```
> df[5:16, ]
    output revenue   costs price     MC    MR
 1:      4    91.0  87.576 22.75 11.432 21.75
 2:      5   112.5  98.625 22.50 10.675 21.25
 3:      6   133.5 108.944 22.25  9.972 20.75
 4:      7   154.0 118.587 22.00  9.323 20.25
 5:      8   174.0 127.608 21.75  8.728 19.75
 6:      9   193.5 136.061 21.50  8.187 19.25
 7:     10   212.5 144.000 21.25  7.700 18.75
 8:     11   231.0 151.479 21.00  7.267 18.25
 9:     12   249.0 158.552 20.75  6.888 17.75
10:     13   266.5 165.273 20.50  6.563 17.25
11:     14   283.5 171.696 20.25  6.292 16.75
12:     15   300.0 177.875 20.00  6.075 16.25
```

The inverse demand function is

$$P = 23.75 - 0.25Q$$

Let's solve for Q to find the demand function.

$$Q = 95 - 4P$$

Let's verify if this is correct by plugging $P = 20$ and $P = 22$.

$$Q = 95 - 4 \cdot 20 = 15$$

$$Q = 95 - 4 \cdot 22 = 7$$

The formula for the elasticity is

$$\varepsilon = \frac{dQ}{dP} \cdot \frac{P}{Q} \tag{4.39}$$

The derivative of $\frac{dQ}{dP} = -4$. Let's substitute this and $P = 20$ and $Q = 15$ in (4.39). Let's build a function, `elas()`, to compute the elasticity.

```
> P20 <- 20
> Q15 <- 15
> Q <- "95 - 4*P"
> elas <- function(Q, p1, q1,
+                  p2 = 0, q2 = 0,
+                  point_elas = TRUE){
+
+   require("Deriv")
+   dQdP <- Deriv(Q, "P")
+   dQdP <- eval(parse(text = dQdP))
+
+   if(point_elas == TRUE){
+
+     e <- dQdP * (p1/q1)
+
+   } else {
+     e <- ((p1 + p2)/
+           (q1 + q2)) * dQdP
+   }
+
+   return(e)
+
+ }
> ELAS <- elas(Q, P20, Q15)
> ELAS
[1] -5.333333
```

$$\varepsilon = -4 \cdot \frac{20}{15} = -5.333333$$

The point price elasticity of demand equals −5.33, i.e. at this point on the demand curve, a 1% price increase causes a 5.3% decrease in quantity demanded.

If we consider the absolute value of the elasticity, given the law of demand, i.e. price and quantity demanded have inverse relation, we can state that

- if $|\varepsilon| < 1$, the demand is inelastic, i.e. quantity is insensitive to a change in price. For example, a price increase does not affect significantly the demand for a good. Consequently, total revenue increases;
- if $|\varepsilon| > 1$, the demand is elastic, i.e. quantity is sensitive to a change in price. For example, a price increase leads consumers to consume significantly less of that good. Consequently, total revenue decreases;
- if $|\varepsilon| = 1$, the demand is unitary, i.e. a percentage change in price leads to the exact same percentage change in the quantity demanded. Consequently, total revenue is unchanged.

Once we know the point price elasticity of demand we can easily compute the marginal revenue:

$$MR = P\left(1 + \frac{1}{\varepsilon}\right) = 20\left(1 + \frac{1}{-5.3333}\right) = 16.25$$

```
> MR <- P20 * (1 + (1/ELAS))
> MR
[1] 16.25
> df[df$price == 20, ]
   output revenue   costs price    MC    MR
1:     15     300 177.875    20 6.075 16.25
```

Finally, note that the `elas()` function can compute the arc elasticity as well. The arc elasticity is defined as follows:

$$\varepsilon = \frac{dQ}{dP} \cdot \frac{P_1 + P_2}{Q_1 + Q_2} \tag{4.40}$$

```
> P2025 <- 20.25
> Q14 <- 14
> ELAS_arc <- elas(Q, P20, Q15, P2025, Q14,
+                  point_elas = F)
> ELAS_arc
[1] -5.551724
```

4.15 Exercise

4.15.1 Exercise 1

In Sect. 4.14.1 we coded `total_cost()` and `marginal_cost()`. In this exercise write a function `cost_fn()` that allows to compute both total cost and marginal cost. Replicate the results in Sect. 4.14.1.

```
> Q10 <- 10
> TC <- cost_fn(Q10, VC1, VC2, FC, VC3)
> TC
[1] 144
> MC <- cost_fn(Q10, VC1, VC2, FC, VC3, n = 1)
> MC
[1] 7.7
```

4.15.2 Exercise 2

In this exercise you are asked to write a function, `profit_max()`, that returns the quantity that maximizes the profit, the corresponding price, and the maximized profit. Make sure to include a step that checks that we reached a maximum. Finally, add an option to plot it.

In my case, the `profit_max()` includes a parameter `w` (by default `w = 50`) to control for the last number in the output sequence; another default value, `Ymax = 50`, to control for the maximum value of the *y* coordinate in `coord_cartesian()`; two default values, `a = 0` and `z = 50`, to control for the lower and upper value of the interval of the `uniroot()` function; finally, `graph = FALSE` by default.

For example, the following code replicates the results from Sect. 4.14.3

```
> R <- function(Q) {40*Q - (2/5)*Q^2}
> C <- function(Q) {0.009*Q^3 - 0.5*Q^2 + 15*Q + 35}
> profit_max(R, C)
$`maximizing output`
[1] 34.35731

$`maximizing price`
[1] 26.25708

$`maximized profit`
[1] 576.9693
```

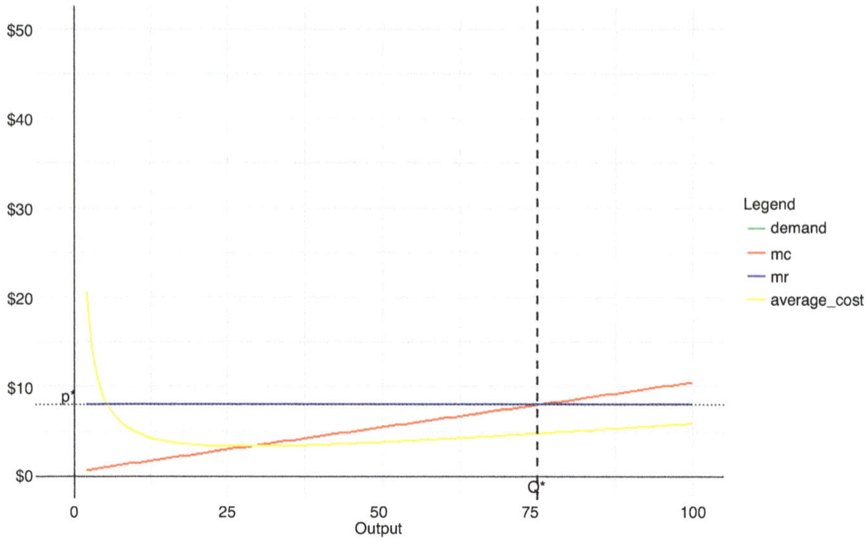

Fig. 4.25 Result of exercise Sect. 4.15

Another example with plot (Fig. 4.25). As you can observe from Fig. 4.25 I made the plot "lighter" by removing most of the labels we included for Fig. 4.21.

```
> R <- function(Q) {8*Q}
> C <- function(Q) {0.05*Q^2 + 0.5*Q + 40}
> profit_max(R, C, w = 100,
+            z = 100, graph = T)
$'maximizing output'
[1] 75

$'maximizing price'
[1] 8

$'maximized profit'
[1] 241.25

[[4]]
```

Another example where we have two critical values. First, we search in the interval [0, 20]. Our test tells us that at the first critical value we reached a minimum.

```
> R <- function(Q) {- 2*Q^2 + 1200*Q }
> C <- function(Q) {Q^3 - 61.25*Q^2 + 1528.5*Q + 2000}
> profit_max(R, C, w = 100, z = 20)
Error in profit_max(R, C, w = 100, z = 20) : you
reached a minimum
```

Let's search in the interval [21, 100].

```
> profit_max(R, C, w = 100, a = 21, z = 100)
$`maximizing output`
[1] 36.5

$`maximizing price`
[1] 1127

$`maximized profit`
[1] 16318.44
```

Therefore the profit maximizing output is 36.5. This last example reproduces the example in Chiang and Wainwright (2005, p. 238).

4.15.3 Exercise 3

Rewrite the `newton()` function by replacing the `dfdx()` function with one of the **R** functions to compute the derivative.

Chapter 5
Integral Calculus

Integration is the other key topic of calculus. Contrary to the derivatives, integration is more difficult. We may have not a *formula-ready-to-apply* to compute the integration process and we may go through a *trial and error* process. Here we present the main cases of integration. We will deal with the broad topic regarding integration by dividing it in two main parts: indefinite integrals and definite integrals. In the first case, we refer to integrals as anti derivatives while, in the second case, we refer to integrals to find the area under a curve.

5.1 Indefinite Integrals

As the word may leave us thinking, anti-derivative is the inverse process of the derivative. Therefore, if a function $G(x)$ has the property that its derivative is $G'(x) = F(x)$, we define $G(x)$ as the anti-derivative of $F(x)$. In mathematical terms,

$$G(x) + c = \int F(x)\, dx \tag{5.1}$$

that is read as "anti-derivative of $F(x)$ with respect to x".

The c in Eq. 5.1 is called *constant of integration*. Let's go through an example to understand the indefinite integral and the meaning of c.

Suppose we want to compute the following integral:

$$\int F(x)\, dx = \int 4x^3\, dx$$

M. Porto, *Introduction to Mathematics for Economics with R*,
https://doi.org/10.1007/978-3-031-05202-6_5

We know that this implies that $G'(x) = F(x)$, i.e. $G'(x) = 4x^3$. In turn, this implies that $G(x) = x^4$. But what about $G(x) = x^4 + 5$? Its derivative is still $G'(x) = 4x^3$. And what about $G(x) = x^4 - 10$? Its derivative is still $G'(x) = 4x^3$ because the derivative of a constant is 0. Therefore, we add c in Eq. 5.1, where c is any arbitrary constant real number.

5.1.1 Anti-derivative Process

5.1.1.1 Fundamental Integrals

5.1.1.1.1 Integration with Power Functions

$$\int x^n \, dx = \frac{1}{n+1} x^{n+1} + c, \quad \text{provided} \quad n \neq -1 \tag{5.2}$$

This is the case we saw in Sect. 5.1. Therefore, applying the rule (5.2)

$$\int 4x^3 \, dx = \frac{4}{3+1} x^{3+1} + c = \frac{4}{4} x^4 + c = x^4 + c$$

Example 5.1.1

$$\int x^{-2} \, dx = \frac{1}{-2+1} x^{-2+1} + c = -x^{-1} + c = -\frac{1}{x} + c$$

Example 5.1.2 But note the following:

$$\int x^{-1} \, dx = \frac{1}{-1+1} x^{-1+1} + c = \frac{1}{0} x^0 + c$$

We have a problem since we cannot divide by 0. Therefore, this integration process is not sustainable. We integrate x^{-1} as follows:

$$\int x^{-1} \, dx = \int \frac{1}{x} dx = \log(|x|) + c, \quad \text{provided} \quad x \neq 0 \tag{5.3}$$

In fact, since $G'(x) = F(x)$, $G'(x) = \frac{1}{x}$. This implies that $G(x) = \log(x)$.

5.1.1.1.2 Integration with a Constant

$$\int k\,dx = k\int dx = kx + c \tag{5.4}$$

Example 5.1.3

$$\int 5\,dx = 5\int dx = 5x + c$$

Note that

$$\int dx = \int x^0\,dx = \frac{1}{0+1}x^{0+1} + c = \frac{1}{1}x^1 + c = x + c$$

$$\int k\cdot F(x)\,dx = k\int F(x)\,dx \tag{5.5}$$

Example 5.1.4

$$\int 6\sqrt{x}\,dx = 6\int x^{\frac{1}{2}}\,dx = 6\cdot\frac{1}{\frac{1}{2}+1}x^{\frac{1}{2}+1} = 6\cdot\frac{1}{\frac{3}{2}}x^{3/2} = 6\cdot\frac{2}{3}x^{3/2} = 4x^{\frac{3}{2}} + c$$

5.1.1.1.3 Sum (Subtraction) Rule

$$\int F(x) + G(x)\,dx = \int F(x)\,dx + \int G(x)\,dx \tag{5.6}$$

Example 5.1.5

$$\int x^2 + \sqrt{x} + 5\,dx = \int x^2\,dx + \int \sqrt{x}\,dx + \int 5\,dx = \frac{1}{3}x^3 + \frac{2}{3}x^{\frac{3}{2}} + 5x + c$$

5.1.1.1.4 Integration with Exponential Functions

$$\int e^{kx}\,dx = \frac{1}{k}e^{kx} + c, \quad \text{where } k \text{ is a constant real number} \tag{5.7}$$

Example 5.1.6

$$\int e^{5x}\,dx = \frac{1}{5}e^{5x} + c$$

$$\int a^x\,dx = \frac{a^x}{\log(a)} + c \tag{5.8}$$

Example 5.1.7

$$\int 5^x\,dx = \frac{5^x}{\log(5)} + c$$

5.1.1.1.5 Integration with Logarithmic Functions

$$\int \log(x)\,dx = x\log(x) - x + c, \quad \text{provided} \quad x > 0 \tag{5.9}$$

5.1.1.1.6 Integration with Rational Functions

$$\int \frac{k}{ax+b}\,dx = \frac{k}{a}\log(|ax+b|) + c, \quad \text{where} \quad a, b, k \quad \text{are constant} \tag{5.10}$$

Example 5.1.8

$$\int \frac{4}{5x-3}\,dx = \frac{4}{5}\int \frac{5}{5x-3}dx = \frac{4}{5}\log(|5x-3|) + c$$

$$\int \frac{dx}{1+x^2}\,dx = \arctan x + c \tag{5.11}$$

where arctan stands for arctangent (we will discuss trigonometric functions in Chap. 8)

$$\int \frac{dx}{1-x^2}\,dx = \log\sqrt{\frac{1+x}{1-x}} + c, \quad \text{provided} \quad |x| < 1 \tag{5.12}$$

$$\int \frac{dx}{x^2-1}\,dx = \log\sqrt{\frac{x-1}{x+1}} + c, \quad \text{provided} \quad |x| > 1 \tag{5.13}$$

Exponential Growth

In Sect. 4.6.7.1, we differentiated (3.29) to compute the population at any time to get the exponential growth function. In this section, we reverse the process.

First, note that we are dealing with a differential equation, i.e. an equation that involves a derivative of a function. We will cover differential equations in Chap. 11. Therefore, let's take the first step and the last steps as given and let's focus on integration.

$$\frac{dN}{dt} = rN$$

Let's separate the variables:

$$\frac{dN}{N} = r\,dt$$

Now let's integrate both sides:

$$\int \frac{1}{N}\,dN = \int r\,dt$$

Let's integrate first the right hand side:

$$\int r\,dt = r\int dt = rt + c$$

Now, let's integrate the left hand side:

$$\int \frac{1}{N}\,dN = \log(|N|) + c$$

Therefore,

$$\log(|N|) = rt + c$$

Let's get rid of the logarithm by taking the exponential of both sides:

$$e^{\log(|N|)} = e^{rt+c}$$

$$|N| = e^{rt+c}$$

And for the properties of exponents:

$$|N| = e^c \cdot e^{rt}$$

Now let's get rid of the absolute value sign:

$$N = \pm e^c \cdot e^{rt}$$

Make the following substitution $\pm e^c = c$.

$$N = ce^{rt}$$

Let's find the value of c when $t = 0$.

$$N(t = 0) = ce^{r0}$$

$$N(t = 0) = c \cdot 1$$

$$N(t = 0) = c$$

Therefore,

$$N(t) = N_0 e^{rt}$$

5.1.1.2 Integration by Substitution

In this section, we see a few examples regarding how to solve integrals applying a method known as integration by substitution. It corresponds to the chain rule for derivatives. Basically, the method consists in substituting a difficult integral with an easier one.

Example 5.1.9

$$\int 4(3x - 5)^3 \, dx \tag{5.14}$$

Substitute what is inside the parenthesis, $3x - 5$, with u, i.e.

$$u = 3x - 5$$

Differentiate u with respect to x:

$$\frac{du}{dx} = 3$$

Solve for dx:

$$du = 3\ dx$$

$$dx = \frac{du}{3}$$

Now let's substitute $3x - 5$ with u and dx with $\frac{du}{3}$ in integral (5.14).

$$\int 4u^3 \frac{du}{3}$$

Bring the constant out of the integral sign:

$$\frac{4}{3}\int u^3\ du$$

Therefore, we have now just to integrate u^3.

$$\frac{4}{3}\frac{1}{4}u^4 \Rightarrow \frac{1}{3}u^4 + c$$

To find the solution substitute back for $u = 3x - 5$:

$$\frac{1}{3}(3x - 5)^4 + c$$

Example 5.1.10

$$\int x^3 e^{x^4+2}\ dx$$

Substitute $x^4 + 2 = u$ and follow the same steps as before.

$$\frac{du}{dx} = 4x^3$$

$$du = 4x^3\ dx$$

$$dx = \frac{du}{4x^3}$$

$$\int x^3 \mathrm{e}^u \frac{du}{4x^3}$$

Simplify x^3 and integrate

$$\frac{1}{4}\int \mathrm{e}^u \, du$$

$$\frac{1}{4}\mathrm{e}^u + c$$

$$\frac{1}{4}\mathrm{e}^{x^4+2} + c$$

Example 5.1.11

$$\int \frac{\log(2x)}{x} \, dx$$

$$\int \log(2x)\frac{1}{x} \, dx$$

Substitute $\log(2x) = u$.

$$\frac{du}{dx} = 2 \cdot \frac{1}{2x} = \frac{1}{x}$$

$$du = \frac{1}{x} \, dx$$

$$dx = x \, du$$

$$\int u \cdot \frac{1}{x} x \, du$$

$$\int u \, du$$

$$\frac{u^2}{2} + c$$

$$\frac{\log^2(2x)}{2} + c$$

Example 5.1.12

$$\int \frac{x}{x+1}\, dx$$

Substitute $x + 1 = u$.

$$\frac{du}{dx} = 1$$

$$du = dx$$

$$\int \frac{x}{u}\, du$$

Here, we have an issue because we have two variables under the integral sign. Let's get rid of x from $x + 1 = u$ by solving for x: $x = u - 1$. Substitute this in the integral.

$$\int \frac{u-1}{u}\, du$$

Rewrite the integral as

$$\int \frac{u}{u} - \frac{1}{u}\, du$$

$$\int du - \int \frac{1}{u}\, du$$

$$u + c - \log(|u|) + c$$

$$u - \log(|u|) + c$$

$$x + 1 - \log(|x+1|) + c$$

Join the constants

$$x - \log(|x+1|) + c$$

5.1.1.3 Integration by Parts

The integration by parts method is based on the following formula:

$$\int u\, dv = uv - \int v\, du \tag{5.15}$$

The left hand side of the formula represents the integral we want to integrate. It represents a multiplication between a function u and a derivative of a function dv. Therefore, to apply an integration by parts we need to identify u and dv in the integral.

Example 5.1.13

$$\int \log(x)\, dx$$

The general strategy is choose dv as to be the easiest to integrate and, consequently, assign u to the remaining element because differentiation is much easier than integration.

Rewrite $\int \log(x)\, dx$ as follows to explicitly highlight the multiplication:

$$\int \log(x) \cdot 1\, dx$$

In this case, $\log(x)$ is easy to differentiate while more complicated to integrate. Therefore, is our candidate to be u. On the other hand, dx is extremely easy to integrate. Therefore, it is our candidate to be dv.

Now that we have identified u and dv in the left hand side, we need to compute du and v that are elements of the right hand side.

Let's start from du. We have $u = \log(x)$. Differentiate u with respect to x.

$$u = \log(x)$$

$$\frac{du}{dx} = \frac{1}{x}$$

$$du = \frac{1}{x}dx$$

Therefore, $u = \log(x)$ and $du = \frac{1}{x}dx$.

Next, let's find v. We have $dv = dx$. Integrate it.

$$dv = dx$$

$$v = \int dx = x$$

Therefore, $dv = dx$ and $v = x$. Note that we will add the constant of integration at the very end.

Substitute $u = \log(x)$, $du = \frac{1}{x}dx$, $dv = dx$ and $v = x$ in the right hand side of formula (5.15). Therefore,

$$\log(x)x - \int x \cdot \frac{1}{x}dx$$

Rearrange the first term and integrate the second term to obtain

$$x\log(x) - \int dx$$

$$x\log(x) - x + c$$

Compare with the integration of the logarithmic function (5.9).

Example 5.1.14

$$\int xe^x\, dx$$

In this case, we choose e^x to be dv because it is very easy to integrate. Consequently, x is u.

Let's start from du. We have $u = x$. Differentiate u with respect to x.

$$u = x$$

$$\frac{du}{dx} = 1$$

$$du = dx$$

Therefore, $u = x$ and $du = dx$.

Next, let's find v. We have $dv = e^x dx$. Integrate it.

$$dv = \int e^x \, dx$$

$$v = \int e^x \, dx = e^x$$

Therefore, $dv = e^x$ and $v = e^x$. Note that we will add the constant of integration at the very end.

Substitute $u = x$, $du = dx$, $dv = e^x \, dx$ and $v = e^x$ in the right hand side of formula (5.15). Therefore,

$$xe^x - \int e^x \, dx$$

$$xe^x - e^x + c$$

$$e^x (x - 1) + c$$

These are quite standard examples for integration by parts. This process can be very complicated. Therefore, it is key to pick up appropriate u and dv. For this last example, pick up $u = e^x$ and $dv = x$ and follow the usual steps. How is the integration process?

5.1.1.4 Partial Fractions

Partial fraction is another method to solve integration when we deal with rational fractions where the numerator and the denominator are polynomials. We can apply this method if the degree of the numerator is smaller than the degree of the denominator.[1] The general strategy is to break, whenever it is possible, the fraction in simpler fractions.

[1] If the degree of the numerator is greater or equal to the degree of the denominator we define the fraction as improper. In this case, that will be not treated here, we need to perform long division first.

Example 5.1.15

$$\int \frac{5}{x^2 + x}\, dx$$

The denominator can be written as $x(x + 1)$.

$$\int \frac{5}{x(x + 1)}\, dx$$

From here we apply the partial fraction method. We decompose the fraction as follows:

$$\frac{A}{x} + \frac{B}{x + 1}$$

where A and B are constants we need to find. We proceed as follows:

$$\frac{5}{x(x + 1)} = \frac{A}{x} + \frac{B}{x + 1}$$

Let's get rid of the fraction on the left hand side:

$$5 = \left(\frac{A}{x} + \frac{B}{x + 1}\right) \cdot x(x + 1)$$

Simplify to obtain

$$5 = A(x + 1) + Bx$$

Now let's choose values for x to find A and B. Let's start with $x = 0$.

$$5 = A(0 + 1) + B \cdot 0$$

$$A = 5$$

For $x = -1$

$$5 = A(-1 + 1) + B \cdot (-1)$$

$$B = -5$$

Therefore, the integral becomes

$$\int \frac{5}{x} - \frac{5}{x+1}\,dx$$

$$\int \frac{5}{x}\,dx - \int \frac{5}{x+1}\,dx$$

$$5\int \frac{1}{x}\,dx - 5\int \frac{1}{x+1}\,dx$$

$$5\log(|x|) - 5\log(|x+1|) + c$$

Finally, applying logarithmic rules we can arrange it as follows:

$$5\log\left(\frac{|x|}{|x+1|}\right) + c$$

Example 5.1.16

$$\int \frac{2x+7}{x^2-5x+5}\,dx$$

First, factor the denominator

$$\int \frac{2x+7}{(x-3)(x-2)}\,dx$$

From here we apply the partial fraction method. We decompose the fraction as follows:

$$\frac{A}{x-3} + \frac{B}{x-2}$$

where A and B are constant we need to find. We proceed as follows:

$$\frac{2x+7}{(x-3)(x-2)} = \frac{A}{x-3} + \frac{B}{x-2}$$

Let's get rid of the fraction on the left hand side:

$$2x+7 = \left(\frac{A}{x-3} + \frac{B}{x-2}\right)(x-3)(x-2)$$

Simplify to obtain

$$2x + 7 = A(x - 2) + B(x - 3)$$

For $x = 3$,

$$2 \cdot 3 + 7 = A(3 - 2) + B(3 - 3)$$

$$13 = A \cdot 1 + B \cdot 0$$

$$A = 13$$

For $x = 2$,

$$2 \cdot 2 + 7 = A(2 - 2) + B(2 - 3)$$

$$11 = A \cdot 0 + B \cdot (-1)$$

$$B = -11$$

Therefore, the integral becomes

$$\int \frac{13}{x-3} - \frac{11}{x-2}\, dx$$

$$\int \frac{13}{x-3}\, dx - \int \frac{11}{x-2}\, dx$$

$$13 \int \frac{1}{x-3}\, dx - 11 \int \frac{1}{x-2}\, dx$$

$$13 \log(|x - 3|) - 11 \log(|x - 2|) + c$$

Example 5.1.17

$$\int \frac{5x}{(x-1)^2}\, dx$$

In this case, care is needed because the denominator contains a repeated line factor, i.e. $(x-1)(x-1)$. The partial fractions are

$$\frac{A}{(x-1)}+\frac{B}{(x-1)^2}$$

$$\frac{5x}{(x-1)^2}=\frac{A}{(x-1)}+\frac{B}{(x-1)^2}$$

$$5x=\left(\frac{A}{(x-1)}+\frac{B}{(x-1)^2}\right)(x-1)^2$$

$$5x=A(x-1)+B$$

For $x=1$,

$$5\cdot 1=A(1-1)+B$$

$$B=5$$

For $B=5$ and $x=0$,

$$5\cdot 0=A(0-1)+5$$

$$A=5$$

$$\int\frac{5}{x-1}+\frac{5}{(x-1)^2}\,dx$$

$$5\int\frac{1}{x-1}\,dx+5\int\frac{1}{(x-1)^2}\,dx$$

The first term becomes

$$5\log(|x-1|)+c$$

For the second term, let's use substitution.

$$x-1=u$$

$$\frac{du}{dx}=1$$

$$du=dx$$

Table 5.1 Integration by partial fractions

Form of the rational function	Form of the partial function
$\frac{px+q}{(x-a)(x-b)}$, $a \neq b$	$\frac{A}{x-a} + \frac{B}{x-b}$
$\frac{px^2+qx+r}{(x-a)(x-b)(x-c)}$, $a \neq b \neq c$	$\frac{A}{x-a} + \frac{B}{x-b} + \frac{C}{x-c}$
$\frac{px+q}{(x-a)^2}$	$\frac{A}{x-a} + \frac{B}{(x-a)^2}$
$\frac{px+q}{(ax+b)^k}$, $k > 0$	$\frac{A_1}{ax+b} + \frac{A_2}{(ax+b)^2} + \cdots + \frac{A_k}{(ax+b)^k}$
$\frac{px^2+qx+r}{(x-a)^2(x-b)}$	$\frac{A}{x-a} + \frac{B}{(x-a)^2} + \frac{C}{x-b}$
$\frac{px^2+qx+r}{ax^2+bx+c}$	$\frac{Ax+B}{ax^2+bx+c}$
$\frac{px^2+qx+r}{(ax^2+bx+c)^k}$, $k > 0$	$\frac{A_1x+B_1}{ax^2+bx+c} + \frac{A_2x+B_2}{(ax^2+bx+c)^2} + \cdots + \frac{A_kx+B_k}{(ax^2+bx+c)^k}$
$\frac{px^2+qx+r}{(a-x)(x^2+bx+c)}$	$\frac{A}{x-a} + \frac{Bx+C}{x^2+bx+c}$

Note: where $x^2 + bx + c$ cannot be further factorised

$$5 \int \frac{1}{u^2}\, du$$

$$5 \int u^{-2} du$$

$$5 \cdot -\frac{1}{-2+1} u^{-2+1}$$

$$-\frac{5}{u}$$

$$-\frac{5}{x-1} + c$$

Putting all together

$$5 \log(|x-1|) - \frac{5}{x-1} + c$$

Table 5.1 sums up integration by partial fractions.

5.1.1.4.1 Logistic Growth

We repeat the same exercise we did for the exponential growth in Sect. 5.1.1.1.6 for the logistic growth.

$$\frac{dN}{dt} = rN\left(1 - \frac{N}{K}\right)$$

Separate the variables.

$$\frac{dN}{N\left(1-\frac{N}{K}\right)} = r\,dt$$

Integrate both sides.

$$\int \frac{dN}{N\left(1-\frac{N}{K}\right)} = \int r\,dt$$

Let's start with the right hand side because it is very easy.

$$\int r\,dt$$

$$r\int dt$$

$$rt + c$$

Now, let's work on the left hand side.

$$\int \frac{1}{N\left(1-\frac{N}{K}\right)}\,dN$$

Let's get rid of the fraction at the denominator by multiply numerator and denominator times K.

$$\int \frac{K}{N(K-N)}\,dN$$

Here, we have to use partial fractions.

$$\frac{A}{N} + \frac{B}{K-N}$$

$$\frac{K}{N(K-N)} = \frac{A}{N} + \frac{B}{K-N}$$

Let's get rid of the fraction on the left side:

$$K = \left(\frac{A}{N} + \frac{B}{K - N}\right) \cdot N(K - N)$$

Multiply out to obtain

$$K = A(K - N) + BN$$

Let's find values for A and B. First, suppose $N = 0$.

$$K = A(K - 0) + B \cdot 0$$

$$K = AK$$

$$A = 1$$

Now, suppose $N = K$.

$$K = A(K - K) + BK$$

$$K = BK$$

$$B = 1$$

Consequently,

$$\int \frac{1}{N} + \frac{1}{K - N}\, dN$$

$$\int \frac{1}{N} dN + \int \frac{1}{K - N}\, dN$$

The integration for the first term is $\log(|N|) + c$.

For the second term we use substitution: $u = K - N$. Therefore, $\frac{du}{dN} = -1$ and $du = -dN$. This leads to $\int -\frac{1}{u} du$ and $-\log(|u|)$ and finally to $-\log(|K - N|) + c$.

Putting all together, with one constant of integration on the right side, we obtain

$$\log(|N|) - \log(|K - N|) = rt + c$$

Multiply both sides by -1.

$$\log(|K - N|) - \log(|N|) = -rt - c$$

By the rules of the logarithms, we write as follows

$$\log\left(\left|\frac{K - N}{N}\right|\right) = -rt - c$$

Let's get rid of the logarithm by taking the exponential of both sides.

$$\mathrm{e}^{\log\left(\left|\frac{K-N}{N}\right|\right)} = \mathrm{e}^{-rt-c}$$

$$\left|\frac{K - N}{N}\right| = \mathrm{e}^{-c} \cdot \mathrm{e}^{-rt}$$

Next, let's get rid of the absolute value.

$$\frac{K - N}{N} = \pm\mathrm{e}^{-c} \cdot \mathrm{e}^{-rt}$$

Let's set $\pm\mathrm{e}^{-c} = A$.

$$\frac{K - N}{N} = A \cdot \mathrm{e}^{-rt}$$

A few algebraic steps:

$$\frac{K}{N} - \frac{N}{N} = A\mathrm{e}^{-rt}$$

$$\frac{K}{N} - 1 = A\mathrm{e}^{-rt}$$

$$\frac{K}{N} = 1 + A\mathrm{e}^{-rt}$$

Solve for N.

$$N = \frac{K}{1 + A\mathrm{e}^{-rt}} \tag{5.16}$$

Find the value of A at $t = 0$

$$N(t = 0) = \frac{K}{1 + A\mathrm{e}^{-r0}}$$

$$N_0 = \frac{K}{1 + A}$$

Solve for A.

$$N_0(1 + A) = K$$

$$N_0 + N_0 A = K$$

$$N_0 A = K - N_0$$

$$A = \frac{K - N_0}{N_0} \tag{5.17}$$

Finally, substitute (5.17) in (5.16)

$$N(t) = \frac{K}{1 + \left(\frac{K - N_0}{N_0}\right) e^{-rt}}$$

5.2 Definite Integrals

5.2.1 Area Under a Curve

In the next lines of code, we plot the area under a curve, $y = x^2$, and above the x axis, over the interval $1 \le x \le 4$. The interval is divided in n subintervals with width Δx. We generate four plots: in the first plot $\Delta x = 1$, in the second plot $\Delta x = 0.5$, in the third plot $\Delta x = 0.1$, and in the fourth plot we fill the area under the plot by assuming that $n \to \infty$, that is that Δx is infinitely small. Figure 5.1 shows that as n approaches infinity, the sum of the area of the rectangles under the curve approaches the area under the curve. Let's investigate the key points of the code to generate Fig. 5.1 before delving into the mathematical definition.

First, we create a data frame, `df`, with only the x values. For y values, we create a function, y, to generate a parabola, `function(x) x^2`.

```
> x <- seq(-10, 10, 0.1)
> df <- data.frame(x)
> y <- function(x) {x^2}
```

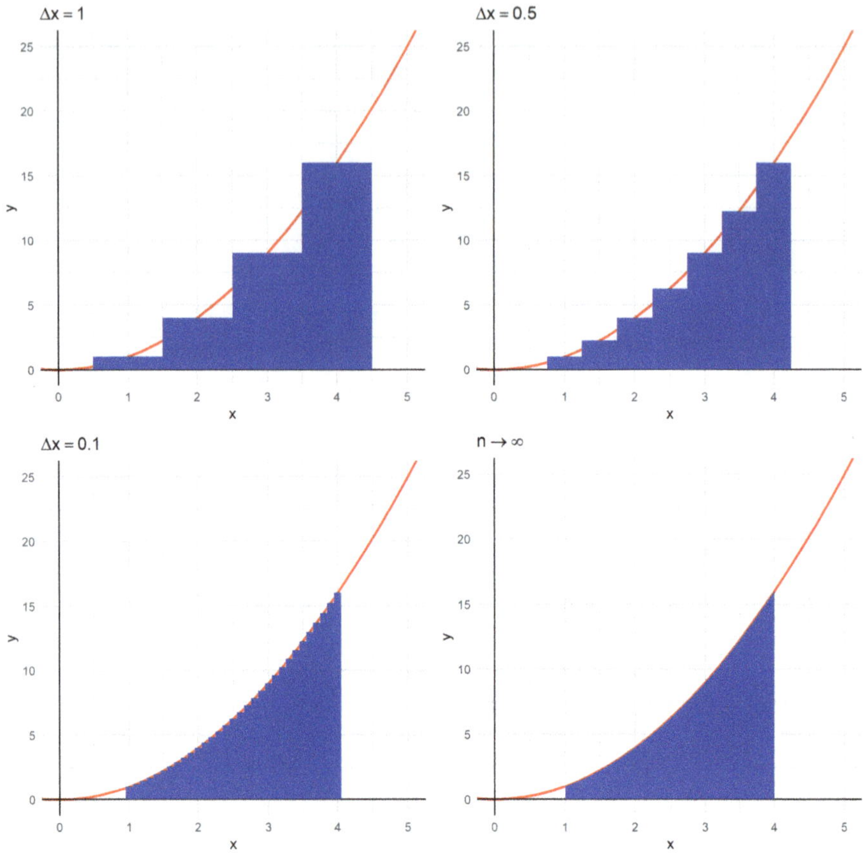

Fig. 5.1 Area under a curve $\left(\int_1^4 x^2\, dx\right)$

Second, we generate a base plot, `pbase`, that we will use as base layer for the following four plots. Note that the plot is generated by `stat_function()` where `fun =` maps to the `y` function we created in the previous step.

```
> pbase <- ggplot() +
+   stat_function(data = df, aes(x),
+                 fun = y,
+                 color = "red",
+                 size = 1) +
+   theme_minimal() +
+   geom_hline(yintercept = 0) +
+   geom_vline(xintercept = 0) +
+   coord_cartesian(xlim = c(0, 5),
+                   ylim = c(0, 25))
```

Next, we generate three different data frames, `df1`, `df2`, and `df3` where `x` is a sequence from 1 to 4, i.e. the length of the interval under the curve we are investigating, but with different delta, 1, 0.5, and 0.1, respectively. We use `geom_bar()` to make a bar chart. In `width =` we use the same number of delta for each plot to remove the space between the bins. We nest `expression()` in `ggtitle()` to write mathematical symbols in the title. Finally, note that the plot is built by adding it to the base plot, `pbase`.

```
> x1 <- seq(1, 4, 1)
> y1 <- x1^2
> df1 <- data.frame(x1, y1)
> p1 <- pbase +
+   geom_bar(data = df1,
+            aes(x = x1, y = y1),
+            fill ="blue",
+            stat = "identity",
+            width = 1) +
+   ggtitle(expression(Delta*x == 1))
> x2 <- seq(1, 4, 0.5)
> y2 <- x2^2
> df2 <- data.frame(x2, y2)
> p2 <- pbase +
+   geom_bar(data = df2,
+            aes(x = x2, y = y2),
+            fill ="blue",
+            stat = "identity",
+            width = 0.5) +
+   ggtitle(expression(Delta*x == 0.5))
> x3 <- seq(1, 4, 0.1)
> y3 <- x3^2
> df3 <- data.frame(x3, y3)
> p3 <- pbase +
+   geom_bar(data = df3,
+            aes(x = x3, y = y3),
+            fill ="blue",
+            stat = "identity",
+            width = 0.1) +
+   ggtitle(expression(Delta*x == 0.1))
```

Finally, we generate the graph under the area by using `stat_function()` as before. However, note that we limit the area, `geom = "area"`, to the interval `xlim = c(1, 4)`.

```
> parea <- pbase +
+   stat_function(data = df, aes(x),
+                 fun = y,
```

```
+                    xlim = c(1, 4),
+                    geom = "area",
+                    fill = "blue") +
+   ggtitle(expression(n %->% infinity))
```

In the last step we combine all the four plots together with `ggarrange()`.

```
> ggarrange(p1, p2,
+           p3, parea,
+           ncol = 2, nrow = 2)
```

From Fig. 5.1, it seems that the area under the graph can be approximated by summing the area of the rectangles under the curve. The area of a rectangle is given by multiplying the base, b, times the height, h.

$$area = b \times h$$

In our case, the base of a single rectangle is equal to the width of delta, Δx, while the height is equal to the function, $F(\Delta x)$. Therefore, the area under the curve is approximated by the sum of all the rectangles.

$$area = \sum_{i=1}^{n} \Delta x \cdot F(x_i)$$

```
> delta_x1 <- 1
> A1 <- sum(delta_x1*df1$y1)
> A1
[1] 30
> delta_x2 <- 0.5
> A2 <- sum(delta_x2*df2$y2)
> A2
[1] 25.375
> delta_x3 <- 0.1
> A3 <- sum(delta_x3*df3$y3)
> A3
[1] 21.855
```

Therefore, as n approaches infinity, Δx gets smaller and smaller, and consequently, the sum of the area of all the rectangles under the curve approximates the area under the curve.

$$area = \lim_{n \to \infty} \sum_{i=1}^{n} \Delta x \cdot F(x_i) \tag{5.18}$$

As for the derivatives, we do not need to apply the general formula to find the area. We will find the area under the curve by using the definite integral, that is defined as

$$\int_a^b F(x)\,dx = \lim_{n\to\infty}\sum_{i=1}^{n} \Delta x \cdot F(x_i) \tag{5.19}$$

where $a \le x \le b$ represent the range of the interval divided into n subintervals each of width $\Delta x = \frac{b-a}{n}$ and $x_i = a + i \cdot \Delta x$ with, naturally, $x_n = a + n \cdot \Delta x = b$.

Let's see practically how we calculate the area under the curve.

For the function $y = x^2,\ 1 \le x \le 4$, we integrate as follows

$$\int_1^4 x^2\,dx$$

We know that $\int x^2\,dx = \frac{x^3}{3} + c$. This is the indefinite integral. Since the definite integral is calculated over an interval and its result is a real number, the area under the curve, we do not need to add the constant of integration. The relation between the concept of the indefinite integration and definite integration is established by the fundamental theorem of calculus.

We have to evaluate the definite integration at $x = 1$ and $x = 4$.

$$\left.\frac{x^3}{3}\right|_{x=1}^{x=4}$$

We first plug in it the upper interval, $x = 4$, and then the lower interval, $x = 1$.

$$\frac{4^3}{3} = \frac{64}{3} \tag{5.20}$$

$$\frac{1^3}{3} = \frac{1}{3} \tag{5.21}$$

Finally, we subtract (5.21) from (5.20).

$$\frac{64}{3} - \frac{1}{3} = \frac{63}{3} = 21$$

Therefore, the area under the function $y = x^2$, with $1 \le x \le 4$, is equal to 21. We see that our approximation was getting closer (`A3 = 21.855`) as Δx was getting smaller and smaller.

An area of study where you will encounter the integrals as tool to find the area under the curve is statistical inference (for example, the area under the curve of the probability density function).

5.2.2 Area Between Two Lines

If a curve $y = G(x)$ is above a curve $y = F(x)$ for all the x in the interval $a \leq x \leq b$, then the total area between these curve in the interval $a \leq x \leq b$ is found by evaluating

$$\int_a^b G(x)\, dx - \int_a^b F(x)\, dx = \int_a^b (G(x) - F(x))\, dx \tag{5.22}$$

Let's see two examples.

In the first example, we show how to compute the area between two lines, $y_{up} = e^x$ and $y_{low} = x^2$ in the interval $1 \leq x \leq 3$ (Fig. 5.2 shows the areas under the two functions while Fig. 5.3 highlights the area between the two functions that we want to compute).[2]

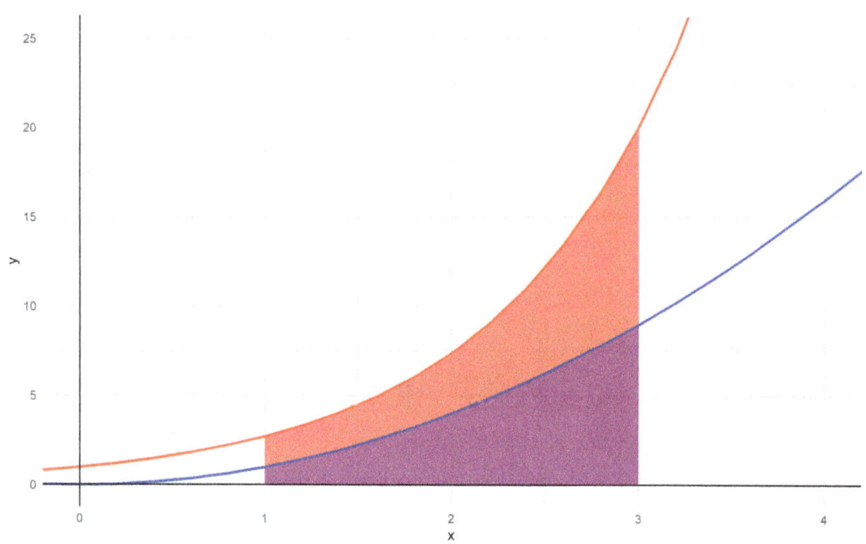

Fig. 5.2 Area under $\int_1^3 e^x\, dx$ and $\int_1^3 x^2\, dx$

[2] The code used to generate Figs. 5.2, 5.3, 5.4, 5.5, 5.6, 5.7, and 5.8 is available in Appendix E.

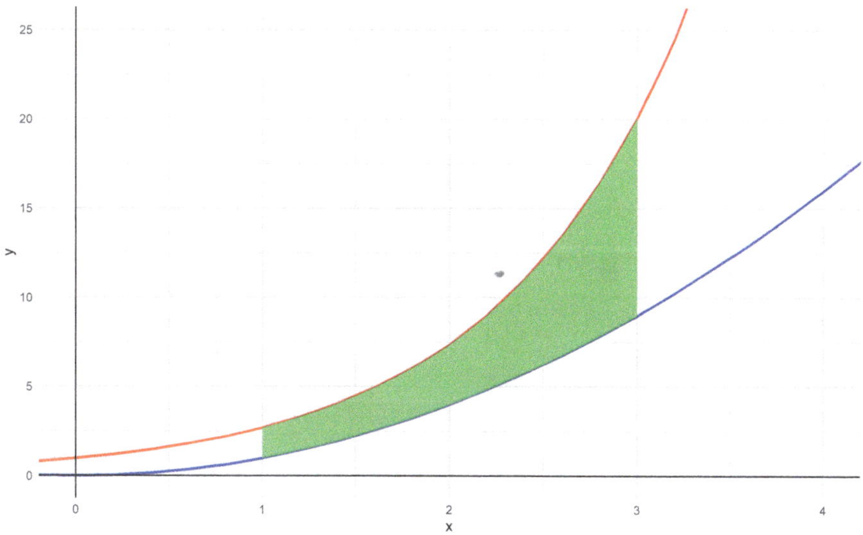

Fig. 5.3 Area between $\int_1^3 (e^x - x^2)\, dx$

The area between the two functions is calculated as follows. First, we integrate the upper function, $y = e^x$, less the lower function, $y = x^2$ between 1 and 3.

$$\int_1^3 (e^x - x^2)\, dx$$

$$\int e^x\, dx - \int x^2\, dx$$

$$e^x - \frac{1}{3}x^3$$

Then, we evaluate it at $x = 1$ and $x = 3$.

$$\left(e^x - \frac{1}{3}x^3\right)\Big|_{x=1}^{x=3}$$

$$e^3 - \frac{1}{3} \cdot (3)^3 = 11.09$$

$$e^1 - \frac{1}{3} \cdot (1)^3 = 2.38$$

$$11.09 - 2.38 = 8.71$$

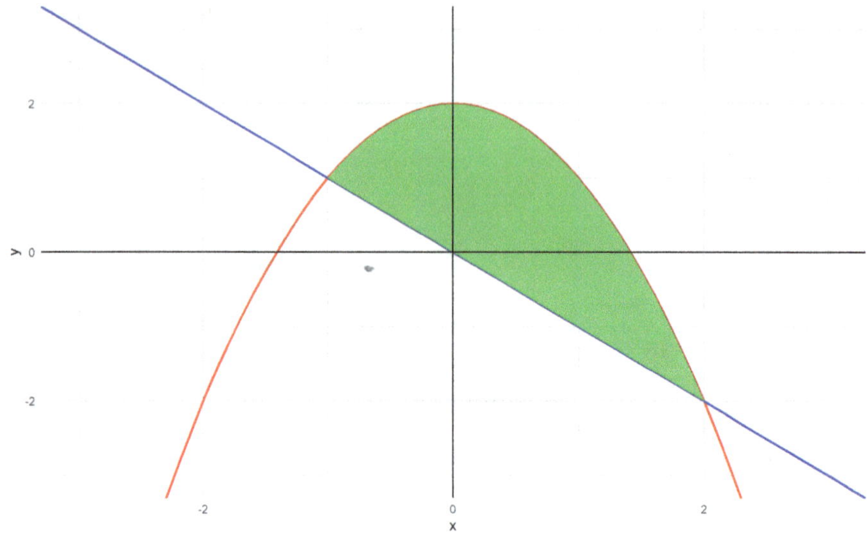

Fig. 5.4 Area between $\int_{-1}^{2}(-x^2+2+x)\,dx$

The area between $y = e^x$ and $y = x^2$ evaluated between 1 and 3 is 8.71.

In the next example, we show how to compute the area between $y_{up} = -x^2 + 2$ and $y_{low} = -x$ (Fig. 5.4).

The area between the two functions is calculated as follows. First, we integrate the upper function, $y = -x^2 + 2$, less the lower function, $y = -x$.

$$\int_{-1}^{2}(-x^2+2+x)\,dx$$

$$\int -x^2\,dx + \int 2\,dx + \int x\,dx$$

$$-\frac{1}{3}x^3 + 2x + \frac{1}{2}x^2$$

Then, we evaluate it at $x = -1$ and $x = 2$ by plugging first the upper .

$$\left(-\frac{1}{3}x^3 + 2x + \frac{1}{2}x^2\right)\Bigg|_{x=-1}^{x=2}$$

$$-\frac{1}{3}(2)^3 + 2\cdot(2) + \frac{1}{2}(2)^2 = \frac{10}{3}$$

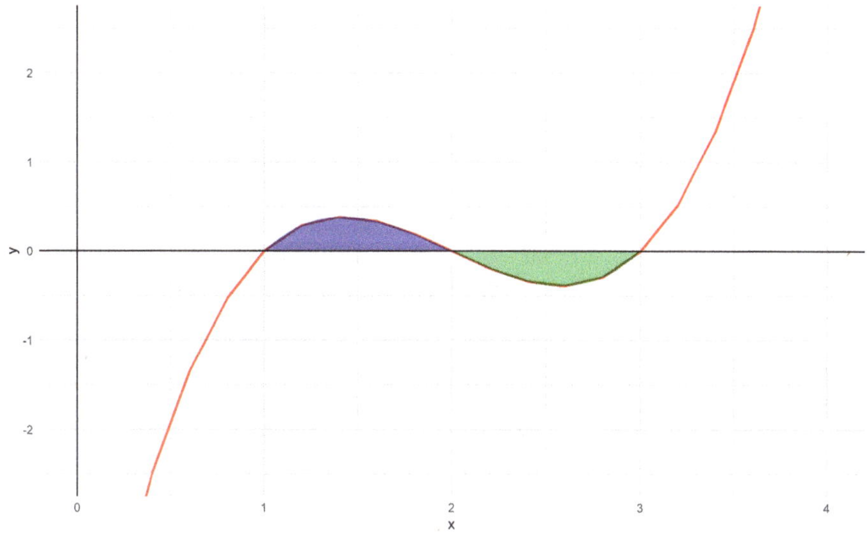

Fig. 5.5 Area under $\int_1^3 x^3 - 6x^2 + 11x - 6\,dx$

$$-\frac{1}{3}(-1)^3 + 2\cdot(-1) + \frac{1}{2}(-1)^2 = -\frac{7}{6}$$

$$\frac{10}{3} - \left(-\frac{7}{6}\right) = \frac{9}{2}$$

The area between $y = -x^2 + 2$ and $y = -x$ evaluated between -1 and 2 is 4.5.

Let's conclude this section on the definite integral with the following example. We want to compute the area below the function $y = x^3 - 6x^2 + 11x - 6$ in the interval $1 \le x \le 3$ (Fig. 5.5).

From Fig. 5.5, we see that the function is positive (blue area) in the interval $1 \le x \le 2$ and negative (green area) in the interval $2 \le x \le 3$.

$$\int_1^3 x^3 - 6x^2 + 11x - 6\,dx$$

$$\frac{x^4}{4} - 2x^3 + \frac{11x^2}{2} - 6x$$

Let's first evaluate the function over the interval $1 \leq x \leq 3$.

$$\left(\frac{x^4}{4} - 2x^3 + \frac{11x^2}{2} - 6x\right)\Bigg|_{x=1}^{x=3}$$

$$\frac{x^4}{4}\Bigg|_{x=1}^{x=3} = \frac{3^4}{4} - \frac{1^4}{4} = 20$$

$$2x^3\Big|_{x=1}^{x=3} = 54 - 2 = 52$$

$$\frac{11x^2}{2}\Bigg|_{x=1}^{x=3} = \frac{99}{2} - \frac{11}{2} = 44$$

$$6x\Big|_{x=1}^{x=3} = 18 - 6 = 12$$

Therefore, the area is

$$20 - 52 + 44 - 12 = 0$$

Let's investigate the function in the interval $1 \leq x \leq 2$ and $2 \leq x \leq 3$.

$$\left(\frac{x^4}{4} - 2x^3 + \frac{11x^2}{2} - 6x\right)\Bigg|_{x=1}^{x=2}$$

$$\frac{x^4}{4}\Bigg|_{x=1}^{x=2} = \frac{2^4}{4} - \frac{1^4}{4} = \frac{15}{4}$$

$$2x^3\Big|_{x=1}^{x=2} = 16 - 2 = 14$$

$$\frac{11x^2}{2}\Bigg|_{x=1}^{x=2} = 22 - \frac{11}{2} = \frac{33}{2}$$

$$6x\Big|_{x=1}^{x=2} = 12 - 6 = 6$$

Therefore, the area in the interval $1 \leq x \leq 2$ is

$$\frac{15}{4} - 14 + \frac{33}{2} - 6 = \frac{1}{4}$$

In the interval $2 \le x \le 3$

$$\left(\frac{x^4}{4} - 2x^3 + \frac{11x^2}{2} - 6x\right)\Bigg|_{x=2}^{x=3}$$

$$\frac{x^4}{4}\Bigg|_{x=2}^{x=3} = \frac{3^4}{4} - \frac{2^4}{4} = \frac{65}{4}$$

$$2x^3\Bigg|_{x=2}^{x=3} = 54 - 16 = 38$$

$$\frac{11x^2}{2}\Bigg|_{x=2}^{x=3} = \frac{99}{2} - \frac{44}{2} = \frac{55}{2}$$

$$6x\Bigg|_{x=2}^{x=3} = 18 - 12 = 6$$

Therefore, the area in the interval $2 \le x \le 3$ is

$$\frac{65}{4} - 38 + \frac{55}{2} - 6 = -\frac{1}{4}$$

As expected, these results are consistent with the area we found over all the interval.

$$\frac{1}{4} + \left(-\frac{1}{4}\right) = 0$$

If a function is negative and positive along an interval, the result that is returned by $\int_a^b F(x)\ dx$ is the *net area*. If we are interested in the *total area*, we need to compute the absolute values

$$\left|\frac{1}{4}\right| + \left|-\frac{1}{4}\right| = \frac{2}{4} = \frac{1}{2}$$

Note, however, that the negative area of a function does not affect the total area when we compute the area between two curves.

5.3 Fundamental Theorem of Calculus

Differential calculus and integral calculus are the two key processes in calculus. As we have seen through the examples in this chapter, there is an implicit reference to derivatives when we compute integrals. In simple words, from one hand, if we differentiate a function over an interval and then we integrate we obtain the original function back. On the other hand, if we first integrate a function and then differentiate it, we get the original function back. Furthermore, from a geometric point of view, differentiation corresponds to finding (slopes of) tangents to curves, while integration corresponds to finding areas under curves. The relation between derivatives (and therefore anti-derivatives) and definite integrals is established by the fundamental theorem of calculus.

Formally:

Let $y = F(x)$ be defined and continuous on the interval $[a, b]$, and let be $G(x)$ be any anti-derivative of $F(x)$, then

$$\int_a^b F(x)\,dx = G(b) - G(a) \tag{5.23}$$

We leave the proof of the fundamental theorem of calculus to more advanced textbooks.

5.4 Improper Integrals and Convergence

In Sect. 5.2, we considered integrals of bounded functions defined on a closed and bounded intervals. What about if the process of integration is applied to functions defined on a semi-infinite interval of the form $[a, \infty)$, where $a \in \mathbb{R}$ or a doubly infinite interval $(-\infty, \infty)$? And what about if the interval is bounded but the function is unbounded? These kinds of integrals are defined as *improper integrals.*

5.4.1 *Case 1: Convergence*

We say that an improper integral $\int_a^\infty F(x)\,dx$ is convergent if the limit

$$\lim_{M\to\infty} G(M) = \lim_{M\to\infty} \int_a^M F(x)\,dx \tag{5.24}$$

exists. If the limit exists it is unique and we write

$$\int_a^\infty F(x)\,dx = L \tag{5.25}$$

where L is a real number. We say that the improper integral $\int_a^\infty F(x)\,dx$ *converges* to L. Furthermore, a convergent integral is still convergent even though we change

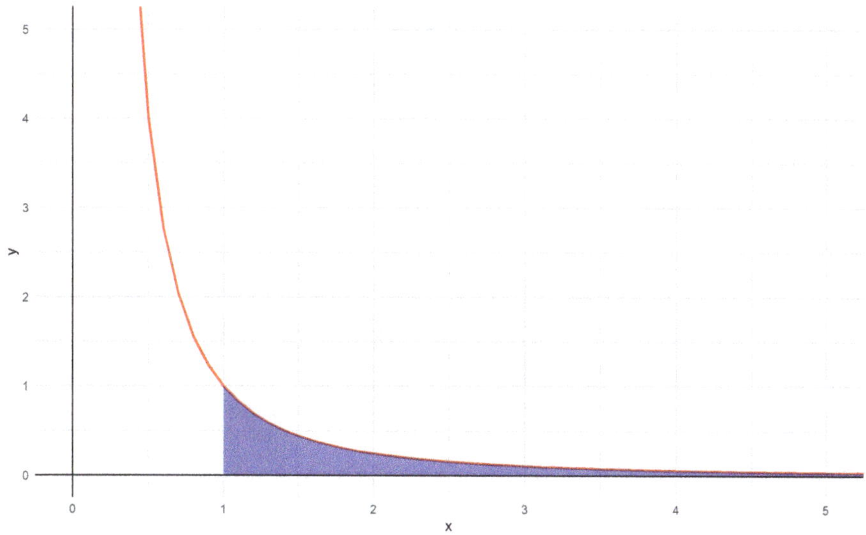

Fig. 5.6 Improper integral: convergence $\left(\int_1^\infty \frac{1}{x^2}\, dx\right)$

the initial point, e.g. to b, where $a \leq b$. In this case the following is true:

$$\int_a^\infty F(x)\, dx = \int_a^b F(x)\, dx + \int_b^\infty F(x)\, dx$$

Let's examine the following improper integral (Fig. 5.6):

$$\int_1^\infty \frac{1}{x^2}\, dx$$

To solve it, let's set an arbitrary upper limit, M.

$$\lim_{M\to\infty} \int_1^M \frac{1}{x^2}\, dx$$

$$\lim_{M\to\infty} \int_1^M x^{-2}\, dx$$

$$\frac{1}{-2+1} x^{-2+1} = -\frac{1}{x}\Big|_{x=1}^{x=M} = -\frac{1}{M} - \left(-\frac{1}{1}\right)$$

$$1 - \frac{1}{M} = 1$$

therefore, the improper integral converges to 1 since $\frac{1}{\infty} = 0$. This means that the area under the curve from 1 to ∞ is 1.

Let's check it. As $M = (2, 4, 6, 8, 10, 50, 100)$ gets larger and larger the area, A, approaches 1.

```
> M <- c(2, 4, 6, 8, 10, 50, 100)
> A <- 1 - 1/M
> round(A, 3)
[1] 0.500 0.750 0.833 0.875 0.900 0.980 0.990
```

Let's change now the initial point to 5 and let's verify the following:

$$\int_1^\infty \frac{1}{x^2}\,dx = \int_1^5 \frac{1}{x^2}\,dx + \int_5^\infty \frac{1}{x^2}\,dx$$

$$\int_1^5 x^{-2}\,dx = -\frac{1}{x}\Big|_{x=1}^{x=5} = -\frac{1}{5} - \left(-\frac{1}{1}\right) = 1 - \frac{1}{5} = \frac{4}{5}$$

$$\lim_{M\to\infty} \int_5^M x^{-2}\,dx = -\frac{1}{x}\Big|_{x=5}^{x=M} = -\frac{1}{M} - \left(-\frac{1}{5}\right)$$

$$\frac{1}{5} - \frac{1}{M} = \frac{1}{5}$$

Therefore,

$$\frac{4}{5} + \frac{1}{5} = 1$$

```
> int1 <- 4/5
> int2 <- 1/5 - 1/M
> A <- int1 + int2
> round(A, 3)
[1] 0.500 0.750 0.833 0.875 0.900 0.980 0.990
```

Let's examine the following improper integral:

$$\int_1^4 \frac{1}{\sqrt{x-1}}\,dx$$

First, let's note that in this example the interval is bounded but the function is unbounded (Fig. 5.7).

From Fig. 5.7, we observe that we have a vertical asymptote at $x = 1$.

The procedure is similar to the one we have already seen. However, in this case we set an arbitrary limit, M, as the function approaches 1.

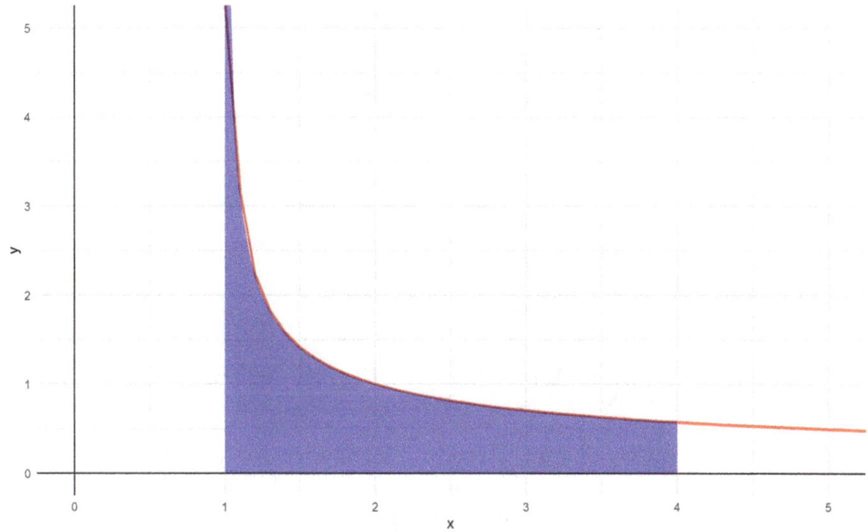

Fig. 5.7 Improper integral: convergence $\left(\int_1^4 \frac{1}{\sqrt{x-1}}\,dx\right)$

$$\lim_{M\to 1}\int_M^4 \frac{1}{\sqrt{x-1}}\,dx$$

Let's substitute $x-1=u$. Therefore, $\frac{du}{dx}=1$ and $dx=du$.

$$\lim_{M\to 1}\int_M^4 \frac{1}{\sqrt{u}}\,du = \lim_{M\to 1}\int_M^4 u^{-\frac{1}{2}}\,du = \frac{1}{-\frac{1}{2}+1}u^{-\frac{1}{2}+1} = 2u^{\frac{1}{2}}$$

Substitute back $u=x-1$

$$2(x-1)^{\frac{1}{2}}\Big|_{x=M}^{x=4} = 2(4-1)^{\frac{1}{2}} - \left[2(1-1)^{\frac{1}{2}}\right] = 2\cdot 3^{\frac{1}{2}}$$

Therefore, the area under the curve from 1 to 4 is $2\cdot 3^{\frac{1}{2}}$.
Let's verify it.

```
> M <- c(1.5, 1.2, 1.1, 1.01, 1.001, 1.0001)
> A <- 2*(4 - 1)^(1/2) - (2*(M - 1)^(1/2))
> round(A, 3)
[1] 2.050 2.570 2.832 3.264 3.401 3.444
```

5.4.2 Case 2: Divergence

We say that an improper integral $\int_a^\infty F(x)\,dx$ is divergent if the limit

$$\lim_{M\to\infty} G(M) = \lim_{M\to\infty} \int_a^M F(x)\,dx \to \infty \tag{5.26}$$

or

$$\lim_{M\to\infty} G(M) = \lim_{M\to\infty} \int_a^M F(x)\,dx \to -\infty \tag{5.27}$$

In these cases, we say that the improper integral *diverges* to infinity (5.26) or to minus infinity (5.27).

Let's examine the following improper integral (Fig. 5.8):

$$\int_1^\infty \frac{1}{x}\,dx$$

We can note that Fig. 5.8 is similar to Fig. 5.6. However, as $x \to \infty$ the function in Fig. 5.8 seems to take more time to gets smaller and smaller. Let's examine what this means.

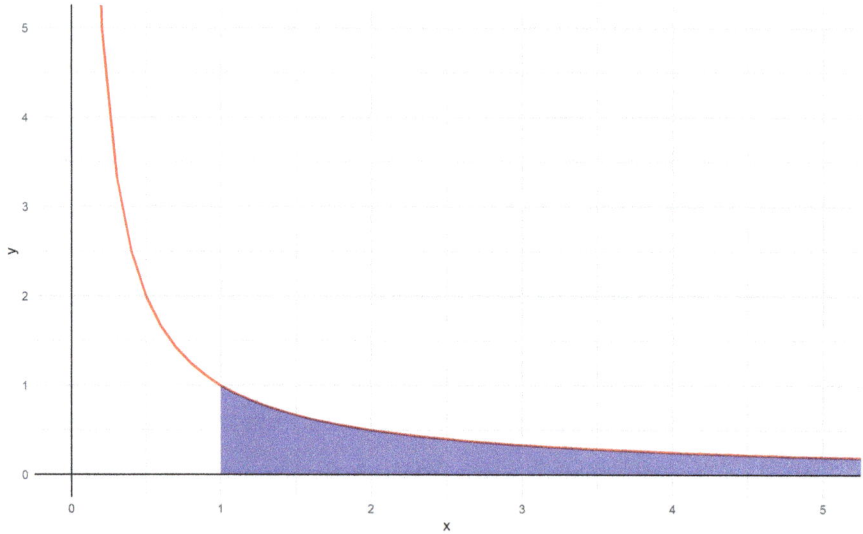

Fig. 5.8 Improper integral: divergence $\left(\int_1^\infty \frac{1}{x}\,dx\right)$

$$\lim_{M\to\infty}\int_1^M \frac{1}{x}\,dx$$

$$\log(x)\Big|_{x=1}^{x=M} = \log(M) - \log(1)$$

Since $\log(1) = 0$, we have $\log(M)$. As M gets larger $\log(M) \to \infty$ therefore this integral diverges to infinity.

```
> M <- c(100, 1000, 10000, 100000)
> A <- log(M) - log(1)
> round(A, 3)
[1]  4.605  6.908  9.210 11.513
```

5.5 Integration with R

We can compute indefinite integrals with the `antiD()` function from the `mosaicCalc` package. It requires an object of type formula to be integrated. It will attempt simple symbolic integration.[3]

For example:

```
> antiD(4*x^3 ~ x)
function (x, C = 0)
1 * x^4 + C
> antiD(x^(-2) ~ x)
function (x, C = 0)
-1 * x^-1 + C
> antiD(6*x^(1/2) ~ x)
function (x, C = 0)
4 * x^(3/2) + C
> antiD(4*(3*x - 5)^3 ~ x)
function (x, C = 0)
1/3 * (3 * x - 5)^4 + C
```

We use the base function `integrate()` to compute definite integrals.

Example 5.5.1 $\int_1^4 x^2\,dx$.

We first store a function object in `integrand`. This object is the first entry in the `integrate()` function. `lower =` and `upper =` are the limits of integration. They can be infinite, `Inf`.

[3] Another package that can be used for symbolic integration is `Ryacas`.

```
> integrand <- function(x) {x^2}
> integrate(integrand, lower = 1, upper = 4)
21 with absolute error < 2.3e-13
```

Example 5.5.2 $\int_1^3 (e^x - x^2)\,dx$:

```
> integrand <- function(x) {exp(x) - x^2}
> integrate(integrand, 1, 3)
8.700588 with absolute error < 9.7e-14
```

Example 5.5.3 $\left(\int_{-1}^{2} (-x^2 + 2 + x)\,dx\right)$:

```
> integrand <- function(x) {(-1*x^2 + 2) + x}
> int <- integrate(integrand, -1, 2)
> int
4.5 with absolute error < 5e-14
> int$value
[1] 4.5
```

Example 5.5.4 $\int_1^3 x^3 - 6x^2 + 11x - 6\,dx$:

```
> integrand <- function(x){x^3 - 6*x^2 + 11*x - 6}
> int <- integrate(integrand, 1, 3)
> int
-1.244068e-15 with absolute error < 5.5e-15
> round(int$value, 1)
[1] 0
> integrand1 <- function(x){x^3 - 6*x^2 + 11*x - 6}
> int1 <- integrate(integrand1, 1, 2)
> int1 <- abs(int1$value)
> integrand2 <- function(x){x^3 - 6*x^2 + 11*x - 6}
> int2 <- integrate(integrand2, 1, 2)
> int2 <- abs(int2$value)
> int1 + int2
[1] 0.5
```

Furthermore, it is possible to compute integrals using the `integral()` function from the `pracma` package. From the last example:

```
> int1 <- abs(integral(integrand1, 1, 2))
> int2 <- abs(integral(integrand2, 2, 3))
> int1 + int2
[1] 0.5
```

Finally, some examples of improper integrals.

```
> integrand <- function(x){1/x^2}
> int <- integrate(integrand, 1, Inf)
> int$value
```

```
[1] 1
> integrand <- function(x){1/sqrt(x - 1)}
> int <- integrate(integrand, 1, 4)
> int$value
[1] 3.464102
> integrand <- function(x) {1/x}
> int <- integrate(integrand, 1, Inf)
Error in integrate(integrand, 1, Inf) :
  maximum number of subdivisions reached
```

5.6 Applications in Economics

5.6.1 Marginal Cost and Cost Function

Let's use integration to find the total cost (TC) function of a firm with $MC = 0.027Q^2 - Q + 15$ and $FC = \$35$.

Since we know that the marginal cost is the derivative of the total cost function, we can integrate the marginal cost function to get the total cost function.

$$TC = \int 0.027Q^2 - Q + 15\, dQ$$

$$TC = \int 0.027Q^2\, dQ - \int Q\, dQ + \int 15\, dQ$$

$$TC = \frac{0.027}{2+1}Q^{2+1} - \frac{1}{1+1}Q^{1+1} + 15Q + c$$

$$TC = 0.009Q^3 - 0.5Q^2 + 15Q + c$$

In addition, since the fixed cost is \$35, then when $Q = 0$, $TC = 35$, so that $c = 35$. Therefore, the total cost function (in dollars) is

$$TC = 0.009Q^3 - 0.5Q^2 + 15Q + 35$$

This is the total cost function in Sect. 4.14.1.

Next let's find the total cost as Q goes from 10 to 20. Therefore, we need to integrate the marginal cost function from 10 to 20.

$$\Delta TC = \int_{10}^{20} 0.027Q^2 - Q + 15\, dQ$$

$$\Delta TC = 0.009Q^3 - 0.5Q^2 + 15Q\Big|_{10}^{20}$$

$$\Delta TC = (0.009 \cdot 20^3 - 0.009 \cdot 10^3) - (0.5 \cdot 20^2 - 0.5 \cdot 10^2) + (15 \cdot 20 - 15 \cdot 10) = 63$$

Let's use R:

```
> MC <- function(Q) {0.027*Q^2 - Q + 15}
> int <- integrate(MC, 10, 20)
> int$value
[1] 63
```

Note that in the data frame df (we built in Sect. 4.14.1) $TC(Q = 20) = 207$ and $TC(Q = 10) = 144$. That is, the difference is 63. Following the print of df from Sect. 4.14.1.

```
> df[11:21, ]
   output total_cost marginal_cost tangent10 tangent45
11     10    144.000         7.700     144.0  -346.000
12     11    151.479         7.267     151.7  -321.325
13     12    158.552         6.888     159.4  -296.650
14     13    165.273         6.563     167.1  -271.975
15     14    171.696         6.292     174.8  -247.300
16     15    177.875         6.075     182.5  -222.625
17     16    183.864         5.912     190.2  -197.950
18     17    189.717         5.803     197.9  -173.275
19     18    195.488         5.748     205.6  -148.600
20     19    201.231         5.747     213.3  -123.925
21     20    207.000         5.800     221.0   -99.250
```

5.6.2 Example: A Problem

The installation of a new equipment will save on the cost of the operation of a firm at the rate of

$$\frac{dS}{dt} = 10000t + 5000, \quad \text{(in dollars per years)}$$

where t is the number of years the firm will have the new equipment and S is the total savings after t years. The savings after the first 10 years after the installation of the new equipment is given by the following integration

$$\int_0^{10} 10000t + 5000 \, dt$$

```
> integrand <- function(t){10000*t + 5000}
> int <- integrate(integrand, 0, 10)
> int$value
[1] 550000
```

So in the first 10 years the firm will save $550,000. The new equipment costs $450,000. To find how long it takes for the savings from its installation to save enough money to pay for it, we set an integration where the upper bound is the *unknown x*

$$\int_0^x 10000t + 5000\, dt = 5000t^2 + 5000t \Big|_0^x = 5000x^2 + 5000x$$

We set the following quadratic equation and solve it. Note that we use the `quadratic_formula()` we built in Sect. 3.3.

$$5000x^2 + 5000x = 450{,}000$$

```
> quadratic_formula(5000, 5000, -450000)
           x1 x2
solutions -10  9
```

$$x_1 = -10, \; x_2 = 9$$

The solution is 9 years. We rule out the negative solution.

5.6.3 The Surplus of Consumer and Producer

The consumer surplus (CS) is given by

$$\int_0^{q_e} D(q)\, dq - p_e q_e \tag{5.28}$$

The producer surplus (PS) is given by

$$p_e q_e - \int_0^{q_e} S(q)\, dq \tag{5.29}$$

Let's assume that the demand and supply functions for a good are, respectively

$$p = D(q) = -2q + 21$$

$$p = S(q) = q + 3$$

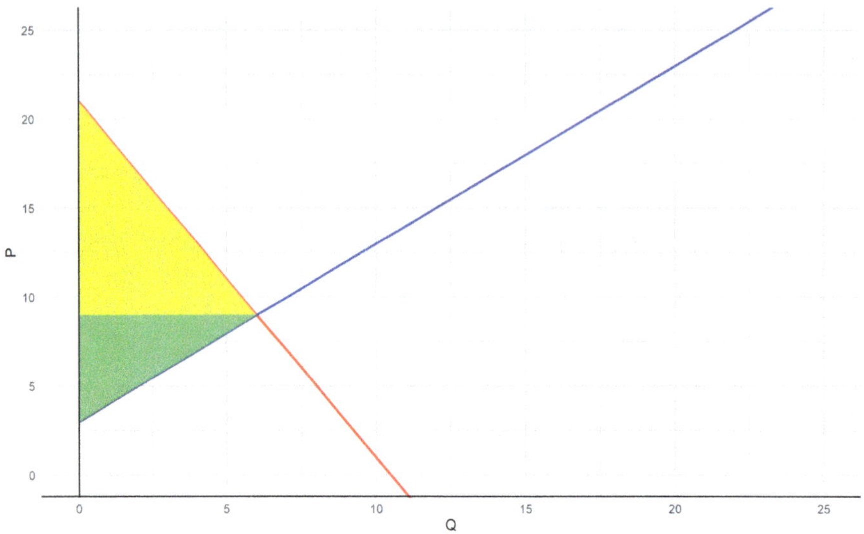

Fig. 5.9 The surplus of consumer and producer

First, let's plot them (Fig. 5.9).

```
> Q <- 0:25
> D <- -2*Q + 21
> S <- Q + 3
> df <- data.frame(Q, D, S)
> demand_fn <- function(Q) {-2*Q + 21}
> supply_fn <- function(Q) {Q + 3}
> Qe <- uniroot(function(Q)
+   {demand_fn(Q) - supply_fn(Q)},
+   c(0, 25))$root
> Qe
[1] 6
> Pe <- Qe + 3
> Pe
[1] 9
> df$Qe <- Qe
> df$Pe <- Pe
> ggplot(df, aes(Q, D)) +
+   geom_line(aes(Q, D),
+             color = "red",
+             size = 1) +
+   geom_line(aes(Q, S),
+             color = "blue",
+             size = 1) +
```

```
+    geom_ribbon(data = subset(df, 0 <= Q &
+                                  Q <= 6),
+                aes(ymin = Pe, ymax = D),
+                fill = "yellow",
+                alpha = 0.8) +
+    geom_ribbon(data = subset(df, 0 <= Q &
+                                  Q <= 6),
+                aes(ymin = S, ymax = Pe),
+                fill = "green",
+                alpha = 0.8) +
+    theme_minimal() +
+    ylab("P") + xlab("Q") +
+    geom_hline(yintercept = -1.2) +
+    geom_vline(xintercept = 0) +
+    coord_cartesian(ylim = c(0, 25))
```

The yellow area represents the consumer surplus while the green area represents the producer surplus.

Then, let's compute the equilibrium quantity:

$$D(q) = S(q)$$

$$-2q + 21 = q + 3$$

$$3q = 18$$

$$q_e = 6$$

The equilibrium price is consequently

$$p_e = 6 + 3 = 9$$

These results correspond to `Qe` and `Pe` that we computed with **R**.

Finally, we can compute the surplus of consumer and producer as, respectively, in (5.28) and (5.29):

$$CS = \int_0^6 -2q + 21 \, dq - (9 \cdot 6)$$

$$CS = -q^2 + 21q \Big|_0^6 - 54$$

$$CS = (-36 + 126) - 54 = 36$$

$$PS = (9 \cdot 6) - \int_0^6 q + 3\, dq$$

$$PS = 54 - \frac{q^2}{2} + 3q \Big|_0^6$$

$$PS = 54 - (18 + 18) = 18$$

```
> CS <- integrate(demand_fn, 0, Qe)$value - (Pe*Qe)
> CS
[1] 36
> PS <- (Pe*Qe) - integrate(supply_fn, 0, Qe)$value
> PS
[1] 18
```

5.7 Exercise

Write a function that computes the area under a curve based on (5.19). Replicate the previous results. For example,

```
> func <- function(x){x^2}
> area_under_curve(func, 1, 4)
[1] 21.00002
> func <- function(x){exp(x) - x^2}
> area_under_curve(func, 1, 3)
[1] 8.700598
> func <- function(x){-x^2 + 2 + x}
> area_under_curve(func, -1, 2)
[1] 4.5
```

Chapter 6
Multivariable Calculus

Until now our treatise has been mainly limited to functions of one variable. However, in real life it is more realistic to consider that an output may depend on more inputs than one. This leads to the discussion of functions of several variables. Indeed, we have already encountered them, for example, when we talked about quadratic forms in Chap. 2.

Before delving into them, we should remark a key point when we move from the analysis of functions of one variable to functions of several variables, that is, we cannot rely anymore on graphical analysis when we work with more than two variables. Until this point, it should be evident how graphical analysis is useful in studying a function. In fact, those plots provided us much of the information we were looking for, such as where the function is increasing or decreasing or the point of maximum or minimum. However, now we know that we can use calculus to study the behaviour of a function. Therefore, the focus of this chapter is on how to apply calculus to functions of several variables. Additionally, we will see how concepts from linear algebra (Chap. 2) apply to calculus analysis.

6.1 Functions of Several Variables

Let's recover our basic definition of a function as an instruction to process inputs to generate a unique output. In Chap. 3, we wrote

$$y = f(x)$$

to formally express a function of one variable x. Now we consider that y depends on more than one variable $x_1, x_2, \cdots, x_n$, that is

M. Porto, *Introduction to Mathematics for Economics with R*,
https://doi.org/10.1007/978-3-031-05202-6_6

$$y = f(x_1, x_2, \cdots, x_n) \tag{6.1}$$

where $(x_1, x_2, \cdots, x_n)$ is called an *n-tuple*, which is an ordered set of n elements. If $n = 1$, we refer to it as a *monad*, that is a set of a single element; if $n = 2$, we refer to it as a *pair*; if $n = 3$, we refer to it as a *triple*. A function of n variables is a function whose domain is some set of *n-tuples* and whose range is some set of real numbers.

In the rest of this chapter, we will mainly work with a function of two variables to keep things simple. For our purpose, except for graphical representation, there will be no difference if we work with 2 or n variables. In the following examples, we will use the notation $z = f(x, y)$ instead of $y = f(x_1, x_2)$ to be consistent with the graphical representation in three dimension where the axes are usually labelled as x, y, z. We need three dimensions to plot the graph of a function of two variables: for each value (x, y) in the domain, we evaluate f at (x, y) and mark the point (x, y, z), where $z = f(x, y)$, in $\mathbb{R}^3$.

We have already seen how to plot a function of two variables in Sect. 2.3.12 with the `plotFun()` function from the `mosaic` package. Load the `manipulate` package to manipulate rotation, elevation and distance of the plot. Let's plot the following functions: $z = x^2 + y^2$ (Fig. 6.1), $z = (x^2 + y^2)/(x^2 + y^2 + 1)$ (Fig. 6.2), and $z = x^4 + y^3$ (Fig. 6.3).

```
> fn <- function(x, y){
+   x^2 + y^2
+ }
> plotFun(fn(x, y) ~ x & y,
+         xlab = "x",
+         ylab = "y",
+         zlab = "f(x, y)",
+         x.lim = range(-10, 10),
+         y.lim = range(-10, 10),
+         surface = T)

> fn2 <- function(x, y){
+    (x^2 + y^2)/(x^2 + y^2 + 1)
+ }
> plotFun(fn2(x, y) ~ x & y,
+         xlab = "x",
+         ylab = "y",
+         zlab = "f(x, y)",
+         x.lim = range(-10, 10),
+         y.lim = range(-10, 10),
+         surface = T)

> fn3 <- function(x, y){
+   x^4 + y^3
```

Fig. 6.1 3D plot of $z = x^2 + y^2$

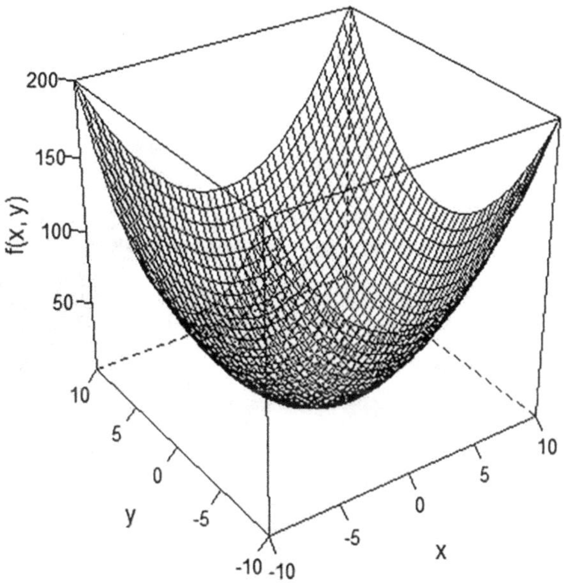

Fig. 6.2 3D plot of $z = (x^2 + y^2)/(x^2 + y^2 + 1)$

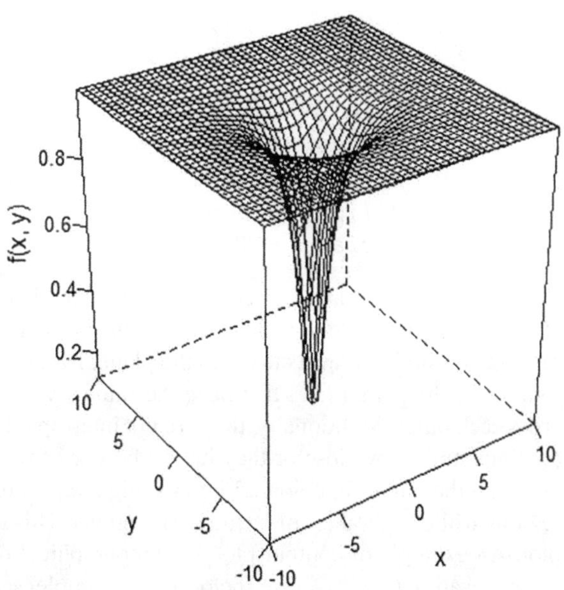

Fig. 6.3 3D plot of $z = x^4 + y^3$

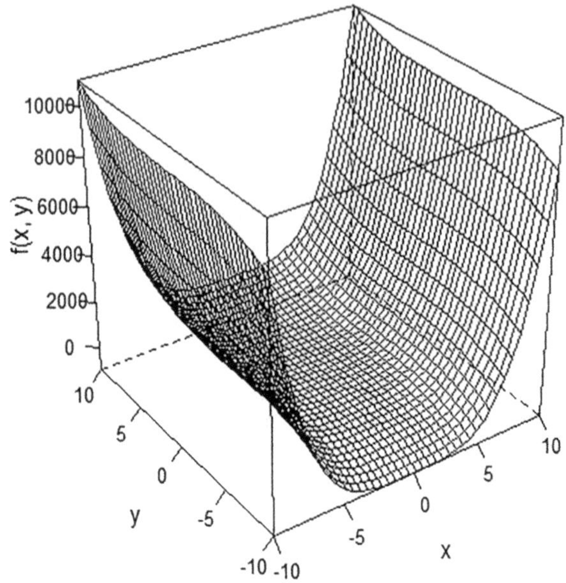


```
+ }
> plotFun(fn3(x, y) ~ x & y,
+           xlab = "x",
+           ylab = "y",
+           zlab = "f(x, y)",
+           x.lim = range(-10, 10),
+           y.lim = range(-10, 10),
+           surface = T)
```

Figures 6.1, 6.2, and 6.3 correspond to our idea of a three dimensional plot. However, it is possible to visualize these three dimensional plots in two dimensions through the study of level curves in the plane. Basically, we draw curves in xy plane joining all the pairs (x, y) that have the same z value. These lines do not touch or cross each other. Additionally, they are not interrupted in the middle of the plot: they continue until they close or they hit the border of the plot. The z value is used for labelling the curve. In coloured figures, high values of z are associated with bright regions while low values of z with dark regions. This kind of plots is called contour plot. An example of contour plot is a topographical map where the lines indicates same elevation (depth) above (below), for example, sea level.

Let's represent the corresponding contour plots of Figs. 6.1, 6.2 and 6.3. In **R**, we use the same function as before, `plotFun()`, with the default value `surface = FALSE`. By setting `filled = FALSE`, we remove the color (Figs. 6.4, 6.5 and 6.6).

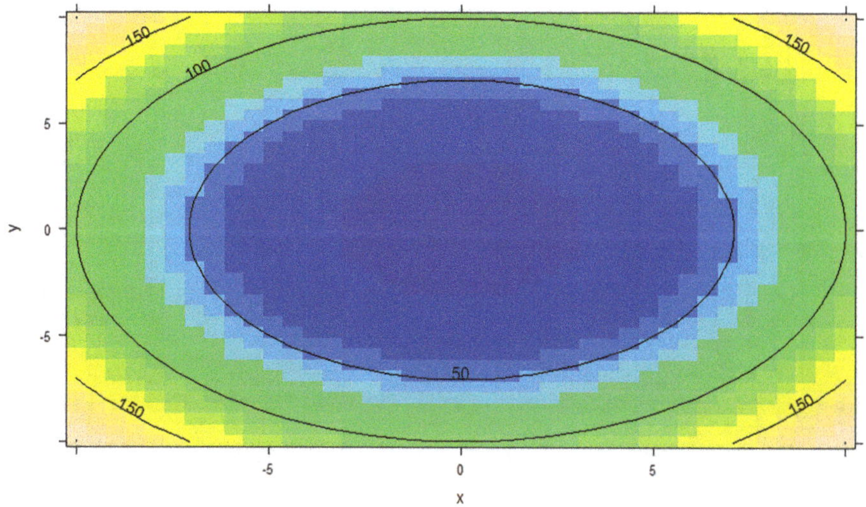

Fig. 6.4 Contour plot of $z = x^2 + y^2$

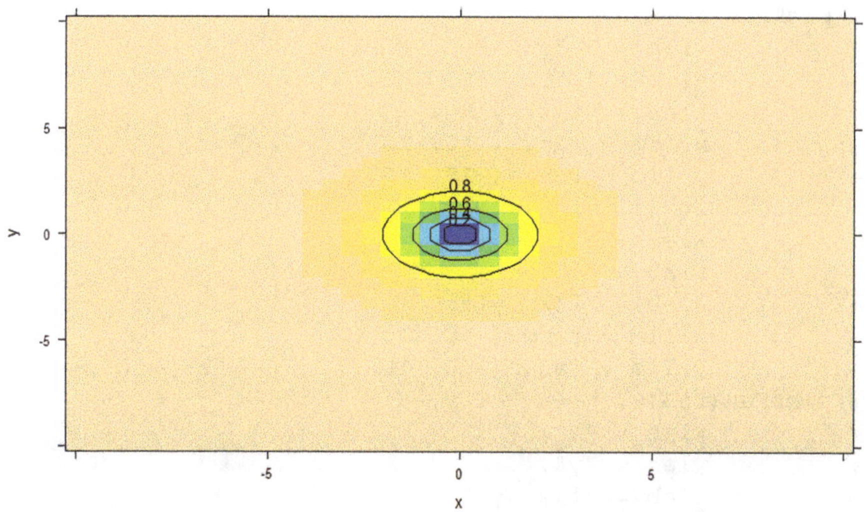

Fig. 6.5 Contour plot of $z = (x^2 + y^2)/(x^2 + y^2 + 1)$

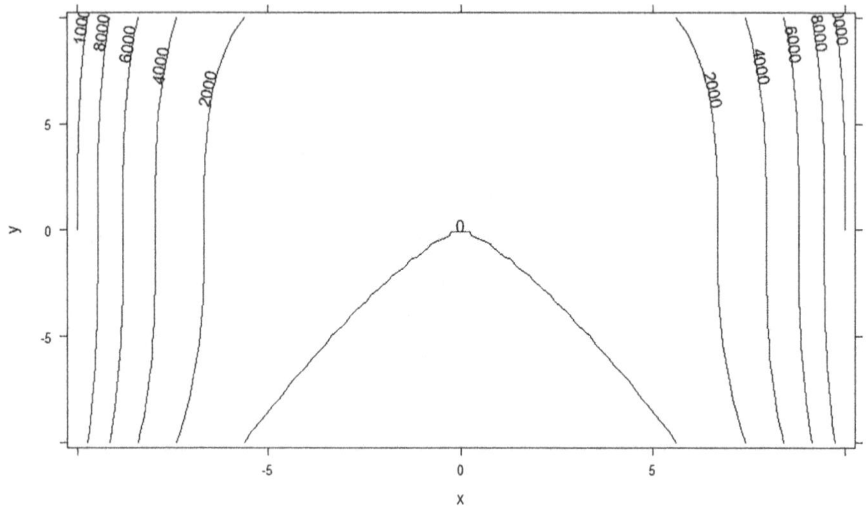

Fig. 6.6 Contour plot of $z = x^4 + y^3$

```
> plotFun(fn(x, y) ~ x & y,
+           xlab = "x",
+           ylab = "y",
+           zlab = "f(x, y)",
+           x.lim = range(-10, 10),
+           y.lim = range(-10, 10))
> plotFun(fn2(x, y) ~ x & y,
+           xlab = "x",
+           ylab = "y",
+           zlab = "f(x, y)",
+           x.lim = range(-10, 10),
+           y.lim = range(-10, 10))
> plotFun(fn3(x, y) ~ x & y,
+           xlab = "x",
+           ylab = "y",
+           zlab = "f(x, y)",
+           x.lim = range(-10, 10),
+           y.lim = range(-10, 10),
+           filled = F)
```

In the case of real-valued functions of two variables operations are defined as follows:

- Addition: $(f + g)(x, y) = f(x, y) + g(x, y)$
- Subtraction: $(f - g)(x, y) = f(x, y) - g(x, y)$
- Multiplication: $(fg)(x, y) = f(x, y) \cdot g(x, y)$

- Constant multiplication: $f(kx, ky) = kf(x, y), k \in \mathbb{R}$
- Division: $(f/g)(x, y) = f(x, y)/g(x, y)$ provided $g(x, y) \neq 0$
- Composition: $(g \circ f)(x, y) = g(f(x, y))$

6.1.1 Applications in Economics

The main functions used in Economics include:

- $y = ax_1 + bx_2$ (linear)
- $y = kx_1^{\alpha}x_2^{\beta}$ (Cobb-Douglas)
- $y = k\left[\delta x_1^{-\rho} + (1-\delta)x_2^{-\rho}\right]^{-\frac{1}{\rho}}$ (constant elasticity of substitution)

6.1.1.1 Complementary Goods and Substitute Goods

Two goods are *complementary* if an increase in the price of a good leads to a decrease in the demand for *both* goods. Two goods are *substitute* if an increase in the price of a good leads to an increase in the demand of the other good.

Let's determine if two goods are complementary or substitute given the following two demand functions

$$Q_1 = 150 - 5p_1 - p_2$$

$$Q_2 = 100 - p_1 - 2p_2$$

If $p_1 = 10$ and $p_2 = 5$, $Q_1 = 150-5(10)-5 = 95$ and $Q_2 = 100-10-2(5) = 80$.

Now let's assume that the price of good 1 increases, $p_1 = 15$. What is the quantity demanded? $Q_1 = 150 - 5(15) - 5 = 70$ and $Q_2 = 100 - 15 - 2(5) = 75$. It results that the increase in p_1 leads to a decrease in the demand for both goods. Consequently, the two goods are complementary.

What about if the demand functions are the following

$$Q_1 = 150 - 5p_1 + p_2$$

$$Q_2 = 100 + p_1 - 2p_2$$

If $p_1 = 10$ and $p_2 = 5$, $Q_1 = 150-5(10)+5 = 105$ and $Q_2 = 100+10-2(5) = 100$. If p_1 increases from 10 to 15, we have $Q_1 = 150 - 5(15) + 5 = 80$ and $Q_2 = 100 + 15 - 2(5) = 105$. It results that the increase in p_1 leads to a decrease in the demand of good 1 and to an increase in the demand of good 2. Consequently, the two goods are substitute.

6.1.1.2 The Cobb-Douglas Function

A Cobb-Douglas production function can be represented as follows

$$Q = f(L, K) = AL^{\alpha}K^{\beta}, \quad A, \alpha, \beta > 0 \tag{6.2}$$

where Q is the total production, A is a positive constant, L is the labour force, K is the capital expenditure and α, β are positive fractions. β may be or may not be equal to $1 - \alpha$.

This production function can exhibit any returns to scale

$$Q = f(tL, tK) = A(tL)^{\alpha}(tK)^{\beta} = At^{\alpha}L^{\alpha}t^{\beta}K^{\beta} = t^{\alpha+\beta}AL^{\alpha}K^{\beta} = t^{\alpha+\beta}f(L, K)$$

- if $\alpha + \beta = 1 \Rightarrow$ constant returns to scale
- if $\alpha + \beta > 1 \Rightarrow$ increasing returns to scale
- if $\alpha + \beta < 1 \Rightarrow$ decreasing returns to scale

Let's represent the following Cobb-Douglas function $Q = 50L^{0.45}K^{0.55}$. Note that in the following code we use the variable names to label the axes. In addition, I set rotation = 45, elevation = 30, and distance = 0.2 in the manipulation option (Fig. 6.7).

```
> CD <- function(L, K){
+   50 * (L^(0.45)) * (K^(0.55))
+   }
> plotFun(CD(L, K) ~ L & K,
+           xlab = "L",
+           ylab = "K",
+           zlab = "Q",
+           L.lim = range(0, 10),
+           K.lim = range(0, 10),
+           surface = T)
```

Figure 6.8 represents the contour plot of the Cobb-Douglas production function.

```
> plotFun(CD(L, K) ~ L & K,
+           xlab = "L",
+           ylab = "K",
+           zlab = "Q",
+           L.lim = range(0, 10),
+           K.lim = range(0, 10),
+           filled = F)
```

From Fig. 6.8, we can see that when $L = 2$ and $K = 2$, the total production $Q = 100$.

Fig. 6.7 The Cobb-Douglas production function $Q = 50L^{0.45}K^{0.55}$

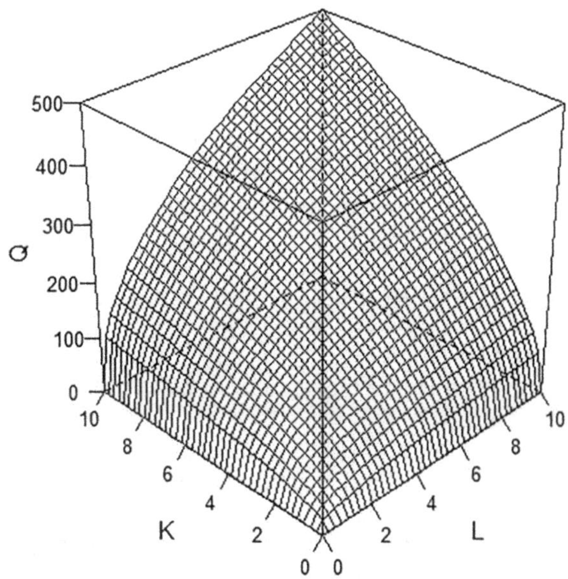

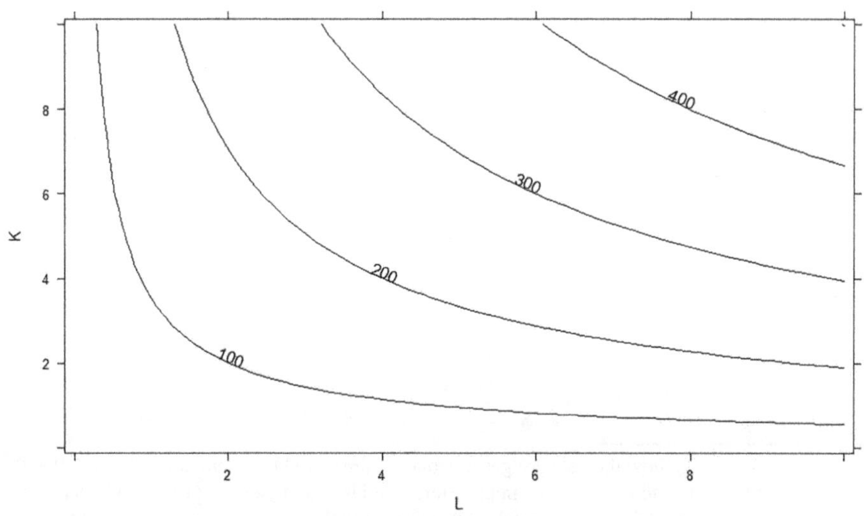

Fig. 6.8 Contour plot of the Cobb-Douglas production function $Q = 50L^{0.45}K^{0.55}$

```
> 50*(2^0.45)*(2^0.55)
[1] 100
```

6.1.1.2.1 Estimation of the Cobb-Douglas Production Function

The following example is for illustration purpose only. Let's build some fake data for labour (in working hours) and capital (in dollars).[1]

```
> l <- 500:1000
> k <- 8000:25000
> set.seed(123)
> L <- sample(l, 100, replace = T)
> head(L)
[1] 914 962 678 513 694 925
> K <- sample(k, 100, replace = T)
> head(K)
[1] 15126 17639 11979 22456 17325 11229
> df <- data.frame(L, K)
> head(df)
    L     K
1 914 15126
2 962 17639
3 678 11979
4 513 22456
5 694 17325
6 925 11229
```

[1] The rules describing how the data are generated are referred to Data Generating Process (DGP). DGP goes beyond the scope of the example. Here, we just use a naive approach to generate the data to estimate the model. You may think of the steps to build a simulated data set as follows:

- specify the model to simulate;
- determine the coefficients of the model;
- build the data for the independent variables and the error term based on probability distributions;
- compute the dependent variable by using the coefficients, the simulated data for the independent variables and the error.

However, in **R** there is the `simstudy` package that allows users to generate simulated data sets to explore modeling techniques or better understand data generating processes. The interested reader may refer to the following link for more details about the `simstudy` package https://cran.r-project.org/web/packages/simstudy/vignettes/simstudy.html.

Now let's compute the total production with the Cobb-Douglas from Sect. 6.1.1.2

```
> df$Q <- with(df, 50*(L^0.45)*(K^0.55))
> head(df)
    L     K        Q
1 914 15126 213916.4
2 962 17639 238209.7
3 678 11979 164495.7
4 513 22456 205000.8
5 694 17325 203634.8
6 925 11229 182566.6
```

Note that we use the `with()` function to evaluate `50*(L^0.45)*(K^0.55)` in `df`.

Now let's suppose that we do not know α and β and we want to estimate them from the data we have collected in `df`.

Clearly, (6.2) is non-linear. However, we can linearise it by using log properties. First, let's take the natural log of both sides of (6.2)

$$\log(Q) = \log(AL^{\alpha}K^{\beta})$$

Now let's apply log properties to the right-hand side

$$\log(Q) = \log(A) + \log(L^{\alpha}) + \log(K^{\beta})$$

$$\log(Q) = \log(A) + \alpha\log(L) + \beta\log(K) \tag{6.3}$$

Now (6.3) is linear in the coefficients.[2] We can use OLS to estimate

$$\log(Q) = \gamma + \alpha\log(L) + \beta\log(K) + u$$

where γ represents the intercept and u represents the error term.

We use the `lm()` function to run the regression.

```
> CD_reg <- lm(log(Q) ~ log(L) + log(K),
+                 data = df)
> coefficients(CD_reg)
(Intercept)      log(L)      log(K)
   3.912023    0.450000    0.550000
```

As expected, the coefficients are 0.45 and 0.55, respectively, our α and β. But what is the intercept? Remember that γ represents $\log(A)$. If we undo the log we find that

[2] Or, in statistical terminology, linear in the parameters, i.e., the *unknown* parameters of the model to be estimated do not appear, for example, as exponent or multiplied by another parameter.

```
> exp(coef(CD_reg)[1])
(Intercept)
         50
```

i.e. our A in (6.2).

Note that as we built the data, this was a deterministic simulation of a Cobb-Douglas production function. In the exercise in Sect. 6.5.1, you are asked to introduce randomness and to estimate again the model.

Now, let's export the results of the regression. We use the `stargazer()` function from `stargazer`. The first entry is the model we want to export. The argument `type =` specifies the type of output we want. In this case, we want the output to be LaTeX (the default value). Other options are `html` and `text`.[3] Then, we set the title of the table and the labels for the dependent and independent variables. The argument `intercept.bottom` places by default the intercept coefficient at the bottom of the table. In our case we set equal to `FALSE` because we want it at the top of the table. The argument `digits =` indicates how many decimal places should be used. The default value is 4. In our case, we set equal to 2. We only keep two statistics, i.e., number of observations `"n"`, and R-squared `"rsq"` (given how we built the data the statistics are not really relevant). The argument `out =` produces a file with the results. In our case it is a LaTeX file. It will be located in your working directory(`Math_R` - refer to Sect. 1.3.1). You can use the output from the file or copy and paste the output that will be printed in the console pane in your LaTeX document. Table 6.1 shows the results of our regression produced by `stargazer`. Investigate the `stargazer` package for more options to present your results.

```
> stargazer(CD_reg,
+           type = "latex",
+           title = "Estimation of the Cobb-Douglas production
            function",
+           dep.var.labels = "natural log of production",
+           covariate.labels = c("natural log of A",
+                                "alpha", "beta"),
+           digits = 2,
+           intercept.bottom = F,
+           keep.stat = c("n", "rsq"),
+           out = "CD_regression.tex")
```

6.1.1.3 The Constant Elasticity of Substitution (CES) Function

Another production function often used in Economics is the constant elasticity of substitution (CES) function that takes the following form

$$Q = A\left[\delta L^{-\rho} + (1-\delta)K^{-\rho}\right]^{-\frac{1}{\rho}} \tag{6.4}$$

[3] If you do not have LaTeX installed on your computer export the results as `text`. In `out =` replace `tex` with `txt`.

Table 6.1 Estimation of the Cobb-Douglas production function

	Dependent variable:
	natural log of production
natural log of A	3.91***
	(0.00)
alpha	0.45***
	(0.00)
beta	0.55***
	(0.00)
Observations	100
R^2	1.00
Note: *p<0.1; **p<0.05; ***p<0.01	

where A, the *efficient parameter*, is an indicator of the state of technology, L and K represent labour and capital, δ is the *distribution parameter* and it concerns the relative factor share in the product, and ρ is the *substitution parameter* that determines the value of the constant elasticity of substitution.

Let's represent the CES function $Q = 5\left[0.6L^{-2} + (1 - 0.6)K^{-2}\right]^{-\frac{1}{2}}$ (Fig. 6.9).

```
> CES <- function(L, K){
+   5 * ((0.6*L^(-2)) + (0.4*K^(-2)))^(-1/2)
+ }
> plotFun(CES(L, K) ~ L & K,
+         xlab = "L",
+         ylab = "K",
+         zlab = "Q",
+         L.lim = range(0, 10),
+         K.lim = range(0, 10),
+         surface = T)
```

Next code produces the contour plot for the CES function (Fig. 6.10).

```
> plotFun(CES(L, K) ~ L & K,
+         xlab = "L",
+         ylab = "K",
+         zlab = "Q",
+         L.lim = range(0, 10),
+         K.lim = range(0, 10),
+         filled = F)
```

From Fig. 6.10 we can see that when $L = 4$ and $K = 4$, the total production $Q = 20$.

Fig. 6.9 The CES production function $Y = 5\left[0.6L^{-2} + (1-0.6)K^{-2}\right]^{-\frac{1}{2}}$

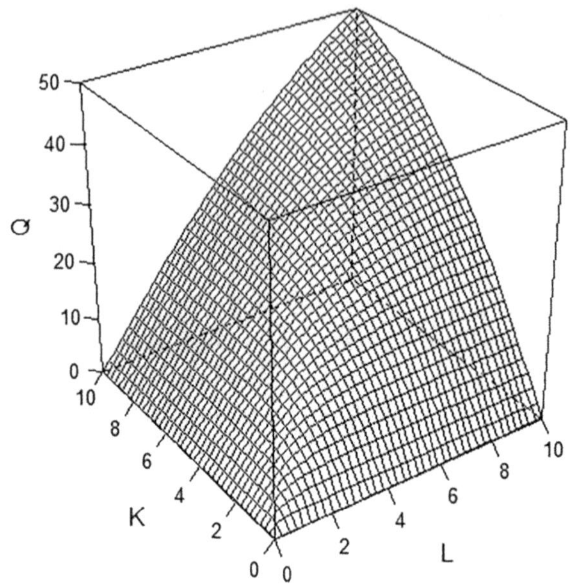

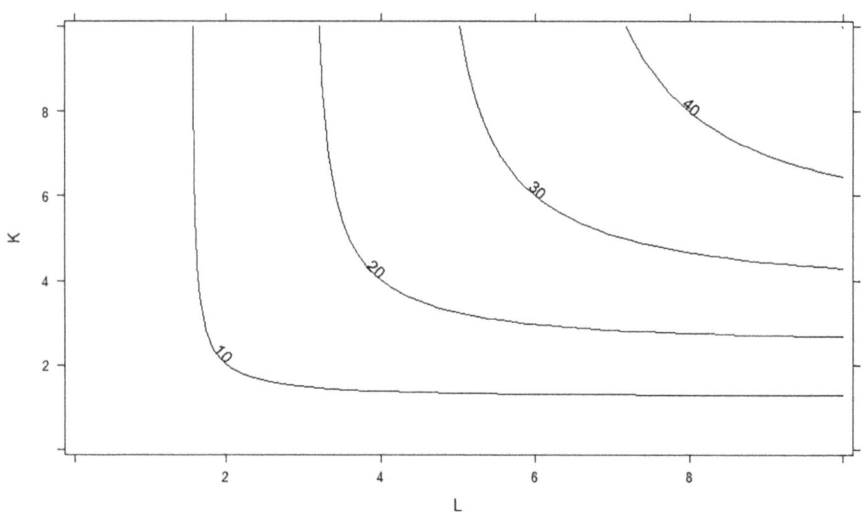

Fig. 6.10 Contour plot of the CES production function $Q = 5\left[0.6L^{-2} + 0.4K^{-2}\right]^{-\frac{1}{2}}$

```
> 5 * ((0.6*4^(-2)) + (0.4*4^(-2)))^(-1/2)
[1] 20
```

6.1.1.4 The Cobb-Douglas Function as a Special Case of the CES Function

The Cobb-Douglas function and the CES function are related. The parameter A plays the same role in both functions. The parameter δ in the CES function is like α in the Cobb-Douglas function. On the other hand ρ in the CES function does not have a counterpart in the Cobb-Douglas function.

In this section we show that the Cobb-Douglas function is a special case of the CES function when $\rho \to 0$ in the CES function.

$$Q = A\left[\delta L^{-\rho} + (1-\delta)K^{-\rho}\right]^{-\frac{1}{\rho}}$$

Let's divide both sides by A

$$\frac{Q}{A} = \left[\delta L^{-\rho} + (1-\delta)K^{-\rho}\right]^{-\frac{1}{\rho}}$$

Let's take the natural log of both sides

$$\log\left(\frac{Q}{A}\right) = \log\left(\left[\delta L^{-\rho} + (1-\delta)K^{-\rho}\right]^{-\frac{1}{\rho}}\right)$$

For the properties of logarithms, we can write the right-hand side as follow

$$\log\left(\frac{Q}{A}\right) = -\frac{1}{\rho}\cdot\log\left(\left[\delta L^{-\rho} + (1-\delta)K^{-\rho}\right]\right)$$

or

$$\log\left(\frac{Q}{A}\right) = \frac{-\log(\left[\delta L^{-\rho} + (1-\delta)K^{-\rho}\right])}{\rho} \tag{6.5}$$

Let's take $\lim_{\rho\to 0}$

$$\lim_{\rho\to 0}\log\left(\frac{Q}{A}\right) = \lim_{\rho\to 0}\frac{-\log(\left[\delta L^{-\rho} + (1-\delta)K^{-\rho}\right])}{\rho}$$

The right-hand side becomes

$$\lim_{\rho\to 0}\frac{-\log([\delta L^{-\rho}+(1-\delta)K^{-\rho}])}{\rho}=\frac{-\log([\delta L^{0}+(1-\delta)K^{0}])}{0}$$
$$=-\frac{\log(\delta+1-\delta)}{0} \tag{6.6}$$
$$=-\frac{\log(1)}{0}=\frac{0}{0}$$

Therefore, we are in the condition to be able to apply L'Hôpital rule (Sect. 4.11). We start by taking the derivative of the denominator in (6.5) with respect to ρ that is 1.

Next, we take the derivative of the numerator with respect to ρ. We use the chain rule. In particular, we use the rule of differentiation for natural log and for the exponents in the case a^x. Refer to Table 4.1. Consequently, we have

$$\frac{1}{\delta L^{-\rho}+(1-\delta)K^{-\rho}}\cdot-\left[-\delta L^{-\rho}\log(L)-(1-\delta)K^{-\rho}\log(K)\right]$$

Therefore,

$$\lim_{\rho\to 0}\frac{f'(\rho)}{g'(\rho)}=\frac{\frac{1}{\delta L^{-\rho}+(1-\delta)K^{-\rho}}\cdot-\left[-\delta L^{-\rho}\log(L)-(1-\delta)K^{-\rho}\log(K)\right]}{1}$$
$$=\frac{-\left[-\delta L^{-\rho}\log(L)-(1-\delta)K^{-\rho}\log(K)\right]}{\delta L^{-\rho}+(1-\delta)K^{-\rho}}$$
$$=\frac{-\left[-\delta L^{0}\log(L)-(1-\delta)K^{0}\log(K)\right]}{\delta L^{0}+(1-\delta)K^{0}}$$
$$=\frac{-\left[-\delta\log(L)-(1-\delta)\log(K)\right]}{\delta+1-\delta}$$
$$=\frac{\left[\delta\log(L)+(1-\delta)\log(K)\right]}{1}$$
$$=\delta\log(L)+(1-\delta)\log(K) \tag{6.7}$$

By using log properties

$$\lim_{\rho\to 0}\log\left(\frac{Q}{A}\right)=\log(L^{\delta})+\log(K^{1-\delta})=\log\left(L^{\delta}K^{1-\delta}\right)$$

By applying the exponential to both sides we undo the log

$$\lim_{\rho\to 0}\frac{Q}{A}=L^{\delta}K^{1-\delta}$$

Finally

$$\lim_{\rho \to 0} Q = AL^{\delta}K^{1-\delta}$$

6.2 Partial and Total Derivatives

Since in the previous chapters we mainly dealt with functions of one variable, we did not need to discuss about the relations among the independent (exogenous) variables. However, in the case of function of several variables as $y = f(x_1, x_2, \cdots, x_n)$ we need to consider whether $x_1, x_2, \cdots, x_n$ are independent of each other. If this is the case, the change of an independent variable will affect the dependent variable but will not produce any effect on other independent variables. Consequently, we can analyse the effect of the change in the independent variable on the dependent variable by using a technique known as *partial derivatives*. On the other hand, if the independent variables are related so that a change in one of them will affect the other independent variables, we can analyse how the changes in all the independent variables affect the dependent variable by using a technique known as *total derivatives*.

6.2.1 Partial Derivatives

Let's continue with a function of two variables, $z = f(x, y)$, that we assume to be continuously differentiable. Finding the partial derivative of z with respect to x consists in taking the derivative of the function $z = f(x, y)$ as a function of x, treating y as a constant.

Therefore, by treating y as constant, we can define the partial derivative of z with respect to x analogously to (4.2)

$$\lim_{\Delta x \to 0} \frac{\Delta z}{\Delta x} = \lim_{\Delta x \to 0} \frac{f(x + \Delta x, y) - f(x, y)}{\Delta x} \tag{6.8}$$

We can interpret the partial derivative of z with respect to x as the rate of change of z at (a, b) along the x axis. Naturally, the reverse applies to y with x treated as constant. Additionally, it can be extended to more than two independent variables provided that they are independent of each other.

For the notation used in multi-variable calculus refer to Sect. 4.4.

Following some examples.

Example 6.2.1 $z = x^2 + y$

First, let's find the partial derivative of z with respect to x, i.e., we are treating y as a constant.

$$\frac{\partial z}{\partial x} = 2x$$

Second, let's find the partial derivative of z with respect to y, i.e., we are treating x as a constant.

$$\frac{\partial z}{\partial y} = 1$$

Example 6.2.2 $z = x^2 + xy^2 + 5$

First, let's find the partial derivative of z with respect to x, i.e., we are treating y as a constant.

$$\frac{\partial z}{\partial x} = 2x + y^2$$

Second, let's find the partial derivative of z with respect to y, i.e., we are treating x as a constant.

$$\frac{\partial z}{\partial y} = 2xy$$

The second partial derivatives are

$$\frac{\partial^2 z}{\partial x^2} = 2$$

$$\frac{\partial^2 z}{\partial y^2} = 2x$$

Example 6.2.3 $(2x + y^2)(x^2 + y^3)$

In this case we have to use the product rule

$$\frac{\partial z}{\partial x} = 2(x^2 + y^3) + 2x(2x + y^2) = 2y^3 + 6x^2 + 2xy^2$$

$$\frac{\partial z}{\partial y} = 2y(x^2 + y^3) + 3y^2(2x + y^2) = 5y^4 + 2x^2y + 6xy^2$$

Example 6.2.4 $(2x + y^2)/(x^2 + y^3)$

In this case we have to use the quotient rule

$$\frac{\partial z}{\partial x} = \frac{2y^3 - 2x^2 - 2xy^2}{(x^2 + y^3)^2}$$

$$\frac{\partial z}{\partial y} = \frac{-y^4 + 2x^2y - 6xy^2}{(x^2 + y^3)^2}$$

6.2.1.1 Gradient Vector

The *gradient vector* (or only *gradient*), ∇ (read as "del"), collects the first partial derivatives of a function $y = f(x_1, x_2, \cdots, x_n)$ and it is denoted as follows

$$\nabla f(x_1, x_2, \cdots, x_n) = (f_1, f_2, \cdots, f_n) \tag{6.9}$$

From Example 6.2.2, the gradient is

$$\nabla z = \nabla(x, y) = (2x + y^2, 2xy)$$

If we evaluate these partial derivatives at point $(1, 2)$ we have a vector of specific derivatives values $(6, 4)$.

Since the gradient is a vector, it has a magnitude and a direction. In particular, ∇f points in the direction in which the function f increases most rapidly, and its magnitude is the rate of this increase (Moore & Siegel 2013, p. 362).

6.2.1.2 Jacobian Matrix

Another mathematical entity that collects first partial derivatives of a function of several variables is called *Jacobian*.[4]

In this section, we are interested in building the *Jacobian matrix*. The determinant of a Jacobian matrix provides us with information about the (linear or non-linear) dependence of functions of several variables. Let's see an example.

Let's suppose we want to test the dependence between the following two functions

[4] The gradient is associated with the *storage* of partial derivatives of a *scalar* function, i.e., a function that assigns a scalar (real number) to a set of real variables, whereas the Jacobian is associated with the *storage* of partial derivatives of a *vector* function, i.e., a function that assigns a vector value to a set of real variables. For a clear and concise explanation of vector functions the reader may refer to Moore and Siegel (2013).

$$y_1 = f(x_1, x_2) = x_1 + x_2$$

$$y_2 = g(x_1, x_2) = x_1^2 + 2x_1x_2 + x_2^2$$

First, let's find the partial derivatives and store them in a matrix, J, in the given order.
$\frac{\partial y_1}{\partial x_1} = 1$
$\frac{\partial y_1}{\partial x_2} = 1$
$\frac{\partial y_2}{\partial x_1} = 2x_1 + 2x_2$
$\frac{\partial y_2}{\partial x_2} = 2x_1 + 2x_2$

$$J = \begin{bmatrix} \frac{\partial y_1}{\partial x_1} & \frac{\partial y_1}{\partial x_2} \\ \frac{\partial y_2}{\partial x_1} & \frac{\partial y_2}{\partial x_2} \end{bmatrix} \tag{6.10}$$

$$J = \begin{bmatrix} 1 & 1 \\ 2x_1 + 2x_2 & 2x_1 + 2x_2 \end{bmatrix}$$

The J matrix is known as the Jacobian matrix.

Second, by investigating its determinant (Sect. 2.3.8) we find whether the two functions are dependent, $|J| = 0$, or are independent, $|J| \neq 0$

$$|J| = \begin{vmatrix} 1 & 1 \\ 2x_1 + 2x_2 & 2x_1 + 2x_2 \end{vmatrix} = 2x_1 + 2x_2 - (2x_1 + 2x_2) = 0$$

Consequently, the two functions are dependent. We can add that the two functions are non-linear dependent since y_2 is just the square of y_1.

6.2.1.3 Hessian Matrix

The *Hessian matrix*, H, collects the second partial derivatives of function of several variables.

Let's consider the function $z = x^2 + y^4$. First, we compute the first partial derivatives and store in J (note that this step of storing the partial derivatives in J is not necessary but I think it may be helpful at the beginning to remember how to compute the Hessian matrix).

$$J = \begin{bmatrix} 2x & 4y^3 \end{bmatrix}$$

Next, we populate H with the second partial derivatives

$$H = \begin{bmatrix} \frac{\partial^2 z}{\partial x^2} & \frac{\partial^2 z}{\partial xy} \\ \frac{\partial^2 z}{\partial yx} & \frac{\partial^2 z}{\partial y^2} \end{bmatrix} \tag{6.11}$$

that is, we differentiate the first term in J with respect to x and then to y and we place the results in the first row; then, we differentiate the second term in J with respect to x and then to y and we place the results in the second row.

$$H = \begin{bmatrix} 2 & 0 \\ 0 & 12y^2 \end{bmatrix}$$

Note that the Hessian matrix is symmetric (Sect. 2.3.2). In fact, generally $\frac{\partial^2 z}{\partial xy} = \frac{\partial^2 z}{\partial yx}$ by Young's theorem. $\frac{\partial^2 z}{\partial xy}$ and $\frac{\partial^2 z}{\partial yx}$ are called *cross partial derivatives* or *mixed partial derivatives*.[5]

We will return to the interpretation of the Hessian matrix in Sect. 6.3.

Example 6.2.5 Write the Hessian matrix of $w = f(x, y, z) = x^2 + y^4 + 2xyz^2$.

Following the previous steps

$$J = \begin{bmatrix} 2x + 2yz^2 & 4y^3 + 2xz^2 & 4xyz \end{bmatrix}$$

$$H = \begin{bmatrix} \frac{\partial^2 w}{\partial x^2} & \frac{\partial^2 w}{\partial xy} & \frac{\partial^2 w}{\partial xz} \\ \frac{\partial^2 w}{\partial yx} & \frac{\partial^2 w}{\partial y^2} & \frac{\partial^2 w}{\partial yz} \\ \frac{\partial^2 w}{\partial zx} & \frac{\partial^2 w}{\partial zy} & \frac{\partial^2 w}{\partial z^2} \end{bmatrix} = \begin{bmatrix} 2 & 2z^2 & 4yz \\ 2z^2 & 12y^2 & 4xz \\ 4yz & 4xz & 4xy \end{bmatrix}$$

6.2.2 Total Derivatives

Let's consider the following function $z = f(x, y) = x^2+y$. The total differentiation is given by

$$dz = \frac{\partial z}{\partial x}dx + \frac{\partial z}{\partial y}dy \tag{6.12}$$

[5] Refer to an advanced textbook for a proof of the Young's theorem.

that is, the total change in z, i.e. the total differential dz, is approximated by the sum of the partial differentials in the right-hand side of (6.12). Therefore

$$dz = 2x\ dx + 1\ dy = 2x\ dx + dy$$

Example 6.2.6 $z = f(x, y) = x^2y^3$
We have that

$$dz = 2xy^3\ dx + 3x^2y^2\ dy$$

Let's plug some numbers, for example $x = 2$, $y = 4$. By replacing these numbers in the initial function it results that $z = 2^2 4^3 = 256$.

Let's suppose that x and y change to $x = 2.1$ and $y = 4.1$. By replacing these in the initial function it results that $z = 2.1^2 4.1^3 = 303.9$. Consequently, the change in z is $dz = 303.9 - 256 = 47.9$.

Additionally, this means that $dx = 2.1 - 2 = 0.1$ and $dy = 4.1 - 4 = 0.1$. Consequently,

$$dz = 2(2)(4)^3(0.1) + 3(2)^2(4)^2(0.1) = 44.8$$

approximates the total change.

What about if x and y change to $x = 2.01$, $y = 4.01$. By replacing these in the initial function it results that $z = 2.01^2 4.01^3 = 260.5$. Consequently, the change in z is $dz = 260.5 - 256 = 4.5$.

Now, by replacing in the total differentiation formula we find that

$$dz = 2(2)(4)^3(0.01) + 3(2)^2(4)^2(0.01) = 4.48$$

Now let's suppose that only x changes to $x = 2.01$. This means that $dx = 0.01$ while $dy = 0$ because y does not change. Following the previous steps we have that $z = 2.01^2 4^3 = 258.5664$. Consequently, the change in z is $dz = 258.5664 - 256 = 2.5664$.

Now, by replacing in the total differentiation formula we find that

$$dz = 2(2)(4)^3(0.01) + 3(2)^2(4)^2(0) = 2.56$$

We can observe that the approximation gets better as the differentials approach 0.

Now we need to consider how to find the total derivative in the case where the independent variables are not independent of each other. For example, let's consider the following function

$$z = f(x, y) \tag{6.13}$$

where, in turn, $x = g(y)$.

Consequently, we can write the function z as follows

$$z = f(g(y), y)$$

It is evident that in this case would make not much sense to take the partial derivative of z with respect to y by treating x as a constant given that x if function of y. In fact, we need to consider that in this case y affects z *directly* through f and *indirectly* through g.

To find the total derivative of z with respect to y, let's first get the total differentiation of z as in (6.12)

$$dz = \frac{\partial z}{\partial x}dx + \frac{\partial z}{\partial y}dy$$

Next let's divide it through dy

$$\frac{dz}{dy} = \frac{\partial z}{\partial x}\frac{dx}{dy} + \frac{\partial z}{\partial y}\frac{dy}{dy}$$

and, consequently

$$\frac{dz}{dy} = \frac{\partial z}{\partial x}\frac{dx}{dy} + \frac{\partial z}{\partial y} \tag{6.14}$$

where $\frac{\partial z}{\partial y}$ represents the direct effect of y and $\frac{\partial z}{\partial d}\frac{dx}{dy}$ represents the indirect effect of y.

Example 6.2.7 Let's consider again the function $z = f(x, y) = x^2 + y$ but this time we add that x is function of y, $x = g(y) = 3y^2 + y$. By applying (6.14), first we compute the partial derivatives $\frac{\partial z}{\partial x}$ and $\frac{\partial z}{\partial y}$ and replace them in (6.14)

$$\frac{dz}{dy} = 2x\frac{dx}{dy} + 1$$

Next, we find the derivative of x with respect to y, $\frac{dx}{dy}$ and we replace it in (6.14)

$$\frac{dz}{dy} = 2x(6y + 1) + 1 = 12xy + 2x + 1$$

and given that $x = 3y^2 + y$

$$\frac{dz}{dy} = 12y(3y^2 + y) + 2(3y^2 + y) + 1 = 36y^3 + 12y^2 + 6y^2 + 2y + 1$$

Example 6.2.8 $z = f(x, y) = x^2 - xy - 2y^2, x = g(y) = 2 - 7y$
Following the previous steps

$$\frac{dz}{dy} = (2x - y)\frac{dx}{dy} - x - 4y$$

$$\frac{dz}{dy} = (2x - y)(-7) - x - 4y = -14x + 7y - x - 4y = -15x + 3y$$

$$\frac{dz}{dy} = -15(2 - 7y) + 3y = -30 + 105y + 3y = 108y - 30$$

6.2.3 Derivatives with R

We can compute derivatives of functions of several variables in **R** with the `deriv()` function as follows

```
> f <- expression(x^2 + y)
> deltafdeltax <- deriv(f, "x")
> deltafdeltax
expression({
    .value <- x^2 + y
    .grad <- array(0, c(length(.value), 1L), list(NULL,
     c("x")))
    .grad[, "x"] <- 2 * x
    attr(.value, "gradient") <- .grad
    .value
})
> deltafdeltay <- deriv(f, "y")
> deltafdeltay
expression({
    .value <- x^2 + y
    .grad <- array(0, c(length(.value), 1L), list(NULL,
     c("y")))
    .grad[, "y"] <- 1
    attr(.value, "gradient") <- .grad
    .value
})
> tot_diff <- deriv(f, c("x", "y"))
> tot_diff
expression({
    .value <- x^2 + y
```

```
    .grad <- array(0, c(length(.value), 2L), list(NULL,
     c("x", "y")))
    .grad[, "x"] <- 2 * x
    .grad[, "y"] <- 1
    attr(.value, "gradient") <- .grad
    .value
})
```

Now, let's see some examples with the `Deriv()` function from the `Deriv` package.

```
> f <- "x^2 + y"
> deltafdeltax <- Deriv(f, "x")
> deltafdeltax
[1] "2 * x"
> deltafdeltay <- Deriv(f, "y")
> deltafdeltay
[1] "1"
> tot_diff <- Deriv(f)
> tot_diff
[1] "c(x = 2 * x, y = 1)"
```

We can use the `grad()` function from the `pracma` package to numerically compute the gradient

```
> f <- function(x){
+   x[1]^2 + x[1]*x[2]^2 + 5
+   }
> grad(f, c(1, 2))
[1] 6 4
```

We can use the `jacobian()` function from the `pracma` package to numerically compute the Jacobian matrix

```
> f <- function(x){
+   c(x[1] + x[2],
+     x[1]^2 + 2*x[1]*x[2] + x[2]^2)
+   }
> J <- jacobian(f, c(1, 1))
> J
     [,1] [,2]
[1,]    1    1
[2,]    4    4
> det(J)
[1] 0
```

We can use the `hessian()` function from the `pracma` package to numerically compute the Hessian matrix

```
> f <- function(x){
+   x[1]^2 + x[2]^4
+   }
> hessian(f, c(1, 1))
     [,1] [,2]
[1,]    2    0
[2,]    0   12
```

6.2.4 Applications in Economics

6.2.4.1 Marginal Product of Labour and Capital

We can use partial derivatives to compute the marginal product of labour (MPL) and the marginal product of capital (MPK). Given the following function $Q = f(L, K)$, the marginal product of labour

$$MPL = \frac{\partial Q}{\partial L} \tag{6.15}$$

represents the rate at which output changes with respect to labour L while treating capital K as a constant.

Similarly, the marginal product of capital

$$MPK = \frac{\partial Q}{\partial K} \tag{6.16}$$

represents the rate at which output changes with respect to capital K while treating labour L as a constant.

For example, by considering the production function $Q = 13L^{0.3}K^{0.7}$, we find that when $L = 800$ and $K = 20{,}000$, $Q = 13 \cdot 800^{0.3} \cdot 20000^{0.7} = 98{,}990$.

Now let's compute MPL and MPK

$$MPL = 13 \cdot 0.3 \cdot L^{0.3-1}K^{0.7} = 13 \cdot 0.3 \cdot 800^{-0.7} \cdot 20000^{0.7} = 37.1$$

$$MPK = 13 \cdot 0.7 \cdot L^{0.3}K^{0.7-1} = 13 \cdot 0.7 \cdot 800^{0.3} \cdot 20000^{-0.3} = 3.46$$

Consequently, if K is held constant and L increases by ΔL, Q will approximately increase to

$$Q = Q + MPL \cdot \Delta L$$

For example, if L increases by 1 unit, that is, if $\Delta L = 1$,

$$Q = 98990 + 37.1 \cdot 1 = 99027.1$$

We can check the approximation by replacing $L = 801$ in the initial function $Q = 13 \cdot 801^{0.3} \cdot 20{,}000^{0.7} = 99{,}027.11$.

Similarly, if L is held constant and K increased by ΔK, Q will approximately increase to

$$Q = Q + MPK \cdot \Delta K$$

For example, if K increased by 5 units, that is, if $\Delta K = 5$,

$$Q = 98{,}990 + 3.46 \cdot 5 = 99{,}007.3$$

We can check the approximation by replacing $K = 20{,}005$ in the initial function $Q = 13 \cdot 800^{0.3} \cdot 20{,}005^{0.7} = 99{,}007.33$.

6.2.4.2 The Law of Diminishing Marginal Productivity

Suppose that you decide to open a restaurant with 120 seats. At the beginning you are the chef and the waiter. It will be more than challenging to cook and serve customers at the table. Therefore, you decide to hire a waiter. Now you can focus on cooking. Luckily, your restaurant is always full and you think one chef and one waiter are not enough. Consequently, you hire another chef and another waiter. Now you are more productive than before because you can serve more customers in less time. But what about if you continue to hire waiters? For example, you hire one waiter for table in the restaurant. It can happen that when the restaurant is full the waiters will get in each other way. On the other hand, if the restaurant has a few customers, most of the waiters will be idle. Consequently, the benefit of adding an extra waiter will decrease as more waiters are hired. In other words, the first derivative of Q with respect to L, that is, MPL, is positive and the second derivative of Q with respect to L is negative. Analogously, the example applies to capital as well. The fact that the second partial derivative of a production function is negative is known as the *law of diminishing marginal productivity*.

6.2.4.3 An Application with the Jacobian

Suppose that the demand functions for good 1, Q_1, and good 2, Q_2, are the following

$$Q_1 = 4P_1^{3/2}P_2^{1/2}Y$$

$$Q_2 = 2P_1^{1/2}P_2^{1/2}Y$$

Given that the current prices are $P_1^* = 4$, $P_2^* = 6$, and the current income $Y^* = 2000$, we want to analyse the impact on the demand of the two goods of a reduction of income by 0.1, $dY = -0.1$.

First, we set the Jacobian

$$J = \begin{bmatrix} \frac{\partial Q_1}{\partial P_1} & \frac{\partial Q_1}{\partial P_2} & \frac{\partial Q_1}{\partial Y} \\ \frac{\partial Q_2}{\partial P_1} & \frac{\partial Q_2}{\partial P_2} & \frac{\partial Q_2}{\partial Y} \end{bmatrix} = \begin{bmatrix} 4 \cdot \frac{3}{2} P_1^{3/2-1} P_2^{1/2} Y & 4 \cdot \frac{1}{2} P_1^{3/2} P_2^{1/2-1} Y & 4 P_1^{3/2} P_2^{1/2} \\ 2 \cdot \frac{1}{2} P_1^{1/2-1} P_2^{1/2} Y & 2 \cdot \frac{1}{2} P_1^{1/2} P_2^{1/2-1} Y & 2 P_1^{1/2} P_2^{1/2} \end{bmatrix}$$

We evaluate J at the current prices and income. Let's use **R** for this task by using the `jacobian()` function from the `pracma` package.

```
> f <- function(x){
+    c(4*x[1]^(3/2)*x[2]^(1/2)*x[3],
+      2*x[1]^(1/2)*x[2]^(1/2)*x[3])
+    }
> J <- jacobian(f, c(4, 6, 2000))
> J
          [,1]       [,2]      [,3]
[1,] 58787.75 13063.945 78.383672
[2,]   2449.49   1632.993  9.797959
```

In the next step we multiply J evaluated at $P_1^* = 4$, $P_2^* = 6$, $Y^* = 2000$ by a vector of changes in prices and income. Since income drops by 0.1, $dY = -0.1$, while prices are unchanged, $dP_1 = dP_2 = 0$, we have that

```
> D <- matrix(c(0, 0, -0.1),
+               nrow = 3, ncol = 1)
> D
     [,1]
[1,]  0.0
[2,]  0.0
[3,] -0.1
> J %*% D
           [,1]
[1,] -7.8383672
[2,] -0.9797959
```

that is, $dQ_1 = -7.8$ and $dQ_2 = -0.98$.

6.3 Unconstrained Optimization

In Chap. 4, we used calculus to find the *extreme* values of a function, a *maximum* or a *minimum*. Formally, we can write the definition of maximum and minimum for a real-valued function of n variables, $f : D \to \mathbb{R}^1$, where domain D is a subset of $\mathbb{R}^n$, as follows:

- $\mathbf{x}^* \in D$ is a maximum (minimum) value of f on D if $f(\mathbf{x}^*) \geq f(\mathbf{x})\ \forall \mathbf{x} \in D$ $(f(\mathbf{x}^*) \leq f(\mathbf{x})\ \forall \mathbf{x} \in D)$
- $\mathbf{x}^* \in D$ is a strict maximum (minimum) value if $\mathbf{x}^*$ is a maximum (minimum) and $f(\mathbf{x}^*) > f(\mathbf{x})\ \forall \mathbf{x} \neq \mathbf{x}^* \in D$ $(f(\mathbf{x}^*) < f(\mathbf{x})\ \forall \mathbf{x} \neq \mathbf{x}^* \in D)$

If $\mathbf{x}^*$ is a maximum (minimum) value of f on the whole domain D, we refer to it as a *global max* or *absolute max* (*global min* or *absolute min*).[6] If we want to stress that there are no *nearby* points to $\mathbf{x}^*$ where f takes a larger (smaller) value, we refer to $\mathbf{x}^*$ as a *local max* (*local min*).

When we translate these concepts from Mathematics to Economics, we refer to them as *optimization* problems. In these optimization problems, the first task is to identify the *objective function* where the dependent variable is the object we want to maximize or minimize and the independent variables, also referred to as *choice variables* or *policy variables*, represent the economic values that lead to the optimization of the objective function. Consequently, the solution of an optimization problem is a set of values of independent variables that maximizes or minimizes the value of the dependent variable.

6.3.1 First Order Condition

The first order condition of a function of one variable is

$$f'(x^*) = 0 \tag{6.17}$$

where x^* is a critical value of f. Additionally, we require that the critical point lie in the interior of the domain of f (*interior max* or *interior min*) rather than lie at the endpoint of the interval under consideration (*boundary max* or *boundary min*). (6.17) is referred to as a *necessary* condition since it has to be satisfied in order to have either a maximum or a minimum.

The same condition applies to functions of several variables. However, we need to consider the first partial derivatives of the function of several variables

$$\frac{\partial f}{\partial x_i}(\mathbf{x}^*) = 0 \quad \text{for } i = 1, ..., n. \tag{6.18}$$

Consequently, for a function of n variables we need to consider n first partial derivatives.

Example 6.3.1 Find the critical values of the following function

$$z = -2x^2 - y^2 + 2xy + 4x$$

[6] *max* and *min* are abbreviations for *maximum* and *minimum*.

Step 1
Find the partial derivatives

$$\begin{aligned}\frac{\partial z}{\partial x} &= -4x + 2y + 4\\ \frac{\partial z}{\partial y} &= -2y + 2x\end{aligned} \tag{6.19}$$

Step 2
Set the partial derivatives equal to 0

$$\begin{aligned}-4x + 2y + 4 &= 0\\ -2y + 2x &= 0\end{aligned} \tag{6.20}$$

Step 3
Solve the system of equations in Step 2

Here we proceed by backsolving the system (you may use a different approach). Solve the second one for y (choosing which equation and which variable to solve for is discretionary)

$$-2y + 2x = 0 \rightarrow y = x$$

Substitute the solution in the other equation. In this case, substitute it in $-4x + 2y + 4 = 0$ to find x

$$-4x + 2(x) + 4 = 0 \rightarrow -2x = -4 \rightarrow x = 2$$

Substitute the result for x

$$y = 2$$

Step 4
Define the critical values to evaluate as max or min of the function.

The critical values are (2, 2).

6.3.2 Second Order Condition

To determine if the critical values correspond to a maximum or a minimum of the function, we need to compute the second derivatives. If $f'(x^*) = 0$, the second order (*sufficient*) conditions (but not *necessary*) for a function of one variable maintain that if

- $f''(x^*) < 0$, then x^* is a relative max of f
- $f''(x^*) > 0$, then x^* is a relative min of f

If $f'(x^*) = 0$ and instead of a strict inequality we have a weak inequality, the second order (*necessary*) condition (but not *sufficient*) for a function of one variable maintain that if

- $f''(x^*) \leq 0$, then x^* is a relative max of f
- $f''(x^*) \geq 0$, then x^* is a relative min of f

To be remarked that if $f'(x^*) = 0$ and $f''(x^*) = 0$, a possible inflection point may exist.[7]

In the case of a function of several variables, we need to consider the second partial derivatives. We can store them in the Hessian matrix

$$H = \begin{bmatrix} \frac{\partial^2 f}{\partial x_1^2}(\mathbf{x}^*) & \cdots & \frac{\partial^2 f}{\partial x_n \partial x_1}(\mathbf{x}^*) \\ \vdots & \ddots & \vdots \\ \frac{\partial^2 f}{\partial x_1 \partial x_n}(\mathbf{x}^*) & \cdots & \frac{\partial^2 f}{\partial x_n^2}(\mathbf{x}^*) \end{bmatrix} \tag{6.21}$$

Consequently, we need to study the definiteness of the Hessian matrix to be able to determine if $\mathbf{x}^*$ is a maximum or a minimum (refer to Sect. 2.3.12 for definiteness of a matrix). If $\frac{\partial f}{\partial x_i}(\mathbf{x}^*) = 0$, the *sufficient* conditions are the following

- if the Hessian is a negative definite symmetric matrix, then $\mathbf{x}^*$ is a strict local max of f
- if the Hessian is a positive definite symmetric matrix, then $\mathbf{x}^*$ is a strict local min of f
- if the Hessian is indefinite, then $\mathbf{x}^*$ is neither a local max or a local min of f (saddle point)

If $\frac{\partial f}{\partial x_i}(\mathbf{x}^*) = 0$, the *necessary* conditions for a max or min of a function of several variables require the Hessian to be

[7] It may be helpful to think about $f(x) = x^4$. This function has a minimum at $x^* = 0$. The first order condition, $4x^3 = 0$ implies that $x^* = 0$. The second order condition, $12x^2$, evaluated at x^* is 0. Therefore, despite $f''(x^*) = 0$ we reached a minimum. Plot $f(x) = x^4$ to visualize the function.

- a negative semidefinite symmetric matrix at a local max of f
- a positive semidefinite symmetric matrix at a local min of f

Let's continue with Example 6.3.1.

Step 5
Form the Hessian

$$J = \begin{bmatrix} -4x + 2y + 4 & -2y + 2x \end{bmatrix}$$

$$H = \begin{bmatrix} -4 & 2 \\ 2 & -2 \end{bmatrix}$$

Step 6
Compute the leading principal minors

$$|H_1| = -4$$

$$|H_2| = 4$$

Step 7
Evaluate the leading principal minors at the critical values

	(2, 2)
$\lvert H_1 \rvert$	−4
$\lvert H_2 \rvert$	4

Since $|H_1| < 0$ and $|H_2| > 0$, H is negative definite and at the critical values $(2, 2)$ we have a strict local max.

Example 6.3.2 Find the critical values of the following function:

$$z = x^3 + 8y^3 - 12xy$$

Step 1

$$\begin{aligned} \frac{\partial z}{\partial x} &= 3x^2 - 12y \\ \frac{\partial z}{\partial y} &= 24y^2 - 12x \end{aligned} \tag{6.22}$$

Step 2

$$\begin{aligned} 3x^2 - 12y &= 0 \\ 24y^2 - 12x &= 0 \end{aligned} \tag{6.23}$$

Step 3

$$24y^2 - 12x = 0 \rightarrow x = 2y^2$$

$$3(2y^2)^2 - 12y = 0 \rightarrow 12y^4 - 12y = 0 \rightarrow 12y(y^3 - 1) = 0$$

Consequently, the real solutions are $y_1 = 0$, $y_2 = 1$.

$$x_1 = 2(0)^2 \rightarrow x_1 = 0$$

$$x_2 = 2(1)^2 \rightarrow x_2 = 2$$

Step 4
Critical values are (0, 0) and (2, 1).

Step 5

$$J = \begin{bmatrix} 3x^2 - 12y & 24y^2 - 12x \end{bmatrix}$$

$$H = \begin{bmatrix} 6x & -12 \\ -12 & 48y \end{bmatrix}$$

Step 6

$$|H_1| = 6x$$

$$|H_2| = 288xy - 144$$

Step 7

	(0, 0)	(2, 1)
$\|H_1\|$	0	12
$\|H_2\|$	−144	432

From the leading principal minors we can conclude that at critical values (0, 0) we do not have neither a max nor a min (saddle point);[8] at critical values (2, 1) we have a strict local min (the Hessian matrix is positive definite).

Let's implement Example 6.3.2 with **R**. We identify x with `x[1]` and y with `x[2]` (we will return to their meaning in Sect. 7.4.4). Additionally, note that we use the `LPM()` function we built in Sect. 2.3.8.2.1

```
> f <- function(x){
+   x[1]^3 + 8*x[2]^3 -12 *x[1]*x[2]
+   }
> # at point (0, 0)
> H_00 <- hessian(f, c(0, 0))
> H_00
      [,1] [,2]
[1,]     0  -12
[2,]   -12    0
> LPM(H_00)
[1]     0 -144
> # at point (2, 1)
> H_21 <- hessian(f, c(2, 1))
> H_21
```

[8] In case of a 2×2 H as in the example, $|H_2| = |H|$. If $|H| < 0$, then H is indefinite. Refer to an advanced textbook for the proof of this theorem.

```
      [,1] [,2]
[1,]   12  -12
[2,]  -12   48
> LPM(H_21)
[1]  12 432
```

6.3.2.1 Concavity and Convexity

In Sect. 3.1.3, we introduced the concepts of concavity and convexity with regard to a function of one variable. We limited our discussion to a graphic analysis. In this section, we define concavity and convexity of a function by using the second derivative of a twice continuously differentiable function.

In the case of a function of one variable $f(x)$,

- f is concave if and only if $f^{''}(x) \leq 0$. If $f^{''}(x) < 0$, then f is strictly concave
- f is convex if and only if $f^{''}(x) \geq 0$. If $f^{''}(x) > 0$, then f is strictly convex

In the case of a function of several variables $f(x_1, x_2, \cdots, x_n)$,

- f is concave if and only if the Hessian $H(\mathbf{x})$ is negative semidefinite. If $H(\mathbf{x})$ is negative definite, then f is strictly concave
- f is convex if and only if the Hessian $H(\mathbf{x})$ is positive semidefinite. If $H(\mathbf{x})$ is positive definite, then f is strictly convex

6.3.3 Optimization with R

In this section we introduce optimization with **R**. We will return to this topic in Sect. 7.3.

Let's solve the previous two examples with the `optim()` function. This function requires initial values for the parameters to be optimized over, a function to be minimized (or maximized), and a function to return the gradient. Note that this function by default performs minimization. To maximize it we set `control=list(fnscale=-1)`. Additionally, we set `hessian = TRUE` to get the Hessian matrix.

Example 6.3.1:

```
> fn <- function(x){
+    -2*x[1]^2 -x[2]^2 + 2*x[1]*x[2] + 4*x[1]
+    }
> gr <- function(x){
+    c(-4*x[1] + 2*x[2] + 4,
+       -2*x[2] + 2*x[1])
+    }
> optim(c(0, 0), fn, gr, hessian = T,
```

```
+         control=list(fnscale=-1))
$par
[1] 2 2

$value
[1] 4

$counts
function gradient
     133       NA

$convergence
[1] 0

$message
NULL

$hessian
     [,1] [,2]
[1,]   -4    2
[2,]    2   -2
```

`par` returns the best set of parameters found while `value` returns the value of the function corresponding to `par`.

In Example 6.3.2, we write `NULL` instead of the gradient. In this case the function will use a finite-difference approximation.

```
> fn <- function(x){
+   x[1]^3 + 8*x[2]^3 -12*x[1]*x[2]
+   }
> optim(c(0, 0), fn, NULL, hessian = T)
$par
[1] 2 1

$value
[1] -8

$counts
function gradient
     143       NA

$convergence
[1] 0

$message
NULL
```

```
$hessian
      [,1] [,2]
[1,]   12  -12
[2,]  -12   48
```

6.3.4 *Applications in Economics*

6.3.4.1 Multi-product Firm

Let's consider an example where a firm that produces two goods wants to maximizes its level of output. Clearly, we are in the case of a function of two variables and we need to use partial derivatives to find the solution of this problem.

As we know, the first task is to identify the objective function. In this case it is the profit function. We know that the profit equals revenue minus costs. However, in this case we need to consider that we have the revenues from the sales of product one, $R_1 = P_1Q_1$, and the revenues from the sales of product two, $R_2 = P_2Q_2$. Given that the cost is function of the quantities produced of the two goods, $C = C(Q_1, Q_2)$, the objective function of this problem is

$$\pi = R_1 + R_2 - C \tag{6.24}$$

Let's suppose that for our problem

$$\begin{aligned} P_1 &= 38 - Q_1 - 2Q_2 \\ P_2 &= 90 - 2Q_1 - 4Q_2 \\ C &= 3Q_1^2 - 2Q_1Q_2 + 2Q_2^2 + 100 \end{aligned} \tag{6.25}$$

where all the quantities are in thousand per month.

Consequently, the objective function to maximize is

$$\pi = (38 - Q_1 - 2Q_2)Q_1 + (90 - 2Q_1 - 4Q_2)Q_2 - (3Q_1^2 - 2Q_1Q_2 + 2Q_2^2 + 100)$$

$$\pi = -4Q_1^2 - 6Q_2^2 - 2Q_1Q_2 + 38Q_1 + 90Q_2 - 100$$

Once we defined the objective function, we can apply the seven steps.

Step 1

$$\begin{aligned}\frac{\partial \pi}{\partial Q_1} &= -8Q_1 - 2Q_2 + 38 \\ \frac{\partial \pi}{\partial Q_2} &= -2Q_1 - 12Q_2 + 90\end{aligned} \tag{6.26}$$

Step 2

$$\begin{aligned}-8Q_1 - 2Q_2 + 38 &= 0 \\ -2Q_1 - 12Q_2 + 90 &= 0\end{aligned} \tag{6.27}$$

Step 3

$$-2Q_1 - 12Q_2 + 90 = 0 \rightarrow Q_1 = 45 - 6Q_2$$

$$-8(45 - 6Q_2) - 2Q_2 + 38 = 0 \rightarrow Q_2^* = 7$$

$$Q_1^* = 45 - 6(7) = 3$$

and Step 3.5

$$P_1^* = 38 - 3 - 2 \cdot 7 = 21$$

$$P_2^* = 90 - 2 \cdot 3 - 4 \cdot 7 = 56$$

$$\pi^* = -4(3)^2 - 6(7)^2 - 2(3)(7) + 38(3) + 90(7) - 100 = 278$$

Step 4

The critical point is (3, 7)

Step 5

$$J = \begin{bmatrix} -8Q_1 - 2Q_2 + 38 & -2Q_1 - 12Q_2 + 90 \end{bmatrix}$$

$$H = \begin{bmatrix} -8 & -2 \\ -2 & -12 \end{bmatrix}$$

Step 6

$$|H_1| = -8$$

$$|H_2| = 92$$

Step 7

$$\begin{array}{cc} & (3,7) \\ |H_1| & -8 \\ |H_2| & 92 \end{array}$$

Since the signs of the leading principal minors are independent of where they are evaluated and $|H_1| < 0$ and $|H_2| > 0$, we can conclude that the Hessian is *everywhere* negative definite. Therefore, the solution maximizes the profit (the objective function is strictly concave and it has a unique absolute maximum).

Let's check our results with **R**

```
> profit <- function(Q) {
+       (-4*Q[1]^2 - 6*Q[2]^2 -
+          2*Q[1]*Q[2] + 38*Q[1] + 90*Q[2] - 100)
+ }
> gr <- function(Q) c(-8*Q[1] - 2*Q[2] + 38,
+                     -2*Q[1] -12*Q[2] + 90)
> profit_opt <- optim(c(1, 3), profit, gr,
+                     hessian = T,
+                     control=list(fnscale=-1))
> profit_opt$par
[1] 3.000042 7.000176
```

```
> H_37 <- profit_opt$hessian
> H_37
     [,1] [,2]
[1,]   -8   -2
[2,]   -2  -12
> LPM(H_37)
[1] -8 92
```

6.3.4.2 Ordinary Least Square

In Sect. 2.4.5, we used matrix algebra to estimate a linear model by using ordinary least square (OLS). In this section, we approach the same problem as a minimization problem.

Suppose that we have n observations for the dependent variable y and for the independent variable x, where y and x exhibit a linear relationship

$$y = b + mx$$

The first task is to identify the objective function we want to minimize, that is the sum of squared residuals (6.29).

Residuals are given by the difference between the observed values and the fitted values (6.28)

$$\hat{u}_i = y_i - \hat{b} - \hat{m}x_i \tag{6.28}$$

In our case, we choose $\hat{b}$ and $\hat{m}$ to make (6.29) as small as possible

$$S(\hat{b}, \hat{m}) = \sum_{i=1}^{n} (y_i - \hat{b} - \hat{m}x_i)^2 \tag{6.29}$$

Let's start by setting the first order conditions for (6.29)

$$\frac{\partial S}{\partial \hat{b}} = \sum_{i=1}^{n} 2(y_i - \hat{b} - \hat{m}x_i) \cdot (-1) = 0 \tag{6.30}$$

$$\frac{\partial S}{\partial \hat{m}} = \sum_{i=1}^{n} 2(y_i - \hat{b} - \hat{m}x_i) \cdot (-x_i) = 0 \tag{6.31}$$

Note that we applied the chain rule for (6.30) and (6.31) (Sect. 4.6.4).

Let's divide both sides of (6.30) and (6.31) by 2 and after a few algebraic steps we obtain

$$\begin{aligned}\sum_i \hat{b} + \sum_i \hat{m}x_i - \sum_i y_i &= 0\\ \sum_i \hat{b}x_i + \sum_i \hat{m}x_i^2 - \sum_i x_i y_i &= 0\end{aligned} \tag{6.32}$$

and then

$$\begin{aligned}n \cdot \hat{b} + \left(\sum_i x_i\right)\hat{m} &= \sum_i y_i\\ \left(\sum_i x_i\right)\hat{b} + \left(\sum_i x_i^2\right)\hat{m} &= \sum_i x_i y_i\end{aligned} \tag{6.33}$$

We can find $\hat{b}$ and $\hat{m}$ by applying Cramer's rule to the previous system of equations (Sect. 2.3.8.4)

$$\hat{b} = \frac{\begin{vmatrix}\sum y_i & \sum x_i\\ \sum x_i y_i & \sum x_i^2\end{vmatrix}}{\begin{vmatrix} n & \sum x_i\\ \sum x_i & \sum x_i^2\end{vmatrix}} = \frac{\left(\sum_i x_i^2 \cdot \sum_i y_i\right) - \left(\sum_i x_i \cdot \sum_i x_i y_i\right)}{n\sum_i x_i^2 - \left(\sum_i x_i\right)^2} \tag{6.34}$$

$$\hat{m} = \frac{\begin{vmatrix} n & \sum y_i\\ \sum x_i & \sum x_i y_i\end{vmatrix}}{\begin{vmatrix}\sum x_i^2 & \sum x_i\\ \sum x_i & n\end{vmatrix}} = \frac{n\sum_i x_i y_i - \left(\sum_i x_i \cdot \sum_i y_i\right)}{n\sum_i x_i^2 - \left(\sum_i x_i\right)^2} \tag{6.35}$$

Let's solve the model in Sect. 2.4.5 by using the approach presented here.
First, we need to rebuild the dataset we used

```
> s <- seq(0.1, 40, 0.25)
> pf <- c(rep(0.25, 40), rep(0.3, 30),
+         rep(0.2, 50), rep(0.15, 25),
+         rep(0.05, 15))
> pm <- c(rep(0.1, 15), rep(0.25, 20),
+         rep(0.25, 50), rep(0.25, 30),
+         rep(0.15, 45))
> set.seed(10)
> wage_f <- sample(s, 100, replace = T, prob = pf)
> wage_m <- sample(s, 100, replace = T, prob = pm)
> wage <- c(wage_f, wage_m)
> male <- c(rep(0, 100), rep(1, 100))
```

```
> wages <- data.frame(wage, male)
> head(wages)
   wage male
1  4.35    0
2  9.35    0
3  4.60    0
4 23.60    0
5 12.10    0
6 13.35    0
```

Next, let's estimate again the model by using (6.34) and (6.35)

```
> inter <- with(wages, ((sum(male^2)*sum(wage) -
+                        (sum(male)*sum(male*wage)))/
+                       (nrow(wages)*sum(male^2) -
+                          sum(male)^2)))
> inter
[1] 13.875
> male_hat <- with(wages, ((nrow(wages)*sum(male*wage) -
+                          sum(male)*sum(wage))/
+                         (nrow(wages)*sum(male^2) -
+                            sum(male)^2)))
> male_hat
[1] 4.835
```

Naturally, we obtained the same estimation.

What we obtained is the *regression line*, i.e., the line that best fits our observations. Let's plot the regression line by using `ggplot()`. Note that we use `geom_point()` to generate a scatter plot even though it is less interesting to observe because we have a dummy variable as independent variable. In addition, we generate the regression line with `geom_smooth()` (`stat_smooth()` is an alias). We choose `method = "lm"` for the linear regression. Note that the default formula in `geom_smooth()` is `formula = y ~x`. For example, if you think that your model exhibit a quadratic relationship between the dependent and the independent variable you can write `formula = y ~x + I(x^2)`. Another default value is `se = TRUE` that displays the confidence interval. You can remove it by setting equal to `FALSE`. The output is illustrated in Fig. 6.11.

```
> ggplot(wages, aes(x = male, y = wage)) +
+   geom_point() +
+   geom_smooth(method = "lm") +
+   theme_classic() +
+   xlab("male") + ylab("wage") +
+   annotate("label",
+            x = 0.25, y = 35,
```

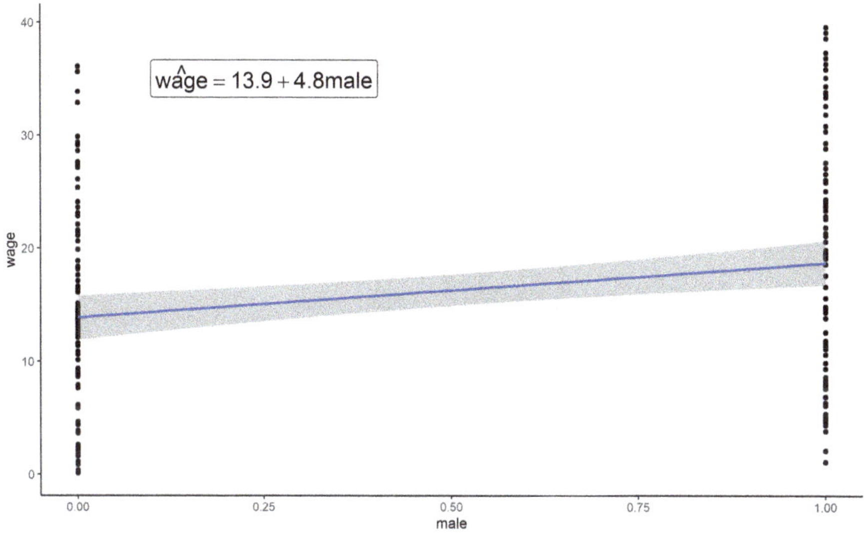

Fig. 6.11 Regression line

```
+                label = "hat(wage) == 13.9 + 4.8*male",
+                parse = TRUE, size = 6)
'geom_smooth()' using formula 'y ~ x'
```

In the exercise in Sect. 6.5.2 you are asked to apply the same approach to the estimation of the Cobb-Douglas production function as in Sect. 6.1.1.2.1.

6.4 Integration with Multiple Variables

We conclude this chapter with integration of a function of multiple variables. Since we are not covering any application with it, we will limit the examples to simple multiple definite integrals just to provide the flavour of the argument.

Example 6.4.1 Solve the following double integral

$$\int_0^1 \int_0^1 2xy^2\, dxdy$$

We proceed piece by piece, i.e. treating one variable as constant. Let's start by integrating over x

$$\int_0^1 2xy^2\, dx = x^2y^2\Big|_{x=0}^{x=1} = y^2$$

Then integrate over y

$$\int_0^1 y^2\,dy = \frac{1}{3}y^3\Big|_{y=0}^{y=1} = \frac{1}{3}$$

Example 6.4.2 Solve the following triple integral

$$\int_1^2 \int_1^2 \int_1^2 2x^2y^2z\,dxdydz$$

We proceed piece by piece, i.e. treating one variable as constant. Let's start by integrating over x

$$\int_1^2 2x^2y^2z\,dx = \frac{2}{3}x^3y^2z\Big|_{x=1}^{x=2} = \frac{14}{3}y^2z$$

Then integrate over y

$$\int_1^2 \frac{14}{3}y^2z\,dy = \frac{14}{3}\frac{1}{3}y^3z\Big|_{y=1}^{y=2} = \frac{98}{9}z$$

Finally, integrate over z

$$\int_1^2 \frac{98}{9}z\,dz = \frac{98}{18}z^2\Big|_{z=1}^{z=2} = \frac{49}{3}$$

Note that if in the previous examples we changed the order of integration we would reach the same conclusion. On the other hand, if one definite integral includes a variable in the bounds, we need to perform integration with a given order so that we remove the integral that has that variable in the bound before integrating over that variable. Let's see an example.

Example 6.4.3 Solve the following double integral

$$\int_0^1 \int_0^x 2xy^2\,dxdy$$

In this integral x appears in the upper bound. Therefore, first we integrate over y

$$\int_0^x 2xy^2\,dy = 2x\frac{1}{3}y^3\Big|_{y=0}^{y=x} = \frac{2}{3}x^4$$

After removing x from the bound, we can integrate over x

$$\int_0^1 \frac{2}{3}x^4\,dx = \frac{2}{15}x^5\Big|_{x=0}^{x=1} = \frac{2}{15}$$

6.5 Exercises

6.5.1 Exercise 1

Rebuild the `df` data frame from Sect. 6.1.1.2.1

```
> head(df)
    L     K
1 914 15126
2 962 17639
3 678 11979
4 513 22456
5 694 17325
6 925 11229
```

This time build `alpha` by randomly select 100 values from a range from 0.45 to 0.55 by increasing the sequence by 0.1 (set `set.seed(123)`). Compute `beta` as $1 - \alpha$. Then, compute again the total production with $A = 50$.

```
> head(df)
    L     K        Q
1 914 15126 213916.4
2 962 17639 238209.7
3 678 11979 164495.7
4 513 22456 140486.4
5 694 17325 203634.8
6 925 11229 142233.4
```

Estimate again the model with OLS. Store the result in `CD_reg2`.

Export the results of `CD_reg` and `CD_reg2` in one table as `text` with `stargazer()`. Compare the result of model 1 and model 2. What are now α, β, A?

```
Estimation of the Cobb-Douglas production function
==============================================
                       Dependent variable:
                   ---------------------------
                    natural log of production
                      Model 1        Model 2
                        (1)            (2)
----------------------------------------------
natural log of A    3.9120***      2.4462***
                     (0.0000)       (0.7115)

alpha               0.4500***      0.6737***
                     (0.0000)       (0.0758)
```

```
beta                    0.5500***        0.5354***
                        (0.0000)         (0.0493)

----------------------------------------------
Observations              100              100
R2                      1.0000           0.6575
==============================================
Note:              *p<0.1; **p<0.05; ***p<0.01
```

6.5.2 Exercise 2

Estimate again Model 2 by minimizing the sum of squared residuals. Use the `cramer()` function you wrote in the exercise in Sect. 2.5.4 to estimate the coefficients.

Your results for the `A` matrix and the `b` column vector (I am using the same notation we used for `cramer()`) should be

```
> A
         [,1]     [,2]      [,3]
[1,] 100.0000  658.335  970.3103
[2,] 658.3350 4338.179 6387.5232
[3,] 970.3103 6387.523 9424.7789
> b
[1]  1207.588  7952.559 11722.328
```

Next use the `cramer()` function to estimate the coefficients

```
> cramer(A, b)
       x1        x2        x3
2.4462265 0.6736610 0.5353657
```

Chapter 7
Constrained Optimization

In Chaps. 4 and 6, we learnt how to find the extrema of a function of one variable and of several variables, respectively. We defined those problems as *unconstrained* optimization problems. The reason why they are unconstrained optimization problems is because we said nothing about the value the variables can take. That is, the variables can take any value of the domain of the function.

Unfortunately, this possibility turns to be not very realistic in Economics. Indeed, this is explicitly implied by the often used definition of Economics as the science of optimal use of scarce resources. This is just another way to say that we are dealing with *constrained* optimization problems where the constraint is given by the scarcity of the resources. From a mathematical point of view, the constraint limits the domain and, consequently, the range of the objective function. This in turn means that generally the constrained maximum (minimum) is lower (greater) than the free maximum (minimum) even though in special circumstances constrained maximum (minimum) and free maximum (minimum) can be the same.

In Sect. 2.4.1, we showed that the combination of seven pizzas and seven cinema tickets $(7, 7)$ was not possible for the consumer because the cost was beyond her available budget. If the consumer had an unlimited budget, the optimal quantities would be determined by the extrema of the function. However, since it happens that the consumer has a limited budget, we should maximize the utility function (Sect. 3.8.2.1) *subject to* (*s.t.*) the budget constraint. This is the so-called *utility maximization* problem and it is one of the first problems a student of Microeconomics encounters (we will return to this problem in Sect. 7.4.1).

From a conceptual point of view, solving a constrained problem does not differ much from solving an unconstrained problem. First, we need to set the objective function. Then, the first order condition will determine the extrema and, finally, the second order conditions will identify if we found a minimum or a maximum. What it differs is the tool we need to use: the *Lagrangian* function.

M. Porto, *Introduction to Mathematics for Economics with R*,
https://doi.org/10.1007/978-3-031-05202-6_7

7.1 Equality Constraints

Suppose we have to maximize the following function of two variables $z = z(x, y) = xy$ and we are told that $g(x, y) = c = x + y = 4$, where c is the constant. Compared with the cases we dealt with in Chap. 6, we find that the two independent variables, x and y, are *constrained* in the values they can take because their sum must be equal to 4. This means that as x gets larger and larger, y needs to be smaller and smaller. Naturally, the reverse holds true as well. This means that the constraint is introducing a dependence between the two choice variables. Additionally, we can say that in this case the function we have to maximize is subject to a single equality constraint because of the equality sign.

We write this problem in general terms as follows

$$max \quad z = z(x, y) \tag{7.1}$$

$$s.t. \quad g(x, y) = c \tag{7.2}$$

7.1.1 First-Order Condition

The first step towards the solution of this problem is always the identification of the objective function. In this kind of problems the objective function is known as the *Lagrangian function*, $\mathcal{L}$, and it is built as follows

$$\mathcal{L} = z(x, y) + \lambda\,[c - g(x, y)] \tag{7.3}$$

where λ is known as the *Lagrange multiplier*.[1] In other words, we set up the objective function so that it is now a function of three variables $\mathcal{L} = \mathcal{L}(x, y, \lambda)$.

Next step consists in setting up the first order conditions, that is, in taking the partial derivative of $\mathcal{L}$ with respect to x, y, λ and setting equal to zero

$$\frac{\partial \mathcal{L}}{\partial x} = 0 \tag{7.4}$$

$$\frac{\partial \mathcal{L}}{\partial y} = 0 \tag{7.5}$$

$$\frac{\partial \mathcal{L}}{\partial \lambda} = 0 \tag{7.6}$$

[1] Note that you may find the Lagrangian set as $\mathcal{L} = z(x, y) - \lambda\,[g(x, y) - c]$. Both lead to the same optimal solution. Usually, in Economics the Lagrangian it is set up with $+\lambda$ for the economic meaning that we can attribute to the multiplier (refer to Sect. 7.1.3.2).

The solutions of this system of three equations in three unknowns x^*, y^*, λ^* will provide the stationary value $\mathcal{L}^*$.

Example 7.1.1 Let's follow these steps to solve the maximization problem

$$\begin{aligned} max \quad & z = xy \\ s.t. \quad & x + y = 4 \end{aligned} \tag{7.7}$$

Step 1
Set up the Lagrangian function.

The main point of this step is to rewrite the constrain as $c - g(x, y)$ and substitute it in the Lagrangian. In this case, we write $4 - x - y$. Consequently the Lagrangian is

$$\mathcal{L} = xy + \lambda(4 - x - y)$$

Step 2
First order condition

$$\begin{aligned} \frac{\partial \mathcal{L}}{\partial x} &= 0 \rightarrow y - \lambda = 0 \\ \frac{\partial \mathcal{L}}{\partial y} &= 0 \rightarrow x - \lambda = 0 \\ \frac{\partial \mathcal{L}}{\partial \lambda} &= 0 \rightarrow 4 - x - y = 0 \end{aligned} \tag{7.8}$$

Step 3
Solve the system of equations

$$y = \lambda$$

$$x = \lambda$$

Substitute the values for x and y in $\frac{\partial \mathcal{L}}{\partial \lambda} = 0$

$$4 - \lambda - \lambda = 0 \rightarrow 2\lambda = 4 \rightarrow \lambda^* = 2$$

and consequently

$$x^* = 2$$

$$y^* = 2.$$

Step 4
Find the stationary value

$$\mathcal{L}^* = x^* y^* + \lambda^*(4 - x^* - y^*) = 2 \cdot 2 + 2(4 - 2 - 2) = 4$$

7.1.2 *Multiple Equality Constraints*

Let's now suppose that the maximization of the function $z = xy$ is subject not only to the constraint $x + y = 4$ but also to the constraint $x = 1$. We are in the case of multiple constraints.

Adding a new constraint does not change the nature of the problem or the steps we have to follow. We just need to add another Lagrange multiplier that we can call μ. Therefore, the Lagrangian function will be a function of four variables in this case $\mathcal{L} = \mathcal{L}(x, y, \lambda, \mu)$.

Example 7.1.2 By following the previous steps we have

Step 1

$$\mathcal{L} = xy + \lambda(4 - x - y) + \mu(1 - x)$$

Step 2

$$\begin{aligned} \frac{\partial \mathcal{L}}{\partial x} &= 0 \rightarrow y - \lambda - \mu = 0 \\ \frac{\partial \mathcal{L}}{\partial y} &= 0 \rightarrow x - \lambda = 0 \\ \frac{\partial \mathcal{L}}{\partial \lambda} &= 0 \rightarrow 4 - x - y = 0 \\ \frac{\partial \mathcal{L}}{\partial \mu} &= 0 \rightarrow 1 - x = 0 \end{aligned} \tag{7.9}$$

Step 3
From the last equation we know that

$$x^* = 1$$

Consequently, by substituting it in the second equation we find that

$$\lambda^* = 1$$

Therefore, the first equation becomes

$$y = 1 + \mu$$

and the third equation

$$4 - 1 - 1 - \mu = 0 \rightarrow \mu^* = 2$$

and finally

$$y^* = 3$$

Step 4

$$\mathcal{L}^* = 1 \cdot 3 + 1(4 - 1 - 3) + 2(1 - 1) = 3$$

This was a very naive example of a multiple constraint problem. In fact, we could have found the solutions directly from the constraints without the need of setting up the Lagrangian function.

Generally, in a multiple constraint optimization problem the number of choice variables is greater than the number of constraints and the number of multipliers needed is equal to the number of constraints.

Let's consider another example.

Example 7.1.3 The function to be optimized is $z = 2wx + xy$ that is subject to two constraints, $x + y = 4$ and $w + x = -8$. Let's follow the same steps as before.

Step 1

$$\mathcal{L} = 2wx + xy + \lambda(4 - x - y) + \mu(-8 - w - x)$$

Step 2

$$\begin{aligned}
\frac{\partial \mathcal{L}}{\partial w} &= 0 \rightarrow 2x - \mu = 0 \\
\frac{\partial \mathcal{L}}{\partial x} &= 0 \rightarrow 2w + y - \lambda - \mu = 0 \\
\frac{\partial \mathcal{L}}{\partial y} &= 0 \rightarrow x - \lambda = 0 \\
\frac{\partial \mathcal{L}}{\partial \lambda} &= 0 \rightarrow 4 - x - y = 0 \\
\frac{\partial \mathcal{L}}{\partial \mu} &= 0 \rightarrow -8 - w - x = 0
\end{aligned} \tag{7.10}$$

Step 3
Since this is a large system of linear equations let's solve it by using the Gauss-Jordan elimination. We use the `echelon()` function from the `matlib` package (Sect. 2.3.7.2).

First, let's take the constant to the right-hand side of the equations.

$$\begin{aligned}
2x - \mu &= 0 \\
2w + y - \lambda - \mu &= 0 \\
x - \lambda &= 0 \\
-x - y &= -4 \\
-w - x &= 8
\end{aligned} \tag{7.11}$$

Second, let's write it in matrix form

$$\begin{bmatrix} 0 & 2 & 0 & 0 & -1 \\ 2 & 0 & 1 & -1 & -1 \\ 0 & 1 & 0 & -1 & 0 \\ 0 & -1 & -1 & 0 & 0 \\ -1 & -1 & 0 & 0 & 0 \end{bmatrix} \begin{bmatrix} w \\ x \\ y \\ \lambda \\ \mu \end{bmatrix} = \begin{bmatrix} 0 \\ 0 \\ 0 \\ -4 \\ 8 \end{bmatrix}$$

```
> A <- matrix(c(0, 2, 0, 0, -1,
+               2, 0, 1, -1, -1,
+               0, 1, 0, -1, 0,
+               0, -1, -1, 0, 0,
+               -1, -1, 0, 0, 0),
+             nrow = 5,
+             ncol = 5,
+             byrow = T)
> A
     [,1] [,2] [,3] [,4] [,5]
[1,]    0    2    0    0   -1
[2,]    2    0    1   -1   -1
[3,]    0    1    0   -1    0
[4,]    0   -1   -1    0    0
[5,]   -1   -1    0    0    0
> b <- c(0, 0, 0, -4, 8)
> echelon(A, b)
     [,1] [,2] [,3] [,4] [,5] [,6]
[1,]    1    0    0    0    0   -6
[2,]    0    1    0    0    0   -2
[3,]    0    0    1    0    0    6
[4,]    0    0    0    1    0   -2
[5,]    0    0    0    0    1   -4
```

Therefore, the solutions are

$$w^* = -6 \quad x^* = -2 \quad y^* = 6 \quad \lambda^* = -2 \quad \mu^* = -4$$

Step 4

$$\mathcal{L}^* = 2(-6)(-2) + -2 \cdot 6 + -2(4 + 2 - 6) + -4(-8 + 6 + 2) = 12$$

7.1.3 *Lagrange Multiplier*

7.1.3.1 A Mathematical Interpretation

In all three examples, you may have noticed that when we compute $\mathcal{L}^*$ the values in the parenthesis multiplied by the Lagrange multipliers become zero. Consequently, regardless the value of the Lagrange multipliers, the constrained terms will vanish at the optimal values of the choice variables.

This is a consequence of the first-order condition. In fact, by adding the Lagrange multiplier to the objective function and by considering it as a choice variable, its first-order condition (7.6) is just a restatement of the constraint. Therefore, by setting the constraint equal to 0, the solutions of the system of equations will make the constraint vanish.

Now let's approach the optimization problem (7.1) from a different perspective.

Let's take the gradient of the Lagrangian function and set equal to the zero vector

$$\nabla \mathcal{L} = \mathbf{0} \tag{7.12}$$

that is

$$\begin{bmatrix} \frac{\partial \mathcal{L}}{\partial x_1} \\ \frac{\partial \mathcal{L}}{\partial x_2} \\ \frac{\partial \mathcal{L}}{\partial \lambda} \end{bmatrix} = \begin{bmatrix} 0 \\ 0 \\ 0 \end{bmatrix}$$

This in turn means that

$$\frac{\partial \mathcal{L}}{\partial x_i} = 0 \rightarrow \frac{\partial z}{x_i} = \lambda \frac{\partial g}{\partial x_i}, \quad i = \{1, 2\}$$

We can rewrite it as follows

$$\nabla z(x_1^*, x_2^*) = \lambda^* \nabla g(x_1^*, x_2^*) \tag{7.13}$$

that is, the gradients are scalar multiples of each other, where the multiplier is the Lagrange multiplier.

Let's see these concepts with a new example.

Example 7.1.4 Let's optimize the function $z = xy + 2x$ subject to $2x + 5y = 90$.

Step 1

$$\mathcal{L} = xy + 2x + \lambda(90 - 2x - 5y)$$

Step 2

$$\begin{aligned} \frac{\partial \mathcal{L}}{\partial x} &= y + 2 - 2\lambda = 0 \rightarrow y = 2\lambda - 2 \\ \frac{\partial \mathcal{L}}{\partial y} &= x - 5\lambda = 0 \rightarrow x = 5\lambda \\ \frac{\partial \mathcal{L}}{\partial \lambda} &= 90 - 2x - 5y = 0 \end{aligned} \tag{7.14}$$

Step 3

$$y = 2\lambda - 2$$

$$x = 5\lambda$$

$$90 - 2(5\lambda) - 5(2\lambda - 2) = 0 \rightarrow \lambda^* = 5$$

and consequently

$$x^* = 25$$

$$y^* = 8$$

Step 4
We know that at the optimized values the constraint will vanish. In fact, $90 - (2 \cdot 25) - (5 \cdot 8) = 0$. Therefore, we just need x^* and y^* to find the stationary value of $\mathcal{L}$

$$\mathcal{L}^* = (25 \cdot 8) + (2 \cdot 25) + 0 = 250$$

This in turn implies that $z^* = \mathcal{L}^*$. All these steps turned a constrained optimization problem in two variables, $z(x, y)$, $s.t.$ $g(x, y)$, into an unconstrained optimization problem in three variables, $\mathcal{L}(x, y, \lambda)$.

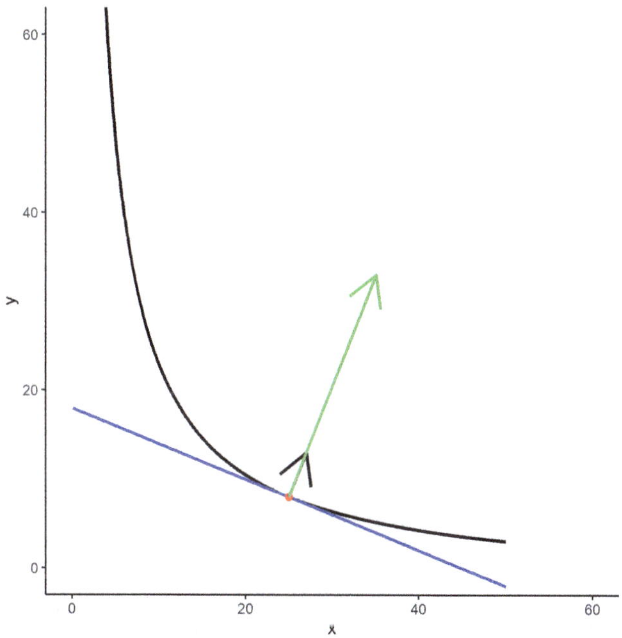

Fig. 7.1 Constrained optimization and gradient vectors (1)

Step 4.5
In this step, we verify (7.13).

$$\begin{bmatrix} y+2 \\ x \end{bmatrix} = \lambda \begin{bmatrix} 2 \\ 5 \end{bmatrix}$$

By evaluating it at x^*, y^*, λ^*

$$\begin{bmatrix} 10 \\ 25 \end{bmatrix} = 5 \begin{bmatrix} 2 \\ 5 \end{bmatrix}$$

Figure 7.1 represents the geometric solution of the problem in Example 7.1.4.[2] As expected, it shows that the constrained extremum is located at the tangent point with the constraint, that the gradient vectors are multiple of each other, and that the gradient vectors are perpendicular to the level curve (refer to an advanced textbook for insights about the related theorem).

Example 7.1.5 Now let's assume that the constant in the constraint is increased to 130 so that $z(x, y) = xy + 2x$ is subject to $g(x, y) = 2x + 5y = 130$.

[2] The code used to generate Fig. 7.1, 7.2, and 7.3 is available in the Appendix F.

Step 1

$$\mathcal{L} = xy + 2x + \lambda(130 - 2x - 5y)$$

Step 2
From the objective function it is evident that the first-order conditions for x and y are the same as in Example 7.1.4. On the other hand, the first-order condition with respect to λ is changed by the new constant

$$\frac{\partial \mathcal{L}}{\partial \lambda} = 130 - 2x - 5y = 0$$

Step 3
Let's substitute the values for x and y we found in the previous example in this constraint (you can verify they are the same)

$$130 - 2(5\lambda) - 5(2\lambda - 2) = 0 \rightarrow 140 - 20\lambda = 0 \rightarrow \lambda^* = 7$$

Consequently,

$$x^* = 35$$

$$y^* = 12$$

Step 4

$$\mathcal{L}^* = 35 \cdot 12 + 2 \cdot 35 = 490$$

Step 4.5

$$\begin{bmatrix} y + 2 \\ x \end{bmatrix} = \lambda \begin{bmatrix} 2 \\ 5 \end{bmatrix}$$

By evaluating it at x^*, y^*, λ^*

$$\begin{bmatrix} 14 \\ 35 \end{bmatrix} = 7 \begin{bmatrix} 2 \\ 5 \end{bmatrix}$$

Let's add the geometric representation of this problem to the plot in Fig. 7.1.

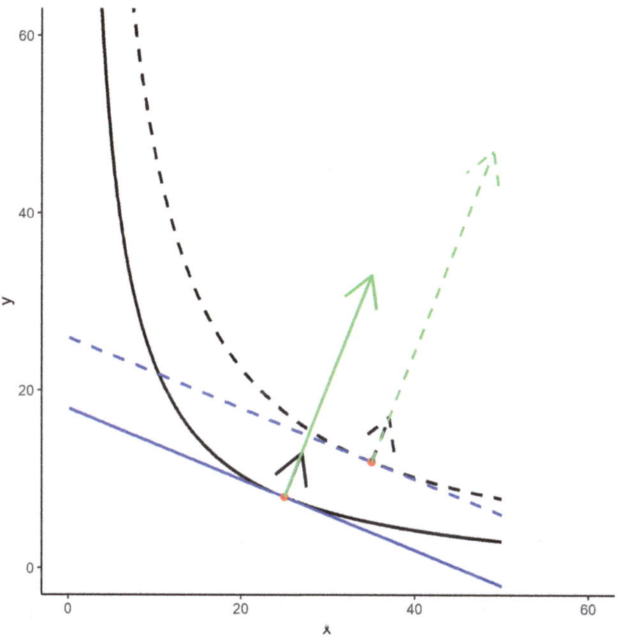

Fig. 7.2 Constrained optimization and gradient vectors (2)

In Example 7.1.5, the increased value of the constant in the constraint, from 90 to 130, relaxed the constraint. Figure 7.2 indicates how the optimal solution is affected by this change in the value of the constant in the constraint. The measure of this effect is captured by the Lagrange multiplier.

Therefore, we could ask how the optimal value changes with an infinitesimal change in the constant. That is, we do not treat c as a constant anymore. Additionally, by thinking how the optimal solution changes with a change in c, we can treat x^*, y^*, and λ^* as implicit functions of the constraint parameter c. Since at the optimal value $\mathcal{L}^*$ depends on x^*, y^*, and λ^*, we can rewrite $\mathcal{L}^*$ as follows

$$\mathcal{L}^* = z(x^*(c), y^*(c)) + \lambda^* \left[c - g(x^*(c), y^*(c))\right] \tag{7.15}$$

that is, we can consider $\mathcal{L}^*$ to be only function of c. Consequently, by total differentiating (Sect. 6.2.2) $\mathcal{L}^*$ with respect to c we find

$$\frac{d\mathcal{L}^*}{dc} = \frac{\partial z}{\partial x^*}\frac{dx^*}{dc} + \frac{\partial z}{\partial y^*}\frac{dy^*}{dc} + \left[c - g(x^*(c), y^*(c))\right]\frac{d\lambda^*}{dc} + \lambda^*\left(1 - \frac{\partial g}{\partial x^*}\frac{dx^*}{dc} - \frac{\partial g}{\partial y^*}\frac{dy^*}{dc}\right)$$

Let's rearrange it by collecting the terms with the same $\frac{dx^*}{dc}$ and $\frac{dy^*}{dc}$

$$\frac{d\mathcal{L}^*}{dc} = \left(\frac{\partial z}{\partial x^*} - \lambda^* \frac{\partial g}{\partial x^*}\right)\frac{dx^*}{dc} + \left(\frac{\partial z}{\partial y^*} - \lambda^* \frac{\partial g}{\partial y^*}\right)\frac{dy^*}{dc} + \left[c - g(x^*(c), y^*(c))\right]\frac{d\lambda^*}{dc} + \lambda^*$$

Since the only term that does not vanish is λ^*, we can simplify it to

$$\frac{d\mathcal{L}^*}{dc} = \lambda^* \tag{7.16}$$

meaning that the Lagrange multiplier measures the effect of an infinitesimal change in the constant of the constraint on the optimal solution.

7.1.3.2 An Economic Interpretation

In Sect. 7.1.3.1, we have discussed about the Lagrange multiplier in general terms. However, we can attribute a special meaning in Economics to the result from (7.16). The Lagrange multiplier at the optimal solution is known in Economics as the *shadow price*, representing the infinitesimal change in the objective function due to an infinitesimal change in the constant of the constraint. For example, in the consumer choice problem the Lagrange multiplier is interpreted as the marginal utility of income (the interested reader may refer to Dixit (1990) for a detailed explanations of shadow prices).

7.1.4 Second-Order Conditions

Let's continue with the analysis of the constrained optimization problem.

In the previous examples, we found the extrema of the constrained function. The next step consists in determining if the extrema correspond to a maximum or a minimum. As for the unconstrained optimization problem, we need to verify the second-order conditions. However, for the constrained optimization problem we need to introduced a new tool, the *bordered Hessian*, $|\overline{H}|$.

What we need to set up the bordered Hessian is the Hessian of the Lagrangian function (refer to Sect. 6.2.1.3 to review the Hessian matrix) and the first partial derivatives of the constraint.

Let's start by considering the case of a function of two variables, $z(x, y)$, subject to a single constraint, $g(x, y) = c$. In this case, the bordered Hessian will take the following form

$$|\overline{H}| = \left|\begin{array}{c:cc} 0 & \frac{\partial g}{\partial x} & \frac{\partial g}{\partial y} \\ \hdashline \frac{\partial g}{\partial x} & & \\ & H & \\ \frac{\partial g}{\partial x} & & \end{array}\right| \tag{7.17}$$

The partitioned matrix (7.17) gives an idea of why it is called bordered Hessian. Let's continue Example 7.1.1.

Step 5

Set-up of the bordered Hessian.

Let's populate the first row by taking the partial derivative of g with respect to x and y

$$|\overline{H}| = \left|\begin{array}{c:cc} 0 & 1 & 1 \\ \hdashline & & \\ & & \end{array}\right|$$

You may have already noticed that we are working with a symmetric matrix. Consequently, the first column becomes

$$|\overline{H}| = \left|\begin{array}{c:cc} 0 & 1 & 1 \\ \hdashline 1 & & \\ 1 & & \end{array}\right|$$

Finally, let's add the Hessian. From the first-order condition we can easily see that

$$|\overline{H}| = \left|\begin{array}{c:cc} 0 & 1 & 1 \\ \hdashline 1 & 0 & 1 \\ 1 & 1 & 0 \end{array}\right|$$

Step 6

Compute the determinant of the bordered Hessian.

By computing the determinant we find that $|\overline{H}| = 2$.

```
> bH <- matrix(c(0, 1, 1,
+                1, 0, 1,
+                1, 1, 0),
+              nrow = 3,
+              ncol = 3,
+              byrow = T)
> bH
     [,1] [,2] [,3]
[1,]    0    1    1
[2,]    1    0    1
[3,]    1    1    0
> det(bH)
[1] 2
```

Since $|\overline{H}| > 0$, the value $z^* = 4$ is a maximum. On the other hand, if $|\overline{H}| < 0$, the stationary value would be a minimum.

The bordered Hessian for the n-variable case is built as in the two variables case. For example, given the function $z(w, x, y)$ subject to $g(w, x, y) = c$, the bordered Hessian takes the following form

$$|\overline{H}| = \begin{vmatrix} 0 & \vdots & \frac{\partial g}{\partial w} & \frac{\partial g}{\partial x} & \frac{\partial g}{\partial y} \\ \cdots & & \cdots & \cdots & \cdots \\ \frac{\partial g}{\partial w} & \vdots & & & \\ \frac{\partial g}{\partial x} & \vdots & & H & \\ \frac{\partial g}{\partial y} & \vdots & & & \end{vmatrix} \tag{7.18}$$

Naturally, this can be extended to n-variables.

The main difference with the previous case is that we need to analyse the bordered leading principal minors. In this example, we would have

$$|\overline{H_2}| = \begin{vmatrix} 0 & \vdots & \frac{\partial g}{\partial w} & \frac{\partial g}{\partial x} \\ \cdots & & \cdots & \cdots \\ \frac{\partial g}{\partial w} & \vdots & & \\ \frac{\partial g}{\partial x} & \vdots & & H \end{vmatrix}$$

and

$$|\overline{H_3}| = \begin{vmatrix} 0 & \vdots & \frac{\partial g}{\partial w} & \frac{\partial g}{\partial x} & \frac{\partial g}{\partial y} \\ \cdots & \cdots & \cdots & \cdots & \cdots \\ \frac{\partial g}{\partial w} & \vdots & & & \\ \frac{\partial g}{\partial x} & \vdots & & H & \\ \frac{\partial g}{\partial y} & \vdots & & & \end{vmatrix}$$

where in this case $|\overline{H_3}| = |\overline{H}|$. Consequently, with n-variables we would have $|\overline{H_n}| = |\overline{H}|$.

Note that $|\overline{H_2}|$ refers to two variables, $|\overline{H_3}|$ refers to three variables, and so on. This means that $|\overline{H_1}|$ refers to one variable. This last case, in turn, means that $|\overline{H_1}| < 0$ because in the determinant formula $ad - bc$, $ad = 0$ and c, d are the same. Therefore, the second-order sufficient condition for a maximum is given by $|\overline{H_2}| > 0$; $|\overline{H_3}| < 0$; $|\overline{H_4}| > 0$; ... and for a minimum is given by $|\overline{H_2}|, |\overline{H_3}|, \ldots, |\overline{H_n}| < 0$.

In the case of multiple constraints, the border around the Hessian becomes thicker. Given the function $z(w, x, y)$ and two constraints $g(w, x, y) = c$ and $h(w, x, y) = k$, the bordered Hessian takes the following form

$$|\overline{H}| = \begin{vmatrix} 0 & 0 & \vdots & \frac{\partial g}{\partial w} & \frac{\partial g}{\partial x} & \frac{\partial g}{\partial y} \\ 0 & 0 & \vdots & \frac{\partial h}{\partial w} & \frac{\partial h}{\partial x} & \frac{\partial h}{\partial y} \\ \cdots & \cdots & \cdots & \cdots & \cdots & \cdots \\ \frac{\partial g}{\partial w} & \frac{\partial h}{\partial w} & \vdots & & & \\ \frac{\partial g}{\partial x} & \frac{\partial h}{\partial x} & \vdots & & H & \\ \frac{\partial g}{\partial y} & \frac{\partial h}{\partial y} & \vdots & & & \end{vmatrix} \tag{7.19}$$

Naturally, this extends to the case with m-constraints. In the multiple constraint case as well we need to evaluate the bordered leading principal minors. The sufficient condition for a maximum is that the bordered leading principal minors alternate in sign, with the sign of $|\overline{H_{m+1}}|$ being that of $(-1)^{m+1}$, while the sufficient condition for a minimum is that the bordered leading principal minors take the same sign of $(-1)^m$.

Let's continue Example 7.1.3.

Step 5

Let's populate the bordered Hessian step by step. First, let's take the partial derivative of the first constraint $x + y = 4$ in the first row

$$|\overline{H}| = \left|\begin{array}{cc|ccc} 0 & 0 & 0 & 1 & 1 \\ & & & & \\ \hline & & & & \\ & & & & \\ & & & & \end{array}\right|$$

Next, let's take the partial derivative of the second constraint $w + x = -8$ in the second row

$$|\overline{H}| = \left|\begin{array}{cc|ccc} 0 & 0 & 0 & 1 & 1 \\ 0 & 0 & 1 & 1 & 0 \\ \hline & & & & \\ & & & & \\ & & & & \end{array}\right|$$

Consequently, the first two columns are

$$|\overline{H}| = \left|\begin{array}{cc|ccc} 0 & 0 & 0 & 1 & 1 \\ 0 & 0 & 1 & 1 & 0 \\ \hline 0 & 1 & & & \\ 1 & 1 & & & \\ 1 & 0 & & & \end{array}\right|$$

Finally, we compute the Hessian of the Lagrangian

$$|\overline{H}| = \left|\begin{array}{cc|ccc} 0 & 0 & 0 & 1 & 1 \\ 0 & 0 & 1 & 1 & 0 \\ \hline 0 & 1 & 0 & 2 & 0 \\ 1 & 1 & 2 & 0 & 1 \\ 1 & 0 & 0 & 1 & 0 \end{array}\right|$$

Step 6

We compute the bordered leading principal minors. I use the `bLPM()` function that is a modified version of the `LPM()` function. The code for this function is left as exercise.

```
> bH <- matrix(c(0, 0, 0, 1, 1,
+                0, 0, 1, 1, 0,
+                0, 1, 0, 2, 0,
+                1, 1, 2, 0, 1,
+                1, 0, 0, 1, 0),
+              nrow = 5,
+              ncol = 5,
+              byrow = TRUE)
> bH
     [,1] [,2] [,3] [,4] [,5]
[1,]    0    0    0    1    1
[2,]    0    0    1    1    0
[3,]    0    1    0    2    0
[4,]    1    1    2    0    1
[5,]    1    0    0    1    0
> bLPM(bH, m = 2)
[1]  1 -6
```

where $|\overline{H_{m+1}}|$ is $|\overline{H_3}| = -6$ with the sign as $(-1)^{2+1} \rightarrow -$.

Consequently, the value $z^* = 12$ is a maximum.

7.2 Inequality Constraints

Optimization problems with inequality constraints is the last topic of Part I. Since this topic is more complex than optimization with equality constraints, in this book we limit the exposition to an introductory presentation of the topic, to the steps of the solution of a simple example, and to a practical setting and solution of the problem with **R**.

Suppose that now the problem is the following

$$max \quad z = z(x, y) \tag{7.20}$$

$$s.t. \quad h = h(x, y) \leq c \tag{7.21}$$

When we worked with the equality case, we found that the constrained optimal solution lied on the boundary of the constraint, at the tangent point with the function. By working with inequality constraints such as (7.21), the constrained maximum may lie on the boundary of the constraint or below the boundary of the constraint (in the interior of the constraint set). In the first case we say that the constraint is *binding* (or *active*) while in the second case we say that the constraint is not *binding* (or *inactive*). Let's set the Lagrangian as always for further insight on this last point.

$$\mathcal{L} = z(x, y) + \lambda [c - h(x, y)]$$

If we assume that the constraint is not binding, then $\lambda = 0$. In this way the constraint function vanishes. On the other hand, if we assume that the constraint is binding, then $\lambda \geq 0$ and $c - h(x, y) = 0$. In this way as well, the constraint function vanishes. In other words, we need that

$$\lambda \cdot [c - h(x, y)] = 0 \tag{7.22}$$

that is or $\lambda = 0$ or $c - h(x, y) = 0$ (in rare case it may happen that both are zero). Condition such as (7.22) is called *complementary slackness condition.*

7.2.1 Kuhn-Tucker Conditions

Let's suppose we want to maximize

$$\begin{aligned} max \quad & z = z(x, y) \\ s.t. \quad & g = g(x, y) \leq c \end{aligned} \tag{7.23}$$

where the choice variables are non-negative, i.e. $x, y \geq 0$.

We can solve this kind of problems with inequality constraints by relying on the *Kuhn-Tucker conditions.* Given the Lagrangian

$$\mathcal{L} = z(x, y) + \lambda [c - g(x, y)]$$

the Kuhn-Tucker conditions in terms of the Lagrangian are

$$\frac{\partial \mathcal{L}}{\partial x} \leq 0 \quad x \geq 0 \quad \text{and} \quad x\frac{\partial \mathcal{L}}{\partial x} = 0 \ \left[\text{complementary slackness}\right] \tag{7.24}$$

$$\frac{\partial \mathcal{L}}{\partial y} \leq 0 \quad y \geq 0 \quad \text{and} \quad y\frac{\partial \mathcal{L}}{\partial y} = 0 \ \left[\text{complementary slackness}\right] \tag{7.25}$$

$$\frac{\partial \mathcal{L}}{\partial \lambda} \geq 0 \quad \lambda \geq 0 \quad \text{and} \quad \lambda\frac{\partial \mathcal{L}}{\partial \lambda} = 0 \ \left[\text{complementary slackness}\right] \tag{7.26}$$

The solution of this kind of problems is not immediate as in the equality case but require some trials and errors. Let's consider an example to see concretely how to tackle it.

Example 7.2.1

$$\begin{aligned} max \quad & z = xy \\ s.t. \quad & 10x + 5y \leq 100 \end{aligned} \tag{7.27}$$

with $x, y \geq 0$.

Step 1
Set the Lagrangian

$$\mathcal{L} = xy + \lambda(100 - 10x - 5y)$$

Step 2
Find acceptable solutions

Step 2 is where we depart from the equality case. We have to start with an assumption and test if the outcome satisfy the Kuhn-Tucker conditions as described by (7.24)–(7.26). If they violate any of them we have to start again from another assumption and check again if the results satisfy the Kuhn-Tucker conditions. In other words, unless the result based on the assumption satisfy the Kuhn-Tucker conditions we have to start again. Naturally, if the solutions do not violate any of the Kuhn-Tucker conditions we have found the solutions that maximize the function z. Let's consider the first assumption.

Assumption 1: the constraint is not binding, i.e. $\lambda = 0$.
Consequently,

$$\frac{\partial \mathcal{L}}{\partial x} = y = 0$$

$$\frac{\partial \mathcal{L}}{\partial y} = x = 0$$

The solutions $x, y = 0$ imply that $z^* = 0$. These solutions can be ruled out since they do not make much sense given the nature of the problem. In general, the mathematical nature of the function or the economic nature of the problem can help us to rule out some possible assumptions.[3]

Assumption 2: the constraint is binding, i.e. $100 - 10x - 5y = 0$.
Consequently,

[3] The interested reader may refer to Dixit (1990) for detailed examples.

$$
\begin{aligned}
\frac{\partial \mathcal{L}}{\partial x} &= y - 10\lambda = 0 \\
\frac{\partial \mathcal{L}}{\partial y} &= x - 5\lambda = 0 \\
\frac{\partial \mathcal{L}}{\partial \lambda} &= 100 - 10x - 5y = 0
\end{aligned}
\tag{7.28}
$$

By solving this system we find that $\lambda^* = 1$, $x^* = 5$, and $y^* = 10$. Let's check if these solutions satisfy the Kuhn-Tucker conditions.

$$
\begin{aligned}
\frac{\partial \mathcal{L}}{\partial x} &\leq 0 \rightarrow 10 - 10 = 0 \quad \checkmark \\
\frac{\partial \mathcal{L}}{\partial y} &\leq 0 \rightarrow 5 - 5 = 0 \quad \checkmark \\
\frac{\partial \mathcal{L}}{\partial \lambda} &\geq 0 \rightarrow 100 - 50 - 50 = 0 \quad \checkmark \\
x &\geq 0 \rightarrow x = 5 \quad \checkmark \\
y &\geq 0 \rightarrow y = 10 \quad \checkmark \\
\lambda &\geq 0 \rightarrow \lambda = 1 \quad \checkmark
\end{aligned}
\tag{7.29}
$$

and consequently

$$
\begin{aligned}
x\frac{\partial \mathcal{L}}{\partial x} &= 0 \quad \checkmark \\
y\frac{\partial \mathcal{L}}{\partial y} &= 0 \quad \checkmark \\
\lambda\frac{\partial \mathcal{L}}{\partial \lambda} &= 0 \quad \checkmark
\end{aligned}
\tag{7.30}
$$

Therefore, $x^* = 5$ and $y^* = 10$ are acceptable solutions for this problem.

In the case of multiple constraints

$$
\begin{aligned}
max \quad & z = z(x, y) \\
s.t. \quad & g = g(x, y) \leq c \\
& h = h(x, y) \leq k
\end{aligned}
\tag{7.31}
$$

and with $x, y \geq 0$, the Lagrangian is

$$
\mathcal{L} = z(x, y) + \lambda\,[c - g(x, y)] + \mu\,[k - h(x, y)]
$$

The Kuhn-Tucker conditions in terms of the Lagrangian are

$$\frac{\partial \mathcal{L}}{\partial x} \leq 0 \quad x \geq 0 \quad \text{and} \quad x\frac{\partial \mathcal{L}}{\partial x} = 0 \ \left[\text{complementary slackness}\right] \tag{7.32}$$

$$\frac{\partial \mathcal{L}}{\partial y} \leq 0 \quad y \geq 0 \quad \text{and} \quad y\frac{\partial \mathcal{L}}{\partial y} = 0 \ \left[\text{complementary slackness}\right] \tag{7.33}$$

$$\frac{\partial \mathcal{L}}{\partial \lambda} \geq 0 \quad \lambda \geq 0 \quad \text{and} \quad \lambda\frac{\partial \mathcal{L}}{\partial \lambda} = 0 \ \left[\text{complementary slackness}\right] \tag{7.34}$$

$$\frac{\partial \mathcal{L}}{\partial \mu} \geq 0 \quad \mu \geq 0 \quad \text{and} \quad \mu\frac{\partial \mathcal{L}}{\partial \mu} = 0 \ \left[\text{complementary slackness}\right] \tag{7.35}$$

Example 7.2.2

$$max \quad z = xy$$

$$s.t. \quad x + y \leq 40$$

and

$$s.t. \quad x \leq 10$$

with $x, y \geq 0$.

Step 1

$$\mathcal{L} = xy + \lambda(40 - x - y) + \mu(10 - x)$$

Step 2
In this problem, we can rule out both $x, y = 0$ because this would imply $z^* = 0$. Let's consider the first assumption.

Assumption 1: the first constraint is binding but the second constraint is not binding, i.e. $\mu = 0$
Consequently,

$$\frac{\partial \mathcal{L}}{\partial x} = y - \lambda = 0$$

$$\frac{\partial \mathcal{L}}{\partial y} = x - \lambda = 0$$

$$\frac{\partial \mathcal{L}}{\partial \lambda} = 40 - x - y = 0$$

By solving this system we find that $\lambda = 20$, $x = 20$, $y = 20$. However, $x = 20$ violates the second constraint that states that $x \leq 10$. Consequently, these solutions are not feasible and we have to start with another assumption.

Assumption 2: the first constraint and the second constraint are binding.

Then, the second constraint implies that $x = 10$. Consequently, from the first constraint $y = 30$. Additionally, the complementary slackness in (7.32) and (7.33) state that $x\frac{\mathcal{L}}{\partial x} = 0$ and $y\frac{\mathcal{L}}{\partial y} = 0$. That is, $10 \cdot \frac{\mathcal{L}}{\partial x} = 0$ and $30 \cdot \frac{\mathcal{L}}{\partial y} = 0$ to be true require, respectively, that

$$\frac{\partial \mathcal{L}}{\partial x} = y - \lambda - \mu = 0$$

$$\frac{\partial \mathcal{L}}{\partial y} = x - \lambda = 0$$

By replacing $x = 10$ and $y = 30$ we find that $\lambda = 10$ and $\mu = 20$. Let's check if these solutions satisfy the Kuhn-Tucker conditions.

$$\begin{aligned}
\frac{\partial \mathcal{L}}{\partial x} &\leq 0 \rightarrow 30 - 10 - 20 = 0 \quad \checkmark \\
\frac{\partial \mathcal{L}}{\partial y} &\leq 0 \rightarrow 10 - 10 = 0 \quad \checkmark \\
\frac{\partial \mathcal{L}}{\partial \lambda} &\geq 0 \rightarrow 40 - 10 - 30 = 0 \quad \checkmark \\
\frac{\partial \mathcal{L}}{\partial \mu} &\geq 0 \rightarrow 10 - 10 = 0 \quad \checkmark \\
x &\geq 0 \rightarrow x = 10 \quad \checkmark \\
y &\geq 0 \rightarrow y = 30 \quad \checkmark \\
\lambda &\geq 0 \rightarrow \lambda = 10 \quad \checkmark \\
\mu &\geq 0 \rightarrow \mu = 20 \quad \checkmark
\end{aligned} \tag{7.36}$$

and consequently

$$\begin{aligned}
x\frac{\partial \mathcal{L}}{\partial x} &= 0 \quad \checkmark \\
y\frac{\partial \mathcal{L}}{\partial y} &= 0 \quad \checkmark \\
\lambda\frac{\partial \mathcal{L}}{\partial \lambda} &= 0 \quad \checkmark \\
\mu\frac{\partial \mathcal{L}}{\partial \mu} &= 0 \quad \checkmark
\end{aligned} \tag{7.37}$$

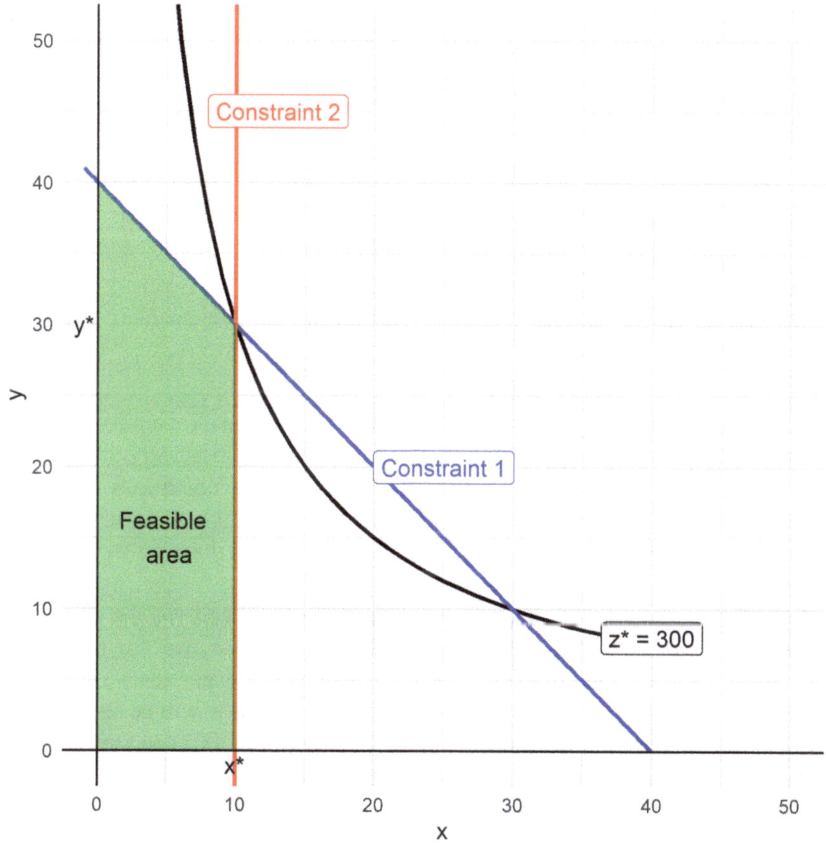

Fig. 7.3 Feasible area in the Kuhn-Tucker problem (Example 7.2.2)

Therefore, $x^* = 10$ and $y^* = 30$ are acceptable solutions for this problem.

Figure 7.3 gives a graphical representation of Example 7.2.2.

Let's now express the Kuhn-Tucker conditions in terms of the Lagrangian for a general case with n-variables and m-constraints. Given the following Lagrangian function

$$\mathcal{L} = f(x_1, x_2, \ldots, x_n) + \sum_{i=1}^{m} \lambda_i \left[(c_i - g_i(x_1, x_2, \ldots, x_n)\right]$$

the Kuhn-Tucker conditions in terms of the Lagrangian for a maximization problem are expressed as follows

$$\frac{\partial \mathcal{L}}{\partial x_i} \leq 0 \quad x_i \geq 0 \quad \text{and} \quad x_i \frac{\partial \mathcal{L}}{\partial x_i} = 0 \ \left[\text{complementary slackness}\right] \tag{7.38}$$

$$\frac{\partial \mathcal{L}}{\partial \lambda_j} \geq 0 \quad \lambda_j \geq 0 \quad \text{and} \quad \lambda_j \frac{\partial \mathcal{L}}{\partial \lambda_j} = 0 \text{ [complementary slackness]} \tag{7.39}$$

while the Kuhn-Tucker conditions in terms of the Lagrangian for a minimization problem are expressed as follows[4]

$$\frac{\partial \mathcal{L}}{\partial x_i} \geq 0 \quad x_i \geq 0 \quad \text{and} \quad x_i \frac{\partial \mathcal{L}}{\partial x_i} = 0 \text{ [complementary slackness]} \tag{7.40}$$

$$\frac{\partial \mathcal{L}}{\partial \lambda_j} \leq 0 \quad \lambda_j \geq 0 \quad \text{and} \quad \lambda_j \frac{\partial \mathcal{L}}{\partial \lambda_j} = 0 \text{ [complementary slackness]} \tag{7.41}$$

where $i = 1, 2, \ldots, n$ and $j = 1, 2, \ldots, m$.

Before concluding this section we need to touch upon some regularity conditions known as the *constraint qualification*. The issue is that boundary irregularities at the optimal solution may invalidate the Kuhn-Tucker conditions. Therefore, the fulfillment of the Kuhn-Tucker conditions depends on the satisfaction of the constraint qualification, that consists in certain restrictions on the constraint functions.

Additionally, to be noted, the constraint qualification concerns the constrained optimization with equality constraints as well. In our case, we did not need to worry about the constraint qualification because in all our examples we used linear constraints. With linear constraints the constraint qualification will be automatically satisfied. The reader may refer to Chiang and Wainwright (2005) and to Simon and Blume (1994) to investigate this topic in details.

7.3 Constrained Optimization with R

A comprehensive list of packages for solving optimization problems in **R** is available at the CRAN website: https://cran.r-project.org/web/views/Optimization.html. In this section we will use functions from the `lpSolve` package, the `nloptr` package and the `constrOptim()` function.

The `lpSolve` package is applied to linear programming problems, that is an optimization problem with a linear objective function and linear constraints. For example,

[4] Other textbooks may introduce constrained optimization with inequalities in general terms without using the Kuhn-Tucker formulation. In that case, pay attention to how the signs and the inequalities are formulated. We will return on the signs and the inequalities when we solve the constrained optimization problems with **R** in Sect. 7.3.

$$
\begin{aligned}
max \quad & 15x + 22y \\
s.t. \quad & 11x + 17y \leq 5400 \\
& 23x + 19y \leq 4100 \\
& x \geq 100 \\
& y \geq 50
\end{aligned}
\tag{7.42}
$$

In **R**, we write this problem as follows. First, we store the coefficients of the objective function in an object, `f.obj`. Second, we store the coefficients of the variables of the constraints in a matrix with one row for constraint and one column per variable (`f.con`). Third, we determine the direction of the constraints. In this example, we are working with inequality constraints, `"<="` and `">="`. Other options include: `"=="`, `"<"`, `">"`. Fourth, we generate a vector of numeric values for the right-hand sides of the constraints. Finally, we use the `lp()` function to solve the problem. We choose `"max"` for a maximization problem and `"min"` for a minimization problem.

```
> f.obj <- c(15, 22)
> f.con <- matrix (c(11, 17,
+                    23, 19,
+                    1, 0,
+                    0, 1),
+                  nrow = 4,
+                  ncol = 2,
+                  byrow=TRUE)
> f.dir <- c("<=", "<=", ">=", ">=")
> f.rhs <- c(5400, 4100, 100, 50)
> lp("max", f.obj, f.con, f.dir, f.rhs)
Success: the objective function is 3584.211
> lp("max", f.obj, f.con, f.dir, f.rhs)$solution
[1] 100.00000  94.73684
```

Therefore, $f(x^*, y^*) = 3584.2$, with $x^* = 100$ and $y^* = 94.7$. In Sect. 7.4.3, we will implement a special case of linear programming problem known as the *transportation problem*.

Next, let's consider the case where the objective function is not linear. In this case, we can use the `nloptr` package or the `constrOptim()` function that is a base **R** function .

For example, we can solve Example 7.1.1 with `nloptr` as follows. First, we generate a function that contains in a `list()` the objective function and its gradient. Second, we generate another function for the constraint. In this case, we have an equality constraint. We again set a `list()` with the constraint and its jacobian. Third, we set the algorithm options. `local_opts` is required with equality constraints. Finally, we use the `nloptr()` function. We set some initial values, `x0`, and lower and upper bounds, `lb` and `ub`. Note that this function solves a minimization problem. In optimization, we can convert a maximization problem into a minimization problem (and vice versa) considering that

$$max\ f(x) = -min\ -\ f(x) \tag{7.43}$$

Note, however, that the properties of the function may be changed by this transformation.

```
> eval_f <- function(x){
+   return(list("objective" = -1*(x[1]*x[2]),
+               "gradient" = c(-1, -1)))
+ }
> eval_g_eq <- function(x){
+   return(list("constraints" = c(4 - x[1] - x[2]),
+               "jacobian" = c(-1, -1)))
+ }
> local_opts <- list("algorithm" = "NLOPT_LD_MMA",
+                    "xtol_rel"  = 1.0e-7 )
> opts <- list("algorithm" = "NLOPT_LD_AUGLAG",
+              "xtol_rel"  = 1.0e-7,
+              "maxeval"   = 1000,
+             "local_opts" = local_opts )
> res0 <- nloptr(x0 = c(0, 0),
+               eval_f=eval_f,
+               lb = c(0, 0),
+               ub = c(4, 4),
+               eval_g_eq = eval_g_eq,
+               opts = opts)
> res0

Call:
nloptr(x0 = c(0, 0), eval_f = eval_f, lb = c(0, 0),
   ub = c(4,4), eval_g_eq = eval_g_eq, opts = opts)


Minimization using NLopt version 2.4.2

NLopt solver status: 4 ( NLOPT_XTOL_REACHED:
Optimization stopped because xtol_rel or
xtol_abs (above) was reached. )

Number of Iterations....: 580
Termination conditions:  xtol_rel: 1e-07 maxeval: 1000
Number of inequality constraints:  0
Number of equality constraints:    1
```

```
Optimal value of objective function:  -4.00000000194742
Optimal value of controls: 2 2
```

The optimal choice variables are $x^* = 2$ and $y^* = 2$ as expected. To get the optimal value of the objective function we need to multiply by -1

```
> -1*res0$objective
[1] 4
```

Next, we solve Example 7.1.3. This a maximization problem with two equality constraints.

```
> eval_f <- function(x){
+   return(list("objective" = -1*(2*x[1]*x[2] + x[2]*x[3]),
+               "gradient" = c(-2*x[2],
+                              -2*x[1] - 1*x[3],
+                              -1*x[2])))
+ }
> eval_g_eq <- function(x){
+   return(list("constraints" = rbind(c(4 - x[2] - x[3]),
+                                     c(-8 - x[1] - x[2])),
+               "jacobian" = rbind(c(0, -1, -1),
+                                  c(-1, -1, 0))))
+ }
> local_opts <- list("algorithm" = "NLOPT_LD_MMA",
+                    "xtol_rel"  = 1.0e-7 )
> opts <- list("algorithm" = "NLOPT_LD_AUGLAG",
+              "xtol_rel"  = 1.0e-7,
+              "maxeval"   = 1000,
+              "local_opts" = local_opts )
> res0 <- nloptr(x0 = c(0, 0, 0),
+                eval_f=eval_f,
+                lb = c(-8, -8, 0),
+                ub = c(Inf, Inf, Inf),
+                eval_g_eq = eval_g_eq,
+                opts = opts)
> res0

Call:
nloptr(x0 = c(0, 0, 0), eval_f = eval_f, lb = c(-8, -8, 0),
   ub = c(Inf, Inf, Inf), eval_g_eq = eval_g_eq, opts = opts)


Minimization using NLopt version 2.4.2

NLopt solver status: 4 ( NLOPT_XTOL_REACHED:
Optimization stopped because xtol_rel or
xtol_abs (above) was reached. )

Number of Iterations....: 591
Termination conditions:  xtol_rel: 1e-07 maxeval: 1000
Number of inequality constraints:  0
```

```
Number of equality constraints:    2
Optimal value of objective function:  -12.0000000181514
Optimal value of controls: -6 -2 6


> -1*res0$objective
[1] 12
```

Let's solve a minimization problem before moving to the case with inequality constraints. The following minimization problem is described in Sect. 7.4.2.[5]

```
> eval_f <- function(x){
+   return(list("objective" = c(21*x[1] + 3*x[2]),
+               "gradient" = c(21, 3)))
+ }
> eval_g_eq <- function(x){
+   return(list("constraints" = c(90 - x[1]^(0.7)*x[2]^(0.3)),
+               "jacobian" = c(-0.7*x[1]^(-0.3)*x[2]^0.3,
+                              -0.3*x[1]^(0.7)*x[2]^(-0.7))))
+ }
> local_opts <- list("algorithm" = "NLOPT_LD_MMA",
+                    "xtol_rel"  = 1.0e-7 )
> opts <- list("algorithm" = "NLOPT_LD_AUGLAG",
+              "xtol_rel"  = 1.0e-7,
+              "maxeval"   = 1000,
+              "local_opts" = local_opts )
> res0 <- nloptr(x0 = c(10, 10),
+                eval_f = eval_f,
+                lb = c(1, 1),
+                ub = c(Inf, Inf),
+                eval_g_eq = eval_g_eq,
+                opts = opts)
> res0

Call:
nloptr(x0 = c(10, 10), eval_f = eval_f, lb = c(1, 1), ub = c(Inf,
    Inf), eval_g_eq = eval_g_eq, opts = opts)


Minimization using NLopt version 2.4.2

NLopt solver status: 4 ( NLOPT_XTOL_REACHED: Optimization stopped
because xtol_rel or xtol_abs (above) was reached. )

Number of Iterations....: 179
Termination conditions:  xtol_rel: 1e-07 maxeval: 1000
Number of inequality constraints:  0
Number of equality constraints:    1
Optimal value of objective function:  1941.90235203495
Optimal value of controls: 64.73008 194.1902
```

[5] Note that in this example the constraint is non linear. We assume that the constraint qualification holds.

In the next example, we will solve optimization problems with inequality constraint as in Sect. 7.2. First, we use the `nloptr()` function. Then, we solve the same problem with the `constrOptim()` function.

This time we code only the function and the constraint. The gradients will be computed by the algorithm.

The following code solves Example 7.2.2.

```
> # re-formulate constraints to be of form g(x) <= 0
> # -40 + x1 + x2 <= 0
> # -10 + x1 <= 0
> eval_f <- function(x){
+   return(-1*(x[1]*x[2]))
+ }
> # gradient of objective function
> eval_g_ineq <- function(x){
+   return(c(-40 + x[1] + x[2],
+            -10 +x[1]))
+ }
> res0 <- nloptr(x0 = c(0.1, 0.1),
+                eval_f = eval_f,
+                lb = c(0, 0),
+                ub = c(Inf, Inf),
+                eval_g_ineq = eval_g_ineq,
+                opts = list("algorithm"="NLOPT_LN_COBYLA",
+                            "xtol_rel"  = 1.0e-7))
> res0

Call:
nloptr(x0 = c(0.1, 0.1), eval_f = eval_f, lb = c(0, 0), ub = c(Inf,
    Inf), eval_g_ineq = eval_g_ineq,
    opts = list(algorithm = "NLOPT_LN_COBYLA", xtol_rel = 1e-07))


Minimization using NLopt version 2.4.2

NLopt solver status: 4 ( NLOPT_XTOL_REACHED:
Optimization stopped because xtol_rel or
xtol_abs (above) was reached. )

Number of Iterations....: 73
Termination conditions:  xtol_rel: 1e-07
Number of inequality constraints:  2
Number of equality constraints:    0
Optimal value of objective function:  -300
Optimal value of controls: 10 30


> -1*res0$objective
[1] 300
```

The following code solves Example 7.2.1.

```
> # re-formulate constraints to be of form g(x) <= 0
> # -100 + 10*x[1] + 5*x[2] <= 0
> eval_f <- function(x){
```

```
+   return(-1*(x[1]*x[2]))
+ }
> eval_g_ineq <- function(x){
+   return(-100 + 10*x[1] + 5*x[2])
+ }
> res0 <- nloptr(x0 = c(0.1, 0.1),
+                eval_f = eval_f,
+                lb = c(0, 0),
+                ub = c(Inf, Inf),
+                eval_g_ineq = eval_g_ineq,
+                opts = list("algorithm"="NLOPT_LN_COBYLA",
+                            "xtol_rel"  = 1.0e-7))
> res0

Call:
nloptr(x0 = c(0.1, 0.1), eval_f = eval_f, lb = c(0, 0), ub = c(Inf,
    Inf), eval_g_ineq = eval_g_ineq,
    opts = list(algorithm = "NLOPT_LN_COBYLA", xtol_rel = 1e-07))


Minimization using NLopt version 2.4.2

NLopt solver status: 5 ( NLOPT_MAXEVAL_REACHED:
Optimization stopped because maxeval
(above) was reached. )

Number of Iterations....: 100
Termination conditions:  xtol_rel: 1e-07
Number of inequality constraints:  1
Number of equality constraints:    0
Current value of objective function:  -49.9999999987485
Current value of controls: 4.999975 10.00005


> -1*res0$objective
[1] 50
```

The `constrOptim()` function uses a minimization algorithm as well. However, in this case we can set `control = list(fnscale = -1)` in the function to convert it into a maximization problem. This functions needs a function as objective function, a matrix with the coefficients of the variables in the constraints, a vector with the constants in the constraints, and initial values. We replicate again Examples 7.2.2 and 7.2.1.

We need to reformulate the constraints $x_1 + x_2 \leq 40$ as $-x_1 - x_2 \geq -40$ and $x_1 \leq 10$ as $-x_1 \geq -10$.

```
> # max x1*x2
> # st x1 >= 0
> # st x2 >= 0
> # st x1 + x2 <= 40 -> -x1 - x2 >= - 40
> # st x1 <= 10 -> -x1 >= -10
> fn <- function(x) x[1]*x[2]
```

```
> ui <- matrix(c(1, 0,
+                 0, 1,
+                 -1, -1,
+                 -1, 0),
+               nrow = 4,
+               ncol = 2,
+               byrow = T)
> ci <- c(0, 0, -40, -10)
> constrOptim(c(0.1, 0.1), fn, NULL, ui = ui, ci = ci,
+              control=list(fnscale=-1))
$par
[1] 10.00000 29.99962

$value
[1] 299.9962

$counts
function gradient
     474       NA

$convergence
[1] 0

$message
NULL

$outer.iterations
[1] 3

$barrier.value
[1] 0.01350571
```

For Example 7.2.1, we reformulate the constraint $10x_1 + 5x_2 <= 100$ as $-(10x_1 + 5x_2) >= -100$.

```
> # max x1*x2
> # st x1 >= 0
> # st x2 >= 0
> # st 10x1 + 5x2 <= 100 -> -10x1 -5x2 >= -100
> fn <- function(x) x[1]*x[2]
> ui <- matrix(c(1, 0,
+                 0, 1,
+                 -10, -5),
+               nrow = 3,
```

```
+                 ncol = 2,
+                 byrow = T)
> ci <- c(0, 0, -100)
> constrOptim(c(0.1, 0.1), fn, NULL, ui = ui, ci = ci,
+                 control=list(fnscale=-1))
$par
[1]  4.999502 10.000996

$value
[1] 50

$counts
function gradient
     276       NA

$convergence
[1] 0

$message
NULL

$outer.iterations
[1] 3

$barrier.value
[1] 0.01160745
```

7.4 Applications in Economics

7.4.1 Utility Maximization Problem

One of the first maximization problems a student of Economics faces is the utility maximization problem. We started to build it in Sect. 2.4.1 where we defined the constraint of a consumer and in Sect. 3.8.2.1 where we defined an utility function and plot for three possible values 25, 50, 100.

In this section, we are going to investigate which of these values is the solution of the following maximization problem

$$\begin{aligned} max \quad & U(x, y) = xy \\ s.t. \quad & 10x + 5y = 100 \end{aligned} \tag{7.44}$$

We follow the previous steps: 1–4 to find the stationary value and 5–6 to confirm that the value indeed is a maximum.

Step 1

$$\mathcal{L} = xy + \lambda(100 - 10x - 5y)$$

Step 2

$$\frac{\partial \mathcal{L}}{\partial x} = y - 10\lambda = 0$$

$$\frac{\partial \mathcal{L}}{\partial y} = x - 5\lambda = 0$$

$$\frac{\partial \mathcal{L}}{\partial \lambda} = 100 - 10x - 5y = 0$$

Step 3

$$y = 10\lambda$$

$$x = 5\lambda$$

$$100 - 50\lambda - 50\lambda = 0 \rightarrow \lambda^* = 1$$

$$x^* = 5$$

$$y^* = 10$$

Step 4

$$U(x^*, y^*) = 50$$

Consequently, the stationary value is $U^* = 50$. Let's confirm this is indeed a maximum.

Step 5

$$|\overline{H}| = \begin{vmatrix} 0 & \vdots & 10 & 5 \\ \cdots & \vdots & \cdots & \cdots \\ 10 & \vdots & 0 & 1 \\ 5 & \vdots & 1 & 0 \end{vmatrix}$$

Step 6

```
> bH <- matrix(c(0, 10, 5,
+                10, 0, 1,
+                5, 1, 0),
+              nrow = 3,
+              ncol = 3,
+              byrow = T)
> bH
     [,1] [,2] [,3]
[1,]    0   10    5
[2,]   10    0    1
[3,]    5    1    0
> det(bH)
[1] 100
> bLPM(bH, m = 1)
[1] 100
```

This confirms that we found a maximum. Figure 7.4 gives a representation of this problem.

```
> L <- 50
> x <- seq(0, 25, 1)
> y <- L/x
> Y <- 20 - 2*x
> ggplot() +
+   geom_line(map = aes(x = x, y = y), size = 1) +
+   geom_line(map = aes(x = x, y = Y), size = 1,
+             color = "blue") +
+   geom_point(aes(x = 5, y = 10),
+              color = "red",
+              size = 2) +
+   coord_fixed(xlim = c(0, 25),
+               ylim = c(0, 25)) +
+   theme_classic() +
```

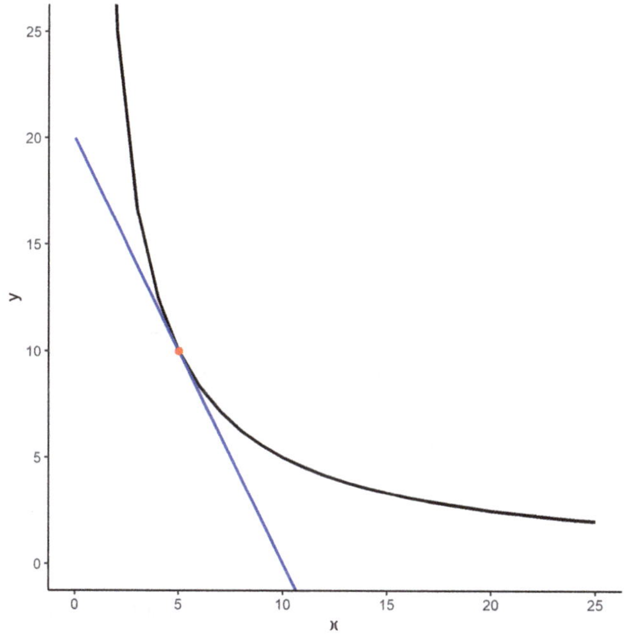

Fig. 7.4 Utility maximization with one constraint

```
+    xlab("x") + ylab("y")
```

Let's solve the utility maximization problem analytically. The utility function we want to maximize is given by the following CES function

$$U = \left[\alpha^{\frac{1}{\sigma}} X^{\frac{\sigma-1}{\sigma}} + \beta^{\frac{1}{\sigma}} Y^{\frac{\sigma-1}{\sigma}}\right]^{\frac{\sigma}{\sigma-1}} \tag{7.45}$$

subject to the following budget constraint

$$pX + qY = I \tag{7.46}$$

where X and Y are two goods, α and β are share parameters, σ is the substitution elasticity, p is the price of good X, q is the price of good Y and I is the income.

We set the Lagrangian and take the first derivative with respect to X, Y, and λ. Note that for the first terms in (7.48) and (7.49) we apply the chain rule.

$$\mathcal{L} = \left[\alpha^{\frac{1}{\sigma}} X^{\frac{\sigma-1}{\sigma}} + \beta^{\frac{1}{\sigma}} Y^{\frac{\sigma-1}{\sigma}}\right]^{\frac{\sigma}{\sigma-1}} + \lambda\left[I - pX - qY\right] \tag{7.47}$$

$$\frac{\partial \mathcal{L}}{\partial X} = \frac{\sigma}{\sigma-1}\frac{\sigma-1}{\sigma}\alpha^{\frac{1}{\sigma}} X^{\frac{\sigma-1}{\sigma}-1}\left[\alpha^{\frac{1}{\sigma}} X^{\frac{\sigma-1}{\sigma}} + \beta^{\frac{1}{\sigma}} Y^{\frac{\sigma-1}{\sigma}}\right]^{\frac{\sigma}{\sigma-1}-1} - \lambda p = 0 \tag{7.48}$$

$$\frac{\partial \mathcal{L}}{\partial Y} = \frac{\sigma}{\sigma-1}\frac{\sigma-1}{\sigma}\beta^{\frac{1}{\sigma}}Y^{\frac{\sigma-1}{\sigma}-1}\left[\alpha^{\frac{1}{\sigma}}X^{\frac{\sigma-1}{\sigma}} + \beta^{\frac{1}{\sigma}}Y^{\frac{\sigma-1}{\sigma}}\right]^{\frac{\sigma}{\sigma-1}-1} - \lambda q = 0 \tag{7.49}$$

$$\frac{\partial \mathcal{L}}{\partial \lambda} = I - pX - qY = 0 \tag{7.50}$$

Now, to make our life easier the "trick" is to divide (7.48) by (7.49). Thus, we set (note that the first two terms cancelled out)

$$\frac{\alpha^{\frac{1}{\sigma}}X^{\frac{\sigma-1}{\sigma}-1}\left[\alpha^{\frac{1}{\sigma}}X^{\frac{\sigma-1}{\sigma}} + \beta^{\frac{1}{\sigma}}Y^{\frac{\sigma-1}{\sigma}}\right]^{\frac{\sigma}{\sigma-1}-1}}{\beta^{\frac{1}{\sigma}}Y^{\frac{\sigma-1}{\sigma}-1}\left[\alpha^{\frac{1}{\sigma}}X^{\frac{\sigma-1}{\sigma}} + \beta^{\frac{1}{\sigma}}Y^{\frac{\sigma-1}{\sigma}}\right]^{\frac{\sigma}{\sigma-1}-1}} = \frac{\lambda p}{\lambda q}$$

and by cancelling out the same terms we are left with

$$\frac{\alpha^{\frac{1}{\sigma}}X^{-\frac{1}{\sigma}}}{\beta^{\frac{1}{\sigma}}Y^{-\frac{1}{\sigma}}} = \frac{p}{q}$$

Now we can proceed with the usual steps. First, let's solve for X

$$X^{-\frac{1}{\sigma}} = \frac{p}{q}\left(\frac{\beta}{\alpha}\right)^{\frac{1}{\sigma}} Y^{-\frac{1}{\sigma}}$$

$$X^{-\frac{1}{\sigma}\cdot -\sigma} = \left(\frac{p}{q}\right)^{-\sigma}\left(\frac{\beta}{\alpha}\right)^{\frac{1}{\sigma}\cdot -\sigma} Y^{-\frac{1}{\sigma}\cdot -\sigma}$$

$$X = \left(\frac{p}{q}\right)^{-\sigma}\left(\frac{\beta}{\alpha}\right)^{-1} Y$$

$$X = \frac{p^{-\sigma}}{q^{-\sigma}}\frac{\alpha}{\beta}Y \tag{7.51}$$

Similarly, we obtain Y

$$Y = \frac{q^{-\sigma}}{p^{-\sigma}}\frac{\beta}{\alpha}X \tag{7.52}$$

Now let's plug (7.51) in a rearranged (7.50) and solve for Y

$$I = p \cdot \frac{p^{-\sigma}\alpha}{q^{-\sigma}\beta}Y + qY$$

$$I = \frac{pp^{-\sigma}\alpha Y + qq^{-\sigma}\beta Y}{q^{-\sigma}\beta}$$

$$I = Y\left(\frac{p^{1-\sigma}\alpha + q^{1-\sigma}\beta}{q^{-\sigma}\beta}\right)$$

$$Y = \frac{q^{-\sigma}\beta I}{p^{1-\sigma}\alpha + q^{1-\sigma}\beta}$$

$$Y^* = \beta\frac{I}{q^{\sigma}\left(\alpha p^{1-\sigma} + \beta q^{1-\sigma}\right)} \tag{7.53}$$

By plugging (7.53) in (7.51) we obtain

$$X = \frac{p^{-\sigma}}{q^{-\sigma}}\frac{\alpha}{\beta}\cdot\beta\frac{I}{q^{\sigma}\left(\alpha p^{1-\sigma} + \beta q^{1-\sigma}\right)}$$

$$X = \frac{q^{\sigma}}{p^{\sigma}}\frac{\alpha}{\beta}\cdot\beta\frac{I}{q^{\sigma}\left(\alpha p^{1-\sigma} + \beta q^{1-\sigma}\right)}$$

$$X^* = \alpha\frac{I}{p^{\sigma}\left(\alpha p^{1-\sigma} + \beta q^{1-\sigma}\right)} \tag{7.54}$$

This complete the derivation of the demand functions. X^* and Y^* are also known as *Marshallian* demand functions. In Sect. 7.4.4 we will see a practical application.

7.4.2 Firm's Cost Minimization Problem

In this section, we will deal with the firm's cost minimization problem, i.e. produce a given level of output with the minimum cost.

Let's suppose that the firms has to produce 90 units of output Q. The cost for this firm is given by \$21 (wage) per unit of labour L and \$3 (price of capital) per unit of capital K: $C(L, K) = 21L + 3K$. We assume that the output is produced according to the following Cobb-Douglas function: $Q(L, K) = L^{0.7}K^{0.3}$. We can set this problem as follows

$$\begin{aligned} min \quad & 21L + 3K \\ s.t. \quad & 90 = L^{0.7}K^{0.3} \end{aligned} \tag{7.55}$$

Step 1

$$\mathcal{L} = 21L + 3K + \lambda(90 - L^{0.7}K^{0.3})$$

Step 2

$$\frac{\partial \mathcal{L}}{\partial L} = 21 - 0.7\lambda L^{-0.3} K^{0.3} = 0$$
$$\frac{\partial \mathcal{L}}{\partial K} = 3 - 0.3\lambda L^{0.7} K^{-0.7} = 0 \tag{7.56}$$
$$\frac{\partial \mathcal{L}}{\partial \lambda} = 90 - L^{0.7} K^{0.3} = 0$$

Step 3

$$0.7\lambda L^{-0.3} K^{0.3} = 21 \rightarrow \lambda = \frac{21}{0.7} \frac{L^{0.3}}{K^{0.3}} \rightarrow \lambda = 30\frac{L^{0.3}}{K^{0.3}}$$

$$0.3\lambda L^{0.7} K^{-0.7} = 3 \rightarrow \lambda = \frac{3}{0.3} \frac{K^{0.7}}{L^{0.7}} \rightarrow \lambda = 10\frac{K^{0.7}}{L^{0.7}}$$

$$30\frac{L^{0.3}}{K^{0.3}} = 10\frac{K^{0.7}}{L^{0.7}}$$

$$3\frac{L^{0.3}}{K^{0.3}} = \frac{K^{0.7}}{L^{0.7}}$$

$$3L^{0.3}L^{0.7} = K^{0.7}K^{0.3} \rightarrow 3L = K$$

$$90 - L^{0.7}(3L)^{0.3} = 0 \rightarrow L^* = 64.73$$

$$K^* = 3 \cdot 64.73 = 194.19$$

Step 4

$$C(L^*, K^*) = 21 \cdot 64.73 + 3 \cdot 194.19 = 1941.9$$

The input combination (L^*, K^*) represents the optimal input combination that the firm should use to produce the given amount of output at the minimum cost.

We solved this problem with **R** in Sect. 7.3. Now let's give a graphic representation of this result.

Let's rearrange the objective function and the constraint.

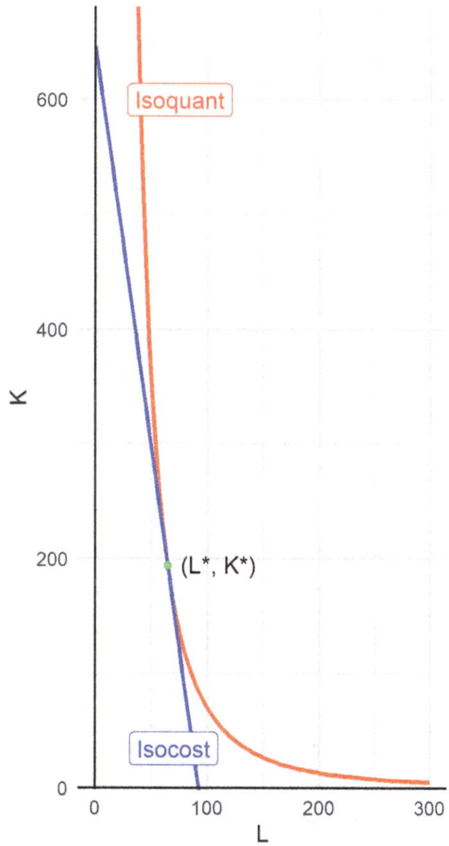

Fig. 7.5 Cost minimization with one constraint

$$1941.9 = 21L + 3K \rightarrow K = \frac{1941.9}{3} - 7L$$

$$90 = L^{0.7}K^{0.3} \rightarrow K = \left(\frac{90}{L^{0.7}}\right)^{\frac{1}{0.3}}$$

Figure 7.5 shows the output of the following code. We add two labels: *isocost*, the line that shows all combinations of inputs that cost the same total amount, and *isoquant*, that is the contour line that shows the same amount of output produced with different combinations of inputs.

```
> dfL <- data.frame(L = seq(0, 300, 1))
> isoquant <- function(L){(90/L^(0.7))^(1/0.3)}
> isocost <- function(L){1941.9/3 - 7*L}
> ggplot(data = dfL) +
+       stat_function(aes(L),
+                     fun = isoquant,
```

```
+                      color = "red",
+                      size = 1) +
+       stat_function(aes(L),
+                      fun = isocost,
+                      color = "blue",
+                      size = 1) +
+       geom_point(aes(x = 64.73, y = 194.19),
+                   color = "green", size = 1.5) +
+       geom_hline(yintercept = 0) +
+       geom_vline(xintercept = 0) +
+       coord_fixed(xlim = c(0, 300),
+                    ylim = c(30, 650)) +
+       theme_minimal() +
+       xlab("L") + ylab("K") +
+       annotate("label", x = c(70, 75),
+                 y = c(35, 600),
+                 label = c("Isocost", "Isoquant"),
+                 color = c("blue", "red")) +
+       annotate("text", x = 110, y = 195,
+                 label = "(L*, K*)")
```

7.4.3 Transportation Problem

The transportation problem consists in finding the minimum cost to transport products from supply locations to destinations where the products are demanded.

In the following example, we suppose that a firm, *XYZ*, has two plants, one in Milan and one in Marseille, and it needs to supply four markets: Rome, Paris, Amsterdam, and Berlin.

We have the following information

- the supply capacity of the plant in Milan is 700 units while the production capacity of the plant in Marseille is 500 units.
- the demand for the *XYZ* products is 250 from Rome, 300 from Paris, 150 from Amsterdam, and 500 from Berlin.
- the distance in km between suppliers and markets is:
  - 600 for Milan—Rome and 900 for Marseille—Rome
  - 850 for Milan—Paris and 750 for Marseille—Paris
  - 1000 for Milan—Amsterdam and 1200 for Marseille—Amsterdam
  - 1000 for Milan—Berlin and 1500 for Marseille—Berlin
- the freight cost to transport the goods is 0.1 euro per km.

Let's organize this info in a transportation matrix with the suppliers on the rows and the final markets on the columns (Table 7.1).

Table 7.1 Transportation matrix

	Rome	Paris	Amsterdam	Berlin	*Supply*
Milan	60	85	100	100	700
Marseille	90	75	120	150	500
Demand	250	300	150	500	

Before setting up the problem, let's represent all the possible connections between suppliers and final markets on a geographical map by using the `leaflet` package. The `leaflet()` function generates an interactive map.

First, we need latitude and longitude of the cities. The geo-coordinates could be obtain with the `geocode()` function from the `ggmap` package. However, it requires that the user to agree to the Google Maps API Terms. For this exercise, I searched for the coordinates manually.

Note that I generate three object: `lat`, `lng`, `df`. The first two objects contain the coordinates, latitude and longitude respectively, to locate the cities on the map; the last one is a data frame that is organized to draw the connection lines on the map.

```
> MLN_lat <- 45.46578
> MLN_lng <- 9.194975
> MRS_lat <- 43.296398
> MRS_lng <- 5.370000
> ROM_lat <- 41.902569
> ROM_lng <- 12.494091
> PRS_lat <- 48.864716
> PRS_lng <- 2.349014
> AMS_lat <- 52.377956
> AMS_lng <- 4.897070
> BRL_lat <- 52.498263
> BRL_lng <- 13.368727
> lat <- c(MLN_lat, MRS_lat, ROM_lat,
+          PRS_lat, AMS_lat, BRL_lat)
> lng <- c(MLN_lng, MRS_lng, ROM_lng,
+          PRS_lng, AMS_lng, BRL_lng)
> df <- data.frame(lat = c(MLN_lat, ROM_lat,
+                          MLN_lat, PRS_lat,
+                          MLN_lat, AMS_lat,
+                          MLN_lat, BRL_lat,
+                          MRS_lat, ROM_lat,
+                          MRS_lat, PRS_lat,
+                          MRS_lat, AMS_lat,
+                          MRS_lat, BRL_lat),
+                  lng = c(MLN_lng, ROM_lng,
+                          MLN_lng, PRS_lng,
+                          MLN_lng, AMS_lng,
+                          MLN_lng, BRL_lng,
```

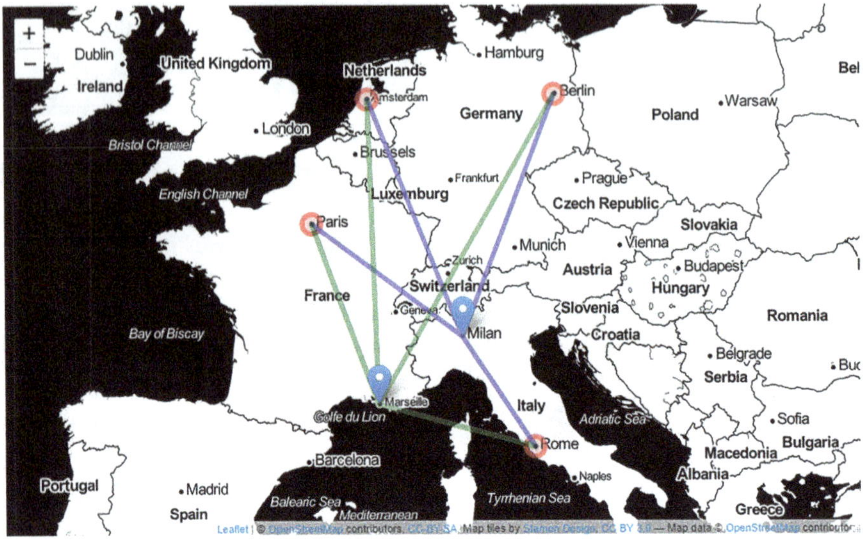

Fig. 7.6 Transportation problem: geo-spatial network

```
+                                          MRS_lng, ROM_lng,
+                                          MRS_lng, PRS_lng,
+                                          MRS_lng, AMS_lng,
+                                          MRS_lng, BRL_lng))
```

Now we are ready to plot the map with `leaflet()`. We use `addMarkers()` to add the marker at the given latitude and longitude of the suppliers and `addCircleMarkers()` to add a circle marker at the latitude and longitude of the final markets. This is an interactive map. When we click on the marker, the info we added about the plant and the final market pop up. With `addPolylines()` we add the connection lines between the plants and the final markets.[6] Finally, we set a different layout for the map with `addProviderTiles()`. Figure 7.6 shows the output.

```
> leaflet() %>%
+   addTiles() %>%
+   addMarkers(lng = lng[1:2], lat = lat[1:2],
+              popup = c("Plant: 700",
+                        "Plant: 500")) %>%
+   addCircleMarkers(lng = lng[3:6], lat = lat[3:6],
+                    popup = c("Final market: 250",
+                              "Final market: 300",
```

[6] We repeat it twice to distinguish the connection lines of Milan and Marseille by color. A more compact and efficient way to do it consists in setting up a `for()` loop for this task.

```
+                                "Final market: 150",
+                                "Final market: 500"),
+                      color = "red") %>%
+   addPolylines(lng = df$lng[1:8], lat = df$lat[1:8],
+                color = "blue") %>%
+   addPolylines(lng = df$lng[9:16], lat = df$lat[9:16],
+                color = "green") %>%
+   addProviderTiles(provider = "Stamen")
```

Let's continue with the set-up of this problem. Let's indicate with i the suppliers and with j the destinations. Consequently, x_{ij}, choice variables, represents the units to be shipped from suppliers to destinations, and c_{ij} the cost for shipment from suppliers to destinations. We can now write down the objective function to minimize as

$$\sum_i \sum_j c_{ij} x_{ij} \tag{7.57}$$

where $x_{ij} \geq 0$.

Next step is to define the constraints.

By indicating with a_i the supply capacity at plant i and by b_j the demand at market j, the constraints are

$$\sum_j x_{ij} \leq a_i, \forall i \tag{7.58}$$

$$\sum_i x_{ij} \geq b_j, \forall j \tag{7.59}$$

where constraint (7.58) means that supplies from Milan and Marseille to Rome, Paris, Amsterdam, and Berlin cannot overcome their production capacity, while constraint (7.59) means that supplies from Milan and Marseille need to satisfy the demand from the final markets.

Let's solve this problem with **R**. First, we build a matrix, `dist`, the contains the distance in km. On the row, we place the suppliers and on the columns the destinations.

```
> suppliers <- c("Milan", "Marseille")
> destinations <- c("Rome", "Paris",
+                   "Amsterdam", "Berlin")
> dist <- matrix(c(600, 850, 1000, 1000,
+                  900, 750, 1200, 1500),
+                nrow = 2,
+                ncol = 4, byrow = TRUE)
> rownames(dist) <- suppliers
> colnames(dist) <- destinations
```

```
> dist
          Rome Paris Amsterdam Berlin
Milan      600   850      1000   1000
Marseille  900   750      1200   1500
```

We generate a new variable, `fc`, to store the freight cost of 0.1 euro per km. The `costs` matrix stores the costs of transportation from suppliers to destinations.

```
> fc <- 0.1
> costs <- fc*dist
> costs
          Rome Paris Amsterdam Berlin
Milan       60    85       100    100
Marseille   90    75       120    150
```

Then, we add the info about the production capacity and the final market demand. At the same time we define the direction of the row constraints and of the column constraints. The `row` objects indicates that the production capacities cannot be higher than 700 for Milan and that 500 for Merseille (constraint (7.58)). On the other hand, the `col` objects indicates the minimum values that needs to be supplied to satisfy the final markets (constraint (7.59)).

```
> row.rhs <- c(700, 500)
> row.signs <- rep("<=", 2)
> col.rhs <- c(250, 300, 150, 500)
> col.signs <- rep(">=", 4)
```

Finally, we use the `lp.transport()` function from `lpSolve` to solve this problem. We add `min` to specify that this is a minimization problem (the default value). We save the solution in `sol` and `sol_mtx`.

```
> sol <- lp.transport(costs, "min",
+                      row.signs, row.rhs,
+                      col.signs, col.rhs)
> sol
Success: the objective function is 107000
> sol_mtx <- sol$solution
> rownames(sol_mtx) <- suppliers
> colnames(sol_mtx) <- destinations
> sol_mtx
          Rome Paris Amsterdam Berlin
Milan      200     0         0    500
Marseille   50   300       150      0
```

The minimized cost for this problem is 107,000 euro.

Additionally, the solution matrix displays the optimal shipments. From the solution we find that *XYZ* firm should supply the Berlin market only from the Milan plant and the Paris and Amsterdam markets only from the Marseille plant. Finally, it should supply the Rome market with 50 units from the Marseille plant and 200 units from the Milan plant.

7.4.4 CGE Model with R

Computable general equilibrium (CGE) models are a class of models widely used in Economics. CGE models simulate the impact of policy changes on the economy. Consequently, they became an important tool to support policy decisions.

In this section, we provide a method to solve a CGE model with **R** that consists in tackling a CGE model based on the mathematical nature of the problem, i.e. as a solution of a system of non-linear equations. We apply this method to the Shoven-Whalley (Shoven and Whalley 1984) model without taxes. The same approach has been applied by Cheah (2003) to solve the Shoven-Whalley model with SAS.

In Sect. 7.4.4.1 we introduce the Shoven-Whalley model without taxes. In Sect. 7.4.4.2 we replicate the results with **R**.

7.4.4.1 Shoven-Whalley Model Without Taxes

The Shoven-Whalley model without taxes is a model with two final goods (manufacturing and non-manufacturing), two factors of production (capital and labor), and two classes of consumers, rich households, that own all the capital, and poor households that own all the labor. The model is specified as follows.

First, it is described the production side of the model, where a constant-elasticity of substitution (CES) is used to represent the production of both goods

$$Q_i = \Phi_i \left[\delta_i L_i^{\frac{\sigma_i - 1}{\sigma_i}} + (1 - \delta_i) K_i^{\frac{\sigma_i - 1}{\sigma_i}} \right]^{\frac{\sigma_i}{\sigma_i - 1}} \tag{7.60}$$

where $i = \{\text{manufacturing} = 1, \text{non-manufacturing} = 2\}$, Q_i is the output of the ith industry, Φ_i is the scale parameter, δ_i is the distribution parameter, K_i and L_i are, respectively, the capital and labor factor inputs, and σ_i is the elasticity of factor substitution.

From (7.60), the following factor demands are derived as the solution of a cost minimization problem

$$L_i = \Phi_i^{-1} Q_i \left[\delta_i + (1 - \delta_i) \left[\frac{\delta_i r}{(1 - \delta_i) w} \right]^{1 - \sigma_i} \right]^{\frac{\sigma_i}{1 - \sigma_i}} \tag{7.61}$$

$$K_i = \Phi_i^{-1} Q_i \left[\delta_i \left[\frac{(1-\delta_i)w}{\delta_i r} \right]^{1-\sigma_i} + (1-\delta_i) \right]^{\frac{\sigma_i}{1-\sigma_i}} \tag{7.62}$$

where w and r are the factor prices.

Subsequently, the consumption side of the model is described with a CES utility function

$$U^c = \left[\sum_{i=1}^{2} (\alpha_i^c)^{\frac{1}{\mu_c}} \cdot (X_i^c)^{\frac{\mu_c - 1}{\mu_c}} \right]^{\frac{\mu_c}{\mu_c - 1}} \tag{7.63}$$

where X_i^c is the quantity of good i demanded by consumer c, α_i^c are share parameters, μ_c is the substitution elasticity in consumer c's CES utility function. The demand functions are derived from the maximization of (7.63) subject to the budget constraint $p_1 X_1^c + p_2 X_2^c \leq I^c$, where p_1 and p_2 are the consumer prices for the two goods, and I^c is the income of consumer c that is equal to $r\overline{K}^c + w\overline{L}^c$, with $\overline{K}^c$ and $\overline{L}^c$ being the consumer c's endowment of capital and labor

$$X_i^c = \alpha_i^c \frac{r\overline{K}^c + w\overline{L}^c}{p_i^{\mu_c} \left(\alpha_1^c p_i^{1-\mu_c} + \alpha_2^c p_2^{1-\mu_c} \right)} \tag{7.64}$$

Finally, the model is completed with the following equilibrium conditions for the factors market ((7.65)–(7.66)), for the goods market ((7.67)–(7.68)), and the zero profit conditions ((7.69)–(7.70))

$$\sum_{i=1}^{2} K_i(r, w, Q_i) = \sum_{c=R,P} \overline{K}^c \tag{7.65}$$

$$\sum_{i=1}^{2} L_i(r, w, Q_i) = \sum_{c=R,P} \overline{L}^c \tag{7.66}$$

$$X_1^1(p_1, p_2, r, w) + X_1^2(p_1, p_2, r, w) = Q_1 \tag{7.67}$$

$$X_2^1(p_1, p_2, r, w) + X_2^2(p_1, p_2, r, w) = Q_2 \tag{7.68}$$

$$rK_1(r, w, Q_1) + wL_1(r, w, Q_1) = P_1 Q_1 \tag{7.69}$$

$$rK_2(r, w, Q_2) + wL_2(r, w, Q_2) = P_2 Q_2 \tag{7.70}$$

The parameters of the model with the numerical values for replication are reported in Table 7.2. Additionally, w has been chosen as the numeraire.

Table 7.2 Model parameters

Production parameter	Value	Demand parameter	Value	Endowment	Value
Φ_1	1.5	α_1^R	0.5	$\overline{K}^R$	25
Φ_2	2.0	α_2^R	0.5	$\overline{K}^P$	0
δ_1	0.6	α_1^P	0.3	$\overline{L}^R$	0
δ_2	0.7	α_2^P	0.7	$\overline{L}^P$	60
σ_1	2.0	μ^R	1.5	–	–
σ_2	0.5	μ^P	0.75	–	–

Source: Shoven and Whalley (1984, p. 1011)

This model turns to be a system of non-linear equations with 13 unknowns. The equations we include in the system are (7.61), (7.62), (7.64), (7.65), (7.66), (7.67), (7.69), and (7.70). In the next section we provide the solution with **R**.

7.4.4.2 Solving the Model with R

We will solve this system of non-linear equations in **R** by using the `nleqslv` package. The `nleqslv` package provides two algorithms, Broyden and Newton, for solving (dense) nonlinear systems of equations.

First we define the parameters. We store them in matrices and vectors.

```
> # Demand values ####
> ALPHA <- matrix(c(0.5, 0.5,
+                   0.3, 0.7),
+                 nrow = 2,
+                 byrow = T)
> colnames(ALPHA) <- c("manufacturing",
+                      "non-manufacturing")
> rownames(ALPHA) <- c("rich", "poor")
> ALPHA
     manufacturing non-manufacturing
rich           0.5               0.5
poor           0.3               0.7
> FACTORS <- matrix(c(25, 0,
+                      0, 60),
+                   nrow = 2,
+                   byrow = T)
> colnames(FACTORS) <- c("K", "L")
> rownames(FACTORS) <- c("rich", "poor")
> FACTORS
      K  L
rich 25  0
poor  0 60
```

```
> MU <- matrix(c(1.5,
+                0.75),
+              nrow = 2,
+              byrow = T)
> rownames(MU) <- c("rich", "poor")
> MU
     [,1]
rich 1.50
poor 0.75
> # Production values ####
> phi <- c(phi1 = 1.5, phi2 = 2)
> phi
phi1 phi2
 1.5  2.0
> delta <- c(delta1 = 0.6, delta2 = 0.7)
> delta
delta1 delta2
   0.6    0.7
> sigma <- c(sigma1 = 2, sigma2 = 0.5)
> sigma
sigma1 sigma2
   2.0    0.5
> w <- 1
```

Next step consists in writing a function that contains the equations with the unknowns we want to solve for. We name this function `SWmodel()`. Here a bit of explanation is needed. We set `SWmodel()` as a function of `x`. The trick is that we identify the 13 unknowns by using the square brackets operator `[ ]`. This operator has the function to subset, extract, or replace a part of an object such as a vector, a matrix or a data frame. By setting `x[1]` for the first unknown, `x[2]` for the second unknown and so on, **R** will consider them as elements of the same vector. For clarity, at the beginning of the function we describe which variable corresponds to each element of x. Since the lines are preceded by # they are treated as a comment by **R** and consequently they are not run.

Now the real coding starts. We initialize an object, `y`, with the `numeric()` function. The number 13 corresponds to the number of unknowns. We are taking advantage of **R**'s vectorization to code a minimum number of equations. This allows us to code only seven equations instead of 13. However, it should be remarked that extra care is needed with vectorization.

```
> SWmodel <- function(x){
+
+   #r => x[1]
+   #p1 => x[2]
+   #p2 => x[3]
+   #X1_r => x[4]
+   #X2_r => x[5]
```

```
+   #X1_p => x[6]
+   #X2_p => x[7]
+   #L1 => x[8]
+   #L2 => x[9]
+   #K1 => x[10]
+   #K2 => x[11]
+   #Q1 => x[12]
+   #Q2 => x[13]
+
+
+   # functions
+   y <- numeric(13)
+
+
+   # Factor demand functions
+   ## Equation 2
+   y[1:2] <- (c(x[8], x[9]) -
+               ((1/phi*c(x[12], x[13]))*(
+                 (delta + ((1-delta)*(
+                   ((delta*x[1])/
+                      ((1-delta)*w))^(1-sigma))
+                 )^(sigma/(1-sigma)))))
+
+   ## Equation 3
+   y[3:4] <- (c(x[10], x[11]) -
+               ((1/phi*c(x[12], x[13]))*(((
+                 delta*((((1-delta)*w)/
+                          (delta*x[1]))^(1-sigma))) +
+                   (1-delta))^(sigma/(1-sigma)))))
+
+
+   # Demand functions
+   ## Equation 5
+   ### Rich
+   y[5:6] <- (c(x[4], x[5]) -
+               (ALPHA["rich", ]*(sum(
+                 c(x[1], w)*FACTORS["rich", ])/
+                   ((c(x[2], x[3])^MU["rich",])*sum(
+                     ALPHA["rich", ]*c(x[2],x[3]
+                                   )^(1 - MU["rich",]))))))
+   ## Equation 5
+   ### Poor
+   y[7:8] <- (c(x[6], x[7]) -
+               (ALPHA["poor", ]*(sum(
+                 c(x[1], w)*FACTORS["poor", ])/
+                   ((c(x[2], x[3])^MU["poor",])*sum(
+                     ALPHA["poor", ]*c(x[2],x[3]
+                                   )^(1 - MU["poor",]))))))
+
+
+   # Demands equal supply for factors
+   ## Equation 6 and 7
+   y[9:10] <-  c((x[10] + x[11]), (x[8] + x[9])) - colSums
       (FACTORS)
```

```
+
+
+    # Zero profit conditions hold in both industries
+    ## Equation 10 and 11
+    y[11:12] <- c(x[2], x[3]) - c((w*x[8]/x[12]) + (x[1]*x[10]/x[12]),
+                                  (w*x[9]/x[13]) + (x[1]*x[11]/x[13]))
+
+    # Demands equal supply for goods
+    ## Equation 8
+    y[13] <- (x[12] - (x[6] + x[4]))
+
+
+    return(y)
+
+ }
```

Now that the model has been built we can solve it with the `nleqslv()` function. The first argument of `nleqslv()` is a numeric vector with an initial guess of the root of the function. We store it in `xstart`. The second argument is the function of `x` returning a vector of function values with the same length as the vector `x`. In this case it is the `SWmodel()` function. Finally, we set the method equal to Newton to solve the system of non-linear equations. We store the results in `sol`.

```
> xstart <- c(1, 1, 1, 5, 10, 10, 15, 20, 25, 2, 10, 15, 30)
> sol <- nleqslv(xstart, SWmodel, method = "Newton")
```

The optimal solutions are

```
> sol$x
 [1]    1.373471   1.399111   1.093076 11.514649 16.674506
 [6]   13.427824 37.703664 26.365584 33.634416  6.211776
[11]   18.788224 24.942473 54.378170
```

In **R** the order is very important. This means that

```
> sol$x[1]
[1] 1.373471
```

is the optimal value for r. Table 7.3 reports the results.

We can assign the name of the variables for clarity

Table 7.3 Equilibrium solution

r	1.373471	L_1	26.365584
p_1	1.399111	L_2	33.634416
p_2	1.093076	K_1	6.211776
X_1^R	11.514649	K_2	18.788224
X_2^R	16.674506	Q_1	24.942473
X_1^P	13.427824	Q_2	54.378170
X_2^P	37.703664	–	–

```
> opt_sol <- sol$x
> names(opt_sol) <- c("r", "p1", "p2",
+                     "X1_r", "X2_r", "X1_p", "X2_p",
+                     "L1", "L2", "K1", "K2",
+                     "Q1", "Q2")
> opt_sol
        r        p1        p2      X1_r      X2_r      X1_p      X2_p
 1.373471  1.399111  1.093076 11.514649 16.674506 13.427824 37.703664
       L1        L2        K1        K2        Q1        Q2
26.365584 33.634416  6.211776 18.788224 24.942473 54.378170
```

Consequently, if we want to compute the revenue for the manufacturing sector

```
> RevMan <- opt_sol[["p1"]] * opt_sol[["Q1"]]
> RevMan
[1] 34.89728
```

Finally, by running `sol` we have access to the full report of `nleqslv()`

```
> sol
$x
 [1]  1.373471  1.399111  1.093076 11.514649 16.674506
 [6] 13.427824 37.703664 26.365584 33.634416  6.211776
 [11] 18.788224 24.942473 54.378170

$fvec
 [1]  4.327205e-12  2.131628e-13 -4.435563e-12 -1.023182e-12 5.329071e-15
 [6]  1.090683e-12 -2.678746e-12 -1.449507e-12 -2.486900e-14 3.552714e-14
 [11] -5.351275e-14 -3.108624e-15 -3.552714e-15

$termcd
[1] 1

$message
[1] "Function criterion near zero"

$scalex
 [1] 1 1 1 1 1 1 1 1 1 1 1 1 1

$nfcnt
[1] 5

$njcnt
[1] 5

$iter
[1] 5
```

7.5 Exercise

Write a function to compute the bordered leading principal minors (Sect. 7.1.4). Test your function by replicating the results in this chapter.

Part II
Introduction to Mathematics for Dynamic Economics

Chapter 8
Trigonometry

8.1 Right Triangles and Angles

In this section we start by reviewing some key concepts of geometry.

Let's draw two rays, l^1 and l^2, from a point A. Then, from a point B along l^2 let's draw a perpendicular line to l^1. This perpendicular line intersects l^1 at point C. The triangle ABC is a right triangle since γ is a 90° (*degree*) angle (Fig. 8.1).[1]

We recall that the sum of the angles in a triangle equals 180°. In turn, this means that in the right triangle the sum of angle θ and ϕ is 90°, i.e. θ and ϕ are *complementary* angles. We can express this last concept as

$$\theta = \frac{\pi}{2} - \phi \tag{8.1}$$

where $\frac{\pi}{2}$ is the measure of the 90° angle expressed in *radians*. As we can express, for example, the measure of distance in different ways, such as metres, centimetres, inches and so on, we can express the unit of measurement of an angle in degree or radians. The advantage to express the angle in radians is that radians are real numbers. In fact, $\frac{\pi}{2} = 1.570796$ and this is the unit of measurement in radians associated with the 90° angle.

Before explaining where the measurement in radians comes from, let's build a function, `angle_conversion()`, that converts the measurement of an angle in degree to radians (default) and vice versa, based on the following relation

$$\theta_{\text{rad}} : \theta_{\text{deg}} = 2\pi : 360° \tag{8.2}$$

[1] The code used to generate Figs. 8.1, 8.2, 8.3, 8.4, 8.5, and 8.6 is available in Appendix G.

M. Porto, *Introduction to Mathematics for Economics with R*,
https://doi.org/10.1007/978-3-031-05202-6_8

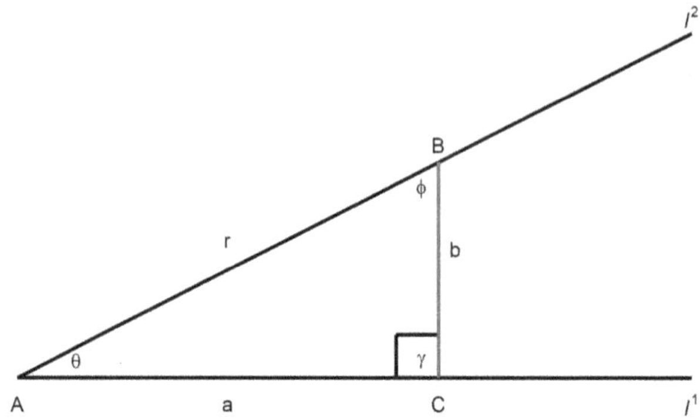

Fig. 8.1 Right triangle

```
> angle_conversion <- function(theta, degree = TRUE){
+
+   if(degree == TRUE){
+
+     angle_radians <- (theta*2*pi)/360
+     return(angle_radians)
+
+   } else{
+
+     angle_degree <- (theta*360)/(2*pi)
+     return(angle_degree)
+
+   }
+
+ }
```

A 45° angle in radians is 0.7853982, or $\frac{\pi}{4}$. Let's check it

```
> pi/4
[1] 0.7853982
> pi4 <- angle_conversion(45)
> pi4
[1] 0.7853982
> angle_conversion(pi4, degree = FALSE)
[1] 45
```

To grasp where radians come from and what *exactly* radians measure, let's inscribe the right triangle in a circle. To comply with the convention used for the trigonometric functions, let's draw a *unit circle*, that is a circle with *radius* equal 1, $r = 1$, centred in the origin of a Cartesian system. This means that point B is located 1 unit away from the origin on the circumference of the circle (Fig. 8.2).

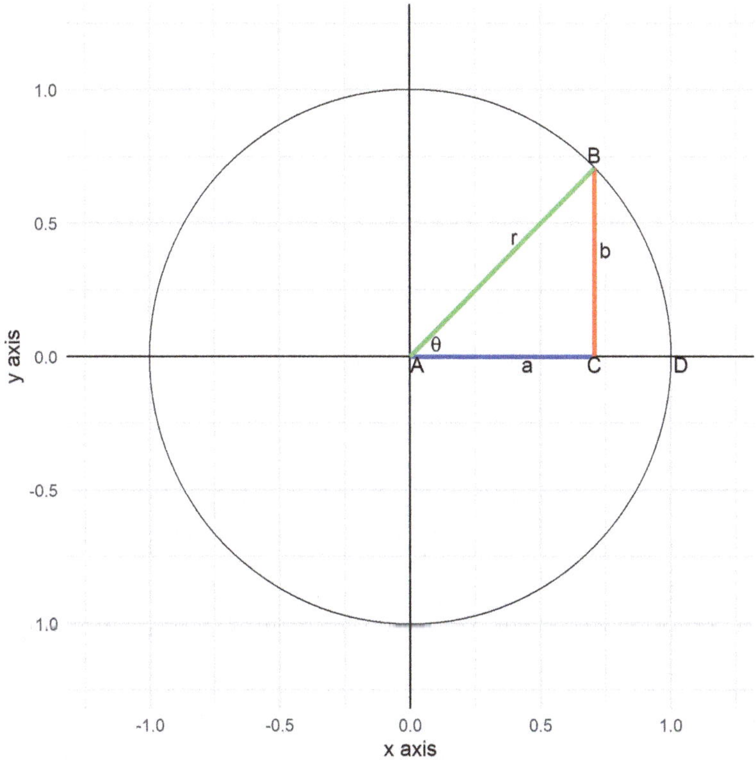

Fig. 8.2 Right triangle inscribed in a unit circle with $\theta = 45°$

The radians measure an angle by the *length of the arc* of the circle. In the example in Fig. 8.2 it measures the angle at the center of the circle subtended by the arc DB. Let's see how to calculate the size of such an angle subtended by an arc L of a circle (not necessary a unit circle) in radians. The radians of L is calculated as the ratio between the length of the arc and the radius, expressed in the same unit of measurement

$$radians_L = \frac{L}{r} \tag{8.3}$$

In our example with $\theta = 45°$, the arc DB is $1/8$ of the circumference, i.e. $DB = \frac{1}{8}2\pi r$, where $2\pi r$ is the length of the circumference. By replacing it in (8.3) for L

$$radians_{DB} = \frac{\frac{1}{8}2\pi r}{r} = \frac{\pi}{4}$$

If the angle were a 90° angle, the length of the arc L would be $1/4$ of the entire circumference. In other words, a 90° angle in radians is

Table 8.1 Angle in degree and radians

Degree	Radians
0	0
30°	$\pi/6$
45°	$\pi/4$
60°	$\pi/3$
90°	$\pi/2$
180°	π
270°	$3\pi/2$
360°	2π

$$radians_L = \frac{\frac{1}{4}2\pi r}{r} = \frac{\pi}{2}$$

An interesting fact to observe is that r in the formula cancels out. This means that, regardless the length of r, a 45° angle measures $\frac{\pi}{4}$ radians and a 90° angle measures $\frac{\pi}{2}$ radians and so on. From this fact we derive the formula as in (8.2). Table 8.1 reports the main angles in degree and radians.

Now let's add $\theta = 30°$ and $\theta = 60°$ to Fig. 8.2.

As we can observe from Fig. 8.3, where the solid lines represent the right triangle with $\theta = 45°$, the dot-dashed lines represent the right triangle with $\theta = 30°$, and the dotted lines represent the right triangle with $\theta = 60°$, the angle θ increases by a *counterclockerwise* rotation. This is the convention adopted in Mathematics.

Finally, to conclude this review let's recall that in a right triangle, $\overline{AB}$ is called *hypotenuse*, $\overline{BC}$ is called the *opposite leg* relative to the angle θ, and $\overline{AC}$ is called the *adjacent leg* relative to the angle θ.

This leads us to the Pythagorean Theorem that states that the sum of the squares of the legs of a right triangle equals the square of the length of the hypotenuse

$$a^2 + b^2 = r^2 \tag{8.4}$$

We will return to this theorem in next section.

8.2 Trigonometric Functions

The code to replicate Figs. 8.2 and 8.3 makes use of sine, `sin()`, and cosine, `cos()`, as part of a formula to calculate the sides of the opposite and adjacent legs to θ. Sine and cosine are two of the trigonometric functions that also include tangent, cotangent, secant, and cosecant. These trigonometric functions are defined as ratio of the sides of the triangle ABC

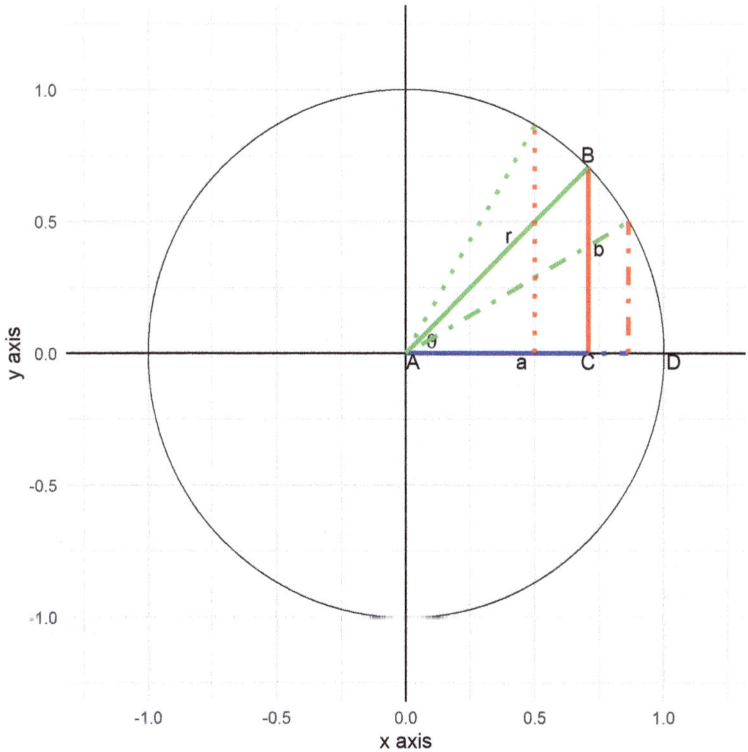

Fig. 8.3 Right triangle inscribed in a unit circle with $\theta = 30°, 45°, 60°$

$$\begin{aligned}\text{sine } \theta &= \frac{b}{r}\\ \text{cosine } \theta &= \frac{a}{r}\\ \text{tangent } \theta &= \frac{b}{a}\\ \text{cotangent } \theta &= \frac{a}{b}\\ \text{secant } \theta &= \frac{r}{a}\\ \text{cosecant } \theta &= \frac{r}{b}\end{aligned} \tag{8.5}$$

Additionally, note that

$$\text{tangent } \theta = \frac{b}{a} = \frac{\frac{b}{r}}{\frac{a}{r}} = \frac{\text{sine } \theta}{\text{cosine } \theta}$$

We can derive all the trigonometric functions in terms of sine and cosine

$$\begin{aligned} \text{cotangent } \theta &= \frac{\text{cosine } \theta}{\text{sine } \theta} \\ \text{secant } \theta &= \frac{1}{\text{cosine } \theta} \\ \text{cosecant } \theta &= \frac{1}{\text{sine } \theta} \end{aligned} \tag{8.6}$$

Finally, note that in the unit circle $r = 1$, consequently sine $\theta = b$ and cosine $\theta = a$. We used these relations to compute the sides of the ABC triangle in Figs. 8.2 and 8.3 by knowing the angle and the length of the hypotenuse that in our case is 1. Additionally, note that the `sin()` and `cos()` functions require the angles to be in radians.

With an hypotenuse of length 1, we can rewrite the Pythagorean Theorem as

$$a^2 + b^2 = 1 \tag{8.7}$$

and, consequently, as

$$cos^2\theta + \sin^2\theta = 1 \tag{8.8}$$

In turn, (8.8) means that $-1 < \sin\theta < 1$ and $-1 < \cos\theta < 1$.

Additionally, by dividing (8.7) through a^2

$$\frac{a^2}{a^2} + \frac{b^2}{a^2} = \frac{1}{a^2} \rightarrow 1 + \frac{b^2}{a^2} = \frac{1}{a^2} \rightarrow 1 + \tan^2\theta = \sec^2\theta$$

Analogously, by dividing (8.7) through b^2

$$\frac{a^2}{b^2} + \frac{b^2}{b^2} = \frac{1}{b^2} \rightarrow \frac{a^2}{b^2} + 1 = \frac{1}{b^2} \rightarrow \cot^2\theta + 1 = \csc^2\theta$$

Figure 8.4 represents the sine and cosine functions.

Let's refer to Fig. 8.3 to describe Fig. 8.4. In Fig. 8.3, we should consider what happens to the sides $\overline{BC}$ and $\overline{AC}$ of the triangle ABC as θ (x in Fig. 8.4) goes from 30° to 45° and 60°. As we can observe, this increase corresponds to a longer $\overline{BC}$ and a shorter $\overline{AC}$. Let's stay in the first quadrant in Fig. 8.3 and let's consider what the length of $\overline{BC}$ and $\overline{AC}$ would be if $\theta = 0$ and $\theta = 90°$. We can figure out that when $\theta = 0$, $\overline{BC} = 0$ and $\overline{AC} = 1$. On the other hand, we can figure out that when $\theta = 90°$, $\overline{BC} = 1$ and $\overline{AC} = 0$.

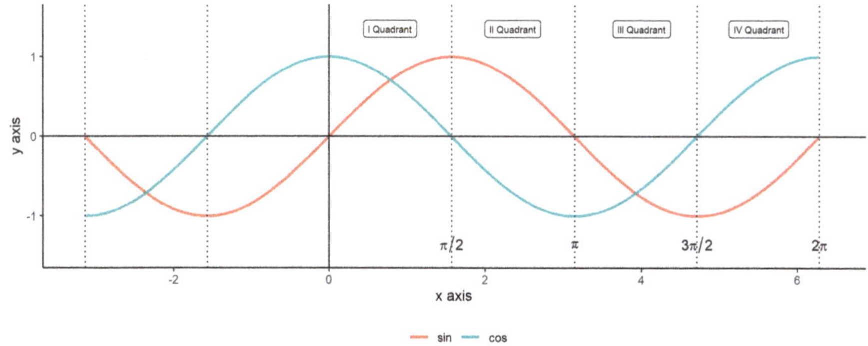

Fig. 8.4 Sine and cosine functions

Recall that we said that in the unit circle $\sin\theta = b = \overline{BC}$ and $\cos\theta = a = \overline{AC}$. In fact,

```
> sin(0)
[1] 0
> cos(0)
[1] 1
> sin(pi/2)
[1] 1
> cos(pi/2) # zero
[1] 6.123032e-17
```

With these considerations in mind let's move to comment Fig. 8.4. We can observe that when $x = 0$, $\sin x = 0$ and $\cos x = 1$, and when $x = \pi/2$, $\sin x = 1$ and $\cos x = 0$. What about $x = \pi$? We can observe that in this case $\sin x = 0$ and $\cos x = -1$. If we return to Fig. 8.3, we could observe point B moving to the II Quadrant until $\theta = 180°$. If we track the sides of the triangle ABC, we can see that $\overline{BC} = 0$ and $\overline{AC} = -1$.[2] Therefore, we generate the graph of sine and cosine by keeping track of b and a as point B moves around the unit circle.

Additionally, if point B moves *clockwise* around the unit circle, we refer to negative angles by definition. On the other hand, point B can move *counterclockwise* around the unit circle for an angle greater than 360°. However, referring to an angle of 390°, for example, would be the same as referring to an angle of 30°. Consequently, as we can see from Fig. 8.4, the functions repeat their pattern towards $-\infty$ and ∞ with 2π periodicity.

Now let's consider the representation of the tangent in the unit circle. In Fig. 8.5, we add a tangent to the circumference at point D, i.e. the vertical line. Then, we extend r until it intersects the tangent. In the example in Fig. 8.5 with $\theta = 45°$, the

[2] Note that the length is a positive measure. Therefore, it is more appropriate to refer to $|\overline{AC}| = 1$ and then make considerations about the sign.

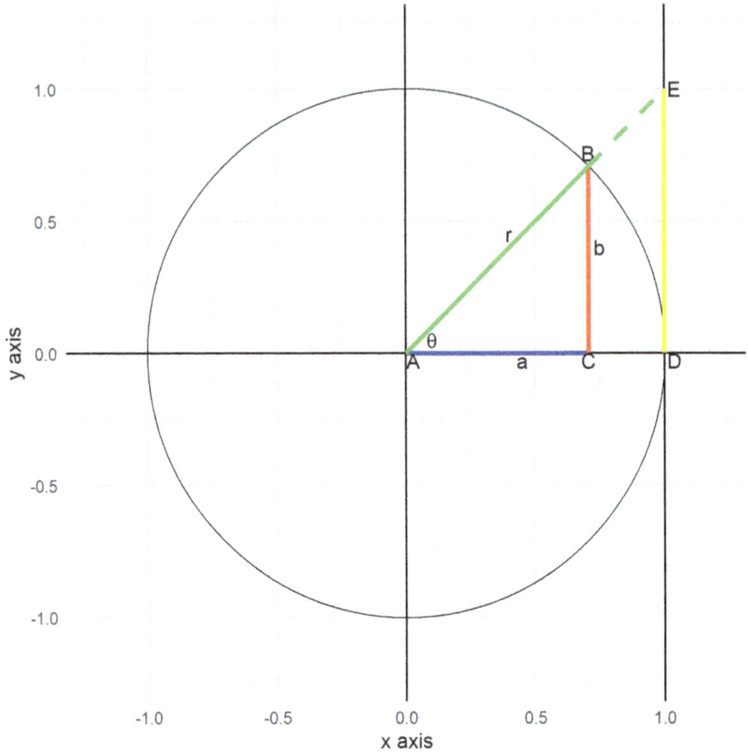

Fig. 8.5 Tangent in the unit circle with $\theta = 45°$

tangent equals 1, the y coordinate. By extending the reasoning for sine and cosine, we can associate the tangent to $\overline{ED}$.

At the beginning of this section we learnt that we can define the tangent in terms of sine and cosine

$$\tan\theta = \frac{\sin\theta}{\cos\theta}$$

Consequently, it is important to consider when $\cos\theta = 0$. Let's observe this fact in Fig. 8.6.

In Fig. 8.6, the tangent function is represented by the green line. As in the case of sine and cosine functions, we see that the pattern of the tangent function repeats. However, the periodicity is π. Additionally, we have asymptotes, the blue lines, that occur when $\theta = -\frac{pi}{2}, \theta = \frac{\pi}{2}$, and $\theta = \frac{3\pi}{2}$, i.e. when the cosine is zero. In fact, when the cosine is zero the tangent is not defined because we cannot divide by zero. We can reach the same conclusion from Fig. 8.5. In fact, if point B moves to $\theta = 90°$, $\overline{AE}$ becomes parallel to the tangent to the circumference and, consequently, it never intersects it.

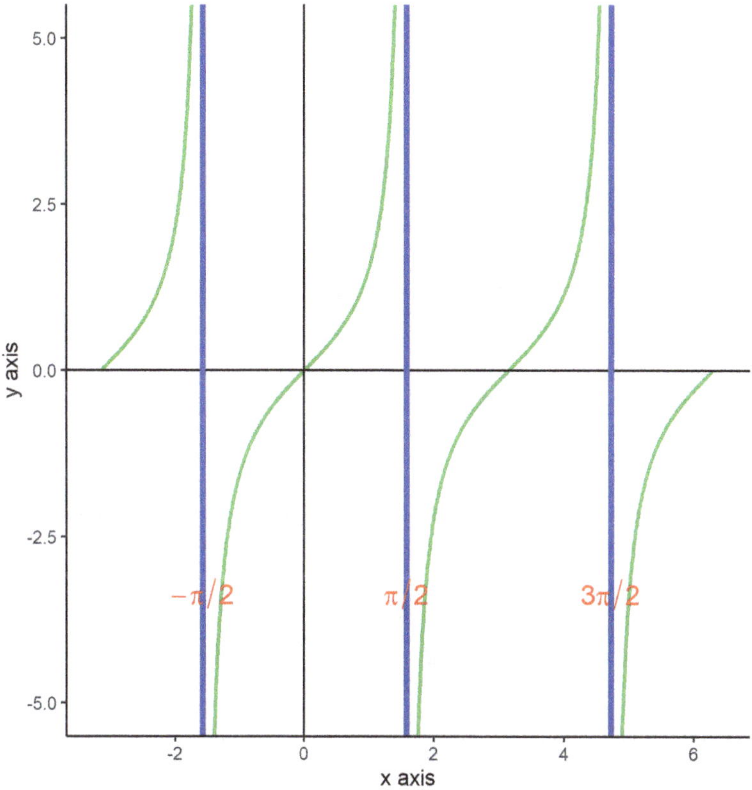

Fig. 8.6 Tangent function

The regular pattern that emerges from the trigonometric functions, as we saw from the sine, cosine, and tangent functions, makes these functions a good instrument to model regular periodic patterns that we observe, for example, in business cycles and agricultural seasons.

We conclude this section with two examples.

Example 8.2.1 Given that $\sin\theta = 0.819152$, find θ in degree.

$$\theta = \sin^{-1}\theta$$

where $\sin^{-1}$ is the inverse function of the sine, also known as arcsine. The solution with **R** is the following. First, we use the arcsine function, `asin()`, to find θ measured in radians. Then, we use the `angle_conversion()` function to express its measurement in degree.

```
> theta <- asin(0.819152)
> theta
[1] 0.959931
```

```
> theta_deg <- angle_conversion(theta, degree = F)
> theta_deg
[1] 55
```

We conclude that $\theta = 55°$.

Example 8.2.2 Find θ and ϕ in the right triangle in Fig. 8.1.

We know that $\overline{AC} = a = 8$, $\overline{BC} = b = 4$,[3] and $\gamma = 90°$. We can proceed as follows.

First, we find the hypotenuse $\overline{AB} = r$ with the Pythagorean Theorem

```
> a <- 8
> b <- 4
> r <- sqrt(a^2 + b^2)
> r
[1] 8.944272
```

By using the definition of trigonometric functions as ratio of the sides of the right triangle we know that

$$\cos\theta = \frac{a}{r}$$

```
> cosin_theta <- a/r
> cosin_theta
[1] 0.8944272
```

Therefore, $\theta = \cos^{-1}\theta$, where $\cos^{-1}$ is the inverse function of cosine, also known as arccosine.

```
> theta <- acos(cosin_theta)
> theta
[1] 0.4636476
> theta_deg <- angle_conversion(theta, degree = F)
> theta_deg
[1] 26.56505
```

Therefore, $\theta = 26.6°$. Since θ and ϕ are complementary, they sum to $90°$

```
> phi_deg <- 90 - theta_deg
> phi_deg
[1] 63.43495
```

Consequently, $\phi = 63.4°$. As expected the sum of the angles γ, θ, ϕ is $180°$.

```
> gamma_deg <- 90
> gamma_deg + theta_deg + phi_deg
[1] 180
```

[3] Refer to the code for Fig. 8.1 in Appendix G.

Note that instead of using the cosine we could have used $\sin\theta = \frac{b}{r}$ to find θ

```
> sin_theta <- b/r
> sin_theta
[1] 0.4472136
> theta <- asin(sin_theta)
> theta
[1] 0.4636476
> theta_deg <- angle_conversion(theta, degree = F)
> theta_deg
[1] 26.56505
```

Alternatively, we could have found ϕ before θ. In this case, note that $\overline{BC} = b$ becomes the adjacent side to ϕ and $\overline{AC} = a$ the opposite side to ϕ. This means that

```
> sin_phi <- a/r
> sin_phi
[1] 0.8944272
> phi <- asin(sin_phi)
> phi
[1] 1.107149
> phi_deg <- angle_conversion(phi, degree = F)
> phi_deg
[1] 63.43495
```

A faster alternative would have been to find θ from the tangent

$$\tan\theta = \frac{b}{a}$$

$$\theta = \tan^{-1}\theta$$

where $\tan^{-1}$ is the inverse function of the tangent, also known as arctangent.

After finding θ we can compute $\phi = 90° - \theta$. Note that in this case we do not need to compute the hypotenuse.

```
> tan_theta <- b/a
> tan_theta
[1] 0.5
> theta <- atan(tan_theta)
> theta
[1] 0.4636476
> theta_deg <- angle_conversion(theta, degree = F)
> theta_deg
[1] 26.56505
```

In alternative, we could have started from ϕ

```
> tan_phi <- a/b
> tan_phi
[1] 2
> phi <- atan(tan_phi)
> phi
[1] 1.107149
> phi_deg <- angle_conversion(phi, degree = F)
> phi_deg
[1] 63.43495
```

8.3 Sum and Differences of Angles

For any two angles α and β, we have

$$
\begin{aligned}
\sin(\alpha+\beta) &= \sin\alpha\cos\beta + \cos\alpha\sin\beta \\
\sin(\alpha-\beta) &= \sin\alpha\cos\beta - \cos\alpha\sin\beta \\
\cos(\alpha+\beta) &= \cos\alpha\cos\beta - \sin\alpha\sin\beta \\
\cos(\alpha-\beta) &= \cos\alpha\cos\beta + \sin\alpha\sin\beta
\end{aligned}
\tag{8.9}
$$

In the case $\alpha = \beta$,

$$
\begin{aligned}
\sin 2\alpha &= 2\sin\alpha\cos\alpha \\
\cos 2\alpha &= \cos^2\alpha - \sin^2\alpha
\end{aligned}
\tag{8.10}
$$

8.4 Derivatives of Trigonometric Functions

Table 8.2 reports the derivatives of trigonometric functions.

Table 8.2 Derivatives of trigonometric functions

$f(x)$	$f'(x)$
$\sin(x)$	$\cos(x)$
$\cos(x)$	$-\sin(x)$
$\tan(x)$	$\sec^2(x)$
$\cot x$	$-\csc^2(x)$
$\sec(x)$	$\sec(x)\tan(x)$
$\csc(x)$	$-\csc(x)\cot(x)$
$\arcsin(x)$	$\frac{1}{\sqrt{1-x^2}}$
$\arccos(x)$	$-\frac{1}{\sqrt{1-x^2}}$
$\arctan(x)$	$\frac{1}{x^2+1}$

Chapter 9
Complex Numbers

9.1 Set of Complex Numbers

We first referred to complex numbers at the very beginning of this textbook (Sect. 2.1). In particular, in Sect. 2.1 we introduced the set of complex numbers $\mathbb{C}$. To grasp the need for complex numbers, let's resume and continue the example in Sect. 2.1. We said that $5^{-1} = \frac{1}{5} \notin \mathbb{Z}$. However, $5^{-1} = \frac{1}{5} = 0.2 \in \mathbb{Q}$. On the other hand, $\sqrt{5} = 2.23606797\ldots \notin \mathbb{Q}$ but $\sqrt{5} \in \mathbb{R}$.

Now, what about $\sqrt{-25}$? We know that both 5^2 and $(-5)^2$ equal 25. Therefore, there is no real solution for this operation. We can conclude that $\sqrt{-25} \notin \mathbb{R}$. Then, what should the solution to $\sqrt{-25}$ be? And why should we want to compute $\sqrt{-25}$? To answer the second question first, we saw that a square root of a negative number is a possible outcome in the quadratic formula when the discriminant D is less than zero (Sect. 3.3.2). Consequently, the concept of numbers is extended with the complex numbers where the solution to $\sqrt{-25} \in \mathbb{C}$.

9.2 Complex Numbers: Real Part and Imaginary Part

From Sect. 3.3.2 we know that the symbol i plays a key role in this extension. The symbol i stands for $\sqrt{-1}$ so that $i^2 = -1$. This allows us to write

$$\sqrt{-25} = \sqrt{25 \cdot -1} = \sqrt{25} \cdot \sqrt{-1} = 5i$$

In **R**,

```
> z <- sqrt(as.complex(-25))
> z
[1] 0+5i
```


M. Porto, *Introduction to Mathematics for Economics with R*,
https://doi.org/10.1007/978-3-031-05202-6_9

We see that **R** returns the solution as $0 + 5i$, where 0 is the *real part* of the complex number and 5 is the *imaginary part* of the complex number.

```
> Re(z)
[1] 0
> Im(z)
[1] 5
```

Since the real part in this case is 0, the solution to $\sqrt{-25}$ is said to be an *imaginary number*.

Generally the complex number is indicated with z and takes the following form

$$z = a + bi \tag{9.1}$$

where a and b are real numbers and a represents the real part of z and b the imaginary part of z.

For example, in

$$z = 2 + 3i$$

2 and 3 are real numbers, 2 represents the real part of z and 3 represents the imaginary part of z. In **R**

```
> z <- 2 + 3i
> Re(z)
[1] 2
> Im(z)
[1] 3
```

The complex number

$$\bar{z} = a - bi \tag{9.2}$$

is called the *complex conjugate* of z. In **R**

```
> z_bar <- Conj(z)
> z_bar
[1] 2-3i
> Re(z_bar)
[1] 2
> Im(z_bar)
[1] -3
```

9.3 Arithmetic Operations

Following the arithmetic operations with complex numbers:
Addition

$$(a + bi) + (c + di) = a + c + bi + di = (a + c) + (b + d)i \tag{9.3}$$

```
> z1 <- 1 + 3i
> z2 <- 4 + 15i
> z1 + z2
[1] 5+18i
```

Subtraction

$$(a + bi) - (c + di) = a - c + bi - di = (a - c) + (b - d)i \tag{9.4}$$

```
> z1 - z2
[1] -3-12i
```

Multiplication

$$(a+bi)(c+di) = (a\cdot c)+(a\cdot di)+(bi\cdot c)+(bi\cdot di) = (ac-bd)+(ad+cb)i \tag{9.5}$$

Note that we have $-bd$ because $bi \cdot di = bdi^2$ where $i^2 = -1$

```
> z1 * z2
[1] -41+27i
> i <- sqrt(as.complex(-1))
> i
[1] 0+1i
> i2 <- i^2
> i2
[1] -1+0i
```

Additionally,

$$(a + bi)^2 = (a + bi)(a + bi) = (a^2 - b^2) + 2abi \tag{9.6}$$

and

$$(a + bi)(a - bi) = a^2 + b^2 \tag{9.7}$$

```
> z1^2
[1] -8+6i
> z1 * Conj(z1)
[1] 10+0i
```

Division

$$\frac{z_1}{z_2} = \frac{z_1}{z_2} \cdot \frac{\overline{z_2}}{\overline{z_2}} = \tag{9.8}$$

$$= \frac{a+bi}{c+di} \cdot \frac{c-di}{c-di} = \frac{(ac+bd)+(cb-ad)i}{c^2+b^2} = \left(\frac{ac+bd}{c^2+b^2}\right) + \left(\frac{cb-ad}{c^2+b^2}\right)i$$

```
> z2 / z1
[1] 4.9+0.3i
```

9.4 Geometric Interpretation and Polar Form

A complex number $a + bi$ can be represented in the *complex plane* where the x axis is called the *real axis* and the y axis is called the *imaginary axis* (Fig. 9.1).[1]

We can use the Pythagorean Theorem to compute the distance from the origin (0, 0) to the point $z = a + bi$. Let's call this distance r. Therefore,

$$r = \sqrt{a^2 + b^2}$$

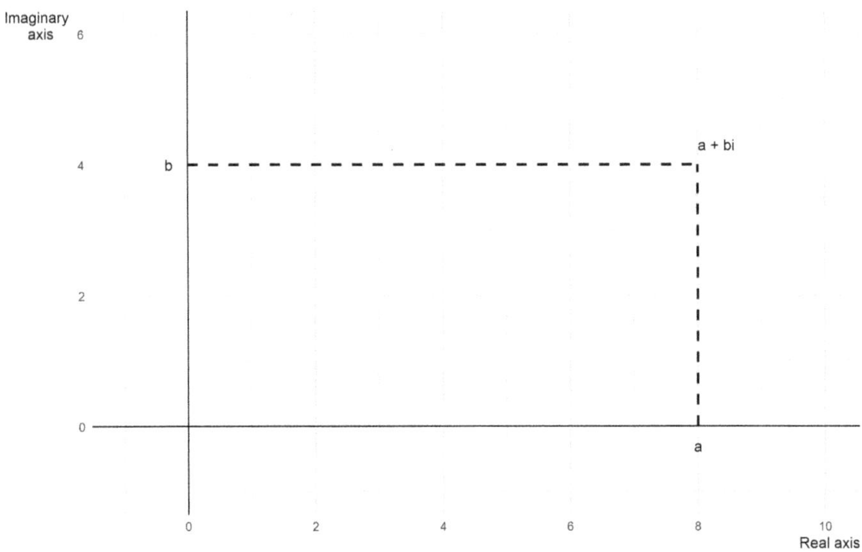

Fig. 9.1 Geometric representation of complex numbers

[1] The code used to generate Figs. 9.1 and 9.2 is available in Appendix H.

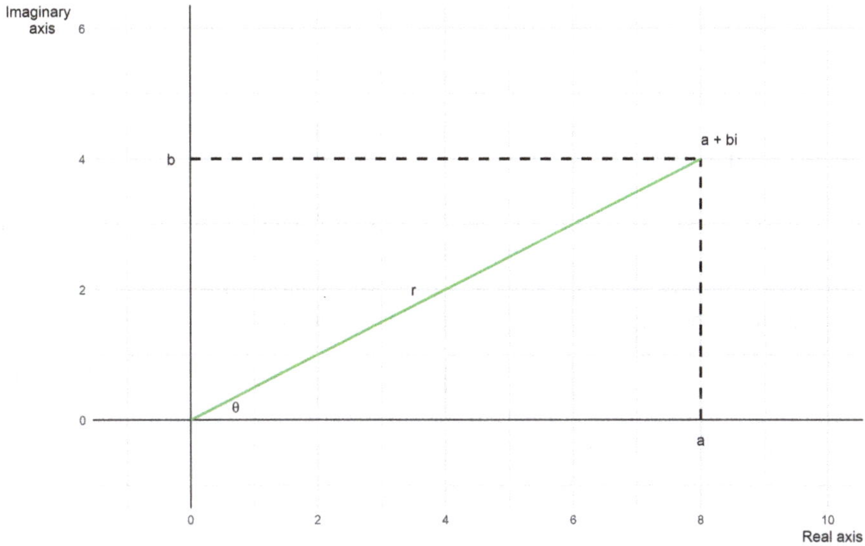

Fig. 9.2 Polar coordinate representation of complex numbers

By (9.7), (9.1), and (9.2), we can rewrite it as

$$r = \sqrt{(a + bi)(a - bi)} = \sqrt{z\bar{z}} \tag{9.9}$$

```
> z <- 8 + 4i
> z
[1] 8+4i
> r <- sqrt(z*Conj(z))
> r
[1] 8.944272+0i
```

By drawing r we find that it makes an angle θ with the positive real axis (Fig. 9.2). This angle is called the *argument* of the complex number.

```
> theta <- Arg(z)
> theta
[1] 0.4636476
> theta_deg <- angle_conversion(theta, degree = F)
> theta_deg
[1] 26.56505
```

Compare this result for angle θ with the result for θ from Example 8.2.2. If you replicated these figures, you may have already noticed that we used the same real values for a and b that we used to build the right triangle in Fig. 8.1. By using trigonometric relations from Chap. 8, we find that r is

```
> a/cos(theta)
[1] 8.944272
```

```
> b/sin(theta)
[1] 8.944272
```

that corresponds to the result from (9.9). In turn, this means that by using trigonometric relations we can write $a = r\cos\theta$ and $b = r\sin\theta$. Therefore, we can rewrite the complex number $a + bi$ as follows

$$a + bi = (r\cos\theta) + (r\sin\theta)i = r(\cos\theta + i\sin\theta) \tag{9.10}$$

Equation 9.10 is the *polar form* of $a + bi$. The polar form is particularly useful to compute the powers of $a + bi$. By De Moivre's theorem, we have that

$$(a + bi)^n = r^n(\cos n\theta + i\sin n\theta) \tag{9.11}$$

where n is a positive integer.

```
> z
[1] 8+4i
> z^3
[1] 128+704i
> i <- sqrt(as.complex(-1))
> i
[1] 0+1i
> r
[1] 8.944272+0i
> r^3 *(cos(3*theta) + i*sin(3*theta))
[1] 128+704i
```

9.5 Exponential Form

The values of sine and cosine can be computed by using the Taylor series. For the sine function the Taylor series is

$$\sin x = x - \frac{1}{3!}x^3 + \frac{1}{5!}x^5 - \frac{1}{7!}x^7 + \frac{1}{9!}x^9 - \cdots = \sum_{n=0}^{\infty}\frac{(-1)^n x^{2n+1}}{(2n+1)!} \tag{9.12}$$

For the cosine function, the Taylor series is

$$\cos x = 1 - \frac{1}{2!}x^2 + \frac{1}{4!}x^4 - \frac{1}{6!}x^6 + \frac{1}{8!}x^8 + \cdots = \sum_{n=0}^{\infty}\frac{(-1)^n x^{2n}}{(2n)!} \tag{9.13}$$

Next, we build a function, `trig_taylor()`, based on (9.12) and (9.13) to compute the values of sine and cosine.

```
> trig_taylor <- function(x, n = 0:5, sin = TRUE){
+
+   if(sin == TRUE){
+     app_trig <- sum(((-1)^n * x^(2*n+1))/
+                       factorial(2*n+1))
+
+   } else {
+     app_trig <- sum(((-1)^n * x^(2*n))/
+                       factorial(2*n))
+
+   }
+   return(app_trig)
+ }
```

First, let's test it with $\theta = 55°$.

```
> theta_deg <- 55
> theta <- angle_conversion(theta_deg)
> theta
[1] 0.9599311
> sin(theta)
[1] 0.819152
> trig_taylor(theta)
[1] 0.819152
> cos(theta)
[1] 0.5735764
> trig_taylor(theta, sin = FALSE)
[1] 0.5735764
```

For $\theta = 120°$ we need to expand the terms of the Taylor series to obtain a better approximation.

```
> theta_deg <- 120
> theta <- angle_conversion(theta_deg)
> theta
[1] 2.094395
> sin(theta)
[1] 0.8660254
> trig_taylor(theta)
[1] 0.8660231
> trig_taylor(theta, 0:9)
[1] 0.8660254
> cos(theta)
[1] -0.5
> trig_taylor(theta, sin = FALSE)
[1] -0.5000145
```

```
> trig_taylor(theta, 0:9, sin = FALSE)
[1] -0.5
```

Let's substitute (9.12) and (9.13) in (9.10)

$$a + bi = r(\cos\theta + i\sin\theta) =$$

$$= r\left[\left(1 - \frac{\theta^2}{2!} + \frac{\theta^4}{4!} - \frac{\theta^6}{6!} + \frac{\theta^8}{8!} + \cdots\right) + i\left(\theta - \frac{\theta^3}{3!} + \frac{\theta^5}{5!} - \frac{\theta^7}{7!} + \frac{\theta^9}{9!} - \cdots\right)\right]$$

Let's reorder the terms by the powers

$$= r\left(1 + i\theta - \frac{\theta^2}{2!} - \frac{i\theta^3}{3!} + \frac{\theta^4}{4!} + \frac{i\theta^5}{5!} - \frac{\theta^6}{6!} - \frac{i\theta^7}{7!} + \frac{\theta^8}{8!} + \frac{i\theta^9}{9!} - \cdots\right)$$

By noting the i when raised to the power $n = 1, 2, 3, 4, 5, 6, ...$ follows this pattern

```
> n <- 1:8
> i <- sqrt(as.complex(-1))
> i
[1] 0+1i
> i^n
[1]  0+1i -1+0i  0-1i  1+0i  0+1i -1+0i  0-1i  1+0i
```

we can rewrite the previous as

$$= r\left(\frac{(i\theta)^0}{0!} + \frac{(i\theta)^1}{1!} + \frac{(i\theta)^2}{2!} + \frac{(i\theta)^3}{3!} + \frac{(i\theta)^4}{4!} + \cdots\right)$$

By setting $\Theta = i\theta$, we can write

$$= f(\Theta) = r\left(\frac{(\Theta)^0}{0!} + \frac{(\Theta)^1}{1!} + \frac{(\Theta)^2}{2!} + \frac{(\Theta)^3}{3!} + \frac{(\Theta)^4}{4!} + \cdots\right)$$

If we take the first derivative we have that $f'(\Theta) = f(\Theta)$. Since we know that the exponential function is the derivative of itself (Sect. 4.6.7)

$$f(\Theta) = re^{\Theta} = re^{i\theta} \tag{9.14}$$

(9.14) is known as the *exponential form* of $a + bi$.

Finally, by setting $r = 1$ we can write

$$e^{i\theta} = \cos\theta + i \sin\theta \tag{9.15}$$

Equation 9.15 is known as *Euler's equation*. Additionally, the following identity holds true as well

$$e^{-i\theta} = \cos\theta - i \sin\theta \tag{9.16}$$

If $\theta = \pi$, that is if it is a 180° angle, $\cos\pi = -1$ and $\sin\pi = 0$. By replacing these in (9.15) we have

$$e^{i\pi} = -1 \quad \text{or} \quad e^{i\pi} + 1 = 0$$

To conclude this section, by the properties of exponentiation and by (9.15) we have

$$e^{a+bi} = e^a \cdot e^{bi} = e^a \cdot (\cos b + i \sin b)$$

Chapter 10
Difference Equations

Difference equations are equations where the time change of a variable y only occurs between integer values, for example from $t = 1$ to $t = 2$ but not in the meantime between the integers. Therefore, difference equations are suitable to model dynamic problems where the time is to be taken as a *discrete* variable. Consequently, we refer to this analysis as *discrete-time* analysis.

The notation used to describe the change in a variable between two periods is Δ. Therefore, Δy_t means the change in y between two consecutive periods. Technically, we should write $\frac{\Delta y}{\Delta t}$ but since the difference between two consecutive periods is one, we end up only writing Δy_t (refer to Shone (2002, p. 10) for an interesting insight on this point). Consequently,

$$\Delta y_t \equiv y_{t+1} - y_t \tag{10.1}$$

This means that, for example,

$$\Delta y_t = 1$$

can be written as

$$y_{t+1} - y_t = 1 \tag{10.2}$$

or

$$y_{t+1} = y_t + 1 \tag{10.3}$$

Additionally, note that writing (10.1) as $\Delta y \equiv y_t - y_{t-1}$ or $\Delta y \equiv y_{t+2} - y_{t+1}$ would keep the meaning of a one period change. You may also find some textbooks to use $y(t), y(t+1), y(t+2), \ldots$ as notation instead of subscripts.

Example 10.0.1 Convert $\Delta y_t = -0.2y_t$ into form (10.2) and (10.3).

M. Porto, *Introduction to Mathematics for Economics with R*,
https://doi.org/10.1007/978-3-031-05202-6_10

$$\Delta y = -0.2y_t$$

$$y_{t+1} - y_t = -0.2y_t$$

$$y_{t+1} = y_t - 0.2y_t \rightarrow y_{t+1} = 0.8y_t$$

Solving a difference equation consists in finding a time path for y_t such that the solution does not contain any lag terms Δ.

We encounter the following terminology associated with difference equations:

- linear/non-linear
  - linear: no y term is raised to the second or higher power, or is multiplied by a y term of another period (e.g. $y_{t+1} = 1.2y_t + 1$)
  - non-linear: y term is raised to the second or higher power or is multiplied by a y term of another period (e.g. $y_{t+1} = 1.2y_t(1 - y_t)$)
- homogeneous/nonhomogeneous
  - homogeneous: after collecting all the y terms in the left-hand side, we have zero in the right-hand side (e.g. $y_{t+1} - 2y_t = 0$)
  - nonhomogeneous: after collecting all the y terms in the left-hand side, we have non-zero in the right-hand side (e.g. $y_{t+1} - 2y_t = 1$)
- first-order difference equation/second-order (or higher) difference equation
  - first-order difference equation: the difference equation only includes one period time lag (e.g. $y_{t+1} = 2y_t + 1$)
  - second order difference equation: the difference equation includes two period time lag (e.g. $y_{t+2} - 2y_{t+1} + 2y_t = 4$)
- constant coefficient and constant term/variable terms
  - constant coefficient and constant term: they are constant (e.g. $y_{t+1} - 2y_t = 1$)
  - variable terms: coefficients and/or constant are functions of t (e.g. $y_{t+1} - 2y_t = 4^t$)

10.1 First-Order Linear Difference Equations

$$y_{t+1} - 2y_t = 4 \tag{10.4}$$

is an example of a first-order linear non-homogeneous difference equation. We can solve it by iteration or by using a more general approach.

10.1.1 Solution by Iteration

Solving a difference equation by iteration consists in finding y_1 given an initial condition y_0. Once we obtained y_1 we can use it to find y_2 and so on by iteration. The iteration allows us to infer the time path of y_t.

Let's apply the iterative method to (10.4).

Step 1
Convert (10.4) into the form (10.3).

$$y_1 = 2y_0 + 4$$

Step 2
Start iterating

$$y_2 = 2y_1 + 4 = 2(2y_0 + 4) + 4$$

We replaced the value for y_1. Continue iterating

$$y_3 = 2y_2 + 4 = 2(2y_1 + 4) + 4 = 2(2(2y_0 + 4) + 4) + 4$$

We replaced the value for y_2 and so on. Assuming an initial value $y_0 = 2$, the time path of $y_{t+1} = 2y_t + 4$ is the following

t	0	1	2	3	...
y	2	8	20	44	...

Let's build a function, `iter_de()`, that solves difference equations by iteration. The function takes five arguments

- `rhs`: the right-hand side of a difference equation as in (10.3)
- `y0`: a vector of initial conditions
- `order`: the order of the difference equation. By default 1
- `periods`: the periods of the time path. By default 100
- `graph`: if the function has to generate a plot of the time path. By default `FALSE`

By now the reader should be able to grasp the content of this code. In reading this code, just keep in mind that **R** start indexing from 1, i.e, the initial condition y_0 will be stored in `y[1]`.

```
> iter_de <- function(rhs, y0, order = 1,
+                      periods = 100, graph = FALSE){
```

```
+
+   y <- numeric(periods + 1)
+   y[1:order] <- y0
+
+   for(t in 1:(periods - order + 1)){
+
+      y[t+order] <- eval(parse(text = rhs))
+
+   }
+   if(graph == FALSE){
+
+     return(y)
+
+   } else{
+
+     require("ggplot2")
+     require("scales")
+
+     df <- data.frame(Time = 0:(length(y)-1), y)
+     p <- ggplot(df, aes(x = Time, y = y)) +
+       geom_point(size = 1, color = "red") +
+       theme_classic() +
+       scale_y_continuous(breaks = pretty_breaks()) +
+       scale_x_continuous(breaks = pretty_breaks())
+     l <- list(results = y,
+               graph_simulation = p)
+     return(l)
+
+   }
+
+ }
```

Let's solve the difference equation in Example 10.4. Figure 10.1 represents the time path for the first 10 periods. Note that I chose a scatter plot (`geom_point()` in the `ggplot()` function) instead of a line plot to represent the concept that "nothing happens" to y_t in the between of integer values, for example between y_1 and y_2.

```
> RHS <- "2*y[t] + 4"
> iter_de(RHS, y0 = 2, periods = 10, graph = T)
$results
 [1]    2    8   20   44   92  188  380  764 1532 3068 6140

$graph_simulation
```

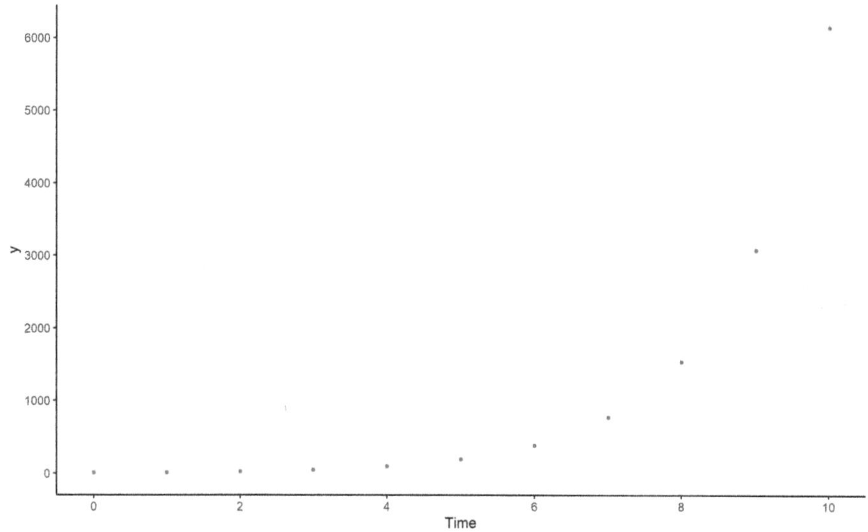

Fig. 10.1 Time path difference equation $y_1 = 2y_0 + 4 \quad (y_0 = 2)$

Example 10.1.1 Solve $y_{t+1} = 0.8y_t$ by iteration.

Step 1
The difference equation is already in form (10.3).

Step 2

$$y_1 = 0.8y_0$$

$$y_2 = 0.8y_1 = 0.8(0.8)y_0$$

$$y_3 = 0.8y_3 = 0.8(0.8)y_1 = 0.8(0.8)(0.8)y_0$$

Assuming an initial value $y_0 = 4$, the time path of $y_{t+1} = 0.8y_t$ is the following

t	0	1	2	3	...
y	4	3.2	2.56	2.048	...

With **R**

```
> RHS <- "0.8*y[t]"
> iter_de(RHS, y0 = 4, periods = 10)
 [1] 4.0000000 3.2000000 2.5600000 2.0480000 1.6384000 1.3107200
 [7] 1.0485760 0.8388608 0.6710886 0.5368709 0.4294967
```

Example 10.1.2 Solve $2y_{t+1} - y_t = 4$ by iteration.

Step 1

$$y_{t+1} = \frac{y_t}{2} + 2$$

Step 2

$$y_1 = \frac{y_0}{2} + 2$$

$$y_2 = \frac{y_1}{2} + 2 = \frac{\frac{y_0}{2} + 2}{2} + 2$$

$$y_3 = \frac{y_2}{2} + 2 = \frac{\frac{\frac{y_0}{2}+2}{2} + 2}{2} + 2$$

Assuming an initial value $y_0 = 1$, the time path of $2y_{t+1} - y_t = 4$ is the following

t	0	1	2	3	...
y	1	2.5	3.25	3.625	...

With **R**

```
> RHS <- "y[t]/2 + 2"
> iter_de(RHS, y0 = 1, periods = 5)
[1] 1.00000 2.50000 3.25000 3.62500 3.81250 3.90625
```

10.1.2 Solution by General Method

Let's observe the solution of Example 10.1.1. At $t = 1$, we have $0.8y_0$. At $t = 2$,we have $0.8(0.8)y_0 = 0.8^2 y_0$. At $t = 3$, we have $0.8(0.8)(0.8)y_0 = 0.8^3 y_0$. This means that at $t = 6$, we have $0.8^6 y_0$, and given the initial value $y_0 = 4$, our solution is 1.048576.

The difference equation in Example 10.1.1 is a homogeneous first-order difference equation. We can rewrite it as

$$y_{t+1} - 0.8y_t = 0$$

This suggests that for a homogeneous first-order difference equation, the general solution can be written as Ab^t, where b stands for *base* (0.8 in the example) and A is a general multiplicative constant in place of y_0 (4 in the example).

As expected this produces the same results as in Example 10.1.1

```
> t <- 0:10
> A <- 4
> b <- 0.8
> A*b^t
 [1] 4.0000000 3.2000000 2.5600000 2.0480000 1.6384000 1.3107200
 [7] 1.0485760 0.8388608 0.6710886 0.5368709 0.4294967
```

Next we investigate how to find a general solution with a nonhomogeneous equation. We can write the solution to a nonhomogeneous equation as

$$y_t = y_c + y_p \tag{10.5}$$

where y_c is the *complementary function*, which represents the deviations from the equilibrium, and y_p is the *particular solution* which represents the inter-temporal equilibrium level of y.

y_c is the reduced form of (10.5), i.e. the homogeneous equation associated with the nonhomogeneous equation while y_p is *any* solution of the complete nonhomogeneous equation (Chiang and Wainwright 2005, p. 548).

Let's see how to find the solution to (10.4) by following the general approach.

Step 1
Write the homogeneous equation associated to (10.4).

$$y_{t+1} - 2y_t = 0$$

Step 2
Since the solution of a homogeneous equation takes the form $y_t = Ab^t$, consequently $y_{t+1} = Ab^{t+1}$. Replace them in the homogeneous equation

$$Ab^{t+1} - 2Ab^t = 0$$

Factor out Ab^t

$$Ab^t(b-2) = 0 \quad \left[Ab^t \neq 0\right]$$

Divide both sides by Ab^t

$$b - 2 = 0$$
$$b = 2$$

Replace $b = 2$ in $y_c = Ab^t$

$$y_c = A2^t$$

Therefore

$$y_t = A2^t + y_p$$

Step 3
Find a particular solution y_p. Since a particular solution y_p is *any* solution of the non-homogeneous equation, we can try to assume the solution to be a constant value k. If the solution is a constant, this means that $y_t = k$ but also that $y_{t+1} = k$. Replace them in the non-homogeneous equation

$$k - 2k = 4$$

Solve for k

$$k = -4$$

Therefore,

$$y_p = -4$$

Step 4
Write the general solution $y_t = y_c + y_p$

$$y_t = A2^t - 4$$

Step 5
Determine the value for A. We need an initial condition. In the example $y_0 = 2$. This means that at $t = 0$, $y_t = 2$. Replace them in the general solution.

$$y_0 = A(2)^0 - 4$$

$$2 = A(1) - 4$$

$$A = 6$$

Step 6
Write the particular solution

$$y_t = 6(2)^t - 4$$

Let's check this solution with **R**.

```
> 6*2^t - 4
 [1]    2    8   20   44   92  188  380  764 1532 3068 6140
```

You can check that this is the same time path we found by iteration.

Example 10.1.3 Solve Example 10.1.2 by following the general approach.

Step 1

$$y_{t+1} - \frac{1}{2}y_t = 0$$

Step 2

$$Ab^{t+1} - \frac{1}{2}Ab^t = 0$$

$$Ab^t\left(b - \frac{1}{2}\right) = 0 \quad \left[Ab^t \neq 0\right]$$

$$b - \frac{1}{2} = 0$$

$$b = \frac{1}{2}$$

$$y_c = A\left(\frac{1}{2}\right)^t$$

$$y_t = A\left(\frac{1}{2}\right)^t + y_p$$

Step 3

$$k - \frac{1}{2}k = 2$$

$$\frac{1}{2}k = 2$$

$$k = 4$$

Step 4

$$y_t = A\left(\frac{1}{2}\right)^t + 4$$

Step 5
At $t = 0$, $y_0 = 1$

$$1 = A\left(\frac{1}{2}\right)^0 + 4$$

$$1 = A + 4$$

$$A = -3$$

Step 6

$$y_t = -3\left(\frac{1}{2}\right)^t + 4$$

```
> -3*(1/2)^t + 4
 [1] 1.000000 2.500000 3.250000 3.625000 3.812500 3.906250
 [7] 3.953125 3.976562 3.988281 3.994141 3.997070
```

Now let's consider the general case

$$y_{t+1} = ay_t + c \tag{10.6}$$

and let's solve it with the general method.

Step 1

$$y_{t+1} - ay_t = 0$$

Step 2

$$Ab^{t+1} - aAb^t = 0$$

$$Ab^t(b - a) = 0\left[Ab^t \neq 0\right]$$

$$b - a$$

$$y_c = A(a)^t$$

Step 3
Let's try the solution $y_t = k$. Therefore,

$$k - ak = c$$

$$k(1 - a) = c$$

$$k = \frac{c}{1 - a}$$

Reached this point, we need to consider the value of a. If $a \neq 1$, we can follow the steps as in the previous example. However, clearly, if $a = 1$, the particular solution is not defined. Therefore, in this case we cannot accept the solution $y_t = k$.

Let's consider the solution to be $y_t = kt$. In turn, this means that $y_{t+1} = k(t+1)$. By substituting them into (10.6), we find

$$k(t + 1) = akt + c$$

$$k(t + 1) - akt = c$$

$$k(t + 1 - at) = c$$

$$k = \frac{c}{t + 1 - at} \tag{10.7}$$

Since we reached this point by assuming the case $a = 1$, the denominator of (10.7) is 1 meaning that

$$k = c$$

Additionally, since we set $y_t = kt$, this means that the particular solution when $a = 1$ is

$$y_p = ct$$

Now let's continue by distinguishing the cases $a \neq 1$ and $a = 1$.

Step 4 (Case of $a \neq 1$)

$$y_t = y_c + y_p$$

$$y_t = A(a)^t + \frac{c}{1 - a}$$

Step 5 (Case of $a \neq 1$)
By setting $y_t = y_0$ when $t = 0$, we have

$$y_0 = A(a)^0 + \frac{c}{1 - a}$$

$$y_0 = A + \frac{c}{1 - a}$$

$$A = y_0 - \frac{c}{1 - a}$$

Step 6 (Case of $a \neq 1$)
The particular solution when $a \neq 1$ is

$$y_t = \left(y_0 - \frac{c}{1 - a}\right)(a)^t + \frac{c}{1 - a}$$

Step 4 (Case of $a = 1$)

$$y_t = y_c + y_p$$

$$y_t = A + ct$$

Step 5 (Case of $a = 1$)
By setting $y_t = y_0$ when $t = 0$, we have

$$y_0 = A + c \cdot 0$$

$$A = y_0$$

Step 6 (Case of $a = 1$)
The particular solution when $a = 1$ is

$$y_t = y_0 + ct$$

This last result can be clearly observed by solving (10.6) by iteration. Therefore, by considering $a = 1$

$$y_1 = y_0 + c$$

$$y_2 = y_1 + c = (y_0 + c) + c = y_0 + 2c$$

$$y_3 = y_2 + c = y_0 + 2c + c = y_0 + 3c$$

By following this pattern we consequently have

$$y_t = y_0 + ct$$

as expected, the same solution by applying the general method.

Example 10.1.4 Solve the following difference equation by applying the general method

$$y_{t+1} = y_t + 2 \quad (y_0 = 5)$$

Step 1

$$y_{t+1} - y_t = 0$$

Step 2

$$Ab^{t+1} - Ab^t = 0$$

$$Ab^t(b-1) = 0 \quad \left[Ab^t \neq 0\right]$$

$$b = 1$$

$$y_c = A(1)^t$$

Step 3
In step 3, if we followed the usual approach we would end up with

$$k - k = 2$$

that is, the particular solution would be not defined. Therefore, by following the case of $a = 1$, we set $y_t = kt$ and $y_{t+1} = k(t+1)$. By substituting them into the complete nonhomogeneous difference equation we have

$$k(t+1) = kt + 2$$

$$k(t+1) - kt = 2$$

$$k = 2$$

Because we set $y_t = kt$, the particular solution becomes

$$y_p = 2t$$

Step 4
Therefore, the general solution is

$$y_t = A + 2t$$

Step 5
At $t = 0$, $y_t = 5$,

$$5 = A + (2 \cdot 0)$$

$$A = 5$$

Step 6
The particular solution is

$$y_t = 5 + 2t$$

Let's check the solution with **R**

```
> RHS <- "y[t] + 2"
> iter_de(RHS, y0 = 5, periods = 10)
 [1]  5  7  9 11 13 15 17 19 21 23 25
```

10.1.3 Time Path and Equilibrium

The nature of the time path of y_t depends on the Ab^t term in the complementary function, and in particular on the value and sign of the base b. Let's assume $A = 1$ and let's focus only on b. We have the following cases:

- $b > 1$: b^t increases with t at an increasing pace and consequently the series gets larger and larger over time, tending to infinity in the limit (top left panel in Fig. 10.2)[1]
- $b = 1$: b^t will remain at unity regardless the value of t and consequently the series is a straight line with the y intercept equal to 1 (top right panel in Fig. 10.2)
- $0 < b < 1$: b^t decreases with t at an increasing pace and consequently the series gets smaller and smaller over time, tending to zero in the limit (middle left panel in Fig. 10.2)
- $-1 < b < 0$: b is a negative fraction and the series alternates between positive and negative values, tending to zero in the limit (middle right panel in Fig. 10.2)
- $b = -1$: the series alternates between $+1$ and -1 (bottom left panel in Fig. 10.2)
- $b < -1$: the series alternates between positive and negative values but, contrary to the case $-1 < b < 0$, it tends to explode over time (bottom right panel in Fig. 10.2)

[1] The code used to generate Figs. 10.2, 10.3, 10.4, and 10.5 is available in Appendix I.

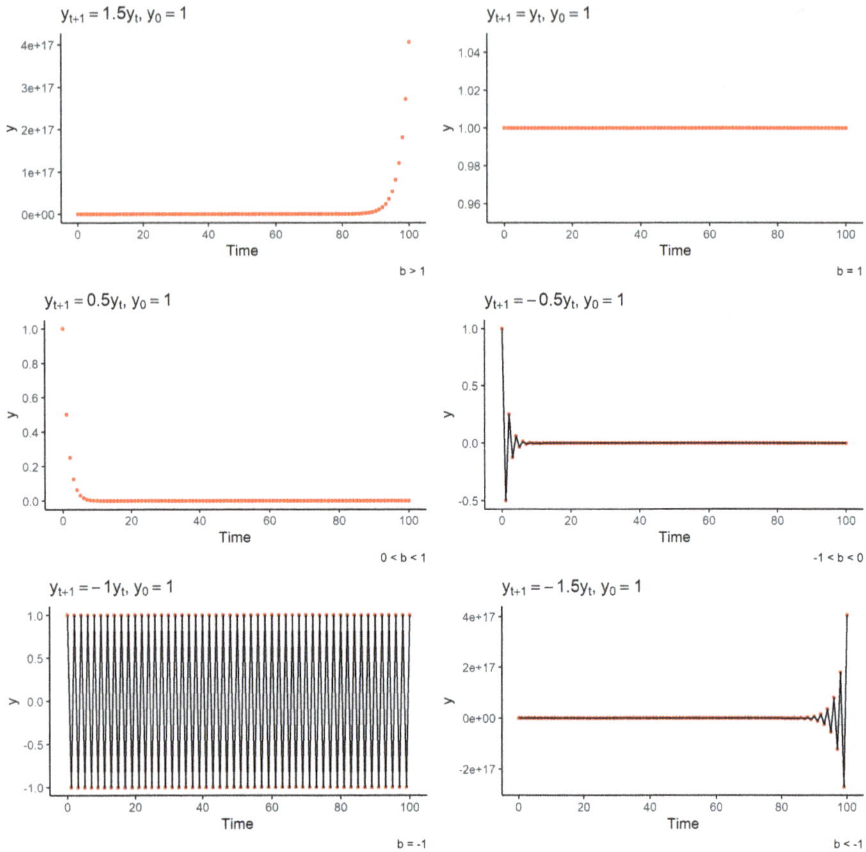

Fig. 10.2 Time path of y_t: the role of b

Additionally, based on the magnitude and sign of b we can state that the time path is

- Non-oscillatory if $b > 0$
- Oscillatory if $b < 0$
- Divergent if $|b| > 1$
- Convergent if $|b| < 1$

Next we consider the role of A in Ab^t. The multiplicative constant A has two main effects: a *scale effect* and a *mirror effect*

- $A > 1$: scale up the series while maintaining the same time path shape (*scale effect*) (top panel in Fig. 10.3)
- $0 < A < 1$: scale down the series while maintaining the same time path shape (*scale effect*) (middle panel in Fig. 10.3)

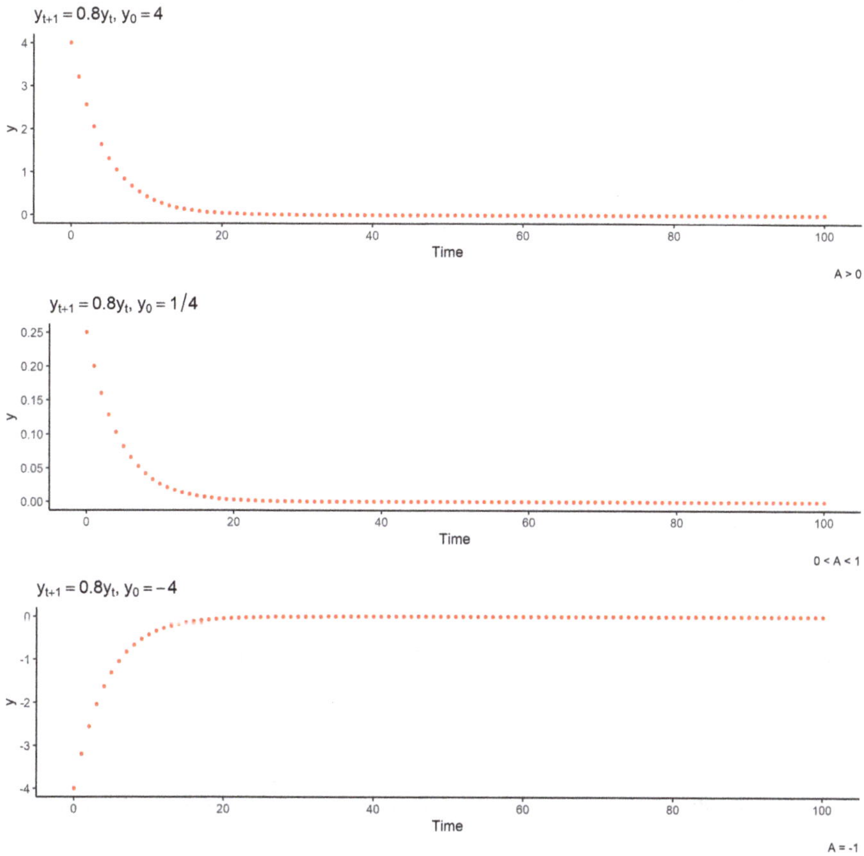

Fig. 10.3 Time path of y_t: the role of A

- $A = -1$: if b^t is multiplied by -1 the shape to the time path is reverted as in a mirror (*mirror effect*) (bottom panel in Fig. 10.3)

  In commenting the time path of the general solution

$$y_t = y_c + y_p = Ab^t + y_p \tag{10.8}$$

the nature of the time path resides in b, which is convergent if and only if $|b| < 1$. The role of y_p is to shift up or down the series depending on the sign but it does not affect the nature of the path, i.e. if convergent or divergent. However, what is affected by including y_p is the level reference of the convergent or divergent time path. In case we only analyse y_c this level reference is 0; in case we analyse a general solution as (10.8), the reference level is given by y_p.

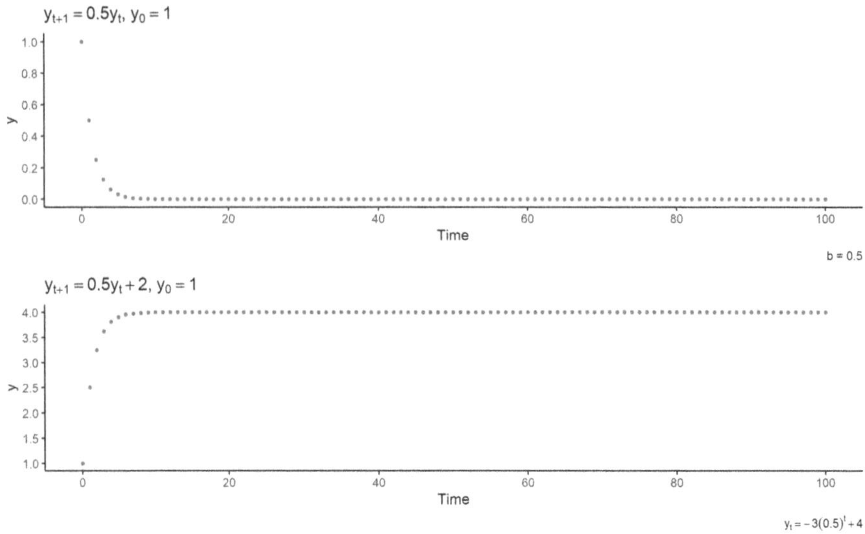

Fig. 10.4 Time path of Example 10.1.3

Let's consider the solution in Example 10.1.3. We have that

$$b = \frac{1}{2} \rightarrow |b| < 1$$

therefore we can conclude that the time path is convergent. $y_p = 4$ and the particular solution is

$$y_t = -3\left(\frac{1}{2}\right)^t + 4$$

that does not affect the conclusion about the nature of the path. Figure 10.4 shows in the top panel the time path of the homogeneous equation with $b = 0.5$. We observe that the time path is convergent to zero. In the bottom panel, we consider the time path of the nonhomogeneous equation. We can observe that the shape of the time path is affected by $A = -3$ (*scale effect* and *mirror effect*) but still the time path is convergent. However, it converges to the level value 4.

10.2 Second-Order Linear Difference Equations

In a second-order linear difference equation the variable of interest depends on two-period time lag. The notation used to describe the change in the variable of interest is $\Delta^2 y_t$. Therefore, we have

$$
\begin{aligned}
\Delta^2 y_t &= \Delta(\Delta y_t) \\
&= \Delta(y_{t+1} - y_t) \\
&= \Delta y_{t+1} - \Delta y_t \\
&= (y_{t+2} - y_{t+1}) - (y_{t+1} - y_t) \\
&= y_{t+2} - 2y_{t+1} + y_t
\end{aligned}
\tag{10.9}
$$

We will work with this last form.

10.2.1 Solution to Second-Order Linear Homogeneous Difference Equation

Let's consider the case of a second-order linear homogeneous difference equation

$$y_{t+2} + a_1 y_{t+1} + a_2 y_t = 0 \tag{10.10}$$

We will follow the same approach used for the first-order linear difference equation by trying $y_t = Ab^t$ as solution. In the case of a second-order difference equation this implies $y_{t+1} = Ab^{t+1}$ and $y_{t+2} = Ab^{t+2}$. By substituting them into (10.10)

$$Ab^{t+2} + a_1 Ab^{t+1} + a_2 Ab^t = 0$$

$$Ab^t(b^2 + a_1 b + a_2) = 0 \quad \left[Ab^t \neq 0\right]$$

$$b^2 + a_1 b + a_2 = 0 \tag{10.11}$$

Equation 10.11 is known as *characteristic equation*. Basically, this is a quadratic equation. We can find the roots—*characteristic roots*—with the quadratic formula[2]

$$b_1, b_2 = \frac{-a_1 \pm \sqrt{a_1^2 - 4a_2}}{2} \tag{10.12}$$

We know that the type of roots depends on the discriminant D (Sect. 3.3.2). Consequently, we examine the three cases based on $D \lesseqgtr 0$.

[2] The quadratic formula is in the normalized form, i.e. the coefficient of b^2 needs to be 1.

10.2.1.1 Two Distinct Real Roots (Case of $D > 0$)

If $D > 0$, we have two distinct real roots and y_c can be written as a linear combination of b_1^t and b_2^t, that are linearly independent

$$y_c = A_1 b_1^t + A_2 b_2^t \tag{10.13}$$

where A_1 and A_2 are two arbitrary constants whose values can be obtained given the initial conditions y_0 and y_1

$$y_0 = A_1 b_1^0 + A_2 b_2^0 = A_1 + A_2$$

$$y_1 = A_1 b_1^1 + A_2 b_2^1 = A_1 b_1 + A_2 b_2$$

By solving this system of equations for A_1 and A_2, we find that

$$A_1 = \frac{y_1 - b_2 y_0}{b_1 - b_2}, \quad A_2 = \frac{y_1 - b_1 y_0}{b_2 - b_1}$$

Example 10.2.1 Find the solution to the following second-order homogeneous difference equation

$$y_{t+2} - 3y_{t+1} + 2y_t = 0$$

Step 1
Substitute $y_t = Ab^t$, $y_{t+1} = Ab^{t+1}$, and $y_{t+2} = Ab^{t+2}$ into the homogeneous difference equation

$$Ab^{t+2} - 3Ab^{t+1} + 2Ab^t = 0$$

$$Ab^t\left(b^2 - 3b + 2\right) = 0 \quad \left[Ab^t \neq 0\right]$$

Step 2
Find the characteristic roots

$$b_1, b_2 = \frac{-(-3) \pm \sqrt{(-3)^2 - 4 \cdot 2}}{2}$$

$$b_1 = 2, \quad b_2 = 1$$

Step 3
Write the solution to the homogeneous difference equation

$$y_t = A_1(2)^t + A_2(1)^t$$

Step 4
Given the initial conditions $y_0 = 2$ and $y_1 = 5$, find the constants

$$2 = A_1 + A_2$$

$$5 = 2A_1 + A_2$$

$$A_1 = 2 - A_2$$

$$5 = 2(2 - A_2) + A_2 \rightarrow 5 = 4 - 2A_2 + A_2 \rightarrow A_2 = -1$$

$$A_1 = 3$$

Step 5
Write the particular solution

$$y_t = 3 \cdot 2^t + (-1) \cdot 1^t$$

Check the solution with **R**

```
> t <- 0:10
> b1 <- 2
> b2 <- 1
> A1 <- 3
> A2 <- -1
> A1*b1^t + A2*b2^t
 [1]    2    5   11   23   47   95  191  383  767 1535 3071
```

Verify the solution with the `iter_de()` function

```
> RHS <- "3*y[t+1] - 2*y[t]"
> iter_de(RHS, y0 = c(2, 5), order = 2, periods = 10)
 [1]    2    5   11   23   47   95  191  383  767 1535 3071
```

10.2.1.2 One Real Root (or Repeated Real Roots) (Case of $D = 0$)

If $D = 0$, $b_1 = b_2 \equiv b$. Consequently,

$$y_c = A_1 b^t + A_2 b^t = (A_1 + A_2) b^t = A_3 b^t$$

where we set $A_3 = A_1 + A_2$. Additionally, if $A_3 b$ is a solution, $A_4 t b$ is a solution as well. Consequently,

$$y_c = A_3 b^t + A_4 t b^t \tag{10.14}$$

Example 10.2.2 Find the solution to the following second-order homogeneous difference equation

$$y_{t+2} - 6y_{t+1} + 9y_t = 0$$

Step 1

$$Ab^{t+2} - 6Ab^{t+1} + 9Ab^t = 0$$

$$Ab^t(b^2 - 6b + 9) = 0 \quad \left[Ab^t \neq 0\right]$$

Step 2

$$b_1 = b_2 = b = 3$$

Step 3

$$y_t = A_3(3)^t + A_4 t(3)^t$$

Step 4
Given $y_0 = 6$ and $y_1 = 4$

$$6 = A_3(3)^0 + A_4 0 \cdot (3)^0 \rightarrow A_3 = 6$$

$$4 = A_3(3)^1 + A_4 1 \cdot (3)^1 \rightarrow A_4 = -\frac{14}{3}$$

Step 5

$$y_t = 6 \cdot 3^t - \frac{14}{3} t(3)^t$$

```
> t <- 0:10
> b <- 3
> A3 <- 6
> A4 <- -(14/3)
> A3*b^t + A4*t*b^t
 [1]        6        4      -30     -216    -1026    -4212   -16038
 [8]   -58320  -205578  -708588 -2401326
> RHS <- "6*y[t+1] - 9*y[t]"
> iter_de(RHS, y0 = c(6, 4), order = 2, periods = 10)
 [1]        6        4      -30     -216    -1026    -4212   -16038
 [8]   -58320  -205578  -708588 -2401326
```

10.2.1.3 Complex Roots (Case of $D < 0$)

If $D < 0$, the characteristic roots are complex roots. The De Moivre theorem plays a key role in order to go from complex roots to real solutions. Here we will only present the solution. The interested reader may refer to Chiang and Wainwright (2005, p. 572) and Simon and Blume (1994, p. 613) for more details.

Step 1

$$Ab^{t+2} - a_1 Ab^{t+1} + a_2 Ab^t = 0$$

$$Ab^t(b^2 - a_1 b + a_2) = 0 \quad \left[Ab^t \neq 0\right]$$

Step 2
With the discriminant less than zero, $a_1^2 - 4a_2 < 0$, the characteristic roots are complex roots

$$b_1 = \alpha + \beta i$$

$$b_2 = \alpha - \beta i$$

Step 3
Keep the values of α and β. Additionally, use them to find r

$$r = \sqrt{\alpha^2 + \beta^2}$$

Use trigonometric relations to find θ. By using cos

$$\cos\theta = \frac{\alpha}{r}$$

$$\theta = \cos^{-1}\theta$$

Step 4
Write the general solution

$$y_t = A_5 r^t \cos(\theta t) + A_6 r^t \sin(\theta t)$$

Step 5
Given the initial conditions y_0 and y_1, find A_5 and A_6

$$A_5 = y_0$$

$$A_6 = \frac{y_1 - y_0 r \cos\theta}{r \sin\theta}$$

Write the solution

$$y_t = A_5 \cdot r^t \cos(\theta t) + \left(\frac{y_1 - y_0 r \cos\theta}{r \sin\theta}\right) \cdot r^t \sin(\theta t)$$

Example 10.2.3 Find the solution to the following second-order homogeneous difference equation

$$y_{t+2} - 3y_{t+1} + 3y_t = 0$$

Step 1

$$Ab^{t+2} - 3Ab^{t+1} + 3Ab^t = 0$$

$$Ab^t(b^2 - 3b + 3) = 0 \quad \left[Ab^t \neq 0\right]$$

Step 2

$$b_1 = \frac{3}{2} + \frac{\sqrt{3}}{2}i$$

$$b_2 = \frac{3}{2} - \frac{\sqrt{3}}{2}i$$

Step 3

$$\alpha = \frac{3}{2}$$

$$\beta = \frac{\sqrt{3}}{2}$$

$$r = \sqrt{\alpha^2 + \beta^2} = \sqrt{\left(\frac{3}{2}\right)^2 + \left(\frac{\sqrt{3}}{2}\right)^2} = \sqrt{3}$$

$$\cos\theta = \frac{\alpha}{r} = 0.8660254$$

$$\theta = \cos^{-1}\theta = 0.5235988$$

Step 4

$$y_t = A_5 r^t \cos(\theta t) + A_6 r^t \sin(\theta t)$$

$$y_t = A_5 \sqrt{3}^t \cos(0.5235988t) + A_6 \sqrt{3}^t \sin(0.5235988t)$$

Step 5
Given $y_0 = 2$ and $y_1 = 3$

$$A_5 = 2$$

$$A_6 = \frac{y_1 - y_0 r \cos\theta}{r \sin\theta} = \frac{3 - 2\sqrt{3}\cos 0.5235988}{\sqrt{3}\sin 0.5235988} = 0$$

$$y_t = 2 \cdot \sqrt{3}^t \cos(0.5235988t) + 0 \cdot \sqrt{3}^t \sin(0.5235988t)$$

```
> t <- 0:20
> y0 <- 2
> y1 <- 3
> r <- sqrt(3)
> alpha <- 3/2
> beta <- (sqrt(3)/2)
> cos_theta <- alpha/r
> sin_theta <- beta/r
> theta <- acos(cos_theta)
> theta
[1] 0.5235988
> asin(sin_theta)
[1] 0.5235988
> A5 <- y0
> A6 <- ((y1 - y0*r*cos(theta))/
+           (r*sin(theta)))
> round(A5*(r^t)*(cos(theta*t)) + A6*(r^t)*
(sin(theta*t)), 1)
 [1]      2      3      3      0     -9    -27
 [7]    -54    -81    -81      0    243    729
[13]   1458   2187   2187      0  -6561 -19683
[19] -39366 -59049 -59049
> RHS <- "3*y[t+1] - 3*y[t]"
> iter_de(RHS, y0 = c(2, 3), order = 2, periods = 20)
 [1]      2      3      3      0     -9    -27
 [7]    -54    -81    -81      0    243    729
[13]   1458   2187   2187      0  -6561 -19683
[19] -39366 -59049 -59049
```

10.2.2 Solution to Second-Order Linear Nonhomogeneous Difference Equation

Let's consider a second-order linear nonhomogeneous difference equation

$$y_{t+2} + a_1 y_{t+1} + a_2 y_t = c \tag{10.15}$$

As before we can identify the two components of the solution of (10.15)

$$y_t = y_c + y_p$$

where y_c is the solution to the homogeneous part of (10.15) (Steps 1–3 in Sect. 10.2.1).

We follow the same approach as for the first-order to find y_p. Let's substitute $y_t = k$, $y_{t+1} = k$, $y_{t+2} = k$ into (10.15)

$$k + a_1 k + a_2 k = c$$

and solve for k

$$k = \frac{c}{1 + a_1 + a_2}$$

In this case as well, we need to consider the value of the denominator.

If $1 + a_1 + a_2 \neq 0$, i.e. $a_1 + a_2 \neq -1$,

$$y_p = \frac{c}{1 + a_1 + a_2}$$

If $1 + a_1 + a_2 = 0$, i.e. $a_1 + a_2 = -1$, we need to try a solution of the form $y_t = kt$, implying $y_{t+1} = k(t + 1)$ and $y_{t+2} = k(t + 2)$. By substituting these in (10.15)

$$k(t + 2) + a_1 k(t + 1) + a_2 kt = c$$

$$k(t + 2 + a_1 t + a_1 + a_2 t) = c$$

$$k = \frac{c}{t(1 + a_1 + a_2) + a_1 + 2} \tag{10.16}$$

Since we are investigating this solution because we are in the case of $1 + a_1 + a_2 = 0$, (10.16) leads to

$$y_p = \frac{c}{a_1 + 2} t$$

If $1 + a_1 + a_2 = 0$ and $a_1 = -2$, we need to try a solution of the form $y_t = kt^2$, implying $y_{t+1} = k(t+1)^2$ and $y_{t+2} = k(t+2)^2$. By substituting these into (10.15) the solution is

$$y_p = \frac{c}{2}t^2$$

This case corresponds to the difference equation $y_{t+2} - 2y_{t+1} + y_t = c$ (Chiang and Wainwright 2005, p. 570).

Example 10.2.4 Find the solution to the following second-order linear nonhomogeneous difference equation

$$y_{t+2} - 3y_{t+1} + 2y_t = 6$$

The complementary component is the homogeneous equation in Example 10.2.1. At Step 3 we found

$$y_c = A_1(2)^t + A_2(1)^t$$

Now let's continue by considering the particular component

Step 4
Let's check the coefficients $a_1 = -3$ and $a_2 = 2$. Since $a_1 + a_2 = -3 + 2 = -1$ we exclude the trial solution $y_t = k$ and adopt a trial solution of the form $y_t = kt$. Consequently,

$$k(t+2) - 3k(t+1) + 2kt = 6$$

$$k(t + 2 - 3t - 3 + 2t) = 6$$

$$k = -6$$

$$y_p = -6t$$

Step 5

$$y_t = A_1(2)^t + A_2(1)^t - 6t$$

Step 6
Given the initial conditions $y_0 = 2$ and $y_1 = 5$, find the constants

$$2 = A_1 + A_2$$

$$A_1 = 2 - A_2$$

$$5 = A_1 2 + A_2 - 6 \rightarrow 5 = (2 - A_2)2 + A_2 - 6$$

$$A_2 = -7$$

$$A_1 = 9$$

Step 7
Write the solution

$$y_t = 9 \cdot 2^t - 7 \cdot 1^t - 6t$$

Check the solution with **R**

```
> t <- 0:10
> b1 <- 2
> b2 <- 1
> A1 <- 9
> A2 <- -7
> A1*b1^t + A2*b2^t - 6*t
 [1]    2    5   17   47  113  251  533 1103 2249 4547 9149
> RHS <- "3*y[t+1] - 2*y[t] + 6"
> iter_de(RHS, y0 = c(2, 5), order = 2, periods = 10)
 [1]    2    5   17   47  113  251  533 1103 2249 4547 9149
```

10.2.3 Time Path and Equilibrium

As in the case of the first-order linear difference equation, the base b plays the key role in determining the time path of y_t. However, in this case we need to consider that we have two bases, i.e. the two characteristic roots, b_1 and b_2. If $|b_1| > |b_2|$, b_1 is known as the *dominant root*.

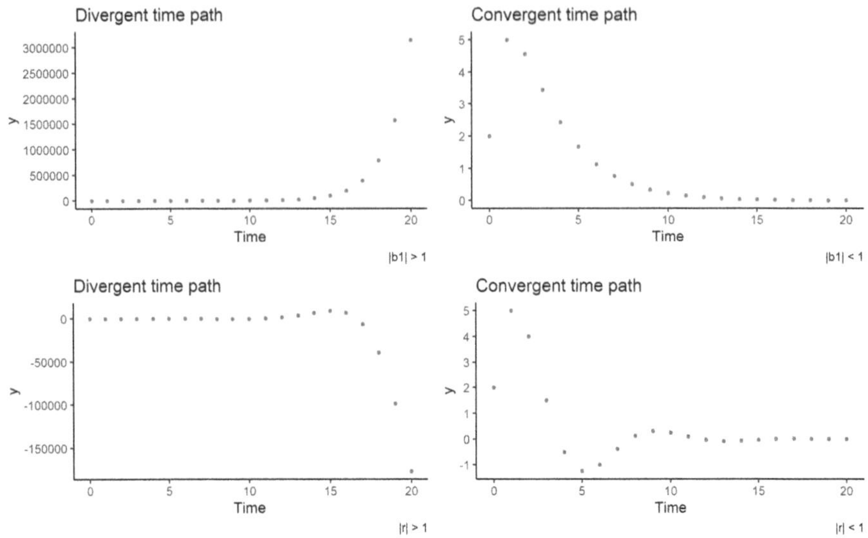

Fig. 10.5 Time path: second-order linear difference equations

If $b_1 \neq b_2$, and

- $|b_1| > 1$ and $|b_2| > 1$, the time path is divergent
- $|b_1| > 1$ and $|b_2| < 1$, the time path is divergent
- $|b_1| < 1$ and $|b_2| < 1$, the time path is convergent

If $b_1 = b_2 \equiv b$, and

- $|b| > 1$, the time path is divergent
- $|b| < 1$, the time path is convergent

In the case of complex roots, $b = \alpha \pm \beta i$, and

- $|r| > 1$,[3] the time path is divergent
- $|r| < 1$, the time path is convergent

Figure 10.5 provides some examples of divergent and convergent paths.

10.3 System of Linear Difference Equations

In this section, we introduce systems of linear difference equations.

[3] r by definition is the absolute value of the conjugate complex roots. Refer to Eqs. 9.7 and 9.9.

10.3.1 Equilibrium

The following linear homogeneous system

$$x_{t+1} = ax_t + by_t$$
$$y_{t+1} = cx_t + dy_t \tag{10.17}$$

can be represented in matrix form as

$$\begin{bmatrix} x_{t+1} \\ y_{t+1} \end{bmatrix} = \begin{bmatrix} a & b \\ c & d \end{bmatrix} \begin{bmatrix} x_t \\ y_t \end{bmatrix} \tag{10.18}$$

that can be written as

$$\mathbf{z}_{t+1} = A\mathbf{z}_t \tag{10.19}$$

In equilibrium $x_t = x_{t+1} = x^*$ and $y_t = y_{t+1} = y^*$. Therefore, (10.18) and (10.19) become

$$\begin{bmatrix} x^* \\ y^* \end{bmatrix} = \begin{bmatrix} a & b \\ c & d \end{bmatrix} \begin{bmatrix} x^* \\ y^* \end{bmatrix}$$

and

$$\mathbf{z}^* = A\mathbf{z}^*$$

Therefore, if

$$\mathbf{z}^* = A\mathbf{z}^*$$
$$\mathbf{z}^* - A\mathbf{z}^* = 0$$
$$(I - A)\mathbf{z}^* = 0$$
$$\mathbf{z}^* = (I - A)^{-1}0 = 0$$

an equilibrium solution exists.

Similarly, the first-order linear nonhomogeneous system

$$x_{t+1} = ax_t + by_t + j$$
$$y_{t+1} = cx_t + dy_t + k \tag{10.20}$$

can be written in matrix form as

$$\begin{bmatrix} x_{t+1} \\ y_{t+1} \end{bmatrix} = \begin{bmatrix} a & b \\ c & d \end{bmatrix} \begin{bmatrix} x_t \\ y_t \end{bmatrix} + \begin{bmatrix} j \\ k \end{bmatrix} \tag{10.21}$$

that can be written as

$$\mathbf{z}_{t+1} = A\mathbf{z}_t + \mathbf{b} \tag{10.22}$$

In equilibrium we have

$$\begin{bmatrix} x^* \\ y^* \end{bmatrix} = \begin{bmatrix} a & b \\ c & d \end{bmatrix} \begin{bmatrix} x^* \\ y^* \end{bmatrix} + \begin{bmatrix} j \\ k \end{bmatrix}$$

or

$$\mathbf{z}^* = A\mathbf{z}^* + \mathbf{b}$$

Therefore, if

$$\mathbf{z}^* = A\mathbf{z}^* + \mathbf{b}$$

$$\mathbf{z}^* - A\mathbf{z}^* = \mathbf{b}$$

$$(I - A)\mathbf{z}^* = \mathbf{b}$$

$$\mathbf{z}^* = (I - A)^{-1}\mathbf{b}$$

an equilibrium solution exists.

Therefore, for a linear homogeneous system the equilibrium exists if $\mathbf{z}^* = 0$; for a linear nonhomogeneous system the equilibrium exists if $(I - A)$ is invertible.

10.3.2 Solution with the Powers of a Matrix

We can solve systems of difference equations by iteration as well.

By applying the iteration method, the solution to (10.19) is

$$\mathbf{z}_t = A^t\mathbf{z}_0 \tag{10.23}$$

By applying the iteration method, the solution to (10.22) is

$$\mathbf{z}_t = A^t\mathbf{z}_0 + (I + A + A^2 + \cdots + A^{t-1})\mathbf{b} \tag{10.24}$$

Based on Eqs. 10.23 and 10.24, let's write a function, `sys_folde()`, to numerically solve system of first-order linear difference equations. The function takes four arguments

- `A`: a matrix with the coefficients
- `A0`: a column vector of initial values
- `b`: a column vector with constant values. By default `NULL`, i.e. it is a homogeneous system
- `periods`: the value for the period to be returned. By default 10

Note that `%^%` computes the power of a matrix. It is a function from the `expm` package.

```
> sys_folde <- function(A, A0, b = NULL, periods = 10){
+
+   require("expm")
+
+   Id <- diag(nrow(A))
+
+   if(is.null(b)){
+
+     sol <- A%^%periods %*% A0
+
+   } else if(periods == 1){
+
+     sol <- A%^%periods %*% A0 + (Id%*%b)
+
+     return(sol)
+
+   } else if(periods == 2){
+
+     sol <- A%^%periods %*% A0 + (Id + A)%*%b
+
+   } else {
+
+     int1 <- A%^%periods %*% A0
+     int2 <- Id + A
+
+     for(t in 3:(periods)){
+
+       int2 <- int2 + A%^%(t-1)
+
+     }
+
+     int3 <- int2 %*% b
+     sol <- int1 + int3
```

```
+
+     }
+
+     return(sol)
+
+ }
```

10.3.3 Eigenvalues Method

In this section we write the general solution in terms of eigenvalues and eigenvectors. Additionally, let's considering the following. By subtracting the equilibrium vector $\mathbf{z}^* = A\mathbf{z}^* + \mathbf{b}$ from $\mathbf{z}_{t+1} = A\mathbf{z}_t + \mathbf{b}$, that is

$$\mathbf{z}_{t+1} - \mathbf{z}^* = A\mathbf{z}_t + \mathbf{b} - \left(A\mathbf{z}^* + \mathbf{b}\right)$$

$$\mathbf{z}_{t+1} - \mathbf{z}^* = A\mathbf{z}_t - A\mathbf{z}^*$$

$$\mathbf{z}_{t+1} - \mathbf{z}^* = A\left(\mathbf{z}_t - \mathbf{z}^*\right)$$

$$\mathbf{w}_{t+1} = A\mathbf{w}_t$$

where $\mathbf{w}_t = \mathbf{z}_t - \mathbf{z}^*$, and consequently, $\mathbf{w}_{t+1} = \mathbf{z}_{t+1} - \mathbf{z}^*$, we can reduce a linear nonhomogeneous system to a linear homogeneous system in terms of deviations from the equilibrium. Therefore, in this section we will focus exclusively on linear homogeneous systems.

We will consider three cases:

1. distinct real eigenvalues
2. repeated eigenvalues
3. complex eigenvalues

10.3.3.1 Case 1: Distinct Real Eigenvalues

Consider the following system

$$\begin{aligned} x_{t+1} &= 2x_t + 4y_t \\ y_{t+1} &= x_t + 5y_t \end{aligned} \tag{10.25}$$

It can be written in matrix form as

$$\begin{bmatrix} x_{t+1} \\ y_{t+1} \end{bmatrix} = \begin{bmatrix} 2 & 4 \\ 1 & 5 \end{bmatrix} \begin{bmatrix} x_t \\ y_t \end{bmatrix}$$

Let's find the eigenvalues and eigenvectors of matrix

$$A = \begin{bmatrix} 2 & 4 \\ 1 & 5 \end{bmatrix}$$

by following the steps in Example 2.3.1.

Step 1
Set the characteristic polynomial

$$\begin{vmatrix} 2-\lambda & 4 \\ 1 & 5-\lambda \end{vmatrix} = 0$$

$$(2-\lambda)(5-\lambda) - 4 = 0$$

$$10 + \lambda^2 - 7\lambda - 4 = 0$$

$$\lambda^2 - 7\lambda + 6 = 0$$

Step 2
Find the eigenvalues

$$\lambda = \frac{-b \pm \sqrt{b^2 - 4ac}}{2a}$$

$$\lambda = \frac{7 \pm \sqrt{49-24}}{2} = \frac{7 \pm 5}{2}$$

$$\lambda_1 = 6, \quad \lambda_2 = 1$$

Step 3
Find the eigenvectors.
For $\lambda = 6$

$$\begin{bmatrix} 2-6 & 4 \\ 1 & 5-6 \end{bmatrix} \begin{bmatrix} v_1 \\ v_2 \end{bmatrix} = 0$$

$$\begin{bmatrix} -4 & 4 \\ 1 & -1 \end{bmatrix} \begin{bmatrix} v_1 \\ v_2 \end{bmatrix} = 0$$

The system of equations is

$$\begin{cases} -4v_1 + 4v_2 = 0 \\ v_1 - v_2 = 0 \end{cases}$$

Note that the first equation is equal to −4 times the second equation. If we solve the second equation, we find that

$$v_1 = v_2$$

If $v_1 = 1$, $v_2 = 1$. Therefore, an eigenvector is $\mathbf{v}_1 = \begin{bmatrix} 1 \\ 1 \end{bmatrix}$.

For $\lambda = 1$

$$\begin{vmatrix} 2-1 & 4 \\ 1 & 5-1 \end{vmatrix} \begin{bmatrix} v_1 \\ v_2 \end{bmatrix} = 0$$

$$\begin{vmatrix} 1 & 4 \\ 1 & 4 \end{vmatrix} \begin{bmatrix} v_1 \\ v_2 \end{bmatrix} = 0$$

The system of equations is

$$\begin{cases} v_1 + 4v_2 = 0 \\ v_1 + 4v_2 = 0 \end{cases}$$

If we solve the first equation, we find that

$$v_1 = -4v_2$$

If $v_2 = 1$, $v_1 = -4$. Therefore, an eigenvector is $\mathbf{v}_2 = \begin{bmatrix} -4 \\ 1 \end{bmatrix}$.

Step 4
Write the general solution.

Now that we have found the eigenvalues and eigenvectors we can write the general solution.

In case of distinct real eigenvalues, the solution of the system $\mathbf{z}_{t+1} = A\mathbf{z}_t$, where A is a $k \times k$ matrix, is

$$\mathbf{z}_t = c_1\lambda_1^t\mathbf{v}_1 + c_2\lambda_2^t\mathbf{v}_2 + \cdots + c_k\lambda_k^t\mathbf{v}_k \tag{10.26}$$

where $c_k, k = \{1, \cdots, k\}$, $\lambda_k, k = \{1, \cdots, k\}$ and $\mathbf{v}_k, k = \{1, \cdots, k\}$ are constants, eigenvalues and eigenvectors, respectively (you may refer to Simon and Blume (1994, p. 593) for the related theorem).

Consequently, the general solution for our example is

$$\mathbf{z}_t = c_1\lambda_1^t\mathbf{v}_1 + c_2\lambda_2^t\mathbf{v}_2$$

$$\mathbf{z}_t = c_1(6)^t\begin{bmatrix}1\\1\end{bmatrix} + c_2(1)^t\begin{bmatrix}-4\\1\end{bmatrix}$$

Step 5

Find the constants given initial values and write the particular solution.

Given $x_0 = 4$, $y_0 = 5$,

$$4 = c_1(6)^0 \cdot 1 + c_2(1)^0 \cdot (-4) \rightarrow 4 = c_1 - 4c_2$$

$$5 = c_1(6)^0 \cdot 1 + c_2(1)^0 \cdot (1) \rightarrow 5 = c_1 + c_2 \rightarrow c_1 = 5 - c_2$$

$$4 = (5 - c_2) - 4c_2 \rightarrow c_2 = \frac{1}{5}$$

$$c_1 = 5 - \frac{1}{5} \rightarrow c_1 = \frac{24}{5}$$

Therefore, given the initial conditions, the solution is

$$\mathbf{z}_t = \frac{24}{5}(6)^t\begin{bmatrix}1\\1\end{bmatrix} + \frac{1}{5}(1)^t\begin{bmatrix}-4\\1\end{bmatrix}$$

Let's verify our solution with **R**. At $t = 10$

```
> l1 <- 6
> l2 <- 1
> c1 <- (24/5)
> c2 <- (1/5)
> v1 <- matrix(c(1, 1), nrow = 2, ncol =1, byrow = T)
> v1
     [,1]
[1,]    1
[2,]    1
> v2 <- matrix(c(-4, 1), nrow = 2, ncol =1, byrow = T)
> v2
     [,1]
```

```
[1,]    -4
[2,]     1
> t <- 10
> (c1*l1^t)*v1 + (c2*l2^t)*v2
              [,1]
[1,] 290237644
[2,] 290237645
```

Let's check the solution with `sys_folde()`

```
> A <- matrix(c(2, 4,
+                  1, 5),
+                nrow = 2, ncol = 2,
+                byrow = T)
> A
     [,1] [,2]
[1,]    2    4
[2,]    1    5
> A0 <- matrix(c(4, 5),
+                 ncol = 1, nrow = 2,
+                 byrow = T)
> sys_folde(A, A0)
              [,1]
[1,] 290237644
[2,] 290237645
```

The solution of this system can be approached with eigenvalues in a different way by considering the Jordan canonical form of the original matrix A. Let's go through the steps in Sect. 2.3.9.1 for a review. We have already found the eigenvectors of matrix A to be

$$\mathbf{v}^{\lambda_1} = \begin{bmatrix} 1 \\ 1 \end{bmatrix} \quad \mathbf{v}^{\lambda_2} = \begin{bmatrix} -4 \\ 1 \end{bmatrix}$$

Let's form the P matrix.

$$P = \begin{bmatrix} \mathbf{v}^{\lambda_1} \; \mathbf{v}^{\lambda_2} \end{bmatrix} = \begin{bmatrix} 1 & -4 \\ 1 & 1 \end{bmatrix}$$

```
> P <- matrix(c(1, -4,
+                  1, 1),
+                nrow = 2, ncol = 2,
+                byrow = T)
> P
     [,1] [,2]
[1,]    1   -4
[2,]    1    1
```

Then, compute P^{-1} and find D

```
> P1 <- solve(P)
> P1
     [,1] [,2]
[1,]  0.2  0.8
[2,] -0.2  0.2
> D <- P1%*%A%*%P
> round(D, 1)
     [,1] [,2]
[1,]    6    0
[2,]    0    1
```

The solution to the system $\mathbf{z}_{t+1} = A\mathbf{z}_t$ can be written as

$$\mathbf{z}_t = P \begin{bmatrix} \lambda_1^t & 0 \\ 0 & \lambda_2^t \end{bmatrix} P^{-1}\mathbf{z}_0 \tag{10.27}$$

where $\mathbf{z}_0$ is the initial vector.

```
> t <- 10
> D <- diag(c(l1^t, l2^t))
> D
         [,1] [,2]
[1,] 60466176    0
[2,]        0    1
> P%*%D%*%P1%*%A0
          [,1]
[1,] 290237644
[2,] 290237645
```

Exercise 10.6.2 asks you to write a function that implements this process.

We conclude with the stability of the system. If λ_1 and λ_2 are two distinct and real eigenvalues of matrix A for the system $\mathbf{z}_{t+1} = A\mathbf{z}_t$, then

- the system is dynamically stable if $|\lambda_1| < 1$ and $|\lambda_2| < 1$;
- the system is dynamically unstable if $|\lambda_1| > 1$ and $|\lambda_2| > 1$;
- the system is dynamically unstable if, say, $|\lambda_1| > 1$ and $|\lambda_2| < 1$;

10.3.3.2 Case 2: Repeated Real Eigenvalues

Consider the following system

$$\begin{aligned} x_{t+1} &= 3x_t + y_t \\ y_{t+1} &= -x_t + y_t \end{aligned} \tag{10.28}$$

It can be written in matrix form as

$$\begin{bmatrix} x_{t+1} \\ y_{t+1} \end{bmatrix} = \begin{bmatrix} 3 & 1 \\ -1 & 1 \end{bmatrix} \begin{bmatrix} x_t \\ y_t \end{bmatrix}$$

Let's find the eigenvalues and eigenvectors of matrix

$$A = \begin{bmatrix} 3 & 1 \\ -1 & 1 \end{bmatrix}$$

by following the steps in Example 2.3.1.

Step 1
Set the characteristic polynomial

$$\begin{vmatrix} 3-\lambda & 1 \\ -1 & 1-\lambda \end{vmatrix} = 0$$

$$(3-\lambda)(1-\lambda) - (-1) = 0$$

$$3 + \lambda^2 - 4\lambda + 1 = 0$$

$$\lambda^2 - 4\lambda + 4 = 0$$

Step 2
Find the eigenvalues

$$\lambda = \frac{-b \pm \sqrt{b^2 - 4ac}}{2a}$$

$$\lambda = \frac{4 \pm \sqrt{16-16}}{2} = \frac{4}{2} = 2$$

$$\lambda^* = 2 \quad [\text{with multiplicity of } 2]$$

where λ^* denote the unique eigenvalue of A.

Step 3
Find the eigenvectors.

For $\lambda^* = 2$

$$\begin{bmatrix} 3-2 & 1 \\ -1 & 1-2 \end{bmatrix} \begin{bmatrix} v_1 \\ v_2 \end{bmatrix} = 0$$

$$\begin{bmatrix} 1 & 1 \\ -1 & -1 \end{bmatrix} \begin{bmatrix} v_1 \\ v_2 \end{bmatrix} = 0$$

The system of equations is

$$\begin{cases} v_1 + v_2 = 0 \\ -v_1 - v_2 = 0 \end{cases}$$

If we solve the second equation, we find that

$$-v_1 = v_2$$

If $v_2 = 1$, $v_1 = -1$. Therefore, an eigenvector is $\mathbf{v}_1 = \begin{bmatrix} -1 \\ 1 \end{bmatrix}$.

The matrix A has one independent eigenvector. A matrix with eigenvalue of multiplicity $m > 1$ but without m independent eigenvectors is called *non diagonalizable* or *defective* (refer to Sect. 2.3.9.1).

It is necessary to compute the *generalized eigenvector* for the solution of the system.

Step 3.5
Compute the generalized eigenvector.

A generalized eigenvector is a non-zero vector such as $(A - \lambda^* I)\,\mathbf{v} \neq 0$ but $(A - \lambda^* I)^m\,\mathbf{v} = 0$, with some integer $m > 1$ (refer to Simon and Blume (1994, p. 603)).

Set $(A - \lambda^* I)\,\mathbf{v}_2 = \mathbf{v}_1$

$$\begin{bmatrix} 3-2 & 1 \\ -1 & 1-2 \end{bmatrix} \begin{bmatrix} v_{21} \\ v_{22} \end{bmatrix} = \begin{bmatrix} -1 \\ 1 \end{bmatrix}$$

The system of equations is

$$\begin{cases} v_{21} + v_{22} = -1 \\ -v_{21} - v_{22} = 1 \end{cases}$$

Therefore, if $v_{22} = 1$, $v_{21} = -2$. The generalized eigenvector is $\mathbf{v}_2 = \begin{bmatrix} -2 \\ 1 \end{bmatrix}$.

To check if this is correct, we need that $P^{-1}AP$ to be as simple as possible. The simplest matrix is the diagonal matrix $\begin{bmatrix} \lambda^* & 0 \\ 0 & \lambda^* \end{bmatrix}$. If this matrix is not achievable, the next simplest matrix is

$$P^{-1}AP = \begin{bmatrix} \lambda^* & 1 \\ 0 & \lambda^* \end{bmatrix} \tag{10.29}$$

where $P = [\mathbf{v}_1 \mathbf{v}_2]$ is a matrix formed with independent eigenvectors of matrix A. Since in the case of repeated eigenvalues the matrix A has only one independent eigenvector we found its generalized eigenvector to compensate for its "defectiveness". In this case, the columns of P must be formed with the eigenvector of A (first column) and the generalized eigenvector (second column), both corresponding to eigenvalue λ^*. Note that matrices as in (2.21) and (10.29) are called the Jordan canonical form of the original matrix A. The process to compute the generalized eigenvector for a 2×2 matrix can be similarly extended to larger matrix with repeated eigenvalues. You may refer to Simon and Blume (1994, p. 604) for an explanation and an example.

Now let's verify it with **R**

```
> A <- matrix(c(3, 1,
+                 -1, 1),
+               nrow = 2, ncol = 2,
+               byrow = T)
> A
     [,1] [,2]
[1,]    3    1
[2,]   -1    1
> P <- matrix(c(-1, -2,
+                 1, 1),
+               nrow = 2, ncol = 2,
+               byrow = T)
> P
     [,1] [,2]
[1,]   -1   -2
[2,]    1    1
> P1 <- solve(P)
> P1
     [,1] [,2]
[1,]    1    2
[2,]   -1   -1
> P1 %*% A %*% P
     [,1] [,2]
```

```
[1,]    2    1
[2,]    0    2
```

Step 4

Write the general solution

Now that we have found the eigenvalues and eigenvectors we can write the general solution.

In case of repeated eigenvalues, the general solution of the system $\mathbf{z}_{t+1} = A\mathbf{z}_t$, where A is a 2×2 matrix, is

$$\mathbf{z}_t = \left(c_1\lambda^t + tc_2\lambda^{t-1}\right)\mathbf{v}_1 + c_2\lambda^t\mathbf{v}_2 \tag{10.30}$$

where c, λ and $\mathbf{v}$ are constants, eigenvalues and eigenvectors, respectively (you may refer to Simon and Blume (1994, p. 607) for the related theorem).

Consequently, the general solution for our example is

$$\mathbf{z}_t = \left(c_1 2^t + tc_2 2^{t-1}\right)\begin{bmatrix}-1\\1\end{bmatrix} + c_2 2^t\begin{bmatrix}-2\\1\end{bmatrix}$$

Step 5

Find the constants given initial values and write the particular solution.

Given $x_0 = 4$, $y_0 = 5$,

$$4 = -c_1 2^0 - 0 \cdot c_2 2^{0-1} + c_2 2^0(-2) \rightarrow 4 = -c_1 - 2c_2$$

$$5 = c_1 2^0 + 0 \cdot c_2 2^{0-1} + c_2 2^0(1) \rightarrow 5 = c_1 + c_2 \rightarrow c_1 = 5 - c_2$$

$$4 = -(5 - c_2) - 2c_2 \rightarrow c_2 = -9$$

$$c_1 = 5 - (-9) = 14$$

Therefore, given the initial conditions, the solution is

$$\mathbf{z}_t = \left(14 \cdot 2^t + t(-9)2^{t-1}\right)\begin{bmatrix}-1\\1\end{bmatrix} + (-9)2^t\begin{bmatrix}-2\\1\end{bmatrix}$$

Let's verify our solution with **R**. At $t = 10$

```
> l <- 2
> c1 <- 14
> c2 <- -9
```

```
> v1 <- matrix(c(-1, 1), nrow = 2, ncol =1, byrow = T)
> v1
     [,1]
[1,]   -1
[2,]    1
> v2 <- matrix(c(-2, 1), nrow = 2, ncol =1, byrow = T)
> v2
     [,1]
[1,]   -2
[2,]    1
> t <- 10
> (c1*l^t + t*c2*l^(t-1))*v1 + c2*l^t*v2
       [,1]
[1,]  50176
[2,] -40960
```

Let's check the solution with `sys_folde()`

```
> sys_folde(A, A0)
       [,1]
[1,]  50176
[2,] -40960
```

With a 2 × 2 A matrix with repeated eigenvalues, the solution to the system $\mathbf{z}_{t+1} = A\mathbf{z}_t$ can be written as

$$\mathbf{z}_t = P \begin{bmatrix} \lambda^t & t\lambda^{t-1} \\ 0 & \lambda^t \end{bmatrix} P^{-1}\mathbf{z}_0 \tag{10.31}$$

where $\mathbf{z}_0$ is the initial vector. Let's check the solution with **R**

```
> D <- matrix(c(l^t, t*l^(t-1),
+                0, l^t),
+              nrow = 2, ncol = 2,
+              byrow = T)
> D
     [,1] [,2]
[1,] 1024 5120
[2,]    0 1024
> P%*%D%*%P1%*%A0
       [,1]
[1,]  50176
[2,] -40960
```

We conclude with the stability of the system. If λ is a repeated eigenvalue of matrix A for the system $\mathbf{z}_{t+1} = A\mathbf{z}_t$, then

- the system is asymptotically stable if $|\lambda| < 1$;
- the system is asymptotically unstable if $|\lambda| > 1$.

10.3.3.3 Case 3: Complex Eigenvalues

Consider the following system

$$\begin{aligned} x_{t+1} &= x_t - 5y_t \\ y_{t+1} &= x_t + 3y_t \end{aligned} \tag{10.32}$$

It can be written in matrix form as

$$\begin{bmatrix} x_{t+1} \\ y_{t+1} \end{bmatrix} = \begin{bmatrix} 1 & -5 \\ 1 & 3 \end{bmatrix} \begin{bmatrix} x_t \\ y_t \end{bmatrix}$$

Let's find the eigenvalues and eigenvectors of matrix

$$A = \begin{bmatrix} 1 & -5 \\ 1 & 3 \end{bmatrix}$$

by following the steps in Example 2.3.1.

Step 1

$$\begin{vmatrix} 1-\lambda & -5 \\ 1 & 3-\lambda \end{vmatrix} = 0$$

$$(1-\lambda)(3-\lambda) - (-5) = 0$$

$$3 - \lambda^2 - 4\lambda + 5 = 0$$

$$\lambda^2 - 4\lambda + 8 = 0$$

Step 2

$$\lambda = \frac{-b \pm \sqrt{b^2 - 4ac}}{2a}$$

$$\lambda = \frac{4 \pm \sqrt{16-32}}{2} = \frac{4 \pm \sqrt{-16}}{2} = \frac{4 \pm \sqrt{16}\cdot\sqrt{-1}}{2} = \frac{4 \pm 4i}{2} = 2 \pm 2i$$

$$\lambda_1 = 2 + 2i, \quad \lambda_2 = 2 - 2i$$

Step 3
For $\lambda = 2 + 2i$

$$\begin{bmatrix} 1-(2+2i) & -5 \\ 1 & 3-(2+2i) \end{bmatrix} \begin{bmatrix} v_1 \\ v_2 \end{bmatrix} = 0$$

$$\begin{bmatrix} -1-2i & -5 \\ 1 & 1-2i \end{bmatrix} \begin{bmatrix} v_1 \\ v_2 \end{bmatrix} = 0$$

The system of equations is

$$\begin{cases} (-1-2i)\,v_1 - 5v_2 = 0 \\ v_1 + (1-2i)\,v_2 = 0 \end{cases}$$

If we solve the first equation, we find that

$$(-1-2i)v_1 = 5v_2$$

Therefore, if $v_1 = 1$, $v_2 = -\frac{1}{5} - \frac{2}{5}i$. The eigenvector is $\mathbf{v} = \begin{bmatrix} 1 \\ -\frac{1}{5} - \frac{2}{5}i \end{bmatrix}$.
We can write it as

$$\begin{bmatrix} 1 \\ -\frac{1}{5} \end{bmatrix} + i \begin{bmatrix} 0 \\ -\frac{2}{5} \end{bmatrix}$$

where we set

$$\mathbf{u} = \begin{bmatrix} 1 \\ -\frac{1}{5} \end{bmatrix} \quad \mathbf{w} = \begin{bmatrix} 0 \\ -\frac{2}{5} \end{bmatrix}$$

Therefore, we can write it as $\mathbf{v} = \mathbf{u} + i\mathbf{w}$.

By a theorem, if for an eigenvalue $\alpha + i\beta$ we have $\mathbf{v} = \mathbf{u} + i\mathbf{w}$ as eigenvector, for $\alpha - i\beta$ we have $\overline{\mathbf{v}} = \mathbf{u} - i\mathbf{w}$. If A is a $k \times k$ and k is odd, A must have at least one real eigenvalue (refer to Simon and Blume (1994, p. 610)). Thus,

$$\overline{\mathbf{v}} = \begin{bmatrix} 1 \\ -\frac{1}{5} + \frac{2}{5}i \end{bmatrix}$$

Let's verify if it is correct

```
> A <- matrix(c(1, -5,
+                 1, 3),
+               nrow = 2, ncol = 2,
+               byrow = T)
> A
     [,1] [,2]
[1,]    1   -5
[2,]    1    3
> P <- matrix(c(1, 1,
+                 -(1/5)- (2i/5), -(1/5)+ (2i/5)),
+               nrow = 2, ncol = 2,
+               byrow = T)
> P
          [,1]       [,2]
[1,]  1.0+0.0i  1.0+0.0i
[2,] -0.2-0.4i -0.2+0.4i
> P1 <- solve(P)
> P1
          [,1]     [,2]
[1,] 0.5+0.25i 0+1.25i
[2,] 0.5-0.25i 0-1.25i
> P1 %*% A %*% P
     [,1] [,2]
[1,] 2+2i 0+0i
[2,] 0+0i 2-2i
```

Step 4

Now that we have found the eigenvalues and eigenvectors we can write the general solution.

In case of complex eigenvalues, the general solution of the system $\mathbf{z}_{t+1} = A\mathbf{z}_t$, where A is a 2×2 matrix, is

$$\mathbf{z}_t = r^t \left[(c_1 \cos(t\theta) - c_2 \sin(t\theta))\,\mathbf{u} - (c_2 \cos(t\theta) + c_1 \sin(t\theta))\,\mathbf{w} \right] \tag{10.33}$$

where $r = \sqrt{\alpha^2 + \beta^2}$, α and β come from the complex eigenvalue written as $\alpha \pm \beta i$, $\cos\theta = \frac{\alpha}{r}$ and $\sin\theta = \frac{\beta}{r}$ (you may refer to Simon and Blume (1994, p. 613) for the related theorem).

```
> alpha <- 2
> beta <- 2
> r <- sqrt(alpha^2 + beta^2)
> r
```

```
[1] 2.828427
> cos_theta <- alpha/r
> sin_theta <- beta/r
> theta <- acos(cos_theta)
> theta
[1] 0.7853982
> asin(sin_theta)
[1] 0.7853982
```

Consequently, the general solution for our example is

$$\mathbf{z}_t = 2.83^t\left[(c_1\cos(t0.78) - c_2\sin(t0.78))\begin{bmatrix}1\\-\frac{1}{5}\end{bmatrix} - (c_2\cos(t0.78) + c_1\sin(t0.78))\begin{bmatrix}0\\-\frac{2}{5}\end{bmatrix}\right]$$

Step 5
Given $x_0 = 4$, $y_0 = 5$,

$$4 = 2.83^0\left[(c_1\cos(0\cdot 0.78) - c_2\sin(0\cdot 0.78))\cdot 1 - (c_2\cos(0\cdot 0.78) + c_1\sin(0\cdot 0.78))\cdot 0\right]$$

$$4 = c_1$$

$$5 = 2.83^0\Bigg[(c_1\cos(0\cdot 0.78) - c_2\sin(0\cdot 0.78))\cdot\left(-\frac{1}{5}\right) - (c_2\cos(0\cdot 0.78) + c_1\sin(0\cdot 0.78))\cdot\left(-\frac{2}{5}\right)\Bigg]$$

$$5 = -\frac{1}{5}c_1 - c_2\left(-\frac{2}{5}\right) \rightarrow 5 = -\frac{1}{5}c_1 + \frac{2}{5}c_2 \rightarrow 5 = -\frac{4}{5} + \frac{2}{5}c_2$$

$$c_2 = \frac{29}{2}$$

Therefore, given the initial conditions, the solution is

$$\mathbf{z}_t = 2.83^t\left[\left(4\cos(t0.78) - \frac{29}{2}\sin(t0.78)\right)\begin{bmatrix}1\\-\frac{1}{5}\end{bmatrix} - \left(\frac{29}{2}\cos(t0.78) + 4\sin(t0.78)\right)\begin{bmatrix}0\\-\frac{2}{5}\end{bmatrix}\right]$$

Let's verify our solution with **R**. At $t = 10$

```
> c1 <- 4
> c2 <- 29/2
```

```
> u <- matrix(c(1, -1/5), nrow = 2,
+                ncol = 1, byrow = T)
> u
      [,1]
[1,]  1.0
[2,] -0.2
> w <- matrix(c(0, -2/5), nrow = 2,
+                ncol = 1, byrow = T)
> w
      [,1]
[1,]  0.0
[2,] -0.4
> r^t * ((c1*cos(theta*t) - c2*sin(theta*t))*u -
+           (c2*cos(theta*t) + c1*sin(theta*t))*w)
         [,1]
[1,] -475136
[2,]  147456
```

Let's check the solution with `sys_folde()`

```
> sys_folde(A, A0)
         [,1]
[1,] -475136
[2,]  147456
```

With a 2×2 A matrix with complex eigenvalues, the solution to the system $\mathbf{z}_{t+1} = A\mathbf{z}_t$ can be written as

$$\mathbf{z}_t = P \begin{bmatrix} (\alpha + \beta i)^t & 0 \\ 0 & (\alpha - \beta i)^t \end{bmatrix} P^{-1}\mathbf{z}_0 \tag{10.34}$$

where $\mathbf{z}_0$ is the initial vector. Let's check the solution with **R**

```
> D <- matrix(c((2 + 2i)^t, 0,
+                  0, (2 - 2i)^t),
+                nrow = 2, ncol = 2,
+                byrow = T)
> D
          [,1]      [,2]
[1,] 0+32768i 0+     0i
[2,] 0+     0i 0-32768i
> P%*%D%*%P1%*%A0
             [,1]
[1,] -475136+0i
[2,]  147456+0i
```

A system with complex eigenvalues

- is an *asymptotically stable focus* if $|r| < 1$;
- is an *unstable focus* if $|r| > 1$;
- has a *centre* if $|r| = 1$.

10.3.4 Graphing Trajectory of a Discrete System

In this section, we give a graphical representation of a system of linear difference equations by extending the capabilities of the `sys_folde()` function. The `sys_folde()` function only returns the value for a single period. Our goal is to modify the function such that it returns all the values up to the desired period. Let's name the function `trajectory_de()`. The main structure of the function is naturally based on `sys_folde()`. I mainly added loops. After I stored all the needed matrices in a list, I proceeded to unlist it and store the results in a data frame with two columns, `xt` and `yt`. The values of these two columns are mapped to the `x` and `y` in `ggplot()`. I leave as exercise part of the replication of the function.

```
> trajectory_de <-function(A,A0, b = NULL, periods = 10,
+                                    graph = TRUE){
+
+   require("expm")
+

COMPLETION OF THE CODE LEFT AS EXERCISE

+
+   if(graph == TRUE){
+
+     if(nrow(A) != 2){
+       stop("Graphing trajectory: \n
+            A must be a 2x2 matrix for the plot")
+     }
+
+     require("ggplot2")
+
+     g <- ggplot(M, aes(x = xt, y = yt)) +
+       geom_segment(aes(xend = c(tail(xt, n = -1), NA),
+                    yend = c(tail(yt, n = -1), NA))) +
+       geom_point(size = 1, color = "red") +
+       xlab("") + ylab("") + ggtitle("") +
+       theme_minimal() +
+       geom_hline(yintercept = 0) +
+       geom_vline(xintercept = 0)
```

```
+
+       l <- list(simulation = M,
+                  graph = g)
+       return(l)
+
+    } else{
+
+       return(M)
+
+    }
+
+ }
```

To test the function I will replicate examples 5.8, 5.14 and 5.15 in Shone (2002). Given the system of difference equations in example 5.8 in Shone (2002, p. 220)

$$x_{t+1} = -5 + 0.25x_t + 0.4y_t$$
$$y_{t+1} = 10 - x_t + y_t \tag{10.35}$$

with $x_0 = 10$ and $y_0 = 5$, plot the trajectory of the system (Fig. 10.6).

```
> # example 5.8 in Shone 2002
> A <- matrix(c(0.25, 0.4,
+                 -1, 1),
```

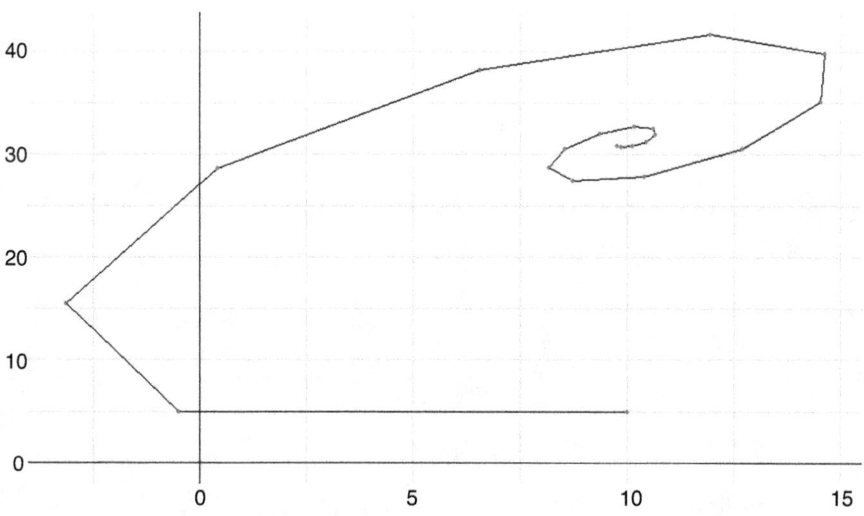

Fig. 10.6 Graphing trajectory of a discrete system: asymptotically stable focus

```
+                nrow = 2, ncol = 2,
+                byrow = T)
> A
      [,1] [,2]
[1,]  0.25  0.4
[2,] -1.00  1.0
> eigen(A)$values
[1] 0.625+0.5092887i 0.625-0.5092887i
> lambda <- eigen(A)$values[1]
> lambda
[1] 0.625+0.5092887i
> r <- sqrt(Re(lambda)^2 + Im(lambda)^2)
> r
[1] 0.8062258
```

Since $|r| < 1$ the system is an asymptotically stable focus.

```
> A0 <- matrix(c(10, 5),
+                 nrow = 2, ncol = 1,
+                 byrow = T)
> A0
     [,1]
[1,]   10
[2,]    5
> b <- matrix(c(-5, 10),
+                nrow = 2, ncol = 1,
+                byrow = T)
> b
     [,1]
[1,]   -5
[2,]   10
> trajectory_de(A, A0, periods = 20, b = b)
$results
          xt       yt
1  10.000000  5.00000
2  -0.500000  5.00000
3  -3.125000 15.50000
4   0.418750 28.62500
5   6.554688 38.20625
6  11.921172 41.65156
7  14.640918 39.73039
8  14.552386 35.08947
9  12.673885 30.53709
10 10.383306 27.86320
11  8.741107 27.47990
12  8.177235 28.73879
```

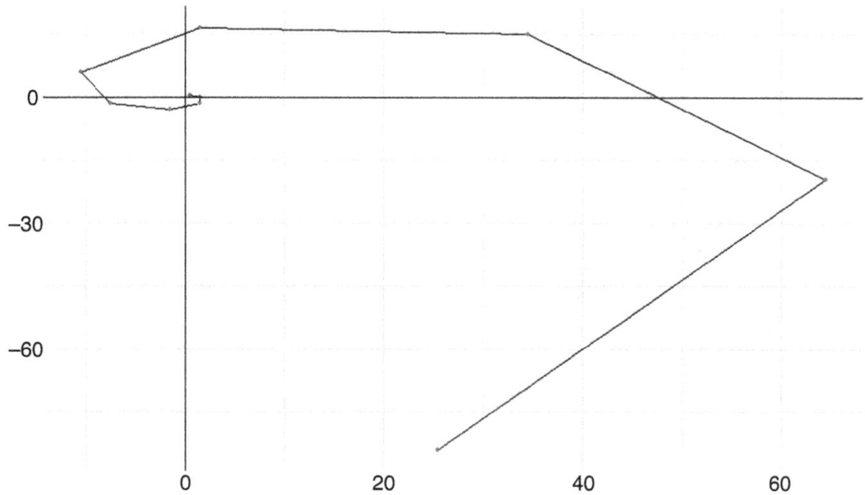

Fig. 10.7 Graphing trajectory of a discrete system: unstable focus

```
13   8.539824 30.56155
14   9.359577 32.02173
15 10.148586 32.66215
16 10.602007 32.51357
17 10.655928 31.91156
18 10.428606 31.25563
19 10.109404 30.82702
20   9.858161 30.71762
21   9.751589 30.85946

$graph

Warning message:
Removed 1 rows containing missing values (geom_segment).
```

Given the system of difference equations in example 5.14 in Shone (2002, p. 234)

$$\begin{aligned} x_{t+1} &= x_t + 2y_t \\ y_{t+1} &= -x_t + y_t \end{aligned} \tag{10.36}$$

with $x_0 = 0.5$ and $y_0 = 0.5$, plot the trajectory of the system (Fig. 10.7).[4]

[4] Even though the conclusion for the system is the same, the plot of my function slightly differs from that in Shone (2002). However, by reproducing his result with Excel as illustrated in Shone (2002, p. 220) I obtain the same simulation as with `trajectory_de()`.

```
> A <- matrix(c(1, 2,
+               -1, 1),
+             nrow = 2, ncol = 2,
+             byrow = T)
> A
     [,1] [,2]
[1,]    1    2
[2,]   -1    1
> eigen(A)$values
[1] 1+1.414214i 1-1.414214i
> lambda <- eigen(A)$values[1]
> lambda
[1] 1+1.414214i
> r <- sqrt(Re(lambda)^2 + Im(lambda)^2)
> r
[1] 1.732051
```

Since $|r| > 1$ the system is an unstable focus.

```
> A0 <- matrix(c(0.5, 0.5),
+              nrow = 2, ncol = 1,
+              byrow = T)
> A0
     [,1]
[1,]  0.5
[2,]  0.5
> trajectory_de(A, A0, periods = 9)
$simulation
      xt    yt
1    0.5   0.5
2    1.5   0.0
3    1.5  -1.5
4   -1.5  -3.0
5   -7.5  -1.5
6  -10.5   6.0
7    1.5  16.5
8   34.5  15.0
9   64.5 -19.5
10  25.5 -84.0

$graph

Warning message:
Removed 1 rows containing missing values (geom_segment).
```

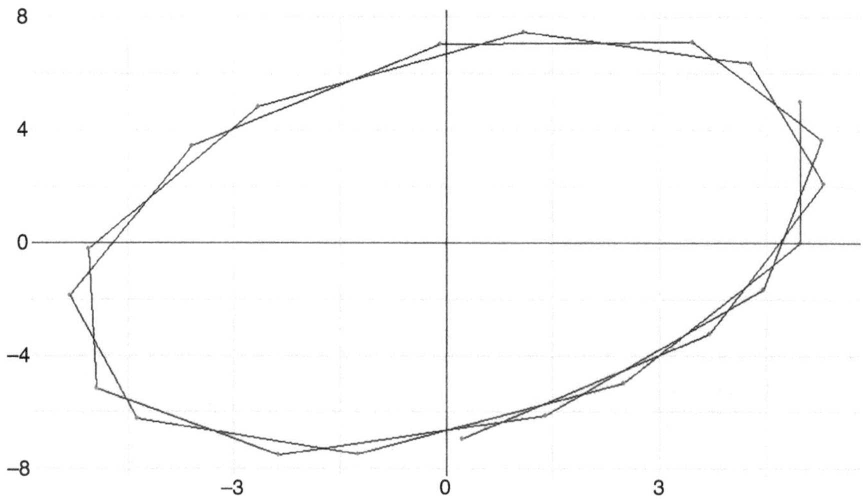

Fig. 10.8 Graphing trajectory of a discrete system: centre

Given the system of difference equations in example 5.15 in Shone (2002, p. 234)

$$
\begin{aligned}
x_{t+1} &= 0.5x_t + 0.5y_t \\
y_{t+1} &= -x_t + y_t
\end{aligned}
\tag{10.37}
$$

with $x_0 = 5$ and $y_0 = 5$, plot the trajectory of the system (Fig. 10.8).

```
> A <- matrix(c(0.5, 0.5,
+                   -1, 1),
+                nrow = 2, ncol = 2,
+                byrow = T)
> A
     [,1] [,2]
[1,]  0.5  0.5
[2,] -1.0  1.0
> eigen(A)$values
[1] 0.75+0.6614378i 0.75-0.6614378i
> lambda <- eigen(A)$values[1]
> lambda
[1] 0.75+0.6614378i
> r <- sqrt(Re(lambda)^2 + Im(lambda)^2)
> r
[1] 1
```

Since $|r| = 1$, the system oscillates around a centre.

```
> A0 <- matrix(c(5, 5),
+              nrow = 2, ncol = 1,
+              byrow = T)
> A0
     [,1]
[1,]    5
[2,]    5
> trajectory_de(A, A0, periods = 20)
$simulation
          xt         yt
1   5.0000000  5.0000000
2   5.0000000  0.0000000
3   2.5000000 -5.0000000
4  -1.2500000 -7.5000000
5  -4.3750000 -6.2500000
6  -5.3125000 -1.8750000
7  -3.5937500  3.4375000
8  -0.0781250  7.0312500
9   3.4765625  7.1093750
10  5.2929688  3.6328125
11  4.4628906 -1.6601562
12  1.4013672 -6.1230469
13 -2.3608398 -7.5244141
14 -4.9426270 -5.1635742
15 -5.0531006 -0.2209473
16 -2.6370239  4.8321533
17  1.0975647  7.4691772
18  4.2833710  6.3716125
19  5.3274918  2.0882416
20  3.7078667 -3.2392502
21  0.2343082 -6.9471169

$graph

Warning message:
Removed 1 rows containing missing values (geom_segment).
```

10.4 Transforming High-Order Difference Equations

In this book we limited our discussion to first-order and second order linear difference equations. In this section we learn how to transform a nth-order linear difference equation into an equivalent system of n linear difference equations.

Let's consider an example with a third-order difference equation. We can transform it into a system of three first-order difference equations by building two artificial variables. For example, given the following third-order linear difference equation (10.38)

$$y_{t+3} = 2y_{t+2} - y_{t+1} + 3y_t \tag{10.38}$$

we can build two variables, $x_t \equiv y_{t+1}$, and consequently, $x_{t+1} \equiv y_{t+2}$, and $w_t \equiv x_{t+1}$, and consequently, $w_{t+1} \equiv x_{t+2}$. With this information we can set a system of equations

$$\begin{aligned} y_{t+1} &= x_t \\ x_{t+1} &= w_t \\ w_{t+1} &= 3y_t - x_t + 2w_t \end{aligned} \tag{10.39}$$

where the first two equations derive from $x_t = y_{t+1}$ and $w_t = x_{t+1}$, while the third equation is the result of substitutions into the third-order equation. Therefore, we have transformed a third-order equation into a system of first-order equations.

In matrix form,

$$\begin{bmatrix} y_{t+1} \\ x_{t+1} \\ w_{t+1} \end{bmatrix} = \begin{bmatrix} 0 & 1 & 0 \\ 0 & 0 & 1 \\ 3 & -1 & 2 \end{bmatrix} \begin{bmatrix} y_t \\ x_t \\ w_t \end{bmatrix}$$

Let's check the solution with the functions `iter_de()` and `sys_folde()`.

```
> RHS <- "2*y[t+2] - y[t+1] + 3*y[t]"
> iter_de(RHS, y0 = c(1, 2, 3), order = 3, periods = 8)
[1]   1   2   3   7  17  36  76 167 366
> A <- matrix(c(0, 1, 0,
+               0, 0, 1,
+               3, -1, 2),
+             nrow = 3, ncol = 3,
+             byrow = T)
> A
     [,1] [,2] [,3]
[1,]    0    1    0
[2,]    0    0    1
[3,]    3   -1    2
> A0 <- matrix(c(1, 2, 3),
+              nrow = 3, ncol = 1,
+              byrow = T)
```

```
> A0
     [,1]
[1,]    1
[2,]    2
[3,]    3
> sys_folde(A, A0, periods = 6)
     [,1]
[1,]   76
[2,]  167
[3,]  366
```

Let's consider another example. Let's find the solution to the Fibonacci sequence. The Fibonacci Sequence is the series of numbers: 0, 1, 1, 2, 3, 5, 8, 13, 21, 34, 55, 89, 144, ... where the next number is found by adding up the two numbers before it. For example, $2 = 1 + 1$, $3 = 2 + 1$, $5 = 3 + 2$ and so on.

The Fibonacci sequence is represented by the following equation

$$y_{t+2} = y_{t+1} + y_t \tag{10.40}$$

Equation 10.40 is a second-order linear difference equation. To transform it into a system of two first-order linear difference equations we need to build an artificial variable $x_t \equiv y_{t+1}$, and consequently $x_{t+1} \equiv y_{t+2}$. Let's write the system

$$\begin{aligned} y_{t+1} &= x_t \\ x_{t+1} &= y_t + x_t \end{aligned} \tag{10.41}$$

In matrix form,

$$\begin{bmatrix} y_{t+1} \\ x_{t+1} \end{bmatrix} = \begin{bmatrix} 0 & 1 \\ 1 & 1 \end{bmatrix} \begin{bmatrix} y_t \\ x_t \end{bmatrix} \tag{10.42}$$

In the Fibonacci sequence, the initial values are 0 and 1.[5] Let's check the solution with **R**

[5] Note that we wrote (10.41) to be consistent with the previous example. However, you may find (10.42) with 0 and 1 inverted on the main diagonal, implying that the equations in (10.41) are written with a different order. However, the interpretation of the results does not change. To be noted that as we arranged the equations and consequently the matrix and the column vectors, `periods` in `sys_folde()` returns the desired period at index [1, 1]. That is, in the example, 89 corresponds to $t = 11$, and consequently 144 corresponds to $t = 12$. For example, if you set `periods = 0`, the values 0 and 1, i.e. the initial values, are returned at index [1, 1] and [2, 1], respectively. Naturally the function also works if you appropriately rewrite (10.41) and consequently rewrite (10.42). However, make sure you correctly interpret the results.

```
> RHS <- "y[t+1] + y[t]"
> iter_de(RHS, y0 = c(0, 1), order = 2, periods = 12)
 [1]   0   1   1   2   3   5   8  13  21  34  55  89 144
 > M <- matrix(c(0, 1,
+                1, 1),
+              nrow = 2, ncol = 2,
+              byrow = T)
> M
     [,1] [,2]
[1,]    0    1
[2,]    1    1
> M0 <- matrix(c(0, 1),
+               nrow = 2, ncol = 1,
+               byrow = T)
> M0
     [,1]
[1,]    0
[2,]    1
> sys_folde(M, M0, periods = 11)
     [,1]
[1,]   89
[2,]  144
```

Let's conclude this section by applying the general method to (10.40)

$$y_{t+2} - y_{t+1} - y_t = 0$$

$$Ab^t\left(b^2 - b - 1\right) = 0 \quad \left[Ab^t \neq 0\right]$$

$$b^2 - b - 1 = 0$$

$$b = \frac{1 \pm \sqrt{5}}{2}$$

$$y_t = A_1 b_1^t + A_2 b_2^t$$

Given $y_0 = 0$ and $y_1 = 1$

$$A_1 = \frac{y_1 - b_2 y_0}{b_1 - b_2}$$

$$A_2 = \frac{y_1 - b_1 y_0}{b_2 - b_1}$$

$$y_t = \left(\frac{y_1 - b_2 y_0}{b_1 - b_2}\right) b_1^t + \left(\frac{y_1 - b_1 y_0}{b_2 - b_1}\right) b_2^t$$

Let's check the solution with **R**

```
> b1 <- (1 + sqrt(5))/2
> b2 <- (1 - sqrt(5))/2
> y0 <- 0
> y1 <- 1
> A1 <- (y1 - b2*y0)/(b1 - b2)
> A1
[1] 0.4472136
> A2 <- (y1 - b1*y0)/(b2 - b1)
> A2
[1] -0.4472136
> t <- 0:12
> A1*b1^t + A2*b2^t
 [1]   0   1   1   2   3   5   8  13  21  34  55  89 144
```

10.5 Applications in Economics

10.5.1 A Problem with Interest Rate

A student has \$5000 in her bank account. She decides to invest it. The interest rate compounded annually on her investment is 5%. Additionally, her part-time job allows her to put aside some money. Thus, she decides to add \$1000 to her investment at the end of each year. Compute the accumulated amount after 5 year investment.

Let's write this problem as a difference equation

$$y_{t+1} = 1.05 y_t + 1000$$

and let's solve it using the `iter_de()` function.

```
> RHS <- "1.05*y[t] + 1000"
> iter_de(RHS, y0 = 5000, periods = 5)
[1]  5000.000  6250.000  7562.500  8940.625 10387.656 11907.039
```

The amount accumulated after 5 years is \$11,907.

Now let's derive a general solution for this problem.

$$y_{t+1} = y_t + r y_t + a$$

where y_t is the amount invested at time t, r is the annual interest rate and a is the additional deposit at the end of each period. We can rewrite it as

$$y_{t+1} = (1 + r)y_t + a$$

Let's set $R = 1 + r$.

$$y_{t+1} = Ry_t + a$$

From now let's solve with the general method.

Step 1

$$y_{t+1} - Ry_t = 0$$

Step 2

$$Ab^{t+1} - RAb^t = 0$$

$$Ab^t(b - R) = 0 \quad \left[Ab^t \neq 0\right]$$

$$b = R$$

Step 3

$$y_c = AR^t$$

Step 4

$$k - Rk = a$$

$$k(1 - R) = a$$

$$k = \frac{a}{1 - R}$$

$$y_p = \frac{a}{1 - R}$$

Step 5

$$y_t = AR^t + \frac{a}{1 - R}$$

Step 6
At $t = 0$, $y_t = y_0$

$$y_0 = A + \frac{a}{1 - R}$$

$$A = y_0 - \frac{a}{1 - R}$$

Step 7

$$y_t = \left(y_0 - \frac{a}{1 - R}\right) R^t + \frac{a}{1 - R}$$

$$y_t = y_0 R^t - \frac{aR^t}{1 - R} + \frac{a}{1 - R}$$

$$y_t = y_0 R^t + a\left(\frac{1 - R^t}{1 - R}\right)$$

```
> y0 <- 5000
> a <- 1000
> r <- 0.05
> R <- 1 + r
> t <- 5
> y0*R^t + a*(1 - R^t)/(1 - R)
[1] 11907.04
```

10.5.2 *The Cobweb Model*

The cobweb model is a market model where the demand depends on the current price while the supply depends on the price of the preceding time period.[6] This specification is based on the consideration that the producer has to take a decision on the output level one period in advance of the actual sale. Equation 10.43 represents the demand function

$$Q_{dt} = \alpha - \beta p_t \tag{10.43}$$

and Eq. 10.44 represents the "lagged" supply function

$$Q_{st} = \gamma + \delta p_{t-1} \tag{10.44}$$

Since the market is cleared in any period we have

$$Q_{dt} = Q_{st} \tag{10.45}$$

Here we provide the solution to this model by applying the steps in Sect. 10.1.2. To be consistent with the previous notation, we move one period forward.

Let's start by replacing (10.43) and (10.44) in (10.45). Then, let's rearrange it.

$$\alpha - \beta p_{t+1} = \gamma + \delta p_t$$

$$\beta p_{t+1} = \alpha - \gamma - \delta p_t$$

$$p_{t+1} = \frac{\alpha - \gamma}{\beta} - \frac{\delta}{\beta} p_t$$

Step 1

$$p_{t+1} + \frac{\delta}{\beta} p_t = 0$$

Step 2
By setting $p_t = Ab^t$ and consequently $p_{t+1} = Ab^{t+1}$

[6] This is the simplest assumption about expected price. Other possible specifications include *adaptive expectations* and *Goodwin expectations*.

$$Ab^{t+1} + \frac{\delta}{\beta} Ab^t = 0$$

$$Ab^t \left(b + \frac{\delta}{\beta} \right) = 0 \quad \left[Ab^t \neq 0 \right]$$

$$b + \frac{\delta}{\beta} = 0$$

$$b = -\frac{\delta}{\beta}$$

$$p_c = A \left(-\frac{\delta}{\beta} \right)^t$$

Step 3
For the particular solution, we try $p_t = k$ and consequently $p_{t+1} = k$.

$$k + \frac{\delta}{\beta} k = \frac{\alpha - \gamma}{\beta}$$

$$k \left(1 + \frac{\delta}{\beta} \right) = \frac{\alpha - \gamma}{\beta}$$

$$k \left(\frac{\beta + \delta}{\beta} \right) = \frac{\alpha - \gamma}{\beta}$$

$$k = \frac{\alpha - \gamma}{\beta + \delta}$$

$$p_p = \frac{\alpha - \gamma}{\beta + \delta}$$

Step 4

$$p_t = A \left(-\frac{\delta}{\beta} \right)^t + \frac{\alpha - \gamma}{\beta + \delta}$$

Step 5
At $t = 0$, $p_t = p_0$

$$p_0 = A\left(-\frac{\delta}{\beta}\right)^0 + \frac{\alpha - \gamma}{\beta + \delta}$$

$$p_0 = A + \frac{\alpha - \gamma}{\beta + \delta}$$

$$A = p_0 - \frac{\alpha - \gamma}{\beta + \delta}$$

Step 6

$$p_t = \left(p_0 - \frac{\alpha - \gamma}{\beta + \delta}\right)\left(-\frac{\delta}{\beta}\right)^t + \frac{\alpha - \gamma}{\beta + \delta}$$

Let's make a simulation with the following demand and supply functions

$$Q_{dt} = 22 - 3p_t$$

$$Q_{st} = 2 + p_{t-1}$$

Let's assume an initial price $p_0 = 10$ and let's plug the values for α, β, γ, δ, p_0 into the solution at step 6.

```
> alpha <- 22
> beta <- 3
> gamma <- 2
> delta <- 1
> p0 <- 10
> t <- 0:20
> ((p0- (alpha - gamma)/(beta + delta))*(-delta/beta)^t+
+    (alpha - gamma)/(beta + delta))
 [1] 10.000000  3.333333  5.555556  4.814815  5.061728 4.979424
 [7]  5.006859  4.997714  5.000762  4.999746  5.000085 4.999972
 [13] 5.000009  4.999997  5.000001  5.000000  5.000000 5.000000
 [19] 5.000000  5.000000  5.000000
```

The simulation shows that the price tends to equilibrium. Could we have figured it out? Yes. In fact, from step 2 we know that the *base* is $-\frac{\delta}{\beta}$. In this simulations

```
> abs(-delta/beta) < 1
[1] TRUE
```

$\left|-\frac{\delta}{\beta}\right| < 1$ the system is convergent. We can verify this result by using iter_de()

```
> ALPHA <- (alpha - gamma)/beta
> BETA <- -delta/beta
> cw <- "ALPHA + BETA*y[t]"
> iter_de(cw, y0 = 10, periods = 20)
 [1] 10.000000  3.333333  5.555556  4.814815  5.061728 4.979424
 [7]  5.006859  4.997714  5.000762  4.999746  5.000085 4.999972
 [13] 5.000009  4.999997  5.000001  5.000000  5.000000 5.000000
 [19] 5.000000  5.000000  5.000000
```

Let's conclude this section by giving a graphical representation of p_t and Q_t. We design a function for this task that we name cobweb().

```
> cobweb <- function(alpha, beta, gamma, delta, p0,
+                    periods = 20){
+
+   require("tidyr")
+   require("ggplot2")
+   require("scales")
+
+   pstar <- (alpha - gamma)/(beta + delta)
+   qstar <- (alpha*delta + beta*gamma)/(beta + delta)
+
+   pt <- numeric(periods + 1)
+   pt[1] <- p0
+   Qt <- numeric(periods + 1)
+   Qt[1] <- NA
+
+   for(t in 1:(periods)){
+
+     pt[t+1] <- ((alpha - gamma)/beta) - (delta/beta)
            *pt[t]
+     Qt[t+1] <- gamma + delta*pt[t]
+
+   }
+
+   t <- 0:periods
+   df <- data.frame(t = t,
+                    pt = pt,
+                    Qt = Qt)
+
+   df_l <- df %>%
+     pivot_longer(!t)
+
+   g <- ggplot(df_l, aes(x = t, y = value,
```

```
+                                group = name,
+                                color = name)) +
+     geom_line(size = 1) +
+     theme_classic() + ylab("pt, Qt") +
+     scale_y_continuous(breaks = pretty_breaks()) +
+     scale_x_continuous(breaks = pretty_breaks()) +
+     theme(legend.position = "bottom",
+           legend.title = element_blank())
+
+   equilibrium <- c(pstar = pstar, qstar = qstar)
+   l <- list(equilibrium = equilibrium,
+             data = df,
+             plot = g)
+
+   return(l)
+
+ }
```

The function returns the equilibrium price, `pstar`, and quantity, `qstar`, the simulated data and the plot (the quantities traded Q_t are taken from the supply curve). Let's run it for the model under investigation

```
> cobweb(22, 3, 2, 1, 10)
$equilibrium
pstar qstar
    5     7

$data
    t        pt        Qt
1   0 10.000000        NA
2   1  3.333333 12.000000
3   2  5.555556  5.333333
4   3  4.814815  7.555556
5   4  5.061728  6.814815
6   5  4.979424  7.061728
7   6  5.006859  6.979424
8   7  4.997714  7.006859
9   8  5.000762  6.997714
10  9  4.999746  7.000762
11 10  5.000085  6.999746
12 11  4.999972  7.000085
13 12  5.000009  6.999972
14 13  4.999997  7.000009
15 14  5.000001  6.999997
16 15  5.000000  7.000001
17 16  5.000000  7.000000
```

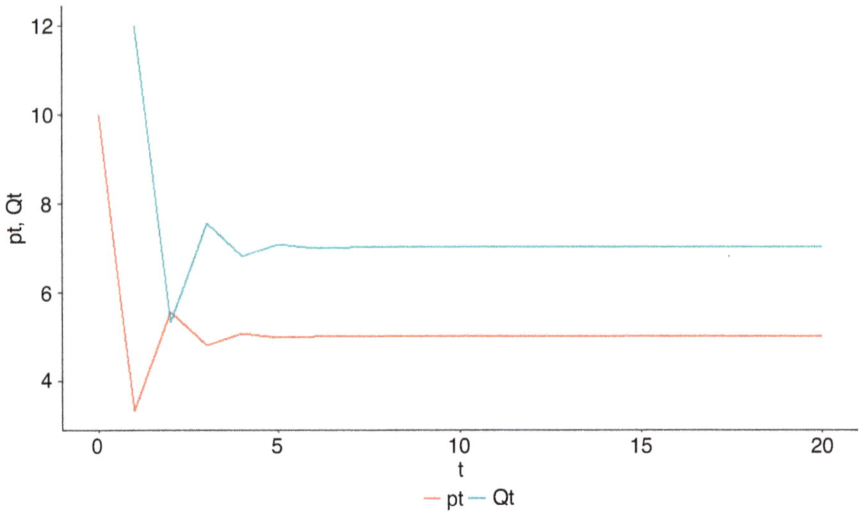

Fig. 10.9 The cobweb model

```
18 17   5.000000   7.000000
19 18   5.000000   7.000000
20 19   5.000000   7.000000
21 20   5.000000   7.000000

$plot

Warning message:
Removed 1 row(s) containing missing values (geom_path).
```

Figure 10.9 shows that after an initial oscillation the price and quantity converge to the equilibrium price and quantity.

10.5.3 The Harrod-Domar Growth Model

In a similar fashion we can solve the Harrod-Domar growth model in discrete time. The model is specified as follows

$$S_t = sY_t \tag{10.46}$$

$$I_t = v(Y_t - Y_{t-1}) \tag{10.47}$$

$$S_t = I_t \tag{10.48}$$

where S, savings, is assumed proportional to income Y, and I, investment, is proportional to the change in income between time periods. In equilibrium, savings is equal to investment. Again, to be consistent with the previous notation, we move one period forward.

$$sY_{t+1} = v(Y_{t+1} - Y_t)$$

$$sY_{t+1} = vY_{t+1} - vY_t$$

$$sY_{t+1} - vY_{t+1} + vY_t = 0$$

$$Y_{t+1}(s - v) + vY_t = 0$$

$$Y_{t+1} + \frac{v}{s-v}Y_t = 0$$

$Y_t = Ab^t$, $Y_{t+1} = Ab^{t+1}$

$$Ab^{t+1} + \frac{v}{s-v}Ab^t = 0$$

$$Ab^t\left(b + \frac{v}{s-v}\right) = 0 \quad \left[Ab^t \neq 0\right]$$

$$b + \frac{v}{s-v} = 0$$

$$b = -\frac{v}{s-v}$$

$$Y_t = A\left(-\frac{v}{s-v}\right)^t$$

At $t = 0$, $Y_t = Y_0$

$$Y_0 = A\left(-\frac{v}{s-v}\right)^0$$

$$A = Y_0$$

$$Y_t = Y_0\left(-\frac{v}{s-v}\right)^t$$

10.5.4 Law of Motion for Public Debt

In this section we use difference equations to describe the dynamics of public debt.

To keep things simple we will not consider inflation. The law of motion for public debt is

$$b_t = \frac{1+r}{1+g} b_{t-1} + d \tag{10.49}$$

where $b_t = \frac{B_t}{Y_t}$ denotes the debt to GDP ratio, r denotes the interest rate the government pays, g denotes the GDP growth rates, and $d = \frac{G_t - T_t}{Y_t}$ denotes the deficit to GDP ratio, where $G_t - T_t$, government spending minus taxes, denotes the primary deficit. Additionally, we take r, g, and d as exogenous variables.

Let's consider the case where the primary surplus is zero. Equation 10.49 becomes

$$b_t = \frac{1+r}{1+g} b_{t-1} \tag{10.50}$$

Let's find the general solution to this difference equation. Let's change the period notation to be consistent with the previous examples.

$$b_{t+1} - \frac{1+r}{1+g} b_t = 0$$

and for convenience let's set $\frac{1+r}{1+g} = \alpha$.

$$b_{t+1} - \alpha b_t = 0$$

This is a homogeneous first-order difference equation. Let's practice with the general method.

Let's set $b_t = AB^t$ (we are picking capital B to avoid confusion with b in the law of motion equation), and consequently, $b_{t+1} = AB^{t+1}$. By replacing them

$$AB^{t+1} - \alpha AB^t = 0$$

$$AB^t(B - \alpha) = 0 \quad \left[AB^t \neq 0\right]$$

$$B = \alpha$$

Therefore,

$$b_t = A\alpha^t$$

Given the initial condition $b_t = b_0$ at time $t = 0$

$$b_0 = A\alpha^0$$

$$A = b_0$$

Then

$$b_t = b_0\alpha^t$$

and by replacing α

$$b_t = b_0\left(\frac{1+r}{1+g}\right)^t$$

Its stability is determined by $\frac{1+r}{1+g}$. If

- $r < g$, b_t goes to zero (convergent).
- $r = g$, b_t is constant.
- $r > g$, b_t goes to infinity (divergent).

Let's verify these results by plotting the path by using `iter_de()` (Fig. 10.10).

```
> r <- 2
> g <- 5
> alpha <- (1 + r)/(1 + g)
> RHS1 <- "alpha*y[t]"
> p1 <- iter_de(RHS1, y0 = 1, order = 1,
+              periods = 20, graph = TRUE)$graph_simulation
+   labs(caption = "r < g")
> r <- 2
> g <- 2
> alpha <- (1 + r)/(1 + g)
> RHS2 <- "alpha*y[t]"
> p2 <- iter_de(RHS2, y0 = 1, order = 1,
+              periods = 20, graph = TRUE)$graph_simulation
+   labs(caption = "r = g")
> r <- 5
> g <- 2
> alpha <- (1 + r)/(1 + g)
> RHS3 <- "alpha*y[t]"
> p3 <- iter_de(RHS3, y0 = 1, order = 1,
+              periods = 20, graph = TRUE)$graph_simulation
+   labs(caption = "r > g")
> ggarrange(p1, p2, p3,
+               nrow = 3, ncol = 1)
```

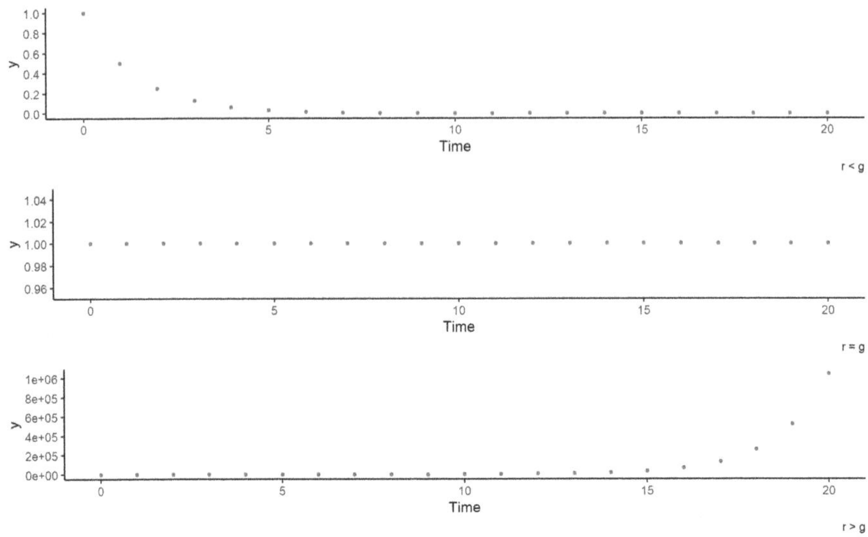

Fig. 10.10 Simulation of law motion of public debt

Next let's write a function, `debt_path()`, based on Eq. 10.49. This function presents two main differences with `iter_de()`. First, the model is embedded in the body of the function. Second, data will be returned as a spreadsheet style.

```
> debt_path <- function(B0, r, g, d, period = 500,
+                            graph = TRUE, data = TRUE){
+
+   s <- c(B0, numeric(period))
+   df <- data.frame(t = 0:(length(s)-1), Bt = s)
+
+   for(t in 1:(period)){
+
+     df$Bt[t+1] <- ((1 + r) / (1 + g))*df$Bt[t] + d
+
+   }
+
+   if(graph == TRUE & data == TRUE){
+
+     library("ggplot2")
+
+     gr <- ggplot(df, aes(x = df$t,
+                           y = df$Bt)) +
+       geom_point(color = "red") +
+       ggtitle("Debt path") +
+       xlab("period") + ylab("Debt/GDP") +
+       theme_classic()
```

```
+
+     l <- list(gr, df)
+
+     return(l)
+
+   } else if(graph == TRUE & data == FALSE){
+
+     library("ggplot2")
+
+     gr <- ggplot(df, aes(x = t,
+                          y = Bt)) +
+       geom_point(color = "red") +
+       ggtitle("Debt path") +
+       xlab("period") + ylab("Debt/GDP") +
+       theme_classic()
+
+     return(gr)
+
+   } else if(graph == FALSE & data == TRUE){
+
+     return(df)
+
+   }
+
+ }
```

Let's test it by comparing its output with that of `iter_de()`.

```
> r <- 2
> g <- 5
> alpha <- (1 + r)/(1 + g)
> RHS <- "alpha*y[t]"
> iter_de(RHS, y0 = 1, order = 1, periods = 10)
 [1] 1.0000000000 0.5000000000 0.2500000000 0.1250000000
 [5] 0.0625000000 0.0312500000 0.0156250000 0.0078125000
 [9] 0.0039062500 0.0019531250 0.0009765625
> debt_path(1, 2, 5, 0, graph = F, period = 10)
   t           Bt
1  0 1.0000000000
2  1 0.5000000000
3  2 0.2500000000
4  3 0.1250000000
5  4 0.0625000000
6  5 0.0312500000
7  6 0.0156250000
8  7 0.0078125000
9  8 0.0039062500
```

```
10  9 0.0019531250
11 10 0.0009765625
> d <- 4
> RHS <- "alpha*y[t] + d"
> iter_de(RHS, y0 = 1, order = 1, periods = 10)
 [1] 1.000000 4.500000 6.250000 7.125000
 [5] 7.562500 7.781250 7.890625 7.945312
 [9] 7.972656  7.986328 7.993164
> debt_path(1, 2, 5, 4, graph = F, period = 10)
    t       Bt
1   0 1.000000
2   1 4.500000
3   2 6.250000
4   3 7.125000
5   4 7.562500
6   5 7.781250
7   6 7.890625
8   7 7.945312
9   8 7.972656
10  9 7.986328
11 10 7.993164
```

Now let's make some simulations. Let's assume an initial government debt of 60% of GDP, an interest of 2%, and a deficit of 3% of GDP. Let's assume different growth rates: 1%, 3%, 5%, and 8% (Fig. 10.11).

```
> g01 <- debt_path(0.6, 0.02, 0.01, 0.03, data = FALSE) +
+   labs(caption = "growth rate of GDP: 1%")
> g03 <- debt_path(0.6, 0.02, 0.03, 0.03, data = FALSE) +
+   labs(caption = "growth rate of GDP: 3%")
> g05 <- debt_path(0.6, 0.02, 0.05, 0.03, data = FALSE) +
+   labs(caption = "growth rate of GDP: 5%")
> g08 <- debt_path(0.6, 0.02, 0.08, 0.03, data = FALSE) +
+   labs(caption = "growth rate of GDP: 8%")
> ggarrange(g01, g03, g05, g08,
+           nrow = 2, ncol = 2)
```

Let's make another simulation with the same values for `B0` and `r` but this time we fix `g` to 5% and try different simulations with `d`: 5%, 4%, 2%, and 1% (Fig. 10.12).

```
> d05 <- debt_path(0.6, 0.02, 0.05, 0.05, data = FALSE) +
+   labs(caption = "growth rate of deficit: 5%")
> d04 <- debt_path(0.6, 0.02, 0.05, 0.04, data = FALSE) +
+   labs(caption = "growth rate of deficit: 4%")
> d02 <- debt_path(0.6, 0.02, 0.05, 0.02, data = FALSE) +
+   labs(caption = "growth rate of deficit: 2%")
> d01 <- debt_path(0.6, 0.02, 0.05, 0.01, data = FALSE) +
+   labs(caption = "growth rate of deficit: 1%")
> ggarrange(d05, d04, d02, d01,
+           nrow = 2, ncol = 2)
```

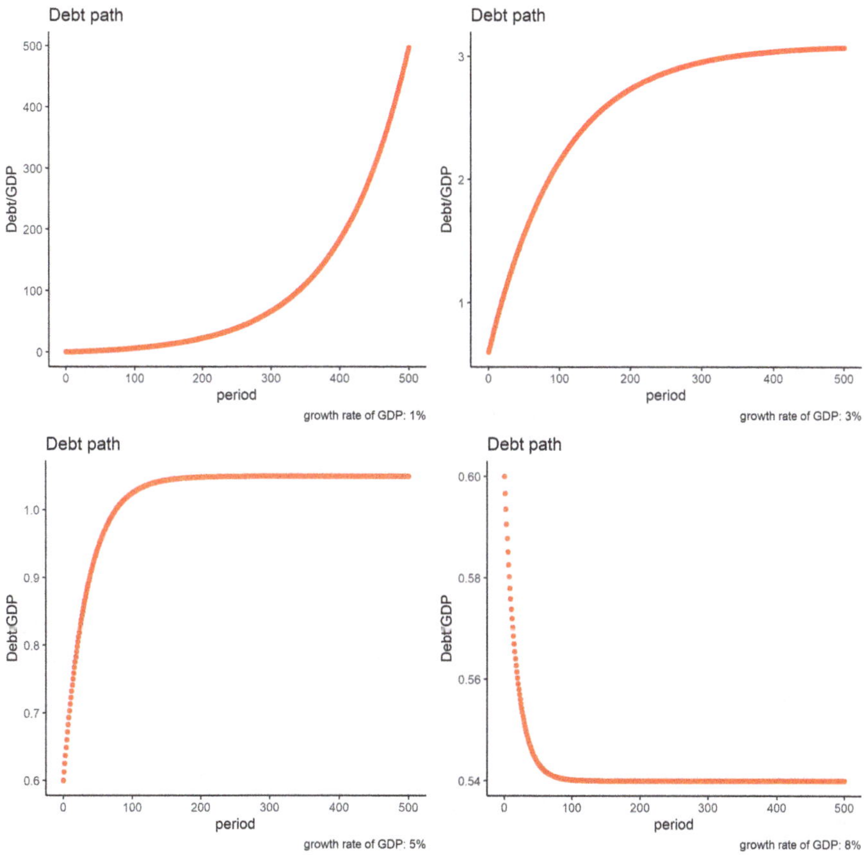

Fig. 10.11 Simulation of law motion of public debt with different GDP growth rates

10.5.5 Linear Difference Equations and Autoregressive Process

We have the following second-order linear difference equation

$$y_{t+2} = 0.7y_{t+1} - 0.45y_t \tag{10.51}$$

We know how to solve (10.51) with the usual approach.

$$y_{t+2} - 0.7y_{t+1} + 0.45y_t = 0$$

$$Ab^t(b^2 - 0.7b + 0.45) = 0 \quad [Ab^t \neq 0]$$

$$b^2 - 0.7b + 0.45 = 0$$

$$b_{1,2} = \frac{0.7}{2} \pm \frac{i\sqrt{1.31}}{2}$$

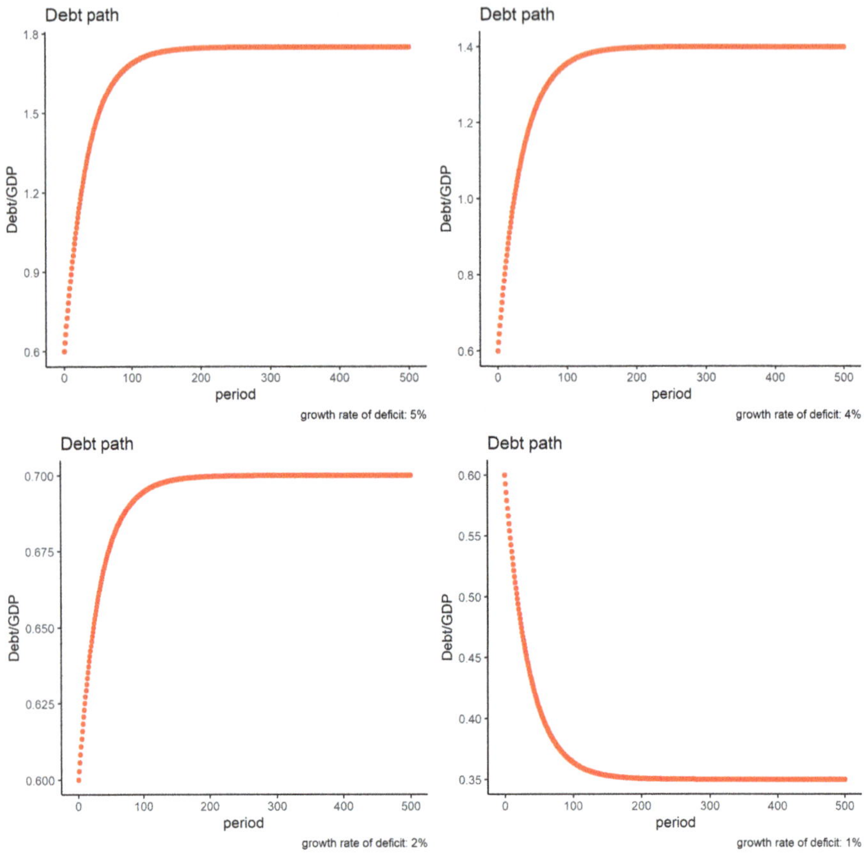

Fig. 10.12 Simulation of law motion of public debt with different deficit growth rates

We have complex roots $b_{1,2} = \alpha \pm i\beta$. Hence

$$r = \sqrt{\left(\frac{0.7}{2}\right)^2 + \left(\frac{\sqrt{1.31}}{2}\right)^2} = 0.6705$$

Since $|r| < 1$ we conclude that the path of (10.51) is convergent. This is our usual analysis. Now let's compute the following:

$$(1 - b_1 L) \cdot (1 - b_2 L) = 0 \tag{10.52}$$

that in our case is

$$\left[1-\left(\frac{0.7}{2}+\frac{i\sqrt{1.31}}{2}\right)L\right]\cdot\left[1-\left(\frac{0.7}{2}-\frac{i\sqrt{1.31}}{2}\right)L\right]=0$$

$$1-0.7L+0.45L^2=0 \tag{10.53}$$

What does (10.53) represent?

Before answering this question, let's consider (10.51) from another perspective. Let's consider the following second-order autoregressive process AR(2)

$$y_t=c+\phi_1 y_{t_1}+\phi_2 y_{t-2}+\epsilon_t \tag{10.54}$$

where the current period's value y_t is explained by the two previous period's values, a constant c, and an error process ϵ_t that is assumed to be a *Gaussian white noise process*, i.e. ϵ_t is assumed to be normally distributed: $\epsilon_t \sim N(0,\sigma^2)$.

Additionally, let's say that $\phi_1=0.7$ and $\phi_2=-0.45$. That is, (10.54) is

$$y_t=c+0.7y_{t-1}-0.45y_{t-2}+\epsilon_t \tag{10.55}$$

Our objective is to determine if (10.55) is *stationary*. For this task we need to consider the homogeneous difference equation of (10.55), i.e.

$$y_t-0.7y_{t-1}+0.45y_{t-2}=0 \tag{10.56}$$

and observe the roots of the characteristic equation obtained by expressing the AR(2) process in lag polynomial notation. The lag operator L, operating on y_t, has the effect to lag the data. That is

$$Ly_t=y_{t-1} \quad \text{and} \quad L(Ly_t)=L^2y_t=y_{t-2} \tag{10.57}$$

Let's substitute (10.57) into (10.56)

$$y_t-0.7Ly_t+0.45L^2y_t=0$$

and factor out y_t to obtain

$$(1-0.7L+0.45L^2)y_t=0 \tag{10.58}$$

where the term in parenthesis is what we obtained in (10.53).

Next we replace the lag operator L with a variable z and set the corresponding polynomial equation equal to zero

$$1-0.7z+0.45z^2=0 \tag{10.59}$$

and solve for z

$$z_{1,2} = \frac{7}{9} \pm \frac{i\sqrt{131}}{9} = 0.\bar{7} \pm 1.271725i \tag{10.60}$$

y_t is stationary if all the roots "lie outside the unit circle". If the roots are complex, as in our case, the modulus needs to be greater than one. With $z = \alpha + i\beta$, the modulus is $|z| = \sqrt{\alpha^2 + \beta^2}$. If the roots are all real numbers, y_t is stationary if the absolute values of all the real roots are greater than one. On the other hand, we have a *unit root* if a root equals one or minus one. If there is at least one unit root, or if any root lies between plus and minus one, then the series is not stationary.

These conclusions can be easily seen with an AR(1) process: $y_t = \phi y_{t-1} + \epsilon_t$. Applying the lag operator and making the z variable substitution, the characteristic equation of this AR(1) process is $1 - \phi z = 0$ and the root is $z = \frac{1}{\phi}$. This leads to $|z| = |\frac{1}{\phi}| > 1$ when $|\phi| < 1$ (For theory, concepts, and applications with **R** related to the autoregressive process the reader is referred to Pfaff (2008)).

By placing restrictions on the values of the parameters, we restrict an autoregressive model to stationarity:

- AR(1) model: $-1 < \phi < 1$
- AR(2) model: $-1 < \phi_2 < 1$, $\phi_1 + \phi_2 < 1$, and $\phi_2 - \phi_1 < 1$ (Hyndman & Athanasopoulos 2021)

In our case we set $\phi_1 = 0.7$ and $\phi_2 = -0.45$. In our example, the modulus is

$$|z| = \sqrt{\left(\frac{7}{9}\right)^2 + \left(\frac{\sqrt{131}}{9}\right)^2} = 1.490712 \tag{10.61}$$

confirming that y_t is stationary.

Next we simulate this AR(2) process in **R**. First, we generate an AR(2) process with `arima.sim()`.

```
> set.seed(12345)
> yt <- arima.sim(n = 1000, list(ar = c(0.7, -0.45)),
+                 innov = rnorm(1000))
```

Second, we fit the AR(2) model to the univariate time series `yt`

```
> ar2 <- arima(yt, order = c(2, 0, 0))
> ar2$coef
       ar1         ar2   intercept
 0.70745968 -0.46034765  0.05412489
```

We can observe that we included an intercept in the model (c in (10.54)) and that the estimates for ϕ_1 and ϕ_2 are close to their theoretical values.

Third, we use the `polyroot()` function to retrieve the roots of the characteristic polynomial equation (10.59). Note that we exclude the estimated coefficient for the intercept and we reverse the signs of the estimated coefficients ϕ_1 and ϕ_2 to correspond to (10.59)

```
> polyroot(c(1, -ar2$coef[1:2]))
[1] 0.768397+1.257711i 0.768397-1.257711i
```

By using the `Mod()` function the moduli of the characteristic equation are retrieved

```
> Mod(polyroot(c(1, -ar2$coef[1:2])))
[1] 1.473863 1.473863
```

We can compute the modulus manually and check that is greater than one

```
> root.real <- Re(polyroot(c(1, -ar2$coef[1:2])))
> root.real
[1] 0.7683972 0.7683972
> root.com <- Im(polyroot(c(1, -ar2$coef[1:2])))
> root.com
[1]  1.257711 -1.257711
> alpha <- root.real[1]
> beta <- root.com[1]
> sqrt(alpha^2 + beta^2) > 1
[1] TRUE
```

Finally, we plot the roots in a Cartesian coordinate system with a unit circle. Figure 10.13 shows that the roots lie outside the unit circle.

```
> x <- seq(-1, 1, length = 1000)
> y1 <- sqrt(1 - x^2)
> y2 <- -sqrt(1 - x^2)
> plot(c(x, x), c(y1, y2),
+       type = "l",
+       xlab = "Real part",
+       ylab = "Complex part",
+       main = "Unit circle",
+       ylim = c(-2, 2),
+       xlim = c(-2, 2))
> abline(h = 0)
> abline(v = 0)
> points(root.real, root.com, pch = 19)
> legend(-1.5, -1.5, legend = "Roots of AR(2)", pch = 19)
```

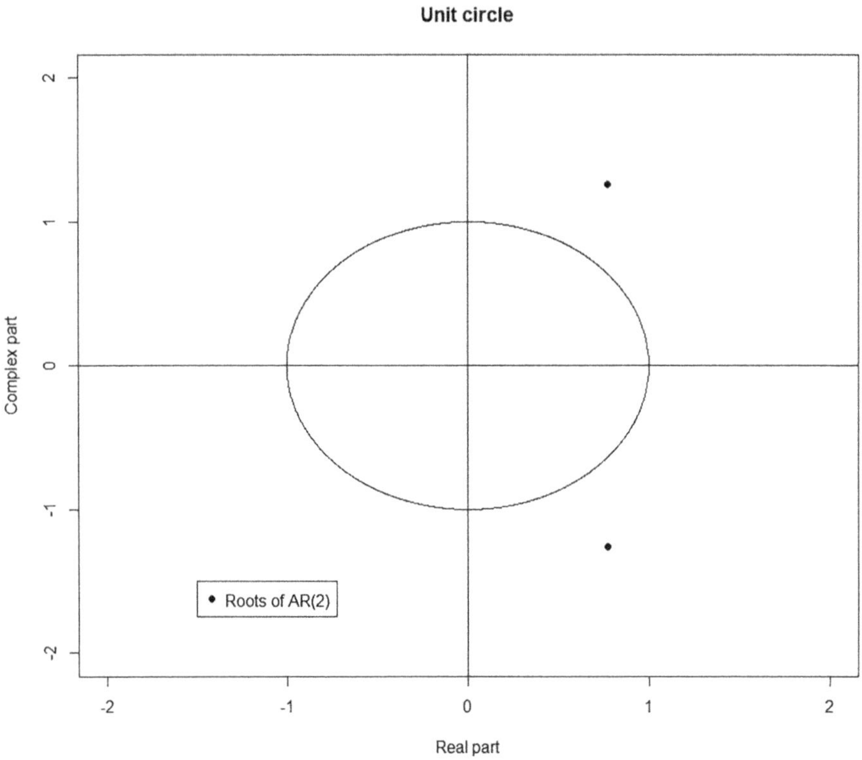

Fig. 10.13 Unit circle and roots of a stable AR(2) process with $\phi_1 = 0.7$ and $\phi_2 = -0.45$

10.6 Exercises

10.6.1 Exercise 1

Rewrite `iter_de()` so that it returns a spreadsheet style result as in `debt_path()`.

10.6.2 Exercise 2

Write a function, `sys_folde_diag()`, that solves system of first-order linear equations by applying the diagonalization process as described in Sect. 10.3.3.1. Replicate the result in Sect. 10.3.3.1

```
> A <- matrix(c(2, 4,
+                1, 5),
+              nrow = 2, ncol = 2,
+              byrow = T)
```

```
> A
     [,1] [,2]
[1,]    2    4
[2,]    1    5
> A0 <- matrix(c(4, 5),
+               ncol = 1, nrow = 2,
+               byrow = T)
> A0
     [,1]
[1,]    4
[2,]    5
> sys_folde_diag(A, A0, t = 10)
           t10
[1,] 290237644
[2,] 290237645
```

Add a level of complexity to the function by making it return results for multiple periods. Replicate the results for the Fibonacci sequence

```
> M <- matrix(c(0, 1,
+                1, 1),
+              nrow = 2,
+              ncol = 2,
+              byrow = T)
> M
     [,1] [,2]
[1,]    0    1
[2,]    1    1
> M0 <- matrix(c(0, 1),
+               nrow = 2,
+               ncol = 1,
+               byrow = T)
> M0
     [,1]
[1,]    0
[2,]    1
> sys_folde_diag(M, M0, t = 0:11)
               t0 t1 t2 t3 t4 t5 t6 t7 t8 t9 t10 t11
[1,] 1.110223e-16  1  1  2  3  5  8 13 21 34  55  89
[2,] 1.000000e+00  1  2  3  5  8 13 21 34 55  89 144
```

10.6.3 Exercise 3

Complete the code for `trajectory_de()` and test your function by replicating the examples in Sect. 10.3.4.

Chapter 11
Differential Equations

In Chap. 10 the dynamic analysis described a discrete-time context, where the time variable t takes only integer values. In the present chapter, we modify the time context of the dynamic analysis by considering a continuous-time context where the variable t changes continuously. Consequently, we cannot rely on difference equations to set up and solve continuous dynamic models. We need to introduce differential equations for this task. We have already referred to differential equations in terms of notation in Sect. 4.4 and we have already solved differential equations in Sects. 5.1.1.1.6 and 5.1.1.4.1. However, in the case of the solution of differential equations in Sects. 5.1.1.1.6 and 5.1.1.4.1, the main focus was on integration techniques and not on the differential equations *per se*. Thus, we can anticipate that integration techniques are fundamental to find a solution to differential equations. This is also the reason why the "solution of a differential equation is often referred to as the *integral* of that solution" (Chiang & Wainwright, 2005, p. 475).

We denote with $y = y(t)$ the function that describes the state of a system at any time t, where y is the dependent variable of the system and t is the independent variable of the system. y is also known as the *state* variable of the system that varies with t. In a dynamic system we find $y(t)$ related to some of its derivatives. An equation that relates the unknown function to any of its derivatives is known as a differential equation. By solving differential equations we learn about the state of the system with the change of time.

We encounter the following terminology associated with differential equations:

- ordinary/partial
  - ordinary: the unknowns function depends only on a single independent variable and consequently only ordinary derivatives appear in the differential equation
  - partial: the unknowns function depends on several independent variables and consequently partial derivatives appear in the differential equation

M. Porto, *Introduction to Mathematics for Economics with R*,
https://doi.org/10.1007/978-3-031-05202-6_11

- linear/non-linear
- homogeneous/nonhomogeneous
- first-order/second-order (or higher)
  - first-order: the first derivative is the highest derivative that appears in the differential equation
  - second-order: the second derivative is the highest derivative that appears in the differential equation
  - *nth*-order: the *nth*-derivative is the highest derivative that appears in the differential equation
- constant coefficient and constant term/variable terms
- autonomous/nonautonomous
  - autonomous: the differential equation does not explicitly depend on the independent variable (*time-invariant* in case of time as independent variable; that is, “time can be shifted with no effect” (Logan, 2011, p. 11))
  - nonautonomous: the differential equation explicitly depends on the independent variable (*time-variant* in case of time as independent variable)

11.1 On the Solution of Differential Equations

11.1.1 Existence and Uniqueness

A first-order ordinary differential equation (ODE) takes the following general form

$$y' = f(t, y) \tag{11.1}$$

that can be written as

$$\frac{dy}{dt} = f(t, y) \tag{11.2}$$

The solution of the differential equation (11.1) is a function $y(t)$. In other words, we have to find a function that solves (11.1).

In this section we assume that in Eq. 11.1 $f(t, y)$ depends linearly on the dependent variable y. That is, Eq. 11.1 is a first-order linear equation. It can be written as

$$y' + p(t)y = g(t) \tag{11.3}$$

where p and g are given function and they are continuous on some interval $\alpha < t < \beta$.

Before showing the methods to solve first-order linear differential equations, we will address the following two questions:

1. Does an equation of the form (11.3) have a solution? (question of *existence*)
2. If Eq. 11.3 has a solution, does it have other solutions? (question of *uniqueness*)

Theorem of existence and uniqueness for a first-order linear differential equation states that if p and g are continuous on an open interval $I : \alpha < t < \beta$ containing the point $t = t_0$, then there exists a unique function $y = y(t)$ that satisfies Eq. 11.3 for each t in I, and that also satisfies the initial condition $y(t_0) = y_0$ where y_0 is a prescribed initial value (the reader may refer to Boyce and DiPrima (1992, p. 23) for the proof).

11.1.2 Implicit and Explicit Solutions

Let's add some comments on the solution of a differential equation by solving the following differential equation (we will return to the following method to find the solution in Sect. 11.2.3)

$$\frac{dy}{dt} = 1 - t + 4y \tag{11.4}$$

$$\int \frac{d}{dt} e^{-4t} y = \int e^{-4t} - e^{-4t} t \, dt$$

$$e^{-4t} y = -\frac{1}{4} e^{-4t} + \frac{1}{4} t e^{-4t} + \frac{1}{16} e^{-4t} + c \tag{11.5}$$

Equation 11.5 is known as the implicit solution of the differential equation (11.4). To get the explicit solution we need to solve (11.5) for y in terms of t

$$y = -\frac{1}{4} + \frac{1}{4} t + \frac{1}{16} + \frac{c}{e^{-4t}}$$

$$y = \frac{1}{4} t - \frac{3}{16} + c e^{4t} \tag{11.6}$$

11.1.3 Complementary and Particular Solutions

As in the case of difference equations, we may refer to *complementary solution*, the solution that satisfies the homogeneous equation, and to *particular solution*, the solution to the nonhomogeneous equation.

For example, in (11.6), ce^{4t} is the complementary solution. In fact,

$$\frac{dy}{dt} = 4y$$

$$\frac{dy}{y} = 4\,dt$$

$$\int \frac{dy}{y} = 4\int dt$$

$$\log \mid y \mid = 4t + c$$

$$y = e^{4t+c}$$

$$y = e^{4t} \cdot e^{c}$$

$$y = ce^{4t}$$

To be noted that we used a different method to solve this differential equation. We will return to this method in Sect. 11.2.1.

11.1.4 Verification of the Solution

To verify if our solution is correct, we can check that the left side and right side of (11.4) are equal.

Step 1
Find $\frac{dy}{dt}$ of the explicit solution (11.6)

$$\frac{dy}{dt} = \frac{1}{4} + 4ce^{4t}$$

Step 2
Plug the explicit solution (11.6) into the right-hand side of (11.4)

$$1 - t + 4\left(\frac{1}{4}t - \frac{3}{16} + ce^{4t}\right) = \frac{1}{4} + 4ce^{4t}$$

Step 3
Compare the two sides. If they are equal we found a solution to the differential equation. In this example, the two sides are equal therefore we found a solution.

11.1.5 Initial Value Problem

In solution (11.6) an *arbitrary constant*, c, appears. This means that we have a solution for each value of c, i.e. there is an infinity of solutions. Solution (11.6) is also called the *general solution* of the differential equation. As in the case of difference equations, we set an *initial condition* to find the value of c. For this example, we plot (11.6) with $y_0 = \{-2, -1, 1, 2\}$ implying $c = \{-\frac{29}{16}, -\frac{13}{16}, \frac{19}{16}, \frac{35}{16}\}$ (Fig. 11.1).[1]

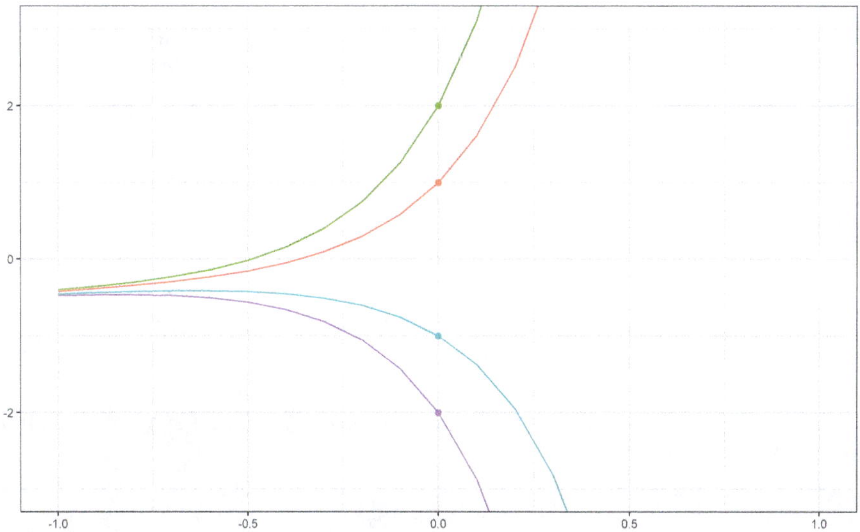

Fig. 11.1 Plot of general solution with $-2 \leq y_0 \leq 2$

[1] The code used to generate Figs. 11.1, 11.7, and 11.8 is available in Appendix J.

11.1.6 Analytical Solution and Numerical Solution

In Sect. 11.2, we will learn how to find an *analytical solution* to a differential equation. In other words, we will learn the steps that leads to an exact expression for the solution. However, it should be stressed that in most of real-world applications it is not often possible to obtain an analytical solution. If it is not possible to solve the differential equation analytically, we can approximate the solution *numerically* by using algorithms. In this case, the solution is represented by a table of numbers or a plot.

In the next section, we investigate two algorithms to numerically solve a differential equation. The first algorithm is the Euler algorithm, that is the simplest algorithm to approximate a solution of a differential equation. The second algorithm is the Runge-Kutta algorithm that is the most popular algorithm to approximate a solution of a differential equation. We will build two functions, `ode_euler()` and `ode_RungeKutta()` that apply the respective algorithms to numerically solve a differential equation. We will apply the algorithms to (11.4) and compare the numerical solution to the analytical solution. To be noted that the differential equation (11.4) is used in Boyce and DiPrima (1992) to compare different numerical methods. I use this differential equation in Boyce and DiPrima (1992) to test whether the two functions properly work. The following functions are built for pedagogic purpose only. In Sect. 11.7 we will use the functions of the `deSolve` package to numerically solve differential equations.

11.1.6.1 The Euler Method

The algorithm presented in this section is known as *Euler method* or *tangent line method*. This algorithm is based on the intuition that the slope of the tangent line at $y' = y(t_0, y_0)$ is known since it is known that at $t = 0$, $y = y_0$. By finding the tangent line to the solution at t_0, it becomes possible to approximate the solution at y_1 by moving t from t_0 to t_1 and then approximate the solution at y_2 by moving t from t_1 to t_2 and so on

$$y_1 = y_0 + y'(t_0, y_0)(t_1 - t_0)$$

$$y_2 = y_1 + y'(t_1, y_1)(t_2 - t_1)$$

The Euler method can be expressed as

$$y_{n+1} = y_n + hy'_n, n = 0, 1, 2, \ldots \tag{11.7}$$

where $h = t_{n+1} - t_n$ is a uniform step size between the points $t_0, t_1, t_2, \ldots$ and $y' = f(t_n, y_n)$.

Let's apply the Euler method to the differential equation (11.4).

At $n = 0$, with $f(t_0 = 0, y_0 = 1)$ we have that $y_0' = 1 - t_0 + 4y_0 = 5$. Consequently, with $h = 0.01$ we have

$$y_1 = y_0 + hf(t_0, y_0) = 1 + 0.01 \cdot 5 = 1.05$$

At $n = 1$, with $f(t_1 = 0.01, y_1 = 1.05)$ we have that $y_1' = 1 - t_1 + 4y_1 = 5.19$. Consequently

$$y_2 = y_1 + hf(t_1, y_1) = 1.05 + 0.01 \cdot 5.19 = 1.1019$$

At $n = 2$, with $f(t_2 = 0.02, y_2 = 1.1019)$ we have that $y_2' = 1 - t_2 + 4y_2 = 5.3876$. Consequently

$$y_3 = y_2 + hf(t_2, y_2) = 1.1019 + 0.01 \cdot 5.3876 = 1.155776$$

and so on.

Now it is time to write in **R** a function that uses the Euler method. We use a loop to implement (11.7). Let's name this function `ode_euler()`.[2] The function takes five arguments

- `dy`: a first-order differential equation written as character. If it is a nonautonomous differential equation, the variable time needs to be written as `T`. This will be replaced by `h*(t - 1)` in the function. The reason for this depends on the fact the the initial value in **R** is stored at index 1. So we replace `T` with `t-1` to represent t_0 when the loop starts. On the other hand, we need to multiply by `h` because we are representing continuous time
- `y0`: the initial condition
- `h`: the step size (by default 0.01)
- `periods`: the length of the time (by default 100)
- `actual_solution`: the actual solution, if available, to compare the result of the approximation (by default `NULL`). Note that the actual solution needs to be written as character with t written as `t*h`.

The function returns a table of numbers and a graph as solution.

```
> ode_euler <- function(dy, y0, h = 0.01, periods = 100,
+                        actual_solution = NULL){
+
+   require("tidyr")
+   require("ggplot2")
+   require("scales")
+
```

[2] In Sect. 11.7 we will use a different approach to code the Euler method.

```
+   dy <- gsub("T", "(h*(t-1))", dy)
+   y <- numeric(periods)
+   y[1] <- y0
+
+   for(t in seq_along(y)){
+
+     y[t+1] <- y[t] + eval(parse(text = dy))*h
+
+     }
+
+   times <- 0:(length(y) - 1)*h
+   df <- data.frame(t = times, yt = y)
+
+   if(is.null(actual_solution)){
+
+     colnames(df) <- c("t", "Euler approximation")
+
+     } else{
+
+       sol <- actual_solution
+       y <- numeric(periods)
+       y[1] <- y0
+
+       for(t in seq_along(y)){
+
+         y[t+1] <- eval(parse(text = sol))
+
+         }
+
+       df$sol <- y
+       colnames(df) <- c("t", "Euler approximation",
+                              "Actual solution")
+       }
+
+   df_l <- df %>%
+     pivot_longer(!t,
+                  names_to = "variable",
+                  values_to = "value")
+
+   g <- ggplot(df_l, aes(x = t, y = value,
+                          group = variable,
+                          color = variable)) +
+     geom_line(size = 1) +
+     theme_bw() + ylab("") +
+     theme(legend.position = "bottom",
```

```
+          legend.title = element_blank()) +
+     scale_y_continuous(breaks = pretty_breaks()) +
+     scale_x_continuous(breaks = pretty_breaks())
+
+   l <- list(graph_results = g,
+             results = df)
+
+   return(l)
+
+ }
```

Let's use step size $h = 0.05$ and 0.01 for the following example.

```
> RHS <- "1 - T + 4*y[t]"
> sol <- "(1/4)*(t*h) - (3/16) + (19/16)*exp(4*t*h)"
> df <- ode_euler(RHS, 1, h = 0.05,
+                 actual_solution = sol)$results
> head(df, 11)
      t Euler approximation Actual solution
1  0.00            1.000000        1.000000
2  0.05            1.250000        1.275416
3  0.10            1.547500        1.609042
4  0.15            1.902000        2.013766
5  0.20            2.324900        2.505330
6  0.25            2.829880        3.102960
7  0.30            3.433356        3.830139
8  0.35            4.155027        4.715550
9  0.40            5.018533        5.794226
10 0.45            6.052239        7.108956
11 0.50            7.290187        8.712004
> df2 <- ode_euler(RHS, 1, h = 0.01,
+                  actual_solution = sol)
> head(df2$results, 11)
      t Euler approximation Actual solution
1  0.00            1.000000        1.000000
2  0.01            1.050000        1.050963
3  0.02            1.101900        1.103903
4  0.03            1.155776        1.158903
5  0.04            1.211707        1.216044
6  0.05            1.269775        1.275416
7  0.06            1.330066        1.337108
8  0.07            1.392669        1.401217
9  0.08            1.457676        1.467839
10 0.09            1.525183        1.537079
11 0.10            1.595290        1.609042
> df2$graph_results
```

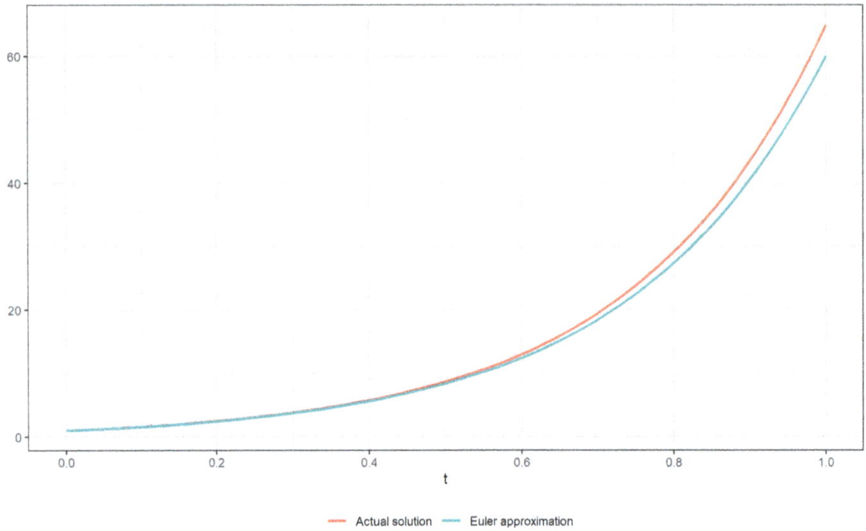

Fig. 11.2 Solution of $y' = 1 - t + 4y,\ y(0) = 1,\ h = 0.01$ with the Euler method

Figure 11.2 represents the numerical solution and the analytical solution with $h = 0.01$.

Next we compute the absolute error. Note that in the following code we use `filter()` from the `dplyr` package to subset; we use ` to generate new columns in the data frame because we write the column name with a space; `DF[, c(1, 2, 4, 3)]` reorders the columns in the data frame.

```
> df$t <- round(df$t, 2)
> df05 <- df %>%
+   filter(t == 0.0 | t == 0.1 | t == 0.2 |
+          t == 0.3 | t == 0.4 | t == 0.5 |
+          t == 0.6 | t == 0.7 | t == 0.8 |
+          t == 0.9 | t == 1.0)
> df01 <- df2$results
> df01$t <- round(df01$t, 2)
> df01 <- df01 %>%
+   filter(t == 0.0 | t == 0.1 | t == 0.2 |
+          t == 0.3 | t == 0.4 | t == 0.5 |
+          t == 0.6 | t == 0.7 | t == 0.8 |
+          t == 0.9 | t == 1.0)
> DF <- df05
> colnames(DF)[2] <- c("h = 0.05")
> DF$`h = 0.01` <- df01$`Euler approximation`
> DF <- DF[, c(1, 2, 4, 3)]
> DF$`Abs Err (h = 0.05)` <- abs(DF$`h = 0.05` -
```

```
+                                    DF$'Actual solution')
> DF$'Abs Err (h = 0.01)' <- abs(DF$'h = 0.01' -
+                                    DF$'Actual solution')
> round(DF[, c(1, 5, 6)], 4)
      t Abs Err (h = 0.05) Abs Err (h = 0.01)
1  0.0              0.0000             0.0000
2  0.1              0.0615             0.0138
3  0.2              0.1804             0.0409
4  0.3              0.3968             0.0911
5  0.4              0.7757             0.1805
6  0.5              1.4218             0.3353
7  0.6              2.5022             0.5980
8  0.7              4.2815             1.0367
9  0.8              7.1774             1.7607
10 0.9             11.8452             2.9437
11 1.0             19.3094             4.8607
```

By computing the absolute error, it results that by reducing h we get a better approximation. We may think to further reduce h to get a better approximation. However, it is not recommended because it is not considered efficient. To produce better approximations it is recommended to use higher order methods (Soetaert et al., 2012, p. 15).

11.1.6.2 The Runge-Kutta Method

The Runge-Kutta formula is

$$y_{n+1} = y_n + \frac{h}{6}\left(k_{n1} + 2k_{n2} + 2k_{n3} + k_{n4}\right) \tag{11.8}$$

where

$$k_{n1} = f(t_n, y_n)$$

$$k_{n2} = f\left(t_n + \frac{1}{2}h, y_n + \frac{1}{2}hk_{n1}\right)$$

$$k_{n3} = f\left(t_n + \frac{1}{2}h, y_n + \frac{1}{2}hk_{n2}\right)$$

$$k_{n4} = f\left(t_n + h, y_n + hk_{n3}\right)$$

Here we show the steps for the implementation of the Runge-Kutta method. For details about this method the reader may refer to Boyce and DiPrima (1992, pp. 406–409) or other advanced textbook on differential equations.

Let's consider the example with (11.4). With $h = 0.01$ and $y(0) = 1$, at $n = 0$ we have

$$k_{01} = f(0, 1) = 1 - 0 + 4 \cdot 1 = 5$$

$$hk_{01} = 0.01 \cdot 5 = 0.05$$

$$k_{02} = f\left(0 + \frac{0.01}{2}, 1 + \frac{0.05}{2}\right) = 1 - 0.005 + 4 \cdot 1.025 = 5.095$$

$$hk_{02} = 0.01 \cdot 5.095 = 0.05095$$

$$k_{03} = f\left(0 + \frac{0.01}{2}, 1 + \frac{0.05095}{2}\right) = 1 - 0.005 + 4 \cdot 1.025475 = 5.0969$$

$$hk_{03} = 0.01 \cdot 5.0969 = 0.050969$$

$$k_{04} = f\left(0 + 0.01, 1 + 0.050969\right) = 1 - 0.01 + 4 \cdot 1.050969 = 5.193876$$

Thus

$$y_1 = 1 + \frac{0.01}{6}\left(5 + 2 \cdot 5.095 + 2 \cdot 5.0969 + 5.193876\right) = 1.050963$$

At $n = 0.01$

$$k_{11} = f(0.01, 1.050963) = 1 - 0.01 + 4 \cdot 1.050963 = 5.193852$$

$$hk_{11} = 0.01 \cdot 5.193852 = 0.05193852$$

$$k_{12} = f\left(0.01 + \frac{0.01}{2}, 1.050963 + \frac{0.05193852}{2}\right) = 1 - 0.015 + 4 \cdot 1.076932 = 5.292729$$

$$hk_{12} = 0.01 \cdot 5.292729 = 0.05292729$$

$$k_{13} = f\left(0.01 + \frac{0.01}{2}, 1.050963 + \frac{0.05292729}{2}\right) = 1 - 0.015 + 4 \cdot 1.077427 = 5.294707$$

$$hk_{13} = 0.01 \cdot 5.294707 = 0.05294707$$

$$k_{14} = f\,(0.01 + 0.01, 1.050963 + 0.05294707) = 1 - 0.02 + 4 \cdot 1.10391 = 5.39564$$

Thus

$$y_2 = 1.050963 + \frac{0.01}{6}(5.193852 + 2 \cdot 5.292729 + 2 \cdot 5.294707 + 5.39564) = 1.103904$$

Now let's code the `ode_RungeKutta()` function to apply the Runge-Kutta algorithm. We follow the same approach that we used for `ode_euler()`.[3]

```
> ode_RungeKutta <- function(dy, y0, h = 0.01, periods = 100,
+                                   actual_solution = NULL){
+
+   require("tidyr")
+   require("ggplot2")
+   require("scales")
+
+   y <- numeric(periods)
+   K1 <- numeric(periods)
+   K2 <- numeric(periods)
+   K3 <- numeric(periods)
+   K4 <- numeric(periods)
+   y[1] <- y0
+
+   k1 <- gsub("T", "(h*(t-1))", dy)
+
+   k2 <- gsub("T", "(h*(t-1) + (1/2)*h)", dy)
+   k2 <- gsub("y\\[t]", "(y[t] + (1/2)*hk1)", k2)
+
+   k3 <- gsub("k1", "k2", k2)
+
+   k4 <- gsub("T", "(h*(t-1) + h)", dy)
+   k4 <- gsub("y\\[t]", "(y[t] + hk3)", k4)
+
+   for(t in seq_along(y)){
+
+     K1[t] <- eval(parse(text = k1))
+     hk1 <- h*K1[t]
+
+     K2[t] <- eval(parse(text = k2))
```

[3] In Sect. 11.7 we will use a different approach to code the Runge-Kutta algorithm.

```
+     hk2 <- h*K2[t]
+
+     K3[t] <- eval(parse(text = k3))
+     hk3 <- h*K3[t]
+
+     K4[t] <- eval(parse(text = k4))
+
+     y[t+1] <- y[t] + (h/6) * (K1[t] + 2*K2[t] + 2*K3[t] + K4[t])
+
+     }
+
+   times <- 0:(length(y) - 1)*h
+   df <- data.frame(t = times, yt = y)
+
+   if(is.null(actual_solution)){
+     colnames(df) <- c("t", "Runge-Kutta approximation")
+   } else{
+
+     sol <- actual_solution
+     y <- numeric(periods)
+     y[1] <- y0
+
+     for(t in seq_along(y)){
+
+       y[t+1] <- eval(parse(text = sol))
+
+       }
+
+     df$sol <- y
+     colnames(df) <- c("t", "Runge-Kutta approximation",
+                       "Actual solution")
+     }
+
+   df_l <- df %>%
+     pivot_longer(!t,
+                  names_to = "variable",
+                  values_to = "value")
+
+   g <- ggplot(df_l, aes(x = t, y = value,
+                         group = variable,
+                         color = variable)) +
+     geom_line(size = 1) +
+     theme_bw() + ylab("") +
+     theme(legend.position = "bottom",
+           legend.title = element_blank()) +
+     scale_y_continuous(breaks = pretty_breaks()) +
+     scale_x_continuous(breaks = pretty_breaks())
+
+     l <- list(graph_results = g,
+               results = df)
+
+     return(l)
+ }
```

The first two examples with $h = 0.1$ and $h = 0.2$ replicate the results in Boyce and DiPrima (1992, p. 408).

```
> RHS <- "1 - T + 4 * y[t]"
> sol <- "(1/4)*(t*h) - (3/16) + (19/16)*exp(4*t*h)"
> df1 <- ode_RungeKutta(RHS, 1, h = 0.1,
+                        actual_solution = sol,
+                        periods = 10)$results
> df1
     t Runge-Kutta approximation Actual solution
1  0.0                  1.000000        1.000000
2  0.1                  1.608933        1.609042
3  0.2                  2.505006        2.505330
4  0.3                  3.829415        3.830139
5  0.4                  5.792785        5.794226
6  0.5                  8.709318        8.712004
7  0.6                 13.047713       13.052522
8  0.7                 19.507148       19.515518
9  0.8                 29.130609       29.144880
10 0.9                 43.473954       43.497903
11 1.0                 64.858107       64.897803
> df2 <- ode_RungeKutta(RHS, 1, h = 0.2,
+                        actual_solution = sol,
+                        periods = 10)$results
> df2
     t Runge-Kutta approximation Actual solution
1  0.0                  1.000000        1.000000
2  0.2                  2.501600        2.505330
3  0.4                  5.777636        5.794226
4  0.6                 12.997178       13.052522
5  0.8                 28.980768       29.144880
6  1.0                 64.441579       64.897803
7  1.2                143.188565      144.406121
8  1.4                318.134748      321.293859
9  1.6                706.874024      714.903482
10 1.8               1570.747070     1590.836533
11 2.0               3490.557409     3540.200110
```

In the next example, we set $h = 0.01$ and plot the graphs of the Runge-Kutta approximation and the exact result (Fig. 11.3). From the results and the plot we can observe that the Runge-Kutta algorithm essentially produces the same result of the actual solution.

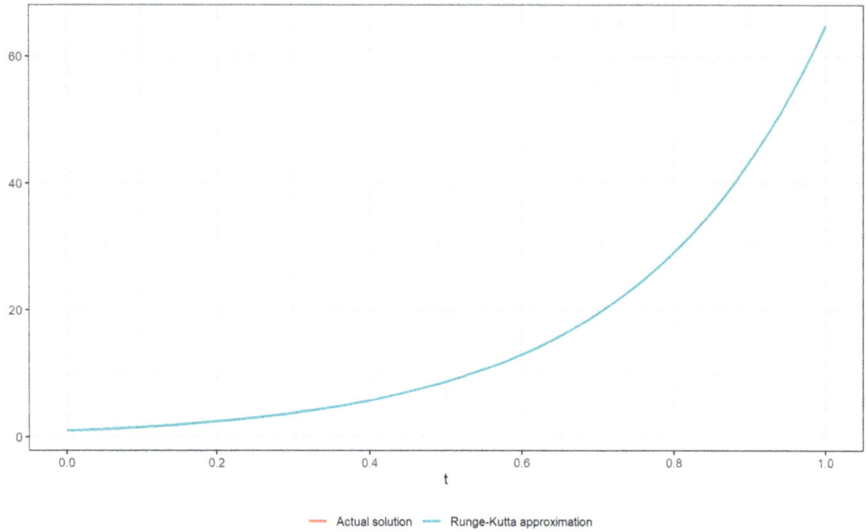

Fig. 11.3 Solution of $y' = 1 - t + 4y,\ y(0) = 1,\ h = 0.01$ with the Runge-Kutta method

```
> df3 <- ode_RungeKutta(RHS, 1, h = 0.01,
+                         actual_solution = sol)
> head(df3$results, 11)
      t Runge-Kutta approximation Actual solution
1  0.00                  1.000000        1.000000
2  0.01                  1.050963        1.050963
3  0.02                  1.103903        1.103903
4  0.03                  1.158903        1.158903
5  0.04                  1.216044        1.216044
6  0.05                  1.275416        1.275416
7  0.06                  1.337108        1.337108
8  0.07                  1.401217        1.401217
9  0.08                  1.467839        1.467839
10 0.09                  1.537079        1.537079
11 0.10                  1.609042        1.609042
> df3$graph_results
```

11.1.7 Geometric Interpretation

Differential equations can be interpreted from a geometric point of view. Geometrically, the differential equation

$$y' = f(t, y)$$

says that at any point (t, y), the slope y' of the solution curve $y = y(t)$ at that point is given by $f(t, y)$. By drawing a short line segment through the point (t, y) with slope $f(t, y)$ we can graphically approximate solution curves for a first-order differential equation. For example, at the point (1, 1) for (11.4), the slope of the line segment is $1 - 1 + 4 \cdot 1 = 4$; at the point (1, 2) the slope of the line segment is $1 - 1 + 4 \cdot 2 = 8$ and so on. The *direction field* or *slope field* represents the collection of all such line segments.

In **R**, we can use the phaseR package to represent a direction field of an autonomous system of ordinary differential equations. Let's consider an example by plotting the slope field for the logistic growth equation. The logistic growth equation is already present in the phaseR package as logistic(). Here, we write it from scratch as in Grayling (2014, p. 46) but using the notation in Sect. 5.1.1.4.1

$$\frac{dN}{dt} = rN\left(1 - \frac{N}{K}\right)$$

The lgst() function takes as arguments the current time (t), the value of the dependent variable (N), and a parameter vector (parms). Note that the derivative is returned as a list. Additionally, to be noted that the function is written in a style compatible with the deSolve package (we will discuss deSolve package in Sect. 11.7).

```
> lgst <- function(t, N, parms){
+   r <- parms[1]
+   K <- parms[2]
+   dN <- r*N*(1 - N/K)
+   list(dN)
+ }
```

With flowField() we plot the direction field. The first argument is a function computing the derivative at a point for the ordinary differential equation; xlim and ylim set the limit of the independent and dependent variable, respectively; parameters are the parameters to be passed to the function, in our case 1 to r and 2 to K in lgst(); points sets the density of the line segments to be plotted; system indicate whether it is a system in one or two dimensions; add determines if the direction field plot is added to an existing plot; xlab and ylab set the label for the corresponding axis.

```
> lgst_flowField <- flowField(lgst,
+                              xlim = c(0, 5),
+                              ylim = c(-1, 3),
+                              parameters = c(1, 2),
+                              points = 21,
+                              system = "one.dim",
+                              add = FALSE,
+                              xlab = "t",
+                              ylab = "N")
```

With the `nullclines()` function we add the *nulliclines* to the plot. The nulliclines are the sets of points where the slope field is zero. To find the nullclines we set $\frac{dN}{dt} = 0$. Thus,

$$rN\left(1 - \frac{N}{K}\right) = 0$$

Consequently, the nullclines are

$$rN = 0 \rightarrow N = 0$$

and

$$1 - \frac{N}{K} = 0 \rightarrow N = K$$

In our case, $N = 2$.

To be noted, additionally, that the sets of points with the same numerical value are called *isoclines*.

```
> lgst_nullclines <- nullclines(lgst,
+                               xlim = c(0, 5),
+                               ylim = c(-1, 3),
+                               parameters = c(1, 2),
+                               system = "one.dim",
+                               state.names = "N")
```

Then, we define a vector with initial conditions (`N0`). Finally, with `trajectory()` we plot the trajectories in the plane. Figure 11.4 represents the direction field of the logistic growth.

```
> N0 <- c(-0.5, 0.5, 1.5, 2.5)
> lgst_trajectory <- trajectory(lgst,
+                               y0 = N0,
+                               tlim = c(0, 5),
+                               parameters = c(1, 2),
+                               system = "one.dim")
Note: col has been reset as required
```

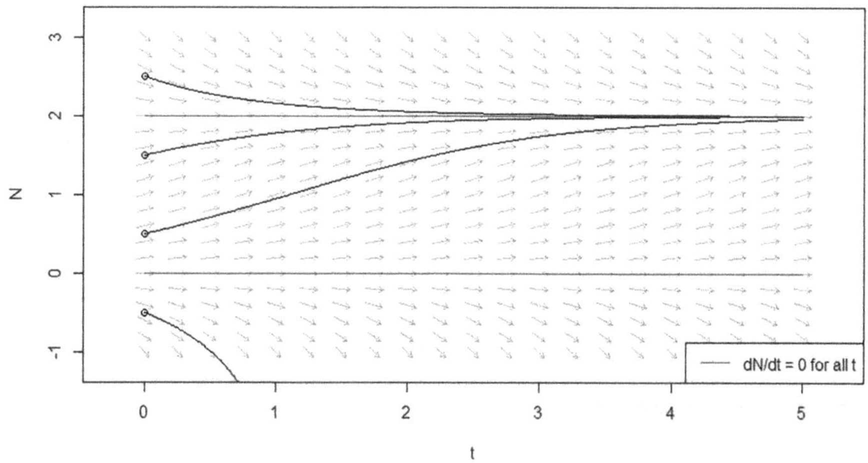

Fig. 11.4 Direction field of the logistic growth

11.2 Methods to Solve First-Order Differential Equations

11.2.1 Separation of Variables

The simplest method to solve first-order differential equations is the method of separation of variables.

This method can be applied when the differential equation takes the following form

$$y' = g(t)p(y) \tag{11.9}$$

For this method it is convenient to write (11.9) as

$$\frac{dy}{dt} = g(t)p(y)$$

This method is called separation of variables because we collect the term with y on the left side and the term with t on the right side.

Step 1
Collect the term with y on the left side and the term with t on the right side.

$$\frac{dy}{p(y)} = g(t)dt$$

Step 2
Integrate both sides

$$\int \frac{dy}{p(y)} = \int g(t)dt$$

Step 3
Solve for y

$$P(y) = G(t) + c$$

This is the method we applied in Sect. 11.1.3. Let's consider another example.

Example 11.2.1 Let's solve the following differential equation

$$\frac{dy}{dt} = 2y^2 t \tag{11.10}$$

We recognize that it can be solved by the method of separation of variables.

Step 1

$$\frac{dy}{y^2} = 2t\ dt$$

Step 2

$$\int y^{-2}\ dy = 2\int t\ dt$$

$$\frac{y^{-1}}{-1} + c_1 = 2\frac{t^2}{2} + c_2$$

$$-\frac{1}{y} = t^2 + c$$

This equation is the implicit solution of the differential equation (11.10).

Step 3
To get the explicit solution we need to solve it for y in terms of t

$$y = -\frac{1}{t^2 + c}$$

As this example shows, this method can be applied to nonlinear differential equations in the form of (11.9).

Let's verify our solution as in Sect. 11.1.4.

Step 1

$$\frac{dy}{dt} = \frac{2t}{(t^2 + c)^2}$$

Step 2

$$2\left(-\frac{1}{t^2 + c}\right)^2 t = \frac{2t}{(t^2 + c)^2}$$

Step 3
The two sides are equal therefore we found a solution.

11.2.2 Substitution Method for Homogeneous-Type Equations

Homogeneous differential equations can be solved by using the method of separation of variables upon a change of variables.

Let's consider the following example

$$\frac{dy}{dt} = \frac{t + y}{t} \tag{11.11}$$

In the form (11.11) we cannot proceed with the method of separation of variables. However, since this is a homogeneous equations we can make a change of variable to reduce it to a separable form. First of all, let's confirm that it is a homogeneous equation by replacing kt for t and ky for y. If it is homogeneous it results that $f(kt, ky) = f(t, y)$.

$$\frac{dy}{dt} = \frac{(kt) + (ky)}{(kt)}$$

$$\frac{dy}{dt} = \frac{k(t+y)}{kt}$$

We see that k cancels out and we are back to the initial equation (11.11).

The next step is to recognize that the right-hand side can be expressed as a function of $\frac{y}{t}$.

Example 11.2.2 Let's go through the steps of differential equation (11.11).

Step 1
Divide (11.11) by t with the highest power, in our case it is just t

$$\frac{dy}{dt} = \frac{\frac{t}{t} + \frac{y}{t}}{\frac{t}{t}}$$

$$\frac{dy}{dt} = 1 + \frac{y}{t} \tag{11.12}$$

Step 2
Set $v = \frac{y}{t}$ and replace it in (11.12)

$$\frac{dy}{dt} = 1 + v \tag{11.13}$$

Step 3
Write $y = tv$ and compute the derivative $\frac{dy}{dt}$

$$\frac{dy}{dt} = t\frac{dv}{dt} + v \tag{11.14}$$

Step 4
Set (11.14) equal to (11.13)

$$t\frac{dv}{dt} + v = 1 + v$$

$$t\frac{dv}{dt} = 1 \tag{11.15}$$

Step 5
Now we are in the condition to apply the method of separation of variables to (11.15)

$$dv = \frac{1}{t}dt$$

$$\int dv = \int \frac{1}{t}dt$$

$$v = \log \mid t \mid + c \tag{11.16}$$

Step 6
Replace (11.16) into $v = \frac{y}{t}$ and rearrange

$$\frac{y}{t} = \log \mid t \mid + c$$

$$y = t\left(\log t + c\right)$$

Let's verify the solution

Step 1

$$\frac{dy}{dt} = 1 \cdot (\log t + c) + t\left(\frac{1}{t}\right) = \log t + c + 1$$

Step 2

$$\frac{t + (t(\log t + c))}{t} = \frac{t}{t} + \frac{t(\log t + c)}{t} = 1 + \log t + c$$

Step 3
The two sides are equal. Therefore we found a solution.

11.2.3 Integrating Factor

The method described in this section is known as *integrating factor*. Given a first-order linear differential equation in the standard form (11.3)

$$y' + p(t)y = g(t)$$

we must find a function $\mu(t)$, called *integrating factor*, that multiplies both sides of the differential equation. A suitable integrating factor must turn the left-hand side of the differential equation into the total derivative of a quantity. Another key point is that the differential equation needs to be in the standard form, and, in particular, the coefficient of y' needs to be 1. Otherwise the calculation for the integrating factor will be wrong.

Now let's go through the steps.

Step 1
Make sure that the differential equation is in the standard form

Step 2
Compute the integrating factor

$$\mu(t) = e^{\int p(t)\, dt} \tag{11.17}$$

Step 3
Multiply both sides of the differential equation by the integrating factor

$$\mu(t)\left[y' + p(t)y\right] = \mu(t)g(t)$$

$$\mu(t)y' + \mu(t)p(t)y = \mu(t)g(t)$$

where the left-hand side is

$$\frac{d}{dt}\left[\mu(t)y\right] \quad \left[\text{by the product rule}\right]$$

Consequently,

$$\frac{d}{dt}\left[\mu(t)y\right] = \mu(t)g(t) \tag{11.18}$$

Step 4
Integrate both sides of (11.18)

$$\int \frac{d}{dt}[\mu(t)y]\,dt = \int \mu(t)g(t)\,dt$$

$$\mu(t)y = G(t) + c$$

Step 5
Solve for y

$$y = \frac{G(t)}{\mu(t)} + \frac{c}{\mu(t)}$$

Example 11.2.3 Let's apply these steps to (11.4).

Step 1
Let's rearrange (11.4) in the standard form

$$y' - 4y = 1 - t$$

Step 2
In this differential equation $p(t) = -4$. Consequently,[4]

$$\mu(t) = e^{\int -4\,dt} = e^{-4t}$$

Step 3

$$e^{-4t}\left[y' - 4y\right] = e^{-4t}[1 - t]$$

$$\frac{d}{dt}e^{-4t}y = e^{-4t}[1 - t]$$

[4] Usually, the constant of integration is omitted from the integrating factor. This is a choice to make the procedure less burdensome when it is known that the constant of integration will be absorbed by another constant in the following steps. As you have noticed sometimes we wrote the constant of integration on the left-hand side as c_1 and on the right-hand side as c_2. Then, we combined the constant of integration as c. In this sense, to make the procedure less burdensome we just write c directly on the right-hand side.

Step 4

$$\int \frac{d}{dt} e^{-4t} y \, dt = \int e^{-4t} \left[1 - t\right] dt$$

The integration of the left-hand side is

$$e^{-4t} y$$

The right-hand side has been integrated by parts (Sect. 5.1.1.3) by setting $u = 1 - t$ and $dv = e^{-4t}$ (steps to the solution left as exercise)

$$-\frac{1}{4} e^{-4t} + \frac{1}{4} t e^{-4t} + \frac{1}{16} e^{-4t} + c$$

Let's put all together

$$e^{-4t} y = -\frac{1}{4} e^{-4t} + \frac{1}{4} t e^{-4t} + \frac{1}{16} e^{-4t} + c$$

Step 5

$$y = \frac{1}{4} t - \frac{1}{4} + \frac{1}{16} + \frac{c}{e^{-4t}}$$

$$y = \frac{1}{4} t - \frac{3}{16} + c e^{4t}$$

Let's verify the solution.

Step 1

$$\frac{dy}{dt} = \frac{1}{4} + 4 c e^{4t}$$

Step 2

$$1 - t + 4\left(\frac{1}{4}t - \frac{3}{16} + ce^{4t}\right)$$

$$1 - \frac{3}{4} + 4ce^{4t} \rightarrow \frac{1}{4} + 4ce^{4t}$$

Step 3
The two sides are equal. This confirms that we found a solution.

Let's continue the example by finding the constant c when $y(0) = 1$.

$$1 = \frac{1}{4} \cdot 0 - \frac{3}{16} + ce^{4 \cdot 0}$$

$$1 = -\frac{3}{16} + c$$

$$c = \frac{19}{16}$$

Therefore, the particular solution becomes

$$y = \frac{1}{4}t - \frac{3}{16} + \frac{19}{16}e^{4t}$$

This is the actual solution that we plotted with `ode_euler()` and `ode_RungeKutta()` (Figs. 11.2 and 11.3).

11.2.4 Exact Equations

The method described in this section can be applied to first-order nonlinear differential equations in the form

$$M(t, y) + N(t, y)y' = 0 \tag{11.19}$$

Let's write (11.19) as

$$M(t, y) + N(t, y)\frac{dy}{dt} = 0$$

and let's multiply all by dt

$$M(t, y)dt + N(t, y)dy = 0 \tag{11.20}$$

If there is a function $\phi(t, y)$ such that

$$\frac{\partial \phi}{\partial t} = M(t, y) \quad \text{and} \quad \frac{\partial \phi}{\partial y} = N(t, y)$$

then (11.20) is said to be an *exact differential equation* (for more details the reader may refer to Giordano and Weir (1991, pp. 81–91)).

Let's go through the steps to find a solution to this kind of differential equations.

Step 1
Write the differential equation in the standard form as (11.20).

Step 2
Test for exactness:

$$\frac{\partial M}{\partial y} = \frac{\partial N}{\partial t}$$

that is, take the partial derivative of M with respect to y and take the partial derivative of N with respect to t. If they are equal it passes the test and we can continue with this method.

Step 3
If it passes the test, we need to integrate or M with respect to t or N with respect to y. Let's go for M

$$\phi(t, y) = \int M\, dt + g(y)$$

Step 4
Find the unknown function $g(y)$ by

- differentiating ϕ with respect to y and equate the result to N: $N = \frac{\partial}{\partial y}\left(\int M\, dt\right) + g'(y)$
- and by integrating $g'(y)$ to find g

Step 5
Write the implicit solution to the first-order equation $\phi(t, y) = c$

Example 11.2.4 Let's solve the following differential equation

$$y' = -\frac{t+2y}{y^2+2t}$$

Step 1
Let's write the equation in the standard form

$$\frac{dy}{dt} = -\frac{t+2y}{y^2+2t}$$

$$(y^2+2t)dy = -(t+2y)dt$$

$$(t+2y)dt + (y^2+2t)dy = 0$$

where $M = (t+2y)$ and $N = (y^2+2t)$.
Let's test for exactness

$$\frac{\partial M}{\partial y} = 2$$

$$\frac{\partial N}{\partial t} = 2$$

This confirms that it is an exact equation.

Step 3

$$\phi = \int (t+2y)dt + g(y)$$

$$\phi = \frac{1}{2}t^2 + 2yt + g(y)$$

Step 4
Let's find $g(y)$ by setting $\frac{\partial \phi}{\partial y} = N$ where

$$\frac{\partial \phi}{\partial y} = 2t + \frac{dg}{dy}$$

and

$$N = y^2 + 2t$$

Therefore,

$$2t + \frac{dg}{dy} = y^2 + 2t$$

$$g'(y) = y^2$$

By integration

$$g(y) = \frac{y^3}{3} + c$$

Note that the constant can be omitted since it will be absorbed in the final solution.

Step 5
Let's replace $g(y)$ in Step 3 and write the implicit solution

$$\frac{y^3}{3} + 2yt + \frac{t^2}{2} = c$$

11.2.5 Reduction to Linearity: Bernoulli Equation

Bernoulli equation of the form

$$y' + p(t)y = q(t)y^n \tag{11.21}$$

is a special type of nonlinear differential equation that can be turned into a linear equation by a change of variable.

Let's first observe that if $n = 1$, the Bernoulli equation is separable; if $n = 0$, it is linear. If $n \neq 0$ and $n \neq 1$, we can make the following change of variable to turn (11.21) into a linear equation

$$v = y^{1-n}$$

Then, by chain rule

$$\frac{dv}{dt} = \frac{dv}{dy} \cdot \frac{dy}{dt}$$

where

$$\frac{dv}{dy} = (1-n)y^{1-n-1}$$

and let's write

$$\frac{dy}{dt} = y'$$

Let's put all together

$$\frac{dv}{dt} = (1-n)y^{-n}y'$$

and solve for y'

$$y' = \frac{1}{1-n}y^n\frac{dv}{dt} \tag{11.22}$$

Now let's substitute (11.22) into (11.21)

$$\frac{1}{1-n}y^n\frac{dv}{dt} + p(t)y = q(t)y^n$$

Let's set the coefficient of $\frac{dv}{dt}$ to 1 by multiplying both sides by $(1-n)y^{-n}$

$$\frac{dv}{dt} + (1-n)p(t)y^{1-n} = (1-n)q(t)$$

By replacing $v = y^{1-n}$ we obtain

$$\frac{dv}{dt} + (1-n)p(t)v = (1-n)q(t) \tag{11.23}$$

that is linear in v. Now it can be solved by the method of integrating factor.

Example 11.2.5 Let's consider the following differential equation

$$N' - rN = -\frac{r}{K}N^2$$

This is a Bernoulli equation where $n = 2$. Let's make the following change of variable $v = N^{1-2} \rightarrow v = N^{-1}$. Then, by chain rule

$$\frac{dv}{dt} = -N^{-2}N'$$

Let's solve for N'

$$N' = -N^2\frac{dv}{dt}$$

Let's substitute for N' in the initial equation

$$-N^2\frac{dv}{dt} - rN = -\frac{r}{K}N^2$$

Let's set the coefficient of v' equal to 1 by multiplying both sides by $-N^{-2}$

$$\frac{dv}{dt} + rN^{-1} = \frac{r}{K}$$

By replacing $v = N^{-1}$ we obtain

$$\frac{dv}{dt} + rv = \frac{r}{K}$$

that is now linear in v. Let's solve by using the method of integrating factor. The integrating factor is $\mu(t) = e^{\int r\,dt} = e^{rt}$. Then

$$\int \frac{d}{dt}e^{rt}v = \int e^{rt}\frac{r}{K}\,dt$$

$$e^{rt}v = \frac{1}{K}e^{rt} + A$$

where A is the constant of integration. Let's solve for v

$$v = \frac{1}{K} + Ae^{-rt}$$

Since we set $v = N^{-1} = \frac{1}{N}$, this implies that $N = \frac{1}{v}$. Then, by replacing v we find that

$$N = \frac{K}{1 + Ae^{-rt}}$$

Compare with (5.16). This example shows that the logistic equation is a Bernoulli equation.

11.3 Time Path and Equilibrium

The solution for the following autonomous differential equation

$$\frac{dy}{dt} = -y + 7$$

is $y = -ce^{-t} + 7$ (check it). Now let's plot it by considering the following initial values at $t = 0$: 1, -1, 10, -10.

```
> t <- seq(-1, 10, 0.1)
> C <- c(6, 8, -3, 17)
> df <- sapply(C, FUN = function(C) -C*exp(-t) + 7)
> df <- as.data.frame(df)
> df <- cbind(t, df)
> tail(df)
        t       V1       V2       V3       V4
106   9.5 6.999551 6.999401 7.000225 6.998728
107   9.6 6.999594 6.999458 7.000203 6.998849
108   9.7 6.999632 6.999510 7.000184 6.998958
109   9.8 6.999667 6.999556 7.000166 6.999057
110   9.9 6.999699 6.999599 7.000151 6.999147
111  10.0 6.999728 6.999637 7.000136 6.999228
```

The first observation is that as $t \to \infty$, $y \to 7$ regardless of the initial condition. This is also evident from Fig. 11.5.

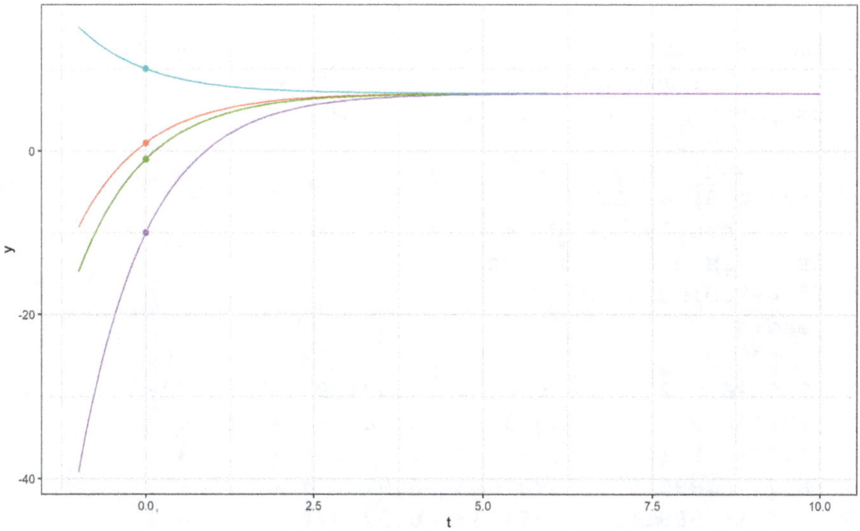

Fig. 11.5 Convergent time path of $y' = -y + 7$

```
> df_l <- df %>%
+   pivot_longer(!t,
+                names_to = "variable",
+                values_to = "value")
> df_o <- df[df$t == 0, ]
> df_o
   t V1 V2 V3  V4
11 0  1 -1 10 -10
> df_ol <- df_o %>%
+   pivot_longer(!t,
+                 names_to = "variable",
+                 values_to = "value")
> ggplot() +
+   geom_line(dat = df_l, aes(x = t, y = value,
+                             group = variable,
+                             color = variable)) +
+   geom_point(dat = df_ol, aes(x = t, y = value,
+                               group = variable,
+                               color = variable),
+              size = 2) +
+   theme_bw() + xlab("t") + ylab("y") +
+   theme(legend.position = "none")
```

Now, let's slightly modify the previous differential equation by changing the sign of the coefficient in front of y, that is

$$\frac{dy}{dt} = y + 7$$

The solution is $y = ce^t - 7$ (check it). Now let's plot it by considering the following initial values at $t = 0 : 1, -1, 10, -10$. For this example, let's modify the time sequence of t by setting the initial value equal to -7.

```
> t <- seq(-7, 3, 0.1)
> C <- c(8, 6, 17, -3)
> df <- sapply(C, FUN = function(C) C*exp(t) - 7)
> df <- as.data.frame(df)
> df <- cbind(t, df)
> head(df)
     t        V1        V2        V3        V4
1 -7.0 -6.992705 -6.994529 -6.984498 -7.002736
2 -6.9 -6.991938 -6.993953 -6.982868 -7.003023
3 -6.8 -6.991090 -6.993317 -6.981066 -7.003341
4 -6.7 -6.990153 -6.992615 -6.979074 -7.003693
5 -6.6 -6.989117 -6.991838 -6.976874 -7.004081
6 -6.5 -6.987972 -6.990979 -6.974442 -7.004510
```

```
> tail(df)
      t        V1        V2       V3        V4
96  2.5  90.45995  66.09496 200.1024 -43.54748
97  2.6 100.70990  73.78243 221.8835 -47.39121
98  2.7 112.03785  82.27839 245.9554 -51.63920
99  2.8 124.55717  91.66788 272.5590 -56.33394
100 2.9 138.39316 102.04487 301.9605 -61.52244
101 3.0 153.68430 113.51322 334.4541 -67.25661
```

From the head of the data frame we can observe that the values are extremely close to -7. On the other hand, the tail of the data frame shows that the values are diverging as $t \to \infty$. Let's represent it (Fig. 11.6).

```
> df_l <- df %>%
+   pivot_longer(!t,
+                names_to = "variable",
+                values_to = "value")
> df_o <- df[t == 0, ]
> df_o
   t V1 V2 V3  V4
71 0  1 -1 10 -10
> df_ol <- df_o %>%
+   pivot_longer(!t,
+                names_to = "variable",
+                values_to = "value")
> ggplot() +
+   geom_line(dat = df_l, aes(x = t, y = value,
+                             group = variable,
+                             color = variable)) +
+   geom_point(dat = df_ol, aes(x = t, y = value,
+                               group = variable,
+                               color = variable),
+              size = 2) +
+   theme_bw() + xlab("t") + ylab("y") +
+   theme(legend.position = "none") +
+   coord_cartesian(ylim = c(-40, 20),
+                   xlim = c(-7, 4))
```

We did a small modification to the differential equations, that is we changed the coefficient of y from -1 to 1 and the conclusions about the time path completely changed. Let's observe again the solutions of these two differential equations. For the convergent case, e is raised to a negative exponent; for the divergent case, e is raised to a positive exponent. This e term in the solution governs the time path.

Let's make a different representation of these two differential equations. Figures 11.5 and 11.6 are time series plot showing $y(t)$ versus t for different initial conditions. Another graphical tool used to analyse differential equations is the *phase*

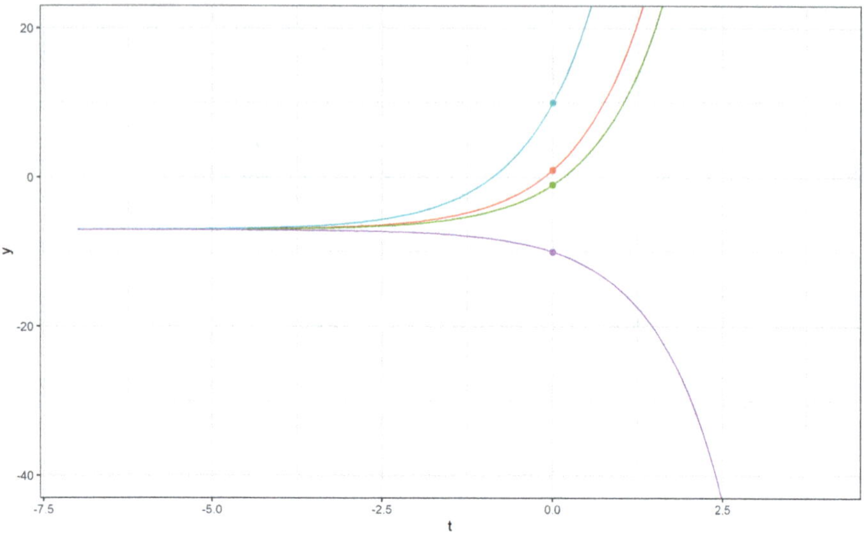

Fig. 11.6 Divergent time path of $y' = y + 7$

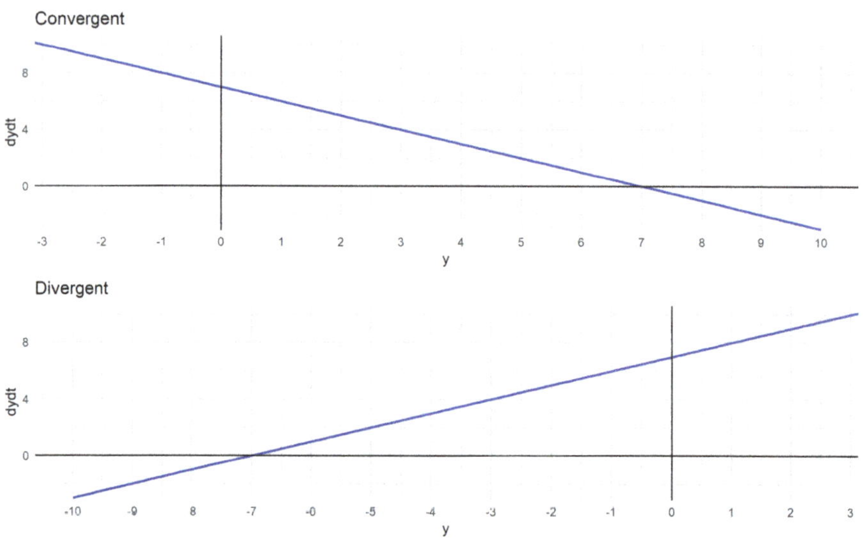

Fig. 11.7 Phase diagrams of $y' = -y + 7$ and $y' = y + 7$

diagram. In the phase diagram we plot dy/dt versus y. Let's plot and comment the phase diagrams for $y' = -y + 7$ and $y' = y + 7$ (Fig. 11.7).

What could we say by just observing Fig. 11.7?

1. the intercept on the vertical axis is the same, i.e. 7;
2. the slope is different. In the convergent phase diagram the slope is negative and in the divergent phase diagram the slope is positive. But what is the slope? The coefficient of y that is -1 in the convergent case and 1 in the divergent case (does it ring a bell?);
3. in the convergent case, the blue line, i.e. $y' = -y + 7$, crosses the horizontal axis at $y^* = 7$. Let's consider the point when $y = 1$. Will the point move to the right (i.e. towards $y^* = 7$) or to the left (i.e. further away from $y^* = 7$)? As we can observe, at $y = 1$, $dy/dt > 0$. This means that y will increase over time, i.e. it will move to the right towards $y^* = 7$. Let's consider now that point when $y = 9$. Will the point move to the right (i.e. further away $y^* = 7$) or to the left (i.e. towards $y^* = 7$)? As we can observe, at $y = 9$, $dy/dt < 0$. This means that y will decrease over time, i.e. it will move to the left towards $y^* = 7$. In this case y^* is said to be an *attractor*;
4. in the divergent case, the blue line, i.e. $y' = y + 7$, crosses the horizontal axis at $y^* = -7$. Let's consider the point when $y = 1$. Will the point move to the right (i.e. further away from $y^* = -7$) or to the left (i.e. towards $y^* = -7$)? As we can observe, at $y = 1$, $dy/dt > 0$. This means that y will increase over time, i.e. it will move to the right further away from $y^* = -7$. Let's consider now that point when $y = -9$. Will the point move to the right (i.e. towards $y^* = -7$) or to the left (i.e. further away from $y^* = -7$). As we can observe, at $y = -9$, $dy/dt < 0$. This means that y will decrease over time, i.e. it will move to the left further away from $y^* = -7$. In this case y^* is said to be a *repellor*.

These are the same conclusions that we reached by observing the time series plots (Figs. 11.5 and 11.6). However, by commenting the phase diagram we did not need to solve the differential equations. That is, we obtain insights about the dynamic properties of the differential equations without solving them. This the great advantage of the *quality analysis* from observing the phase diagram.[5]

Before moving to the next example, let's give some more details. The phase diagram is feasible when dy/dt is function of y alone, that is the differential equation is autonomous. The point y^* is known as *critical point*, *fixed point*, *rest point*, *equilibrium point*, or *steady-state solution*. Therefore, if the equilibrium level of y exists, it occurs at the intersection of the horizontal axis with the *phase line*. The path of solutions as t varies is called a *trajectory*, *path*, or *orbit*. In addition to attractor and repellor, there are two intermediate cases where the trajectory moves towards the fixed point and then after passing the fixed point it moves away from it. This can happen from the right to the left and from the left to the right. These fixed points are called *shunt* (Fig. 11.8).

Let's consider again the logistic growth equation

[5] Note that with the due modifications, the phase diagram analysis applies to difference equations as well.

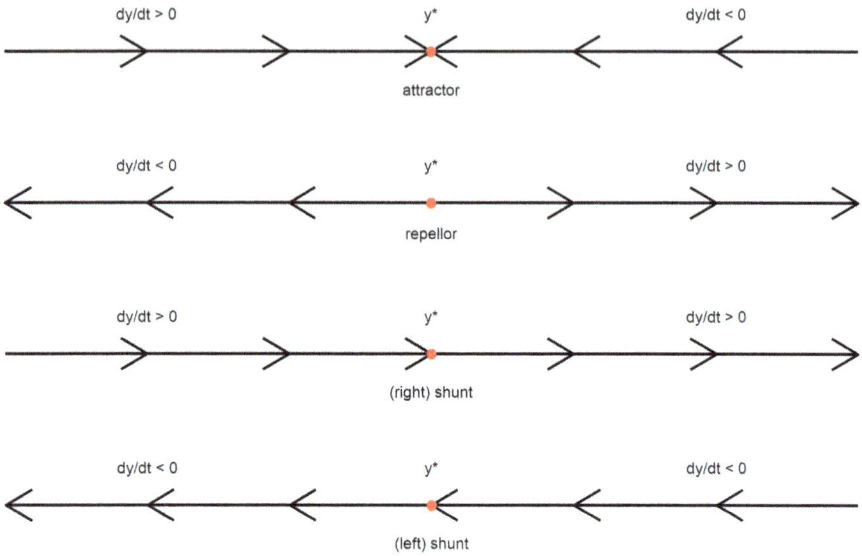

Fig. 11.8 Fixed points, attractor, repellor

$$\frac{dN}{dt} = rN\left(1 - \frac{N}{K}\right)$$

Let's plot the phase diagram by using the same values for the parameters r and K that we used to represent the direction field, i.e. $r = 1$ and $K = 2$ (Fig. 11.9).

```
> r <- 1
> K <- 2
> N <- seq(-1, 3, 0.1)
> dNdt <- r*N*(1 - N/K)
> df_lgst <- data.frame(N, dNdt)
> ggplot(df_lgst, aes(x = N, y = dNdt)) +
+   geom_line(size = 1, color = "blue") +
+   geom_vline(xintercept = 0) +
+   geom_hline(yintercept = 0) +
+   theme_minimal() +
+   coord_cartesian(ylim = c(-0.25, 0.75)) +
+   annotate("text", y = 0.05, x = 2.1,
+              label = "K")
```

The first consideration we can make by observing Fig. 11.9 is that there are two equilibrium points, one at $N_1^* = 0$ and the other one at $N_2^* = K$. We find these two points by setting the right-hand side of the logistic growth equation equal to zero (i.e. as we found the nullclines). Let's consider the nature of these two points. If $N > K, dN/dt < 0$. This means that N decreases over time, i.e. it moves to the left

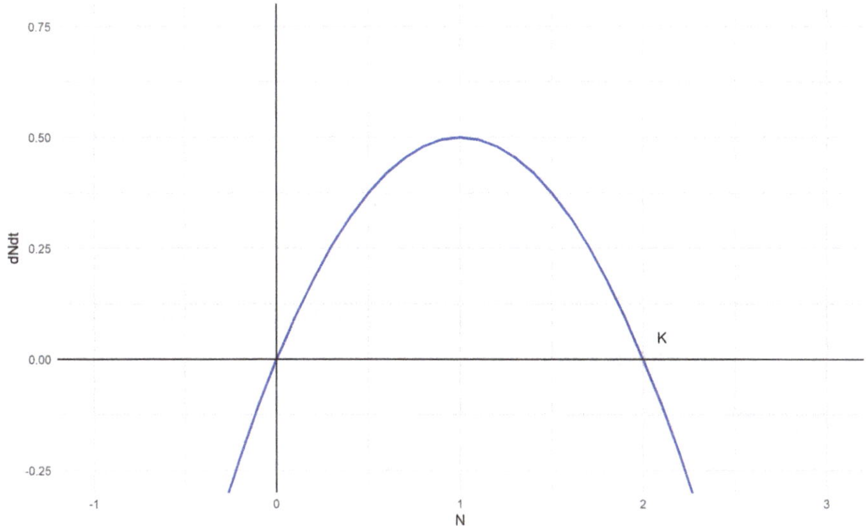

Fig. 11.9 Phase diagrams of the logistic growth equation

towards $N_2^* = K$. On the other hand, if $0 < N < K, dN/dt > 0$. This means that N increases over time, i.e. it moves to the right towards $N_2^* = K$. We can conclude that $N_2^* = K$ is an attractor.

What about $N_1^* = 0$? We have already said that for $0 < N < K, dN/dt > 0$. That is, for values close to zero N moves away from N_1^* towards N_2^*. We can conclude that $N_1^* = 0$ is a repellor.[6] Therefore, the phase diagram for the logistic growth equation tells us that regardless the initial value (if positive), N moves towards K, or the population approaches the carrying capacity. This is the same conclusion drawn by observing the direction field of the logistic growth (Fig. 11.4)

11.4 Second-Order Linear Differential Equations

The following differential equations

$$y''(t) + a_1 y'(t) + a_2 y = b \tag{11.24}$$

is a second-order linear differential equations with constant coefficients (a_1, a_2) and constant term (b). If b is zero, the equation is homogeneous; otherwise, it

[6] The logistic growth equation is used to model population growth, where N represents the population. If this is the case, we can omit the analysis for $N < 0$, that is we only consider positive populations.

is nonhomogeneous. We will concentrate on second-order linear equations with constant coefficients and constant term. However, in Sect. 11.4.4 we will consider an example with a non-constant term.

In the next two sections we will see that the approach and the steps to the solution of a second-order linear differential equation with constant coefficients and constant term is very similar to the approach and steps we went through to solve second-order linear difference equations.

11.4.1 Solution to Second-Order Linear Homogeneous Differential Equation

Let's start with a second-order linear homogeneous differential equation with constant coefficients

$$y''(t) + a_1 y'(t) + a_2 y = 0 \tag{11.25}$$

We approach it by considering $y = Ae^{rt}$ as a trial solution, where A is an arbitrary constant. By adopting this solution, it follows that

$$\frac{dy}{dt} = rAe^{rt} \quad \text{and} \quad \frac{d^2y}{dt^2} = r^2Ae^{rt} \tag{11.26}$$

By replacing $y = Ae^{rt}$ and (11.26) into (11.25)

$$r^2Ae^{rt} + a_1 rAe^{rt} + a_2 Ae^{rt} = 0$$

and by factoring out Ae^{rt}, we have

$$Ae^{rt}(r^2 + a_1 r + a_2) = 0 \tag{11.27}$$

If the values of A and r satisfy (11.27), the trial solution $y = Ae^{rt}$ is feasible. This in turns means that r needs to satisfy

$$r^2 + a_1 r + a_2 = 0 \tag{11.28}$$

because e^{rt} can never be zero and because the value of A is determined by the initial conditions.

Equation 11.28 is known as *characteristic equation*. We can find the roots—*characteristic roots*—with the quadratic formula[7]

[7] The quadratic formula is in the normalized form, i.e. the coefficient of r^2 needs to be 1.

$$r_1, r_2 = \frac{-a_1 \pm \sqrt{a_1^2 - 4a_2}}{2} \tag{11.29}$$

As we did for difference equations, we need to consider three cases depending on whether $D \lesseqgtr 0$.

11.4.1.1 Two Distinct Real Roots (Case of $D > 0$)

If $D > 0$, y_c can be written as a linear combination of $e^{r_1 t}$ and $e^{r_2 t}$, that are linearly independent

$$y_c = A_1 e^{r_1 t} + A_2 e^{r_2 t} \tag{11.30}$$

where A_1 and A_2 are two arbitrary constants whose values can be obtained given the initial conditions $y(0)$ and $y'(0)$

$$y(0) = A_1 e^{r_1 0} + A_2 e^{r_2 0} = A_1 + A_2$$

For $y'(0)$, let's first compute $\frac{dy}{dt}$

$$\frac{dy}{dt} = r_1 A_1 e^{r_1 t} + r_2 A_2 e^{r_2 t}$$

Then

$$y'(0) = r_1 A_1 e^{r_1 0} + r_2 A_2 e^{r_2 0} = r_1 A_1 + r_2 A_2$$

By solving this system of equations for A_1 and A_2, we find that

$$A_1 = \frac{y'(0) - r_2 y(0)}{r_1 - r_2}, \quad A_2 = \frac{y'(0) - r_1 y(0)}{r_2 - r_1} \tag{11.31}$$

Example 11.4.1 Find the solution to the following second-order homogeneous differential equation

$$y''(t) - 3y'(t) + 2y = 0$$

Step 1
Substitute $y = Ae^{rt}$, $y'(t) = rAe^{rt}$, and $y''(t) = r^2 Ae^{rt}$ in the homogeneous differential equation

$$r^2 Ae^{rt} - 3rAe^{rt} + 2Ae^{rt} = 0$$

$$Ae^{rt}\left(r^2 - 3r + 2\right) = 0$$

Step 2
Find the characteristic roots

$$r_1, r_2 = \frac{-(-3) \pm \sqrt{(-3)^2 - 4 \cdot 2}}{2}$$

$$r_1 = 2, \quad r_2 = 1$$

Step 2.5
We can check our calculation by verifying that

$$r_1 + r_2 = -a_1 \quad \text{and} \quad r_1 \cdot r_2 = a_2$$

$$2 + 1 = 3 = -a_1$$

$$2 \cdot 1 = 2 = a_2$$

Step 3
Write the solution to the homogeneous differential equation

$$y_c = A_1 e^{2t} + A_2 e^t$$

Step 4
Given the initial conditions $y(0) = 2$ and $y'(0) = 5$, find the constants. Let's use (11.31)

$$A_1 = \frac{5 - (1 \cdot 2)}{2 - 1} = 3$$

$$A_2 = \frac{5 - (2 \cdot 2)}{1 - 2} = -1$$

Step 5
Write the particular solution

$$y_c = 3e^{2t} + (-1)e^t \tag{11.32}$$

Step 6
Verification of the solution
Find $y'(t)$ and $y''(t)$ of (11.32)

$$y'(t) = 6e^{2t} - e^t$$

$$y''(t) = 12e^{2t} - e^t$$

Substitute y_c, i.e. $y(t)$, $y'(t)$, and $y''(t)$ in the given differential equation. If the identity holds, we found a solution.

$$12e^{2t} - e^t - 3(6e^{2t} - e^t) + 2(3e^{2t} - e^t) = 0$$

$$12e^{2t} - e^t - 18e^{2t} + 3e^t + 6e^{2t} - 2e^t = 0$$

$$0 = 0$$

This confirms that we found a solution.

11.4.1.2 One Real Root (or Repeated Real Roots) (Case of $D = 0$)

If $D = 0, r_1 = r_2 \equiv r$. The solution is

$$y_c = A_3e^{rt} + A_4te^{rt} \tag{11.33}$$

Example 11.4.2 Find the solution to the following second-order homogeneous differential equation

$$y''(t) - 6y'(t) + 9y = 0$$

Step 1
Substitute $y = Ae^{rt}$, $y'(t) = rAe^{rt}$, and $y''(t) = r^2Ae^{rt}$ in the homogeneous differential equation

$$r^2Ae^{rt} - 6rAe^{rt} + 9Ae^{rt} = 0$$

$$Ae^{rt}\left(r^2 - 6r + 9\right) = 0$$

Step 2
Find the characteristic roots

$$r_1, r_2 = \frac{-(-6) \pm \sqrt{(-6)^2 - 4 \cdot 9}}{2}$$

$$r_1 = r_2 = 3$$

Step 3
Write the solution to the homogeneous differential equation

$$y_c = A_3e^{3t} + A_4te^{3t}$$

Step 4
Given the initial conditions $y(0) = 6$ and $y'(0) = 4$, find the constants

$$6 = A_3e^{3 \cdot 0} + A_4 0 \cdot e^{3 \cdot 0} \rightarrow A_3 = 6$$

$$y'(t) = 3A_3e^{3t} + A_4e^{3t} + 3A_4te^{3t}$$

$$4 = 3A_3e^{3 \cdot 0} + A_4e^{3 \cdot 0} + 3A_4 0 \cdot e^{3 \cdot}$$

$$4 = 3A_3 + A_4 \rightarrow 4 = 18 + A_4 \rightarrow A_4 = -14$$

Step 5
Write the particular solution

$$y_c = 6e^{3t} + (-14)te^{3t} \tag{11.34}$$

Step 6
Verification of the solution
Find $y'(t)$ and $y''(t)$ of (11.34)

$$y'(t) = 18e^{3t} - 14e^{3t} - 42te^{3t}$$

$$y''(t) = 54e^{3t} - 42e^{3t} - 42e^{3t} - 126te^{3t}$$

Substitute y_c, i.e. $y(t)$, $y'(t)$, and $y''(t)$ in the given differential equation. If the identity holds, we found a solution.

$$54e^{3t} - 42e^{3t} - 42e^{3t} - 126te^{3t} - 6(18e^{3t} \quad 14e^{3t} - 42te^{3t}) + 9(6e^{3t} - 14te^{3t}) = 0$$

$$54e^{3t} - 84e^{3t} - 126te^{3t} - 108e^{3t} + 84e^{3t} + 252te^{3t} + 54e^{3t} - 126te^{3t} = 0$$

$$0 = 0$$

11.4.1.3 Complex Roots (Case of $D < 0$)

If $D < 0$, the characteristic roots are complex roots, where $r_1 = \alpha + \beta i$ and $r_2 = \alpha - \beta i$. The solution is

$$y_c = A_5 e^{\alpha t}\cos(\beta t) + A_6 e^{\alpha t}\sin(\beta t) \tag{11.35}$$

Example 11.4.3 Find the solution to the following second-order homogeneous differential equation

$$y''(t) - 3y'(t) + 3y = 0$$

Step 1

$$Ae^{rt}(r^2 - 3r + 3) = 0$$

Step 2

$$r = \frac{-(-3) \pm \sqrt{(-3)^2 - 4 \cdot 3}}{2}$$

$$r_1 = \frac{3}{2} + \frac{\sqrt{3}}{2}i$$

$$r_2 = \frac{3}{2} - \frac{\sqrt{3}}{2}i$$

Step 3
Obtain α and β

$$\alpha = \frac{3}{2} \quad \beta = \frac{\sqrt{3}}{2}$$

Step 4

$$y_c = A_5 e^{\frac{3}{2}t} \cos\left(\frac{\sqrt{3}}{2}t\right) + A_6 e^{\frac{3}{2}t} \sin\left(\frac{\sqrt{3}}{2}t\right)$$

Step 5
$y(0) = 2$, $y'(0) = 3$

$$2 = A_5 e^{\frac{3}{2} \cdot 0} \cos\left(\frac{\sqrt{3}}{2} \cdot 0\right) + A_6 e^{\frac{3}{2} \cdot 0} \sin\left(\frac{\sqrt{3}}{2} \cdot 0\right)$$

$$A_5 = 2$$

$$y'(0) = (\alpha A_5 + \beta A_6)e^{\alpha t}\cos(\beta t) + (\alpha A_5 - \beta A_6)e^{\alpha t}\sin(\beta t)$$

$$y'(0) = (\alpha A_5 + \beta A_6)e^{\alpha 0}\cos(\beta 0) + (\alpha A_5 - \beta A_6)e^{\alpha 0}\sin(\beta 0)$$

$$y'(0) = \alpha A_5 + \beta A_6$$

$$3 = \frac{3}{2}2 + \frac{\sqrt{3}}{2}A_6 \rightarrow A_6 = 0$$

Step 6
Verification of the solution

$$y'(t) = \frac{3}{2}2e^{\frac{3}{2}t}\cos\left(\frac{3}{2}t\right) - \sqrt{3}e^{\frac{3}{2}t}\sin\left(\frac{\sqrt{3}}{2}t\right)$$

$$y''(t) = 3e^{\frac{3}{2}t}\cos\left(\frac{\sqrt{3}}{2}t\right) - \frac{3\sqrt{3}e^{\frac{3}{2}t}\sin\left(\frac{\sqrt{3}}{2}t\right)}{2} - \frac{3\sqrt{3}e^{\frac{3}{2}t}\sin\left(\frac{\sqrt{3}}{2}t\right)}{2}$$

By substituting y_c, i.e. $y(t)$, $y'(t)$, and $y''(t)$ in the given differential equation we find that the identity holds (check it!).

11.4.2 Solution to Second-Order Linear Nonhomogeneous Differential Equation

Let's consider a second-order linear nonhomogeneous differential equation as (11.24), where now $b \neq 0$. The general solution of (11.24) is given by the sum of the *complementary function* y_c, i.e. the solution of the reduced (homogeneous) equation of (11.24), and the *particular integral* y_p, i.e. any particular solution with no arbitrary constant of (11.24)

$$y(t) = y_c + y_p$$

The steps we applied in Sect. 11.4.1 to find the solution of the homogeneous equation apply to the reduced form of (11.24).

For the particular integral, we follow an approach similar to the approach for difference equations. That is, since y_p is any particular solution, we start by trying the simplest one, $y = k$, where k is a constant. Since k is a constant, this in turn means that

$$\frac{dy}{dt} = 0 \quad \text{and} \quad \frac{d^2y}{dt^2} = 0$$

By replacing all of them in (11.24), we have

$$a_2 k = b$$

$$k = \frac{b}{a_2}$$

and consequently

$$y_p = \frac{b}{a_2}$$

If $a_2 = 0$, the trial solution is not feasible. We need to try a non-constant solution such as $y = kt$. This in turn means that

$$\frac{dy}{dt} = k \quad \text{and} \quad \frac{d^2y}{dt^2} = 0$$

Since we are investigating this solution because of $a_2 = 0$, by replacing all of them in (11.24), we have

$$a_1 k = b$$

$$k = \frac{b}{a_1}$$

and consequently

$$y_p = \frac{b}{a_1}t \quad (\text{case of } a_2 = 0)$$

If it happens that also $a_1 = 0$, we may try a solution of the form $y = kt^2$. With $a_1 = a_2 = 0$, this means

$$\frac{d^2y}{dt^2} = 2k$$

By replacing it in (11.24)

$$2k = b$$

$$k = \frac{b}{2}$$

and consequently,

$$y_p = \frac{b}{2}t^2 \quad (\text{case of } a_1 = a_2 = 0)$$

With y_c and y_p we can write the general solution, where the former represents the deviation from the equilibrium and the latter represents the intertemporal equilibrium. Let's consider an example.

Example 11.4.4 Find the solution to the following second-order linear nonhomogeneous differential equation

$$y''(t) - 3y'(t) + 2y = 6$$

The complementary function is the equation in Example 11.4.1.1. At step 3 we found

$$y_c = A_1 e^2 t + A_2 e^t$$

Now let's continue by considering the particular integral.

Step 4
The coefficient $a_2 = 2$, therefore we can apply $y_p = \frac{b}{a_2}$

$$y_p = \frac{6}{2} = 3$$

Step 5

$$y = y_c + y_p$$

$$y = A_1 e^{2t} + A_2 e^t + 3$$

Step 6
Given the initial conditions $y(0) = 2$ and $y'(0) = 5$, find the constants

$$2 = A_1 e^{2 \cdot 0} + A_2 e^0 + 3$$

$$A_1 = -1 - A_2$$

$$y'(t) = 2A_1 e^{2t} + A_2 e^t$$

$$5 = 2A_1 e^{2 \cdot 0} + A_2 e^0$$

$$5 = 2A_1 + A_2 \rightarrow 5 = 2(-1 - A_2) + A_2$$

$$A_2 = -7$$

$$A_1 = 6$$

Step 7
Write the particular solution

$$y(t) = 6e^{2t} + (-7)e^t + 3$$

Step 8
Verification of the solution.

$$y'(t) = 12e^{2t} - 7e^t$$

$$y''(t) = 24e^{2t} - 7e^t$$

$$24e^{2t} - 7e^t - 3(12e^{2t} - 7e^t) + 2(6e^{2t} - 7e^t + 3) = 6$$

$$24e^{2t} - 7e^t - 36e^{2t} + 21e^t + 12e^{2t} - 14e^t + 6 = 6$$

$$6 = 6$$

11.4.3 The Dynamic Stability of the Equilibrium

The equilibrium is dynamically stable ($y_c \to 0$ as $t \to \infty$) if

- case of two distinct real roots: r_1 and r_2 are *both* less than zero
- case of repeated real roots: $r < 0$
- case of complex roots: $\alpha < 0$

11.4.4 Method of Undetermined Coefficients

Let's consider the case with a non-constant term. That is, we want to find a solution to a second-order linear differential equation of the following form

$$y''(t) + a_1 y'(t) + a_2 y = g(t) \tag{11.36}$$

where $g(t)$ is some function of t. Let's see its solution through an example.

Example 11.4.5 Find the solution to the following second-order linear differential equations

$$y''(t) - 3y'(t) + 2y = 6t^2 \tag{11.37}$$

where we have a quadratic term on the right-hand side.

First of all, note that the reduced form (i.e. its homogeneous part) of (11.37) is the same of Examples 11.4.1 and 11.4.4. Therefore, we can jump directly to the steps to find the integral part.

Step 4
Given that the variable term on the right-hand side is a quadratic term, let's find a particular solution that is also quadratic in t. Let's try

$$y_p = B_1 t^2 + B_2 t + B_3 \tag{11.38}$$

where B_1, B_2, B_3 are coefficients to be determined.

Step 5
Differentiate (11.38) and plug into (11.37)

$$y' = 2B_1 t + B_2 \tag{11.39}$$

$$y'' = 2B_1 \tag{11.40}$$

Let's plug (11.38), (11.39), and (11.40) into (11.37) and rearrange

$$2B_1 - 3(2B_1t + B_2) + 2(B_1t^2 + B_2t + B_3) = 6t^2$$

$$(2B_1)t^2 + (2B_2 - 6B_1)t + (2B_1 - 3B_2 + 2B_3) = 6t^2 \tag{11.41}$$

Step 6
Equate the left-hand side and the right-hand side of (11.41) term by term and solve the corresponding system

$$\begin{cases} 2B_1 = 6 \\ 2B_2 - 6B_1 = 0 \\ 2B_1 - 3B_2 + 2B_3 = 0 \end{cases}$$

The solutions are $B_1 = 3$, $B_2 = 9$, $B_3 = \frac{21}{2}$

Step 7
Write the particular integral by substituting $B_1 = 3$, $B_2 = 9$, $B_3 = \frac{21}{2}$ into (11.38)

$$y_p = 3t^2 + 9t + \frac{21}{2}$$

Step 8
Write the general solution $y(t) = y_c + y_p$

$$y(t) = A_1e^{2t} + A_2e^t + 3t^2 + 9t + \frac{21}{2}$$

Be aware that complications may arise with this approach. Let's consider an example.

Example 11.4.6 Find the solution of the following second-order linear differential equations

$$y''(t) - 3y'(t) = 6t^2 \tag{11.42}$$

In (11.42) the y term is missing. This entails that if we try a quadratic solution as in Example 11.4.5 we will end up with no quadratic term upon differentiation (i.e. no B_1t^2). This implies that the trial solution in Example 11.4.5 is not feasible in this situation.

Let's see how we can deal with such a situation. First of all we need to find the complementary function.

The reduced form of (11.42) is $y''(t) - 3y'(t) = 0$. The characteristic equations become $r^2 - 3r = 0$ giving as solutions $r_1 = 3$ and $r_2 = 0$. Consequently,

$$y_c = A_1 e^{3t} + A_2$$

Let's compute the particular integral. We need to consider a trial solution that upon differentiation will produce a quadratic term. We can try

$$y_p = t(B_1 t^2 + B_2 t + B_3) \tag{11.43}$$

This means that

$$y'(t) = 3B_1 t^2 + 2B_2 t + B_3$$

$$y''(t) = 6B_1 t + 2B_2$$

By replacing $y'(t)$ and $y''(t)$ into (11.42) and rearranging

$$6B_1 t + 2B_2 - 3(3B_1 t^2 + 2B_2 t + B_3) = 6t^2$$

$$(-9B_1)t^2 + (6B_1 - 6B_2)t + (2B_2 - 3B_3) = 6t^2$$

From now we set the system and replace the solutions into (11.43)

$$\begin{cases} -9B_1 = 6 \\ 6B_1 - 6B_2 = 0 \\ 2B_2 - 3B_3 = 0 \end{cases}$$

$$B_1 = -\frac{2}{3} \quad B_2 = -\frac{2}{3} \quad B_3 = -\frac{4}{9}$$

$$y_p = t\left(-\frac{2}{3}t^2 - \frac{2}{3}t - \frac{4}{9}\right)$$

$$y_p = -\frac{2}{3}t^3 - \frac{2}{3}t^2 - \frac{4}{9}t$$

$$y(t) = A_1 e^{3t} + A_2 - \frac{2}{3}t^3 - \frac{2}{3}t^2 - \frac{4}{9}t$$

11.5 System of Linear Differential Equations

In this section we discuss the solution to systems of first-order linear differential equations such as

$$\begin{aligned} \dot{x} &= ax + by \\ \dot{y} &= cx + dy \end{aligned} \tag{11.44}$$

This is a system of linear equations. It is autonomous since the variable t does not appear explicitly in the system and homogeneous because there is no additional constant. This is the type of system we will discuss.

A solution to the system consists of a pair of functions $x = x(t)$ and $y = y(t)$ that when substituted in the equations reduce the equations to identities.

Before delving into the analytical solution, let's consider the numerical solution of the system. The Euler method and the Runge-Kutta method apply to system of first-order differential equations as well. We will write two functions to solve systems of two first-order differential equations, `system_ode_euler()` and `system_ode_RungeKutta()` (the last one left as exercise).

The Euler method is given by

$$x_{n+1} = x_n + hf(t_n, x_n, y_n) = x_n + hx'_n$$

and

$$y_{n+1} = y_n + hg(t_n, x_n, y_n) = y_n + hy'_n$$

This requires a slight modification to the code of `ode_euler()`

```
> system_ode_euler <- function(dx, dy, iv, h = 0.01,
+                              periods = 100){
+
+   dx <- gsub("T", "(h*(t-1))", dx)
+   dy <- gsub("T", "(h*(t-1))", dy)
+   x <- numeric(periods)
+   x[1] <- iv[1]
+   y <- numeric(periods)
+   y[1] <- iv[2]
+
+   for(t in seq_along(y)){
+
+     x[t+1] <- x[t] + eval(parse(text = dx))*h
+     y[t+1] <- y[t] + eval(parse(text = dy))*h
+
+   }
```

```
+
+     results <- data.frame(xt = x, yt = y)
+
+     return(results)
+
+ }
```

The algorithm for the Runge-Kutta method is presented in Sect. 11.9.[8]

11.5.1 Eigenvalues Method

In this section we present the eigenvalues method. Since the study of the eigenvalues and eigenvectors is the same of the eigenvalues method from the analysis of the system of linear first-order difference equations, we will go straight to the solution of the system (the interested reader may refer to any of the cited book in this chapter for more details about systems of differential equations).

The system presented earlier can be represented in matrix form as follows

$$\begin{bmatrix} \dot{x} \\ \dot{y} \end{bmatrix} = \begin{bmatrix} a & b \\ c & d \end{bmatrix} \begin{bmatrix} x \\ y \end{bmatrix}$$

Given the matrix $A = \begin{bmatrix} a & b \\ c & d \end{bmatrix}$, we follow the usual steps to the characteristic equations, eigenvalues and eigenvectors. The characteristic equation leads to three different cases:

1. distinct and real eigenvalues
2. repeated eigenvalues
3. complex eigenvalues

11.5.1.1 Case 1: Distinct and Real Eigenvalues

Consider the following system of differential equations

$$\begin{aligned} \dot{x} &= 2x + 4y \\ \dot{y} &= x + 5y \end{aligned} \tag{11.45}$$

It can be written in matrix form as

$$\begin{bmatrix} \dot{x} \\ \dot{y} \end{bmatrix} = \begin{bmatrix} 2 & 4 \\ 1 & 5 \end{bmatrix} \begin{bmatrix} x \\ y \end{bmatrix}$$

[8] For `system_ode_RungeKutta()` I retain the possibility to plot the results.

Now, the eigenvalues and eigenvectors of matrix

$$A = \begin{bmatrix} 2 & 4 \\ 1 & 5 \end{bmatrix}$$

are the same of the corresponding example for the system of difference equations, i.e.

$$\lambda_1 = 6 \quad \lambda_2 = 1$$

$$v_1 = \begin{bmatrix} 1 \\ 1 \end{bmatrix} \quad v_2 = \begin{bmatrix} -4 \\ 1 \end{bmatrix}$$

Consequently, we jump directly to Step 4, i.e., write the general solution.

Step 4
Write the general solution
For a system of linear differential equations with an $n \times n$ A matrix with distinct and real eigenvalues the solution takes the following form

$$\mathbf{z} = c_1 e^{\lambda_1 t}\mathbf{v}_1 + c_2 e^{\lambda_2 t}\mathbf{v}_2 + \cdots + c_n e^{\lambda_n t}\mathbf{v}_n \tag{11.46}$$

Consequently, the general solution for this example is

$$\mathbf{z} = c_1 e^{\lambda_1 t}\mathbf{v}_1 + c_2 e^{\lambda_2 t}\mathbf{v}_2$$

$$\mathbf{z} = c_1 e^{6t}\begin{bmatrix} 1 \\ 1 \end{bmatrix} + c_2 e^{t}\begin{bmatrix} -4 \\ 1 \end{bmatrix}$$

Step 5
Find the constants given the initial values and write the particular solution.
Given $x_0 = 4$ and $y_0 = 5$,

$$4 = c_1 e^0 \cdot 1 + c_2 e^0 \cdot (-4) \rightarrow 4 = c_1 - 4c_2 \rightarrow c_1 = 4 + 4c_2$$

$$5 = c_1 e^0 \cdot 1 + c_2 e^0 \cdot 1 \rightarrow 5 = c_1 + c_2 \rightarrow 5 = 4 + 4c_2 + c_2 \rightarrow c_2 = \frac{1}{5}$$

$$c_1 = \frac{24}{5} \quad c_2 = \frac{1}{5}$$

Therefore, given the initial conditions, the solution is

$$\mathbf{z} = \frac{24}{5}e^{6t}\begin{bmatrix}1\\1\end{bmatrix} + \frac{1}{5}e^{t}\begin{bmatrix}-4\\1\end{bmatrix}$$

Let's verify the solution with **R**.

```
> t <- seq(0, 1, 0.01)
> l1 <- 6
> l2 <- 1
> c1 <- (24/5)
> c2 <- (1/5)
> v11 <- 1
> v12 <- 1
> v21 <- -4
> v22 <- 1
> xt <- c1*exp(l1*t)*v11 + c2*exp(l2*t)*v21
> yt <- c1*exp(l1*t)*v12 + c2*exp(l2*t)*v22
> head(xt)
[1] 4.000000 4.288775 4.595824 4.922280 5.269347
    5.638305
> head(yt)
[1] 5.000000 5.298825 5.616025 5.952734 6.310158
    6.689576
```

Let's check the results with the Euler method and the Runge-Kutta method.

```
> dx <- "2*x[t] + 4*y[t]"
> dy <- "x[t] + 5*y[t]"
> case1_euler <- system_ode_euler(dx, dy, iv = c(4,5))
> head(case1_euler)
        xt       yt
1 4.000000 5.000000
2 4.280000 5.290000
3 4.577200 5.597300
4 4.892636 5.922937
5 5.227406 6.268010
6 5.582675 6.633685
> case1_rk <- system_ode_RungeKutta(dx, dy, iv = c(4,5))
> head(case1_rk$results)
        xt       yt
1 4.000000 5.000000
2 4.288775 5.298825
3 4.595824 5.616025
```

```
4 4.922280 5.952734
5 5.269347 6.310158
6 5.638305 6.689576
```

11.5.1.2 Case 2: Repeated Real Eigenvalues

Consider the following system of differential equations

$$\begin{aligned} \dot{x} &= 3x + y \\ \dot{y} &= -x + y \end{aligned} \tag{11.47}$$

It can be written in matrix form as

$$\begin{bmatrix} \dot{x} \\ \dot{y} \end{bmatrix} = \begin{bmatrix} 3 & 1 \\ -1 & 1 \end{bmatrix} \begin{bmatrix} x \\ y \end{bmatrix}$$

Now, the eigenvalues and eigenvectors of matrix

$$A = \begin{bmatrix} 3 & 1 \\ -1 & 1 \end{bmatrix}$$

are the same of the corresponding example for the system of difference equations, i.e.

$$\lambda = 2 \quad \left[\text{with multiplicity of } 2\right]$$

$$v_1 = \begin{bmatrix} 1 \\ 1 \end{bmatrix} \quad v_2 = \begin{bmatrix} -2 \\ 1 \end{bmatrix}$$

Consequently, we jump directly to Step 4, i.e., write the general solution.

Step 4
Write the general solution
In the case A is a 2×2 matrix with repeated real eigenvalues with only one associated eigenvector, the solution takes the following form

$$\mathbf{z} = \left(c_1 e^{\lambda t} + t c_2 e^{\lambda t}\right) \mathbf{v}_1 + c_2 e^{\lambda t} \mathbf{v}_2 \tag{11.48}$$

Consequently, the general solution for this example is

$$\mathbf{z} = \left(c_1 e^{2t} + t c_2 e^{2t}\right) \begin{bmatrix} 1 \\ 1 \end{bmatrix} + c_2 e^{2t} \begin{bmatrix} -2 \\ 1 \end{bmatrix}$$

Step 5

Find the constants given the initial values and write the particular solution. Given $x_0 = 4$ and $y_0 = 5$, the constants are $c_1 = 14$ and $c_2 = -9$. Therefore, given the initial conditions, the solution is

$$\mathbf{z} = \left(14e^{2t} + t(-9)e^{2t}\right)\begin{bmatrix}1\\1\end{bmatrix} + (-9)e^{2t}\begin{bmatrix}-2\\1\end{bmatrix}$$

Let's verify our solution with **R**.

```
> t <- seq(0, 1, 0.01)
> l <- 2
> c1 <- 14
> c2 <- -9
> v11 <- -1
> v12 <- 1
> v21 <- -2
> v22 <- 1
> xt <- (c1*exp(l*t) + t*c2*exp(l*t))*v11 + c2*exp(l*t)*v21
> yt <- (c1*exp(l*t) + t*c2*exp(l*t))*v12 + c2*exp(l*t)*v22
> head(xt)
[1] 4.000000 4.172623 4.350589 4.534042 4.723132 4.918011
> head(yt)
[1] 5.000000 5.009189 5.016708 5.022487 5.026452 5.028528
> dx <- "3*x[t] + y[t]"
> dy <- "-x[t] + y[t]"
> case2_euler <- system_ode_euler(dx, dy, iv = c(4, 5))
> head(case2_euler)
        xt       yt
1 4.000000 5.000000
2 4.170000 5.010000
3 4.345200 5.018400
4 4.525740 5.025132
5 4.711764 5.030126
6 4.903418 5.033310
> case2_rk <- system_ode_RungeKutta(dx, dy, iv = c(4, 5))
> head(case2_rk$results)
        xt       yt
1 4.000000 5.000000
2 4.172623 5.009189
3 4.350589 5.016708
4 4.534042 5.022487
5 4.723132 5.026452
6 4.918011 5.028528
```

11.5.1.3 Case 3: Complex Eigenvalues

Consider the following system of differential equations

$$\begin{aligned} \dot{x} &= x - 5y \\ \dot{y} &= x + 3y \end{aligned} \tag{11.49}$$

It can be written in matrix form as

$$\begin{bmatrix} \dot{x} \\ \dot{y} \end{bmatrix} = \begin{bmatrix} 1 & -5 \\ 1 & 3 \end{bmatrix} \begin{bmatrix} x \\ y \end{bmatrix}$$

Now, the eigenvalues and eigenvectors of matrix

$$A = \begin{bmatrix} 1 & -5 \\ 1 & 3 \end{bmatrix}$$

are the same of the corresponding example for the system of difference equations, i.e.

$$\lambda_1 = 2 + 2i \quad \lambda_2 = 2 - 2i$$

$$\mathbf{v} = \begin{bmatrix} 1 \\ -\frac{1}{5} - \frac{2}{5}i \end{bmatrix} \quad \overline{\mathbf{v}} = \begin{bmatrix} 1 \\ -\frac{1}{5} + \frac{2}{5}i \end{bmatrix}$$

with

$$\mathbf{u} = \begin{bmatrix} 1 \\ -\frac{1}{5} \end{bmatrix} \quad \mathbf{w} = \begin{bmatrix} 1 \\ -\frac{2}{5} \end{bmatrix}$$

Consequently, we jump directly to Step 4, i.e., write the general solution.

Step 4
Write the general solution
In the case A is a 2×2 real matrix with complex eigenvalues, the general solution is

$$\mathbf{z} = e^{\alpha t} \left(\cos(\beta t)(c_1 \mathbf{u} - c_2 \mathbf{w}) - \sin(\beta t)(c_2 \mathbf{u} + c_1 \mathbf{w}) \right) \tag{11.50}$$

In our example, the general solution is

$$\mathbf{z} = e^{2t} \left(\cos(2t) \left(c_1 \begin{bmatrix} 1 \\ -\frac{1}{5} \end{bmatrix} - c_2 \begin{bmatrix} 1 \\ -\frac{2}{5} \end{bmatrix} \right) - \sin(2t) \left(c_2 \begin{bmatrix} 1 \\ -\frac{1}{5} \end{bmatrix} + c_1 \begin{bmatrix} 1 \\ -\frac{2}{5} \end{bmatrix} \right) \right)$$

Step 5

Given $x_0 = 4$, $y_0 = 5$ the constants are $c_1 = 4$ and $c_2 = \frac{29}{2}$. Consequently, the particular solution is

$$\mathbf{z} = e^{2t}\left(\cos(2t)\left(4\begin{bmatrix}1\\-\frac{1}{5}\end{bmatrix} - \frac{29}{2}\begin{bmatrix}1\\-\frac{2}{5}\end{bmatrix}\right) - \sin(2t)\left(\frac{29}{2}\begin{bmatrix}1\\-\frac{1}{5}\end{bmatrix} + 4\begin{bmatrix}1\\-\frac{2}{5}\end{bmatrix}\right)\right)$$

Let's verify the solution with **R**.

```
> t <- seq(0, 1, 0.01)
> alpha <- 2
> beta <- 2
> u1 <- 1
> u2 <- -(1/5)
> w1 <- 0
> w2 <- -(2/5)
> c1 <- 4
> c2 <- (29/2)
> xt <- (exp(alpha*t)*(cos(beta*t)*(c1*u1 - c2*w1) -
+                            sin(beta*t)*(c2*u1 + c1*w1)))
> yt <- (exp(alpha*t)*(cos(beta*t)*(c1*u2 - c2*w2) -
+                            sin(beta*t)*(c2*u2 + c1*w2)))
> head(xt)
[1] 4.000000 3.784151 3.556404 3.316460 3.064017 2.798770
> head(yt)
[1] 5.000000 5.191799 5.387187 5.586153 5.788679 5.994747
> dx <- "x[t] - 5*y[t]"
> dy <- "x[t] + 3*y[t]"
> case3_euler <- system_ode_euler(dx, dy, iv = c(4, 5))
> head(case3_euler)
        xt       yt
1 4.000000 5.000000
2 3.790000 5.190000
3 3.568400 5.383600
4 3.334904 5.580792
5 3.089213 5.781565
6 2.831027 5.985904
> case3_rk <- system_ode_RungeKutta(dx, dy,iv = c(4, 5),
+                                        periods = 200)
> head(case3_rk$results)
        xt       yt
1 4.000000 5.000000
2 3.784151 5.191799
3 3.556404 5.387187
4 3.316460 5.586153
5 3.064017 5.788679
6 2.798770 5.994747
```

11.5.2 Equilibrium

Now that we learnt how to find the solution of a system of linear first-order differential equations, we want to further investigate the dynamics of the system.

Therefore the next steps consists in finding the equilibrium point, (or fixed point, steady steady, stationary solution, rest point) and in investigating if the point is stable or unstable.

Let's consider the system from Sect. 11.5.1.1

$$\begin{aligned} \dot{x} &= 2x + 4y \\ \dot{y} &= x + 5y \end{aligned} \tag{11.51}$$

We establish the equilibrium point by setting $\dot{x} = 0$ and $\dot{y} = 0$

$$\begin{aligned} 2x + 4y &= 0 \\ x + 5y &= 0 \end{aligned} \tag{11.52}$$

and then solve the system for x and y. Thus, the system has solution $x^* = 0$ and $y^* = 0$. Indeed, it results that the origin $(0, 0)$ is the equilibrium point of independent homogeneous linear equation systems.

In general terms, given a first order system of differential equations

$$\begin{aligned} \dot{y}_1 &= f_1(y_1, \ldots, y_n) \\ &\vdots \quad \ldots \\ \dot{y}_n &= f_n(y_1, \ldots, y_n) \end{aligned}$$

since for a steady state solution $\dot{y}_i = 0, i = \{1, \ldots, n\}$, a point $\mathbf{y}^* = (y_1^*, \ldots, y_n^*)$ is a steady state of the system if and only if

$$\begin{aligned} f_1(y_1^*, \ldots, y_n^*) &= 0 \\ \vdots \quad &\vdots \\ f_n(y_1^*, \ldots, y_n^*) &= 0 \end{aligned}$$

Once we have established that an equilibrium point exists, we need to investigate if it is stable or unstable.

Let $\mathbf{y}^*$ be an equilibrium for the system. Then we can have the following cases:

- $\mathbf{y}^*$ is an *asymptotically stable equilibrium* if every solution $y(t)$ which starts near[9] $\mathbf{y}^*$ converges to $\mathbf{y}^*$ as $t \to \infty$. Additionally, $\mathbf{y}^*$ is
  - *globally asymptotically stable* if every trajectory approaches the equilibrium point
  - *locally asymptotically stable* if only trajectories that satisfy a set of initial conditions (called *basin of attraction*) approach the equilibrium point
- $\mathbf{y}^*$ is *neutrally stable* if $\mathbf{y}^*$ is stable but not asymptotically stable, i.e. as $t \to \infty$ the solutions which start near $\mathbf{y}^*$ remain close to $\mathbf{y}^*$ without approaching it
- $\mathbf{y}^*$ is *unstable* if it is neither asymptotically stable nor neutrally stable.

From the solutions with the eigenvalues method we can establish the dynamics of the system.

- In the case of the A matrix with real eigenvalues
  - if one $\lambda > 0$ then it is unstable; if $\lambda_1 > 0$ and $\lambda_2 < 0$, i.e. the real eigenvalues have opposite signs, the origin is called *saddle point* (more on saddle points in Sect. 11.5.2.1)
  - if all $\lambda < 0$ it is asymptotically stable
  - if $\lambda_1 = 0$ and $\lambda_2 \neq 0$ the solution is of the form $c_1\mathbf{v}_1 + c_2 e^{\lambda_2 t}\mathbf{v}_2$, i.e. $c_1\mathbf{v}_1$ is constant and the stability depends on λ_2 ($\lambda_2 < 0$ stable, $\lambda_2 > 0$, unstable)
- In the case of repeated eigenvalues
  - if $\lambda < 0$ it is stable, $\lambda > 0$ it is unstable
  - if $\lambda = 0$ and $c_2 \neq 0$, then the solution tends to infinity
- In the case of complex eigenvalues, the stability of the system is determined by real part of the complex eigenvalue α
  - if $\alpha < 0$ then the solution is asymptotically stable
  - if $\alpha > 0$ then the solution is unstable
  - if $\alpha = 0$ then it is neutrally stable

Therefore, in the previous examples we have

- Case 1: with $\lambda_1 = 6$ and $\lambda_1 = 1$ then the solution is unstable
- Case 2: with $\lambda = 2$ then the solution is unstable
- Case 3: with $\alpha = 2$ then the solution is unstable

[9] Clearly, the term "near" is very approximative. There are rigorous definition for this measure of distance, such as that of Liapunov. We leave this concept to more advanced books.

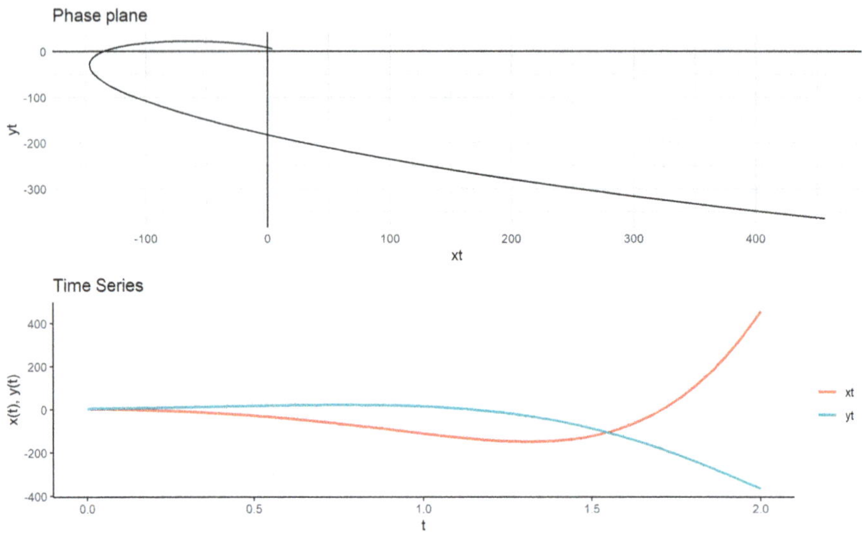

Fig. 11.10 Phase plane and time series plots of solution of Case 3

11.5.2.1 Geometric Interpretation

The solution can be represented in two ways: as a trajectory in a *xy*-phase plane and as a time series plot.

Let's consider the solution of Case 3. In the function `system_ode_RungeKutta()` I retained the function to plot. Therefore, it is possible to extract the trajectory plot. We add a title and stored it in `xyplane`. Then we plot the time series plot, `tsplot`. We arrange the two plots in one figure. Figure 11.10 shows the graphical representation of solution of Case 3.

```
> xyplane <- case3_rk$graph_results +
+   ggtitle("Phase plane")
> times <- seq(0, by = 0.01,
+              length.out = length(case3_rk$results[[1]]))
> case3_rk$results$times <- times
> df <- case3_rk$results
> df_l <- df %>%
+   pivot_longer(!times)
> head(df_l)
# A tibble: 6 x 3
  times name  value
  <dbl> <chr> <dbl>
1  0    xt     4
2  0    yt     5
3  0.01 xt     3.78
```

```
4  0.01 yt     5.19
5  0.02 xt     3.56
6  0.02 yt     5.39
> tsplot <- ggplot(df_l, aes(x = times,
+                     y = value,
+                     group = name,
+                     color = name)) +
+   geom_line(size = 1) +
+   ylab("x(t), y(t)") + xlab("t") +
+   ggtitle("Time Series") +
+   theme_classic() +
+   scale_y_continuous(breaks = pretty_breaks()) +
+   scale_x_continuous(breaks = pretty_breaks()) +
+   theme(legend.title = element_blank())
> ggarrange(xyplane, tsplot,
+           nrow = 2, ncol = 1)
Warning message:
Removed 1 rows containing missing values (geom_segment).
```

Let's now represent the phase diagram of Case 3 with `phaseR`.

```
> case3_fn <- function(t, y, parameters){
+  x <- y[1]
+  y <- y[2]
+  dy <- numeric(2)
+  dy[1] <- x - 5*y
+  dy[2] <- x + 3*y
+  list(dy)
+ }
> case3_flowField <- flowField(case3_fn,
+                              xlim = c(-150, 400),
+                              ylim = c(-300, 50),
+                              parameters = NULL,
+                              add = FALSE)
> grid()
> case3_nullclines <- nullclines(case3_fn,
+                                xlim = c(-150, 400),
+                                ylim = c(-300, 50),
+                                parameters = NULL)
> y0 <- matrix(c(4, 5), ncol = 2, nrow = 1,byrow = TRUE)
> case3_trajectory <- trajectory(case3_fn, y0 = y0,
+                                tlim = c(0, 10),
+                                parameters = NULL)
```

Figure 11.11 shows the output of this code.

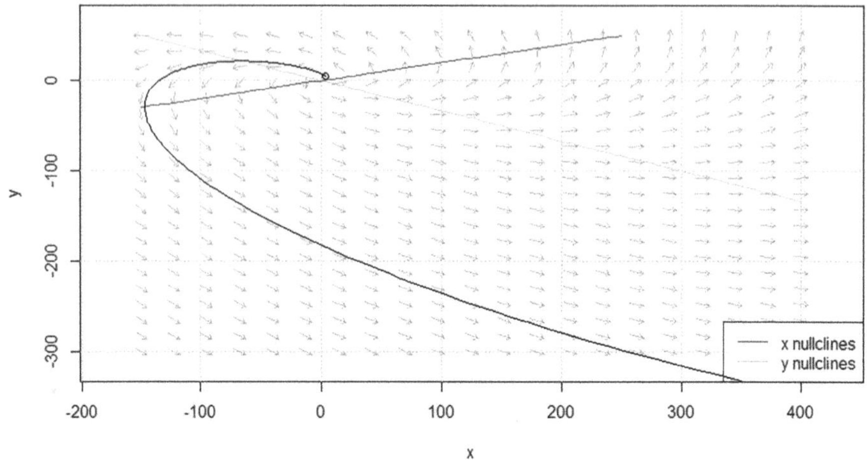

Fig. 11.11 Phase diagram of Case 3

We can use the `stability()` function to classify the equilibrium points. It is classified as an unstable focus, confirming our previous analysis.

```
> case3_stability <- stability(case3_fn, ystar = c(4,5),
+                                    parameters = NULL)
tr = 4, Delta = 8, discriminant = -16, classification = Unstable focus
```

Before continuing, a word of warning. We built the examples for the system of differential equations by using the same A matrix as in the examples of the system for difference equations. Now we may think that since the characteristic equation, the eigenvalues and eigenvectors are the same, the conclusion about the convergence/divergence could be the same. However, this may not be the case.

Let's consider the corresponding example with differential equations of the first example in Sect. 10.3.4.

$$\begin{aligned} \dot{x} &= -5 + 0.25x + 0.4y \\ \dot{y} &= 10 - x + y \end{aligned} \tag{11.53}$$

```
> dx <- "- 5+ 0.25*x[t] + 0.4*y[t]"
> dy <- "10 -x[t] + y[t]"
> res1 <- system_ode_RungeKutta(dx, dy, iv = c(10, 5),
+                                      periods = 1000)
> head(res1$results)
         xt       yt
1 10.000000 5.000000
2  9.995094 5.050276
3  9.990379 5.101105
4  9.985856 5.152491
5  9.981529 5.204439
```

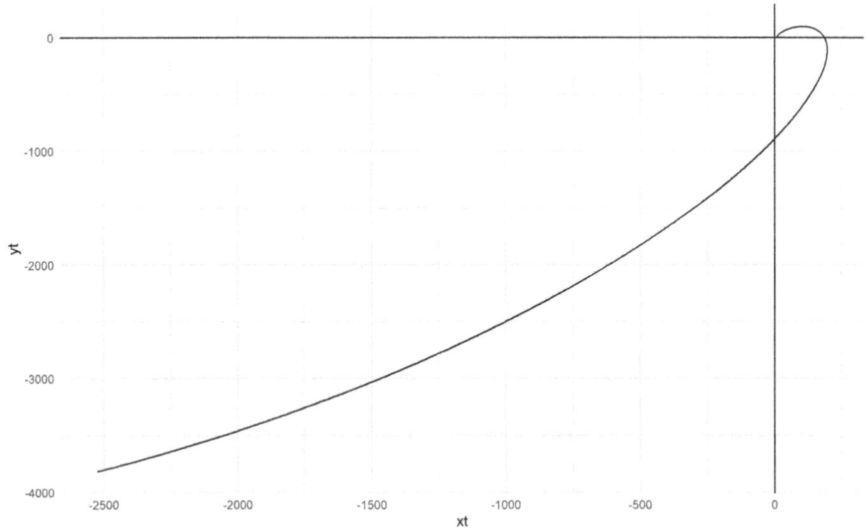

Fig. 11.12 Graphing trajectory: unstable focus

```
6  9.977400 5.256951
> res1$graph_results
Warning message:
Removed 1 rows containing missing values (geom_segment).
```

As we can observe, Figs. 11.12 and 10.6 produce two different results.

If we check again the eigenvalues of the matrix A (Sect. 10.3.4), we see that $\alpha = 0.625$ is greater than 0. On the other hand, the conclusion for the dynamics of system of difference equations with complex eigenvalues was based on the value of $|r|$. To quote Professor Shone, "This acts as a warning not to attribute the properties of one (model) to the other without further investigation" (Shone, 2001, p. 126).[10]

Let's consider the following system

$$\begin{aligned}\dot{x} &= -3x + 2y \\ \dot{y} &= 2x - 6y\end{aligned} \tag{11.54}$$

In matrix form

$$\begin{bmatrix}\dot{x} \\ \dot{y}\end{bmatrix} = \begin{bmatrix}-3 & 3 \\ 2 & -6\end{bmatrix}\begin{bmatrix}x \\ y\end{bmatrix}$$

[10] In particular, Professor Shone is discussing about the inflation-unemployment dynamics with a discrete model and a continuous model. The word model in parenthesis added here.

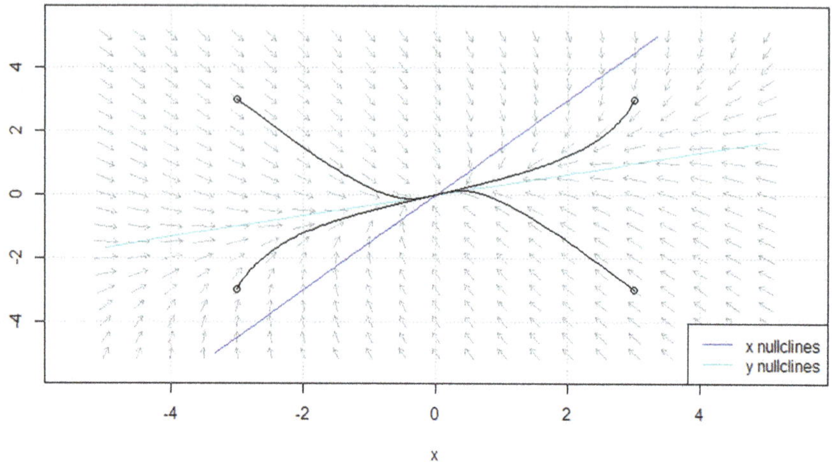

Fig. 11.13 Stable node

The A matrix has eigenvalues -2 and -7. We know this because it is the negative definite matrix that we used in Sect. 2.3.12. Therefore we expect that the system is asymptotically stable. With phaseR we confirm that it is a stable node (Fig. 11.13).

```
> fn1 <- function(t, y, parameters){
+   x <- y[1]
+   y <- y[2]
+   dy <- numeric(2)
+   dy[1] <- -3*x + 2*y
+   dy[2] <- 2*x - 6*y
+   list(dy)
+ }
> fn1_flowField <- flowField(fn1, xlim = c(-5, 5),
+                               ylim = c(-5, 5),
+                               parameters = NULL,
+                               add = FALSE)
> grid()
> fn1_nullclines <- nullclines(fn1, xlim = c(-5, 5),
+                                ylim = c(-5, 5),
+                                parameters = NULL)
> y0 <- matrix(c(-3, 3,
+                3, -3,
+                3, 3,
+                -3, -3),
+              ncol = 2,
+              nrow = 4,
+              byrow = TRUE)
> fn1_trajectory <- trajectory(fn1, y0 = y0,
+                                tlim = c(0, 5),
+                                parameters = NULL)
Note: col has been reset as required
> fn1_stability <- stability(fn1, ystar = c(3, -3),
+                               parameters = NULL)
tr = -9, Delta = 14, discriminant = 25, classification = Stable node
```

Let's consider the following system

$$\begin{aligned}\dot{x} &= -3x + 2y \\ \dot{y} &= -4x + y\end{aligned} \tag{11.55}$$

In matrix form

$$\begin{bmatrix}\dot{x} \\ \dot{y}\end{bmatrix} = \begin{bmatrix}-3 & 2 \\ -4 & 1\end{bmatrix}\begin{bmatrix}x \\ y\end{bmatrix}$$

Let's check the eigenvalues of matrix A

```
> A <- matrix(c(-3, 2,
+               -4, 1),
+             nrow = 2, ncol = 2,
+             byrow = TRUE)
> eigen(A)$values
[1] -1+2i -1-2i
```

The complex eigenvalues have $\alpha < 0$. Therefore we expect that it is asymptotically stable. This is confirmed with phaseR (Fig. 11.14).

```
> fn2 <- function(t, y, parameters){
+   x <- y[1]
+   y <- y[2]
+   dy <- numeric(2)
+   dy[1] <- -3*x + 2*y
+   dy[2] <- -4*x + y
+   list(dy)
```

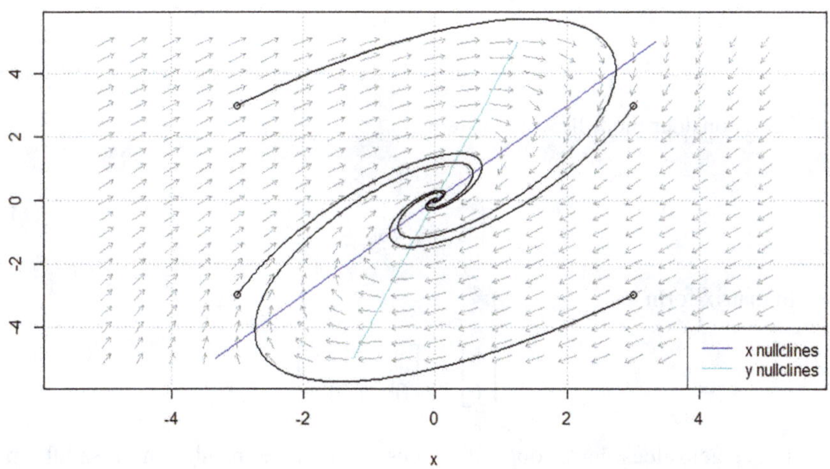

Fig. 11.14 Stable focus

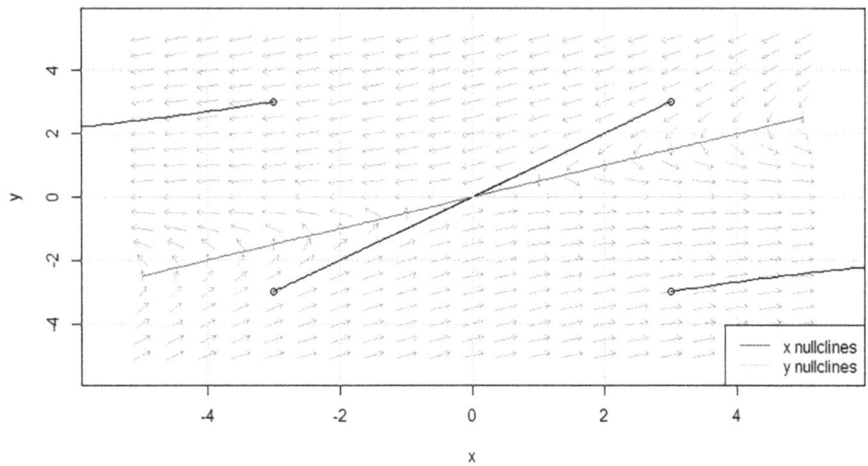

Fig. 11.15 Saddle point

```
+ }
> fn2_flowField <- flowField(fn2, xlim = c(-5, 5),
+                            ylim = c(-5, 5),
+                            parameters = NULL,
+                            add = FALSE)
> grid()
> fn2_nullclines <- nullclines(fn2, xlim = c(-5, 5),
+                              ylim = c(-5, 5),
+                              parameters = NULL)
> fn2_trajectory <- trajectory(fn2, y0 = y0,
+                              tlim = c(0, 5),
+                              parameters = NULL)
Note: col has been reset as required
> fn2_stability <- stability(fn2, ystar = c(3, -3),
+                            parameters = NULL)
tr = -2, Delta = 5, discriminant = -16, classification = Stable focus
```

Let's consider the following system

$$
\begin{aligned}
\dot{x} &= x - 2y \\
\dot{y} &= -y
\end{aligned} \tag{11.56}
$$

In matrix form

$$
\begin{bmatrix} \dot{x} \\ \dot{y} \end{bmatrix} = \begin{bmatrix} 1 & -2 \\ 0 & -1 \end{bmatrix} \begin{bmatrix} x \\ y \end{bmatrix}
$$

The eigenvalues have opposite signs. This case results in a saddle point (Fig. 11.15).

```
> A <- matrix(c(1, -2,
+               0, -1),
+             nrow = 2, ncol = 2,
+             byrow = TRUE)
> eigen(A)$values
[1]  1 -1
> fn3 <- function(t, y, parameters){
+   x <- y[1]
+   y <- y[2]
+   dy <- numeric(2)
+   dy[1] <- x - 2*y
+   dy[2] <- -y
+   list(dy)
+ }
> fn3_flowField <- flowField(fn3, xlim = c(-5, 5),
+                             ylim = c(-5, 5),
+                             parameters = NULL,
+                             add = FALSE)
> grid()
> fn3_nullclines <- nullclines(fn3, xlim = c(-5, 5),
+                               ylim = c(-5, 5),
+                               parameters = NULL)
> fn3_trajectory <- trajectory(fn3, y0 = y0,
+                               tlim = c(0, 5),
+                               parameters = NULL)
Note: col has been reset as required
> fn3_stability <- stability(fn3, ystar = c(3, -3),
+                             parameters = NULL)
tr = 0, Delta = -1, discriminant = 4, classification = Saddle
```

Let's consider the following system

$$\begin{aligned} \dot{x} &= 3x + 5y \\ \dot{y} &= -5x - 3y \end{aligned} \tag{11.57}$$

In matrix form

$$\begin{bmatrix} \dot{x} \\ \dot{y} \end{bmatrix} = \begin{bmatrix} 3 & 5 \\ -5 & -3 \end{bmatrix} \begin{bmatrix} x \\ y \end{bmatrix}$$

The matrix A has pure imaginary eigenvalues. This case results in a centre (Fig. 11.16)

```
> A <- matrix(c(3, 5,
+               -5, -3),
+             nrow = 2, ncol = 2,
+             byrow = TRUE)
> eigen(A)$values
[1] 0+4i 0-4i
> fn4 <- function(t, y, parameters){
+   x <- y[1]
```

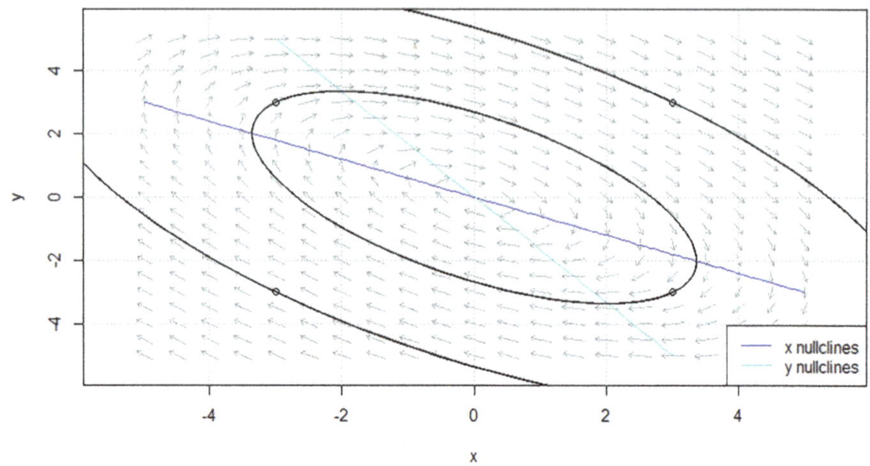

Fig. 11.16 Centre

```
+   y <- y[2]
+   dy <- numeric(2)
+   dy[1] <- 3*x + 5*y
+   dy[2] <- -5*x -3*y
+   list(dy)
+ }
> fn4_flowField <- flowField(fn4, xlim = c(-5, 5),
+                            ylim = c(-5, 5),
+                            parameters = NULL,
+                            add = FALSE)
> grid()
> fn4_nullclines <- nullclines(fn4, xlim = c(-5, 5),
+                              ylim = c(-5, 5),
+                              parameters = NULL)
> fn4_trajectory <- trajectory(fn4, y0 = y0,
+                              tlim = c(0, 5),
+                              parameters = NULL)
Note: col has been reset as required
> fn4_stability <- stability(fn4, ystar = c(3, -3),
+                            parameters = NULL)
tr = 0, Delta = 16, discriminant = -64, classification = Centre
```

Let's sum up the classification of the types of equilibrium

- node
  - stable node: equilibrium where trajectories flow noncyclically toward it
  - unstable node: equilibrium where trajectories flow noncyclically away from it

- focus
  - stable focus: equilibrium where whirling trajectories flow cyclically toward it
  - unstable focus: equilibrium where whirling trajectories flow cyclically away from it
- saddle point
  - from Fig. 11.15 it is possible to identify *stable arms* that flow directly to the equilibrium and *unstable arms* that flow directly away from it. Only the solutions that start on the stable arms approach the origin. Solutions that start close but not on the stable arms flow away from it. Therefore, generically the saddle point is classified as unstable
- centre
  - from Fig. 11.16 it is possible to observe that the solutions are closed curves encircling the origin

We conclude this section with a non-linear system. We did not discuss how to solve non-linear systems but we can still solve them numerically and graphically.

Let's consider the well-known *Lotka-Volterra* model, also known as the *predator-prey* system

$$\dot{x} = ax - bxy$$

$$\dot{y} = dxy - cy$$

where x denote the size of the prey population, y denote the size of the predator population, and the term xy denote the number of interactions between the two species, i.e. prey and predator. The equations of the system tell us that x grows at a rate a that is proportional to the size of x and it decays at a rate b that is proportional to the number of encounters between prey and predator xy; on the other hand y grows at a rate d that is proportional to the number of encounters between prey and predator xy and it decays at a rate c that is proportional to its size.[11] Or put in simple words, the rate of growth of the preys x depends positively on its size and negatively on the the encounter with the predator because it increases the possibilities to be hunted; on the other hand the rate of growth of the predators depends positively on the encounter with the preys because it increases the possibility to hunt them and negatively on the predator size itself because more predators means less food for all of them.

[11] As this model is specified, in the absence of the predator ($y = 0$) the growth rate of the prey x is $\dot{x} = ax$, i.e. the population of the prey will grow without bound. This led to further enhancement of the model that will be not considered here.

Let's start by setting the x and y nullclines and finding the equilibrium points, i.e. $\dot{x} = 0$ and $\dot{y} = 0$

$$ax - bxy = 0$$

$$dxy - cy = 0$$

Both can be rewritten as

$$x(a - by) = 0$$

$$y(dx - c) = 0$$

and from here we find that one equilibrium point is $(0, 0)$ and the other one is $\left(\frac{c}{d}, \frac{a}{b}\right)$.

We can add that

- on the positive x axis $y = 0$. Then $\dot{x} = ax$ and, as a result, $x(t)$ is always increasing;
- on the positive y axis $x = 0$. Then $\dot{y} = -cy$ and, as a result, $y(t)$ is always decreasing;
- the vertical line $x = \frac{c}{d}$ and the horizontal line $y = \frac{a}{b}$ divide the xy plane into four panes. In particular,
  - along the vertical line $x = \frac{c}{d}$, $\dot{y} = 0$. The vertical line divide the xy plane in two half planes. On the left of $x = \frac{c}{d}$, $\dot{y}$ is negative; on the right of $x = \frac{c}{d}$, $\dot{y}$ is positive;
  - along the horizontal line $y = \frac{a}{b}$, $\dot{x} = 0$. The horizontal line divide the xy plane in two half planes. Above $y = \frac{a}{b}$, $\dot{x}$ is negative; below $y = \frac{a}{b}$, $\dot{x}$ is positive

With these considerations in mind, let's represent a numerical example

$$\begin{aligned} \dot{x} &= 2x - xy \\ \dot{y} &= 0.5xy - 2y \end{aligned} \tag{11.58}$$

Therefore, in this example $a = 2$, $b = 1$, $c = 2$, $d = 0.5$. The nullclines are

$$2x - xy = 0 \rightarrow x(2 - y) = 0 \rightarrow x_1 = 0;\ y_2 = 2$$

$$0.5xy - 2y = 0 \rightarrow y(0.5x - 2) = 0 \rightarrow y_1 = 0;\ x_2 = 4$$

The equilibrium points are $(0, 0)$ and $(4, 2)$.

Let's represent the phase diagram with `phaseR`. The Lotka-Volterra model is already provided in the package as `lotka.Volterra()`

```
> lotkaVolterra.flowField <- flowField(lotkaVolterra,
+                                       xlim = c(0, 10),
+                                       ylim = c(0, 5),
```

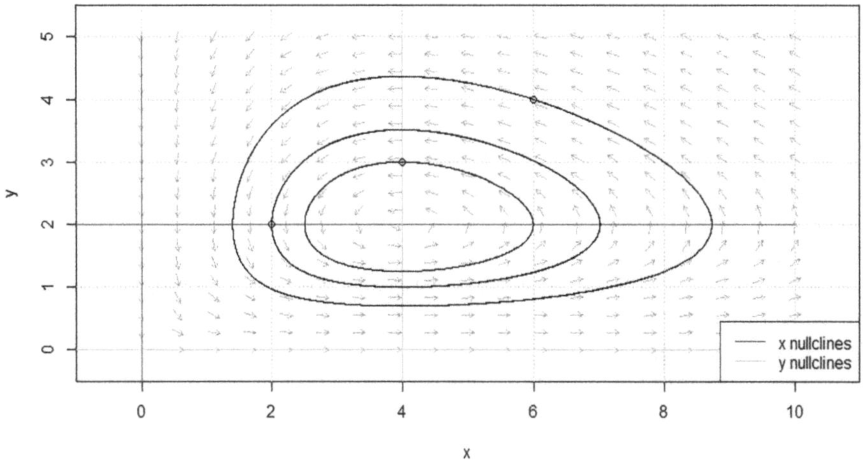

Fig. 11.17 Lotka-Volterra model

```
+                                         parameters = c(2, 1, 0.5, 2),
+                                         points = 19, add = FALSE)
> grid()
> lotkaVolterra.nullclines <- nullclines(lotkaVolterra,
+                                         xlim = c(-1, 10),
+                                         ylim = c(-1, 5),
+                                         parameters = c(2, 1, 0.5, 2),
+                                         points = 500)
> y0 <- matrix(c(2, 2, 4, 3, 6, 4), ncol = 2, nrow = 3, byrow = TRUE)
> lotkaVolterra.trajectory <- trajectory(lotkaVolterra, y0 = y0,
+                                         tlim = c(0, 10),
+                                         parameters = c(2, 1, 0.5, 2))
Note: col has been reset as required
```

The vertical line $x = 4$ and the horizontal line $y = 2$ divide the xy plane into four panes (Fig. 11.17). On the left of $x = 4$, $\dot{y}$ is negative; on the right of of $x = 4$, $\dot{y}$ is positive. On the other hand, along the xy plane is divide in two panes. Above $y = 2$, $\dot{x}$ is negative; below $y = 2$, $\dot{x}$ is positive.

Next, we use the `stability()` function to investigate the type of equilibrium of point (0, 0) and point (4, 2). It results that (0, 0) is a saddle point and (4, 2) is a centre.

```
> lotkaVolterra.stability <- stability(lotkaVolterra,
+                                       ystar = c(0, 0),
+                                       parameters = c(2,1,0.5,2))
tr = 0, Delta = -4, discriminant = 16, classification = Saddle
> lotkaVolterra.stability <- stability(lotkaVolterra,
+                                       ystar = c(4, 2),
+                                       parameters = c(2,1,0.5,2))
tr = 0, Delta = 4, discriminant = -16, classification = Centre
```

We can represent the Lotka-Volterra model as a time series plot. For this task we solve the model with `system_ode_RungeKutta()`. We use as initial values $x_0 = 6$ and $y_0 = 4$.

```
> dx <- "2*x[t] - x[t]*y[t]"
> dy <- "0.5*x[t]*y[t] - 2*y[t]"
> LV <- system_ode_RungeKutta(dx, dy, iv = c(6, 4),
+                                           periods = 1000)
> times <- seq(0, by = 0.01,
+                length.out = length(LV$results[[1]]))
> LV$results$t <- times
> df <- LV$results
> head(df)
        xt       yt    t
1 6.000000 4.000000 0.00
2 5.880036 4.038989 0.01
3 5.760283 4.075914 0.02
4 5.640945 4.110719 0.03
5 5.522217 4.143354 0.04
6 5.404284 4.173777 0.05
> colnames(df)[c(1, 2)] <- c("prey", "predator")
> df_l <- df %>%
+   pivot_longer(!t)
> head(df_l)
# A tibble: 6 x 3
      t name     value
  <dbl> <chr>    <dbl>
1  0    prey      6
2  0    predator  4
3  0.01 prey      5.88
4  0.01 predator  4.04
5  0.02 prey      5.76
6  0.02 predator  4.08
> tsplot <- ggplot(df_l, aes(x = t,
+                            y = value,
+                            group = name,
+                            color = name)) +
+   geom_line(size = 1) +
+   ylab("prey, predator") + xlab("t") +
+   ggtitle("Time Series") +
+   theme_classic() +
+   scale_y_continuous(breaks = pretty_breaks()) +
+   scale_x_continuous(breaks = pretty_breaks()) +
+   theme(legend.title = element_blank(),
+         legend.position = "bottom")
> tsplot
```

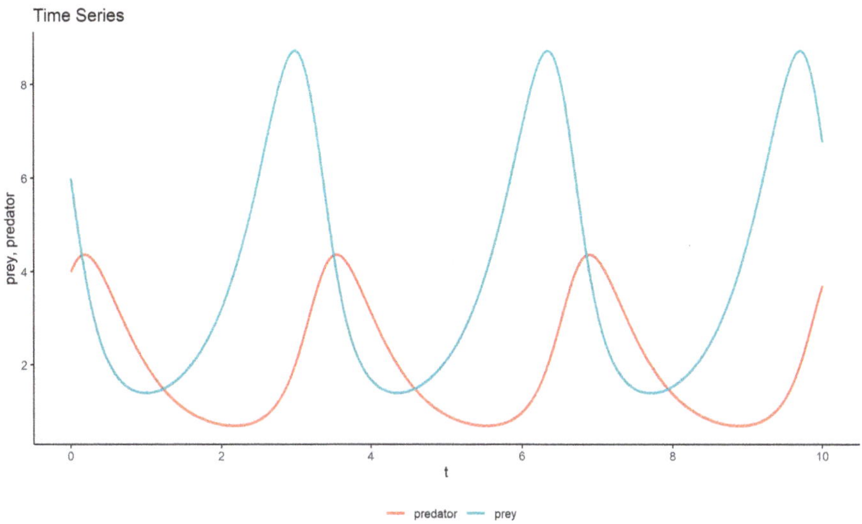

Fig. 11.18 Lotka-Volterra model - time series plot

From Fig. 11.18 we can observe that $x(t)$ (Prey) and $y(t)$ (Predator) are periodic functions of t. Additionally, we can observe that the predator population lags behind the prey population. The prey population increases when there are few predators. However, when the prey population becomes abundant there are more encounters between preys and predators, and, consequently, it is easier for the predators to hunt them. This leads to the growth of the predator population. However, a large number of predators causes a decrease in the number of preys. This causes a scarcity of food for predators and consequently a reduction of its population. With fewer predators the prey population can grow again and the cycle restarts.

11.6 Transforming High-Order Differential Equations

In Sect. 10.4 we learnt how to transform a high-order difference equation into a system of first-order difference equations. A similar procedure applies to high-order differential equations as well. Let's consider a second order differential equation

$$y''(t) + a_1 y'(t) + a_2 y = 0, \quad y(0) = y_0, y'(0) = v_0 \tag{11.59}$$

By introducing a new variable $v = y'(t)$, implying $v' = y''(t)$, we can rewrite (11.59) as a system of two first-order differential equations

$$
\begin{aligned}
y' &= v \\
v' &= -a_1 v - a_2 y
\end{aligned}
\tag{11.60}
$$

with initial conditions $y(0) = y_0$ and $v(0) = v_0$.

We can numerically solve system (11.60) by using the Euler method or the Runge-Kutta method. Here, we will build a function, `ode2nd_euler()`, that uses the Euler method. The Runge-Kutta method is left as exercise.

The Euler method applied to (11.60) is

$$y_{n+1} = y_n + hv_n$$

$$v_{n+1} = v_n + h(-a_n v - a_n y)$$

The following code for `ode2nd_euler()` is very similar to the code of `ode_euler()`. We just added a new equation. Note that it requires the same notation as in (11.60).

```
> ode2nd_euler <- function(dy, dv, iv, h = 0.01,
+                          periods = 100,
+                          actual_solution = NULL){
+
+   require("tidyr")
+   require("ggplot2")
+   require("scales")
+
+   dv <- gsub("T", "(h*(t-1))", dv)
+
+   y <- numeric(periods)
+   y[1] <- iv[1]
+   v <- numeric(periods)
+   v[1] <- iv[2]
+
+   for(t in seq_along(y)){
+
+     y[t+1] <- y[t] + v[t]*h
+     v[t+1] <- v[t] + eval(parse(text = dv))*h
+
+   }
+
+   times <- 0:(length(y) - 1)*h
+   df <- data.frame(t = times, yt = y)
+
+   if(is.null(actual_solution)){
+
+     colnames(df) <- c("t", "Euler approximation")
+
+   } else{
+
+       sol <- actual_solution
```

```
+       y <- numeric(periods)
+       times <- 0:(length(y))
+
+       for(t in times){
+         y[t+1] <- eval(parse(text = sol))
+         }
+
+       df[["sol"]] <- y
+       colnames(df) <- c("t", "Euler approximation",
+                         "Actual solution")
+       }
+
+   df_l <- df %>%
+     pivot_longer(!t,
+                  names_to = "variable",
+                  values_to = "value")
+
+   g <- ggplot(df_l, aes(x = t, y = value,
+                        group = variable,
+                        color = variable)) +
+               geom_line(size = 1) +
+               theme_bw() + ylab("") +
+               theme(legend.position = "bottom",
+                     legend.title = element_blank()) +
+               scale_y_continuous(breaks = pretty_breaks()) +
+               scale_x_continuous(breaks = pretty_breaks())
+
+   l <- list(graph_results = g,
+             results = df)
+
+   return(l)
+ }
```

Let's test it by solving the second order differential equation from Example 11.4.1.

Example 11.6.1 Transform the following second-order differential equation into a system of two first-order differential equations

$$y''(t) - 3y'(t) + 2y = 0$$

By setting $v = y'$, and consequently $v' = y''$, the system becomes

$$\begin{aligned} y' &= v \\ v' &= 3v - 2y \end{aligned} \tag{11.61}$$

We compare the results of the approximation with the actual solution (Fig. 11.19).

```
> dy <- "v[t]"
> dv <- "3*v[t] -2*y[t]"
> sol <- "3*exp(2*t*h) - exp(t*h)"
> res <- ode2nd_euler(dy, dv, iv = c(2, 5),
```

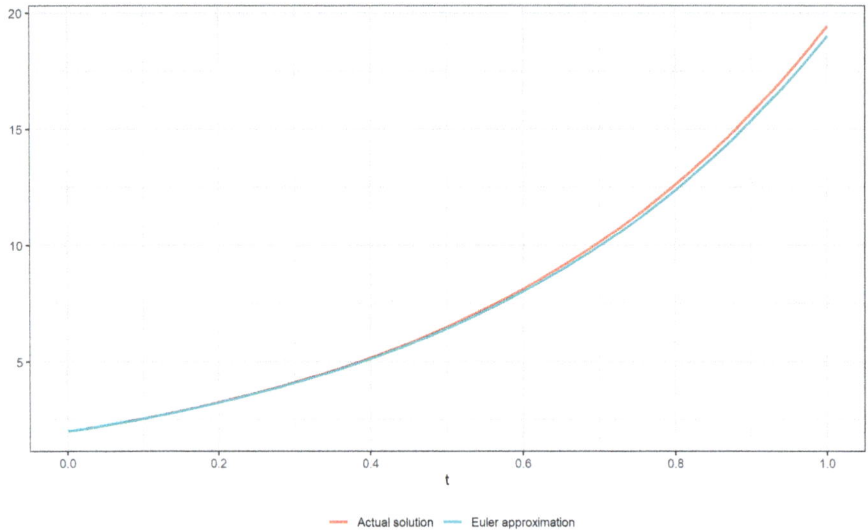

Fig. 11.19 Solution of $y''(t) - 3y'(t) + 2y = 0$, $y = 2$, $v = 5$ with the Euler method

```
+                          h = 0.01,
+                          actual_solution = sol)
> head(res$results)
     t Euler approximation Actual solution
1 0.00            2.000000        2.000000
2 0.01            2.050000        2.050554
3 0.02            2.101100        2.102231
4 0.03            2.153323        2.155055
5 0.04            2.206692        2.209050
6 0.05            2.261232        2.264242
> res$graph_results
```

With the Runge-Kutta method

```
> res <- ode2nd_RungeKutta(dy,dv, iv = c(2,5), h = 0.01,
+                          actual_solution = sol)
> head(res$results)
     t Runge-Kutta approximation Actual solution
1 0.00                  2.000000        2.000000
2 0.01                  2.050554        2.050554
3 0.02                  2.102231        2.102231
4 0.03                  2.155055        2.155055
5 0.04                  2.209050        2.209050
6 0.05                  2.264242        2.264242
```

11.7 Differential Equations with R

In this section we use the `deSolve` package to solve differential equations. Let's start with $y' = 1 - t + 4y$. First, we define the function. We can write as we wrote the logistic function `lgst()` or as follows

```
fn <- function(t, y, parms){list(1 - t + 4*y)}
```

We have two possibilities to implement the Euler algorithm: `euler()` and `ode()`. `y` is the initial (state) values for the ODE system; `times` is times at which explicit estimates for y are desired. The first value in times must be the initial time; `func` is the function with the differential equation we want to solve; `parms` is a vector or list of parameters used in `func`. In the second function we need to choose `method = "euler"`. Other arguments are available for both functions.

```
> out_eu <- euler(y = 1, times = seq(0, 100, by = 0.01),
+                 func = fn, parms = NULL)
> head(out_eu, 11)
      time        1
 [1,] 0.00 1.000000
 [2,] 0.01 1.050000
 [3,] 0.02 1.101900
 [4,] 0.03 1.155776
 [5,] 0.04 1.211707
 [6,] 0.05 1.269775
 [7,] 0.06 1.330066
 [8,] 0.07 1.392669
 [9,] 0.08 1.457676
[10,] 0.09 1.525183
[11,] 0.10 1.595290
> out_eu_b <- ode(y = 1, times = seq(0, 100, by = 0.01),
+                func = fn, parms = NULL,
+                method = "euler")
> head(out_eu_b, 11)
      time        1
 [1,] 0.00 1.000000
 [2,] 0.01 1.050000
 [3,] 0.02 1.101900
 [4,] 0.03 1.155776
 [5,] 0.04 1.211707
 [6,] 0.05 1.269775
 [7,] 0.06 1.330066
 [8,] 0.07 1.392669
 [9,] 0.08 1.457676
[10,] 0.09 1.525183
[11,] 0.10 1.595290
```

With the Runge-Kutta algorithm we have two options as well: `rk4()` and `ode()` with `method = "rk4"`.

```
> out_rk <- rk4(y = 1, times = seq(0, 100, by = 0.01),
+               func = fn, parms = NULL)
> head(out_rk, 11)
      time        1
 [1,] 0.00 1.000000
 [2,] 0.01 1.050963
 [3,] 0.02 1.103903
 [4,] 0.03 1.158903
 [5,] 0.04 1.216044
 [6,] 0.05 1.275416
 [7,] 0.06 1.337108
 [8,] 0.07 1.401217
 [9,] 0.08 1.467839
[10,] 0.09 1.537079
[11,] 0.10 1.609042
> out_rk_b <- ode(y = 1, times = seq(0, 100, by = 0.01),
+               func = fn, parms = NULL,
+               method = "rk4")
> head(out_rk_b, 11)
      time        1
 [1,] 0.00 1.000000
 [2,] 0.01 1.050963
 [3,] 0.02 1.103903
 [4,] 0.03 1.158903
 [5,] 0.04 1.216044
 [6,] 0.05 1.275416
 [7,] 0.06 1.337108
 [8,] 0.07 1.401217
 [9,] 0.08 1.467839
[10,] 0.09 1.537079
[11,] 0.10 1.609042
```

We can plot these results with the `plot()` function. `lwd` stands for line width while `lty` stands for line type (Fig. 11.20).

```
> plot(out_eu_b, out_rk_b,
+      main = "Differential equations with deSolve",
+      lwd = 2, lty = c("solid", "dashed"),
+      col = c("red", "blue"),
+      xlim = c(0, 1),
+      ylim = c(0, 60))
> legend("bottomright",
+        legend = c("Euler approximation",
```

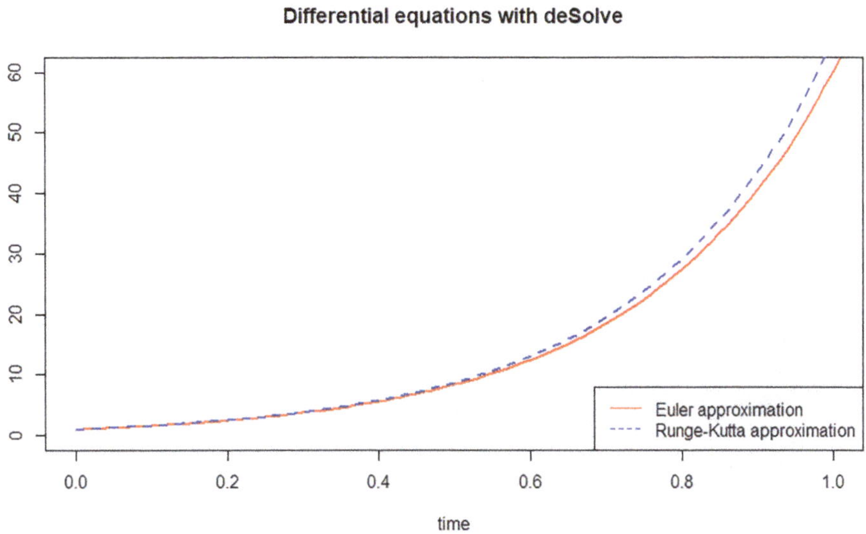

Fig. 11.20 Plot of $y' = 1 - t + 4y,\ y(0) = 1, h = 0.01$ with deSolve

```
+                        "Runge-Kutta approximation"),
+          lty = c("solid", "dashed"),
+          col = c("red", "blue"))
```

For the next examples we use only ode(). We will compare the results with the functions we built. The next example solves the differential equation in Sect. 11.2.1.

```
> fn <- function(t, y, parms){
+   a <- parms[1]
+   dy <- a*(y^2)*t
+   list(dy)
+ }
> out_eu <- ode(y = 3, times = seq(0, 0.2, by = 0.02),
+               func = fn, parms = 2,
+               method = "euler")
> out_eu
   time        1
1  0.00 3.000000
2  0.02 3.000000
3  0.04 3.007200
4  0.06 3.021669
5  0.08 3.043582
6  0.10 3.073225
7  0.12 3.111004
8  0.14 3.157460
9  0.16 3.213290
10 0.18 3.279371
```

```
11 0.20 3.356802
> out_rk <- ode(y = 3, times = seq(0, 0.2, by = 0.02),
+                  func = fn, parms = 2,
+                  method = "rk4")
> out_rk
   time        1
1  0.00 3.000000
2  0.02 3.003604
3  0.04 3.014469
4  0.06 3.032754
5  0.08 3.058728
6  0.10 3.092784
7  0.12 3.135452
8  0.14 3.187420
9  0.16 3.249567
10 0.18 3.322995
11 0.20 3.409091
> RHS <- "2*y[t]^2*T"
> res_eu <- ode_euler(RHS, 3, h = 0.02,
+                      periods = 10)$results
> res_eu
      t       yt
1  0.00 3.000000
2  0.02 3.000000
3  0.04 3.007200
4  0.06 3.021669
5  0.08 3.043582
6  0.10 3.073225
7  0.12 3.111004
8  0.14 3.157460
9  0.16 3.213290
10 0.18 3.279371
11 0.20 3.356802
> res_kr <- ode_RungeKutta(RHS, 3, h = 0.02,
+                             periods = 10)
> res_kr$results
      t       yt
1  0.00 3.000000
2  0.02 3.003604
3  0.04 3.014469
4  0.06 3.032754
5  0.08 3.058728
6  0.10 3.092784
7  0.12 3.135452
8  0.14 3.187420
```

```
9  0.16 3.249567
10 0.18 3.322995
11 0.20 3.409091
```

Let's see some other examples:

$$y' = \sqrt{t+y},\ y(0) = 5$$

```
> fn <- function(t, y, parms){
+   dy <- sqrt(t + y)
+   list(dy)
+ }
> out_eu <- ode(y = 5, times = seq(0, 1, by = 0.1),
+                func = fn, parms = NULL,
+                method = "euler")
> out_eu
   time        1
1   0.0 5.000000
2   0.1 5.223607
3   0.2 5.454336
4   0.3 5.692125
5   0.4 5.936913
6   0.5 6.188645
7   0.6 6.447269
8   0.7 6.712736
9   0.8 6.985000
10  0.9 7.264016
11  1.0 7.549743
> out_rk <- ode(y = 5, times = seq(0, 1, by = 0.1),
+                func = fn, parms = NULL,
+                method = "rk4")
> out_rk
   time        1
1   0.0 5.000000
2   0.1 5.227213
3   0.2 5.461593
4   0.3 5.703074
5   0.4 5.951597
6   0.5 6.207103
7   0.6 6.469541
8   0.7 6.738859
9   0.8 7.015011
10  0.9 7.297952
11  1.0 7.587639
> RHS <- "sqrt(T + y[t])"
```

```
> res_eu <- ode_euler(RHS, 5, h = 0.1,
+                     periods = 10)$results
> res_eu
     t       yt
1  0.0 5.000000
2  0.1 5.223607
3  0.2 5.454336
4  0.3 5.692125
5  0.4 5.936913
6  0.5 6.188645
7  0.6 6.447269
8  0.7 6.712736
9  0.8 6.985000
10 0.9 7.264016
11 1.0 7.549743
> res_kr <- ode_RungeKutta(RHS, 5, h = 0.1,
+                          periods = 10)
> res_kr$results
     t       yt
1  0.0 5.000000
2  0.1 5.227213
3  0.2 5.461593
4  0.3 5.703074
5  0.4 5.951597
6  0.5 6.207103
7  0.6 6.469541
8  0.7 6.738859
9  0.8 7.015011
10 0.9 7.297952
11 1.0 7.587639
```

$$y' = \frac{y^2 + 2ty}{3 + t^2},\ y(0) = -3$$

```
> fn <- function(t, y, parms){
+   dy <- (y^2 + 2*y*t)/(3 + t^2)
+   list(dy)
+ }
> out_eu <- ode(y = -3, times = seq(0, 1, by = 0.1),
+               func = fn, parms = NULL,
+               method = "euler")
> out_eu
  time         1
1  0.0 -3.000000
2  0.1 -2.700000
```

```
3    0.2 -2.475748
4    0.3 -2.306701
5    0.4 -2.179295
6    0.5 -2.084171
7    0.6 -2.014645
8    0.7 -1.965799
9    0.8 -1.933930
10   0.9 -1.916188
11   1.0 -1.910345
> out_rk <- ode(y = -3, times = seq(0, 1, by = 0.1),
+                 func = fn, parms = NULL,
+                 method = "rk4")
> out_rk
  time         1
1    0.0 -3.000000
2    0.1 -2.736364
3    0.2 -2.533333
4    0.3 -2.376922
5    0.4 -2.257142
6    0.5 -2.166666
7    0.6 -2.099999
8    0.7 -2.052940
9    0.8 -2.022221
10   0.9 -2.005262
11   1.0 -1.999999
> RHS <- "((y[t]^2 + 2*y[t]*T)/(3 + T^2))"
> res_eu <- ode_euler(RHS, -3, h = 0.1,
+                       periods = 10)$results
> res_eu
    t        yt
1  0.0 -3.000000
2  0.1 -2.700000
3  0.2 -2.475748
4  0.3 -2.306701
5  0.4 -2.179295
6  0.5 -2.084171
7  0.6 -2.014645
8  0.7 -1.965799
9  0.8 -1.933930
10 0.9 -1.916188
11 1.0 -1.910345
> res_kr <- ode_RungeKutta(RHS, -3, h = 0.1,
+                            periods = 10)
> res_kr$results
    t        yt
```

```
1   0.0 -3.000000
2   0.1 -2.736364
3   0.2 -2.533333
4   0.3 -2.376922
5   0.4 -2.257142
6   0.5 -2.166666
7   0.6 -2.099999
8   0.7 -2.052940
9   0.8 -2.022221
10  0.9 -2.005262
11  1.0 -1.999999
```

Let's rewrite `ode_euler()` and `ode_RungeKutta()` in a `deSolve` "fashion".

```
> ode_euler_deSolve <- function(y0, t, func, parms){
+
+   y <- numeric(length(t)-1)
+   y[1] <- y0
+   h <- t[2] - t[1]
+
+   for(i in seq_along(y)){
+
+     t[i+1] <- t[i] + h
+     y[i+1] <- y[i] + func(t[i], y[i], parms)*h
+
+   }
+
+   out <- data.frame(time = t,
+                     yt = y)
+
+   return(out)
+
+ }
> ode_rk_deSolve <- function(y0, t, func, parms){
+
+   y <- numeric(length(t)-1)
+   y[1] <- y0
+   h <- t[2] - t[1]
+
+   K1 <- numeric(length(t)-1)
+   K2 <- numeric(length(t)-1)
+   K3 <- numeric(length(t)-1)
+   K4 <- numeric(length(t)-1)
+
+   for(i in seq_along(y)){
+
```

```
+     K1[i] <- func(t[i], y[i], parms)
+
+     K2[i] <- func(t[i] + (1/2)*h, y[i] + (1/2)*h*K1[i], parms)
+
+     K3[i] <- func(t[i] + (1/2)*h, y[i] + (1/2)*h*K2[i], parms)
+
+     K4[i] <- func(t[i] + h, y[i] + h*K3[i], parms)
+
+     y[i+1] <- y[i] + (h/6) * (K1[i] + 2*K2[i] + 2*K3[i] + K4[i])
+
+   }
+
+   out <- data.frame(time = t, yt = y)
+   return(out)
+
+ }
```

Now let's test them with $y' = 1 - t + 4y$.

```
> fn <- function(t, y, parms){
+   a <- parms[1]
+   b <- parms[2]
+   dy <- a - t + b*y
+   return(dy)
+ }
> res_eu <- ode_euler_deSolve(y0 = 1,
+                             t = seq(0, 0.1, by = 0.01),
+                             func = fn, parms = c(1, 4))
> res_eu
   time       yt
1  0.00 1.000000
2  0.01 1.050000
3  0.02 1.101900
4  0.03 1.155776
5  0.04 1.211707
6  0.05 1.269775
7  0.06 1.330066
8  0.07 1.392669
9  0.08 1.457676
10 0.09 1.525183
11 0.10 1.595290
> res_rk <- ode_rk_deSolve(y0 = 1,
+                          t = seq(0, 0.1, by = 0.01),
+                          func = fn, parms = c(1, 4))
> res_rk
   time       yt
1  0.00 1.000000
2  0.01 1.050963
```

```
3  0.02 1.103903
4  0.03 1.158903
5  0.04 1.216044
6  0.05 1.275416
7  0.06 1.337108
8  0.07 1.401217
9  0.08 1.467839
10 0.09 1.537079
11 0.10 1.609042
```

Similarly, we can solve a system of differential equations in deSolve. As an example, let's solve the Lotka-Volterra model as in Sect. 11.5.2.1

```
> LV_model <- function(t, y, parms){
+    x <- y[1]
+    y <- y[2]
+    a <- parms[1]
+    b <- parms[2]
+    d <- parms[3]
+    c <- parms[4]
+    dy <- numeric(2)
+    dy[1] <- a*x - b*x*y
+    dy[2] <- d*x*y - c*y
+    list(dy)
+ }
> times <- seq(0, 1, by = 0.01)
> yini <- c(6, 4)
> out <- ode(y = yini, times = times, func = LV_model,
+              parms = c(2, 1, 0.5, 2), method = "rk4")
> head(out)
     time        1        2
[1,] 0.00 6.000000 4.000000
[2,] 0.01 5.880036 4.038989
[3,] 0.02 5.760283 4.075914
[4,] 0.03 5.640945 4.110719
[5,] 0.04 5.522217 4.143354
[6,] 0.05 5.404284 4.173777
```

Finally, we solve the second order differential equation from Sect. 11.6

```
> ode2_model <- function(t, y, parms){
+   v <- y[2]
+   y <- y[1]
+   a <- parms[1]
+   b <- parms[2]
+   c <- parms[3]
+   dy <- numeric(2)
+   dy[1] <- a*v
```

```
+   dy[2] <- b*v - c*y
+   list(dy)
+ }
> times <- seq(0, 1, by = 0.01)
> yini <- c(2, 5)
> out_eu <- ode(y = yini, times = times, func = ode2_model,
+              parms = c(1, 3, 2), method = "euler")
> head(out_eu)
     time        1        2
[1,] 0.00 2.000000 5.000000
[2,] 0.01 2.050000 5.110000
[3,] 0.02 2.101100 5.222300
[4,] 0.03 2.153323 5.336947
[5,] 0.04 2.206692 5.453989
[6,] 0.05 2.261232 5.573475
> out_rk <- ode(y = yini, times = times, func = ode2_model,
+              parms = c(1, 3, 2), method = "rk4")
> head(out_rk)
     time        1        2
[1,] 0.00 2.000000 5.000000
[2,] 0.01 2.050554 5.111158
[3,] 0.02 2.102231 5.224663
[4,] 0.03 2.155055 5.340565
[5,] 0.04 2.209050 5.458912
[6,] 0.05 2.264242 5.579754
```

11.8 Applications in Economics

11.8.1 A Problem with Interest Rate

The growth of a principal P in a bank account where the interest rate r is compounded continuously can be described by the following differential equation

$$\frac{dP}{dt} = rP$$

where $\frac{dP}{dt}$ is the rate of change of the value of the principal. This quantity is equal to the rate at which the interest accrues , i.e. the interest rate times the current value of the principal.

We can solve this differential equation with the method of separation of variables

$$\frac{dP}{P} = r\ dt$$

$$\int \frac{1}{P} dP = r \int dt$$

$$\log|P| = rt + c$$

$$e^{\log|P|} = e^{rt+c}$$

$$P = ce^{rt}$$

Let A denote the principal at $t = 0$, meaning that $c = A$. Consequently,

$$P(t) = Ae^{rt} \tag{11.62}$$

Compare (11.62) with (3.26).

Let's now assume that deposits take place at a constant rate d. The differential equation becomes

$$\frac{dP}{dt} = rP + d$$

We can solve it with the method of integrating factor.

Step 1
Rewrite the differential equation in the standard form

$$\frac{dP}{dt} - rP = d$$

Step 2
Compute the integrating factor

$$\mu(t) = e^{\int -r\,dt} = e^{-rt}$$

Step 3
Multiply both sides of the differential equation by the integrating factor

$$e^{-rt}\left[\frac{dP}{dt} - rP = d\right]$$

Step 4
Integrate both sides

$$e^{-rt}P = -\frac{de^{-rt}}{r} + c$$

$$P = -\frac{d}{r} + ce^{rt}$$

Let P_0 denote the principal at $t = 0$

$$P(t) = -\frac{d}{r} + \left(P_0 + \frac{d}{r}\right)e^{rt}$$

that can be rewritten as

$$P(t) = P_0 e^{rt} + \frac{d}{r}\left(e^{rt} - 1\right) \tag{11.63}$$

where the first term of (11.63) is the part of $P(t)$ due to the interest rate paid on the initial amount P_0, while the second term of $P(t)$ is the part of $P(t)$ due to the deposit rate d.

Let's check our solution with **R**

```
> P0 <- 5000
> d <- 1000
> r <- 0.08
> t <- seq(0, 40, 0.01)
> Pt <- P0*exp(r*t) + (d/r)*(exp(r*t) - 1)
> tail(Pt)
[1] 415105.4 415447.7 415790.1 416132.9 416476.0 416819.3
> invest <- function(t, P, parms){
+   d <- parms[1]
+   r <- parms[2]
+   dP <- r*P + d
+   list(dP)
+ }
> out <- ode(y = P0, times = t, func = invest,
+            parms = c(1000, 0.08),
+            method = "rk4")
> tail(out)
         time        1
[3996,] 39.95 415105.4
[3997,] 39.96 415447.7
[3998,] 39.97 415790.1
[3999,] 39.98 416132.9
```

```
[4000,] 39.99 416476.0
[4001,] 40.00 416819.3
```

that is after 40 years of investment the amount accumulated is $P(40) =$ \$416,819, composed of

```
> P0*exp(r*40)
[1] 122662.7
> (d/r)*(exp(r*40) - 1)
[1] 294156.6
```

i.e. \$122,663 due to the interest paid on the initial amount and \$294,157 due to the deposit rate.

11.8.2 Advertising Model

A producer to sell its products needs to inform consumers about it. Advertising can accomplish this task. Thus, let's investigate the effect of advertising on sales. First, we set up a simple model of sales in the absence of advertising. Then, we consider that the producer invests in an advertising campaign.

By assuming that without advertising sales decrease at a constant rate r which is proportional to the sales S at that time, we can write a differential equation that describes the decrease in sales

$$\dot{S} = -rS \tag{11.64}$$

whose solution is $S(t) = S_0 e^{-rt}$, where S_0 denotes initial sales. Figure 11.22 shows the results of (11.64) with $S_0 = 1000$ and $r = 0.05$. We observe that sales in the case of no advertising decline to zero over time. Indeed, zero is the equilibrium point of this model.

```
> no_adv_model <- function(t, S, parms){
+   r <- parms[1]
+   dS <- -r*S
+   list(dS)
+ }
> S0 <- 1000
> t <- seq(0, 50, by = 0.01)
> no_adv_sales <- ode(y = S0, times = t, func = no_adv_model,
+                      parms = 0.05,
+                      method = "rk4")
> no_adv_stability <- stability(no_adv_model, ystar = 0,
+                      parameters = 0.05,
+                      system = "one.dim")
discriminant = -0.05, classification = Stable
```

Therefore, to keep up sales, the producer decides to invest in advertising. To rewrite the model we make two assumptions

1. the rate of increase in sales due to advertising is directly proportional to the rate of advertising
2. given M the maximum value of the market for sales of the product, the increase in sales due to advertising affects only the portion of the market that has not purchased the product yet $\frac{M-S}{M}$

   Therefore, the differential equation becomes

$$\dot{S} = -rS + \alpha A\left(\frac{M-S}{M}\right) \tag{11.65}$$

where α is the proportion of sales improved by advertising and A is the constant rate of advertising (say in US dollar).

It can be rearranged as follows

$$\dot{S} = -\left(r + \frac{\alpha A}{M}\right)S + \alpha A$$

Let's solve (11.65) with the method of integrating factor.

$$\dot{S} + \left(r + \frac{\alpha A}{M}\right)S = \alpha A$$

For convenience let's set $b = r + \frac{\alpha A}{M}$. Therefore

$$\dot{S} + bS = \alpha A$$

$$\mu(t) = e^{bt}$$

$$e^{bt}S = \alpha A \int e^{bt}\,dt$$

After integrating the right-hand side by substitution we get

$$e^{bt}S = \frac{\alpha A}{b}e^{bt} + c$$

$$S = \frac{\alpha A}{b} + ce^{-bt}$$

At $t = 0$, $S = S_0$

$$c = S_0 - \frac{\alpha A}{b}$$

The solution is

$$S(t) = \frac{\alpha A}{b} + \left(S_0 - \frac{\alpha A}{b} \right) e^{-bt}$$

that we can rewrite as

$$S(t) = S_0 e^{-bt} + \frac{\alpha A}{b} \left(1 - e^{-bt} \right)$$

Let's check our solution with **R** where we set $\alpha = 0.2$, $A = 10$, $M = 5000$

```
> r <- 0.05
> alpha <- 0.2
> A <- 10
> M <- 5000
> b <- (r + (alpha*A)/M)
> St <- S0*exp(-b*t) +
+    ((alpha*A)/b)*(1 - exp(-b*t))
> head(St)
[1] 1000.0000  999.5161  999.0325  998.5491  998.0660
     997.5830
> adv_model <- function(t, S, parms){
+    r <- parms[1]
+    alpha <- parms[2]
+    A <- parms[3]
+    M <- parms[4]
+    dS <- -r*S + (alpha*A)*((M - S)/M)
+    list(dS)
+ }
> adv_sales <- ode(y = S0, times = t, func = adv_model,
+                   parms = c(0.05, 0.2, 10, 5000),
+                   method = "rk4")
> head(adv_sales)
     time         1
[1,] 0.00 1000.0000
[2,] 0.01  999.5161
[3,] 0.02  999.0325
[4,] 0.03  998.5491
[5,] 0.04  998.0660
[6,] 0.05  997.5830
```

Let's find the equilibrium point, i.e. $\dot{S} = 0$

$$-\left(r + \frac{\alpha A}{M} \right) S + \alpha A = 0$$

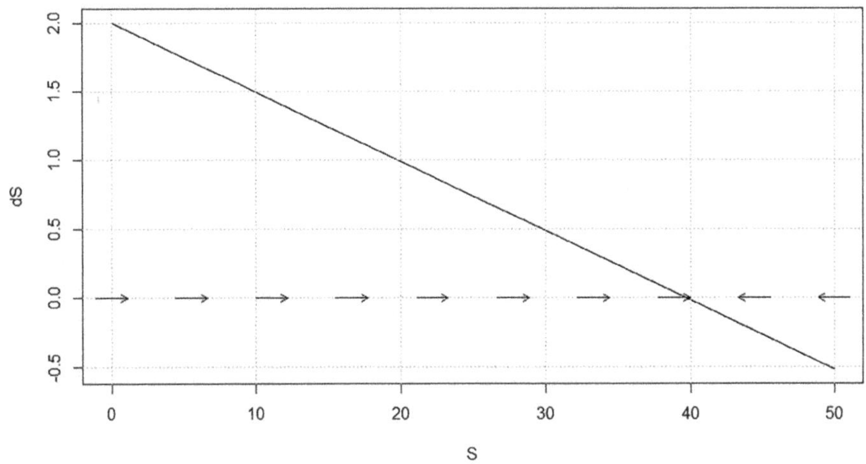

Fig. 11.21 Advertising model - phase diagram

$$S^* = \frac{\alpha AM}{rM + \alpha A}$$

```
> Sstar <- (alpha*A*M)/(r*M + alpha*A)
> Sstar
[1] 39.68254
> adv_stability <- stability(adv_model, ystar = Sstar,
+                            parameters = c(0.05, 0.2, 10, 5000),
+                            system = "one.dim")
discriminant = -0.0504, classification = Stable
```

Figure 11.21 shows that S^* is an attractor.

```
> adv_phasePortrait <- phasePortrait(adv_model,
+                                   ylim = c(0, 50),
+                                   parameters = c(0.05, 0.2,10,5000),
+                                   points = 10, frac = 0.4,
+                                   state.names = "S")
```

Let's plot the solution for the model without advertising and the model with advertising. Figure 11.22 shows that advertising curbs the decline in sales.

```
> plot(no_adv_sales, adv_sales, lwd = 2, main = " ")
> legend("topright",
+        legend = c("with no advertising",
+                   "with advertising"),
+        lwd = 2,
+        lty = c("solid", "dashed"),
+        col = c("black", "red"))
```

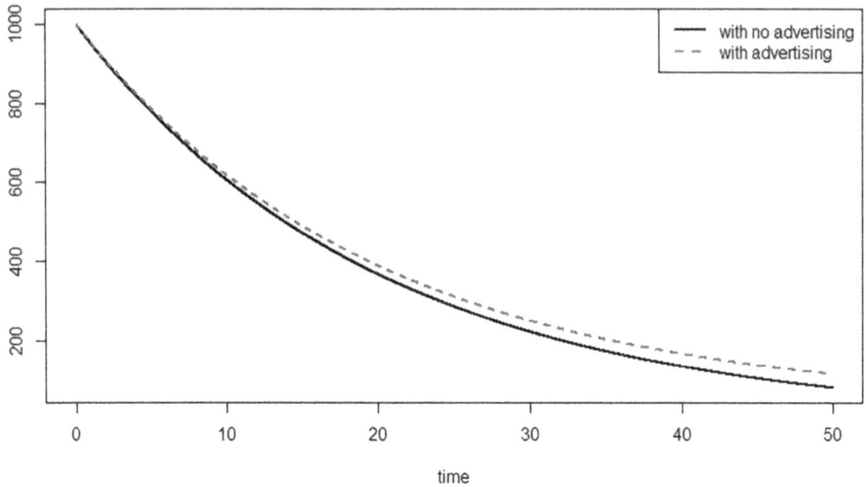

Fig. 11.22 Advertising model

Indeed, advertising prevents sales from falling below S^*. Let's check it by setting a longer time sequence.

```
> t <- seq(0, 500, by = 0.01)
> adv_sales2 <- ode(y = S0, times = t, func = adv_model,
+                   parms = c(0.05, 0.2, 10, 5000),
+                   method = "rk4")
> tail(adv_sales2)
          time        1
[49996,] 499.95 39.68254
[49997,] 499.96 39.68254
[49998,] 499.97 39.68254
[49999,] 499.98 39.68254
[50000,] 499.99 39.68254
[50001,] 500.00 39.68254
```

11.8.3 The Harrod-Domar Growth Model

In this section we solve the Harrod-Domar growth model in continuous time specified as follows

$$S = sY \tag{11.66}$$

$$I = \dot{K} = v\dot{Y} \tag{11.67}$$

$$I = S \tag{11.68}$$

where S, savings, is assumed proportional to income Y, and I, investment, that is the change in capital stock K, is proportional to the change in income between time periods. In equilibrium, investment is equal to savings.

Let's replace (11.66) and (11.67) in (11.68)

$$v\dot{Y} = sY$$

Let's divide both sides through v

$$\dot{Y} = \frac{s}{v}Y$$

This is a first-order differential equation. Let's use the notation $\frac{dY}{dt}$ instead of $\dot{Y}$

$$\frac{dY}{dt} = \frac{s}{v}Y \tag{11.69}$$

Now it is clearer that we can solve it with the method of separation of variables

$$\frac{dY}{Y} = \frac{s}{v}dt$$

$$\int \frac{dY}{Y} = \int \frac{s}{v}dt$$

$$\log Y = \frac{s}{v}t + c$$

$$Y = e^{\frac{s}{v}t+c}$$

$$Y = e^{\frac{s}{v}t} \cdot e^{c}$$

$$Y = ce^{\frac{s}{v}t}$$

At $t = 0$, $Y = Y_0$

$$Y_0 = ce^{\frac{s}{v}\cdot 0}$$

$$c = Y_0$$

$$Y(t) = Y_0 e^{\frac{s}{v}t} \tag{11.70}$$

Verification of the solution

Step 1
Find $\frac{dY}{dt}$ of (11.70)

$$\frac{dY}{dt} = \frac{s}{v} Y_0 e^{\frac{s}{v}t}$$

Step 2
Plug (11.70) in the right-hand side of (11.69)

$$\frac{s}{v}\left(Y_0 e^{\frac{s}{v}t}\right)$$

Step 3
The two sides are equal therefore we found a solution.

Equilibrium
The equilibrium point of this model is

$$\dot{Y} = 0 \rightarrow \frac{s}{v} Y = 0 \rightarrow Y^* = 0$$

11.8.4 The Solow Growth Model

The Solow growth model is one of the main models students learn in a course of Macroeconomics.

Briefly, we specify the model as follows

1. production function $Y = f(K, L)$: continuous, twice differentiable and homogeneous of degree one
2. labour force L: L grows at a constant rate n, $\dot{L} = nL$
3. savings S: S is constant fraction of output $S = sY$
4. investment I: I is equal to the sum of the change in capital stock and the replacement of capital $I = \dot{K} + \delta K$
5. savings equal investment $S = I$

Let's assume a Cobb-Douglas production function (Sect. 6.1.1.2)

$$Y = AK^{\alpha} L^{1-\alpha}, \quad 0 < \alpha < 1 \tag{11.71}$$

Divide both sides by L

$$\frac{Y}{L} = \frac{AK^{\alpha}L^{1-\alpha}}{L}$$

$$\frac{Y}{L} = AK^{\alpha}L^{-\alpha}$$

$$\frac{Y}{L} = A\left(\frac{K}{L}\right)^{\alpha}$$

Let $y = \frac{Y}{L}$ denote the output/labour ration and $k = \frac{K}{L}$ the capital/labour ratio

$$y = f(k) = Ak^{\alpha} \tag{11.72}$$

Next, we take the derivative of k with respect to time, i.e.

$$\frac{dk}{dt} = \dot{k} = \frac{L\frac{dK}{dt} - K\frac{dL}{dt}}{L^2}$$

Rearrange and simplify

$$\dot{k} = \left(\frac{1}{L}\right)\frac{dK}{dt} - \left(\frac{K}{L}\right)\left(\frac{1}{L}\right)\frac{dL}{dt}$$

Substitute $\frac{1}{L} = \frac{K}{L}\frac{1}{K}$

$$\dot{k} = \left(\frac{K}{L}\right)\left(\frac{1}{K}\right)\frac{dK}{dt} - \left(\frac{K}{L}\right)\left(\frac{1}{L}\right)\frac{dL}{dt}$$

Substitute $k = \frac{K}{L}$, $\dot{K} = \frac{dK}{dt}$, and $\dot{L} = \frac{dL}{dt}$ and rearrange

$$\dot{k} = k\left(\frac{\dot{K}}{K} - \frac{\dot{L}}{L}\right) \tag{11.73}$$

From the investment equation

$$\dot{K} = I - \delta K$$

and since $S = I$ we have

$$\dot{K} = sY - \delta K \tag{11.74}$$

Therefore, $\frac{\dot{K}}{K}$ in (11.73) can be rewritten as

$$\frac{sY - \delta K}{K} = \frac{sY}{L}\left(\frac{L}{K}\right) - \delta = \frac{sf(k)}{k} - \delta \tag{11.75}$$

Replace (11.72) in (11.75)

$$\frac{sAk^{\alpha}}{k} - \delta \tag{11.76}$$

By replacing (11.76) and $n = \frac{\dot{L}}{L}$ in (11.73) we have

$$\dot{k} = sAk^{\alpha} - \delta k - nk$$

$$\dot{k} = sAk^{\alpha} - (\delta + n)k \tag{11.77}$$

Rewrite (11.77) as

$$\dot{k} + (\delta + n)k = sAk^{\alpha} \tag{11.78}$$

This is a Bernoulli equation. Therefore, we can solve it as in Sect. 11.2.5

$$v = k^{1-\alpha}$$

$$\frac{dv}{dt} = (1-\alpha)k^{-\alpha}\dot{k}$$

$$\dot{k} = \frac{k^{\alpha}}{1-\alpha}\frac{dv}{dt} \tag{11.79}$$

Substitute (11.79) in (11.78)

$$\frac{k^{\alpha}}{1-\alpha}\frac{dv}{dt} + (\delta + n)k = sAk^{\alpha}$$

Divide it through $\frac{k^{\alpha}}{1-\alpha}$

$$\frac{dv}{dt} + \frac{k^{\alpha}}{1-\alpha}(\delta + n)k = \frac{k^{\alpha}}{1-\alpha}sAk^{\alpha}$$

$$\frac{dv}{dt} + (1-\alpha)(\delta + n)k^{1-\alpha} = s(1-\alpha)A$$

Replace $v = k^{1-\alpha}$

$$\frac{dv}{dt} + (1-\alpha)(\delta+n)v = s(1-\alpha)A$$

Now it is linear in v. We can solve it with the method of integrating factor. The integrating factor is

$$\mu(t) = e^{\int (1-\alpha)(\delta+n)dt} = e^{(1-\alpha)(\delta+n)t}$$

$$e^{(1-\alpha)(\delta+n)t}\left[v' + (1-\alpha)(\delta+n)\right] = e^{(1-\alpha)(\delta+n)t}s(1-\alpha)A$$

After integrating both sides we obtain

$$e^{(1-\alpha)(\delta+n)t}v = \frac{s(1-\alpha)A}{(1-\alpha)(\delta+n)}e^{(1-\alpha)(\delta+n)t} + c$$

$$v = \frac{sA}{\delta+n} + ce^{-(1-\alpha)(\delta+n)t}$$

At $t = 0$, $v = v_0$

$$v_0 = \frac{sA}{\delta+n} + ce^{-(1-\alpha)(\delta+n)\cdot 0}$$

$$v_0 = \frac{sA}{\delta+n} + c \to c = v_0 - \frac{sA}{\delta+n}$$

$$v(t) = \frac{sA}{\delta+n} + \left(v_0 - \frac{sA}{\delta+n}\right)e^{-(1-\alpha)(\delta+n)t}$$

Substitute $v = k^{1-\alpha}$ and $v_0 = k_0^{1-\alpha}$

$$k^{1-\alpha} = \frac{sA}{\delta+n} + \left(k_0^{1-\alpha} - \frac{sA}{\delta+n}\right)e^{-(1-\alpha)(\delta+n)t}$$

and solve for k

$$k(t) = \left[\frac{sA}{\delta+n} + \left(k_0^{1-\alpha} - \frac{sA}{\delta+n}\right)e^{-(1-\alpha)(\delta+n)t}\right]^{\frac{1}{1-\alpha}} \tag{11.80}$$

Let's check our solution

```
> A <- 1
> alpha <- 0.3
> delta <- 0.05
> n <- 0.01
> s <- 0.4
> k0 <- 0.1
> t <- seq(0, 1, by = 0.01)
> kt <- ((s*A)/(n + delta) +
+          exp(-(1 - alpha)*(n + delta)*t)*
+          (k0^(1 - alpha) - (s*A)/(n + delta)))^(1/(1 - alpha))
> res <- data.frame(t, kt)
> head(res)
     t        kt
1 0.00 0.1000000
2 0.01 0.1019500
3 0.02 0.1039104
4 0.03 0.1058812
5 0.04 0.1078622
6 0.05 0.1098533
> tail(res)
       t        kt
96  0.95 0.3221114
97  0.96 0.3247683
98  0.97 0.3274307
99  0.98 0.3300984
100 0.99 0.3327715
101 1.00 0.3354499
```

With deSolve

```
> solow_model <- function(t, k, parms){
+   A <- parms[1]
+   alpha <- parms[2]
+   delta <- parms[3]
+   n <- parms[4]
+   s <- parms[5]
+   dk <- s*A*k^(alpha) - (n + delta)*k
+   list(dk)
+ }
> out <- ode(y = k0, times = t, func = solow_model,
+            parms = c(1, 0.3, 0.05, 0.01, 0.4),
+            method = "rk4")
> head(out)
     time         1
[1,] 0.00 0.1000000
[2,] 0.01 0.1019500
[3,] 0.02 0.1039104
[4,] 0.03 0.1058812
```

```
[5,] 0.04 0.1078622
[6,] 0.05 0.1098533
> tail(out)
       time         1
 [96,] 0.95 0.3221114
 [97,] 0.96 0.3247683
 [98,] 0.97 0.3274307
 [99,] 0.98 0.3300984
[100,] 0.99 0.3327715
[101,] 1.00 0.3354499
```

Let's find the equilibrium points. We set $\dot{k} = 0$, i.e.

$$sAk^{\alpha} - (\delta + n)k = 0$$

$$k\left[sAk^{\alpha}k^{-1} - (\delta + n)\right] = 0$$

$$k_1^* = 0$$

$$sAk^{\alpha-1} - (\delta + n) = 0$$

$$k_2^* = \left(\frac{sA}{\delta + n}\right)^{-\frac{1}{\alpha-1}}$$

```
> k2star <- ((s*A)/(n + delta))^(-(1/(alpha - 1)))
> k2star
[1] 15.03185
> solow_stabilty <- stability(solow_model, ystar = k2star,
+                              parameters = c(1, 0.3,0.05,0.01,0.4),
+                              system = "one.dim",
+                              summary = FALSE)
> solow_stabilty$classification
[1] "Stable"
```

Let's conclude this section with graphical representation of the model (Figs. 11.23, 11.24, 11.25).

```
> t <- seq(0, 100, by = 0.01)
> kini1 <- 0.1
> out1 <- ode(y = kini1, times = t, func = solow_model,
+             parms = c(1, 0.3, 0.05, 0.01, 0.4),
+             method = "rk4")
> kini2 <- 5
> out2 <- ode(y = kini2, times = t, func = solow_model,
+              parms = c(1, 0.3, 0.05, 0.01, 0.4),
```

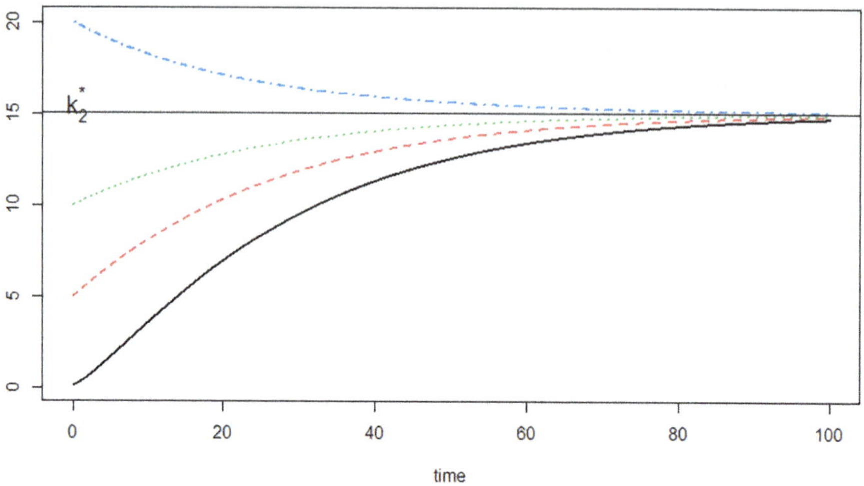

Fig. 11.23 Solow model - time series plot

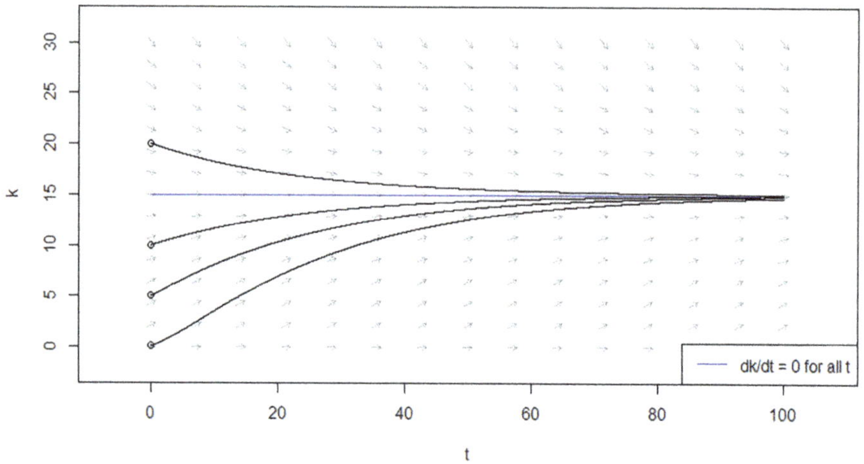

Fig. 11.24 Solow model - direction field

```
+               method = "rk4")
> kini3 <- 10
> out3 <- ode(y = kini3, times = t, func = solow_model,
+               parms = c(1, 0.3, 0.05, 0.01, 0.4),
+               method = "rk4")
> kini4 <- 20
> out4 <- ode(y = kini4, times = t, func = solow_model,
+               parms = c(1, 0.3, 0.05, 0.01, 0.4),
+               method = "rk4")
> plot(out1, out2, out3, out4, lwd = 2, main = " ")
> abline(h = k2star)
```

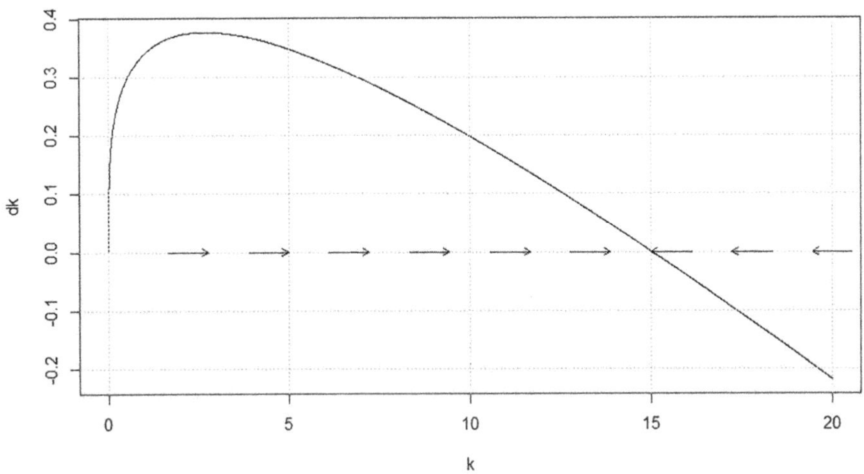

Fig. 11.25 Solow model - phase diagram

```
> text(x = 0.5, y = (k2star + 0.5),
+      expression(k[2]^"*"), cex = 1.5)

> solow_flowField <- flowField(solow_model,
+                              xlim = c(0, 100),
+                              ylim = c(0, 30),
+                              parameters = c(1, 0.3,
+                                             0.05, 0.01, 0.4),
+                              system = "one.dim", points = 15,
+                              state.names = "k",
+                              add = FALSE)
> solow_nullclines <- nullclines(solow_model,
+                                xlim = c(0, 100),
+                                ylim = c(-10, 30),
+                                parameters = c(1, 0.3,
+                                               0.05, 0.01, 0.4),
+                                system = "one.dim",
+                                state.names = "k")
> solow_trajectory <- trajectory(solow_model,
+                                y0 = c(0.1, 5, 10, 20),
+                                tlim = c(0, 100),
+                                parameters = c(1, 0.3,
+                                               0.05, 0.01, 0.4),
+                                system = "one.dim")
Note: col has been reset as required

> solow_phasePortrait <- phasePortrait(solow_model,
+                                      ylim = c(0, 20),
+                                      parameters = c(1, 0.3,
+                                              0.05, 0.01, 0.4),
+                                      points = 10, frac = 0.5,
+                                      state.names = "k")
```

11.9 Exercises

Write a code to implement the Runge-Kutta algorithm to solve systems of first-order differential equations (Sect. 11.5) and second-order differential equations upon transformation into a system of two first-order differential equations (Sect. 11.6).

The Runge-Kutta algorithm for systems of first-order differential equations is the following

$$M_1 = f(t_n, x_n, y_n)$$
$$L_1 = g(t_n, x_n, y_n)$$

$$M_2 = f\left(t_n + \frac{h}{2}, x_n + \frac{hM_1}{2}, y_n + \frac{hL_1}{2}\right)$$

$$L_2 = g\left(t_n + \frac{h}{2}, x_n + \frac{hM_1}{2}, y_n + \frac{hL_1}{2}\right)$$

$$M_3 = f\left(t_n + \frac{h}{2}, x_n + \frac{hM_2}{2}, y_n + \frac{hL_2}{2}\right)$$

$$L_3 = g\left(t_n + \frac{h}{2}, x_n + \frac{hM_2}{2}, y_n + \frac{hL_2}{2}\right)$$

$$M_4 = f(t_n + h, x_n + hM_3, y_n + hL_3)$$

$$L_4 = g(t_n + h, x_n + hM_3, y_n + hL_3)$$

$$x_{n+1} = x_n + \frac{h}{6}(M_1 + 2M_2 + 2M_3 + M_4)$$

$$y_{n+1} = y_n + \frac{h}{6}(L_1 + 2L_2 + 2L_3 + L_4)$$

The reader may refer to Giordano and Weir (1991, pp. 456-460) for the details.

The Runge-Kutta algorithm to solve second-order differential equations upon transformation into a system of two first-order differential equations slightly differs from the previous one

$$M_1 = v_n$$

$$L_1 = g(t_n, y_n, v_n)$$

$$M_2 = v_n + \frac{hL_1}{2}$$

$$L_2 = g\left(t_n + \frac{h}{2}, y_n + \frac{hM_1}{2}, v_n + \frac{hL_1}{2}\right)$$

$$M_3 = v_n + \frac{hL_2}{2}$$

$$L_3 = g\left(t_n + \frac{h}{2}, y_n + \frac{hM_2}{2}, v_n + \frac{hL_2}{2}\right)$$

$$M_4 = v_n + hL_3$$

$$L_4 = g(t_n + h, y_n + hM_3, v_n + hL_3)$$

$$y_{n+1} = y_n + \frac{h}{6}(M_1 + 2M_2 + 2M_3 + M_4)$$

$$v_{n+1} = v_n + \frac{h}{6}(L_1 + 2L_2 + 2L_3 + L_4)$$

where variable v represents the derivative y'. The reader may refer to Giordano and Weir (1991, pp. 274-280) for the details.

Appendix A
Packages Used in Chapters

Load the following packages before starting to replicate the code in the respective chapter.

Chapter 2:

```
> library("RVenn")
> library("ggplot2")
> library("ggpubr")
> library("plot3D")
> library("pracma")
> library("matlib")
> library("zoo")
> library("blockmatrix")
> library("mosaic")
> library("manipulate")
> library("data.table")
> library("tidyr")
> library("igraph")
```

Chapter 3:

```
> library("ggplot2")
> library("ggpubr")
> library("data.table")
> library("polynom")
> library("pracma")
```

Chapter 4:

```
> library("ggplot2")
> library("ggpubr")
> library("scales")
> library("data.table")
> library("tidyr")
> library("Deriv")
> library("gganimate")
> library("gifski")
> library("png")
```


M. Porto, *Introduction to Mathematics for Economics with R*,
https://doi.org/10.1007/978-3-031-05202-6

Chapter 5:

```
> library("pracma")
> library("ggplot2")
> library("ggpubr")
> library("scales")
> library("data.table")
> library("mosaicCalc")
```

Chapter 6:

```
> library("Deriv")
> library("pracma")
> library("mosaic")
> library("manipulate")
> library("stargazer")
> library("ggplot2")
```

Chapter 7

```
> library("matlib")
> library("ggplot2")
> library("pracma")
> library("lpSolve")
> library("nloptr")
> library("leaflet")
> library("nleqslv")
```

Chapter 8

```
> library("ggplot2")
> library("data.table")
```

Chapter 9

```
> library("ggplot2")
```

Chapter 10

```
> library("ggplot2")
> library("scales")
> library("ggpubr")
> library("expm")
> library("tidyr")
```

Chapter 11

```
> library("ggplot2")
> library("scales")
> library("ggpubr")
> library("tidyr")
> library("deSolve")
> library("phaseR")
> library("dplyr")
```

Appendix B
Appendix to Chap. 2

Code to Replicate Fig. 2.3

To build Fig. 2.3, we define the coordinates for the points we want to draw and we define which points to connect. These data are stored in two different data frames. We repeat these operations for the four cases. In addition, we store the title for each of them in an object. We store the information for each of them in a list class object. Finally, we store all the list objects in one list, `DF_l`.

```
> df_a <- data.frame(X = c(6, 20), Y = c(10, 10))
> x_point <- c(20, 5.5, 20, 5.5, 20, 5.5, 20)
> # general
> y_point <- c(6.5, 8.5, 8.5, 10.5, 10.5, 12.5, 12.5)
> df_point_gn <- data.frame(x_point, y_point)
> title_gn <- "General"
> x <- c(5.5, 5.5, 5.5)
> xend <- c(20, 20, 20)
> y <- c(8.5, 12.5, 10.5)
> yend <- c(8.5, 10.5, 10.5)
> df_s_gn <- data.frame(x, xend, y, yend)
> df_gn_list <- list(df_point = df_point_gn,
+                    df_s = df_s_gn,
+                    title = title_gn)
> # bijective
> x_point <- c(5.5, 20, 5.5, 20, 5.5, 20, 5.5, 20)
> y_point <- c(6.5, 6.5, 8.5, 8.5, 10.5, 10.5, 12.5, 12.5)
> df_point_bj <- data.frame(x_point, y_point)
> title_bj <- "Bijective"
> x <- c(5.5, 5.5, 5.5, 5.5)
> xend <- c(20, 20, 20, 20)
> y <- c(6.5, 8.5, 10.5, 12.5)
> yend <- c(6.5, 8.5, 10.5, 12.5 )
> df_s_bj <- data.frame(x, xend, y, yend)
> df_bj_list <- list(df_point = df_point_bj,
+                    df_s = df_s_bj,
```


M. Porto, *Introduction to Mathematics for Economics with R*,
https://doi.org/10.1007/978-3-031-05202-6

```
+                      title = title_bj)
> # injective
> x_point <- c(5.5, 20, 5.5, 20, 20, 5.5, 20)
> y_point <- c(6.5, 6.5, 8.5, 8.5, 10.5, 12.5, 12.5)
> df_point_ij <- data.frame(x_point, y_point)
> title_ij <- "Injective"
> x <- c(5.5, 5.5, 5.5)
> xend <- c(20, 20, 20)
> y <- c(6.5, 8.5, 12.5)
> yend <- c(6.5, 8.5, 12.5)
> df_s_ij <- data.frame(x, xend, y, yend)
> df_ij_list <- list(df_point = df_point_ij,
+                      df_s = df_s_ij,
+                      title = title_ij)
> # surjective
> x_point <- c(5.5, 20, 5.5, 20, 5.5, 20, 5.5)
> y_point <- c(6.5, 6.5, 8.5, 8.5, 10.5, 10.5, 12.5)
> df_point_sj <- data.frame(x_point, y_point)
> title_sj <- "Surjective"
> x <- c(5.5, 5.5, 5.5, 5.5)
> xend <- c(20, 20, 20, 20)
> y <- c(6.5, 8.5, 12.5, 10.5)
> yend <- c(6.5, 8.5, 10.5, 10.5)
> df_s_sj <- data.frame(x, xend, y, yend)
> df_sj_list <- list(df_point = df_point_sj,
+                      df_s = df_s_sj,
+                      title = title_sj)
> DF_l <- list(df_gn_list, df_bj_list,
+                df_ij_list, df_sj_list)
```

Let's have a look at the first list stored in DF_l by using the square brackets operator, DF_l[1].

```
> DF_l[1]
[[1]]
[[1]]$df_point
  x_point y_point
1    20.0     6.5
2     5.5     8.5
3    20.0     8.5
4     5.5    10.5
5    20.0    10.5
6     5.5    12.5
7    20.0    12.5

[[1]]$df_s
    x xend    y yend
1 5.5   20  8.5  8.5
2 5.5   20 12.5 10.5
3 5.5   20 10.5 10.5

[[1]]$title
[1] "General"
```

```
> DF_l[1][[1]][["df_s"]]
    x xend    y yend
1 5.5   20  8.5  8.5
2 5.5   20 12.5 10.5
3 5.5   20 10.5 10.5
> DF_l[1][[1]]$title
[1] "General"
```

We built DF_l in order to loop over it to plot the four plots in Fig. 2.3.

First, we generate a list L that will store the four plots we will plot. We use the for() function to implement the loop. Inside the loop, we write the code to plot with ggplot2.

We use the ggplot() function from the ggplot2 package to initialize the plot. geom_point() is used to generate a scatterplot. Here, we use it to generate two large circles that represent the sets (the data in df_a), and small points that represent the elements of the sets. We control for the size, size = and the type of shape, shape =. Then we use geom_segment() to generate arrows to connect the points of the two sets. x =, y =, xend =, yend = give the starting and ending point of the segment. With arrow = we generate the arrow at the end of the segment. theme_void() produces a blank plot. annotate() is used to write a text over the graph at given coordinates.

```
> L <- list()
> for(i in 1:4){
+
+   g <- ggplot() +
+     geom_point(data = df_a, aes(x = X, y = Y),
+                size = 45, shape = 1) +
+     geom_point(data = DF_l[[i]][["df_point"]],
+                aes(x = x_point, y = y_point),
+                size = 2) +
+     geom_segment(data = DF_l[[i]][["df_s"]],
+                  aes(x = x,
+                      xend = xend,
+                      y = y,
+                      yend = yend),
+                  arrow = arrow(
+                    length = unit(0.3,
+                                  "inches"))) +
+     theme_void() +
+     xlab("") +
+     ylab("") + ggtitle(DF_l[[i]][["title"]]) +
+     coord_cartesian(xlim = c(0, 25),
+                     ylim = c(0, 25)) +
+     annotate("text", x = 5.5, y = 20,
+              label = "S") +
+     annotate("text", x = 20, y = 20,
+              label = "S'")
+
+   L[[i]] <- g
+
+ }
```

After the loop finishes to run, all the plots are stored in `L`. We extract each of the plot and we store them in individual objects. Finally, we use the `ggarrange()` function from the `ggpubr` package to arrange all the plots together in two columns and two rows.

```
> gn <- L[[1]]
> bj <- L[[2]]
> ij <- L[[3]]
> sj <- L[[4]]
> ggarrange(gn, ij,
+           sj, bj,
+           ncol = 2, nrow = 2)
```

Appendix C
Appendix to Chap. 3

Code to Replicate Fig. 3.1

```
> lqc_fn <- function(x, a = 0, b = 0, c = 1, d = 0){
+   # by default linear
+   a*x^3 + b*x^2 + c*x + d
+ }
> log_fn <- function(x, a = 1, b = 1, c = 1, d = 0, e = 0, ...){
+   #  by default natural logarithms
+   b*log(a*x^(c) + d, ...) + e
+   }
> exp_fn <- function(x, a = 1, b = 1, c = 0, d = 0){
+   a*exp(b*x + c) + d
+   }
> radical_fn <- function(x, a = 1, b = 0, c = 0){
+   a*sqrt(x + b) + c
+ }
> x <- seq(-10, 10, 0.1)
> y_lin <- lqc_fn(x)
> y_qdt <- lqc_fn(x, b = 1, c = 0)
> y_cube <- lqc_fn(x, a = 1, c = 0)
> y_log <- log_fn(x)
Warning message:
In log(a * x^(c) + d, ...) : NaNs produced
> y_exp <- exp_fn(x)
> y_rad <- radical_fn(x)
Warning message:
In sqrt(x + b) : NaNs produced
> df <- data.frame(x, y_lin, y_qdt,
+                  y_cube, y_log,
+                  y_exp, y_rad)
```

We will see different ways to plot with `ggplot()`. We start with the complicated way. Why? Because when we learn the easy way will appreciate it more.

M. Porto, *Introduction to Mathematics for Economics with R*,
https://doi.org/10.1007/978-3-031-05202-6

In Sect. 2.4.1 we used `stat_function()` in `ggplot()` to plot the function. Here, we plot the data from the data frame with the input as *x* variable and the output as *y* variable.

We write two loops. With the first loop we build the plots. With the second loop we add the title for each plot.

```
> titles <- c("linear function",
+             "quadratic function",
+             "cubic function",
+             "logarigthmic function",
+             "exponential function",
+             "radical function")
> L <- list()
> item <- names(df)[-1]
> for(i in seq_along(item)){
+   g <- ggplot() +
+     geom_line(data = df,
+               aes_string(x = "x",
+                          y = item[i])) +
+     geom_hline(yintercept = 0) +
+     geom_vline(xintercept = 0) +
+     theme_minimal() +
+     xlab("x") + ylab("y") +
+     ggtitle(titles[i])
+
+
+     L[[titles[i]]] <- g
+
+     }
```

All the plots are now stores in a list, L. We use a `for()` loop to extract all of them. We use the `assign()` function to generate the object that stores the single plot. The `gsub()` function is used to replace the white space in the name of the functions stored in `titles` with an underscore symbol. Finally, we arrange all the plots in a grid with two rows and three columns with the `ggarrange()` function from the `ggpubr` package.

```
> for(i in seq_along(titles)){
+   assign(gsub(" ", "_", titles[i], fixed = TRUE),
+          L[[titles[i]]])
+ }
> ggarrange(linear_function,
+           quadratic_function,
+           cubic_function,
+           logarigthmic_function,
+           exponential_function,
+           radical_function,
+           ncol = 2, nrow = 3)
Warning messages:
1: Removed 100 rows containing missing values (geom_path).
2: Removed 100 rows containing missing values (geom_path).
```

Code to Replicate Fig. 3.2

Note that we are not really drawing a graph of a circle. We are just enlarging one point centred at (0, 0). This trick fits our purpose. However, it may happen that your result will slightly differ from mine. If this is the case, modify the parameters. We will use again this trick in Chap. 8.

```
> circle <- ggplot(data.frame(x = 0, y = 0),
+                  aes(x, y)) +
+   geom_point(size = 100, shape = 1,
+              color = "blue") +
+   geom_hline(yintercept = 0) +
+   geom_vline(xintercept = 0) +
+   theme_minimal() +
+   xlab("x axis") +
+   ylab("y axis") +
+   coord_cartesian(xlim = c(-0.05, 0.05),
+                   ylim = c(-0.05, 0.05))
> circle + geom_vline(xintercept = 0.005,
+                     color = "red")
```

Code to Replicate Fig. 3.3

```
> x <- seq(-10, 10, 0.1)
> y1 <- lqc_fn(x, b = 1, c = 2, d = 3)
> df1 <- data.frame(x, y1)
> df11 <- data.frame(X = c(1, -1, -5, 4),
+                    Y = c(6, 2, 18, 27),
+                    Xend = c(5, 2, 7, -8),
+                    Yend = c(38, 11, 66, 51))
> g1 <- ggplot() +
+   geom_line(data = df1, aes(x, y1)) +
+   geom_segment(data = df11, aes(x = X,
+                                 y = Y,
+                                 xend = Xend,
+                                 yend = Yend)) +
+   theme_classic() +
+   labs(caption = "convex")
> y2 <- lqc_fn(x, b = -1, c = 2, d = 3)
> df2 <- data.frame(x, y2)
> df22 <- data.frame(X = c(-4, 9, 1, -2),
+                    Y = c(-21, -60, 4, -5),
+                    Xend = c(3, 5, 6, 4),
+                    Yend = c(0, -12, -21, -5))
> g2 <- ggplot() +
+   geom_line(data = df2, aes(x, y2)) +
+   geom_segment(data = df22, aes(x = X,
+                                 y = Y,
+                                 xend = Xend,
+                                 yend = Yend)) +
```

```
+   theme_classic() +
+   labs(caption = "concave")
> ggarrange(g1, g2,
+           nrow = 2,
+           ncol =1)
```

Appendix D
Appendix to Chap. 4

Code to Replicate Fig. 4.1

The following code gives a graphical representation of the limit in Fig. 4.1. First, we generate the `x` object as a sequence from -10 to 10. Then, we select the data for `x == 2`. Note that the row for `x == 2` is 1201. Therefore, we select one point to the left (row number 1199) and one point to the right (row number 1203).

```
> x <- seq(-10, 10, 0.01)
> y <- 5*x^3
> df <- data.frame(x, y)
> xy1201 <- df[x == 2, ]
> xy1201
     x  y
1201 2 40
> xy1199 <- df[1199, ]
> xy1199
        x        y
1199 1.98 38.81196
> xy1203 <- df[1203, ]
> xy1203
        x        y
1203 2.02 41.21204
```

We store these data points in `df2`.

```
> x <- c(xy1201$x, 0, xy1199$x, 0, xy1203$x, 0)
> y <- c(xy1201$y, xy1201$y, xy1199$y, xy1199$y,
+        xy1203$y, xy1203$y)
> xend <- c(xy1201$x, xy1201$x, xy1199$x, xy1199$x,
+           xy1203$x, xy1203$x)
> yend <- c(0, xy1201$y, 0, xy1199$y, 0, xy1203$y)
> df2 <- data.frame(x = x, y = y,
+                   xend = xend, yend = yend)
```


M. Porto, *Introduction to Mathematics for Economics with R*,
https://doi.org/10.1007/978-3-031-05202-6

We use `geom_segment()` in `ggplot()` to add line segments to the plot (Fig. 4.1). Try with rows 1200 and 1202 to see how $F(x)$ approaches L.

```
> ggplot(df, aes(x = x, y = y)) +
+      geom_line() +
+      geom_segment(data = df2,
+                   aes(x = x,
+                       y = y,
+                       xend = xend,
+                       yend = yend),
+                   linetype = c(rep("solid", 2),
+                                rep("dashed", 4))) +
+      geom_hline(yintercept = 0) +
+      geom_vline(xintercept = 0) +
+      theme_minimal() +
+      coord_cartesian(xlim = c(0, 2.5),
+                      ylim = c(0, 45))
```

Code to Replicate Fig. 4.2

```
> x <- seq(-10, 10, 0.01)
> Fx <- 2*x^2 + 1
> Gx <- 3*x^2 / 2
> FxplusGx <- Fx + Gx
> FxperGx <- Fx * Gx
> df <- data.frame(x, Fx, Gx,
+                  FxplusGx,
+                  FxperGx)
> head(df)
       x       Fx       Gx FxplusGx  FxperGx
1 -10.00 201.0000 150.0000 351.0000 30150.00
2  -9.99 200.6002 149.7002 350.3003 30029.88
3  -9.98 200.2008 149.4006 349.6014 29910.12
4  -9.97 199.8018 149.1014 348.9032 29790.72
5  -9.96 199.4032 148.8024 348.2056 29671.67
6  -9.95 199.0050 148.5037 347.5087 29552.99
> xy1301 <- df[x == 3, ]
> xy1301
     x Fx   Gx FxplusGx FxperGx
1301 3 19 13.5     32.5   256.5
> xy1299 <- df[1299, ]
> xy1299
        x      Fx      Gx FxplusGx  FxperGx
1299 2.98 18.7608 13.3206  32.0814 249.9051
> xy1303 <- df[1303, ]
> xy1303
        x      Fx      Gx FxplusGx  FxperGx
1303 3.02 19.2408 13.6806  32.9214 263.2257
```

Let's store these points in `df_2` as follows

```
> x <- c(xy1301$x, 0, xy1301$x, 0, xy1301$x, 0, xy1301$x, 0,
```

```
+         xy1299$x, 0, xy1303$x, 0, xy1299$x, 0, xy1303$x, 0,
+         xy1299$x, 0, xy1303$x, 0, xy1299$x, 0, xy1303$x, 0)
> y <- c(xy1301$Fx, xy1301$Fx, xy1301$Gx, xy1301$Gx,
+         xy1301$FxplusGx, xy1301$FxplusGx,
+         xy1301$FxperGx, xy1301$FxperGx,
+         xy1299$Fx, xy1299$Fx, xy1303$Fx, xy1303$Fx,
+         xy1299$Gx, xy1299$Gx,  xy1303$Gx, xy1303$Gx,
+         xy1299$FxplusGx, xy1299$FxplusGx, xy1303$FxplusGx,
+         xy1303$FxplusGx, xy1299$FxperGx, xy1299$FxperGx,
+         xy1303$FxperGx, xy1303$FxperGx)
> xend <- c(xy1301$x, xy1301$x, xy1301$x, xy1301$x, xy1301$x,
+            xy1301$x, xy1301$x, xy1301$x, xy1299$x, xy1299$x,
+            xy1303$x, xy1303$x, xy1299$x, xy1299$x, xy1303$x,
+            xy1303$x, xy1299$x, xy1299$x, xy1303$x, xy1303$x,
+            xy1299$x, xy1299$x, xy1303$x, xy1303$x)
> yend <- c(0, xy1301$Fx, 0, xy1301$Gx, 0, xy1301$FxplusGx,
+            0, xy1301$FxperGx, 0, xy1299$Fx, 0, xy1303$Fx,
+            0, xy1299$Gx, 0, xy1303$Gx, 0, xy1299$FxplusGx,
+            0, xy1303$FxplusGx, 0, xy1299$FxperGx,
+            0, xy1303$FxperGx)
> df2 <- data.frame(x = x, y = y,
+                   xend = xend, yend = yend)
```

Let's turn `df` long by using `melt()` from `data.table`.

```
> df_l <- melt(setDT(df), id.vars = "x",
+              measure.vars = c("Fx", "Gx",
+                               "FxplusGx",
+                               "FxperGx"))
```

Now we are ready to use `ggplot2` package to reproduces Fig. 4.2 where the limits of the individual functions and the limit of the addition and the limit of the multiplication of the functions are reported.

```
> ggplot() +
+   geom_line(data = df_l,
+             aes(x = x, y = value,
+                 group = variable,
+                 color = variable),
+             size = 1.2) +
+   geom_segment(data = df2,
+                aes(x = x,
+                    y = y,
+                    xend = xend,
+                    yend = yend),
+                linetype = c(rep("solid", 8),
+                             rep("dashed", 16))) +
+   geom_hline(yintercept = 0) +
+   geom_vline(xintercept = 0) +
+   theme_minimal() +
+   coord_cartesian(xlim = c(0, 3.5),
+                   ylim = c(0, 300)) +
+   theme(legend.position = "bottom",
+         legend.title = element_blank())
```

Code to Replicate Fig. 4.3

Most of this code should be clear by now. Just note that we store part of the plot in the object p because we are going to use later. In addition, we use `theme_void()` to remove all the background and `coord_fixed()` to fix the ratio of the scale coordinate system.

```
> x <- seq(0, 10, 0.1)
> y <- x
> df <- data.frame(x, y)
> p <- ggplot(df) +
+   geom_curve(aes(x = 2, xend = 7,
+                  y = 1, yend = 6.25),
+              size = 0.5,
+              curvature = 0.4) +
+   geom_point(aes(x = 5, y = 2.17),
+              size = 2.5,
+              color = "red") +
+   geom_hline(yintercept = 0) +
+   geom_vline(xintercept = 0) +
+   geom_segment(aes(x = 3.75,
+                    y = 1.2,
+                    xend = 6.25,
+                    yend = 3.15),
+                linetype = "dashed",
+                size = 1) +
+   coord_fixed() +
+   theme_void() +
+   annotate("text", x = c(7.5, -0.2),
+                    y = c(-0.2, 6.5),
+             label = c("x", "y"))

> p + geom_point(aes(x = 6.85, y = 5),
+                size = 2.5,
+                color = "blue") +
+   geom_segment(aes(x = 6.6,
+                    y = 4,
+                    xend = 7.05,
+                    yend = 6),
+                linetype = "dashed",
+                size = 1)
```

Code to Replicate Fig. 4.4

```
> p + geom_segment(aes(x = 4.1, y = 1.2,
+                      xend = 6.5,yend = 3.8),
+                  linetype = "dashed",
+                  size = 1) +
+     geom_segment(aes(x = 4.3, y = 1.2,
+                      xend = 7.1, yend = 5.2),
```

```
+                     linetype = "dashed",
+                     size = 1) +
+        annotate("text", x = c(4.9, 6.2, 6.7),
+                 y = c(2.3, 3.6, 4.8),
+                 label = c("A", "B", "C"),
+                 color = c("red", "black", "black"))
```

Code to Replicate Fig. 4.5

```
> x <- c(5, 6, 6, 0)
> y <- c(2.17, 2.17, 3, 3)
> xend <- c(5, 0, 6, 6)
> yend <- c(0, 2.17, 0, 3)
> df <- data.frame(x = x, y = y,
+                    xend = xend, yend = yend)
> p + geom_segment(data = df, aes(x = x,
+                        y = y,
+                        xend = xend,
+                        yend = yend),
+                    linetype = "dotted",
+                    size = 1) +
+    annotate("text", x = c(5, 6, -0.2, -0.05,
+                           5.5, 6.2),
+                     y = c(-0.2, -0.2, 2.17, 3,
+                           2, 2.5),
+             label = c("a", "a+dx", "f(a)", "f(a+dx)",
+                       "dx", "dy"))
```

Code to Replicate Fig. 4.6

```
> x <- seq(-10, 10, 1)
> y <- 7*x + 3
> df <- data.frame(x = x,
+                  y = y)
> ggplot(df) +
+    geom_line(aes(x = x, y = y),
+              color = "blue",
+              size = 1) +
+    geom_hline(yintercept = 31, color = "red") +
+    geom_point(aes(x = 4, y = 31), size = 2) +
+    geom_hline(yintercept = 0) +
+    geom_vline(xintercept = 0) +
+    theme_minimal()
```

Code to Replicate Fig. 4.13

```
> x <- seq(1, 5, 0.1)
> y <- -x^3 + 2*x^2 + 4*x
> df <- data.frame(x, y)
> x <- c(2, 0, 5, 5, 1)
> y <- c(0, 8, -55, 0, 5)
> xend <- c(2, 2, 0, 5, 1)
> yend <- c(8, 8, -55, -55, 0)
> df_s <- data.frame(x, y, xend, yend)
> ggplot(df, aes(x = x, y = y)) +
+       geom_line(color = "blue", size = 1) +
+       geom_hline(yintercept = 0) +
+       geom_vline(xintercept = 0) +
+       geom_point(aes(x = 2, y = 8),
+                  color = "green") +
+       geom_point(aes(x = 1, y = 5),
+                  color = "red") +
+       geom_point(aes(x = 5, y = -55),
+                  color = "red") +
+       geom_segment(data = df_s,
+                    aes(x = x,
+                        y = y,
+                        xend = xend,
+                        yend = yend),
+                    linetype = c(rep("dashed", 3),
+                                 rep("dotted", 2)),
+                    size = 1) +
+       theme_minimal() +
+       annotate("text", x = c(1, 5, 2.2, 5.2),
+                y = c(-0.4, 1.5, 10, -56.5),
+                label = c("a", "b", "(2, 8)",
+                          "(5, -55)")) +
+       coord_cartesian(xlim = c(-5, 10),
+                       ylim = c(-60, 15))
```

Appendix E
Appendix to Chap. 5

Code to Replicate Fig. 5.2

```
> x <- seq(-10, 10, 0.1)
> df <- data.frame(x)
```

Generate the two functions.

```
> y_up_fn <- function(x) {exp(x)}
> y_low_fn <- function(x) {x^2}
```

Now plot the area under the two functions (Fig. 5.2). Note that the parameter `alpha =` controls for the transparency of the colour.

```
> ggplot(df, aes(x)) +
+   stat_function(fun = y_up_fn,
+                 color = "red",
+                 size = 1) +
+   stat_function(fun = y_up_fn,
+                 xlim = c(1, 3),
+                 geom = "area",
+                 fill = "red",
+                 alpha = 0.5) +
+   stat_function(fun = y_low_fn,
+                 color = "blue",
+                 size = 1) +
+   stat_function(fun = y_low_fn,
+                 xlim = c(1, 3),
+                 geom = "area",
+                 fill = "blue",
+                 alpha = 0.3) +
+   theme_minimal() +
+   geom_hline(yintercept = 0) +
+   geom_vline(xintercept = 0) +
+   coord_cartesian(xlim = c(0, 4),
+                   ylim = c(0, 25))
```


M. Porto, *Introduction to Mathematics for Economics with R*,
https://doi.org/10.1007/978-3-031-05202-6

Code to Replicate Fig. 5.3

We use `geom_ribbon()` to fill the area between the lines. Basically, we subset the dataset between the values of the interval 1 and 3 and we define the low and up functions in, respectively, `ymin =` and `ymax =`.

```
> y_up <- exp(x)
> y_low <- x^2
> df <- cbind.data.frame(x, y_up, y_low)
> ggplot(df, aes(x, y_up)) +
+   stat_function(fun = y_up_fn,
+                 color = "red",
+                 size = 1) +
+   stat_function(fun = y_low_fn,
+                 color = "blue",
+                 size = 1) +
+   geom_ribbon(data =
+                 subset(df,
+                        1 <= x & x <= 3),
+               aes(ymin = y_low,
+                   ymax = y_up),
+               fill = "green",
+               alpha = 0.8) +
+   theme_minimal() +
+   ylab("y") +
+   geom_hline(yintercept = 0) +
+   geom_vline(xintercept = 0) +
+   coord_cartesian(xlim = c(0, 4),
+                   ylim = c(0, 25))
```

Code to Replicate Fig. 5.4

```
> x <- seq(-10, 10, 0.1)
> y_up <- -1*x^2 + 2
> y_low <- -x
> df <- data.frame(x, y_up, y_low)
```

We need to find where the two functions intersect. We use the `uniroot()` function. Note that we split the interval in two to find the solutions. The interval has been decided based on the shape of the functions in Fig. 5.4.

```
> y_up_fn <- function(x) {-1*x^2 + 2}
> y_low_fn <- function(x) {-x}
> res1 <- uniroot(function(x)
+   {y_up_fn(x) - y_low_fn(x)},
+   c(-2.5, 0))
> r1 <- round(res1$root, 2)
> r1
[1] -1
> res2 <- uniroot(function(x)
```

```
+    {y_up_fn(x) - y_low_fn(x)},
+    c(0, 2.5))
> r2 <- round(res2$root, 2)
> r2
[1] 2
```

Therefore, it results that the solutions are $r_1 = -1$ and $r_2 = 2$.

We use `geom_ribbon()` to fill the area between the lines. Basically, we subset the dataset between the values of our solutions r_1 and r_2 and we define the low and up functions in, respectively, `ymin =` and `ymax =` .

```
> ggplot(df, aes(x, y_up)) +
+    geom_line(aes(x, y_up),
+              color = "red",
+              size = 1) +
+    geom_line(aes(x, y_low),
+              color = "blue",
+              size = 1) +
+    geom_ribbon(data = subset(df, r1 <= x &
+                                  x <= r2),
+                aes(ymin = y_low, ymax = y_up),
+                fill = "green",
+                alpha = 0.8) +
+    theme_minimal() +
+    ylab("y") +
+    geom_hline(yintercept = 0) +
+    geom_vline(xintercept = 0) +
+    coord_cartesian(xlim = c(-3, 3),
+                    ylim = c(-3, 3))
```

Code to Replicate Fig. 5.5

```
> x <- seq(-10, 10, 0.1)
> df <- data.frame(x)
> y <- function(x) {x^3 - 6*x^2 + 11*x - 6}
> ggplot(data = df, aes(x)) +
+    stat_function(fun = y,
+                  color = "red",
+                  size = 1) +
+    stat_function(fun = y,
+                  xlim = c(1, 2),
+                  geom = "area",
+                  fill = "blue",
+                  alpha = 0.5) +
+    stat_function(fun = y,
+                  xlim = c(2, 3),
+                  geom = "area",
+                  fill = "green",
+                  alpha = 0.5) +
+    theme_minimal() +
+    geom_hline(yintercept = 0) +
```

```
+   geom_vline(xintercept = 0) +
+   coord_cartesian(xlim = c(0, 4),
+                   ylim = c(-2.5, 2.5))
```

Code to Replicate Fig. 5.6

```
> x <- seq(0, 10, 0.1)
> df <- data.frame(x)
> y <- function(x) {1/x^2}
> ggplot(data = df, aes(x)) +
+   stat_function(fun = y,
+                 color = "red",
+                 size = 1) +
+   stat_function(fun = y,
+                 xlim = c(1, 10),
+                 geom = "area",
+                 fill = "blue",
+                 alpha = 0.5) +
+   theme_minimal() +
+   geom_hline(yintercept = 0) +
+   geom_vline(xintercept = 0) +
+   coord_cartesian(xlim = c(0, 5),
+                   ylim = c(0, 5))
```

Code to Replicate Fig. 5.7

```
> y <- function(x) {1/sqrt(x - 1)}
> ggplot(data = df, aes(x)) +
+   stat_function(fun = y,
+                 color = "red",
+                 size = 1) +
+   stat_function(fun = y,
+                 xlim = c(1, 4),
+                 geom = "area",
+                 fill = "blue",
+                 alpha = 0.5) +
+   theme_minimal() +
+   geom_hline(yintercept = 0) +
+   geom_vline(xintercept = 0) +
+   coord_cartesian(xlim = c(0, 5),
+                   ylim = c(0, 5))
Warning messages:
1: In sqrt(x - 1) : NaNs produced
2: Removed 10 row(s) containing missing values (geom_path).
```

Let's note that `ggplot()` signals something about $\sqrt{x-1}$. In fact, as we observe from Fig. 5.7, we have a vertical asymptote at $x = 1$.

Code to Replicate Fig. 5.8

```
> y <- function(x) {1/x}
> ggplot(data = df, aes(x)) +
+   stat_function(fun = y,
+                 color = "red",
+                 size = 1) +
+   stat_function(fun = y,
+                 xlim = c(1, 10),
+                 geom = "area",
+                 fill = "blue",
+                 alpha = 0.5) +
+   theme_minimal() +
+   geom_hline(yintercept = 0) +
+   geom_vline(xintercept = 0) +
+   coord_cartesian(xlim = c(0, 5),
+                   ylim = c(0, 5))
```

Appendix F
Appendix to Chap. 7

Code to Replicate Fig. 7.1

The following code reproduces Fig. 7.1. Note that in the first steps we just rearrange the functions to plot by solving for y. Additionally, to avoid overwriting the first `y`, we name the y in the constraint as `Y`. We use `coord_fixed()` to fix the ratio of the scale coordinate system. Finally, note that we store the plot in `p1`.

```
> L <- 250
> x <- seq(0.1, 50, 0.1)
> y <- L/x - 2
> Y <- 90/5 - (2/5)*x
> df_s <- data.frame(x = c(25, 25),
+                    xend = c(25 + 2, 25 + 10),
+                    y = c(8, 8),
+                    yend = c(8 + 5, 8 + 25))
> p1 <- ggplot() +
+   geom_line(map = aes(x = x, y = y), size = 1) +
+   geom_line(map = aes(x = x, y = Y), size = 1,
+             color = "blue") +
+   geom_point(aes(x = 25, y = 8),
+              color = "red",
+              size = 2) +
+   geom_segment(data = df_s, aes(x = x,
+                    xend = xend,
+                    y = y,
+                    yend = yend),
+                size = 1,
+                color = c("black", "green"),
+                arrow = arrow(
+                  length = unit(0.3,
+                                "inches"))) +
+   coord_fixed(xlim = c(0, 60),
+               ylim = c(0, 60)) +
+   theme_classic() +
```


M. Porto, *Introduction to Mathematics for Economics with R*,
https://doi.org/10.1007/978-3-031-05202-6

```
+   xlab("x") + ylab("y")
> p1
```

Code to Replicate Fig. 7.2

```
> L2 <- 490
> y2 <- L2/x - 2
> Y2 <- 130/5 - (2/5)*x
> df_s2 <- data.frame(x = c(35, 35),
+                      xend = c(35 + 2, 35 + 14),
+                      y = c(12, 12),
+                      yend = c(12 + 5, 12 + 35))
> p1 + geom_line(map = aes(x = x, y = y2), size = 1,
+                linetype = "dashed") +
+   geom_line(map = aes(x = x, y = Y2), size = 1,
+             color = "blue",
+             linetype = "dashed") +
+   geom_point(aes(x = 35, y = 12),
+              color = "red",
+              size = 2) +
+   geom_segment(data = df_s2,
+                aes(x = x,
+                    xend = xend,
+                    y = y,
+                    yend = yend),
+                size = c(1, 0.8),
+                color = c("black", "green"),
+                linetype = "dashed",
+                arrow = arrow(
+                  length = unit(0.3,
+                                "inches")))
```

Code to Replicate Fig. 7.3

```
> x <- 0:40
> y <- 40 - x
> df <- data.frame(x, y)
> df$xstar <- 10
> df$ystar <- 30
> df$zstar <- df$xstar*df$ystar
> df$Y <- df$zstar/df$x
> yfun <- function(x){40 - x}
> ggplot(df, aes(x, y)) +
+   geom_line(data = df, aes(x, Y),
+             size = 1) +
+   stat_function(fun = yfun,
+                 color = "blue",
+                 size = 1) +
```

```
+   geom_vline(xintercept = 10,
+              color = "red",
+              size = 1) +
+   geom_ribbon(data = subset(df, x <= 10),
+               aes(ymin = 0, ymax = y),
+               fill = "green",
+               alpha = 0.5) +
+   geom_vline(xintercept = 0) +
+   geom_hline(yintercept = 0) +
+   theme_minimal() +
+   xlab("x") + ylab("y") +
+   annotate("text", x = c(10, -1, 5),
+            y = c(-1, 30, 15),
+            label = c("x*", "y*", "Feasible \n area")) +
+   annotate("label", x = c(25, 13, 40),
+            y = c(20, 45, 8),
+            label = c("Constraint 1",
+                      "Constraint 2",
+                      "z* = 300"),
+            color = c("blue", "red", "black")) +
+   coord_fixed(xlim = c(0, 50),
+               ylim = c(0, 50))
```

Appendix G
Appendix to Chap. 8

Code to Replicate Fig. 8.1

```
> df <- data.frame(X = c(0, 0, 4.5, 4.5, 5),
+                  Y = c(0, 0, 0.5, 0, 0),
+                  XEND = c(8, 8, 5, 4.5, 5),
+                  YEND = c(0, 4, 0.5, 0.5, 2.5))
> df
    X   Y XEND YEND
1 0.0 0.0  8.0  0.0
2 0.0 0.0  8.0  4.0
3 4.5 0.5  5.0  0.5
4 4.5 0.0  4.5  0.5
5 5.0 0.0  5.0  2.5
> ggplot() +
+   geom_segment(data = df,
+                aes(x = X, y = Y,
+                    xend = XEND,
+                    yend = YEND),
+                size = 1,
+                color = c(rep("black", 4), "red")) +
+   theme_void() +
+   coord_fixed(xlim = c(-1, 9),
+               ylim = c(-2, 6)) +
+   annotate("text", x = c(0.7, 4.8, 4.8, 8, 8),
+            y = c(0.2, 0.2, 2.2, -0.3, 4.2),
+            label = c("theta", "gamma", "phi",
+                      "italic(l)^1", "italic(l)^2"),
+            parse = TRUE) +
+   annotate("text", x = c(0, 5, 5, 2.5, 5.2, 2.5),
+            y = c(-0.3, -0.3, 2.7, -0.3, 1.5, 1.6),
+            label = c("A", "C", "B", "a", "b", "r"))
```


M. Porto, *Introduction to Mathematics for Economics with R*,
https://doi.org/10.1007/978-3-031-05202-6

Code to Replicate Fig. 8.2

Note that the circle in Fig. 8.2 is *not* a "real graph" of a circle. We use the same trick used for Fig. 3.2, that is we enlarge a point centred in the origin so that it has $r = 1$. I have to remark that this is not an efficient way to draw a circle. In fact, it may happen that on your device this *circle* can have a slightly different radius from 1. If this is the case, decrease or increase the value of the size in `geom_point()` to set the radius equal to 1 to replicate Fig. 8.2.

```
> r <- 1
> theta45rad <- angle_conversion(45)
> theta45rad
[1] 0.7853982
> b <- sin(theta45rad)*r
> b
[1] 0.7071068
> a <- cos(theta45rad)*r
> a
[1] 0.7071068
> df <- data.frame(X = c(0, a, 0),
+                  Y = c(0, 0, 0),
+                  XEND = c(a, a, a),
+                  YEND = c(0, b, b))
> df
          X Y      XEND      YEND
1 0.0000000 0 0.7071068 0.0000000
2 0.7071068 0 0.7071068 0.7071068
3 0.0000000 0 0.7071068 0.7071068
> trig1 <- ggplot(data.frame(x = 0, y = 0), aes(x, y)) +
+   geom_point(size = 130, shape = 1) +
+   geom_hline(yintercept = 0) +
+   geom_vline(xintercept = 0) +
+   geom_segment(data = df, aes(x = X,
+                               y = Y,
+                               xend = XEND,
+                               yend = YEND),
+                size = 1.2,
+                color = c("blue", "red", "green")) +
+   theme_minimal() +
+   xlab("x axis") + ylab("y axis") +
+   coord_fixed(xlim = c(-1.2, 1.2),
+               ylim = c(-1.2, 1.2)) +
+   annotate("text", x = c(0.1),
+            y = c(0.05),
+            label = c("theta"),
+            parse = TRUE) +
+   annotate("text",
+            x = c(0.03, a, a, 0.45, 0.75, 0.4, 1.04),
+            y = c(-0.03, -0.03, (b+0.05), -0.03, 0.4, 0.45, -0.03),
+            label = c("A", "C", "B", "a", "b", "r", "D"))
> trig1
```

Code to Replicate Fig. 8.3

```
> theta30rad <- angle_conversion(30)
> theta30rad
[1] 0.5235988
> b30 <- sin(theta30rad)*r
> b30
[1] 0.5
> a30 <- cos(theta30rad)*r
> a30
[1] 0.8660254
> theta60rad <- angle_conversion(60)
> theta60rad
[1] 1.047198
> b60 <- sin(theta60rad)*r
> b60
[1] 0.8660254
> a60 <- cos(theta60rad)*r
> a60
[1] 0.5
> df2 <- data.frame(X = c(0, a30, 0, 0, a60, 0),
+                   Y = c(0, 0, 0, 0, 0, 0),
+                   XEND = c(a30, a30, a30, a60, a60, a60),
+                   YEND = c(0, b30, b30, 0, b60, b60))
> df2
          X Y      XEND      YEND
1 0.0000000 0 0.8660254 0.0000000
2 0.8660254 0 0.8660254 0.5000000
3 0.0000000 0 0.8660254 0.5000000
4 0.0000000 0 0.5000000 0.0000000
5 0.5000000 0 0.5000000 0.8660254
6 0.0000000 0 0.5000000 0.8660254
> trig2 <- trig1 +
+   geom_segment(data = df2,
+                aes(x = X, y = Y,
+                    xend = XEND, yend = YEND),
+                size = 1.2, color = rep(c("blue", "red",
+                                         "green"), 2),
+                linetype = c(rep("dotdash", 3),
+                             rep("dotted", 3)))
> trig2
```

Code to Replicate Fig. 8.4

```
> x <- seq(-pi, 2*pi, by = 0.01)
> tail(x)
[1] 6.228407 6.238407 6.248407 6.258407 6.268407 6.278407
> df4 <- data.frame(x, sin = sin(x),
+                   cos = cos(x))
> head(df4)
```

```
          x           sin        cos
1 -3.141593 -1.224606e-16 -1.0000000
2 -3.131593 -9.999833e-03 -0.9999500
3 -3.121593 -1.999867e-02 -0.9998000
4 -3.111593 -2.999550e-02 -0.9995500
5 -3.101593 -3.998933e-02 -0.9992001
6 -3.091593 -4.997917e-02 -0.9987503
> df4_l <- melt(setDT(df4), id.vars = "x",
+               measure.vars = c("sin", "cos"),
+               variable.name = "trig")
> head(df4_l)
           x trig         value
1: -3.141593  sin -1.224606e-16
2: -3.131593  sin -9.999833e-03
3: -3.121593  sin -1.999867e-02
4: -3.111593  sin -2.999550e-02
5: -3.101593  sin -3.998933e-02
6: -3.091593  sin -4.997917e-02
> ggplot(df4_l, aes(x = x, y = value,
+                    group = trig, color = trig)) +
+   geom_line(size = 1) +
+   geom_hline(yintercept = 0) +
+   geom_vline(xintercept = 0) +
+   geom_vline(xintercept = c(-pi/2, -pi, pi/2,
+                             pi, (3/2 * pi), 2*pi),
+              linetype = "dotted") +
+   theme_classic() + xlab("x axis") + ylab("y axis") +
+   theme(legend.position = "bottom",
+         legend.title = element_blank()) +
+   coord_fixed(xlim = c(-3.2, 6.4),
+               ylim = c(-1.5, 1.5)) +
+   annotate("text", x = c(pi/2, pi,
+                          (3/2 * pi), 2*pi),
+            y = rep(-1.35, 4),
+            label = c("pi/2", "pi",
+                      "3*pi/2", "2*pi"),
+            parse = TRUE) +
+   annotate("label",
+            x = c(0.78, 2.35, 4, 5.5),
+            y = rep(1.35, 4),
+            label = c("I Quadrant",
+                      "II Quadrant",
+                      "III Quadrant",
+                      "IV Quadrant"),
+            size = 2.5)
```

Code to Replicate Fig. 8.5

```
> tg45 <- tan(theta45rad)
> tg45
[1] 1
```

```
> df_tg <- data.frame(X = c(a, 1),
+                      Y = c(b, 1),
+                      XEND = c(1, 1),
+                      YEND = c(1, 0))
> df_tg
          X         Y XEND YEND
1 0.7071068 0.7071068    1    1
2 1.0000000 1.0000000    1    0
> trig_tg <- trig1 + geom_vline(xintercept = 1) +
+   geom_segment(data = df_tg,
+                aes(x = X,
+                    y = Y,
+                    xend = XEND,
+                    yend = YEND),
+                size = c(1.2, 1.2),
+                color = c("green", "yellow"),
+                linetype = c("dashed", "solid")) +
+   annotate("text", x = 1.04, y = 1,
+            label = "E")
> trig_tg
```

Code to Replicate Fig. 8.6

```
> df5 <- data.frame(x, tan = tan(x))
> head(df5)
          x          tan
1 -3.141593 1.224647e-16
2 -3.131593 1.000033e-02
3 -3.121593 2.000267e-02
4 -3.111593 3.000900e-02
5 -3.101593 4.002135e-02
6 -3.091593 5.004171e-02
> ggplot(df5, aes(x = x, y = tan)) +
+   geom_line(size = 1, color = "green") +
+   geom_hline(yintercept = 0) +
+   geom_vline(xintercept = 0) +
+   geom_vline(xintercept = c(-pi/2, pi/2,
+                             (3/2 * pi)),
+              linetype = "solid", color = "blue",
+              size = 1.5) +
+   theme_classic() + xlab("x axis") + ylab("y axis") +
+   theme(legend.position = "bottom",
+         legend.title = element_blank()) +
+   coord_fixed(xlim = c(-3.2, 6.4),
+               ylim = c(-5, 5)) +
+   annotate("text", x = c(-pi/2, pi/2,
+                          (3/2 * pi)),
+            y = rep(-3.35, 3),
+            label = c("-pi/2", "pi/2",
+                      "3*pi/2"),
+            color = "red", size = 5,
+            parse = TRUE)
```

Appendix H
Appendix to Chap. 9

Code to Replicate Fig. 9.1

```
> a <- 8
> b <- 4
> df <- data.frame(X = c(0, a),
+                  Y = c(b, 0),
+                  XEND = c(a, a),
+                  YEND = c(b, b))
> df
  X Y XEND YEND
1 0 4    8    4
2 8 0    8    4
> p1 <- ggplot() +
+   geom_segment(data = df,
+                aes(x = X,
+                    y = Y,
+                    xend = XEND,
+                    yend = YEND),
+                size = 1,
+                linetype = "dashed") +
+   geom_vline(xintercept = 0) +
+   geom_hline(yintercept = 0) +
+   theme_minimal() +
+   ylab("Imaginary \n axis") +
+   xlab("Real axis") +
+   theme(axis.title.y = element_text(angle = 360),
+         axis.title.x = element_text(hjust = 1)) +
+   scale_x_continuous(breaks = seq(0, 10, by = 2)) +
+   annotate("text", x = c(a, -0.3, a+0.3),
+            y = c(-0.3, b, b+0.3),
+            label = c("a", "b", "a + bi")) +
+   coord_fixed(xlim = c(-1, 10),
+               ylim = c(-1, 6))
> p1
```


M. Porto, *Introduction to Mathematics for Economics with R*,
https://doi.org/10.1007/978-3-031-05202-6

Code to Replicate Fig. 9.2

```
> p1 + geom_segment(aes(x = 0, y = 0,
+                      xend = 8, yend = 4),
+                      size = 1,
+                      color = "green") +
+   annotate("text", x = c(0.7),
+             y = c(0.2),
+             label = c("theta"),
+             parse = TRUE) +
+   annotate("text", x = c(3.5),
+             y = c(2),
+             label = c("r"))
```

Appendix I
Appendix to Chap. 10

Code to Replicate Fig. 10.2

The following code reproduces Fig. 10.2 by using the `iter_de()` function. Note that the `paste()` function is nested in the `expression()` function to add the comma. The tilde is used to put a space. Additionally, note that for the last three plots I add `geom_line()` to make the time path more evident.

```
> RHS1 <- "1.5*y[t]"
> p1 <- iter_de(RHS1, y0 = 1, graph = T)$graph_simulation +
+   labs(title = expression(
+     paste(y[t+1] == 1.5*y[t], ",", ~ y[0] == 1)),
+        caption = "b > 1")
> RHS2 <- "y[t]"
> p2 <- iter_de(RHS2, y0 = 1, graph = T)$graph_simulation +
+   labs(title = expression(
+     paste(y[t+1] == y[t], ",", ~ y[0] == 1)),
+        caption = "b = 1")
> RHS3 <- "0.5*y[t]"
> p3 <- iter_de(RHS3, y0 = 1, graph = T)$graph_simulation +
+   labs(title = expression(
+     paste(y[t+1] == 0.5*y[t], ",", ~ y[0] == 1)),
+        caption = "0 < b < 1")
> RHS4 <- "-0.5*y[t]"
> p4 <- iter_de(RHS4, y0 = 1, graph = T)$graph_simulation +
+   geom_line() +
+   labs(title = expression(
+     paste(y[t+1] == -0.5*y[t], ",", ~ y[0] == 1)),
+        caption = "-1 < b < 0")
> RHS5 <- "-y[t]"
> p5 <- iter_de(RHS5, y0 = 1, graph = T)$graph_simulation +
+   geom_line() +
+   labs(title = expression(
+     paste(y[t+1] == -1*y[t], ",", ~ y[0] == 1)),
+        caption = "b = -1")
```


M. Porto, *Introduction to Mathematics for Economics with R*,
https://doi.org/10.1007/978-3-031-05202-6

```
> RHS6 <- "-1.5*y[t]"
> p6 <- iter_de(RHS6, y0 = 1, graph = T)$graph_simulation +
+   geom_line() +
+   labs(title = expression(
+     paste(y[t+1] == -1.5*y[t], ",", ~ y[0] == 1)),
+        caption = "b < -1")
> ggarrange(p1, p2, p3,
+           p4, p5, p6,
+           ncol = 2, nrow = 3)
```

Code to Replicate Fig. 10.3

```
> RHSA <- "0.8*y[t]"
> p7 <- iter_de(RHSA, y0 = 4, graph = T)$graph_simulation +
+   labs(title = expression(
+     paste(y[t+1] == 0.8*y[t], ",", ~ y[0] == 4)),
+        caption = "A > 0")
> p8 <- iter_de(RHSA, y0 = 1/4, graph = T)$graph_simulation +
+   labs(title = expression(
+     paste(y[t+1] == 0.8*y[t], ",", ~ y[0] == 1/4)),
+        caption = "0 < A < 1")
> p9 <- iter_de(RHSA, y0 = -4, graph = T)$graph_simulation +
+   labs(title = expression(
+     paste(y[t+1] == 0.8*y[t], ",", ~ y[0] == -4)),
+        caption = "A = -1")
> ggarrange(p7, p8, p9,
+           ncol = 1, nrow = 3)
```

Code to Replicate Fig. 10.4

```
> RHSc <- "0.5*y[t]"
> p10 <- iter_de(RHSc, y0 = 1, graph = T)$graph_simulation +
+   labs(title = expression(
+     paste(y[t+1] == 0.5*y[t], ",", ~ y[0] == 1)),
+        caption = "b = 0.5")
> RHSg <- "0.5*y[t] + 2"
> p11 <- iter_de(RHSg, y0 = 1, graph = T)$graph_simulation +
+   labs(title = expression(
+     paste(y[t+1] == 0.5*y[t] + 2, ",", ~ y[0] == 1)),
+        caption = expression(y[t] == -3(0.5)^t + 4))
> ggarrange(p10, p11,
+           ncol = 1, nrow = 2)
```

Code to Replicate Fig. 10.5

```
> RHS12 <- "3*y[t+1] - 2*y[t]"
> p12 <- iter_de(RHS12, y0 = c(2, 5), order = 2,
+                periods = 20, graph = TRUE)$graph_simulation +
+   labs(title = "Divergent time path",
+        caption = "|b1| > 1")
> RHS13 <- "y[t+1] - (2/9)*y[t]"
> p13 <- iter_de(RHS13, y0 = c(2, 5), order = 2,
+                periods = 20, graph = TRUE)$graph_simulation +
+   labs(title = "Convergent time path",
+        caption = "|b1| < 1")
> RHS14 <- "3*y[t+1] - 3*y[t]"
> p14 <- iter_de(RHS14, y0 = c(2, 5), order = 2,
+                periods = 20, graph = TRUE)$graph_simulation +
+   labs(title = "Divergent time path",
+        caption = "|r| > 1")
> RHS15 <- "y[t+1] - (1/2)*y[t]"
> p15 <- iter_de(RHS15, y0 = c(2, 5), order = 2,
+                periods = 20, graph = TRUE)$graph_simulation +
+   labs(title = "Convergent time path",
+        caption = "|r| < 1")
> ggarrange(p12, p13, p14, p15,
+           nrow = 2, ncol = 2)
```

Appendix J
Appendix to Chap. 11

Code to Replicate Fig. 11.1

```
> t <- seq(-1, 1, 0.1)
> C <- c(-29/16, -13/16, 19/16, 35/16)
> df <- sapply(C, FUN = function(C)
+     (1/4)*t - 3/16 + C*exp(4*t))
> head(df)
           [,1]       [,2]       [,3]        [,4]
[1,] -0.4706971 -0.4523815 -0.4157502 -0.39743454
[2,] -0.4620242 -0.4347005 -0.3800531 -0.35272936
[3,] -0.4613815 -0.4206193 -0.3390949 -0.29833268
[4,] -0.4727182 -0.4119082 -0.2902881 -0.22947799
[5,] -0.5019263 -0.4112083 -0.2297724 -0.13905448
[6,] -0.5577952 -0.4224599 -0.1517894 -0.01645407
> class(df)
[1] "matrix" "array"
> df <- as.data.frame(df)
> class(df)
[1] "data.frame"
> colnames(df) <- c("ym2", "ym1", "y1", "y2")
> df <- cbind(t, df)
> head(df)
     t        ym2        ym1         y1          y2
1 -1.0 -0.4706971 -0.4523815 -0.4157502 -0.39743454
2 -0.9 -0.4620242 -0.4347005 -0.3800531 -0.35272936
3 -0.8 -0.4613815 -0.4206193 -0.3390949 -0.29833268
4 -0.7 -0.4727182 -0.4119082 -0.2902881 -0.22947799
5 -0.6 -0.5019263 -0.4112083 -0.2297724 -0.13905448
6 -0.5 -0.5577952 -0.4224599 -0.1517894 -0.01645407
> df_l <- df %>%
+   pivot_longer(!t,
+                names_to = "variable",
+                values_to = "value")
> head(df_l)
```


M. Porto, *Introduction to Mathematics for Economics with R*,
https://doi.org/10.1007/978-3-031-05202-6

```
# A tibble: 6 x 3
      t variable  value
  <dbl> <chr>     <dbl>
1  -1   ym2      -0.471
2  -1   ym1      -0.452
3  -1   y1       -0.416
4  -1   y2       -0.397
5  -0.9 ym2      -0.462
6  -0.9 ym1      -0.435
> df_o <- df[df$t == 0, ]
> df_o
   t ym2 ym1 y1 y2
11 0  -2  -1  1  2
> df_ol <- df_o %>%
+   pivot_longer(!t,
+                  names_to = "variable",
+                  values_to = "value")
> df_ol
# A tibble: 4 x 3
      t variable value
  <dbl> <chr>    <dbl>
1     0 ym2         -2
2     0 ym1         -1
3     0 y1           1
4     0 y2           2
> ggplot() +
+   geom_line(dat = df_l, aes(x = t, y = value,
+                              group = variable,
+                              color = variable)) +
+   geom_point(dat = df_ol, aes(x = t, y = value,
+                                group = variable,
+                                color = variable),
+              size = 2) +
+   theme_bw() +
+   theme(legend.position = "none",
+         axis.title = element_blank()) +
+   coord_cartesian(ylim = c(-3, 3))
```

Code to Replicate Fig. 11.7

```
> y <- seq(-10, 10, 0.1)
> dydt_conv <- -y + 7
> df_conv <- data.frame(y, dydt_conv)
> y_conv <- ggplot(df_conv, aes(x = y, y = dydt_conv)) +
+   geom_line(size = 1, color = "blue") +
+   geom_vline(xintercept = 0) +
+   geom_hline(yintercept = 0) +
+   theme_minimal() +
+   ylab("dydt") + ggtitle("Convergent") +
+   scale_x_continuous(breaks = pretty_breaks(n = 10)) +
+   coord_cartesian(ylim = c(-2.5, 10),
```

```
+                    xlim = c(-2.5, 10))
> dydt_div <- y + 7
> df_div <- data.frame(y, dydt_div)
> y_div <- ggplot(df_div, aes(x = y, y = dydt_div)) +
+   geom_line(size = 1, color = "blue") +
+   geom_vline(xintercept = 0) +
+   geom_hline(yintercept = 0) +
+   theme_minimal() +
+   ylab("dydt") + ggtitle("Divergent") +
+   scale_x_continuous(breaks = pretty_breaks(n = 10)) +
+   coord_cartesian(ylim = c(-2.5, 10),
+                    xlim = c(-10, 2.5))
> ggarrange(y_conv, y_div,
+           nrow = 2, ncol = 1)
```

Code to Replicate Fig. 11.8

```
> x <- c(2, 4, 6, 8, 14, 12, 10, 8, NA,
+        4, 6, 8, 8, 10, 12, 12, NA,
+        2, 4, 6, 8, 10, 12, NA,
+        14, 12, 10, 8, 6, 4)
> y <- c(0, 0, 0, 0, 0, 0, 0, 0, NA,
+        -2, -2, -2, -2, -2, -2, -2, NA,
+        -4, -4, -4, -4, -4, -4, NA,
+        -6, -6, -6, -6, -6, -6)
> xend <- c(4, 6, 8, 8, 12, 10, 8, 8, NA,
+           2, 4, 6, 10, 12, 14, 14, NA,
+           4, 6, 8, 10, 12, 14, NA,
+           12, 10, 8, 6, 4, 2)
> yend <- c(0, 0, 0, 0, 0, 0, 0, 0, NA,
+           -2, -2, -2, -2, -2, -2, -2, NA,
+           -4, -4, -4, -4, -4, -4, NA,
+           -6, -6, -6, -6, -6, -6)
> df <- data.frame(x, y, xend, yend)
> ggplot() +
+   geom_segment(data = df, aes(x = x, y = y,
+                               xend = xend,
+                               yend = yend),
+                size = 1,
+                arrow = arrow(
+                  length = unit(0.3,
+                                "inches"))) +
+   geom_point(data = data.frame(x = rep(8, 4),
+                                y = c(0, -2, -4, -6)),
+              aes(x, y), size = 3, color = "red") +
+   theme_void() +
+   annotate("text",
+            x = c(rep(8, 4), rep(c(4, 8, 12), 4)),
+            y = c(-0.5, -2.4, -4.5, -6.5, rep(0.5, 3),
+                  rep(-1.5, 3), rep(-3.5, 3), rep(-5.5, 3)),
+            label = c("attractor", "repellor",
```

```
+                        "(right) shunt", "(left) shunt",
+                        "dy/dt > 0", "y*", "dy/dt < 0",
+                        "dy/dt < 0", "y*", "dy/dt > 0",
+                        "dy/dt > 0", "y*", "dy/dt > 0",
+                        "dy/dt < 0", "y*", "dy/dt < 0"))
Warning message:
Removed 3 rows containing missing values (geom_segment).
```

Bibliography

Akyol, T. Y. (2019). *RVenn: Set operations for many sets*. R package version 1.1.0. https://CRAN.R-project.org/package=RVenn

Allaire, J. (2014). *Manipulate: Interactive plots for RStudio*. R package version 1.0.1. https://CRAN.R-project.org/package=manipulate

Berkelaar, M. et al. (2020). *lpSolve: Interface to 'Lp_solve' v. 5.5 to solve linear/integer programs*. R package version 5.6.15. https://CRAN.R-project.org/package=lpSolve

Besanko, D. A., & Braeutigam, R. R. (2011). *Microeconomics* (4th edn.). New York: Wiley.

Bock, T. (2017). Singular value decomposition (SVD): Tutorial using examples in R. Retrieved February 5 2020, from https://www.r-bloggers.com/2017/08/singular-value-decomposition-svd-tutorial-using-examples-in-r/

Borchers, H. W. (2019), *Pracma: Practical numerical math functions*. R package version 2.2.9. https://CRAN.R-project.org/package=pracma

Boyce, W. E., & DiPrima, R. C. (1992), *Elementary differential equations* (5th edn.) New York: Wiley.

Burns, P. (2011). *The R inferno*. Lulu. com

Callahan, J. J. (2010). *Advanced calculus: A geometric view*. Berlin: Springer.

Cheah, B. C. (2003). *Solving Computable General Equilibrium Models with SAS. SAS Conference Proceedings: September 7–10, 2003, Washington*. https://www.lexjansen.com/cgi-bin/xsl_transform.php?x=nesug2003

Cheng, J., Karambelkar, B., & Xie, Y. (2019). *Leaflet: Create interactive web maps with the JavaScript 'Leaflet' library*. R package version 2.0.3. https://CRAN.R-project.org/package=leaflet

Chiang, A. C., & Wainwright, K. (2005). *Fundamental methods of mathematical economics* (4th edn.). New York: McGraw-Hill.

Clausen, A., & Sokol, S. (2019). *Deriv: R-based symbolic differentiation*. Deriv package version 4.0. https://CRAN.R-project.org/package=Deriv

Cordano, E. (2014). *Blockmatrix: Blockmatrix: Tools to solve algebraic systems with partitioned matrices*. R package version 1.0. https://CRAN.R-project.org/package=blockmatrix

Csardi, G., & Nepusz, T. (2006). The igraph software package for complex network research. *InterJournal Complex Systems, 1695(5)*, 1–9. http://igraph.org

Dayal, V. (2020). *Quantitative economics with R*. Berlin: Springer.

Dixit, A. K. (1990). *Optimization in economic theory* (2nd edn.). Oxford: Oxford University Press.

Dowle, M., & Srinivasan, A. (2017). *data.table: Extension of 'data.frame'*. R package version 1.10.4. https://CRAN.R-project.org/package=data.table

Georgakopoulos, H. (2015). *Quantitative trading with R*. London: Palgrave Macmillan.

M. Porto, *Introduction to Mathematics for Economics with R*,
https://doi.org/10.1007/978-3-031-05202-6

Ghorpade, S. R., & Limaye, B. V. (2006). *A course in calculus and real analysis*. Berlin: Springer.

Ghorpade, S. R., & Limaye, B. V. (2010). *A course in multivariable calculus and analysis*. Berlin: Springer.

Giordano, F. R., & Weir, M. D. (1991). *Differential equations*. Boston: Addison-Wesley.

Goulet, V., Dutang, C., Maechler, M., Firth, D., Shapira, M., & Stadelmann, M. (2019). *expm: Matrix exponential, Log, 'etc'*. R package version 0.999-4. https://CRAN.R-project.org/package=expm

Grayling, M. J. (2014). phaseR: An R package for phase plane analysis of autonomous ODE systems. *The R Journal, 6*(2), 43–51. https://doi.org/10.32614/RJ-2014-023

Hady Soliman, S. A., & Al-Kandari, A. M. (2010). 1 - mathematical background and state of the art. In S. A. Hady Soliman & A. M. Al-Kandari (Eds.), *Electrical load forecasting* (pp. 1–44). Boston: Butterworth-Heinemann. http://www.sciencedirect.com/science/article/pii/B9780123815439000014

Hannah, J. (1996). A geometric approach to determinants. *The American Mathematical Monthly, 103*(5), 401–409. http://www.jstor.org/stable/2974931

Hasselman, B. (2018). *nleqslv: Solve systems of nonlinear equations*. R package version 3.3.2. https://CRAN.R-project.org/package=nleqslv

Heiss, A. (2018). Fun with empirical and function-based derivatives in r. Retrieved March 15 2020, from https://www.andrewheiss.com/blog/2018/02/15/derivatives-r-fun/

Hlavac, M. (2018). *stargazer: Well-formatted regression and summary statistics tables*. Central European Labour Studies Institute (CELSI), Bratislava, Slovakia. R package version 5.2.2. https://CRAN.R-project.org/package=stargazer

Hyndman, R. J., & Athanasopoulos, G. (2021). Forecasting: Principles and practice. Retrieved September 27 2021, from https://otexts.com/fpp3/

Johnson, S. G. (2020). The NLopt nonlinear-optimization package. http://github.com/stevengj/nlopt

Kaplan, D. T., Pruim, R, & Horton, N. J. (2017) *mosaicCalc: Function-based numerical and symbolic differentiation and antidifferentiation*. R package version 0.5.0. https://CRAN.R-project.org/package=mosaicCalc

Kassambara, A. (2019). *ggpubr: 'ggplot2' based publication ready plots*. R package version 0.2.1. https://CRAN.R-project.org/package=ggpubr

Lang, S. (2005). *Undergraduate algebra* (3rd edn.). Berlin: Springer.

LeCuyer, E. J. (1978). *Introduction to college mathematics with a programming language*. Berlin: Springer.

Leontief, W. W. (1936). Quantitative input and output relations in the economic systems of the united states. *Review of Economics and Statistics, 18*(3), 105–125.

Leontief, W. W. (1941). *The structure of American economy, 1919–1929*. Cambridge: Harvard University Press.

Lippman, D., Hoffman, D., & Calaway, S. (2016). *Applied calculus*. Pacific Grove: Brooks/Cole.

Logan, J. D. (2011). *A first course in differential equations* (2nd edn.). Berlin: Springer.

Luke, D. A. (2015). *A user's guide to network analysis in R*. Berlin: Springer.

Moore, W. H., & Siegel, D. A. (2013). *A mathematical course for political & social research* (1st edn.). Princeton: Princeton University Press.

Murdoch, D., & Adler, D. (2021). *rgl: 3D visualization using OpenGL*. R package version 0.106.8. https://CRAN.R-project.org/package=rgl

Ooms, J. (2018). *gifski: Highest quality GIF encoder*. R package version 0.8.6. https://CRAN.R-project.org/package=gifski

Ostaszewski, A. (1993). *Mathematics in economics*. Hoboken: Blacwell Publishers.

Pedersen, T. L., & Robinson, D. (2020). *gganimate: A grammar of animated graphics*. R package version 1.0.5. https://CRAN.R-project.org/package=gganimate

Pfaff, B. (2008). *Analysis of integrated and cointegrated time series with R* (2nd edn.). New York: Springer. ISBN 0-387-27960-1. http://www.pfaffikus.de

Pollock, S. (2015). On kronecker products, tensor products and matric differential calculus. Technical report, University of Leicester.

Pruim, R., Kaplan, D. T., & Horton, N. J. (2017). The mosaic package: Helping students to 'think with data' using R. *The R Journal, 9*(1), 77–102. https://journal.r-project.org/archive/2017/RJ-2017-024/index.html

R Core Team. (2020). *R: A language and environment for statistical computing*. R Foundation for Statistical Computing, Vienna. https://www.R-project.org/

RStudio Team. (2020). *RStudio: Integrated development environment for R*. RStudio, PBC, Boston. http://www.rstudio.com/

Schlegel, A. (2020). Singular value decomposition with r. Retrieved 5 February 2020, from https://rpubs.com/aaronsc32/singular-value-decomposition-r

Shone, R. (2001). *An introduction to economic dynamics*. Cambridge: Cambridge University Press.

Shone, R. (2002). *Economic dynamics* (2nd edn.). Cambridge: Cambridge University Press.

Shoven, J. J., & Whalley, J. (1984). Applied general-equilibrium models of taxation and international trade: An introduction and survey. *Journal of Economic Literature, 22*(3), 1007–1051. http://www.jstor.org/stable/2725306

Simon, C. P., & Blume, L. (1994). *Mathematics for economists*. New York: W. W. Norton & Company.

Sirohi, K. (2018). Singular value decomposition with example in R. Retrieved 5 February 2020, from https://towardsdatascience.com/singular-value-decomposition-with-example-in-r-948c3111aa43

Soetaert, K. (2019). *plot3D: Plotting multi-dimensional data*. R package version 1.3. https://CRAN.R-project.org/package=plot3D

Soetaert, K., Cash, J., & Mazza, F. (2012). *Solving differential equations in R*. Berlin: Springer.

Soetaert, K., Petzoldt, T., & Setzer, R. W. (2010). Solving differential equations in R: Package deSolve. *Journal of Statistical Software, 33*(9), 1–25. http://www.jstatsoft.org/v33/i09

Solow, R. M. (1956). A contribution to the theory of economic growth. *The Quarterly Journal of Economics, 70*(1), 65–94.

Strang, G. (1988). *Linear algebra and its applications* (3rd edn.). New York: Harcourt Brace Jovanovich.

Therneau, T. M., & Grambsch, P. M. (2000). *Modeling survival data: Extending the cox model*. New York: Springer.

Theil, H. (1983). Linear algebra and matrix methods in econometrics. In: Z. Griliches & M. D. Intriligator (Eds.), *Handbook of econometrics* (vol. I, chap. 1, pp. 5–65). Amsterdam: North-Holland.

UNCTAD, & WTO. (2012). *A practical guide to trade policy analysis*. Geneva: United Nations Conference on Trade and Development.

Urbanek, S. (2013). *png: Read and write PNG images*. R package version 0.1-7. https://CRAN.R-project.org/package=png

Venables, B., Hornik, K., & Maechler, M. (2019). *polynom: A collection of functions to implement a class for univariate polynomial manipulations*. R package version 1.4-0. S original by Bill Venables, packages for R by Kurt Hornik and Martin Maechler. https://CRAN.R-project.org/package=polynom

Verbeek, M. (2004). *A guide to modern econometrics* (2nd edn.). New York: Wiley.

Wickham, H. (2009). *ggplot2: Elegant graphics for data analysis*. New York: Springer. http://ggplot2.org

Wickham, H. (2018). *scales: Scale functions for visualization*. R package version 1.0.0. https://CRAN.R-project.org/package=scales

Wickham, H. (2019). *Advanced R*. The R Series (2nd edn.). Boca Raton: CRC Press/Taylor & Francis Group.

Wickham, H., François, R., Henry, L., & Müller, K. (2019). *dplyr: A grammar of data manipulation*. R package version 0.8.3. https://CRAN.R-project.org/package=dplyr

Wickham, H., & Henry, L. (2019). *tidyr: Easily tidy data with 'spread()' and 'gather()' functions*. R package version 0.8.3. https://CRAN.R-project.org/package=tidyr

Wooldridge, J. M. (2012). *Introductory econometrics. A modern approach* (5th edn.). Cincinnati: South-Western.

Zeileis, A., & Grothendieck, G. (2005). zoo: S3 infrastructure for regular and irregular time series. *Journal of Statistical Software, 14*(6), 1–27.

Index

M. Porto, *Introduction to Mathematics for Economics with R*,
https://doi.org/10.1007/978-3-031-05202-6

E

S

GPSR Compliance
The European Union's (EU) General Product Safety Regulation (GPSR) is a set of rules that requires consumer products to be safe and our obligations to ensure this.

If you have any concerns about our products, you can contact us on

ProductSafety@springernature.com

In case Publisher is established outside the EU, the EU authorized representative is:

Springer Nature Customer Service Center GmbH
Europaplatz 3
69115 Heidelberg, Germany

www.ingramcontent.com/pod-product-compliance
Lightning Source LLC
Chambersburg PA
CBHW071232230926
51849CB00001B/78
* 9 7 8 3 0 3 1 0 5 2 0 1 9 *